Library and Book Trade Almanac™

formerly **The Bowker Annual**

2023 | 68th Edition

Library and Book Trade Almanac™

formerly **The Bowker Annual**

2023 | 68th Edition

Editor Kathleen Bayer

 **Information Today, Inc.**

Published by Information Today, Inc.
Copyright © 2023 Information Today, Inc.
All rights reserved

International Standard Book Number 978-1-57387-591-2
International Standard Serial Number 2150-5446
Library of Congress Catalog Card Number 55-12434

Information Today, Inc.
143 Old Marlton Pike
Medford, NJ 08055-8750
Phone: 800-300-9868 (customer service)
Fax: 609-654-4309
E-mail (orders): custserv@infotoday.com
Website: http://www.infotoday.com

Typesetting by Amnet Systems

Printed and bound in the United States of America

$319.50
ISBN 978-1-57387-591-2

31950>

9 781573 875912

Contents

v

Part 2
Legislation, Funding, and Grants

Part 3
Library/Information Science Education
and Career Resources

Part 4
Research and Statistics

Part 5
Reference Information

Part 6
Directory of Organizations

Directory of Book Trade and Related Organizations

Preface and Acknowledgments

The staff of Information Today, Inc. presents the latest annual volume of *Library and Book Trade Almanac*.

A few highlights of the 2023 edition:

"Book bans are bad." Those are the first four words of Suzanne LaPierre's Special Report, titled "Book Bans Backfire. That Doesn't Make Them Harmless." Book bans make people curious about books they never would have known about, spur discussions about topics that need to be brought out into the open, and, quite often, even stimulate sales of banned book titles. However, book bans have their dark side as well, including attacks on educators and librarians and the suppression of voices from already marginalized groups. LaPierre explains how authors, independent book stores, and libraries across the country have banded together to fight the forces that are weaponizing books to advance narrow-minded agendas.

Our second Special Report, "The Year of Challenges: Library Digital Content in 2022," is written by Michael Blackwell, director of St. Mary's County Library in Maryland. Using the latest data available, he documents the state of the digital publishing industry and the libraries that provide access to digital collections. He describes the difficulties that face digital publishers, which offer access to thousands of book titles, when certain groups demand that individual titles be removed from their massive digital collections. Why should access to certain titles be denied to thousands of readers when only a few dozen object to the titles in question? Blackwell explains how various digital publishers are dealing with an ever changing political, social, and legal landscape.

Our third Special Report, "What Is the Metaverse, and Why Should You Care?" is written by Chad Mairn, a librarian, teacher, and founder of the Innovation Lab at St. Petersburg College. He documents the origins of the metaverse and the many uses it currently has and will soon have in our daily lives and in education and learning. He believes it is incumbent upon librarians and publishers to be aware of ongoing developments in this quickly evolving field. The metaverse, Mairn says, has the potential to revolutionize the way we access, consume, and create content of all varieties, and it offers opportunities to enhance the primary missions of libraries around the world.

There are many other features to recommend in this 2023/68th edition of *LBTA*—for instance, the extensive directory listings in Part 6. Another annual *LBTA* feature, "Career Resources, Podcasts, and Job Sites for Library and Information Professionals," written by Susanne Markgren and starting on page 193, is a valuable resource for anyone interested in entering the field or migrating to a new position.

Keith Curry Lance and his colleague Debra E. Kachel contributed a report titled "School Librarian Employment in the United States, 2020–2021 to 2021–2022."

Their research is conducted for the SLIDE project. Learn more about this welcome initiative beginning on page 242, and be sure to visit its website.

To close, I want to acknowledge a number of talented individuals who have supported this production with skill and enthusiasm. Without repeating names seen above, special thanks go to contributors Sylvia Orner, Connie Harbison, Carolina Ballester, Kathlin Smith, and Raymond Garcia.

A special thank you to all of those on the *LBTA* team: Terri Koenig; Owen O'Donnell, director of ITI's Reference Division; Jackie Crawford; Tiffany Chamenko; Tom Hogan, Sr., who edited the Special Reports; Vimali Joseph; and Amron Lehte.

To our readers, thank you for using *Library and Book Trade Almanac* in your work.

Part 1
Reports from the Field

Special Reports

Book Bans Backfire.
That Doesn't Make Them Harmless.

Suzanne S. LaPierre

Book bans are bad. No need to belabor this point to library and book publishing professionals. We know that restricting access to books interferes with the right of humans to access information, explore ideas, see themselves and their cultures accurately represented, and develop empathy and understanding for others. So, while our hearts sink when yet another fantastic book is unfairly targeted by people who have never read it, that dismay is often followed by a spark of motivation. Every challenge to a book is an opportunity to talk about reading and intellectual freedom and why these topics are more essential today than ever.

Book bans are bad, but they tend to backfire in a way that can bring about some good. Book challenges make people curious about books they never would have looked at otherwise. They spur discussions of interesting and sometimes controversial topics that need to be brought out in the open. They motivate professionals in library and publishing fields to strengthen their guidelines, policies, advocacy, and partnerships with others in adjacent fields.

Creative abrasion—the intellectual friction that occurs when the need to hash out conflicts spurs innovation—is coming into play. Coping with myriad challenges is birthing new initiatives and generating transformations that may not have happened otherwise. What follows are some reasons that book bans backfire and some ideas that people in library and publishing fields are developing in response.

Voters Oppose Book Bans

Book bans do not sit well with most Americans. According to a study conducted on behalf of the American Library Association (ALA), 71% of voters oppose efforts to remove books from their local libraries. [1] In the same study, 82% of voters agreed with the statement, "We need to protect the ability of young people to have access to books from which they can learn about and understand different perspectives and help them grow into adults who can think for themselves." Only 18% of voters agreed with a converse statement: "We need to protect young people

Suzanne S. LaPierre is a Virginiana Specialist Librarian with Fairfax County Public Library in Virginia and co-author of the book *Desegregation in Northern Virginia Libraries* (The History Press, 2023). She writes The Wired Library column for *Public Libraries Magazine*.

from books they might find upsetting or that reflect ideologies and lifestyles that are outside the mainstream."[2] Politicians using book and curriculum challenges to mobilize voters might galvanize a vociferous minority temporarily, but they are unlikely to reap long-term success from a widely unpopular strategy.

"The politicians who holler and post and draw up their lists of 'harmful' books aren't actually scared of our books. They are using our books to scare people," author David Levithan points out in an essay for the *Washington Post*.[3] PEN America estimates that at least 40% of the bans in its index of 1,109 are connected to proposed or enacted legislation or to political pressure by state officials or elected lawmakers aimed at restricting teaching or access to certain concepts.[4]

"While the censors claim they are protecting children, the focus on black and LGBTQ+ authors and titles reveal the political aim: energizing a radically conservative base to turn out votes and reverse social progress. Far from being grassroots in nature, these efforts are organized and funded by national organizations," explains Michael Blackwell, library director of St. Mary's County Library in Maryland and a member of ALA's Intellectual Freedom Round Table.[5]

In response, strategies to combat book banning include educating and mobilizing voters. The Unite Against Book Bans Action Toolkit[6] includes resources to help voters know where their candidates stand on the issues, what is on their ballots, how to register to vote, and where to vote. If citizens align their votes with their stated opinions against censorship, book banning will backfire at the polls.

Book Bans Sell Books

While removing books from some shelves may hide them from some readers, the publicity resulting from book bans often leads to increased sales of banned titles. Books that might otherwise have been niche titles, such as *Gender Queer*, become bestsellers when book challenges put them in the spotlight. Classics like *Maus* and *The Bluest Eye* are rediscovered by a new generation and hit bestseller lists all over again. Sales of *Maus* exploded 753% in the last week of January 2022 after a Tennessee school district removed the book from its curriculum.[7]

Book challenges pique curiosity. What better way to get people—especially teenagers—to read books than to forbid them? "What do they not want us to see?" they wonder.

Many readers buy extra copies of challenged titles to support authors or gift suppressed titles to those who might not be able to access them. When teenagers at an Austin, Texas, high school started a banned book club after 19 titles were removed from their library (including a graphic novel version of Margaret Atwood's *The Handmaid's Tale*), strangers donated funds to provide books for the group.[8]

While sales of some banned books do skyrocket, this is usually due to the publicity surrounding the banning. However, since the majority of book challenges go unreported to ALA or the media, publicity that propels sales of books like *Gender Queer* or *Maus* doesn't benefit most authors whose books are quietly removed from shelves or reading lists. In a piece for *The Atlantic*, Connor Goodwin uses the example of *The Magic Fish* by debut author Trung Le Nguyen as a book that's likely to suffer after being included on censorship lists (although at the time of this writing, Amazon ranked it #4 in sales of young adult "coming of age" graphic novels).

In addition to reduced sales to individual purchasers, lesser-known authors whose works are suppressed may lose out on bulk purchases by schools and libraries, and their chances of subsequent publishing contracts diminish.[9] This is yet another example of how already marginalized authors and topics are most at risk of harm from book bans. Recent statistics indicate that more than 40% of books challenged are by LGBTQ+ authors or include LGBTQ+ characters or themes, more than 40% are by people of color or address themes of race or racism, and more than 20% include themes of sexuality, puberty, or nudity (even "nude" cartoon mice!). Other frequently challenged books include themes of politics or religion, according to a study by PEN America.[10]

Booksellers and libraries can help boost visibility of at-risk titles by featuring them alongside more famous titles on their displays and lists of challenged books and by including debut and lesser-known authors in programs and panels.

Book Bans Are Backward

Book bans backfire in the 2020s because they are archaic. Oft-censored author Levithan writes, "If you take my book off the shelf, you keep it away from that shelf, but you hardly keep it away from readers."[11] In the age of e-books and social media, pulling paper copies off shelves in certain libraries seems almost quaint. Removing a 200-plus-page book from a school library because of a word, scene, or image buried within its pages seems absurd when almost all U.S. teens have a smartphone with instant access to the Internet.

Brooklyn Public Library (BPL) launched its Books Unbanned program in April 2022, offering free online access to its entire collection of material for teens and young adults ages 13–21 who request an e-card online. The selection of "always available" books includes some of the most frequently banned new titles for young adults, such as *Lawn Boy*, as well as recently challenged classics. The initiative resulted in 5,100 e-cards and 20,000 checkouts within the program as of September 2022. It is available to out-of-state users because it is independently funded.

According to a BPL spokesperson, the library sees spikes in demand for the program in districts where schools are attempting to ban titles.[12] When a high school English teacher in Norman, Oklahoma, posted a QR code linking to BPL's Books Unbanned program and quit after facing repercussions for doing so,[13] the publicity resulted in a surge of applications to the program. The QR code was shared widely online and even posted on yard signs by supporters.

"Censors aren't just going after the freedom to read; they're trying to erase entire identities and histories. Censors claim they are protecting kids from ideology … by imposing their own ideology on whole classrooms and communities," explains Levithan, whose award-winning books for young adults include *Two Boys Kissing* and *Boy Meets Boy*.[14]

Those using book bans as political cudgels must be aware of the futility of their actions in terms of hiding content, which makes the performative nature of book banning more transparent. But resistance to social progress is a losing game long-term. The percentage of Americans who identify as LGBTQ+ has more than doubled in the past decade,[15] indicating society's evolution away from the feats and stigma book banning represents. As each generation becomes more open-minded, book bans targeting marginalized groups are unlikely to gain lasting traction.

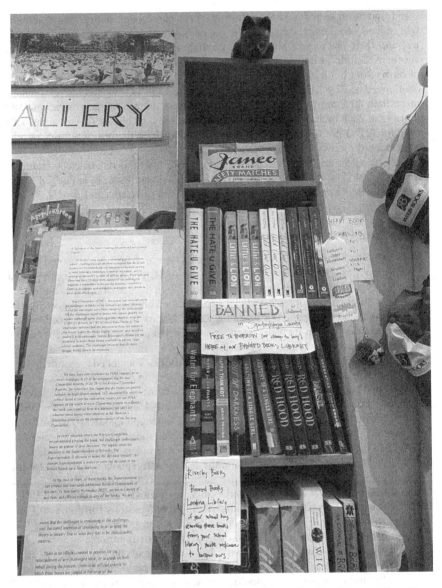

Riverby Books in Fredericksburg, Virginia, provides a lending library of locally banned and challenged books as well as reduced prices on those titles.
(Photo by the author)

Book Bans Spur Creativity and Solidarity

Librarians, authors, teachers, booksellers, publishers, and readers have banded together to launch a multitude of creative responses to the rise in book challenges. The following are just a few examples.

The *Washington Post* brought back Book World, the section devoted to books and reading that had been in hiatus for several years, indicating a commitment to the cause of promoting books and reading even in an era of shrinking print newspaper content. TV news journalist Ali Velshi added a banned book club to his MSNBC weekend show. Many podcasts about banned books have emerged, encouraging critical thinking about titles and themes. National Public Radio released a podcast episode, "Bonus: Banned Books," to discuss challenged titles and the importance of kids' freedom to read.[16]

We Need Diverse Books (WNDB), a nonprofit dedicated to boosting visibility and availability of books by diverse authors, launched the Books Save Lives initiative in December 2022. It offers grants of up to $10,000 for schools to purchase diverse titles, with priority to those located in areas most impacted by censorship. WNDB plans to support grassroots organizations in battleground states by producing resources and assisting educators and media specialists facing book bans. The organization vows to support diverse authors by publicizing their books and arranging school visits to bolster income lost due to censorship.[17]

Several organizations have put together action kits for people who want to support the freedom to read. One is the previously mentioned Unite Against Book Bans Action Toolkit (uniteagainstbookbans.org/toolkit). Many university libraries have created libguides to educate others on the topic, such as Arizona State University (libguides.asu.edu/BannedBooks).

Publishers have reacted to book bans with initiatives such as the Open Books, Open Doors project among Penguin Random House (PRH), *School Library Journal*, PEN America, the National Coalition Against Censorship, the National Council of Teachers of English, and *Library Journal*. The partnership emphasizes the importance of free expression in response to rising book challenges across the country. PRH sponsored artwork for a free poster and created a Banned Books Resource Hub.[18]

Independent bookshops have given away thousands of books to counteract censorship efforts. The Painted Porch Bookshop in Bastrop, Texas, partnered with e-book and audiobook company Scribed to host Banned Bookmobile events in 2022, distributing thousands of free titles to customers.[19]

Students across the country have started banned book clubs in response to attempts to remove books from their schools. Among them are teenagers at Common Ground Teen Center in Washington, Pennsylvania, and students of Vandegrift High School in Austin, Texas.[20]

Authors have banded together to support one another. The Authors Guild, an 11,000-member writer's advocacy group, launched the Authors Guild Banned Book Club. Using the Fable app, it features a monthly book that has recently been barred in one or more U.S. school districts or states. The initiative is supported by a grant from publisher Hachette.

The entire city of Chicago has declared itself a book sanctuary. Along with every branch of Chicago Public Library, city leadership has declared the entire city a sanctuary for the freedom to read. Others are encouraged to create their own book sanctuaries, large or small, using a free toolkit provided by TheBookSanctuary.org. Steps involve collecting and protecting endangered books, making them broadly accessible, hosting book talks and events, and educating others.

While the efforts of these individuals and entities don't compensate for the harm of book censorship falling disproportionately on marginalized authors and disadvantaged readers, the creativity and connections forged are likely to have lasting impact and counteract some of the damage caused by suppression.

Conclusion

There are certainly damaging consequences of book challenges, including attacks against educators and librarians, self-censorship by people in the book business, suppression of voices from already marginalized groups, and barriers falling chiefly on isolated or otherwise disadvantaged people. LGBTQ+ and BIPOC authors have been disproportionately targeted, depriving LGBTQ+ and BIPOC youths of access to books by authors who can relate to their experiences and thwarting all readers' access to diverse points of view. The most vulnerable populations, such as low-income families, are most likely to be roadblocked.

Two recent studies by PEN America and ALA predict that book challenges and bans will increase over the coming year.[21] The last few years, marked by pandemic losses and bitter partisan divisions, have been rough. The angst of this time has been leveraged by politicians who are using books to turn fear into anger and suppression.

"We are in the fight of our lifetime to protect the right to read. That fight can and will be won, but we cannot underestimate the will of those who wish to ban books. We must organize, support writers, librarians, and readers under attack, and be ready for a long campaign," Blackwell asserts.[22] Indeed, we must continue to support inclusive publishing practices that enable works by diverse authors to reach readers of all backgrounds, providing both windows and mirrors. We must promote critical thinking and advocate on behalf of quality works of literature that are unfairly reduced to a line or illustration taken out of context. We need to support legislation on all levels that protects intellectual freedom.

But while book challenges may be at historic levels, so are counteractions celebrating our freedom to read. Escalating threats have forced a refocus on the importance of reading and have strengthened actions to defend diversity of representation and expression. If library and publishing professionals join forces with individual and institutional allies and continue to innovate in defense of intellectual freedom, then book bans of today will only serve to backfire against those of the future.

In the end, because love is stronger than hate, the stamina of booklovers will outlast those who are weaponizing books to advance narrow-minded agendas. We only live once, but through books, readers experience hundreds of lives and thousands of ideas. Booklovers are passionate in defense of this boundless wonder.

Notes

1. Heather Kelly, "You Can Ban a Book, but Can You Stop Teens from Finding It Online?" *Washington Post*. Sept. 22, 2022. washingtonpost.com/technology/2022/09/22/books-banned-libraries.

2. Ibid.

3. David Levithan, "The New Censorship Won't Work, but It's Still Insidious." *Washington Post*. Sept. 25, 2022.

4. PEN America. "Banned in the USA." April 2022. pen.org/banned-in-the-usa.

5. Michael Blackwell, email communication with the author, Dec. 6, 2022.

6. Unite Against Books Bans Action Toolkit. uniteagainstbookbans.org/toolkit.

7. Anna Kaplan, "Sales of 'Maus' Soar 753% in Last Week of January Following Ban by Tennessee School District." *Forbes*. Feb. 4, 2022. forbes.com/sites/annakaplan/2022/02/04/sales-of-maus-soar-753-in-last-week-of-january-following-ban-by-tennessee-school-district/?sh=5f1a6e484cb7.

8. Hannah Natanson, "Teens Fight for the Right to Read with 'Banned-Book Clubs' and Lawsuits." *Washington Post*. May 3, 2022. washingtonpost.com/education/2022/05/03/teens-books-ban-clubs-protest.

9. Connor Goodwin, "The Banned Books You Haven't Heard About." *The Atlantic*. Sept. 20, 2022. theatlantic.com/books/archive/2022/09/banned-books-increased-sales/671479.

10. PEN America. "Banned in the USA." April 2022. pen.org/banned-in-the-usa.

11. David Levithan, "The New Censorship Won't Work, but It's Still Insidious." *Washington Post*. Sept. 25, 2022.

12. Ibid.

13. Jonathan Edwards, "Teacher Quits in Protest after Being Punished for Banned-Books Sign." *Washington Post*. Aug. 25, 2022. washingtonpost.com/nation/2022/08/25/oklahoma-teacher-resigns.

14. David Levithan, "The New Censorship Won't Work, but It's Still Insidious." *Washington Post*. Sept. 25, 2022.

15. Jeffrey M. Jones, "LGBT Identification in U.S. Ticks Up to 7.1%." Gallup. Feb. 17, 2022. news.gallup.com/poll/389792/lgbt-identification-ticks-up.aspx.

16. NPR. "Bonus: Banned Books." *Consider This* podcast. December 2021. npr.org/2021/12/02/1060985607/bonus-banned-books.

17. We Need Diverse Books. Books Save Lives program. 2022. diversebooks.org/programs/bookssavelives.

18. Penguin Random House Banned Books Resource Hub. penguinrandomhouse.com/articles/banned-books-resources.

19. Kelsey Thompson, "Texas Bookshop Shares 1000s of Free Books amid ISD Challenges, Reviews." KXAN News. Feb. 22, 2022 .kxan.com/news/local/bastrop-county/texas-bookshop-shares-1000s-of-free-books-amid-isd-challenges-reviews.

20. Hannah Natanson, "Teens Fight for the Right to Read with 'Banned-Book Clubs' and Lawsuits." *Washington Post*. May 3, 2022. washingtonpost.com/education/2022/05/03/teens-books-ban-clubs-protest.

21. PEN America. "Banned in the USA." April 2022. pen.org/banned-in-the-usa.

22. Michael Blackwell, email communication with the author, Dec. 6, 2022.

The Year of Challenges:
Library Digital Content in 2022

Michael Blackwell

The most significant recent story in libraries has been challenges to the right to read. The challenges have gone beyond the appropriateness of individual book titles. Whole genres, the very way libraries operate to serve all equitably, and, in some cases, even the very existence of libraries are under attack. At least three libraries have been temporarily shuttered or defunded. These attacks take two forms: politically motivated (but as Maurice Cunningham notes in a Network for Public Education blog post, hardly grassroots[1]) citizen efforts and state legislative efforts.

An excellent companion piece in this volume by Suzanne S. LaPierre explores this development at length, but no look at the year in digital can exclude it, especially since librarians are making novel use of digital to expand access to challenged works. Unfortunately, political challenges are not the only ones facing digital libraries. Rising prices, continued poor licensing terms, and changing patron habits combine to make it difficult to offer digital content sustainably. Librarian efforts to meet these difficulties through state laws and innovation have faced some legal setbacks, although efforts are ongoing. While some positive developments have occurred, 2022 can fairly be called The Year of Challenges.

Attacks on Library Books and Libraries

Content challenges, whether by groups or states, were generally not specifically digitally focused. These challenges do, however, often have implications for digital service. At the end of 2022, for example, the Missouri secretary of state introduced a "rule" that would make library service to minors, especially in digital, nearly impossible. The rule would require "every library receiving state funds to publish policies allowing parents to designate which materials their children can access. In addition, children attempting to check out any material would need parental permission."[2] Any library user could also question the library's age designation for materials. Even if the resulting logistical nightmare weren't enough to chill service, digital service would be difficult. Library digital platforms do not allow for blocking individual patron access to titles. Unable to prevent access patron-by-patron, libraries would almost certainly be forced to remove titles, especially titles by and about LGBTQ+ people or that challenge conservative opinion on our nation's racist past.[3]

The Missouri "rule" is being challenged and may or may not be implemented. Already in place, however, is Louisiana's Protecting Minors Tip Line. It encourages "the people of Louisiana to report library workers who engage in 'taxpayer-subsidized sexualization of children,' an accusation made in response to collection development and programming related to LGBTQ+ experiences."[4] A library's

Michael Blackwell is the director of St. Mary's County Library in Maryland, a member of the American Library Association's (ALA) Joint Digital Content Working Group, and the current chair of ALA's Core Ebooks Interest Group.

e-book offerings would be a tempting target for censors. They wouldn't even have to go to a library in person to report a library director who did not have various titles removed from the digital collection.

Some direct attacks have been made on digital content. The county commissioners of Llano, Texas, voted at the end of 2021 to suspend the county library's OverDrive platform, and "More than 17,000 digital books were removed."[5] Digital is a censor's dream: Imagine being able to suppress thousands of books at once. This censorship effort is under a legal challenge that will continue into 2023, with county residents alleging, "Defendants have transformed the County's public libraries from contemplative spaces where residents can explore the marketplace of ideas to battlegrounds in Defendants' political and ideological war." Digital content is more often lost when attempts to defund libraries prevail. John Chrastka of EveryLibrary has warned that such efforts, already shuttering several libraries in 2022, will become more common: "The effort to tie library funding to censorship efforts is likely just beginning in our country. ... If they can't ban the book, will they burn the whole place down?"[6]

Some attempts to remove digital content have come from an unlikely source: librarians themselves. In February 2022 the Library Freedom Project released a "demand for accountability" from two platforms, hoopla and OverDrive, over "fascist propaganda in their digital library collections."[7] At issue initially were Holocaust-denial books such as the opprobrious *Debating the Holocaust*. It is impossible to defend such works as historically accurate and anything other than propaganda. hoopla removed the offending titles; OverDrive did not. The difference is due to access models. hoopla offers a pay-per-use model, with all titles generally visible. Libraries must opt to suppress certain titles if they are not wanted. In OverDrive, only titles selected by the library will be visible. OverDrive has made a decision more in line with traditional library practice: The library is responsible for its collection. To be fair, it is difficult to monitor the hundreds of thousands of titles available through hoopla.

The controversy soon grew beyond books that cannot be defended into value arguments. The Library Freedom Project noted, "There is still a great deal of disinformation to be found on Hoopla. For instance, when you search for e-books about 'homosexuality' and 'abortion,' instead of factual informational content, the search results are largely self-published religious texts designed to misinform and scare library readers about sexual and reproductive topics. There is also an enormous amount of misinformation about vaccines." Demanding "accuracy" certainly seems a laudable stance. This group is not itself a library, but librarians belong. It may not be the best First Amendment optics for librarians, mostly paid with government funding, to be telling a private company what it should and should not offer, especially since the demand is not a wide-ranging insistence on accuracy in every nonfiction subject. Rather, it largely focuses on topics on which libraries are themselves attacked by conservatives.

Demanding removal of content that libraries can't select or suppress internally—and the digital collection is ultimately the individual library's responsibility—is to deny other libraries access, for whatever reason they may wish to offer it, if only to show reprehensible ideas that should be fought. It seems dangerously close to being on the flip side of the censorship coin. Are the group members so rigorous about absolute accuracy in titles they find politically congenial? Most librarians will likely have enough on their hands defending the titles they want in their collections to join an effort to ban other works and open the profession to *tu quoque* arguments. "Librarian, you censor too!" In a time of great polarization, librarians, seeking to provide a range of materials, may find their collections, and themselves, under attack from many perspectives.

The incident certainly underscores how managing collections in varying digital models presents unique challenges not found in print acquisition. One must not only choose what to select but, in some cases, what may need to be suppressed to prevent attacks on funding and library personnel.

A Positive Development: The Growth of New License Models

While censorship efforts complicated digital collecting, some positive developments began or continued in 2022. Many small to medium-sized publishers offer flexible licensing terms, ranging from a perpetual access with unlimited simultaneous use option to a five-download option. The Digital Public Library of America (DPLA) has been particularly successful in inviting publishers to create options.[8] Flexible models allow libraries to make the best use of their dollars while creating more diverse collections. DPLA now offers all of Amazon's unique content through the Palace Project[9] and has begun to integrate all of Amazon's Audible content. A perpetual access license to these titles would have made them even more desirable. Still, four license options offer some flexibility. This content has not been available to libraries before and should make the Palace Project—a nonprofit initiative designed by librarians for libraries—worth a look. A major audiobook producer, Blackstone, dropped its partial embargo on new titles to libraries and now offers three license options on all titles to libraries. A few publishers have even begun to sell, rather than license, e-books to libraries, including Brickhouse, Pressbooks, LibriVox, and Postlight. Work remains to get such books available and thus discoverable in library e-book platforms. However, the ability to treat reasonably priced digital books exactly as we treat print, under copyright, is most welcome.

Continuing Challenges in Big 5 Licensing

Overall use of library digital content continues to rise. Industry leader OverDrive, for example, notes that e-book circulation in schools and public libraries grew 3%, to 331 million. Digital audiobook circulation rose 17%, although numbers were not as high as for e-books, at 191 million. Comics and graphic novel circulation rose to 18%, with 33 million titles checked out.[10] Overall circulation, including digital magazines, grew 10%. That increase, however, is less than in prior years: 16% in 2021, 33% in 2020, and 20% in 2019. COVID created a spike in digital use that is slowing but not shrinking. Despite challenges, many libraries seem to be quietly and efficiently providing content.

This increase, however, masks current difficulties that librarians face in meeting demand. And the public reaction to COVID is not the only reason for slowing growth. When compared to print title costs, the cost of e-books and digital audio has been at issue for years. In 2022 ReadersFirst quantified this cost with its Publisher Price Watch, which identifies publishers that offer better deals."[11] In both licenses that expire and those that do not (although, of course, no license is guaranteed to be permanent), the larger publishers charge at least four times the cost for digital as for the same title in print format. Print brings processing and other costs (staff for shelving, etc.), but, arguably, digital does not bring the return on investment that print does.

Since the release of Publisher Price Watch, ReadersFirst has also tracked e-book price increases.[12] HarperCollins, which had in the past offered some of the better deals, led the way with 31% increases. Scribner was close to 10%, as was Hachette in audio. Recorded Books' prices rose 24%, with its 100 loans license (once again, previously offering some better deals) going up a whopping 128%. Individual titles can be breathtakingly expensive. The most recent Stephen King audiobook is only licensed for two years and at a price of $129.99. Academic print books can run into the hundreds of dollars, but their e-book equivalent might be in the thousands. Increased demand with higher prices is, of course, a formula for trouble for libraries.

Another factor exacerbates the problem. As the COVID pandemic becomes endemic, in-person user visits in libraries are rising, as is print and other physical media circulation. Libraries that have shifted print acquisition funding to digital may have to readjust. The growing number of patrons coming back in person must also be served. Far from seeing an increase in funding, most libraries may be looking at flat funding during a time of inflation, with any increases targeted for employees struggling to make ends meet. Moreover, any 2020 or 2021 American Rescue Plan Act (ARPA) funding that may have gone toward digital will no longer be available.

Perhaps the most challenging issue is the "exploding" metered access license: They expire, rather than being permanent. None of the Big 5 publishers offer a permanent e-book license, and only two offer it for audio. Many other imprints have moved away from the permanent license. The need to constantly relicense older but still high-demand titles while keeping up with new releases puts an intolerable strain on budgets. Digital is becoming difficult to sustain at prior levels. Meanwhile, collections threaten to become less rich and diverse, as high-demand titles take priority. It is impossible for libraries to offer the wealth of titles they can offer in print, even as demand for digital becomes ever higher.

An American Library Association (ALA) Core e-forum, eBook Acquisition and Licensing Issues in Public Libraries,[13] held in December 2022, provides excellent examples of how increased digital demand, rising costs, and unfavorable licensing practices have exacerbated selection challenges. The forum was attended by many collection development librarians across the country. Librarians were unanimous in their reports on digital collections becoming more difficult to sustain. Particularly troubling are the increased costs to replace expired metered access licenses. These are sample attendee comments:

- "In FY [fiscal year] 2021, holds management [providing multiple copies to meet current demand] was 30%, expired licenses were 22%, and new content was 47%. In FY23, holds are 35%, expired licenses were 30%, and new content was 35%. Obviously, this is troubling change in two years."
- "So far this calendar year, the cost of replacing expired licenses has risen to 29.4%"

- "Relicensing costs have risen dramatically for us the last several years—about 300% since 2018."

The year 2018 is significant because four of the Big 5 abandoned perpetual access for e-books, and three of them abandoned it for digital audio. Libraries can work with metered access; however, if metered access costs go up and become more than perpetual access used to be, it is no surprise if simply trying to meet patron demand for older titles cannibalizes budgets. Note that libraries do not typically replace titles simply because they expire. Demand must exist. Many forum participants agreed with one who noted, "We cannot afford to replace expired titles unless they have holds on them." If 25%–30% of a budget is spent simply relicensing what a library already once offered—something that never happens with print titles—maintaining a full and rich collection is impossible.

To provide a more diverse and less costly collection, librarians could turn away from the largest publishers. Patrons have a way of wanting the bestsellers, however, and creating demand for something less well-known is a further challenge. Of course, the patrons are the reason why libraries are fighting for better terms. They are the ones who are disadvantaged under current terms. Those who do not have the wherewithal to buy books, and those seeking titles perhaps lesser known but more diverse than the average best-selling thriller, are disadvantaged most of all.

Legal Challenges: Controlled Digital Lending

Librarians have undertaken efforts to make digital offerings more cost-effective and sustainable. In 2022 two such efforts were faced with legal challenges. The ongoing lawsuit of four large publishers and the publishers' lobbying group, the Association of American Publishers, went from discovery phase into summary judgment phase. Originally started in 2020 *Hachette Book Group, Inc. vs. Internet Archive* was ostensibly over the Internet Archive's National Emergency Library. Begun in response to COVID, this library extended the idea of Controlled Digital Lending (CDL), as practiced in the Internet Archive's long-standing Open Library.[14] CDL is "an emerging method that allows libraries to loan print books to digital patrons in a 'lend like print' fashion."[15] The print title is digitized, but "libraries use technical controls to ensure a consistent 'owned-to-loaned ratio,' meaning the library circulates the exact number of copies of a specific title it owns, regardless of format, putting controls in place to prevent users from redistributing or copying the digitized version." The National Emergency Library may have gone too far to meet the definition of CDL. It abandoned the owned-to-loan ratio and allowed patrons to have unlimited simultaneous access.

That the suit is not really about the National Emergency Library is clear. The Internet Archive actually abandoned the library in 2020, but the publishers continued their suit. In the publishers' statement of summary judgment, almost no mention is made of the National Emergency Library. The suit is a challenge to the very existence of CDL. Although he is not a neutral source, Peter M. Routhier, counsel for the Internet Archive, appears correct when he asserts that "publishers will continue to sue libraries over digital practices that were long considered fair uses in the physical world. ... [T]he publishers argue that digital lending harms markets they claim to own. ... [I]n the digital realm, every non-fee-paying library practice harms the publishers' economic interests as a matter of principle—regardless of libraries' historic practices and their previously-accepted roles."[16]

Little wonder, then, that many scholars, librarians, and even author groups submitted "friend of the court" briefs in support of the Internet Archive.[17] (Full disclosure: This author participated.) CDL is being used worldwide in many libraries, public and academic. One of the most notable related developments in 2022 was the National Information Standards Organization's (NISO) formulation of a group to develop best practices to implement "CDL as a natural extension of existing rights held and practices undertaken by libraries for content they legally hold."[18] (Full disclosure: This author is a member of the group.) The contending briefs ultimately focus on the purpose of copyright. In a *Publishers Weekly* article, Andrew Albanese chooses sections that summarize the dispute well.[19] The publishers claim, "In the end, Internet Archive asks this Court to adopt a radical proposition that would turn copyright law upside down. Since the purpose of copyright is to incentivize the creation of new works, authors and publishers—not [Internet Archive]—hold the exclusive right to publish their books in all formats and distribute them via select channels."

The Internet Archive response is, "All CDL does, and all it can ever do, is offer a limited, digital alternative to physically handing a book to a patron. Libraries deciding how to meet their patrons' needs for digital access to books are not making a choice between paying e-book licensing fees or getting books for free. Libraries pay publishers under either approach [but with CDL], librarians can continue to maintain permanent collections of books, to preserve those books in their original form for future generations, and to lend them to patrons one at time, as they have always done ... to advance the ultimate purpose of copyright: 'the intellectual enrichment of the public.'"

From a library perspective, the Internet Archive may have the upper hand. Libraries do pay for print, upon which any digitization is based. We are allowed to circulate one user at a time under copyright for noncommercial purposes. Copyright is given to Congress under the Constitution "to promote the progress of science and useful arts, by securing for limited times to authors and inventors the exclusive right to their respective writings and discoveries." Knowledge is given at least as much weight as ownership. The publishers' assertion is that digital is different. Whether or not it is different will be up to the judge. Summary judgment should come in 2023. If no sides prevail, a trial will occur. Even if one side prevails—especially if it is the Internet Archive—expect an appeal. The case could go on for a decade. During that time, libraries can and should continue to develop and enter into agreements on CDL. The case may ultimately end with a judgment against the Internet Archive's National Emergency Library practices. But, again, from the library perspective, such a judgment cannot be allowed to result in the end of CDL. CDL is not scalable as a replacement for licensing (or perhaps purchases) through our digital platforms, but, for preservation and limited sharing, it is too valuable an arrow in our quiver to give up. Should the judgment go against CDL in any way, it will be necessary for libraries to seek what is in any case long overdue: a congressional revisitation of copyright under digital with the rights of libraries in mind.

Legal Challenges: Digital Licensing

Copyright, and how current iterations of it hamper libraries, was at the center of the other significant library court case in 2022. The Association of American Publishers brought suit against the state of Maryland over its library e-book law. That law was unanimously passed by the Maryland legislature in 2021. It was not signed by Maryland's governor but took effect on January 1, 2022. [Disclosure: The author was involved with the drafting of an advocacy for the bill that became law.] The law required publishers that license e-books to Maryland consumers to also license them to Maryland public libraries "on reasonable terms." The Maryland attorney general's office defended the law.

The judge in the case noted that "there is inequity and an unfairness on how publishers have treated public libraries."[20] However, while sympathetic to the state's position that "Publishers capitalize on the digital revolution at libraries' expense," the judge ruled that the law as written was unconstitutional. Copyright, she ruled, gives the publishers the right to charge whatever they want for their products and to make or not make their digital products available to libraries. Unlike with print books, which libraries can get from many sources and circulate under copyright, digital copies are controlled. Libraries only have the choice to license the content, however unfair the terms may be, or to forgo the license.

While this ruling might seem a huge setback, the Maryland law had its uses. First, it drew much needed attention to the difficult situation libraries face. Second, it appears to have been instrumental in getting Amazon and Audible to at last license their unique content to libraries, if only on one platform. Most importantly, it provided a case from which library advocates can learn. Librarians cannot count on directly changing licenses, so state laws aiming to create change must work differently.

Two approaches have developed. The first is based on consumer protection law. Kyle Courtney of Harvard University has been instrumental in creating it. The Library Futures group has posted a template for developing an approach of this sort.[21] States that are interested may also work with Library Futures to customize a bill with their unique laws as a guide. A second approach is based on state procurement. It was developed largely by Jonathan Band, counsel for ALA. Basically, to simplify many complex matters, both approaches say that libraries may not enter into unfair contracts, with what is "fair" being determined by each state. In Maryland, for example, what is "fair" would be based on print equivalency. It would be unfair for publishers to charge more for a digital title than the print retail price.

How would such a law work? Unlike with the blocked Maryland law, publishers are not compelled to offer a certain price. If, however, they wanted to license to libraries in a state with such a law, they would have to offer fair terms, or libraries would not be able to license. A publisher might well simply opt not to license in a state at all. That publisher would, however, risk a public relations headache, not to mention financial loss, with libraries all over the country not licensing in sympathy with their fellows.

Librarians intend to rachet up the pressure. In 2023 New York and Massachusetts are expected to move forward with bills of the consumer protection sort. Rhode Island and Connecticut are very likely to introduce bills as well. Maryland has developed draft legislation based on state procurement that is expected to be introduced in 2024. Eight other states may move forward in 2023 or 2024. The aim is not just to compel negotiation by making many state markets problematic. If even three or four states have laws in effect, it is hoped to create enough concern that Congress will need to reconsider copyright in the digital age.

Of course, it is uncertain if Congress would act. The publishers and their lobbyists have money and power. Libraries only have the goodwill of the people, but through that, they have some influence as well. It is a risk for libraries in a state to potentially lose digital access. Patrons may be angered by not getting their favorite e-books. Libraries must refract that anger at the publishers with careful advocacy campaigns. After many years of discontent, though, librarians finally seem to have had enough with publisher e-book practices. Expect contentious years ahead. Digital has become important enough, however, that risks are worth taking. Demand, as well as digital's unique ability to reach widely and to suit homebound and disabled patrons, cannot be met and used sustainably under the terms many large publishers now demand.

Using Digital to Fight Challenges

Digital's unique ability to reach library patrons was imaginatively illustrated by two libraries in 2022 to meet challenges to library books. New York Public Library made four frequently challenged titles available nationally through its Books for All project. The library said it "partnered with publishers Hachette Book Group, Macmillan Publishers, and Scholastic to make a small selection of commonly banned or challenged books available to anyone who chooses to read them—all for free via our e-reader app, SimplyE."[22] The initiative ran during April and May 2022. Brooklyn Public Library (BPL) went further still with its Books Unbanned campaign, offering a library card to teen readers so they could access the entire digital collection. Access was expanded still further: "a selection of frequently challenged books available with no holds or wait times for all BPL cardholders."

Simultaneous access to titles does not come cheaply. It is to be hoped that the publishers gave generous terms. Both publishers and libraries gain by ensuring that reading is a valued activity. BPL should not have to act alone. The organized and politically motivated challenges to intellectual freedom are a danger to democracy. Libraries across the county—or at least those that are better funded and that will not have their budgets cut by vindictive legislators—should join the effort to expand access. Perhaps, if carefully measured, publishers may find that libraries truly do help with discovery and, ultimately, sales of titles, making better licensing terms seem more advantageous. Libraries surely will not be spending less on digital. But we simply cannot afford to spend more on poor licensing terms.

Unfortunately, 2022 will not be the last year of conflict. Can libraries find some way to get better terms? Will publishers work with libraries for the good of reading? Will the majority of Americans who oppose book banning prevail against a smaller, but vocal, even fanatical, minority, with digital expanding access to eager readers in areas where books are challenged?[23] The next years will bring continued challenges, but possibly—dare we hope?—rewards.

Notes

1. Maurice Cunningham, (2021). "Koch Connections and Sham Grassroots of Parents Defending Education." Network for Public Education. https://networkforpubliceducation.org/blog-content/maurice-cunningham-koch-connections-and-sham-grassroots-of-parents-defending-education. Also see Elizabeth A. Harris and Alexandra Alter, (2022). "A Fast-Growing Network of Conservative Groups Is Fueling a Surge in Book Bans." *New York Times.* https://www.nytimes.com/2022/12/12/books/book-bans-libraries.html. Access dates December 29, 2022.

2. Rudi Keller, (2022). "Opposition Growing to Missouri Secretary of State Rules on Library Materials for Children." Missouri Independent. https://missouriindependent.com/2022/11/16/opposition-growing-to-missouri-secretary-of-state-rule-on-library-materials-for-children. Access date December 29, 2022.

3. "The Real Reason for the Attack on Libraries." (2022). Daily Kos. https://www.dailykos.com/stories/2022/12/23/2136462/-The-real-reason-for-the-attack-on-libraries?detail=emaildkre&pm_source=dkre&pm_medium=email. Access date December 29, 2022.

4. Emily Drabinski, (2022). "Louisiana Communities Organize to Defend Libraries from Far Right Censorship." Truthout. https://truthout.org/articles/louisiana-communities-organize-to-defend-libraries-from-far-right-censorship. Access date December 29, 2022.

5. Kelsey Thompson, (2022). "Llano County Residents File Suit after Books Removed from Library System." KXAN. https://www.kxan.com/news/texas/llano-county-residents-file-suit-after-books-removed-from-library-system. Access date December 29, 2022.

6. Andrew Albanese, (2022). "Concerns Linger for Libraries after Mixed Election Results." *Publishers Weekly.* https://www.publishersweekly.com/pw/by-topic/industry-news/libraries/article/90919-concerns-linger-for-libraries-after-mixed-election-results.html. Access date December 29, 2022.

7. "We Demand Accountability from Hoopla Digital and OverDrive Regarding the Platforming of Fascist Propaganda in Their Digital Library Collections." (2022). Library Freedom Project. https://libraryfreedom.medium.com/we-demand-accountability-from-hoopla-digital-and-overdrive-regarding-the-platforming-of-fascist-c47c88e62ddc. Access date December 29, 2022.

8. "Flexible Licensing Models from the DPLA Exchange." (2021). Digital Public Library of America. https://dp.la/news/flexible-licensing-models-from-the-dpla-exchange. Access date December 29, 2022.

9. "The Palace Project: The People's Palace." Lyrasis. https://www.lyrasis.org/programs/Pages/palace-project.aspx. Access date December 29, 2022.

10. David Burleigh, (2022). "OverDrive Releases 2022 Digital Book Circulation Data and Highlights." OverDrive. https://company.overdrive.com/2023/01/06/overdrive-releases-2022-digital-book-circulation-data-and-highlights.

11. "Publisher Price Watch: Comparative Analysis of the Digital Book Prices and License Models Larger Publishers Offer to Libraries." (2022). ReadersFirst. https://www.readersfirst.org/publisher-price-watch. Access date December 29, 2022.

12. "Costs Are Rising (What a Surprise)." (2022). ReadersFirst. https://www.readersfirst.org/news/2022/8/17/costs-are-rising-what-a-surprise. Access date December 29, 2022.

13. Will Stuivenga, (December 23, 2022). "eBook Forum Day 2 Summary Transcript." Email to the author.

14. Internet Archive. (ND). Open Library. https://openlibrary.org. Access date December 29, 2022.

15. "Controlled Digital Lending by Libraries." (2019). Controlled Digital Lending. https://controlleddigitallending.org. Access date December 29, 2022.

16. Peter M. Routhier, (2022). "The CDL Lawsuit and the Future of Libraries." Internet Archive Blogs. http://blog.archive.org/2022/10/17/the-cdl-lawsuit-and-the-future-of-libraries. Access date December 29, 2022.

17. Andrew Albanese, (2022). "Supporters, Opponents Weigh in On Internet Archive Copyright Battle." *Publishers Weekly*. https://www.publishersweekly.com/pw/by-topic/industry-news/libraries/article/89868-supporters-opponents-weigh-in-on-internet-archive-copyright-battle.html. Access date December 29, 2022.

18. "Interoperable System of Controlled Digital Lending." (2022). National Information Standards Organization. https://www.niso.org/standards-committees/is-cdl. Access date December 29, 2022.

19. Andrew Albanese, (2022). "Publishers, Internet Archive Ready for Summary Judgment Hearing in Book Scan Case." *Publishers Weekly*. https://www.publishersweekly.com/pw/by-topic/industry-news/libraries/article/90566-publishers-internet-archive-ready-for-summary-judgment-hearing-in-book-scanning-case.html. Access date December 29, 2022.

20. Shawnda Hines, (2022). "ALA Upholds Maryland E-Books Law and State's Defense as Federal District Court Issues Preliminary Injunction." American Library Association. https://www.ala.org/press-releases/2022/02/ala-upholds-maryland-e-books-law-and-states-defense-federal-district-court#:~:text=Boardman%20stated%2C%20%E2%80%9CIt%20does%20seem,revolution%20at%20libraries'%20expense.%E2%80%9D. Access date December 29, 2022.

21. "Library Futures Draft Legislation (Access to E-Books)" (2022). Library Futures. https://www.libraryfutures.net/draft-ebook-legislation. Access date December 29, 2022.

22. Tony Marx, (2022). "Books For All: NYPL Supports the Right to Read Banned Books." New York Public Library. https://www.nypl.org/blog/2022/04/13/books-for-all-nypl-supports-right-read-banned-books. Access date December 29, 2022.

23. Fred Backus and Anthony Salvanto, (2022). "Big Majorities Reject Book Bans. CBS News. https://www.cbsnews.com/news/book-bans-opinion-poll-2022-02-22. Access date December 29, 2022.

What Is the Metaverse, and Why Should You Care?

Chad Mairn

In 1938 the stereoscope was invented. This device used two separate images (i.e., one from the left eye and one from the right eye) to merge into a single three-dimensional (3D) image. This gave the viewer a sense of depth and presence or the feeling of being inside the image. Fast-forward to 1939 when a simple device called the View-Master was patented to give more people opportunities to immerse themselves in 3D imagery. This basic stereoscopic View-Master concept was later used in Google Cardboard and other virtual reality (VR) headsets. Of course, high-end VR equipment has more functionality than the original View-Master, but the primary concept remains the same today. Researchers started to explore various simulation applications in the 1950s, and that technology has evolved significantly in the last 70-plus years. Most computer scientists agree that Jaron Lanier, founder of VPL Research, coined the term "virtual reality" in 1987.

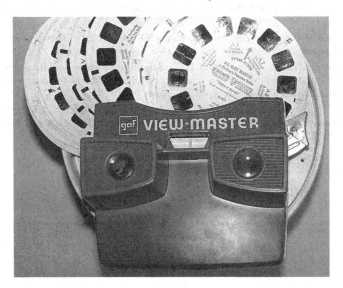

The stereoscopic View-Master (Photo by Enokson/CC BY 2.0 License)

Reality has been questioned since the late sixth century B.C. by Parmenides, and this examination is ongoing. Perception, although not reality, is the process of interpreting and understanding sensory information that influences how people

Chad Mairn is a librarian, teacher, and author who frequently shares his enthusiasm for "all things technology" as a speaker at library and technology conferences. He is an information services librarian, assistant professor, and founder of the Innovation Lab at St. Petersburg College. During his library and information science graduate work at the University of South Florida, Mairn became a technology liaison between the Bill and Melinda Gates Foundation and Florida public libraries.

Author Chad Mairn wearing VR HMD presenting from a New York City hotel to people attending Synapse Summit 2020 in Tampa Bay, Florida

see their own reality. Computer vision applications like Google Lens can "perceive" and identify various objects in the world using machine learning algorithms, and this technology will be used heavily when eye/face/hand/body-tracking technologies are utilized more frequently in virtual spaces. Going further, technologies like VR exist inside computer-generated simulations that are experienced by the user wearing a head-mounted display (HMD). Perception can then be manipulated to create a sense of immersion in that 3D virtual environment, which can be designed to mimic the real world or a world that does not exist yet.

In Stanley G. Weinbaum's 1935 book *Pygmalion's Spectacles,* one of the characters, Professor Albert Ludwig, photographs a "story in a liquid with light-sensitive chromates" then adds "taste chemically and sound electrically," resulting in a solution that is put into "magical spectacles" so that users can view the story with sound, sight, smell, and taste and experience an immersive fictional world.[1] This is becoming more reminiscent of what society now knows as extended reality (XR), in which physical things located in the real world start to blend and interact with digital things inside a 3D simulated world.

XR is an umbrella term that encompasses a range of different technologies, including VR, augmented reality (AR), and mixed reality (MR). VR immerses users in a completely artificial environment, cutting them off from the real world. The HMD typically includes a display for each eye, like the View-Master, as well as sensors and other components that track the user's head movements and adjust the display accordingly. This creates the illusion of being in a different place. 360° VR (e.g., Google Cardboard using a smartphone) provides three degrees of freedom (3DoF) experiences in which the user is stationary and cannot move through 3D space. Users can look left and right (yaw, y-axis) and up and down (pitch, x-axis) and pivot their head from left and right (roll, z-axis). True VR provides six degrees of freedom (6DoF) experiences in which the users are not stationary, and they can move through 3D space. In addition to yaw, pitch, and roll, users can now move left to right (sway, x-axis), up and down (heave, y-axis), and forward and backward (surge, z-axis) through a simulated space. When coupled with stereo-scopic imagery and spatial audio, 6DoF will provide a realistic experience and a sense of presence while inside VR.

AR is a technology that overlays digital information, such as text, images, videos, or 3D models, onto the real world. This information can be accessed through a device such as a smartphone or tablet or through specialized AR glasses. Audi's next-generation SUV has an interactive 3D AR display that replaces the automobile's conventional control panel. It works with AR glasses that superimpose critical navigation information in real time to the driver. Passengers wearing the AR glasses can "browse the web, adjust the interior temperature, or control the music," while eye-tracking technology determines when a passenger is focused on a specific part of the console, which will then provide more detailed information. A passenger's hand gestures are used to interact with the virtual controls.[2]

MR is a more advanced form of AR that merges virtual elements with the real world. This can be achieved using special cameras and sensors that map the user's environment and integrate digital objects into it. All of this is achieved using HMDs or projection systems, allowing users to experience a more seamless blend of the virtual and real worlds while creating an immersive and interactive experience in which digital objects now can appear as if they are a part of the real world.

These XR technologies are gaining traction and are expected to be used in various industries in the future, including entertainment, gaming, education, health care, architecture, and design. And with the evolution of haptic feedback and other sensations occurring via smart fabric (e.g., gloves, bodysuits, etc.), coupled with eye/hand/body tracking, users will have a more responsive tactile experience inside these immersive environments, whether they are AR, VR, MR, or a combination of all of these. This may eventually make it difficult to tell the difference between the digital world and the real world.

What Is the Metaverse?

In 1992 *Snow Crash*, written by Neal Stephenson, introduced the "metaverse" concept. In the book, Hiro Protagonist is a hacker who moves between dystopian Los Angeles and a virtual world called the metaverse to collect all kinds of information, including gossip, videos, audio, data, and documents to then upload to the CIC database, which was originally the Library of Congress. Today the metaverse is a term used to describe a virtual shared space that usually requires Internet connectivity where users can interact with one another as avatars (i.e., digital representations of people) and engage with digital objects in a 3D environment. Ready Player Me is a popular service that creates full-body 3D avatars that can be connected to approximately 100 metaverse applications, such as HiberWorld, Spatial, Atom Universe, VRChat, Immersed, and DeepMotion. Developers using Unity, Unreal Engine, Godot, and other 3D design engines are animating avatars inside virtual spaces to be integrated into various applications and games.

It will not be too far into the future when society starts to see library chat reference and other services using these avatars—which will be powered by artificial intelligence (AI) applications like ChatGPT—incorporate realistic dialogue and other virtual interactions with library users. A few metaverse companies are

Ready Player Me avatar

offering free tools, like Spatial's Creator Toolkit, to build immersive, interactive, and beautiful 3D spaces for these avatars to use. To truly become a "meta"verse, however, there must be a simple way for people (avatars included) to traverse through various VR/MR/AR platforms without being forced to enter, for example, a VR version of Minecraft's metaverse, then enter into an MR version of Microsoft's metaverse, or into an AR version of Amazon's metaverse, and so on. To learn more about interoperability standards for an open metaverse, visit the Metaverse Standards Forum at metaverse-standards.org.

On October 28, 2021 Facebook changed its name to Meta to reflect its new mission, which is to go beyond traditional social media and move into a decentralized "Web 3.0" metaverse platform. Web 3.0 is an umbrella term that includes technologies like blockchain, non-fungible tokens (NFTs), and cryptocurrencies, and it promises to reclaim the Internet from tech giants like Microsoft, Google, and Apple. Mark Zuckerberg, CEO of Meta, uses the term "embodied Internet" for his version of the metaverse, where he imagines a platform that resembles Facebook's ecosystem, but instead of scrolling and looking at content, users will feel as if they are surrounded by various media that was uploaded to Meta.[3]

It is vital to consider how companies and other institutions will handle the metaverse, since society is currently seeing a growing problem with misinformation spreading throughout a variety of social media platforms. This problem will continue to grow exponentially with the popularity of applications like ChatGPT, plus, it is not too difficult to predict how the metaverse will be misused once human-like avatars and digital content look photorealistic. It will not be all bad, however. The metaverse can have therapeutic benefits to help relieve PTSD, anxiety, and pain. For instance, there are programs for burn victims at the University of Washington, women in labor at Cedars-Sinai Medical Center, and others that have all shown that VR can help ease pain once patients can connect with friends and family members in a shared VR space to comfort one another.[4]

Going further, a metaverse platform can provide simulations, good and bad, to demonstrate different experiences that many people have never endured. As a result, a simulation can help foster empathy to develop or strengthen one's moral identity and offer ways for people to examine their own personal values. There is an exhibit at the National Center for Civil and Human Rights where people receive racist jeers and violent threats. It is this type of experience that, again, can provide an empathetic view to help people understand how horrible things can be for others. These types of simulations can help people gain perspective in their own lives and perhaps make a change for the better in other people's lives.

The metaverse is expected to become mainstream in the future, as advancements in VR, AR, MR, and AI continue to improve. Video games and platforms like Minecraft, Fortnite, and Roblox coupled with other virtual places, such as Decentraland, Activeworlds, and Second Life, are essentially building blocks for the metaverse. Interestingly, there are many young kids who are well-versed in this technology, and they will expect these types of environments as they develop into adulthood.

Louis Rosenberg, a pioneer in the fields of AR, VR, and AI, says the metaverse will transform the way we interact with information and that it will remove content from our screens to fit more naturally into our world. People will be able to arrange information to be more conducive to the way they want to perceive it. The world now becomes an interface. It may resemble Weinbaum's notion in which third-person media will become first-person immersive experiences. In other words, the viewer will become the participant. Rosenberg purports that by 2040, AR smart glasses will eventually replace the smartphone as the primary way that people access digital content.[5] Once the metaverse matures, it will resemble the 1990s, when people could start texting anyone no matter what cellphone model they used or what their network provider was. Text messaging is now ubiquitous and device-agnostic. The metaverse will be too.

Why Should We Care?

Although the metaverse concept is still in its infancy, there are many reasons why librarians and other information professionals should care about or at least pay attention to its developments. The metaverse has the potential to revolutionize the way we access, consume, and create educational content. It can provide new and immersive ways for students to interact with course materials. It can offer opportunities for collaboration and community-building, which can help enhance the primary mission of libraries around the world. Students can participate in virtual field trips, attend virtual classes and lectures, and interact with educational

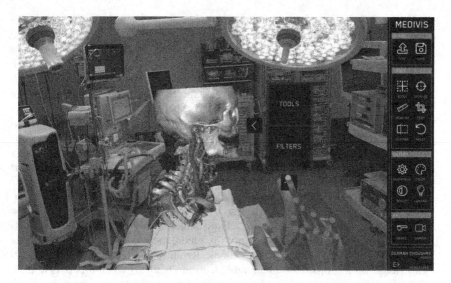

AnatomyX's shared AR learning experience

simulations and games from the comfort of their classrooms or living rooms, with no time or location restrictions.

In time, the metaverse is expected to provide a new dimension for learning while allowing users to experience new ways to fully interact with educational content, offering expanded access to education, and fostering collaboration and community-building among students, educators, and experts in a variety of fields. Research has shown that XR technologies and simulations help deliver experiential and more meaningful learning. In fact, a study showed that 78 percent of student participants preferred VR learning to desktop and hands-on learning, and when describing their reasoning, they used phrases such as VR content was "easier to visualize" and "more realistic," and the lessons were "more immersive," "more fun," "more interesting," and the "most accurate."[6]

We live in a 3D world, but our content supporting various curricula usually only reflects that reality in two dimensions (2D). Reading about a sculpture in a traditional article or research paper, for instance, could be more realistic if a digital 3D scan of the sculpture was embedded into the paper so a user with an appropriate device (e.g., smartphone, tablet, etc.) could lift the 3D object off the page and display it in its actual size into one's physical space instead of viewing a small 2D image copied into the paper. This would give viewers a more realistic view of the sculpture while allowing them to engage more closely with it. Close to 150 years ago, it was like magic to use a camera to capture the 3D world in a realistic 2D image.

Today this is changing. Luma AI is an application that utilizes neural radiance fields (NeRF) to train a neural network to reconstruct objects by converting 2D images into photorealistic 3D scenes without the need to know how to code or to have expensive graphics processing units (GPUs) to do the intense processing.[7] Luma AI does not require high-end LiDAR (light detection and ranging) sensors to capture the objects, so older phones without those sensors can also use the technology to ultimately generate environments and objects for the metaverse and other mediums like high-end video game assets and CGI technologies used in movies. To see an example of aerial drone footage captured using Luma AI's photogrammetry function, which was later processed in the cloud using NeRF technology, visit https://bit.ly/3Y11uM6. Perhaps one day this technology will replace traditional photographs. Regardless, society is now scratching the surface of an exciting new dimension of learning and experience.

AnatomyX, an AR anatomy lab and learning platform, gives students learning experiences that they will not soon forget. Students can interact with various segments of 3D digital anatomy, pull them apart, utilize eye-tracking technology to label the parts while gazing at them, and ultimately see how the body part connects to other systems. This is amazing technology that integrates into course management systems and has embedded assessments, note-taking features, narration, voice, gesture controls, and more.

For this writer, interacting with a large skeleton or some part of human anatomy in an AR application like AnatomyX is a more memorable learning experience than simply reading about it in a textbook. Reading is vital to gain fundamental knowledge on a subject, but memorable learning happens when it occurs in multiple modalities (e.g., visual, auditory, reading/writing, and kinesthetic). Knowing that numerous industries are already using this technology and that many others are on the cusp of using it is important. Libraries are centers for learning. As a result, being able to offer exposure to emerging technologies like the metaverse will help society be prepared for this new world when it fully arrives.

What Will the Future Bring?

Digital twins are like avatars in that they represent exact replicas of physical objects. This technology is being used to help businesses and institutions simulate various processes and product development before they go into production. It saves money and resources to understand how, for example, a factory will function before it is physically built. Moreover, people can virtually walk inside a digital twin and gain a 6DoF perspective of a particular structure while making important decisions before it becomes real. AR technology is also being used to showcase the power of digital twins in which anchored virtual objects can be connected to markers strategically placed around a building to provide interactivity around a physical space. Across the United States, society is seeing declining enrollment and rising tuition, so some universities are partnering with VictoryXR, Meta, and others to use XR technologies to create digital twin campuses or "metaversities" to make online classes more immersive. A student cannot "tear apart a car engine in Zoom," but it is possible in a metaversity.[8]

Imagine reading a book while having an actual conversation with the author and various characters. These characters could start to physically appear right off the page, weaving their ideas and themes in and out of the text and providing more context about the story. In addition to discussing the book's content, this new textual dimension could start to reveal relevant imagery/sounds/smells/tactiles and other senses to float off the pages to bring the story or curriculum into real life like the previously mentioned "magical spectacles" in *Pygmalion's Spectacles.*

Touring a digital twin in VR using the Enscape Architecture plugin

Imagining this today is surreal, but it could be something that is common years from now, especially when XR technologies become more robust and are embedded into the small form factor of eyeglasses and maybe even contact lenses. One day, society may see the metaverse as indistinguishable from reality, and the metaverse becomes a natural part of our lives. Again, we have entered a new dimension of learning and experience, and it is certainly exciting. We all need to be prepared for the time when it arrives.

[Author's Note: *The metaverse has many possibilities for libraries and our society, but the technology is quickly evolving. A "living document" was created to help readers stay up-to-date. It is available at https://bit.ly/3HUOp1j.*]

Notes

1. Stanley G. Weinbaum, *Pygmalion's Spectacles*. Start Publishing, LLC. (2016).
2. Kyle Melnick, "Audi's EV Concept Features Support for AR Glasses." VRScout, (Feb. 1, 2023). https://vrscout.com/news/audis-ev-concept-features-support-for-ar-glasses.
3. John David N. Dionisio, "The Metaverse Could Actually Help People." MIT Technology Review. https://www.technologyreview.com/2021/10/27/1036817/metaverse-facebook-virtual-reality-augmented.
4. Ibid.
5. Louis Rosenberg, "A Better Vision of the Metaverse." https://www.barrons.com/articles/metaverse-dead-ar-augmented-reality-51668188175.
6. J. Madden, et al., "Ready Student One: Exploring the Predictors of Student Learning in Virtual Reality." *PLOS ONE*, vol. 15, no. 3, (March 2020). e0229788. PLOS Journals, https://doi.org/10.1371/journal.pone.0229788.
7. Alan Truly, "I Used an App to Create Incredible 3D Models with My iPhone." Digital Trends, (Nov. 2. 2022). https://www.digitaltrends.com/mobile/luma-ai-iphone-app-create-3d-models-hands-on-review.
8. Bob Violino, "Digital Twins Are Set for Rapid Adoption in 2023." CNBC. https://www.cnbc.com/2023/01/21/digital-twins-are-set-for-rapid-adoption-in-2023.html.

Federal Agency and Federal Library Reports

Library of Congress

10 First St., S.E., Washington, DC 20540
202-707-5000
https://loc.gov

Carla Hayden
Librarian of Congress

The Library of Congress is the largest library in the world. Its mission is to engage, inspire, and inform the U.S. Congress and the American people with a universal and enduring source of knowledge and creativity.

Highlights of 2022

In fiscal year (FY) 2022 the Library of Congress:

- Recorded 174 total petabytes of digital storage in use. The material on the Library's websites alone totals more than 5.3 petabytes.
- Recorded 151.6 million visits to Library of Congress websites
- Recorded 520.3 million webpage views
- Recorded 74 million visits to loc.gov
- Welcomed 370,000 visitors to the historic Jefferson Building
- Circulated more than 22.3 million copies of braille, audio, and large print items to patrons via the National Library Service for the Blind and Print Disabled (NLS) and its network of state and local libraries
- Issued 484,589 copyright registrations and recorded 14,714 documents containing more than 1.1 million works
- Employed 3,172 permanent staff members
- Circulated 243,662 collection items for use inside and outside the Library
- Performed 8.7 million preservation actions on items in the Library's physical collections, with a further 5.7 million pages of materials prepared and shipped to vendors for preservation reformatting services
- Placed 5.9 million items under inventory control in the Library's preservation facility at Fort Meade and more than 2.4 million at the Cabin Branch facility

- Operated with an $838.9 million total budget authority, including $794.019 million in appropriations and $44.974 million in offsetting receipts authority

The Library recorded more than 175.77 million items in its collections, including:

- 25.49 million cataloged books in the Library of Congress Classification system
- 15.87 million items in the nonclassified print collections
- 134.4 million items in the nonclassified (special) collections, consisting of:
  - 4.2 million audio materials
  - 77 million manuscripts
  - 5.8 million maps
  - 17.5 million microforms
  - 8.2 million items of sheet music
  - 1.8 million moving images
  - 15.2 million photographs
  - 864,674 posters, prints, and drawings
  - 1.4 million other
  - 2 million other (including machine-readable items)

Serving Congress

The Library of Congress was established in 1800 to provide resources to members of Congress for use in their work. The Joint Committee on the Library—the oldest continuing joint committee of Congress—was created through legislation in 1802, providing for congressional oversight. The unique collaboration between Congress and the Library has allowed them to serve the nation together for 220-plus years.

In FY 2022 the Library supported members of Congress, their staffs, and constituents in a variety of ways, such as providing reference, research, and analysis on key issues and supplying surplus books to congressional districts.

Legislative Support

The Congressional Research Service (CRS) in the Library serves Congress with the highest-quality research, analysis, information, and confidential consultation to support the exercise of its legislative, representational, and oversight duties in its role as a coequal branch of government. The work of CRS is authoritative, confidential, objective, nonpartisan, and timely. CRS examines pressing legislative issues facing Congress; identifies and assesses policy options; and provides analysis, consultation, and briefings to support Congress throughout the legislative process across the full range of public policy issues.

In FY 2022 CRS responded to more than 73,000 congressional requests. It published nearly 1,100 new products and performed more than 1,900 updates to existing products. More than 8,300 congressional participants attended the 309 webinars offered by CRS during FY 2022.

Congress established the Law Library of Congress in 1832 with the mission of making its resources available to Congress and the U.S. Supreme Court—a mission that expanded to include other branches of government and the global legal community. Librarians and foreign law specialists respond to congressional inquiries about U.S., foreign, comparative, and international legal and legislative research, drawing upon the world's largest collection of legal resources. The collection comprises 2.91 million bound volumes, 3.25 million microforms, 16,100 tangible electronic resources (CD-ROMs and other discs), and 3.9 million digital files.

In FY 2022 the Law Library's Public Services Division and two Foreign, Comparative, and International Law divisions responded to 289 research requests from Congress and legislative branch agencies and provided assistance to congressional offices on 863 reference questions. In total, the Law Library provided 1,152 responses to congressional offices and legislative branch agencies. The Law Library's reference librarians assist congressional staffers any time either chamber of Congress is in session, no matter the hour.

The Researcher and Reference Services Division received and processed more than 12,900 requests for material from members of Congress and congressional staff members during FY 2022. Requests for e-books made up more than half of the requests, with the remaining being physical collection items. Collections Management Division (CMD) staff members serving on Capitol Hill continued to provide on-site support throughout the pandemic to ensure materials were properly charged and delivered to congressional offices.

Library experts provided direct briefings as requested by congressional members and their staffs, on topics such as Internet access, health care and health insurance demographics, redistricting, and social and economic inequity. Other special programs and presentations requested by members of Congress included those on reading room services, European regulation of digital assets, African American genealogical research, and the history of voting rights.

Copyright Law and Policy

The Copyright Claims Board (CCB) opened its doors in June 2022, offering a cheaper, faster alternative to federal court litigation for copyright claims up to $30,000. In 18 months the Copyright Office finalized CCB's entire regulatory framework; completed all hiring; and established an electronic filing and case management system, virtual hearing facilities, and office space. The Copyright Office also produced online materials about CCB, including ccb.gov, a user handbook, educational videos, and FAQs.

The Copyright Office continued its implementation of the Copyright Alternative in Small-Claims Enforcement (CASE) Act of 2020 and provided support and assistance to Congress on various copyright matters. Register Shira Perlmutter testified twice at congressional hearings in FY 2022, and the office supported members of Congress in response to research requests, including on matters related to the Digital Millennium Copyright Act (DMCA) and the Music Modernization Act (MMA).

The Senate requested a study of the effectiveness of current copyright protections for press publishers in the United States. The office held a public roundtable, collected comments, and published a report. It recommended against adopting new copyright protections, since press publishers have significant protections under existing law and the challenges of funding journalism in the Internet era do not appear to be copyright-specific.

The Copyright Office continues work on a Senate request to convene a working group "to achieve the identification and implementation of technical measures" to address technologies for identifying or protecting copyrighted works. As part of a separate Senate request, the Copyright Office sought comments on the interpretation of Section 512(i) of the DMCA and the advisability of potential changes to the "standard technical measures" definition.

The Copyright Office and the World Intellectual Property Organization co-hosted the International Copyright Institute the week of September 26, 2022. Participants from 23 countries came to Washington, D.C., to discuss emerging copyright issues in the digital age.

The Copyright Office closed or issued interim rules in eight rulemaking proceedings, including on digital music providers' reporting requirements under the MMA, the operations of the CCB, and financial matters involving deposits and remitter payments.

The Copyright Office advised the Department of Justice (DOJ) regarding *Andy Warhol Foundation v. Goldsmith*, a pending Supreme Court case considering the application of the Fair Use doctrine as codified in Section 107 of the Copyright Act. The office responded to five requests from district courts to advise whether inaccurate information on an application for registration, if known, would have caused registration to be refused. At the same time, the office assisted DOJ on two cases brought under the Administrative Procedures Act stemming from copyright registration refusals and continued to advise the government in defenses against constitutional challenges to the Copyright Act involving the mandatory deposit requirement and the anti-circumvention provisions.

The Copyright Office collaborated with executive branch agencies on foreign copyright law and policy, including by participating in World Intellectual Property Organization meetings and assisting in preparing the U.S. trade representative's Special 301 Report as well as World Trade Organization trade policy reviews and accessions.

Congressional Preservation Efforts

The Library leads several major preservation initiatives at the behest of Congress to capture and preserve American history and culture for generations to come. Congress passed the National Film Preservation Act of 1988 and the National Recording Preservation Act of 2000 to ensure preservation of the nation's audiovisual heritage. This legislation directs the Librarian of Congress to select "culturally, historically or aesthetically" significant films and sound recordings, respectively, for the National Film Registry and National Recording Registry. To date, the Librarian has selected 825 films and 600 sound recordings for preservation.

In FY 2022, to fulfill mandates in their congressional authorizing legislation, the National Film Preservation Board and the National Recording Preservation Board continued multiyear initiatives to award select starter grants to aid preservation, access, and diversity projects at archives throughout the nation, including the Library. The film board funded a report on the Library's pre-1915 film holdings and several fieldwide projects through the Association of Moving

Image Archivists, including a professional mentorship pilot program and Preservation for Filmmakers webinars. The recording board funded enhancements of the Discography of American Historical Recordings website at the University of California–Santa Barbara, as well as six continuing education webinars with the Association for Recorded Sound Collections.

Established by Congress in 2000, the Veterans History Project (VHP) in the Library's American Folklife Center preserves the memories of those in our nation's armed services who served from World War I through recent conflicts. In October 2021 the Congressional Relations Office (CRO) facilitated a virtual event to introduce VHP to congressional staff. More than 70 members and committee staffers attended the event, which prompted several offices to request individual briefings.

During FY 2022 VHP made 2,255 new acquisitions and now holds more than 114,000 collections from veterans across the nation, including 207 collected under the Gold Star Family Voice Act. In addition, VHP worked with more than 55 congressional offices to promote the project in members' home states and create special video messages featuring the Librarian of Congress.

Congressional Relations Office (CRO)

CRO is the Library's primary point of contact for members of Congress. It responds to congressional inquiries about Library collections, programs, legislative activities, operations, and facilities and informs Congress about Library events and programs.

CRO prepares testimony, briefings, fact sheets, program analysis, and general advice in support of Library officials' meetings with members or testimony at hearings. It also keeps senior management apprised of congressional actions that impact Library programs and operations.

During FY 2022 CRO fully resumed on-site services for Congress, while continuing digital delivery of resources, services, and programming that began during the COVID-19 pandemic. CRO successfully handled more than 14,000 communications (phone calls and emails) in addressing routine congressional requests and business; delivered more than 250,000 targeted outreach emails to congressional offices; facilitated 25 meetings or calls between the Librarian of Congress and members of Congress; provided nearly 200 special tours and live or virtual viewings of collections; and hosted 82 live and 12 virtual congressional events.

CRO coordinated and staffed frequent briefings on Library business for members and congressional staff, including 59 meetings or policy conversations held during FY 2022. Briefing topics included restoration of Library operations; major Library buildings and grounds projects, such as the Visitors Experience Master Plan; CRS core services and mission; agencywide and Copyright Office IT modernization; and many others.

CRO drafted testimony for the Librarian of Congress and staffed and prepared witnesses for the Library, Copyright Office, CRS, and NLS for an October 2021 hearing on information technology modernization before the Senate Rules and Administration Committee. CRO provided hearing preparation to the Financial Services Directorate during the House and Senate appropriations hearings held during the spring and summer.

In FY 2022 the Library resumed the Congressional Dialogue Dinner series and continued the new CRO Virtual Lunchtime Lectures for its congressional users. CRO hosted four dinners, averaging 90 members of Congress in attendance per dinner. The 15 Lunchtime Lectures events attracted a total audience of more than 1,600 members of Congress and congressional staff, with discussions of the war in Ukraine (118 attendees) and the return to on-site operations at the Library (98 attendees) most attended.

In FY 2022 the CRO website recorded more than 9,000 page views through the promotion of Library events and resources such as book loans, digital services, and educational programs. Further, the website was updated in FY 2022 to include enhanced search features, thereby making it easier for staff members to discover, access, and reuse content from loc.gov related to their state.

Supporting the Library

The Consolidated Appropriations Act of 2022 (P.L. 117-103), signed on March 15, 2022, provided the Library with a total budget authority of $838.992 million for FY 2022, including $794.019 million in appropriations and $44.974 million in offsetting receipts authority. The Library operated under four continuing resolutions (CR) at previous FY 2021 funding levels. CR funding was provided from October 1, 2021, to December 3, 2021; December 4, 2021, to February 18, 2022; February 19, 2022, to March 11, 2022; and March 12, 2022, to March 15, 2022. Total Library budget authority increased approximately 4.6 percent over FY 2022 and continued a multiyear strategic modernization in many areas.

New initiatives funded for the Library of Congress included $4.4 million for 5G cellular technology upgrades, $4.4 million for an Integrated Electronic Security System, $6.5 million for the Library Collections Access Platform, and $2.6 million for Microsoft 365 migration. Additionally, the Library received the final $10 million installment to support the Visitor Experience Master Plan initiative, bringing the total federal investment in the project to $40 million. Funding also continued support for VHP ($3.8 million), the Teaching with Primary Sources program ($9.6 million), the surplus books program ($250,000), and the Legislative Branch Financial Management System ($1.4 million).

Librarian of Congress Carla Hayden testified about the Library's FY 2023 budget request on April 27 and May 11, 2022, before the House and Senate Appropriations Subcommittees, respectively. The FY 2023 budget requested to advance public engagement, staff expertise, and modernization of the Library's information technology systems and financial infrastructure. It proposed an increase of $32.8 million, or 3.9 percent, over enacted funding levels for FY 2022, including $24.4 million for new initiatives. These initiatives, Hayden testified, are necessary for the Library to continue to fulfill its mission.

The Library began FY 2023 under a series of continuing resolutions operating at 2022 funding levels, from October 1, 2022, to December 16, 2022; December 17, 2022, to December 23, 2022; and December 24, 2022, to December 30, 2022. The Consolidated Appropriations Act of 2023 (P.L. 117-328) was signed on December. 30, 2022, providing the Library a total budget authority of $875.46 million for FY 2023, including $828.548 million in appropriations and $46.912 million in offsetting receipts authority.

The Library of Congress Trust Fund Board, created in 1925 by an act of Congress, acted as trustee of private funds invested for the benefit of the Library. Its work supports Library literacy programs, exhibitions, acquisitions, scholarly programs and fellowships, concerts, and initiatives.

Restoration of On-Site Operations

More than two years after it closed to the public because of the COVID-19 pandemic, the Library of Congress completed the full restoration of on-site operations on April 11, 2022.

In May 2020, two months into the pandemic, Library administrators announced a multiphase plan to restore on-site operations that would unfold over the next 22 months—employees would gradually return to Library facilities, more work would resume on-site, and reading rooms and exhibitions would reopen. By July 2020 a limited number of staff members began coming to Library facilities on staggered schedules to resume priority activities, such as processing physical collections and responding to congressional loan requests.

But the Library remained quiet, even after phase two of operations restoration began in August and service units identified additional work requiring on-site access. Staff presence gradually increased, but those who could do most of their work remotely continued to do so. Operations continued on this basis for months, as virus variants emerged and Library administrators assessed the safety of bringing more staff on-site.

Then, in June 2021, with COVID-19 indicators improving, some reading rooms opened to researchers—the first step toward resumption of on-site public services. Pandemic protocols, including masking and social distancing, applied in reading rooms, and researchers were required to make appointments to visit to reduce COVID transmission. By mid-July all but one of the 20 reading rooms were open and serving researchers by appointment. Other major milestones included the reopening of public exhibitions on July 15, 2021, and the hosting of a National Book Festival event in the Coolidge Auditorium on September 21—the first public event at the Library in more than a year and a half.

The efforts to reopen culminated on April 11, 2022, when all Library employees were required to report on-site—for some, their first time back in Library buildings in over two years. That day also marked the beginning of new hybrid work schedules that allowed a mix of telework and work in the office—many employees were eligible to telework between one and four days a week. Under the "new normal" of the post-pandemic workplace, 67 percent of staff teleworked, compared to 43 percent before the pandemic.

Collections

The Library of Congress is both the nation's library and the largest library in the world. The institution's vast collections encompass virtually all formats, languages, and subjects. It is perhaps the most comprehensive accumulation of human knowledge ever assembled.

In FY 2022 the Library's collections grew to more than 175.77 million items. Acquisitions came into the Library through a variety of methods and in many formats. The U.S. Copyright Office transferred 626,595 works, with an estimated value of nearly $48 million, to the Library's collections during FY 2022. The Library received more than 468,386 works transferred through mandatory deposit. A total of 257,070 tangible items acquired through transfer—including 75,150 print books, 78,078 print serial issues, 2,762 films, and 13,580 sound recordings—were selected for the permanent collections based on the Library's collection-development policies. The Library also received 87,500 e-serial issues via eDeposits and 43,293 e-books through the Cataloging-in-Publication Program.

The Acquisitions and Bibliographic Access Directorate (ABA) acquired 1,178,121 items for the Library's collections through cost-effective methods, including purchase and exchange. It also facilitated the acquisition of 1,712,514 collection items through gifts to the Special Collections Directorate. Factoring in additional acquisitions, through means such as transfers from other government agencies, the Library's collections increased by more than 3 million items in FY 2022.

The Library has six overseas offices, located in Cairo, Islamabad, Jakarta, Nairobi, New Delhi, and Rio de Janeiro. These offices acquire, catalog, preserve, and distribute library and research materials from regions where such materials are largely unavailable through conventional acquisitions methods. Along with their acquisitions for the Library, the overseas offices in FY 2022 also acquired 188,873 collection items, on a cost-recovery basis, for the more than 100 U.S. libraries participating in the Cooperative Acquisitions Program.

During FY 2022 the web archiving team continued to provide project management and technical support for the acquisition of content for the Library's web archives, spanning collections from 20 Library units. During FY 2022 647.73 terabytes of data were acquired, processed, and added, bringing the total held in the web archives to 3.474 petabytes. Fourteen new web archive collections were proposed, approved, and initiated, bringing the number of active event and thematic archives managed by the web archiving team during FY 2022 to 88.

The team made significant advancements to increase web archives literacy and engagement among the Library's staff. The team developed and launched a new workflow for collection curators to perform quality analysis of the web archive, ensuring a usable and accessible archive. It launched a "getting started" training for Library staff who are new to web archiving.

Collection Development

The Collection Development Office (CDO) supports the Library's strategic goal of acquiring and maintaining a universal collection of knowledge and the record of America's creativity to meet the needs of Congress, researchers, and the American public. It ensures that the Library's physical and digital collections reflect the breadth and depth of knowledge published in all media, languages, and regions of the world.

CDO continued its program to review and update, on a cyclical basis, the Library's collections policy statements and associated supplementary guidelines. Work was completed on 10 documents, including the creation of new social media supplementary guidelines. During the year standard text regarding diverse and inclusive collecting was added, as appropriate, to all collections policy statements and supplementary guidelines. The office continued its general collections assessment program, completing analyses of segments covering U.S. history, naval science, political science, education, military science, and psychology.

Implementation of the Library's new digital collections strategy for 2022–2026 began, led by CDO in partnership with the Digital Services Directorate. This plan incorporates the full life cycle of born-digital materials, from acquisition to preservation and user access, and aligns with the goals prioritized within the Library's strategic plan. During FY 2022 13 targeted actions were undertaken and completed, including pilot work on making Copyright Office registration electronic deposits available to the Library's users and initial steps toward transitioning acquisitions to an electronic-preferred model. In addition, outreach to Library staff and the public about aspects of the digital collections strategy was accomplished.

CMD coordinated the development of the next Library of Congress digitization strategy with a wide range of stakeholders across the institution. This new strategy will guide work to digitize the Library's collections for FY 2023 to FY 2027. As a result of this strategy, the Library will significantly expand online access to a wide range of rare, unique, or distinctive material. By implementing a more systematic approach to analysis of collections, this strategy will enable the Library to determine the resourcing necessary for an even more ambitious future digitization agenda.

Preservation

The Library's mission to provide a "universal and enduring" record of knowledge and creativity guides the work of the Preservation Directorate, which ensures that the Library's historical artifacts and collections remain available in the evolving array of formats needed by users today and in the future. The directorate uses established technologies, practices, and procedures to address risks to these materials and engages in fundamental research to explore new approaches to preserve and enhance our knowledge of Library collections.

The directorate is responsible for millions of preservation actions each year in stewardship of the national collection. Expert staff members perform preventative and corrective treatments and transfer information from obsolete or at-risk media into new formats. They manage secure, environmentally optimized storage facilities and maintain inventory control, enabling the fulfillment of thousands of loans each year to support Congress and serve researchers around the world. The directorate is a center for fundamental research and education, and its insights and innovations set standards and enhance preservation and conservation practices worldwide.

In FY 2022 the directorate performed 8.7 million preservation actions on books, serials, prints, photographs, manuscripts, and other items, with a further 5.7 million pages of materials prepared and shipped to vendors for preservation reformatting services. During FY 2022 113,151 items received new library bindings; 26,471 were treated or repaired in conservation labs; protective containers or housings were provided for 21,185 items; and 54,053 volumes were deacidified. Staff members surveyed the preservation needs of 453,559 items from the general and special collections, monitored 200 environmental data loggers, and continued to play a key role in the Library's security and emergency response programs.

Reformatting is a critical process that ensures the long-term availability of informational content on original media at risk of deterioration, and reformatting via digital transformation was an important focus during FY 2022. The directorate reformatted more than 1.9 million pages, including 818,784 digitized from custodial divisions and 1,006,329 microfilmed from overseas offices.

Off-Site and On-Site Storage

CMD is responsible for safekeeping Library collections through inventory control, storage, and delivery of resources to fulfill user requests. The division operates the general collections stacks on Capitol Hill and off-site preservation storage facilities for all collections. CMD provides the inventory-control systems that ensure items are retrievable; logistics and fulfillment services to deliver materials to their point of use; and chain-of-custody systems to record usage, account for materials while in use, and track the return of materials after use for long-term maintenance.

The Library reached a milestone in its collections-storage program with the opening of Fort Meade Module 6 in late summer of FY 2021 and the subsequent closure of the Landover Center Annex, achieved several months ahead of schedule. Module 6 is the Library's largest storage module to date, providing about 25,000 square feet of secure, high-density, and environmentally optimized storage. By the end of FY 2022 CMD had reached a Module 6 fill rate of 36 percent, including 414,751 trackable items in storage.

CMD continued to prepare and transfer collections material from Capitol Hill to off-site locations at Fort Meade and Cabin Branch. During FY 2022 the division transferred more than 507,341 items into storage across all sites. The transfer process requires the creation of bibliographic and/or inventory records for reassignment of special format materials; stabilization actions, including the removal of acidic enclosures, rehousing, and the creation of finding aids for collections; and accession and verification of items before they are physically moved off-site.

CMD was active in planning for major space and storage projects throughout the year. Several renovation projects will support the Visitor Experience Master Plan project and help provide emergency egress paths. CMD also provided key subject-matter expertise in planning for Fort Meade Module 7, a storage facility to address critical stacks-availability limitations on Capitol Hill.

Newspapers

The National Digital Newspaper Program, jointly sponsored by the Library and the National Endowment for the Humanities (NEH), supports the enhancement of access to American newspapers. Through partnerships, cultural heritage institutions select and digitize representative newspapers from their states or territories for contribution to the Chronicling America collection. In 2022 NEH funded the program's 50th state, New Hampshire.

In FY 2022 the Chronicling America collection recorded 39.4 million page views and 4.3 million visits and celebrated reaching 20 million pages. The collection includes 2,730,873 issues of 3,803 titles from 48 states, two territories, and the District of Columbia. Other publicly available digitized newspaper collections received 1.3 million page views and 721,233 visits.

Audiovisual Collections

The Packard Campus of the National Audio-Visual Conservation Center, located in Culpeper, Virginia, houses the Library's recorded sound and moving image collections—the world's largest and most comprehensive.

In FY 2022 the Moving Image Section acquired 27,970 analog items, 16,983 of which were received by transfer from other Library divisions. The largest purchase was 6,997 reels of film consisting primarily of American features and shorts acquired from Film Archives, Inc. The section also acquired 14,822 born-digital items, 5,256 files via direct transfer from the Senate, 1,030 files from the House recording studio of committee hearings, and 5,694 files from the Vanderbilt Television News Archive. In addition, on December 14, 2021 the Librarian of Congress named 25 films to the National Film Registry, bringing the total to 825.

The Recorded Sound Section is committed to building and enhancing a collection of commercial and noncommercial recordings in all formats from all periods. In FY 2022 the section acquired 40,185 physical audio recordings, 47,325 manuscript items, and 2,912 born-digital recordings. On April 13, 2022 the Librarian announced the addition of 25 sound recordings to the National Recording Registry, bringing the total to 600.

Access

The Library makes its multiformat collections publicly available in its multiple reading rooms and research centers on Capitol Hill; at the Packard Campus for Audio-Visual Conservation in Culpeper, Virginia; and through its website. The library provides discoverability and accessibility to all Library collections by supplying descriptive information (metadata) in English and other languages. These collections are from countries and languages around the world and are accessible through digitization and other technologies.

In FY 2022 the Library's Center for Learning, Literacy and Engagement (CLLE) navigated the challenges of expanding visitation access to the public following the COVID-19 pandemic closures. Public access resumed in July 2021, and in FY 2022 the Library safely welcomed more than 370,000 visitors to the historic Thomas Jefferson Building. After building capacity limits and mask requirements were lifted in the third quarter, the Library returned to normal operations for the visiting public. Beginning in April 2022 5,000 free timed-entry passes were made available to the public each open day, including 1,000 same-day passes for walk-up visitors.

Reference Services

Starting in April 2022 Library reading rooms resumed full service, with appointments encouraged but no longer required, mask wearing optional, and six-foot physical distancing no longer required. The Library continued to require individuals to "avoid close contact," to conduct self-health screening before coming to the Library, and to wash their hands frequently.

Library staff members responded to a total of 143,141 reference requests during FY 2022, including 92,551 requests received online, via email, and through services such as Ask a Librarian. A total of 36,164 reader cards were issued, of which 30,490 were to new readers. The Library circulated 221,067 physical items on-site in FY 2022. More than 50,055 items were circulated off-site to authorized borrowers, and other items were circulated to on-site researchers and staff.

In order to ensure congressional access to collections stored off-site, CMD staff remained available to retrieve material from the Fort Meade and Cabin Branch facilities. Members of Congress and congressional staff members received 5,041 items during FY 2022.

Cataloging

The Library managed 55,063,305 MARC records in its integrated library system. It cataloged 226,551 new works during the year in addition to 1,079,325 manuscript items on 137 bibliographic records. The Cataloging-in-Publication program cataloged 104,263 titles, and the Electronic Cataloging-in-Publication E-book Program prepared cataloging in advance of publication for 43,293 e-books. The Library established 133,261 name authorities, 16,223 subject headings, and 7,105 new Library of Congress Classification numbers.

During the year, the Library's curatorial divisions created 97 new Encoded Archival Description finding aids, bringing the total number of researcher-accessible archival items in the Library's collections to nearly 80 million.

Under contract to the Dewey Program, which supports libraries worldwide that classify their titles in Dewey Decimal Classification, the Library assigned Dewey classification to 124,914 titles.

Bibliographic Framework Initiative

The BIBFRAME initiative began in FY 2011 as a replacement for the cataloging metadata standard known as MARC 21. In FY 2022 the BIBFRAME cataloging pilot continued with 100 participants from all cataloging divisions and four overseas offices. BIBFRAME progress accelerated throughout the year by adding 14,828 descriptions to the publicly shared MARVA Editor database. The pilot increased production through ongoing improvements to the input/update interface of MARVA, the BIBFRAME Editor, and the BIBFRAME database software. In addition, the Library revised the BIBFRAME manual to both reflect the modifications and enable other libraries to access the public version of the MARVA Editor for use in their cataloging.

The Library's BIBFRAME model continued to be used and tested externally by a cohort of libraries under the banner of the Program for Cooperative Cataloging. More than 20 libraries are engaged in these activities. These libraries take advantage of a BIBFRAME input editor that was created by the LD4 group led by Stanford University. This input editor allows the Library and the community to compare the efficacy of two different input editors: the Library's MARVA Editor and LD4's Sinopia editor.

The Library's Network Development and MARC Standards Office continued to refine the BIBFRAME-to-MARC conversion tool and supporting tools. The advances made in FY 2022 improved productivity and helped BIBFRAME progress toward becoming the Library's primary production environment for bibliographic metadata. BIBFRAME databases and software were updated continuously based on feedback from the development team and the pilot participants. In addition, to advance library communities toward the adoption of BIBFRAME, the Library participated in SHARE-VDE, an international, commercially supported cooperative-library project based on BIBFRAME principles. It held regular meetings and telephone conferences with 20 other institutions that experimented with resource description based on BIBFRAME principles.

Access for the Blind and Print Disabled

In FY 2022 NLS added 8,856 talking books and 478 braille books to its collection.

NLS continued its rollout of Duplication on Demand (DoD) to network libraries during FY 2022. The DoD system allows libraries to create their own talking-book cartridges on-site from NLS-produced digital files, making it easy to fill patron requests quickly and reducing costs associated with maintaining large physical collections. DoD also allows libraries to distribute multiple books on a single cartridge, which is a big benefit to patrons. As of September 2022 70 network libraries were using some form of DoD; of those, 61 no longer receive any mass-duplicated cartridges from NLS—a significant cost savings.

NLS began field testing a smart speaker app called My Talking Books that allows users, via voice commands, to connect with Braille and Audio Reading Download (BARD), search the collection, and stream books. Work continued on a next-generation digital talking-book player that will have Internet connectivity, and there were major updates to the BARD Mobile apps for iOS and Android devices. NLS also began to pilot Braille-on-Demand, a program in which patrons can choose each month to have one of the 16,000-plus electronic braille books on BARD embossed in hard-copy braille, to keep indefinitely for personal use.

NLS worked diligently to import accessible content from Marrakesh Treaty partners and export selections from its collection to those partners. In FY 2022 NLS acquired 2,250 works under the treaty—1,375 audiobooks, 567 braille books, and 308 braille music scores—in 14 languages. Works acquired under the treaty were downloaded from BARD nearly 37,000 times. On the other side of the exchange, the World Intellectual Property Organization's Accessible Books Consortium had more than 154,000 books that were originally produced by NLS or its network libraries; those books were downloaded 1,642 times in FY 2022 by readers in 35 countries.

The Library's Website, Congress.gov, and Social Media

The Library's website, loc.gov, provides users with access to the institution's unparalleled resources, such as online catalogs; selected collections in various formats; copyright, legal, and legislative information; exhibitions; and videos and podcasts of events. In FY 2022 the Library recorded nearly 151.6 million unique visits and 520.3 million page views to its websites.

Congress.gov is the official source for legislative information for both Congress and the public. During FY 2022 the Library's Congress.gov team focused on data modernization, enhanced features, and accessibility improvements. The Office of the Chief Information Officer collaborated with CRS, the Law Library, and congressional staff and stakeholders to complete 17 releases of Congress.gov. The Congress.gov sites—the Constitution Annotated, CRS Reports, and Congress .gov—drew 40.8 million visits during FY 2022.

The web archiving team, Researcher and Reference Services, and the Office of the Chief Information Officer, in collaboration with CRO, released an update to the United States Congressional Web Archive. The update added the 115th Congress and 116th Congress and item records for 252 members and six committees. The additions brought the total records available in the collection on loc.gov to 1,413. The Library also expanded efforts to share its blog content and other digital content in new ways, highlighting the institution's depth and breadth of resources in a meaningful, concise, and engaging manner.

Short-form video content featuring celebrities such as Mark Hamill, Alicia Keys, and John Waters for the rollout of the National Film Registry and National Recording Registry announcements boosted the response on social media. A robust rollout of video and photo content following the visit of singer-songwriter Lizzo to the Library in September provided a huge surge of new followers on Facebook, Twitter, and Instagram. Lizzo fans watched video of her visit in record numbers on Twitter (3.4 million views), Facebook (2.8 million views), and Instagram (645,000 views).

In FY 2022 the Library added 12 new digital collections to loc.gov and completed an additional 52 significant upgrades and 14 digital collection migrations. The additions included the Franz Liszt Collection, the Margaret Mead papers and South Pacific Ethnographic Archives, the Toni Frissell Slides, the Jean Lafitte National Historical Park Collection, the Hebraic Manuscript Project, the East Florida Papers, the St. Mark's Poetry Collection, Dun & Bradstreet's Reference Book project, and Historic Sources of Brazilian Law.

In collaboration with WGBH in Boston, the National Audio-Visual Conservation Center launched 11 new online collections and expanded two existing collections as part of the American Archive of Public Broadcasting (AAPB). Among the launches were the Asian American and Pacific Islander Collection, Black Champions Interviews, Inflection Point with Lauren Schiller, the New Jersey Network Collection, and the Soul of Black Identity: Artists Interviews of the Post-Soul Era. AAPB also debuted five new online exhibitions: "Burning with a Deadly Heat": NewsHour Coverage of the Hot Wars of the Cold War, Latino Empowerment through Public Broadcasting, Witnessing New Mexico: The New Mexico Public Media Digitization Project, WRVR Riverside Radio: A Pioneering Noncommercial Station, and ZOOM (1972–1978): Children's Community and Public Television in the 1970s.

By the People continued to increase user engagement and enhancement of digital collections through crowdsourced transcription. During FY 2022 volunteers completed 193,000 transcriptions, and in May 2022 the program achieved the milestone of 500,000 completed transcriptions. By the People launched its first two campaigns from the Music Division: suffrage sheet music and Federal Theatre Project playbills. Seven other new campaigns featured Hannah Arendt, Frederick Law Olmsted, Joseph Holt, Georgia O'Keeffe, African American military history, World War II rumors, and early American books.

The Library maintains 21 blogs that serve as vehicles for sharing collection discoveries and engaging with users. One of them—Unfolding History, produced by the Manuscript Division—debuted during FY 2022. The blogs published 1,348 posts during FY 2022, drawing 6.6 million page views and 5.6 million visits.

The Library also maintains 14 public-facing Twitter accounts and one CRS-protected Twitter account for members of Congress and congressional staff. The public-facing accounts issued 5,901 tweets during FY 2022, earning 138,563 retweets and 11,930 replies. The public accounts also gained 72,534 followers (for a total of more than 1.7 million) and received more than 63.9 million impressions.

In addition to its main Facebook page, the Library offers Facebook pages for the Law Library, the American Folklife Center, Performing Arts, NLS, VHP, and the Library's international collections. The Library posted 2,545 times on those pages during FY 2022, earning more than 390,759 reactions and 36.3 million impressions. Library Facebook accounts have generated more than 6 billion lifetime impressions.

The Library launched its Flickr presence in 2008, featuring historical images organized into two collections: Historic Photographs and Historic Newspapers. In 2019 it created a second Flickr account, Library of Congress Life: Events, Art & Architecture. This account features photos and video coverage of contemporary activity at the Library and views of its beautiful buildings. The accounts combined for 1,742 posts and 2.3 million views during FY 2022 and 448.3 million views over their lifetimes.

The Library's Instagram account continued to share images from events and exhibitions. The account added 30,805 new followers during FY 2022 for a total of 126,372. It received 480,894 likes for a lifetime total of more than 1.2 million.

During FY 2022 the Library made 456 new videos available on its main You-Tube channel, which were liked 103,497 times. The channel's videos, including newly and previously added videos, were viewed more than 15.6 million times during FY 2022. The channel gained 48,341 subscribers. The Copyright Office also made 14 new videos available. The Copyright Office videos, including newly and previously added videos, were viewed 138,097 times during FY 2022. The Library livestreamed 25 events during FY 2022.

The Library's Apple podcast account features selected podcasts, historical films from Library collections, and video and audio recordings from collections and of events at the Library. During FY 2022 the Library added 27 new podcast episodes to Apple podcasts. The account drew 6,794 listeners and 23,470 plays. Since its launch in 2009, the account has added 4,068 files and attracted 66,230 listeners and 227,427 plays.

The Library offers 68 email alerts, including all Library and copyright-related topics for subscription. Loc.gov sent 4,119 bulletins in FY 2022 and recorded 252,172 new subscriptions. Copyright.gov sent 130 bulletins and recorded 108,195 new subscriptions.

Congress.gov's New API

Congress.gov, the official website for U.S. federal legislative information, celebrated its tenth anniversary in September 2022. The site is developed by the Library and provides access to accurate, timely, and complete legislative information for members of Congress, legislative agencies, and the public. Under the Library's agile, continuous software delivery process, Congress.gov is updated with new content and new features every three weeks, based on user feedback and requests.

Just in time for the milestone anniversary in September 2022, the Library collaborated with Congress.gov data partners in the House of Representatives, the

Senate, and the Government Publishing Office to make an application programming interface, or API, publicly available for the site for the first time. The new API allows users to securely download machine-readable datasets from a variety of Congress.gov collections, including bills, amendments, summaries, the Congressional Record, committee reports, nominations, treaties, and House communications. This new feature was one of the most requested enhancements from the enthusiastic Congress.gov user community because of its capacity to facilitate easier access to the treasure trove of congressional and historic legislative data held on the site.

By providing faster and more structured access to Congress.gov data, the API significantly enhances the possibilities for independent computational analysis of this information. Users can apply the API alongside their own automation technologies to pull large amounts of information from the site. They also have more flexibility to rearrange and reorganize this data to discover new insights from both current and historic legislative information.

As with all Congress.gov releases, the team behind the API has made a wealth of user resources available to support researchers in their legislative analysis. Along with user guides and technical documentation, users can find a change log that details updates to the API and opportunities to provide their feedback about the tool and collaborate in real time directly with the development team.

Moving forward, the Library will make even more Congress.gov data collections available through the API in the coming year, ensuring consistent and increasingly sophisticated access to accurate congressional information for the public.

Promoting Creativity

The Library of Congress collections chronicle centuries of human creativity—a rich, diverse, and enduring source of knowledge for the American people and scholars around the world. Through its many public programs, the Library also promotes creativity and cultural literacy.

Public Programs

During the year, the Library presented hundreds of public programs supporting creativity, scholarship, and lifelong learning. Those programs included concerts, author talks, lectures, orientations, workshops, and more. Viewers can watch webcasts of most of these events on the Library's website. The work of CLLE and its various offices—Signature Programs, Literary Initiatives, the Events Office, the Informal Learning Office, and Professional Learning and Outreach Initiatives—play a fundamental role in presenting these programs and in connecting the Library to communities throughout the country.

In FY 2022 the Events Office planned and executed 627 events—a 75 percent increase over FY 2021. More than 300 were held in person. Signature Programs provided leadership in staging major events such as the National Book Festival and the Gershwin Prize concert honoring pop icon Lionel Richie.

The National Book Festival, held September 3 at the Washington Convention Center, was the Library's first in-person book festival since the COVID-19 pandemic began. The festival drew more than 35,000 readers eager to hear from authors such as Mitch Albom, Geraldine Brooks, David Maraniss, and Clint Smith and actor Nick Offerman.

The Library, through the work of CLLE, launched Live! At the Library, a major new program that introduced many visitors to the Library for the first time. Each Thursday night, the Library extended its hours until 8:30 P.M., allowing visitors to enjoy exhibitions, programs, open houses, musical performances, author talks, outdoor movies, and food and drink. Some 55 percent of Live! At the Library guests were attending their first event at the institution.

Concerts

Since 1925 the Library's Coolidge Auditorium has been a venue for world-class performers and world premieres of commissioned works. In FY 2022 the Music Division's Concert Office presented a critically acclaimed series of 87 virtual and in-person events that encompassed chamber music, jazz, pop, and early music. These events included 21 virtual and eight in-person concerts; 26 artist conversations; and panel discussions, educational videos, and two commissioned works: Jeffrey Mumford's "…amid still and floating depths" for string quartet and "Lament. Sing. Arise" for violin and piano by James Lee, III. These events, along with their accompanying digital collections, attracted a global audience of nearly 224,000 views and in-person attendance of more than 1,300 people.

The American Folklife Center hosted 13 virtual concerts in its Homegrown at Home series, sharing traditional American and global music with diverse audiences. The center also produced two on-site and two virtual events for its Benjamin Botkin Folklife Lecture series, including an evening conversation between Oscar-winning actress Frances McDormand and the Kitchen Sisters as part of the Live! At the Library series. The events attracted more than 21,000 viewers and participants.

Exhibitions

The Library's Center for Exhibits and Interpretation (CEI) opened one major new exhibition in FY 2022: Not an Ostrich: & Other Images from America's Library, organized by the Annenberg Space for Photography in Los Angeles in partnership with the Library's Prints and Photographs Division—the new owner of the Annenberg photo collection. The exhibition, which opened on March 23, presented a taste of the Library's spectacular holdings of more than 15 million photographs; the selected images traced the evolution of photography from daguerreotypes and other early processes to contemporary digital technology. Working with curator Nathan Dorn of the Law Library, CEI also continued content and design development for its Join In exhibition.

Lectures, Symposia, and Poetry Readings

On November 9, 2021 the Law Library held a lecture, cosponsored by the American Association of Law Libraries, celebrating the life and legacy of former Law

Librarian of Congress Jane Sanchez. The event brought together leaders from academic, government, and law firm libraries to discuss the future of law libraries and law librarianship. On July 14, 2022 the Law Library celebrated its 190th anniversary with an interview of Harvard Radcliffe Institute dean Tomiko Brown-Nagin by Law Librarian of Congress Aslihan Bulut. This event later was broadcast on C-SPAN.

The John W. Kluge Center hosted 31 events, including virtual programs, in-person events without a virtual component, and hybrid programs. Highlights included the awarding of the John W. Kluge Prize for Achievement in the Study of Humanity to historian George Chauncey; the concluding events of the Pillars of Democracy: Institutions at Risk series examining the public's faith in bedrock institutions of American life; and a series of lunchtime briefings and evening events for congressional staff members, organized in collaboration with CRO. Online views of Kluge Center events continued to average around 2,000, with single events reaching more than 5,000.

With individuals and organizations across the country, the VHP built collections and awareness through an expansion of hybrid and on-site programming as well as attendance at local and national conferences. Collection donations and other events attracted substantial media coverage (including a two-part national radio tour with a reach of nearly 13.7 million people). Hybrid programming inspired focused collections development in underrepresented areas, resulting, for example, in a 1,500 percent increase in collections of native Guam veterans.

Promoting Scholarship

The Library promotes scholarship by offering fellowship and internship opportunities in various disciplines and publications that showcase the Library's unparalleled collections.

The John W. Kluge Center

The John W. Kluge Center was established in 2000 with a gift of $60 million from the late John W. Kluge. The center's goal is to invite eminent and emerging scholars from around the world to make use of the Library's vast collections and to connect their research with the American people and Congress. In FY 2022 the Kluge Center expanded the use of Library collections by offering opportunities for researcher engagement and showcasing the results through programs for the benefit of Congress, policymakers, and the public.

The Kluge Center welcomed and supported 98 scholars. They included 17 chairs and distinguished visiting scholars from a broad array of disciplines, such as sociology, political science, development economics, the Chinese economy, U.S.–Russia relations, U.S. foreign policy, music and art, urban and regional planning, and Middle Eastern politics. The Kluge Center also hosted 81 fellows, many of whom are early career scholars and who are selected based on their potential to use Library collections and develop research in ways that enrich the intellectual life of the Library, Congress, and the nation. Kluge scholars spend four to 12 months in residence at the center.

Throughout the year, Scholars Council members contributed to the work of the Library and the Kluge Center by advising the center on its programming. They also evaluated nominees for the 2022 Kluge Prize for Achievement in the Study of Humanity.

A new Alumni Advisory Group convened its first meeting in FY 2022. This group of 13 diverse Kluge scholars, representing the breadth of disciplines supported by the center, provided valuable feedback for ongoing program development. By activating this significant and growing Library community of more than 1,300 scholars, the center can add a distinguished network of ambassadors for Kluge opportunities and strengthen its outreach, partnerships, and program/event promotion.

The American Folklife Center

The American Folklife Center documents and shares the many expressions of human experience to inspire, revitalize, and perpetuate living traditions. Designated by Congress as the national center for folklife documentation and research, the center stewards archival collections, creates public programs, and exchanges knowledge and expertise. The center's work encourages diversity of expression and fosters community participation in the collective creation of cultural memory. One of the center's major initiatives is VHP.

Poet Laureate

On July 12, 2022 the Library announced the appointment of Ada Limón as the nation's 24th poet laureate consultant in poetry for 2022–2023. Limón is the author of six poetry collections, including *The Hurting Kind*; *The Carrying*, which won the National Book Critics Circle Award for Poetry; *Bright Dead Things*; *Sharks in the Rivers*; *Lucky Wreck*; and *This Big Fake World*. She succeeds Joy Harjo, who served three terms in the position.

Promoting Lifelong Learning

In addition to its fellowships, research services, and collections access, the Library promotes lifelong learning and literacy through CLLE and K–12 educational outreach efforts, which assist the nation's teachers in engaging students through the use of primary sources in the classroom. CLLE sponsors the National Ambassador for Young People's Literature program in collaboration with the Children's Book Council (CBC) and the CBC Foundation and with support from publishers. It also administers the Library of Congress Literacy Awards, which recognize and support organizations and institutions in the United States and abroad that make significant contributions to combating illiteracy.

Professional Learning and Outreach Initiatives

CLLE's Teaching with Primary Sources (TPS) program, administered by the Professional Learning Office, serves educators across the grade spectrum, across the curriculum, and across the country by providing easily accessible, high-quality professional development programs and classroom materials. These opportunities and tools help educators use digitized primary sources, event recordings, and other materials from the Library's online collections in their teaching. In FY 2022 the Library awarded $6.4 million to 46 diverse grantee organizations and TPS regional partners to incorporate Library materials into the educational programs they deliver—growing the TPS national consortium by 23 percent, from 192 to 236 members. FY 2022 grantees include the African American Civil War Museum, the Georgia Council on Economic Education, New Mexico's Peñasco Independent School District, and the University of Arizona libraries.

To strengthen the network of educators, Professional Learning Office staff hosted more than 30 in-person and online professional development events, published new primary source sets, and contributed dozens of articles to professional journals. During FY 2022 TPS consortium members provided 1,133 online and in-person TPS workshops, academic courses, and presentations to more than 21,000 educators. Grantees reported almost 2 million user-downloaded apps, curricular materials, and teaching materials that they created under their TPS grants.

In addition, the Library's suite of online tools and resources for educators at loc.gov/teachers continued to grow and was visited more than 6.5 million times. The "Teaching with the Library of Congress" blog continued to build its audience. In FY 2022 the blog published 91 posts and drew 251,106 visits and 326,383 page views. Over its lifetime, the blog has drawn nearly 25 million visits and more than 34 million page views. The TPS Teachers Network website, a professional networking site for educators using Library of Congress primary sources in their classrooms (hosted by a TPS partner at https://tpsteachersnetwork.org), continued to grow in popularity and use. At the end of FY 2022 13,290 educators had enrolled on the site, sharing teaching ideas and strategies.

Celebrating Achievement

Throughout the year, the Library of Congress celebrates the achievements of the nation's creative and scholarly communities. The Library also recognizes the accomplishments of its staff members. In addition, it sponsors privately endowed programs that honor achievement in the humanities. Through these awards and prizes, the Library honors those who have advanced and embodied the ideals of individuality, conviction, dedication, scholarship, and lifelong learning.

Kluge Prize

Endowed by a great Library benefactor, the John W. Kluge Prize for Achievement in the Study of Humanity rewards achievement in a wide range of disciplines, including history, philosophy, politics, anthropology, sociology, religion, linguistics, and criticism in the arts and humanities. In FY 2022 the Kluge Center awarded the Kluge Prize to George Chauncey, a Columbia University historian of gay life in 20th-century America and of the gay rights movement. Expanded communications efforts meant the prize this year was covered in 345 media stories, for 720 million potential impressions and an advertising equivalence of $18 million, from June through September. In FY 2022 the Kluge Center also began planning an accompanying series of virtual and in-person events that will feature the prize-winner, to be made public between January and June 2023.

Gershwin Prize

The Library of Congress Gershwin Prize for Popular Song was created to honor artists whose lifetime contributions in the field of popular song exemplify the standard of excellence associated with George and Ira Gershwin by bridging musical styles, bringing diverse listeners together, and fostering their mutual respect and appreciation. The 2022 Gershwin Prize was awarded to pop music icon Lionel Richie, known for megahits such as "Endless Love," "Lady," "Truly," "All Night Long," "Penny Lover," "Stuck on You," "Hello," and "Dancing on the Ceiling." Richie was honored with an all-star tribute concert at Constitution Hall in Washington, D.C., on March 9.

Library of Congress Prize for American Fiction

The Library of Congress Prize for American Fiction honors an American literary writer whose body of work is distinguished not only for its mastery of the art but also for its originality of thought and imagination. The 2022 prize was awarded to Jesmyn Ward, the acclaimed author of the novels *Where the Line Bleeds*; *Salvage the Bones*, winner of the 2011 National Book Award; and *Sing, Unburied, Sing*, winner of the 2017 National Book Award. Her nonfiction work includes the memoir *Men We Reaped* and the 2020 work *Navigate Your Stars*. At age 45, Ward was the youngest person ever to receive the prize.

The Library of Congress Lavine/Ken Burns Prize for Film

The National Audio-Visual Conservation Center continued its leadership role in implementing the Library's collaboration with the Better Angels Society on the annual Library of Congress Lavine/Ken Burns Prize for Film. In FY 2022 the prize was awarded to "Gradually, Then Suddenly: The Bankruptcy of Detroit," directed by Sam Katz and James McGovern. "Free Chol Soo Lee," directed by Julie Ha and Eugen Yi, was named runner-up.

Literacy Awards

Created and sponsored by philanthropist and Madison Council Chairman David M. Rubenstein, the Library of Congress Literacy Awards seek to reward organizations that have done exemplary, innovative, and easily replicable work over a sustained period to promote literacy in the United States and abroad.

David M. Rubenstein Prize ($150,000)

The 2022 winner was Street Child, a London-based international charity currently operating in 20 of the world's most vulnerable countries. Street Child works closely with its partners to bring literacy to the forefront of governmental and community discussions.

American Prize ($50,000)

The 2022 winner was Make Way for Books, an organization based in Tucson, Arizona, that provides early literacy programming to young children and their families who may not otherwise have access to books or quality early education.

International Prize ($50,000)

The 2022 winner was Young African Refugees for Integral Development, an educational nonprofit based in Kampala, Uganda. The organization's literacy model follows a phased approach to learning English.

In addition, 12 other organizations were recognized as Successful Practice Honorees and received $5,000 each.

Federal Library and Information Network

Gregory Abraham
Executive Director

The Federal Library and Information Network (FEDLINK) is an organization of federal agencies working together to achieve optimum use of the resources and facilities of federal libraries and information centers by promoting common services, coordinating and sharing available resources, and providing continuing professional education for federal library and information staff.

FEDLINK serves as a forum for discussion of the policies, programs, procedures, and technologies that affect federal libraries and the information services they provide to their agencies, Congress, the federal courts, and the American people.

FEDLINK continued its mission to achieve better utilization of federal library and information resources by providing the most cost-effective and efficient administrative mechanism for delivering necessary services and materials to federal libraries and information centers.

FEDLINK Executive Report

The FEDLINK Advisory Board (FAB) focused its bimonthly meetings on a variety of broad federal information issues, including the return to on-site operations across the federal government, administrative issues related to new federal acquisitions platforms, and related system updates for the FEDLINK-assisted acquisition model. At several sessions, members discussed FEDLINK's customer relations initiatives, including program fee reductions, roles and program goals of the working groups and committees, surveys, directional planning, and sponsored professional education opportunities.

FEDLINK held two expositions in fiscal year (FY) 2022. The Spring Expo, "Mission Critical: Connecting Information to Innovation," featured keynote speakers John Verrico, founder of Share Your Fire, discussing communicating library value and Jennie Rose Halperin, executive director of Library Futures, detailing approaches to building a shared digital future. Additional sessions discussed usage statistics, collection development, AI uses in libraries, and open access. The Fall Expo, "Embracing the Permanence of Change," opened with a keynote address from Dr. Julie Todaro, the dean of library services for Austin Community College, who identified ways to thrive in the information future reality. This was followed by an afternoon keynote presentation from Jason Griffey, director of strategic initiatives at the National Information Standards Organization, who explored the current state of blockchain and the information ecosystem. Other session topics included virtual reference and measuring impact with web metrics data.

FEDLINK Working Group Highlights
FEDLINK Awards Committee

To honor the many innovative ways federal libraries, librarians, and library technicians fulfill the information demands of government, business, research, scholarly communities, and the American public, the Awards Committee administered a series of national awards for federal librarianship.

Winners of the FY 2021 awards, announced in May 2022, were:

2021 Federal Library/Information Center of the Year

Large library/information center (staff of 11 or more federal and/or contract employees): The Goddard Information and Collaboration Center was recognized for its innovative services during the global pandemic to more than 10,000 patrons. The center launched new bibliographic and data visualization services and partnerships with the NASA mission directorates while migrating its consortium catalogs and updating its knowledge management database. Collaborations featured working with agency scientists on bibliographic data capture and data visualization and the development of the Goddard Knowledge Exchange database with the agency's chief knowledge officer. In FY 2021, the center conducted research for senior agency personnel and supported an audit of Goddard authors. As part of a NASA knowledge exchange program, the center mapped the policies of the integrated library system to enhance the center's online public access catalog.

Small library/information center (staff of 10 or fewer federal and/or contract employees): The Andrew W. Breidenbach Environmental Research Center Library was recognized for its role as a lead service center library for the Environmental Protection Agency's (EPA) library network supporting 1,700 EPA staff and the general public in 10 states. In addition to ongoing research and programming, the library implemented radio frequency identification reader scanning for its collection of 48,000 items. This effort increased the efficiency of the library's annual inventory by 93 percent, saving EPA more than $100,000 per year, which allowed it to manage a new repository without increasing staff. In FY 2021, the library began managing EPA's Library Network Dark Archive, which was designed to preserve EPA's publication and scientific history. This collection effectively doubles the library's collection size and makes it the largest EPA network library.

2021 Federal Librarian of the Year

Emily Shohfi, a clinical librarian at Darnall Medical Library in the Defense Health Agency at Walter Reed National Military Medical Center in Bethesda, Maryland, was recognized for her dedication to evidence-based practice, library utilization, and contributions to medical education scholarship. Embedded in nine different medical specialties and training programs, she trained more than 400 physician trainees and 1,000 medical staff in FY 2021. She conducted an additional 275 interactive didactics sessions designed to improve utilization of library resources, search strategies, and appraisal of the literature, empowering trainees to care for approximately 360,000 patients with the best available medical evidence. Shohfi served on three hospital-level committees to address library impact; diversity, equity, and inclusion; and combat trauma research. Beyond her educational role, she responded to 720 questions about patient care, conducted an additional 311 searches for project or research efforts, and tailored databases and strategies for clinical questions, program-level practices, clinical reviews, and/or meta-analyses for original clinical research.

2021 Federal Library Technician of the Year

Reginald A. Stewart, library programmer and environmental officer for the Army Morale, Welfare, and Recreation program's Community Recreation Division at Wiesbaden Library in Germany, was recognized for his dedication to the library's mission, its patrons, and the creation of engaging programs to support literacy and learning. Recipient of the 2002 Federal Library Technician of the Year Award, Stewart continued to design and support inclusive library initiatives to meet the needs of the library's diverse community and cater to the unique developmental stages of children of all age groups. Beyond conducting extensive community programming, Stewart also managed the library's budget and facilities and leveraged the latest library science technology and programming to increase library participation and improve the quality of life and well-being for community members. In FY 2021, Stewart's collaboration with the environmental office to reduce the ecological footprint of the U.S. Army Garrison Wiesbaden's Directorate of Family Morale, Welfare, and Recreation resulted in all 18 of the program's front doors becoming Green Boot certified.

FEDLINK Working Groups

The eResources Working Group hosted a discussion on common federal library datapoints and the role of metrics in reporting to agency management, with speakers from the U.S. Geological Survey and Walter Reed National Military Medical Center. The Research and Metrics Working Group collaborated with the eResources Working Group on identifying metrics to quantify the value of services in individual agencies and joined the Leadership Working Group to discuss revisions to the federal library directory.

FEDLINK Publications and Education Office

FEDLINK continued to develop targeted resources to support the FEDLINK program, including governing body and educational programming support; directional, business, and customer service plans; promotional materials; and supporting materials for both exposition programs and working group projects and events. FEDLINK joined the Military Librarian's Workshop as a presenter and continued brokering information professional conferences for its membership. FEDLINK offered a series of introductory and intermediate catalog training programs, virtual updates on FEDLINK library support services and serials assisted acquisitions programs, and a meeting of current vendors.

New resources for federal librarians included an instructional video, "Establishing Your Interagency Agreement"; updated assisted acquisition resources for customers; virtual exposition and award materials; and a series of newsletters for members and vendors. FEDLINK continued its publication program as a digital communication provider and used its website and community listservs for outreach on critical advocacy and program information to more than 2,000 electronic subscribers.

FEDLINK Contracts and Network Operations

FEDLINK provided assisted acquisition services to the federal information community by procuring publications in a wide variety of formats (print and electronic journals; print and electronic books; sound recordings; audiovisual materials items via document delivery and interlibrary loan; and access to databases of full text, indices, abstracts, and a variety of other data) and library support services (cataloging and related technical processing services, staffing support, information management, resource sharing, integrated library systems, digitization, digital archiving, and preservation services).

FEDLINK remained dedicated to providing cost-effective acquisition services to the federal information community to ensure every member achieves optimum use of agency resources. Early in the year, FEDLINK reduced its Transfer Pay service fees, and by year's end, it announced a tiered pricing structure based on customer-purchasing dollar thresholds.

Through interagency agreements (IAAs), FEDLINK's contracts and network staff members worked on behalf of federal agencies with more than 100 vendors to conduct competitions, issue orders, and resolve issues with vendors. FEDLINK continued to provide assisted-acquisition services to its members, with $68.5 million in Transfer Pay services and $189.4 million in Direct Express.

National Agricultural Library

U.S. Department of Agriculture, Agricultural Research Service
Abraham Lincoln Bldg., 10301 Baltimore Ave., Beltsville, MD 20705-2351
E-mail agref@nal.usda.gov https://www.nal.usda.gov

Paul Wester
Director

The U.S. Department of Agriculture's (USDA) National Agricultural Library (NAL) is one of the world's largest and most accessible agricultural research libraries, offering service directly to the public either on-site in Beltsville, Maryland, or via its website, https://www.nal.usda.gov.

The library was established in 1862 at the same time as the USDA. It became a national library in 1962, when Congress established it as the primary agricultural information resource of the United States (7 USCS § 3125a). Congress assigned to the library the responsibilities to:

- Acquire, preserve, and manage information resources relating to agriculture and allied sciences
- Organize agricultural information products and services and provide them within the United States and internationally
- Plan, coordinate, and evaluate information and library needs relating to agricultural research and education
- Cooperate with and coordinate efforts toward development of a comprehensive agricultural library and information network
- Coordinate the development of specialized subject information services among the agricultural and library information communities

NAL is located in Beltsville, Maryland, near Washington, D.C., on the grounds of USDA's Henry A. Wallace Beltsville Agricultural Research Center. Its 14-story Abraham Lincoln Building is named in honor of the president who created the USDA and signed several of the major U.S. laws affecting agriculture.

The library employs about 100 librarians, information specialists, computer specialists, administrators, and clerical personnel, supplemented by about 50 contract staff and cooperators from NAL partnering organizations.

NAL's reputation as one of the world's foremost agricultural libraries is supported and burnished by its expert staff, ongoing leadership in delivering information services, expanding collaborations with other U.S. and international agricultural research and information organizations, and extensive collection of agricultural information, searchable through AGRICOLA, the library's bibliographic database.

In 2012 NAL reorganized to better align its functions with its overall strategic plan, which includes simplified access to all NAL content, expansion of digital content, and the integration of scientific datasets and discovery tools.

The Collection

The NAL collection dates to the congressionally approved 1839 purchase of books for the Agricultural Division of the Patent Office, predating the 1862 establishment of USDA itself. Today NAL provides access to billions of pages of agricultural information—an immense collection of scientific books, journals, audiovisuals, reports, theses, artifacts, and images—and to a widening array of digital media, as well as databases and other information resources germane to the broad reach of agriculture-related sciences.

The library's collection contains more than 8 million items, dating from the 15th century to the present, including the most complete repository of USDA publications and the world's most extensive set of materials on the history of U.S. agriculture. Publications are selected for the collection based on the National Agricultural Library Collection Development Policy.

Building the Collection

NAL is the only U.S. national library with a legislated mandate to collect in the following disciplines: plant and animal health, welfare, and production; agricultural economics, products, and education; aquaculture; forestry; rural sociology and rural life; family and consumer science; and food science, safety, and nutrition. In addition to collecting as comprehensively as possible in these core subject areas, NAL collects extensively in many related subjects, such as biology, bioinformatics, biochemistry, chemistry, entomology, environmental science, genetics, invasive species, meteorology, natural resources, physics, soil science, sustainability, water quality, and zoology. The library has primary responsibility for collecting and retaining publications issued by USDA and its agencies. As well, NAL collects publications from around the world.

Special Collections

The NAL Special Collections program emphasizes access to and preservation of rare and unique materials documenting the history of agriculture and related sciences. Items in the library's special collections include rare books, manuscripts, nursery and seed trade catalogs, posters, objects, photographs, and other rare materials documenting agricultural subjects. Materials date from the 1500s to the present and include many international sources. Detailed information about these special collections is available on the NAL website at https://specialcollections.nal.usda.gov.

Special Collections of note include the following:

- The U.S. Department of Agriculture History Collection (https://specialcollections.nal.usda.gov/usda-history-collection-introductionindex), assembled over 80 years by USDA historians, includes letters, memoranda, reports, and papers of USDA officials, as well as photographs, oral histories, and clippings covering the activities of the department from its founding through the early 1990s.
- The U.S. Department of Agriculture Pomological Watercolor Collection (https://naldc.nal.usda.gov/usda_pomological_watercolor) includes more

than 7,000 detailed, botanically accurate watercolor illustrations of fruit and nut varieties developed by growers or introduced by USDA plant explorers. Created between 1886 and the 1940s, the watercolors served as official documentation of the work of the Office of the Pomologist and were used to create chromolithographs in publications distributed widely by the department. Although created for scientific accuracy, the works are artistic treasures in their own right.

- The Henry G. Gilbert Nursery and Seed Trade Catalog Collection (https:// specialcollections.nal.usda.gov/guide-collections/henry-g-gilbert-nursery-and-seed-trade-catalog-collection), begun in 1904 by USDA economic botanist Percy L. Ricker, has grown to comprise more than 200,000 U.S. and foreign catalogs. The earliest items date from the late 1700s, but the collection is strongest from the 1890s to the present. Researchers commonly use the collection to document the introduction of plants to the United States, study economic trends, and illustrate early developments in American landscape design.
- The Rare Book Collection (https://specialcollections.nal.usda.gov/guide-collections/rare-book-collection) highlights agriculture's printed historical record. It covers a wide variety of subjects, but is particularly strong in botany, natural history, zoology, and entomology. International in scope, the collection documents early agricultural practices in Britain and Europe, as well as the Americas. Manuscript collections (https://specialcollections .nal.usda.gov/guide-collections/index-manuscript-collections), now numbering more than 400, document the story of American agriculture and its influence on the world.

NAL continues to digitize these and other unique materials to share them broadly via its website and has published detailed indexes to the content of many manuscript collections to improve discovery. AGRICOLA, NAL's catalog, includes bibliographic entries for special collection items, manuscripts, and rare books. The library provides in-house research and reference services for its special collections and offers fee-based duplication services.

Preservation/Digitization

NAL is committed to the preservation of its print and nonprint collections. It continues to monitor and improve the environmental quality of its stacks to extend the longevity of all materials in the collection. The library has instituted a long-term strategy to ensure that the growing body of agricultural information is systematically identified, preserved, and archived.

NAL's digital conversion program has resulted in a growing digital collection of USDA publications and many non-USDA historical materials not restricted by copyright. NAL is in the midst of a large-scale project to digitize agricultural literature and provide online access to the general public. Important and distinctive items were selected from the NAL collection, with an initial focus on USDA-issued publications and nursery and seed trade catalogs. Publications are accessible at NAL's Internet Archive collection (https://archive.org/details/usda nationalagriculturallibrary) and in the National Agricultural Library Digital Collections (https://naldc.nal.usda.gov).

Library Services

Reference Services

NAL serves the agricultural information needs of customers through a combination of web-based and traditional library services, including reference, document delivery, and information centers. The NAL website offers access to a wide variety of full-text resources, as well as online access to reference and document delivery services.

The main reading room in the library's Beltsville facility features a walk-up service desk, access to an array of digital information resources (including full-text scientific journals), current periodicals, and an on-site request service for materials from NAL's collection. Services are available 8:30 A.M. to 4:30 P.M. Monday through Friday, except federal holidays.

NAL's reference services are accessible online using the Ask a Question form on the NAL webpages; by use of e-mail addressed to agref@usda.gov; by telephone at 301-504-5755; or by mail to Research Services, National Agricultural Library ARS/USDA, 10301 Baltimore Avenue, Beltsville, MD 20705. Requesters receive assistance from research services staff in all areas and aspects of agriculture, but staff particularly answer questions, provide research guidance, and make presentations on topics not addressed by the seven subject-focused information centers of the library.

Information Centers and Partnerships

NAL's information centers and partnerships deliver comprehensive, science-based information on key aspects of U.S. agriculture, providing timely, accurate, and in-depth coverage of their specialized subject areas. Their expert staff offers extensive web-based information resources and advanced reference services:

- The Alternative Farming Systems Information Center (AFSIC) (https://www.nal.usda.gov/afsic) specializes in identifying and accessing information relating to farming methods that maintain the health and productivity of the entire farming enterprise, including natural resources. This focus includes sustainable and alternative agricultural systems, crops, and livestock.
- The Animal Welfare Information Center (AWIC) (https://www.nal.usda.gov/awic) provides scientific information and referrals to help ensure the proper care and treatment of animals used in biomedical research, testing, teaching, and exhibitions and by animal dealers. Among its varied outreach activities, the center conducts workshops for researchers on meeting the information requirements of the Animal Welfare Act.
- The Food and Nutrition Information Center (FNIC) (https://www.nal.usda.gov/fnic) provides credible, accurate, and practical resources for nutrition and health professionals, educators, government personnel, and consumers. FNIC maintains a staff of registered dietitians and nutrition experts who can answer questions on food and human nutrition.
- The Food Safety Research Information Office (FSRIO) (https://www.nal.usda.gov/fsrio) delivers information on publicly funded—and, to the extent

possible, privately funded—food safety research initiatives. The Research Projects Database provides more than 17,000 active food safety research projects in a searchable database of U.S. and international agencies. The Research Publications Feed offers access to real-time updates of peer-reviewed publications in food safety.

- The National Invasive Species Information Center (NISIC) (https://www .invasivespeciesinfo.gov) delivers accessible, accurate, referenced, up-to-date, and comprehensive information on invasive species drawn from federal, state, local, and international sources.

- The Rural Information Center (RIC) (https://www.nal.usda.gov/ric) assists local officials, organizations, businesses, and rural residents working to maintain the vitality of rural areas. It collects and disseminates information on such diverse topics as community economic development, small-business development, health care, finance, housing, environment, quality of life, community leadership, and education.

- The Water and Agriculture Information Center (WAIC) (https://www.nal .usda.gov/waic) collects, organizes, and communicates scientific findings, educational methodologies, and public policy issues related to water and agriculture.

In addition to these information centers, NAL manages the popular Nutrition.gov website (http://www.nutrition.gov) in collaboration with other USDA agencies and the Department of Health and Human Services. This site provides evidence-based nutrition information for the general consumer and highlights the latest in nutrition news and tools from across federal government agencies. A team of registered dietitians and nutrition experts at NAL's Food and Nutrition Information Center maintains Nutrition.gov and answers questions on food and nutrition issues.

The Agricultural Law Information Partnership is a collaboration among NAL, the National Agricultural Law Center (NALC), and the Center for Agriculture and Food Systems (CAFS) at Vermont Law School. The partnership supports the dissemination of agricultural and food law information to key audiences, including attorneys, agricultural professionals, and the general public involved in agricultural industries in the United States. Agricultural law is defined broadly to include land-based agriculture, food and fiber production and systems, aquaculture, and energy issues. Explore the partnership at https://www.nal.usda.gov/aglaw/agricultural-law-information-partnership.

Document Delivery Services

NAL's document delivery operation responds to thousands of requests each year from USDA employees and from libraries and organizations around the world. NAL uses the Relais Enterprise document request and delivery system to support document delivery. With Relais fully integrated with the Voyager library system, with DigiTop, and with other Open-URL and ISO ILL-compliant systems, NAL customers can request materials or check on the status of their requests via the web, and the needed materials can easily be delivered electronically. Document requests can also be submitted via OCLC (NAL's symbol is AGL) and DOCLINE

(NAL's libid is MDUNAL). Visit https://www.nal.usda.gov/services/request.shtml for details.

Scientific Research Data Services

In 2012 NAL began including digital scientific research data as part of its mission in support of federal open data and public access requirements. NAL data services help USDA-funded research communities make their data "Findable, Accessible, Interoperable, and Reusable (FAIR)." NAL does this by providing research communities with expert metadata and informatics expertise to help create rich, well-structured, machine-readable metadata; offering a channel to publish data and metadata; and delivering the infrastructure for data preservation. NAL's role is to help the agricultural research community prepare data to be accessed and reused for analytical applications.

NAL services currently support a number of domains, including arthropod genomics, life cycle assessment, geospatial modeling, food and nutrition, and animal welfare. Products that underpin these services include:

- USDA Food Composition Database (https://ndb.nal.usda.gov)
- I5K Workspace@NAL (https://i5k.nal.usda.gov)
- Life Cycle Assessment Commons (LCA Commons) (https://www.lcacommons.gov)
- Dr. Duke's Phytochemical and Ethnobotanical Databases (https://phytochem.nal.usda.gov)
- Geospatial Data Catalog (GeoData) (https://geodata.nal.usda.gov)

Digital Products

NAL's website (https://www.nal.usda.gov) is the primary entry point to all of the following online resources.

AGRICOLA

AGRICOLA is an online catalog of NAL collections, and the article citation database delivers worldwide access to agricultural information through its searchable web interface (http://agricola.nal.usda.gov). Alternatively, users can access AGRICOLA on a fee basis through several commercial vendors, or they can subscribe to the complete AGRICOLA file, also on a fee basis, directly from the library by e-mailing AgricolaPublishers@usda.gov.

The AGRICOLA database covers materials in all formats, including printed works from the 15th century onward. Its records describe publications and resources encompassing all aspects of agriculture and allied disciplines. AGRICOLA, updated daily, includes the following two components:

- NAL Public Access Catalog, containing more than 1 million citations to books, audiovisual materials, serial titles, and other materials in the NAL collection. (The catalog also contains some bibliographic records for items cataloged by other libraries but not held in the NAL collection.)

• NAL Article Citation Database, consisting of more than 6 million citations to journal articles, book chapters, reports, and reprints. NAL has implemented automated indexing/text analytics software to produce this database. This application combines semantic analysis, machine learning, and human rules to automatically assign subject terms to journal articles.

DigiTop

DigiTop, USDA's Digital Desktop Library, delivers the full text of 7,000-plus journals and more than 5,000 newspapers worldwide and provides 27 agriculturally significant citation databases, including AGRICOLA, BIOSIS Previews, Business Source Premier, CAB Abstracts, GEOBASE, GeoRef, Scopus, and Web of Science. DigiTop also supplies a range of digital reference resources and offers focused, personalized services. Navigator is a component of DigiTop that allows cross-searching of multiple bibliographic databases. This discovery service includes citations from academic journals, newspapers, magazines, and nonprint sources. DigiTop is available to on-site visitors and to the entire USDA workforce worldwide—more than 100,000 people—around the clock. NAL staff provides help desk and reference services, continuous user education, and training for DigiTop users.

Ag Data Commons

Ag Data Commons (https://data.nal.usda.gov), a scientific research data catalog and repository, supports USDA's objectives to make USDA-funded research data FAIR. Through Ag Data Commons, NAL provides scientific research data description, publishing, and preservation services for agricultural research communities. Ag Data Commons serves as USDA's central point of access to open agricultural research data. Its catalog, with more than 4,000 records, is a gateway to data from USDA-funded research. Its repository also publishes and preserves data files from intramural and extramural grant programs. Standardized metadata records describe datasets in detail and link them with information, related data, publications, and people, using persistent identifiers. The goal of Ag Data Commons is to enable data reuse to compound the value of USDA science and engender science-based decision making.

Ag Data Commons uses a customized version of the open-source DKAN software, which is compliant with U.S. Project Open Data standards for federal agencies. The system includes both a catalog function describing the data and pointing to its online location and a repository holding and publishing data that's not otherwise available.

National Agricultural Library Digital Collections

National Agricultural Library Digital Collections (NALDC) (https://naldc.nal.usda.govl) offers easy access to collection materials available in digital format. NALDC provides rich searching, browsing, and retrieval of digital materials and collections and delivers reliable, long-term online access to selected publications. NALDC includes historical publications, USDA research, and more.

PubAg

PubAg (https://pubag.nal.usda.gov) provides discovery of and access to full-text articles authored by USDA employees and citations to the peer-reviewed journal literature of agriculture. These citations have been enriched through subject analysis and application of terms from the National Agricultural Library Thesaurus (NALT).

National Agricultural Library Thesaurus (NALT)

Redesigned as part of NAL's NALT for the Machine Age initiative, NALT 2022, 20th edition, is a state-of-the-art multischeme concept space with added structural features for enhanced scalability and machine readability.

2022 Inaugural Schemes

- NALT Core, a trim NALT subscheme with just 13,791 frequently used agricultural concepts, including 4,396 agriculturally important organisms (taxa) and structural updates for a lean and efficient machine-readable agricultural knowledge base
- NALT Full, all NALT concepts and NALT Core plus more than 48,000 additional agricultural related organisms (taxa) and several thousand less-frequently used concepts for a total of 76,933 concepts. NALT Full is a more granular knowledge base.

New NALT 2022 Structural Features

- Streamlined top concepts reflect USDA programs and services to support data linkages and transparency and to enhance agriculture research and information discoverability:
  - Animals, Livestock, One Health
  - Economics, Trade, Law, Business, Industry
  - Farms, Agricultural Production Systems
  - Fields of Study
  - Forestry, Wildland Management
  - Geographical Locations
  - Human Nutrition, Food Safety and Quality
  - Natural Resources, Conservation, Environment
  - Plant Production, Gardening
  - Research, Technology, Methods
  - Rural Development, Communities, Education, Extension
  - Taxonomic Hierarchy
- Maintained natively as a linked data graph, also known as a knowledge graph (SKOS concept scheme)
- The knowledge graph enables linked open data mappings across the Internet, harnessing the power of the semantic web.
- Mapping to other resources: Library of Congress Subject Headings, CAB Thesaurus, AGROVOC, Global Agricultural Concept Space (GACS), and

Wikidata. NALT 2022 mappings have increased since last year by 70 percent to 50,275.

- NALT persistent uniform resource identifiers (URIs) are upgraded to HTTPS (Hypertext Transfer Protocol Secure), ensuring secure access to NALT concept descriptions. Legacy HTTP NALT URIs are currently supported by redirects.
- NALT concept types (Organism, Chemical, Product, Geographical, Topic) express the most salient features of the concept space.
- Product-to-organism relationships are added to capture deeper knowledge of agricultural production from farm to fork.
- The NAL project NALT for the Machine Age, along with interested agricultural subject matter expert communities, is working to create additional subschemes within the NALT concept space.

Networks of Cooperation

The NAL collection and information resources are supplemented by networks of cooperation with other institutions, including arrangements with agricultural libraries at U.S. land-grant universities, other U.S. national libraries, agricultural libraries in other countries, and libraries of the United Nations and other international organizations.

AgNIC

The Agriculture Network Information Collaborative (AgNIC) is a voluntary alliance of member institutions, mostly U.S. land-grant university libraries, dedicated to enhancing collective information and services among the members and their partners for all those seeking agricultural information over the Internet. More information about AgNIC and its activities can be found at https://www.agnic.org.

USAIN

The U.S. Agricultural Information Network (USAIN) is a professional membership organization that provides a forum for members to discuss food and agricultural issues and seeks to take a leadership role in the formation of a national information policy as related to food and agriculture. Central to its mission is cooperation with and support of NAL. Learn more about USAIN at https://usain.org.

AGLINET

Through the Agricultural Libraries Network (AGLINET), NAL serves as the U.S. node of an international agricultural information system that brings together agricultural libraries with strong regional or country coverage and other specialized collections. NAL functions as a gateway to U.S. agricultural libraries and resources, fulfilling requests for information via reciprocal agreements with several other libraries, information centers, and consortia. As an AGLINET member, NAL agrees to provide low-cost interlibrary loan and photocopy service to other

AGLINET libraries. Most materials requested through AGLINET are delivered digitally, although reproductions via fiche or photocopy are used when appropriate. AGLINET is administered by the Food and Agriculture Organization of the United Nations.

Information Management and Information Technology

Over the past quarter century, NAL has applied increasingly sophisticated information technology to support the ever-more complex and demanding information needs of researchers, practitioners, policymakers, and the general public. Technological developments spearheaded by the library date back to the 1940s and 1950s, when NAL director Ralph Shaw invented "electronic machines" such as the photo charger, rapid selector, and photo clerk. Over the years, NAL has made numerous technological improvements, such as automating collections information and delivering full-text and image collections digitally on the Internet.

NAL has fully implemented the Voyager integrated library system from Ex Libris. The system supports ordering, receiving, and invoice processing for purchases; creating and maintaining indexing and cataloging records for AGRICOLA; circulating print holdings; and providing a web-based online catalog for public searching and browsing of the collection. In addition, the system is fully integrated with an automated interlibrary loan and document delivery system by Relais International that streamlines services and provides desktop delivery of needed materials.

NAL has migrated its Voyager and Islandora data to Alma, Ex Libris's library services platform. Alma will allow NAL to integrate AGRICOLA platforms and services and modernize NAL infrastructure. NAL's go-live date for Alma was September 2022.

National Library of Medicine

8600 Rockville Pike, Bethesda, MD 20894
301-496-6308, 888-346-3656, fax 301-496-4450
E-mail nlmcommunications@nlm.nih.gov
http://www.nlm.nih.gov

The National Library of Medicine (NLM) is a leader in biomedical informatics and computational health data science research and the world's largest biomedical library. NLM leads innovation in the development of advanced tools for clinical data interpretation and decision making through its cutting-edge research, training programs, and information services. NLM is distinctive within the National Institutes of Health (NIH) because of the substantial investment in sustainable biomedical information systems that make scientific literature and genomic, clinical, and other types of biomedical data readily available to those who need it.

NLM plays a vital role in biomedical discovery and the translation of biomedical research into practice. NLM builds and employs powerful, sophisticated tools to collect, organize, search, and disseminate data that enable innovation to power new kinds of discovery. NLM is a library for the world, and its work forms the backbone of scientific communication. NLM makes information and knowledge flow—ensuring that scientists, policymakers, clinicians, patients, and the public have access to biomedical information 24 hours a day, 7 days a week.

Advancing Science and Communication to Enhance Human Health

NLM's success is driven in large part by the ability to adapt to changes in science, technology, and society. NLM's genomic and literature resources are vital to helping scientists and clinicians understand biomedical processes and create diagnostic and therapeutic innovations. NLM's technological infrastructure bridges the gap between resources and action and enabled a rapid response to the COVID-19 pandemic in the following ways:

- Accelerated access to coronavirus-related literature
- Partnered with publishers to make coronavirus-related articles freely available
- Created new literature search-and-retrieval strategies
- Expedited deposits, access, and use of SARS-CoV-2 sequence data through its publicly available genetic databases
- Engaged the public to address COVID-19 misinformation
- Conducted key computational research to enhance understanding of the virus' evolution and its impact on human health

In response to the pandemic, NLM reoriented its research programs, which resulted in the development of new methods to characterize the SARS-CoV-2 virus and make readily accessible sequence information. NLM also expanded its literature services, which promoted more rapid access to early COVID-19-related results and clinical guidelines. NLM shared the expertise of its scientific staff across major NIH and government-wide pandemic-related initiatives and leveraged its Network of the National Library of Medicine (NNLM) to support community-based engagement on COVID-19 testing for NIH's Rapid Acceleration of Diagnostics (RADx) advanced testing program, among other major NIH initiatives.

NLM continues to employ computational approaches to advance biomedical discovery and improve human health. Its work helps the scientific and public health communities derive additional knowledge from clinical text and the published literature, model biological systems, understand how viruses evolve and mutate, and extract knowledge from large-scale health databases and medical images. NLM's grantees conduct vital bioinformatics and data science research to support biomedical discovery and clinical care. NLM engages with other NIH institutes and centers, agencies across the government, and external stakeholders to strengthen NLM's infrastructure, reduce redundancy in its information services and operations, promote access to and preservation of its collection, and employ more efficient ways to engage with the public.

To protect the NLM staff while maintaining continuity of operations during the COVID-19 pandemic, NLM engaged in new methods of work to support a remote-capable workforce and leveraged agile, team-oriented product and project management strategies. In fiscal year (FY) 2021 NLM continued efforts to increase staff diversity, equity, and inclusion, and it is active in supporting NIH's UNITE initiative to address structural racism within the NIH-supported and greater scientific community.

Implementing Innovative and Sustainable Solutions

Increased investments in NLM programs and activities have allowed NLM to expand its research portfolio, enhance its information services, and improve its infrastructure to better serve its stakeholders.

Over the past six years NLM has accelerated investments in its intramural and extramural research programs. To build a data science-savvy workforce, NLM has engaged young investigators at the intersection of biology, clinical knowledge, analytics, and visualization across its intramural and extramural research programs. NLM has funded the groundbreaking data science and open science research needed to advance discovery and health. NLM has expanded extramural funding—nearly doubling the number of research project grants—and created the knowledge base to bring the power of data science to scientists, clinicians, and patients.

As the pace and complexity of biomedical research increase, so too does the demand for NLM's biomedical and genomic information services. Sustained investments in information services have allowed NLM to increase capacity, improve functionality, and leverage modern cloud-based technologies. NLM expanded its ability to connect digital objects of research resources, such as linking unique identifiers for genetic sequence records in its databases with the published literature. These investments have improved the resilience of its infrastructure and information services and made research less expensive and more accessible by allowing researchers to bring analysis tools to the data on the cloud. Additionally, through its investments in cloud computing and advanced computational technology, NLM is achieving greater efficiencies in the fields of data science and health care by creating more reliable, secure, and modern computational platforms that foster appropriate and authorized global data sharing to enhance human health.

Accelerating Discovery and Engaging Stakeholders

Science is changing quickly, and NLM is continually adapting to changes in the data science landscape to identify and make new modes of scientific communication widely available. This requires reflecting on what is known and anticipating what needs to be known as NLM builds and maintains its research portfolio, resources, and services. Innovation in the use of computer algorithms is part of NLM's effort to modernize indexing and annotation of journals in MEDLINE, NLM's premier bibliographic database of journal articles in life sciences, with a concentration on biomedicine. These are ways NLM continues to fulfill its mission to maintain, preserve, and make knowledge for medicine and health accessible in perpetuity.

NLM advances its mission by actively engaging and serving a range of stakeholders, including the public, communities, librarians, clinicians, researchers, and public health experts. Leveraging 8,800 points of presence around the country through NNLM, NLM provides data science librarian support to major academic medical schools and centers, brings trusted health information to communities, and provides highly respected community anchors to support awareness and engagement in major NIH initiatives such as the Community Engagement Alliance (CEAL) Against COVID-19 Disparities and the All of Us Research Program.

Advancing NIH and Government-Wide Priorities

NLM advances and supports NIH and government-wide initiatives by contributing expertise to national priorities such as the COVID-19 pandemic response; improving health equity; and advancing data science, artificial intelligence (AI), and open science.

NLM is gathering and sharing variant sequence data through the SARS-CoV-2 Sequencing for Public Health Emergency Response, Epidemiology, and Surveillance (SPHERES) initiative led by the Centers for Disease Control and Prevention (CDC); facilitating standards development by the Public Health Alliance for Genomic Epidemiology (PHA4GE) coalition; and analyzing sequencing data and generating reports for the NIH Accelerating COVID-19 Therapeutic Interventions and Vaccines (ACTIV) Tracking Resistance and Coronavirus Evolution (TRACE) initiative. NLM is making SARS-CoV-2 sequence data freely available to researchers through its Sequence Read Archive (SRA), the world's largest publicly available repository of high-throughput sequencing data, and is also making these data available through commercial cloud platforms.

NLM is the NIH lead in a cross-government effort to ensure a data-driven response to the COVID-19 pandemic and prepare for future public health threats. In collaboration with the CDC, the Office of the National Coordinator for Health Information Technology, and the White House Office of Science and Technology

Policy, NLM is reviewing the effectiveness, interoperability, and connectivity of public health data systems and efforts to advance public health data and analytics. NLM advances NIH's long-standing commitment to make available to the public the results of research it supports and conducts, including publications and scientific data. The PubMed Central (PMC) digital archive provides the public with access to the full text of nearly 7.5 million research articles. Through the launch of the NIH Preprint Pilot, NLM is increasing the discoverability of preprints resulting from NIH-funded scientific research. Since June 2020 NLM has made more than 2,700 preprints reporting NIH-funded COVID-19 research publicly available in PMC and discoverable in PubMed, a database containing more than 33 million citations and abstracts of biomedical literature. NLM is enhancing approaches to help NIH-funded scientists make scientific data and research products findable, accessible, interoperable, and reusable through its information services and data repositories. Nearly two-thirds of articles published in FY 2021 and deposited in PMC under the NIH Public Access Policy include associated supplemental material, such as datasets, images, tables, videos, or files. In FY 2021 NLM added nearly 38,000 new studies to ClinicalTrials.gov, its public registry of clinical trials studies, and added more than 5,000 protocols and statistical analysis plans to registered studies. NLM also made available results summaries for more than 7,000 completed studies. These are just a few examples of the ways in which NLM supports NIH's efforts to promote research transparency and ensure that research findings are contributing to the enhancement of human health.

Future Initiatives

NLM will continue to lead the development of analytics that uncover new patterns and biomedical phenomena from large genetic and literature databases; create innovative ways to reach scientists and society with trustable health information; and develop health data literacy among scientists, clinicians, librarians, and consumers.

Priorities for FY 2023 include efforts to:

- Accelerate biomedical and computational health data science—Through increased investments in intramural and extramural research, NLM will create strategies to support efficient and accurate exploration of large biomedical databases and generate new analytical methods and models to gain new insights from clinical data. NLM will continue to train the next generation of biomedical informatics and data science researchers through its university-based research training programs and accelerate staff training in informatics, data science, and AI.

- Support public accountability and open science—NLM will leverage its expertise in creating high-quality, sustainable, and secure databases to make biomedical research information and data publicly accessible through NLM offerings, including ClinicalTrials.gov, PMC, and SRA. NLM will make biomedical research information and data accessible to support the emerging needs of scientists, clinicians, and the public.

- Modernize NLM's infrastructure and organization—With the support and collaboration of NIH leadership and its institutes and centers, NLM will continue to build a 21st-century digital library that offers literature, data, analytical models, and new approaches to scientific communications that are accessible, sustainable, and available 24 hours a day, 7 days a week. NLM will continue to modernize its computational research infrastructure, improve its operational and organizational efficiency, and facilitate scientific discovery to enhance human health.

- Contribute to NIH and government-wide priorities—NLM will develop new ways to share and apply its scientific, policy, and program expertise in data science, data management, infrastructure, security, and workforce development to support priorities empowered by data science, AI, and open science. NLM will provide critical data management and guidance to support NIH efforts, such as health across the life span and the science of aging, including understanding why and how cells age.

United States Government Publishing Office

732 North Capitol St. N.W., Washington, DC 20401
http://www.gpo.gov

Gary Somerset
Chief Public Relations Officer
202-512-1957, e-mail gsomerset@gpo.gov

The U.S. Government Printing Office (GPO) was created when President James Buchanan signed Joint Resolution 25 on June 23, 1860. GPO opened its doors for business nine months later, on March 4, 1861, the same day Abraham Lincoln took the oath of office to become the 16th president of the United States. On that day, GPO began operation in buildings purchased by Congress, at the same address it occupies today.

A historic moment occurred for GPO in December 2014, when President Barack Obama signed into law a bill changing the agency's name to the U.S. Government Publishing Office. The new name reflects the increasingly prominent role that GPO plays in providing access to government information in digital formats through GPO's GovInfo (govinfo.gov), apps, e-books, and related technologies. The information needs of Congress, federal agencies, and the public have evolved beyond only print, and GPO has transformed itself to meet its customers' needs.

Under Title 44 of the United States Code, GPO is responsible for the production and distribution of information products for all three branches of the federal government. These include the official publications of Congress, federal agencies, and the courts. Today GPO provides products in print and a variety of digital forms, all of which are born digitally. In addition, GPO produces passports for the Department of State and secure credentials for many government agencies.

As the federal government's official resource for gathering, producing, cataloging, providing access to, and preserving published information in all forms, GPO has disseminated millions of publications to the public through its sales and library programs. GPO's Superintendent of Documents and its Library Services and Content Management (LSCM) organizations administer and manage the four programs required by Title 44:

- The Federal Depository Library Program (FDLP)
- Cataloging and indexing
- Distributing government publications to the International Exchange Service
- The By-Law Program, under which certain government publications are distributed to members of Congress and to other government agencies as mandated by law

FDLP dates back to 1813, when Congress first authorized legislation to ensure the provision of certain congressional documents to selected universities, historical societies, and state libraries. At that time, the secretary of state was responsible for distributing publications. In 1857 the secretary of the interior assumed oversight of printing and the designation of depositories. In the Printing Act of 1895, the governance of the depository program was transferred to the Office of the Superintendent of Documents at GPO. Duties remained largely unchanged until 1993, when Public Law 103-40, the Government Printing Office Electronic Information Access Enhancement Act, amended GPO's duties to not only provide public access to printed publications but to Internet-accessible publications as well.

The program continues to serve a vital need of the public through the partnership with federal depository libraries located in nearly every congressional district. GPO is obviously a much different agency in the digital age than it was years ago. While its name has changed, its mission—America Informed—is as important and relevant as ever. GPO's public information programs are examples of the agency's long-standing commitment to free, permanent public access to U.S. government information.

The Superintendent of Documents and LSCM organizations support GPO's continued digital transformation through initiatives to enhance historic and current content on GovInfo and the Catalog of U.S. Government Publications (CGP), as well as through the development of free online tools and resources to help FDLP libraries manage their depository library more effectively and efficiently. LSCM has been working closely with libraries to help preserve tangible government documents in FDLP library collections.

Along with FDLP and an online dissemination system, which are no-fee public access programs, GPO also provides access to official federal information through public sales featuring secure ordering through an online bookstore and partnerships with the private sector that offer federal publications as e-books.

In an effort to further openness and transparency, the Superintendent of Documents seeks comments from the depository library community, interested stakeholders, and the general public on various documents, including draft policies. In fiscal year (FY) 2021 the Superintendent of Documents established a more formal process to obtain, report, and retain comments received. Two new webpages were added to FDLP.gov: Open Requests for Comments and Closed Requests for Comments. When comments are sought, there is an entry on the Open Requests page for the duration of the comment period. The Closed Requests page serves as a record of the comment process, providing an entry for any document for which a call for comments was made.

GPO Welcomes New Superintendent of Documents

GPO director Hugh Halpern named Scott Matheson as the new Superintendent of Documents in September 2022. In this role, Matheson leads GPO in providing public access to government information published by the U.S. Congress, federal agencies, and the federal courts. Matheson will also focus on modernizing FDLP in cooperation with Congress and GPO's library partners. In addition, he oversees GPO's Publication and Information Sales unit and GPO's distribution facilities in Colorado and Maryland. Matheson joined GPO in early October 2022.

National Collection Strategic Plan

The Superintendent of Documents released the National Collection of U.S. Government Public Information: Strategic Plan for FY 2023–FY 2027 on

September 6, 2022. The focus of this strategic plan is building and curating the national collection, thereby ensuring the public's right to free, equitable, and convenient access to past and present public government information resources. Additional focus is given to transforming the LSCM business unit into a primarily digital content and services organization. Comments were received on the draft strategic plan from the depository library community, the Depository Library Council (DLC), and the LSCM team. The comments resulted in revisions to the plan.

Task Force on a Digital FDLP

To contribute to the continued evolution of FDLP, in FY 2021, in response to a recommendation from DLC, GPO director Halpern established a task force to study the feasibility of a digital FDLP. The 23-member task force has representation from DLC, depository libraries of different types and sizes, library associations, federal agencies, and GPO. The task force worked throughout 2022 to investigate whether a digital FDLP is possible, and if so, to define the scope of a digital depository program and make recommendations as to how to implement and operate such a program. The task force's purview included an examination of the current landscape in federal depository libraries, of FDLP-related operations at GPO, and of the dissemination of publications by federal agencies. The task force's draft report was available for public comment from September 14 to October 14, 2022. Public comments were reviewed thoroughly by the task force and evaluated for inclusion in the final report, which was made available to the FDLP community in December 2022. Ultimately, the task force determined that FDLP can and should go digital. Halpern was expected to provide his response to the report in early 2023.

Partnerships and Collaborations

GPO Partnerships

Since 1997 GPO has developed strategic partnerships with federal depository libraries, federal agencies, and other institutions to increase public access to electronic and tangible U.S. government information.

GPO's partner categories are:

- Preservation Steward (for historic tangible content)
- Digital Preservation Steward
- Digital Content Contributor
- Digital Access Partner
- Cataloging and Metadata Contributor
- Other/Specialized

Partnering is an integral part of how GPO is ensuring an "America Informed," and over the past two decades, these partnerships have grown and evolved. At the close of FY 2022 there were 74 official GPO partnerships: 46 Preservation Stewards, 1 Digital Preservation Steward, 7 Digital Content Contributors, 17 Digital Access Partners, and 3 Cataloging and Metadata Contributors.

GPO Collaborations

In FY 2022 the LSCM team contributed to and collaborated with groups in support of the FDLP and Cataloging & Indexing Program:

- In a collaboration with the Law Library of Congress, GPO is cataloging Global Legal Research Directorate Reports to increase public access. In FY 22 GPO cataloged 1,109 of these reports.
- Through its partnership in the Civics Renewal Network (CRN), a consortium of organizations committed to strengthening civic life in the United States by increasing the quality of civics education in our nation's schools, GPO makes available, through the CRN website, K–12 resources that support civics education.
- GPO continues to be a member of the Technical Report Archive & Image Library (TRAIL), which works to ensure that federal technical reports are openly accessible.
- The Digital Public Library of America (DPLA) and GPO continued their collaboration to broaden public access to the information made available via CGP. Through the partnership, more than 266,000 records from CGP are available to the public through the DPLA website. Examples of records include the federal budget; laws; federal regulations; and congressional hearings, reports, and documents.
- GPO has been a member of OCLC since 1976 and contributes bibliographic records for U.S. government information daily to the international database.
- In October 2018 the GPO team began cataloging Congressional Research Service (CRS) reports for CGP and OCLC in an agreement with the Library of Congress.

LSCM Pilot Projects

LSCM Pilot Projects are an opportunity for collaboration between LSCM and federal depository libraries. These jointly conducted projects are envisioned to benefit the larger FDLP community and ultimately to enhance access to the National Collection of U.S. Government Public Information. Two pilot projects are currently underway in LSCM. Pilot Project 1 is proceeding with the Merrill Cazier Library at Utah State University and Pilot Project 2 with the University of North Texas Libraries.

FDLP Academy

The FDLP Academy was launched to support the FDLP community's education and training needs and to advance U.S. government information literacy. The FDLP Academy enhances U.S. government information knowledge through events, conferences, webinars, and webcasts coordinated by GPO that cover a variety of government information topics. Many sessions are presented by the GPO team, while others are presented by staff from other federal agencies and from members of the FDLP community, as recruited and hosted by GPO.

Since its inception in 2012, the FDLP Academy has hosted almost 700 webinars, with more than 78,000 combined registrants and almost 175 recorded webcasts. Training topics cover all aspects of government information resources and librarianship.

Enhancing Content in GovInfo

LSCM has worked closely with GPO's Office of Programs, Strategy, & Technology (PST) throughout the development and ongoing enhancement of GovInfo. Continuing to add to the collections currently available on GovInfo is of the highest priority, with a goal of offering complete and historic holdings to its collections. Notable additions in FY 2022 include:

- The Law Library of Congress and GPO continue to collaborate on digitization of the U.S. Congressional Serial Set. Since the initial public release, 115 additional volumes have been added to the GovInfo collection.
- The ability to browse the U.S. Congressional Serial Set by topic
- The Monthly Catalog browse page is updated to include entry numbers and index contents.
- More than 800 historic congressional hearings
- New publications from digital content contributor Boise State University
- Public Papers of the Presidents of the United States: Barack Obama (2016, Books I and II)
- 2021 Government Manual
- 2020 US Code (United States Code, 2018 Edition, Supplement 2)
- Statutes at Large, Volume 128 (113th Congress, 2nd Session)
- Federal Register Index, 2021
- Code of Federal Regulations Index and Finding Aids, 2021
- Congressional Pictorial Directory: 117th Congress
- Railroad Retirement Board publications
- Seven new courts opted into publishing to the U.S. Courts Opinions collection, bringing the total number of courts participating in the program to 156.

Trustworthy Digital Repository Audit and Certification of GovInfo

Since 2015 GPO has worked to be named as a Trustworthy Digital Repository (TDR) for government information through certification of GovInfo under ISO 16363:2012. In December 2021 GPO was awarded re-certification of GovInfo ISO 16363:2012 TDR compliance. Certification of GovInfo from an accredited certifying body validates GPO's commitment to standards-based digital preservation practices and activities across 109 criteria. GPO underwent its annual surveillance audit required to maintain certification in FY 2022 and was awarded re-certification once again in December 2022.

GPO is also pursuing certification under CoreTrustSeal. CoreTrustSeal offers a core-level certification based on the DSA–WDS Core Trustworthy Data Repositories Requirements catalog and procedures. By participating in the CoreTrustSeal process, GPO may also be better positioned to engage with other federal institutions that have data and information repositories that may have difficulty navigating the ISO 16363:2012 standard and turning its requirements into actionable procedures. GPO's application for certification under CoreTrustSeal was submitted on June 28, 2022.

FDLP LibGuides

FDLP LibGuides is a service provided by GPO for depository libraries and the public. Guides are created by the LSCM team on a variety of topics, including those requested by the FDLP community. All guides are available for free use. Libraries and agencies can also submit their own guides for inclusion on the FDLP LibGuides Community page. In an effort to provide resources that are useful to all FDLP libraries, the LSCM team members continue to review the site and make enhancements to its look and content. FDLP LibGuides has had more than 133,000 views to the 165 guides offered.

Catalog of U.S. Government Publications

CGP (catalog.gpo.gov) is the finding tool for locating publications produced by the federal government, both current and historic. Students, researchers, community leaders, and anyone who needs to find information published by the U.S. government can get help from this online resource. Users can access library catalog records on a wide range of topics, including defense, citizenship, U.S. laws, health, science, and more. There are also direct links to the documents—unless the publication exists only in print. CGP even has a feature called MetaLib, which lets users research and retrieve reports, articles, and citations by searching across multiple U.S. government databases at once. What's more, there's a collection of U.S. government e-books from a variety of federal agencies, all free to access. There were more than 35 million successful searches of CGP in FY 2022.

A service was launched in October 2017 to provide sets of bibliographic records from CGP free of charge on a monthly basis via GPO's CGP on the GitHub repository site. The CGP on GitHub datasets contain records produced by the GPO team according to national standards such as Resource Description and Access (RDA) and Anglo-American Cataloging Rules (AACR2) and include GPO Historic Shelflist project brief bibliographic records and other retrospective records.

Web Archiving

The FDLP Web Archive provides point-in-time captures of U.S. federal agency websites while preserving the functionality of the sites to the greatest extent possible. The aim is to provide permanent public access to federal agency web content. GPO harvests and archives the websites with Archive-It, a subscription-based web harvesting and archiving service offered by the Internet Archive.

LSCM continues to harvest digital publications and websites in order to advance FDLP collection development efforts. Throughout FY 2022 LSCM has:

- Increased the size of the FDLP Web Archive collection to 44.5TB, with more than 454,000,000 URLs crawled
- Made available 217 website collections in the FDLP Web Archive on Archive-It and 269 records available through CGP

FDLP Distribution Facilities

At GPO's distribution facility in Laurel, Maryland, the GPO team continues to distribute publications, fulfill claims, and send special mailings of tangible items to federal depository libraries and international libraries participating in the International Exchange Service. In FY 2022 the team distributed 4,371 titles, totaling 644,874 copies of materials, to FDLP libraries.

At GPO's distribution facility in Pueblo, Colorado, the team distributes FDLP promotional items to FDLP libraries nationwide. As of the end of FY 2022 the Pueblo team managed the inventory and dissemination of 27 different types of FDLP handouts and promotional items.

National Technical Information Service

U.S. Department of Commerce, Alexandria, VA 22312

Wayne Strickland

Director

The National Technical Information Service (NTIS) has long been in the forefront of information collection and retrieval. Established in 1945 as the Publication Board to collect and disseminate government-sponsored research, NTIS became the first major computerized database of scientific and technical information in 1964. In the 1990s NTIS began digitizing the full texts of the reports in its collection and in 2009 began an online subscription service to make those full-text digital copies immediately downloadable.

NTIS manages the largest publicly available U.S. government-sponsored collection of technical and scientific reports, which totals more than 3 million publications. This collection is called the National Technical Reports Library (NTRL), a data dissemination program that involves a multistep process, including document acquisition, indexing, summarizing, and archiving. Through NTRL's online portal, this collection is also made available for comprehensive online bibliographies, commercial database vendors, and document delivery services.

Today almost one-third of NTRL's 3 million federal research documents, (approximately 998,000 documents comprising approximately 3.2 terabytes of data) are available as fully digitized text to download at no charge. The database covers a wide variety of topics, including aeronautics, artificial intelligence, chemistry, energy, the environment, health care, library and information sciences, mathematics, medicine and biology, pandemics, physics, and transportation. In all, there are 39 major subject categories and 375 subcategories. The database is updated weekly, and, historically, more than 10,000 federally funded scientific reports are added every year.

To ensure perpetual access to authentic federally funded scientific research data in a "raw" format for academia, industry, and promoting innovation, Chapter 23 of Title 15 of the United States Code (15 U.S.C. 1151-1157) codified NTIS's basic authority to operate a permanent clearinghouse of scientific and technical information. With this chapter, NTIS was also given authority to charge fees for its products and services and to recover all costs through such fees "to the extent feasible."

This authority was restated in the National Technical Information Act of 1988, codified as 15 U.S.C. 3704b. That act gave NTIS the authority to enter joint ventures and declared the clearinghouse to be a permanent federal function that could not be eliminated or privatized without congressional approval.

The American Technology Preeminence Act of 1992 (Public Law 102-245) (1) required all costs associated with bibliographic control to be recovered by fees, (2) required agencies to make copies of their scientific and technical reports available to NTIS, and (3) directed NTIS to focus on developing new electronic methods and media for disseminating information.

In 2016 NTRL was transitioned to be publicly accessible for free while serving active consumers who include technical professionals and librarians.

Through its stewardship, NTIS recognizes the value of this digital asset and strives to provide a web-friendly NTRL customer experience, which enables straightforward access to such a unique, original, and authenticated collection of scientific, technical, and engineering information. NTIS removed its cost-recovery subscription service and began providing free public access to the entire NTRL clearinghouse. This open access for NTRL publicly expanded the advanced search capabilities for title words, source agency, authors, publication year, and full-text availability. NTIS's Office of the Chief Information Officer (OCIO) team created the infrastructure for a metadata bibliographic database management system (MBS).

The future of NTRL will include exploring open-source publishing technologies and the development of application architecture for automated cataloging and indexing. Such technology modernization will ensure efficiencies for even greater compliance with §3704b, which mandates the transfer of federal scientific and technical information through the encouragement of the head of each federal executive department or agency in a timely manner to NTIS. Ongoing efforts to upgrade the NTRL content management system have become an NTIS priority. A primary focus is to make sure that the public and the research community benefit from the eventual digitization of all tangible formatted legacy documents.

NTIS is collaborating with federal agencies regarding modernization strategies for the submission of future content digitally. Additionally, NTIS has begun investigating and implementing innovative options for automated cataloging and indexing of the new scientific content. As science dictates, NTIS will also ensure updates to researched information categories in NTRL.

The 21st-century goal for NTRL is to continue being at the forefront of promoting economic growth by ensuring perpetual availability to federally funded scientific research in all data formats. NTRL will comprise important information that will be readily reproducible, discoverable, and openly accessible. Establishing trusted relationships with the federal labs, federal agencies, the library community, researchers, industry, and the public will provide an economic growth pipeline for showcasing federal research, authorship, and achievement to better serve the public.

More than 300 U.S. government agencies and federal laboratories contribute to the NTIS collection, including the National Aeronautics and Space Administration; the Environmental Protection Agency; the departments of Agriculture, Commerce, Defense, Energy, Health and Human Services, Homeland Security, Interior, Labor, Treasury, Veterans Affairs, Housing and Urban Development, Education, and Transportation; and numerous other agencies.

National Technical Reports Library (NTRL) on the Web

NTIS offers web-based access to federal information and data on scientific, business, and technical research products at https://ntrl.ntis.gov/NTRL.

Since NTIS discontinued its operating cost-recovery efforts in 2016 for NTRL (which historically utilized a fee-based subscription model), NTIS has been providing the public NTRL service for free while continuously exploring alternative funding models and partnerships to minimize operating loss and modernize maintenance of this valued U.S. government-sponsored collection through automation technologies. In recent years NTIS succeeded in cost-saving efforts that helped dramatically lower operating losses.

Key NTIS/NTRL Contacts

Email

ntrlhelpdesk@ntis.gov

Mail

National Technical Information Service
5301 Shawnee Rd.
Alexandria, VA 22312

National Archives and Records Administration

700 Pennsylvania Ave. NW, Washington, DC 20408
1-86-NARA-NARA or 1-866-272-6272
https://www.archives.gov

The National Archives and Records Administration (NARA), an independent federal agency, is the nation's record keeper. NARA safeguards and preserves the important records of all three branches of the federal government so that the people can discover, use, and learn from this documentary heritage. NARA ensures public access to government records, which strengthens democracy by allowing Americans to claim their rights of citizenship, hold their government accountable, and understand their history so they can participate more effectively in their government.

NARA carries out its mission through a national network of archives and archival field offices and records centers, stretching from Boston to San Francisco and Atlanta to Seattle, in addition to 15 presidential libraries that document administrations back to that of Herbert Hoover—a total of 43 facilities in 17 states, plus the District of Columbia.

The agency includes the National Historical Publications and Records Commission (NHPRC), the grant-making arm of NARA; the Office of the Federal Register, which publishes the official records of the actions of the government; the Information Security Oversight Office (ISOO), which oversees the government's classification programs; the National Declassification Center (NDC), which is streamlining the declassification process; and the Office of Government Information Services (OGIS), which reviews agencies' Freedom of Information Act (FOIA) administration and practices.

NARA also assists federal agencies, the courts, and Congress in documenting their activities by providing records storage, offering reference service, administering records management programs, scheduling records, and retiring noncurrent records to federal records centers. NARA also provides training, advice, and guidance on many issues relating to records management.

NARA's constituents and stakeholders include educators and their students at all levels, a history-minded public, family historians, the media, the archival community, and a broad spectrum of professional associations and researchers in such fields as history, political science, law, library and information services, and genealogy.

The size and breadth of NARA's holdings are staggering. NARA's electronic records holdings amount to 1,265.7 terabytes of data. This consists of records that were "born digital" and managed in a digital form throughout their life cycle.

In addition, NARA maintains traditional holdings that will be converted to digital form for preservation purposes and to ensure access to them far into the future. This, along with the ever-growing quantity of born-digital records, creates a big data challenge for NARA and the federal government. NARA's current traditional holdings include more than 15 billion pages and 44 million photographs.

NARA has issued a new Strategic Plan for fiscal years (FY) 2022 through 2026, setting its long-term objectives. It has four strategic goals: Make Access Happen, Connect with Customers, Maximize NARA's Value to the Nation, and

Build Our Future through Our People. Specific initiatives are underway at NARA to reach each goal.

Records and Access

Information Security Oversight Office (ISOO)

ISOO is responsible to the president for policy and oversight of the government-wide security classification system, the National Industrial Security Program, and the emerging federal policy on "controlled unclassified information" (CUI). ISOO receives policy and program guidance from the assistant to the president for national security affairs and National Security Council staff in the Executive Office of the President.

ISOO oversees the security classification programs (classification, safeguarding, and declassification) in both government and industry. It is also responsible for exercising NARA's authorities and responsibilities as the executive agent for controlled unclassified information. ISOO contributes materially to the effective implementation of the government-wide security classification program and has a direct impact on the performance of thousands of government employees and contract personnel who work with classified national security information. For more information on ISOO, visit archives.gov/isoo.

National Declassification Center (NDC)

In December 2009 Executive Order 13526 established NDC within the National Archives to address declassification of classified federal government records. The focus of this effort was to promote transparency and accountability of records created by the executive branch of the U.S. government.

NDC led a process that streamlined the declassification review processes for classified historical records and eliminated a 350-million-page backlog at the National Archives. NDC is committed to completing QA on all accessioned classified records no later than one year after they have been transferred to our custody. To facilitate public access to these records, NDC established an Indexing on Demand process that allows a researcher to request priority indexing and release for eligible record series.

NDC also processes requests for classified records under the Freedom of Information Act (FOIA) and Mandatory Review Provisions of Executive Order 13526 (MDR). To respond to these requests, NDC works closely with other agencies to ensure exempted records are reviewed by the appropriate equity agency, then processes declassified and redacted records for release. For more information about NDC, go to archives.gov/declassification.

Office of Government Information Services (OGIS)

As the FOIA Ombudsman, OGIS educates stakeholders about the FOIA process, resolves disputes, and assesses agency compliance.

The Open Government Act of 2007 created OGIS within the National Archives. The statute requires that OGIS offer mediation services to help resolve

FOIA disputes and review agency FOIA policies and procedures. FOIA also charges OGIS with identifying methods to improve compliance with the statute. The OGIS director chairs the FOIA Federal Advisory Committee. The committee brings together FOIA experts from inside and outside of government to identify major issues with the implementation of FOIA and develop consensus solutions. The OGIS director also serves as the co-chair of the Chief FOIA Officers Council.

For more information about OGIS, visit archives.gov/ogis or follow OGIS on Twitter @FOIA_Ombuds.

Electronic Records Archives (ERA)

NARA uses the Electronic Records Archives (ERA) system to take in and store electronic records from the White House, Congress, and agencies across the federal government. In addition, since 2012 NARA has required all federal agencies to use ERA to submit records schedules to NARA for approval by the Archivist of the United States, as well as to manage the transfer of all permanent records, electronic and non-electronic, to NARA. The adoption of ERA by federal agencies and the use of ERA to support the transfer of electronic presidential records have led to the transfer of increasing volumes of electronic records to NARA for preservation and eventual access through its public access portal, the National Archives Catalog (NAC).

In late 2018 NARA launched a new system, ERA 2.0, to update and enhance the agency's capabilities to meet the ever-expanding challenges in preserving born-electronic records and digitized material. ERA 2.0 uses cloud services for greater scalability in terms of storage and computer processing to increase NARA's ability to preserve and provide access to greater amounts of digital material over time.

The ERA 2.0 system consists of three major components: a digital processing environment, a digital object repository, and a business object management component. The processing component provides the capability to upload digital material of all types, gives staff a variety of software tools for verification and processing, supports the creation and editing of metadata, and allows users to submit packages of processed digital material to the repository component for preservation. The repository supports the capability to ingest processed digital material to provide for safe archival storage, delivers advanced staff search and discovery capabilities, provides digital material for further processing for preservation, and makes copies of records available for public access through NAC. The business object management component, slated for deployment to federal agencies by early 2023, will provide a redesign of the online forms and approval workflows used by NARA and federal agencies to schedule and transfer records to NARA. For more information about ERA, see archives.gov/era.

Applied Research Division

NARA's Applied Research Division serves as the agency's center for advanced and applied research capabilities in the fields of computer science, engineering, and archival science. The division's staff conducts research on new technologies, both for awareness of new types of electronic record formats that will need to be preserved and to evaluate new technologies that might be incorporated into electronic records management and preservation systems at NARA to increase their effectiveness. The staff also helps NARA managers and employees acquire the knowledge and skills they need to function effectively in e-government through presentations on new technologies. For more information, visit archives.gov/applied-research.

NARA's Website

The online entrance to the National Archives is archives.gov, which provides the most widely available means of electronic access to information about and services available from NARA. Links to various sections provide help to the particular needs of researchers, including veterans and their families, educators and students, and the general public—as well as records managers, journalists, historians, and members of Congress.

The NARA website provides the following:

- Directions on how to contact NARA and conduct research at its facilities around the country
- Direct access to certain archived electronic records at archives.gov/aad
- Digital copies of selected archived documents
- A contact form, at archives.gov/contact, for customer questions, reference requests, comments, and complaints
- Electronic versions of *Federal Register* publications
- Online exhibits
- Classroom resources for students and teachers at archives.gov/education
- Online tools such as eVetRecs (archives.gov/veterans/military-service-records), which allows veterans and their next-of-kin to complete and print, for mail-in submission, requests for their military service records

Public Access Projects

NARA's Office of Innovation is responsible for oversight of the digitization of NARA's holdings and for ensuring public access through NAC (catalog.archives.gov). The Office of Innovation is constantly developing improved tools, techniques, and workflows to accelerate access. In the coming years the Office of Innovation will continue to find new ways to improve digitization and access as we work toward our strategic goal of 500 million pages available in the catalog by the end of FY 2024. For more information, see https://www.archives.gov/about/plans-reports/strategic-plan.

Engagement with "citizen archivists" also represents a critical component to improving access. The tagging, transcribing, and commenting performed by public volunteers help to make NARA's holdings more discoverable to researchers through the addition of critical metadata and searchable text.

The History Hub (History.gov) is another tool that helps expand access to the nation's history and to NARA's holdings. After registering on the History Hub, individuals can submit questions about U.S. history; the platform allows responses from NARA staff, staff at other participating cultural heritage organizations such as the Library of Congress, and the public. This crowdsourced platform helps eliminate the silos that exist between information residing at different organizations and allows researchers, citizen historians, and archival professionals to more easily find answers to their questions.

Social Media

NARA uses multiple social media platforms to increase access to the records in its holdings, which is at the heart of its mission. The main goals of social media at NARA are to increase awareness about archival holdings and programs and to enrich the agency's relationship with the public through conversations about its mission, services, and holdings. In addition to expanding access, use of social media creates a more collaborative work environment and increases communication and knowledge sharing both within NARA and externally with other federal agencies.

NARA has 19 blogs. It also offers historical videos from its holdings and videos of recent public events on its 12 YouTube channels. The agency shares photographs and documents from its collections through Flickr Commons. Across the country, more than 200 NARA staffers contribute actively to the agency's 120-plus social media accounts, including Facebook, Twitter, Tumblr, Instagram, LinkedIn, and others.

Social media also allows NARA's researchers and friends, as well as the public, to become citizen archivists by tagging, sharing, and transcribing documents. For more information, go to archives.gov/citizen-archivist.

Additional information about NARA's social media projects is available at archives.gov/social-media.

National Archives Museum

The National Archives Museum, a set of interconnected resources made possible by a public–private partnership between NARA and the National Archives Foundation, provides a variety of ways to explore the power and importance of the nation's records.

The Rotunda at the National Archives Building in Washington, D.C., is the centerpiece of the National Archives Museum. On display are the Declaration of Independence, the Constitution, and the Bill of Rights. The Public Vaults is a 9,000-square-foot permanent exhibition that conveys the feeling of going beyond the walls of the Rotunda and into the stacks and vaults of the working archives. Dozens of individual exhibits, many of them interactive, reveal the breadth and variety of NARA's holdings.

Complementing the Public Vaults, the Lawrence F. O'Brien Gallery hosts a changing array of topical exhibits based on National Archives records. The 290-seat William G. McGowan Theater is a showplace for NARA's extensive audiovisual holdings and serves as a forum for lectures and discussions.

The David M. Rubenstein Gallery houses a permanent interactive exhibit, Records of Rights, which documents the struggles and debates over civil rights and liberties throughout American history. The Rubenstein Gallery is also home to a 1297 copy of the Magna Carta, owned by Rubenstein.

The Boeing Learning Center is an open and engaging educational space for teachers, parents, and families to explore documents found in the exhibits and in the NARA catalog. The center's education Learning Lab offers an immersive field trip adventure for middle and high school students that links NARA holdings to the curriculum in the classroom. Weekly programs are offered in the Boeing Learning Center for elementary school children as well as families. The center also offers educators professional development opportunities throughout the year as well as weeklong summer workshops.

DocsTeach (docsteach.org) is an education website designed to provide instructional resources to teachers in order to support best practices of teaching with primary sources. Using documents in NARA's holdings as teachable resources, DocsTeach provides teachers with the tools and resources they need to foster civic literacy and civic engagement. This site gives all teachers access to primary sources, instruction in best practices, and opportunities to interact with their counterparts across the nation.

When developing the DocsTeach site, the agency established an online community that serves as a virtual meeting place for NARA's education team and colleagues from schools, institutions, and organizations nationwide to collaborate and share innovative ideas and best practices for this online resource.

The National Archives' New York City field office is located in the Alexander Hamilton U.S. Custom House at the southern tip of Manhattan. There, NARA has a large research center as well as diverse educational and program activities offered for free in the Learning Center. The Learning Center incorporates many of the resources and activities found in the Washington, D.C., building but also includes New York-specific offerings.

At its Kansas City, Missouri, field office at 400 West Pershing Road, NARA also has a welcome center, changing exhibitions, workshops, and other public programs.

A set of webpages now makes the National Archives Museum available anywhere. An illustrated history of the Charters can be found there, as well as information on educational programs, special events, and current exhibits at the National Archives.

Those traveling to Washington, D.C., can bypass the public line during peak tourist season by making online reservations at recreation.gov. For more information, see the National Archives Museum at museum.archives.gov. An online version of the Records of Rights exhibition is available at recordsofrights.org.

National Archives Research Centers

At the Robert M. Warner Research Center in the National Archives Building in Washington, D.C., and the Steny H. Hoyer Research Center at the National Archives at College Park, Maryland, researchers can consult with staff experts on federal records held in each building and submit requests to examine original documents.

The Warner Research Center holds approximately 275,000 rolls of microfilmed records documenting military service prior to World War I, immigration into the United States, the federal census, the U.S. Congress, federal courts in the District of Columbia, the Bureau of Indian Affairs, and the Freedmen's Bureau.

The center also contains an extensive, ever-expanding system of reference reports, helping researchers conduct research in federal documents.

Executive branch records housed in the National Archives Building include those of the Bureau of Indian Affairs and of civilian agencies responsible for maritime affairs. Military records in this building include those of the Army before World War I and the Navy and Marine Corps before World War II. In addition, the National Archives Building holds many records relating to the federal government's interaction with individuals; these are often consulted for genealogical research.

The Steny H. Hoyer Research Center holds textual records of civilian agencies from 1789; investigative records and military holdings that include those from the Army and Army Air Forces dating from World War I; and Navy, Marine Corps, intelligence, defense-related, and seized enemy records dating from World War II. In addition to textual records, special media records include motion pictures, still photographs and posters, sound recordings, maps, architectural drawings, aerial photographs, and electronic records. A research room for accessioned microfilm holds records of the Department of State's Berlin Document Center and other World War II-era captured documents.

Field Archives

NARA has 16 field archives where the public can do research. They are located in or near Boston, New York, Philadelphia, Atlanta, Chicago, St. Louis, Kansas City, Fort Worth, Denver, Riverside (California), San Francisco, Seattle, and Washington, D.C. Archived records of significance, as well as, in some locations, immigration records, are available for use by the public in these field archives.

Presidential Libraries

NARA operates presidential libraries for the 15 most recent U.S. presidents, from Herbert Hoover through Donald J. Trump. Presidential libraries bring together the documents and artifacts of a president and his administration and make them available to the public for study and discussion without regard for political considerations or affiliations. In addition to archiving and preserving presidential papers and objects, presidential libraries bring history to millions of visitors from around the world through public and educational programs, exhibits, and other outreach activities. At archives.gov/presidential-libraries, visitors can learn about the presidential library system as a whole and link to individual library websites to learn about the lives of the presidents and the times in which they served.

Federal Records Centers Program

NARA also serves federal agencies, the courts, and Congress by providing records storage, reference service, life-cycle management, and guidance on many issues relating to records management. A network of 18 Federal Records Centers (FRCs) stores 27 million cubic feet (about 52 billion pages) of noncurrent records for 200 agencies.

The Federal Records Centers program is nationwide. NARA has records centers in or near Atlanta; Boston; Chicago; Dayton, Ohio; Denver; Fort Worth, Texas;

Kansas City, Missouri; Miamisburg, Ohio; Lee's Summit, Missouri; Lenexa, Kansas; Philadelphia; Pittsfield, Massachusetts; Riverside, California; St. Louis; San Francisco; Seattle; Suitland, Maryland; and Valmeyer, Illinois.

Genealogy Research

Genealogy research brings thousands of people to NARA facilities every year. In its holdings, NARA has census records dating back to 1790, records dealing with immigration, land and pension records, and passenger lists from ships arriving from all over the world.

NARA is often considered the first stop in searching for one's ancestry, either at its facilities in the Washington, D.C., area or one of its 16 field archives around the country. At these locations, NARA staffers offer genealogy workshops to show the public how to look through documents dating back to the Revolutionary period.

NARA also offers an annual Genealogy Fair that is now a virtual event at which NARA staffers provide tips and techniques for researching genealogy records at the National Archives. Lectures are designed for experienced genealogy professionals and novices alike. Watch past fairs online at archives.gov/calendar/genealogy-fair.

NARA maintains close relationships with genealogical associations as well as organizations such as Ancestry.com and Fold3, whose online resources can be accessed without charge at any NARA location.

The National Archives has the census schedules from 1790 to 1940 available on microfilm. (Most of the 1890 census was destroyed in a Department of Commerce fire, although partial records are available for some states.)

Archives Library Information Center (ALIC)

The Archives Library Information Center (ALIC) provides access to information on American history and government, archival administration, information management, and government documents. ALIC is located in the National Archives at College Park, Maryland. Customers also can visit ALIC on the Internet at archives.gov/research/alic, where they will find "Reference at Your Desk" Internet links, staff-compiled bibliographies and publications, and an online library catalog. ALIC can be reached by telephone at 301-837-3415.

Government Documents

Government publications are generally available to researchers at many of the 1,250 congressionally designated federal depository libraries throughout the nation. A record set of these publications also is part of NARA's archival holdings. Publications of the U.S. Government (Record Group 287) is a collection of selected publications of government agencies, arranged by the SuDoc classification system devised by the Office of the Superintendent of Documents at the U.S. Government Publishing Office (GPO).

The core of the collection is a library established in 1895 by GPO's Public Documents Division. By 1972, when NARA acquired the library, it included official publications dating from the early years of the federal government and selected publications produced for and by federal government agencies. Since 1972 the

25,000-cubic-foot collection has been augmented periodically with accessions of government publications selected by the Office of the Superintendent of Documents as a by-product of its cataloging activity. As with the federal depository library collections, the holdings in NARA's Record Group 287 comprise only a portion of all U.S. government publications.

NARA Publications

Historically, NARA has published guides and indexes to various portions of its archival holdings. Many of these are still in print, although the most up-to-date information about NARA holdings is now available almost exclusively through online searches at archives.gov. The agency also publishes informational leaflets and brochures.

Some publications appear on NARA's website (archives.gov/publications/online), and many are available from NARA's Customer Service Center in College Park, Maryland, by calling 866-272-6272. The NARA website's publications homepage (archives.gov/publications) provides more detailed information about available publications and ordering.

General-interest books about NARA and its holdings that will appeal to anyone with an interest in U.S. history as well as facsimiles of certain documents are published by the National Archives Foundation. They are for sale at the foundation's National Archives Store in NARA's downtown Washington, D.C., building and through the store's website at nationalarchivesstore.org.

Federal Register

The *Federal Register* is the daily gazette of the U.S. government, containing presidential documents, proposed and final federal regulations, and public notices of federal agencies. It is published by the Office of the Federal Register and printed and distributed by GPO. The two agencies collaborate in the same way to produce the annual revisions of the *Code of Federal Regulations* (*CFR*). Free access to the full text of the electronic version of the *Federal Register* and *CFR*, and to an unofficial, daily-updated electronic *CFR* (the e-CFR), is available via fdsys.gov. *Federal Register* documents scheduled for future publication are available for public inspection at the Office of the Federal Register (7 G Street, N.W., Suite A-734, Washington, DC 20401) or online at the electronic Public Inspection Desk (federalregister.gov/public-inspection). Federalregister.gov provides access to proposed rules, and rules published in the *Federal Register* are open for public comment. (The website federalregister.gov and the multiagency website regulations.gov also provide the means to comment on these documents.)

The full catalog of other Office of the Federal Register publications is posted at ofr.gov and includes the *Compilation of Presidential Documents*, *Public Papers of the Presidents*, slip laws, *United States Statutes at Large*, and the *United States Government Manual*. Printed or microfiche editions of Office of the Federal Register publications also are maintained at federal depository libraries (gpo.gov/libraries).

The Public Law Electronic Notification Service (PENS) is a free subscription email service for notification of recently enacted public laws. Varied subscriptions to the daily *Federal Register* are available from federalregister.gov. Additional information about Office of the Federal Register programs appears on Facebook (facebook.com/federalregister) and Twitter (@FedRegister).

The Office of the Federal Register also publishes information about its ministerial responsibilities associated with the operation of the Electoral College and ratification of constitutional amendments and provides access to related records. Publication information concerning laws, regulations, and presidential documents and services is available from the Office of the Federal Register (telephone 202-741-6070). Information on Federal Register finding aids, the Electoral College, and constitutional amendments is available through archives.gov/federal-register.

Publications can be ordered by contacting GPO at bookstore.gpo.gov or by toll-free telephone at 866-512-1800. To submit orders by fax or by mail, see bookstore.gpo.gov/help-and-contact.

Grants

The National Historical Publications and Records Commission (NHPRC) is the national grants program of the National Archives. The Archivist of the United States chairs the commission and makes grants on its recommendation. NHPRC's 14 other members represent the president (two appointees), the Supreme Court, the Senate and House of Representatives, the departments of State and Defense, the Librarian of Congress, the American Association for State and Local History, the American Historical Association, the Association for Documentary Editing, the National Association of Government Archives and Records Administrators, the Organization of American Historians, and the Society of American Archivists.

NHPRC's mission is to provide opportunities for the American people to discover and use records that increase understanding of the nation's democracy, history, and culture. Through leadership initiatives, grants, and fostering the creation of new tools and methods, the commission connects the work of the National Archives to the work of the nation's archives. NHPRC grants help archives, universities, historical societies, professional organizations, and other nonprofit organizations to establish or strengthen archival programs, improve training and techniques, preserve and process records collections, and provide access to them through finding aids, digitization of collections, and documentary editions of the papers of significant historical figures and movements in American history. The commission works in partnership with a national network of state archives and state historical records advisory boards to develop a national archival infrastructure. For more information about the commission, visit archives.gov/nhprc. For more information about the projects it supports, go to archives.gov/nhprc.

Administration

Former Archivist of the United States, David S. Ferriero, who was appointed in 2009 by President Barack Obama, retired in April 2022. As of September 2022, NARA employed 2,569 people working at NARA locations and remotely around the country.

National Center for Education Statistics

U.S. Department of Education, Institute of Education Sciences
Potomac Center Plaza, 550 12th St. S.W., 4th fl., Washington, DC 20202

Christopher A. Cody and Tara Lawley
Academic Libraries, Integrated Postsecondary Education Data System

Maura Spiegelman
School Library Media Centers, Schools and Staffing Survey/
National Teacher and Principal Survey

In an effort to collect and disseminate more complete statistical information about libraries, the National Center for Education Statistics (NCES) initiated a formal library statistics program in 1989 that included surveys on academic libraries, school library media centers, public libraries, and state libraries. At the end of December 2006 the Public Libraries Survey and the State Library Agencies Survey were officially transferred to the Institute of Museum and Library Services (IMLS). The Academic Libraries Survey (ALS) and the School Library Media Centers Survey continued to be administered and funded by NCES. However, the School Library Media Centers Survey was incorporated into the Schools and Staffing Survey (SASS), and ALS was incorporated into the Integrated Postsecondary Education Data System (IPEDS).

The library surveys conducted by NCES are designed to provide comprehensive nationwide data on the status of libraries. Federal, state, and local officials; professional associations; and local practitioners use these surveys for planning, evaluating, and making policy. These data are also available to researchers and educators.

Past information about elementary and secondary public school library media centers is available on the SASS website, http://nces.ed.gov/surveys/sass. The Library Statistics Program's website, http://nces.ed.gov/surveys/libraries, provides links to data search tools, data files, survey definitions, and survey designs for the complete ALS files from 1996 to 2012. The IPEDS Academic Libraries Information Center, http://nces.ed.gov/ipeds/Section/Alscenter, contains current survey definitions and designs, and the IPEDS Use the Data Website at https://nces.ed.gov/ipeds/Home/UseTheData contains complete data files for the Academic Libraries (AL) component beginning in 2014. The two library surveys conducted by NCES are described next.

Academic Libraries

The AL component provides descriptive statistics from academic libraries in the 50 states, the District of Columbia, and, if applicable, other U.S. jurisdictions (Guam, the Commonwealth of the Northern Mariana Islands, Puerto Rico, and the U.S. Virgin Islands).

NCES surveyed academic libraries on a three-year cycle between 1966 and 1988. From 1988 to 1998, AL was a component of IPEDS collected on a two-year cycle. From 2000 to 2012, ALS separated from IPEDS but remained on a two-year cycle as part of the Library Statistics Program. During this time period, IPEDS and ALS data were still linked by the identification codes of the postsecondary education institutions. In aggregate, these data provide an overview of the status of academic libraries nationally and by state. Beginning with the 2014–2015 collection cycle, AL was reintegrated back into IPEDS, and the AL component became a mandatory, annual survey for all degree-granting Title IV institutions. It was at this time that many questions from the 2012 ALS collections and services sections were removed or revised. Since 2014, the AL component has undergone many changes.

Currently, the AL survey collects data on libraries in the entire universe of degree-granting Title IV postsecondary institutions using a web-based data collection system. The survey component collects the counts and the circulation/usage of books, serials, media, and databases, both in physical and electronic formats. Additionally, academic libraries report on interlibrary loan services. Also, starting in 2020–2021, the AL survey began again collecting information on library staff.

Institutions with reported total library expenditures over zero or institutions that have access to a library collection are required to report collections data, while those with expenditures equal to or greater than $100,000 are required to report collections and detailed expenditures data. Academic libraries report expenditures for salaries, wages, and fringe benefits, if paid from the library budget; materials and services expenditures; operations and maintenance expenditures; and total expenditures.

For the 2020–2021 AL survey, institutions were asked to report data to accurately reflect the time period corresponding with the IPEDS survey component, even if such reporting is seemingly inconsistent with prior-year reporting. NCES expected that some data reported during the 2020–2021 data collection year would vary from established prior trends due to the impacts of the COVID-19 pandemic. Additionally, for the AL survey, institutions were asked to include any library-related expenses that are covered by the Higher Education Emergency Relief Fund (HEERF) grants funded under the Coronavirus Aid, Relief, and Economic Security (CARES) Act, Coronavirus Response and Relief Supplemental Appropriations Act (CRRSAA), and American Rescue Plan (ARP) Act in the appropriate expense sections. These same reporting requirements were required for the AL Survey for the 2021–2022 collection cycle.

For the final 2012 ALS data collection, a First Look report, "Academic Libraries: 2012" (NCES 2014-038), was released on the NCES website in February 2014, as were the final data file and documentation for the 2012 ALS (NCES 2014-039). NCES also has a web-based peer analysis tool for AL called Compare Academic Libraries (https://nces.ed.gov/surveys/libraries/compare) using AL 2012 data. Beginning with the 2014–2015 IPEDS collection cycle and ending with the 2017–2018 IPEDS collection cycle, the following First Look reports were released for AL:

- "Enrollment and Employees in Postsecondary Institutions, Fall 2014; and Financial Statistics and Academic Libraries, Fiscal Year 2014" (NCES 2016-005)
- "Enrollment and Employees in Postsecondary Institutions, Fall 2015; and Financial Statistics and Academic Libraries, Fiscal Year 2015" (NCES 2017-024)

- "Enrollment and Employees in Postsecondary Institutions, Fall 2016; and Financial Statistics and Academic Libraries, Fiscal Year 2016" (NCES 2018-002)
- "Enrollment and Employees in Postsecondary Institutions, Fall 2017; and Financial Statistics and Academic Libraries, Fiscal Year 2017" (NCES 2019-021)

Beginning with the 2018–2019 IPEDS collection cycle, IPEDS no longer produces First Look reports; however, AL data, web reports, and tables from 2014 and on are available via the IPEDS Use the Data website (https://nces.ed.gov/ipeds/Home/UseTheData). Academic library statistics information can be obtained from Christopher A. Cody, Integrated Postsecondary Education Data System, e-mail IPEDS@ed.gov.

School Library Media Centers

National surveys of school library media centers in elementary and secondary schools in the United States were conducted in 1958, 1962, 1974, 1978, and 1986, 1993–1994, 1999–2000, 2003–2004, 2007–2008, and 2011–2012.

NCES, with the assistance of the U.S. Census Bureau, conducted the School Library Media Center Survey as part of SASS. SASS is the nation's largest sample survey of teachers, schools, and principals in K–12 public and private schools. Data from the school library media center questionnaire provide a national picture of public school library staffing, collections, expenditures, technology, and services. Results from the 2011–2012 survey can be found in "Characteristics of Public Elementary and Secondary School Library Media Centers in the United States: Results from the 2011–2012 Schools and Staffing Survey" (NCES 2013-315).

NCES also published a historical report about school libraries titled "Fifty Years of Supporting Children's Learning: A History of Public School Libraries and Federal Legislation from 1953–2000" (NCES 2005-311). Drawn from more than 50 sources, this report gives descriptive data about public school libraries since 1953. Along with key characteristics of school libraries, it also presents national and regional standards and federal legislation affecting school library media centers. Data from sample surveys are provided at the national, regional, and school levels and by state.

NCES recently redesigned SASS as the National Teacher and Principal Survey (NTPS). NTPS focuses on teachers, principals, and the schools in which they work. The 2017–2018 survey counted the number of school library media centers; data on library media center staff were not collected but will be part of the next NTPS. For more information about NTPS or to review data collected in the 2015–2016 and 2017–2018 school years, visit https://nces.ed.gov/surveys/ntps.

Additional information on school library media center statistics can be obtained from Maura Spiegelman, e-mail maura.spiegelman@ed.gov.

NCES has included some library-oriented questions relevant to the library usage and skills of the parent and the teacher instruments of the new Early Childhood Longitudinal Study (ECLS). For additional information, visit http://nces.ed.gov/ecls. Library items also appear in National Household Education Survey

(NHES) instruments. For more information about that survey, visit http://nces. ed.gov/nhes.

NCES included a questionnaire about high school library media centers in the Education Longitudinal Study of 2002 (ELS: 2002). This survey collected data from tenth graders about their schools, their school library media centers, their communities, and their home life. The report, "School Library Media Centers: Selected Results from the Education Longitudinal Study of 2002" (ELS: 2002) (NCES 2005-302), is available on the NCES website. For more information about this survey, visit http://nces.ed.gov/surveys/els2002.

How to Obtain Printed and Electronic Products

Reports are currently published in the First Look format. First Look reports consist of a short collection of tables presenting state and national totals, a survey description, and data highlights. NCES also publishes separate, more in-depth studies analyzing these data.

Internet Access

Many NCES publications (including out-of-print publications) and edited raw data files from the library surveys are available for viewing or downloading at no charge through the Electronic Catalog on the NCES website at http://nces.ed.gov/ pubsearch.

Ordering Printed Products

Many NCES publications are also available in printed format. To order one free copy of recent NCES reports, contact the Education Publications Center (ED Pubs) at https://www.usa.gov/federal-agencies/education-publications-center-edpubs, by e-mail at edpubs@edpubs.ed.gov, by toll-free telephone at 877-4-ED-PUBS (1-877-433-7827) or TTY/TDD 877-576-7734, by fax at 703-605-6794, or by mail at ED Pubs, P.O. Box 22207, Alexandria, VA 22304.

Many publications are available through the Education Resources Information Clearinghouse (ERIC) system. For more information on services and products, visit https://eric.ed.gov.

Out-of-print publications and data files may be available through the NCES Electronic Catalog on the NCES website at http://nces.ed.gov/pubsearch or through one of the 1,250 federal depository libraries throughout the United States (http://catalog.gpo.gov/fdlpdir/FDLPdir.jsp). Use the NCES publication number included in the citations for publications and data files to quickly locate items in the NCES Electronic Catalog. Use the GPO number to locate items in a federal depository library.

Defense Technical Information Center

Fort Belvoir, VA 22060
https://discover.dtic.mil

The Defense Technical Information Center (DTIC) is a Department of Defense (DoD) field activity, under the leadership of the Office of the Under Secretary of Defense for Research and Engineering. DTIC aims to be the premier knowledge resource for defense research, providing a robust science and technology (S&T) knowledge base to enable research and engineering and connect scientific communities.

With more than 4.7 million documents, DTIC is DoD's central resource for scientific and technical information, enabling the entire DoD research community to build on the accumulated knowledge base produced from the department's multibillion-dollar annual investment in S&T. DTIC provides digital applications and services that facilitate search, analysis, and collaboration, making information widely available to decision makers, researchers, engineers, and scientists across DoD.

In this capacity, DTIC has three main focus areas. Collection entails the gathering, preservation, and management of defense technical information. Dissemination involves the distribution of content across DoD to facilitate collaboration and discovery. Finally, the DoD Information Analysis Centers (DoD IACs) help solve DoD's technology challenges through rapid, flexible, and low-cost research services to acquisition program managers, DoD laboratories, Program Executive Offices (PEOs), and Combatant Commands.

Ultimately, DTIC aims to maximize the availability and use of DoD-funded technical information, while balancing information-sharing with information protection.

Reaching across the Federal Government

DTIC offers its capabilities to a broad user base within the federal government. Although some applications are publicly available on https://discover.dtic.mil, many are restricted to registered federal government and contracted personnel. Federal employees and contractors with a public key infrastructure card can access these sites with their credentials. More information about the benefits of and eligibility for restricted access can be found at https://discover.dtic.mil/dtic-registration-benefits.

Who uses DTIC applications and services? Among its registered users are:

- Acquisition personnel
- Active duty military personnel
- Congressional staff
- DoD contractors
- Engineers
- Faculty and students at military schools and universities
- Historians

- Information professionals/librarians
- Program analysts
- Program executive offices
- Researchers
- S&T advisors
- Scientists
- Security managers
- Small-business owners
- Software engineers and developers

Collection

DTIC's holdings include both public and access-controlled documents. Its information collection activities include working with DoD organizations and contractors; other U.S. government organizations and their contractors; and nonprofit organizations on gathering, managing, and preserving the results of DoD-funded scientific, research, and engineering activities. DTIC primarily accepts information electronically and, when necessary, in physical print and digital formats such as CD and DVD. More information about submission and selection is available at https://discover.dtic.mil/submit-documents.

DTIC's holdings include more than 4.7 million documents, such as technical reports on completed research, research summaries of planned and ongoing work, independent research and development summaries, defense technology transfer agreements, DoD planning documents, DoD-funded journal articles, DoD international agreements, conference proceedings, security classification guides, command histories, and special collections dating back to World War II.

Dissemination

The Research and Engineering (R&E) Gateway—accessible only to authorized users via https://www.dtic.mil—is the entry point to DTIC's full suite of applications, some of which are also available on the public website, https://discover.dtic .mil. In an access-controlled environment, the R&E Gateway offers access to DoD research, other scientific and technical information, and collaboration with other subject matter experts.

By providing the highest awareness of relevant information, the R&E Gateway helps the defense research community build on past work and collaborate on current projects. The broad availability of DTIC documents helps avoid duplication of effort and maximize the efficient use of DoD project funds.

DTIC's applications and products include:

- R&E Gateway Search—Available to registered users, Search is DTIC's principal application for discovering scientific and technical information from DTIC's repository of 4.7 million documents. With Search, users can access DoD's body of S&T knowledge to quickly find the most relevant information for their research needs.

- *Journal of DoD Research and Engineering (JDR&E)*—JDR&E is published quarterly for registered users. An access-controlled forum, *JDR&E* advances the development of DoD priority technologies through rigorous peer review of scientific research. The journal provides visibility into controlled defense research and promotes the scientific collaboration that results in new warfighter capabilities.
- PubDefense—In 2013 the White House Office of Science and Technology Policy mandated that federally funded, scholarly journal articles must be made available and free to the public following a 12-month embargo. PubDefense is DTIC's publicly accessible tool to access journal articles, conference papers, and related materials resulting from research funded by DoD and the Office of the Director of National Intelligence/Intelligence Advanced Research Projects Agency. Public datasets associated with these scholarly publications are also available through PubDefense. The application is available at https://publicaccess.dtic.mil/padf_public/#/home.
- Horizons—Horizons is an aggregate tool that enables users to track DoD research across its life cycle. Horizons has recently expanded to show growing technology areas, as well as research and funding sources, including DoD Grant Awards, research clustering, project maturity, and performance tracking. Horizons intends to deliver the information needed to deduplicate similar efforts and provide focus on DoD modernization priorities. The tool will also continue to provide additional datasets, linkages, and functionality over time.
- DTIC Thesaurus—Available to the public at https://discover.dtic.mil/thesaurus, the DTIC Thesaurus provides a broad, multidisciplinary subject-term vocabulary that aids in information search and retrieval. Subject terms, called Descriptors, are organized into hierarchies, where series of narrower terms are linked to broader terms.

DoD Information Analysis Centers

DoD IACs provide research and analysis services to, and develop scientific and technical information products for, the DoD S&T community in the broad domains of cybersecurity and information systems, defense systems, and homeland defense and security. DoD IACs draw on the expertise of scientists, engineers, and information specialists who provide research and analysis to customers with diverse, complex, and challenging requirements.

DoD IACs develop and provide a broad variety of research and analysis products and services, including customer-driven research and analysis; prototyping; answers to scientific and technical inquiries; access to the S&T community's subject matter experts; technical training; and wide-ranging scientific and technical reports, articles, factsheets, State-of-the-Art Reports (SOARs), and other technical information products.

DoD IACs deliver requirements-driven research, development, analysis, prototyping, testing, and concept-design services to DoD and other government agency research challenges requiring up to five years of effort and costing hundreds of millions of dollars. DoD IACs provide access to low-cost research and development contract vehicles with highly qualified, pre-vetted industry leaders across a broad swath of 22 technical areas of interest to DoD: Software and Data Analysis, Cybersecurity, Modeling and Simulation, Knowledge Management and Information Sharing, Advanced Materials, Autonomous Weapon Systems, C4ISR, Directed Energy, Energetics, Military Sensing, Non-Lethal Weapons and Information Operations, RMQSI, Survivability and Vulnerability, Weapons Systems, Homeland Defense and Security, Critical Infrastructure Protection, Weapons of Mass Destruction, CBRN Defense, Biometrics, Medical, Cultural Studies, and Alternative Energy.

Education Resources

National Library of Education

Knowledge Use Division
National Center for Education Evaluation and Regional Assistance
Institute of Education Sciences, U.S. Department of Education
400 Maryland Ave. S.W., Washington, DC 20202
https://ies.ed.gov/ncee/projects/nle

Karen Tate
Director

The U.S. Department of Education's National Library of Education (NLE) is the primary resource center for education information in the federal government, serving the research needs of the Department of Education, the education community, and the public. NLE resides in the Institute of Education Sciences' National Center for Education Evaluation and Regional Assistance.

NLE was created in 1994 by Public Law 103-227, the Educational Research, Development, Dissemination, and Improvement Act of 1994, and reauthorized under Public Law 107-279, the Education Sciences Reform Act of 2002. The act outlines four primary functions of NLE:

1. Collect and archive information, including products and publications developed through, or supported by, the Institute of Education Sciences, and other relevant and useful education-related research, statistics, and evaluation materials, as well as other information, projects, and publications, that are consistent with scientifically valid research or the priorities and mission of the institute and that are developed by the department, other federal agencies, or entities
2. Provide a central location within the federal government for information about education
3. Provide comprehensive reference services on matters relating to education to employees of the Department of Education and its contractors and grantees, other federal employees, and the public
4. Promote greater cooperation and resource-sharing among providers and repositories of education information in the United States

NLE works closely with the Education Resources Information Center (ERIC). ERIC collects and archives information and provides a central location within the federal government for information about education.

The primary responsibility of NLE is to provide information services to agency staff and contractors, other government agencies, and the general public. Located in the agency's headquarters building in Washington, D.C., the library houses current and historical collections and archives of information on education issues, research, statistics, and policy; there is a special emphasis on agency publications and contractor reports, as well as current and historical federal education legislation.

NLE's primary customer base includes about 4,000 department staff nation-wide, department contractors performing research, education organizations, education researchers, and the general public.

Collections

The focus of NLE's collection is on education issues, with an emphasis on research and policy, with some materials on related topics, including law, public policy, economics, urban affairs, sociology, history, philosophy, psychology, and cognitive development. In addition to current materials, the collection has books dating from the early 19th century, including approximately 800 books on education research in the United States and more than 18,000 historical textbooks. Some of these books were donated to the library by Henry Barnard, the first U.S. commissioner of education.

NLE maintains collections of historical documents associated with the Institute of Education Sciences and the U.S. Department of Education and their predecessors. It has a complete collection of ERIC microfiche; research reports reviewed by the What Works Clearinghouse and special panels; and publications of or relating to the department's predecessor agencies, including the U.S. Bureau of Education and the U.S. Office of Education when they were part of the U.S. Department of the Interior, the Federal Security Agency, and the U.S. Department of Health, Education, and Welfare. These collections include reports, studies, manuals, statistical publications, speeches, and policy papers. NLE also serves as a selective federal depository library under the U.S. Government Publishing Office program.

Services

NLE provides reference and other information services to department staff, the education community at large, and the general public, as well as offers document delivery services to department staff and interlibrary loan services to other libraries and government agencies.

Contact Information

The National Library of Education's reference desk is available by e-mail at askalibrarian@ed.gov and by telephone from 9 A.M. to 5 P.M. weekdays, except federal holidays, at 800-424-1616 (toll free) or 202-205-5015. For the hearing-impaired, the toll-free number for the Federal Relay Service is 800-877-8339. The library is open to researchers by appointment from 9 A.M. to 5 P.M. weekdays, except federal holidays.

Education Resources Information Center

Knowledge Use Division
National Center for Education Evaluation and Regional Assistance
Institute of Education Sciences, U.S. Department of Education
550 12th St., S.W., Washington, DC 20208
202-245-8344
https://eric.ed.gov

Erin Pollard
Program Officer
erin.pollard@ed.gov

The Education Resources Information Center (ERIC) is the world's largest and most frequently used digital library of education resources. Since its inception in 1966, ERIC has added 1.9 million records of journal articles, reports, and other materials. More than 1 million records are for peer-reviewed work, and 460,000 records have free full text available to download from ERIC. Each ERIC bibliographic record contains an abstract of a journal article or gray literature document (for example, a technical report or conference paper), along with an abstract, audience, type of report, information on the assessment used, location where the research was conducted, and descriptors that work as keywords to guide users to relevant results.

Background

ERIC is a free, online database of education research that powers more than 23 million searches per year. With more than 50 years of service to the public, ERIC is one of the oldest programs in the U.S. Department of Education. As the world's largest education resource, it is distinguished by two hallmarks: free dissemination of bibliographic records and the collection of gray literature, such as research conference papers and government contractor reports.

The authorizing legislation for ERIC is part of the Education Sciences Reform Act of 2002, Public Law 107-279. This legislation envisioned ERIC subject areas or topics (previously covered by the ERIC Clearinghouses) as part of the totality of enhanced information dissemination to be conducted by the Institute of Education Sciences. In addition, information dissemination includes material on closing the achievement gap and on educational practices that improve academic achievement and promote learning.

Mission of ERIC

ERIC undertakes five major activities:

- It pursues good sources. ERIC reviews journal issues and publications from education-focused programs, organizations, and agencies to locate research in the field of education. A unique feature of ERIC is the inclusion of gray literature, such as work from nonprofits, advocacy organizations, government agencies, or other sources that are typically not indexed by commercial databases. ERIC currently provides content from 2,006 sources, including both journals and non-journal sources, such as organizations and agencies. Ninety-nine percent of ERIC's journals are peer-reviewed.

- It works to make research publicly available. ERIC negotiates with publishers to make as much of its content as freely available as possible. There are 116,000 full-text, peer-reviewed articles available for free download.

- It creates records with supporting information so users know if resources are a good fit. ERIC creates about 48,000 records per year that provide users with information about each article. Information in the record includes an abstract, audience, type of report, information on the assessment used, location where the research was conducted, and descriptors that work as keywords to guide users to relevant results. The metadata gives users the information they need to quickly see if the article will be relevant and useful to them.

- It powers search engines with ERIC metadata to help users find good research, wherever they are searching. ERIC shares its metadata with the public to enable search engines, academic databases, and other information providers to power their searches with ERIC data.

- Ii integrates with other federally funded resources. As applicable, ERIC records are linked with other federally funded resources, including What Works Clearinghouse study pages, Institute of Education Sciences (IES) grant abstracts, and links to federal websites. These interrelationships provide additional information and assist users in finding relevant and valuable IES resources.

Selection Standards

The selection policy provides that all materials added to the ERIC database are rigorous and relevant sources of research directly related to the field of education. The majority of journals indexed in ERIC are peer-reviewed, and peer-reviewed status is indicated for all journals indexed since 2004, when this data began to be documented by the ERIC system. The peer-review status for non-journals is indicated for all sources with a documented peer-review process. The collection scope includes early childhood education through higher education, vocational education, and special education. It also includes teacher education; education administration; assessment and evaluation; counseling; information technology; and the academic areas of reading, mathematics, science, environmental education, languages, and social studies.

To be considered for selection, all submissions must be in digital format and accompanied by author permission for dissemination. For individual document submissions, authors (copyright holders) can upload materials through a link on the ERIC website. Journal publishers, associations, and other entities with multiple documents also submit electronic content following guidance and instructions that are consistent with provider agreements from ERIC.

ERIC Users

About 12 million users search the ERIC website and download more than 7 million full-text documents each year from users all over the world. Approximately half of ERIC's users are driven from a commercial search engine, while 40 percent are driven from academic search engines.

ERIC can be reached at ERICRequests@ed.gov. Questions can also be transmitted via the message box on the Contact Us page on the ERIC website.

National Association and Organization Reports

American Library Association

225 N. Michigan Ave., Suite 1300, Chicago, IL 60601
800-545-2433; http://www.ala.org

Lessa Kanani'opua Pelayo-Lozada
President

The American Library Association (ALA) was founded in 1876 in Philadelphia and later chartered in the commonwealth of Massachusetts. ALA has 49,705 members, including librarians and other library staff, library trustees and friends, and other interested stakeholders from every state in the United States and many other countries. The association serves public, state, school, academic, and governmental libraries, as well as consortia, prison, and special libraries of all types.

ALA is home to eight membership divisions, each focused on a type of library or library function. They are the American Association of School Librarians (AASL); the Association for Library Service to Children (ALSC); the Association of College and Research Libraries (ACRL); Core: Leadership, Infrastructure, Futures; the Public Library Association (PLA); the Reference and User Services Association (RUSA); United for Libraries; and the Young Adult Library Services Association (YALSA).

ALA hosts 19 roundtables for members who share interests that are outside the scope of any of the divisions. A network of affiliates, chapters, and other organizations enables ALA to reach a broad audience.

ALA offices address the broad interests and issues of concern to ALA members. They track issues and provide information, services, and products for members and the public. Current ALA offices are the Chapter Relations Office (CRO); the Communications and Marketing Office (CMO); the Development Office; the Executive/ALA Governance Office; the Human Resources Office; the International Relations Office (IRO); the Library and Research Center (LARC); the Office for Accreditation; the Office for Diversity, Literacy and Outreach Services (ODLOS); the Office for Human Resource Development and Recruitment (HRDR); the Office for Intellectual Freedom (OIF); the Public Policy and Advocacy Office (PPAO); the Public Programs Office (PPO); and Publishing and Media.

While ALA's primary headquarters is in Chicago, PPAO is based in Washington, D.C., and United for Libraries is in Exton, Pennsylvania. ALA also has an editorial office for *Choice*, a review journal for academic libraries, in Middletown, Connecticut.

Leadership

Lessa Kanani'opua Pelayo-Lozada, adult services assistant manager at Palos Verdes Library District in Palos Verdes, California, was inaugurated as 2022–2023 ALA president at the association's 2022 Annual Conference, held in Washington, D.C. Emily Drabinski, critical pedagogy librarian at the Mina Rees Library at the Graduate Center at the City University of New York in New York City, was chosen as the 2023–2024 president-elect. Other officers are Patricia "Patty" Wong, immediate past-president; Peter Hepburn, head librarian at the College of the Canyons in Santa Clarita, California, treasurer for 2022–2025; and Tracie D. Hall, executive director.

Parliamentarian Changes

Adrian Stratton, president of the New York Association of Parliamentarians, accepted the role of ALA parliamentarian. Eli Mina, who had served as ALA's parliamentarian for 20 years, retired at the adjournment of the 2022 Annual Conference. Stratton stepped into this role thereafter. ALA employs a parliamentarian who is not a member of the association for council and membership meetings of the association.

ALA Statements and Anti-Censorship Efforts

The ALA Executive Board issued a statement in response to proposed state legislation that would censor library materials or put library workers who provide access to information, including information on abortion or any aspect of reproductive health care, at risk. The statement reads in part, "ALA stands committed to the free, fair, and unrestricted exchange of ideas, and the right of library patrons to seek information free from observation or unwanted surveillance by the government or other third parties, in accordance with the law and the U.S. Constitution. ALA opposes policies and legislation that ban content, restrict access to information, or compromise library users' right to seek information without the subject matter of their inquiries becoming known to others."

In response to the alarming increase in acts of aggression toward library workers and patrons as reported by the press across the country, the ALA Executive Board released the following statement: "The American Library Association condemns, in the strongest terms possible, violence, threats of violence and other acts of intimidation increasingly taking place in America's libraries, particularly those acts that aim to erase the stories and identities of gay, queer, transgender, Black, Indigenous, persons of color, those with disabilities and religious minorities."

ALA also issued a statement in support of its Iranian colleagues and the people of Iran in their efforts for human rights, including women's rights and freedom of speech and expression. ALA has adopted into its policies Article 19 of the United Nations Declaration of Human Rights, which states, "Everyone has the right to freedom of opinion and expression; this right includes freedom to hold opinions without interference and to seek, receive and impart information and ideas through any media regardless of frontiers."

Letter of Concern to FBI Regarding Threats of Violence in Libraries

During summer and fall 2022, threats directed to public and school libraries and library workers escalated, including the forced temporary closure of five public library systems due to bomb and shooting threats. On September 27, the ALA Executive Board transmitted a letter to FBI director Christopher Wray expressing concerns about the threats directed to public and school libraries and library workers. According to library directors and local officials, there is no evidence at this time showing a direct connection between recent threats and opposition to library materials and programs. However, the letter to Wray does underscore the increasing threats of violence to libraries and library workers nationwide.

Anti-Censorship Efforts and Research

Amid the proliferation of efforts to ban books in every state across the country, a new national poll commissioned by ALA showed that seven in ten voters oppose efforts to remove books from public libraries, including majorities of voters across party lines. Three-quarters of parents of public school children (74 percent) express a high degree of confidence in school librarians to make good decisions about which books to make available to children, and when asked about specific types of books that have been a focus of local debates, large majorities for each party say that they should be available in school libraries on an age-appropriate basis. The new poll is the first to approach the issue of book bans through the lenses of public and school libraries. It also found near-universal high regard for librarians and recognition of the critical role that public and school libraries play in their communities. The findings demonstrated that, far from being a partisan issue, book bans are opposed by large majorities of voters of all parties. The value of libraries and librarians has similar bipartisan support, with strong majorities of voters voicing confidence in libraries and favorability toward librarians.

ALA's OIF has been directly involved in providing legal assistance and strategic guidance in 462 cases. ALA also maintains the LeRoy Merritt Fund, which was established in 1970 to support library professionals who have been "[d]enied employment rights because of defense of intellectual freedom; that is, threatened with loss of employment or discharged because of their stand for the cause of intellectual freedom." In 2022 ALA supported eight individuals through the fund.

Unite Against Book Bans Launch

In 2021 ALA's OIF tracked 729 challenges to library, school, and university materials and services, resulting in more than 1,597 individual book challenges or removals. ALA marked this number of attempts to ban books as the highest since it began its tracking 30 years ago. In response, in spring 2022, ALA and a coalition of more than 25 groups banded together to empower individuals and communities to fight censorship and protect the freedom to read. Organizations such as the American Federation of Teachers and the Authors Guild have joined ALA's Unite Against Book Bans campaign to raise awareness about the rise in book challenges in public libraries and schools. The growing coalition leverages the strength and reach of these national organizations, including advocacy groups, education leaders, businesses, nonprofits, and civil rights groups, which represent a wide range of communities and individuals. These groups are uniting around the principles of intellectual freedom as foundational to democracy, reading as fundamental to learning, the right of readers to access a variety of books, and the need to work together to protect that right.

Events and Celebrations

LibLearnX: The Library Learning Experience

ALA hosted the first LibLearnX: The Library Learning Experience conference online, January 21–24, 2022. LibLearnX is a completely new conference experience, built from the ground up based on years of research, exploration, and, most importantly, input from library professionals. The 2022 conference was intentionally designed as a benefit for ALA members, with an opportunity to learn, network, and celebrate. The event attracted more than 2,100 participants and 66 exhibiting organizations. The conference, originally scheduled to take place in San Antonio, Texas, was redirected to a virtual offering due to the COVID-19 pandemic.

LibLearnX offered education for library professionals by library professionals, with more than 110 live and on-demand education sessions in various learning engagement formats and topics. As a result, attendees were able to learn best practices and gather innovative ideas to promptly take back to their libraries for immediate implementation.

LibLearnX general sessions gave considerable focus to social justice, equality, and advocacy issues. In the opening session, ALA president Patricia "Patty" Wong was joined by U.S. Sen. Mazie K. Hirono (D-Hawaii) in conversation. The motivating session touched on themes of Asian American leadership, the immigrant experience, and the role of women in positions of power. Both women represent important firsts for the organizations they represent. Sen. Hirono is the first female senator to represent Hawaii and the only first-generation immigrant to serve in the Senate; she was born in Japan and came to the United States with her mother when she was eight years old. Wong is the first Asian American president of ALA. Sen. Hirono discussed her memoir, *Heart of Fire: An Immigrant Daughter's Story*, and her unconventional, groundbreaking path that led her to hold one of the country's highest offices.

Wong and ALA executive director Tracie D. Hall hosted and moderated "Innovative Approaches to EDI in Texas Libraries," a live panel session from San Antonio, Texas, on January 23. The panel featured four library leaders from Texas: Tamiko Brown, library coordinator for the Fort Bend International District; Dean Hendrix, dean of libraries for the University of Texas–San Antonio; Shirley Robinson, executive director of the Texas Library Association; and Ramiro Salazar, director of the San Antonio Public Library. An additional highlight was the panel session, "Being a Queer Librarian in Texas: Expectation vs. Reality," presented by the ALA Rainbow RoundTable. The session included LGBTQIA+ librarians who are working in various types of libraries and communities across Texas. The panelists shared their experiences compared to the public assumption of being an out, queer professional in a southern, mostly conservative state.

Colin Kaepernick, activist, athlete, and author of the picture book *I Color Myself Different*, closed LibLearnX with a heartfelt "thank you" message to librarians for being "community anchors" and unshakable stewards of knowledge. In the unforgettable and very well-received session, he challenged librarians to rethink some of the library systems and practices to ensure libraries are spaces where all Black and Brown people feel that they belong.

Annual Conference & Exhibition 2022

ALA's Annual Conference & Exhibition convened in Washington, D.C., June 23–28, 2022. Attendees were informed and updated on trends, policies, and best practices; motivated by celebrity speakers and thought leaders; and entertained by top authors. Conference highlights included the following:

- In the opening general session, ALA president Patricia "Patty" Wong hosted a conversation with Federal Communications Commission chairwoman Jessica Rosenworcel on policymaking and insights into current issues central to the core values of libraries, such as Net Neutrality and challenges and solutions to close the digital divide.
- In a special message to library professionals, Librarian of Congress Carla Hayden discussed the role of libraries and librarians in the misinformation age. Hayden is the first woman and first African American to lead the national library. She was nominated to the position by President Barack Obama.
- In the closing general session, author Luvvie Ajayi Jones was in conversation with Nicole A. Cooke, Augusta Baker Endowed Chair and associate professor at the University of South Carolina's School of Library and Information Science. They discussed Ajayi Jones's book, *Rising Troublemaker: A Fear-Fighter Manual for Teens*.
- In the ALA Leadership Reading and Panel Session, "Defending the Fifth Freedom: Protecting the Right to Read for Incarcerated Individuals," panelists included two formerly incarcerated authors, Reginald Dwayne Betts and Randall Horton, and one formerly incarcerated library staff member, Enrique Rivera. Author Jeanie Austin discussed book and digital access for those who have been incarcerated with ALA's executive director Tracie D. Hall.
- Other speakers included actors Tiffany Haddish and John Cho; journalist Maria Hinojosa; and authors Celeste Ng, Kevin Eastman, and R.L. Stine.

PLA 2022

The PLA biennial national conference was the largest in-person association conference in Portland, Oregon, since the beginning of the COVID-19 pandemic. The event brought more than 4,000 attendees to the Oregon Convention Center March 23–25, 2022. Library professionals attended more than 100 programs focused on shaping the future of U.S. public library service. Conference attendees were inspired by diverse educational sessions, the opportunity to reconnect with colleagues, and the latest in library technology and solutions from more than 100 vendors.

New York Times best-selling author, podcast host, and professional troublemaker Luvvie Ajayi Jones opened the conference by challenging attendees to overcome their fears and get comfortable with being uncomfortable. Her most recent book, *Professional Troublemaker: The Fear-Fighter Manual*, was released in 2021 and was an instant hit. Ajayi Jones is known for her trademark wit, warmth, and perpetual truth-telling.

Kal Penn closed the conference with his entertaining and candid stories of Hollywood, politics, and redefining the American dream. Penn is an actor, writer, producer, and former associate director of the White House Office of Public Engagement.

Core Forum

Core: Leadership, Infrastructure, Futures held its Core Forum 2022 October 13–15 in Salt Lake City, Utah. The forum was an opportunity to reconnect with fellow colleagues and make new connections while celebrating the interconnected library work Core members share. It featured a welcome reception, keynote presentations, more than 45 concurrent sessions, exhibits, and poster sessions. Presentations covered various hot topics and innovative content on access and equity, assessment, buildings and operations, leadership and management, metadata and collections, preservation, and technology. The Core Forum engages the collective expertise of presenters and participants, facilitates enriching conversations, and offers unique learning opportunities.

YALSA Symposium

The 2022 YA Services Symposium took place November 4–6 in Baltimore, Maryland. The theme was Rediscovering Our Charm: Supporting Teens and Each Other in Our Libraries. The symposium offered education sessions and author panels, which included Lamar Giles, Jas Hammonds, Rex Ogle, Francesca Padilla, Nic Stone, Aiden Thomas, and Vincent Tirado.

National Library Week

ALA celebrated National Library Week April 3–9, 2022. The theme was Connect with Your Library. During National Library Week, ALA released its Top 10 List of Most Challenged Books of 2021. The list capped off a record year for attempts to suppress materials with racial and LGBTQIA+ content. More than 330 unique cases were reported to ALA's OIF in the three-month period between September 1 and November 30, 2021. Molly Shannon, Emmy-nominated and Spirit Award-winning actress, comedian, and legendary *Saturday Night Live* cast member, served as the honorary chair of National Library Week.

Grants, Relief, and Funding
COVID Relief Fund

In June 2022 ALA announced grants of $20,000 to 77 libraries that continue to experience substantial economic hardship due to the COVID-19 pandemic. The ALA COVID Library Relief Fund grantees are academic, correctional, public, school, and tribal libraries from 32 states and Puerto Rico. The fund is one of the largest non-federal grant opportunities for libraries. A complete list of grant recipients and project proposals is available on ALA's COVID Library Relief Fund webpage. The fund is supported by Acton Family Giving as part of its ongoing response to the pandemic. The grants will support libraries' ability to provide their users with the information services and digital access they need to retain or secure socioeconomic mobility during a time of shift and upheaval. Libraries serving low income and rural communities, or communities that are predominately Black, Latino, Asian, Indigenous, and people of color, are especially encouraged to apply.

Ukraine Library Relief

With support from more than 150 donors, ALA sent $12,000 to the Ukrainian Library Association. The funds helped purchase computers, software, and other equipment, as well as materials and resources to aid children and adults in over-coming stress. They also helped immediate repair needs to keep libraries open and provided support for librarians and library workers who are in harm's way, wounded, or displaced and in need of financial assistance. In cities and towns throughout Ukraine, dozens of libraries have been severely damaged or destroyed. Librarians have kept libraries open for as long as possible and are improvising to bring services to people.

Support of ALA's Update of Its Standards for Library Services for People Who Are Incarcerated or Detained

A grant from the Andrew W. Mellon Foundation has supported a range of activity related to the update of ALA's Standards for Library Services for People Who Are Incarcerated or Detained, which is projected to be finalized and disseminated by or before the end of 2024. A significant amount of support has come to ALA directly, while other Mellon support has enabled a collaboration between the San Francisco Public Library (SFPL) and ALA to create greater access to information and resources for people in jails and prisons nationwide.

Co-led by SFPL's Jail and Reentry Services team and ALA, the Expanding Information Access for Incarcerated People initiative includes a comprehensive survey of existing models for library services to people in jails and prisons and a revision of outdated standards in collaboration with formerly incarcerated people and librarians. This project will have national visibility and share models for providing resources to people in jails and prisons across the country. To do this, SFPL convened librarians and library staff providing services to the incarcerated population for a half-day meeting prior to the 2022 ALA Annual Conference in Washington, D.C. Additionally, at ALA 2022, the association hosted a hearing on the standards for library services in jails and prisons, which drew more than 150 formerly incarcerated people, library staff members, government officials, advocates, and stakeholders.

Libraries Transforming Communities

ALA's Libraries Transforming Communities project offered more than $7 million in grants to small and rural libraries to increase the accessibility of facilities, services, and programs to better serve people with disabilities. A new phase of the project, funded by a private grant, will mirror previous ALA programs under the Libraries Transforming Communities umbrella. Previous phases have been supported by a private donor and the Institute of Museum and Library Services, with partners such as the Association for Rural and Small Libraries and the National Coalition for Dialogue & Deliberation.

In November 2022 ALA began to accept applications for grants distributed over the next three years, ranging from $10,000 to $20,000. Participating libraries will first conduct community input-gathering sessions to assure that their work aligns with local needs. Libraries will be required to identify the primary audience they are hoping to reach (e.g., homebound seniors, children with autism, deaf community members) and facilitate a community conversation with the impacted populations in order to guide improvement of the library's services.

Federal Funding for Libraries

In December 2022 ALA welcomed substantial increases in federal funding for libraries passed by Congress as part of the Fiscal Year 2023 Omnibus Appropriations bill. The Library Services and Technology Act, administered by the Institute of Museum and Library Services, saw an increase of $13.5 million, raising the program to $211 million as the leading source of federal funding for America's libraries. In addition, Innovative Approaches to Literacy, a Department of Education program designed to support school library literacy initiatives nationwide, saw a $1 million increase, bringing total funding to $30 million.

Initiatives

Civic Imagination Stations

Twelve artists and library staff teams were selected for the pilot cohort of ALA's Civic Imagination Stations program. It is supported by The Estée Lauder Companies' Writing Change, a three-year global literacy initiative in partnership with Amanda Gorman, the youngest inaugural poet in U.S. history, an award-winning writer, and an Estée Lauder Global Changemaker. Libraries will partner with local artists to implement arts programming that builds literacy and digital skills. Teams were selected from a national application process conducted in June and July 2022.

From August 2022 to March 2023, the cohort participated in workshops and coaching led by Civic Imagination Stations lead artists Willa J. Taylor, Goodman Theatre's Walter Director of Education and Engagement, and Michael Rohd, founding artistic director of Sojourn Theatre and co-founder of the Center for Performance and Civic Practice. Civic Imagination Stations cohort teams will culminate their work with the development and implementation of short-term original arts-based projects. In addition, the Civic Imagination Stations program will model processes by which other librarian/artist partnerships can work together to create locally appropriate and meaningful civic imagination projects.

Libraries Build Business Initiative

In July 2022 ALA released a report that showcases the impact of the Libraries Build Business initiative on small businesses and entrepreneurs across the country, as well as the library profession. Libraries Build Business, a $2 million national initiative supported by Google.org, launched in early 2020 and culminated with the release of the Libraries Build Business Playbook in February 2022. The insights, lessons, and outcomes from this initiative can be leveraged for further impact on economic opportunity and advancement in communities across the United States. The "Libraries Build Business Initiative Highlights" report demonstrates the critical role of libraries in the small business and entrepreneurial ecosystem while providing specific examples of impact in urban, suburban, rural, and tribal communities across the country. Because of their reach, information and resources, and strategic and flexible collaboration, libraries are uniquely positioned to be partners, leaders, and connectors in thriving local economies.

ALA Honors

ALA Honorary Memberships

Two recipients were selected to received honorary ALA memberships during the LibLearnX event. Honorary membership is conferred in recognition of outstanding contributions of lasting importance to libraries and librarianship.

The ALA Council elected former ALA president Maureen Sullivan to honorary membership. Sullivan is honored for her lasting contribution to the field of librarianship through her service to the profession and ALA; her work on organizational change and leadership development; and her consulting practice, which has reached thousands of librarians.

The ALA Council also elected former ALA president and treasurer Jim Neal to honorary membership. Neal was nominated in recognition of significant contributions to libraries and the profession of librarianship and his accomplishments as ALA president and treasurer and as a member of the ALA Council. He was a member of the ALA Executive Board when the Spectrum Initiative was launched and has actively raised funds on behalf of the program, as well as advocated for the establishment of diversity, equity, and inclusion as a fourth strategic priority for the association.

Lippincott Award

Kenneth A. Yamashita was the recipient of the 2022 Joseph W. Lippincott Award. Yamashita is the first Asian American to receive it. This award is sponsored by Joseph W. Lippincott III and presented by ALA for distinguished service in the profession of librarianship. The jury for the 2022 Joseph W. Lippincott Award honored Yamashita for his many accomplishments over decades of librarianship in commitment to diversity, mentoring colleagues about equity and inclusion, his dedication to the profession, and a legacy that reflects well on his career.

100th Anniversary of the Newbery Medal

Every year since 1922, lovers of children's literature—children and adults alike—anxiously await the announcement of the Newbery Medal for the "most distinguished contribution to American literature for children." The 100th anniversary in 2022 commemorated not only a century of captivating books, but it also celebrated the longevity and evolution of the award. The world has changed in the last 100 years, and with it, the Newbery Medal seeks to recognize stories that represent and respect all youth.

National Book Foundation Award

ALA executive director Tracie D. Hall received the 2022 Literarian Award for Outstanding Service to the American Literary Community from the National Book Foundation. Given by the foundation's board of directors, the award is traditionally presented to an individual for a lifetime of achievement in expanding the audience for books and reading. The recipients of the Literarian Award represent a variety of literary activists, helping to increase access to and diversity in literature. The award comes with a prize of $10,000. Hall's long history of working toward greater inclusion and opportunity was one of many reasons that she was selected for the honor. Hall received the award on November 16 during the 73rd National Book Awards ceremony in New York City. This was the second consecutive year the Literarian Award was given to a librarian.

ALA News

In January 2022 the Coretta Scott King Book Awards Committee was granted Round Table status by the ALA Council. The Coretta Scott King Book Awards Round Table (CSKBART) honors outstanding African American authors and illustrators of books for children and young adults that demonstrate an appreciation of African American culture and universal human values. The award commemorates the life and work of Dr. Martin Luther King, Jr. and honors his wife, Coretta Scott King, for her courage and determination to continue the work for peace and world brotherhood.

The ALA Council also approved the merger of the Staff Organizations Round Table (SORT) and Library Support Staff Interests Round Table (LSSIRT) to create a Round Table with the new name of the Library Support Staff Round Table (LSSRT). The mission is to provide an arena within ALA for addressing a wide variety of issues of concern to library support staff, including but not limited to basic training programs, education, career development, job duties and responsibilities, and other related issues for the purpose of fostering communication and networking among all levels of library personnel. The Round Table is responsible for the timely dissemination of information to local, regional, state, and national support staff organizations.

Jim Rettig, ALA Past-President, Passes

Jim Rettig, ALA president from 2008 to 2009, died on August 17, 2022. A dedicated library leader, Rettig was awarded a bachelor's and master's degree in English from Marquette University. In 1975 he earned an M.L.S. from University of Wisconsin–Madison. Rettig's career as a reference librarian took him to six different states—Wisconsin, Kentucky, Ohio, Illinois, Virginia, and Maryland. In 1988

Rettig and his family settled in Williamsburg, Virginia, when he became assistant dean of university libraries at the College of William and Mary's Earl Gregg Swem Library. In his most recent position, he served as dean of libraries at the United States Naval Academy in Annapolis, Maryland, from which he retired in May 2017. In addition to his tenure as ALA president, Rettig served on the ALA Executive Board, on the ALA Council as chair of the Committee on Organization, and as president of the Reference and User Services Association.

American Booksellers Association

914-406-7500
www.bookweb.org

For almost 125 years, the American Booksellers Association (ABA) has been the guiding voice for independently owned bookstores. Founded in 1900, ABA is a national not-for-profit trade organization that supports the success of independent bookstores. This success is assisted through education, information dissemination, business services, programming, technology, and advocacy. ABA's membership has evolved over the years, and its members are more diverse, are involved in community, and act as guiding forces in locales around the country. The total number of independent bookstores represented is 2,500-plus.

ABA is governed by a volunteer board of independent booksellers and independent bookstore owners who are elected by the membership. In addition to the board of directors service, booksellers and bookstore owners who belong to ABA also serve on a number of advisory councils, including the ABA Diversity, Equity & Inclusion Committee (DEIC) in support of ABA's commitment to antiracism, representation, equity, and access.

2022

In 2022 independent bookstores continued to rise to the challenge of the COVID-19 pandemic with the spirit, creativity, resilience, and passion that have historically defined this industry. In 2022 ABA continued the prioritization of five key initiatives to support its members: Advocacy (antitrust, small-business issues, publishers), Education, E-Commerce, Freedom of Expression, and Marketing.

Antitrust Advocacy

ABA advocated in support of the American Innovation and Choice Online Act (AICOA), which prohibits gatekeeper platforms from preferencing their own products and services at the expense of smaller online businesses and from making businesses buy other services as a condition of getting good search rankings or placement on their platforms, among other things.

In early 2022 Wisconsin Assistant Attorney General Gwendolyn Lindsay Cooley reached out to ABA's advocacy team to schedule a meeting with other attorney general offices to discuss ABA's white paper, "American Monopoly: Amazon's Anti-Competitive Behavior Is in Violation of Antitrust Laws." Cooley is the Antitrust Task Force chair of the National Association of Attorneys General. The meeting, which occurred in February 2022, was attended by more than 80 people from the attorney general offices of almost all 50 states.

ABA also met with key federal legislative and administrative stakeholders in regard to Amazon's anticompetitive behavior, including the House Committee on Small Business and the Federal Trade Commission's Bureau of Competition. ABA also worked with coalitions in its antitrust efforts, most notably Small Business Rising and the Main Street Competition Coalition. Small Business Rising focuses on protesting Amazon's antitrust violations and lobbying for legislation to protect small business, while the Main Street Competition Coalition works toward changes to, and stronger enforcement of, the Robinson-Patman Act.

Small-Business Advocacy

In 2022 ABA lobbied for the interests of its members by supporting the Credit Card Competition Act, which would enhance competition and choice in the credit card network market that is currently dominated by the Visa-Mastercard duopoly; lobbying for grants and access to capital for booksellers still suffering the ramifications of the COVID-19 pandemic; and supporting bookstores on statewide issues such as bills tackling credit card fraud.

Education

After hosting four major education conferences virtually during the initial years of the pandemic, including Snow Days, the three-day virtual Winter Institute in March 2022, 2022 saw the return of in-person conferences just in time to celebrate the 10th anniversary of ABA's Children's Institute. Nearly 300 booksellers gathered at the historic Arizona Biltmore Resort in Phoenix, along with 200-plus authors, illustrators, publishers, and vendors. During the three-day conference, booksellers participated in two dozen education sessions and workshops, toured Phoenix-area independent bookstores, met more than 70 authors and illustrators, and celebrated the endurance and innovation of independent bookselling in this new era of retail. A one-day virtual Children's Institute capped off the in-person event, ensuring wider accessibility of ABA education.

To further its commitment to member education, ABA created a new position in 2022 to oversee its education initiatives and brought on former bookseller Kim Hooyboer as the director of education. In addition to overseeing ABA conference education and virtual initiatives, Hooyboer traveled to regional bookseller association trade shows in fall 2022 to present education programming on bookstore financial literacy, along with CEO Allison Hill and CFO PK Sindwani, and to meet with booksellers across the country to identify ongoing educational needs among members. In conjunction with the in-person education, ABA continued to provide virtual opportunities for networking and idea-sharing through its ShopTalks, business and best practice webinars, Technology Meetups, Marketing Meetups, dedicated Discord server, bookseller forum, and a newly launched Management Book Club. Looking ahead to 2023, registration for the February 2023 in-person Winter Institute conference sold out in a record-breaking 21 hours when it opened in September 2022, highlighting the enthusiasm for the education programming provided by ABA and the desire to be together as a community again.

E-Commerce

In 2022 ABA continued to provide an e-commerce solution for member bookstores, expanding its offering to become an enterprise-level platform. It's our understanding that we are the only not-for-profit trade organization in the United

States that provides an e-commerce platform that is specifically designed for our trade. Historically, e-commerce sales have represented less than 1 percent of most stores' sales, but in 2020 as COVID shut down stores and consumer buying habits shifted, stores' e-commerce sales spiked to 80–100 percent of their total revenue, depending on the store's circumstances and COVID shutdown status. In 2022 bookstores are still experiencing record online sales representing as much as 25 percent of total gross sales, while in-store sales for many stores have increased to levels that are higher than they were pre-COVID.

ABA is currently completing a two-year, $3 million upgrade to its e-commerce platform, IndieCommerce, for bookstores. The new 2.0 platform is designed to meet the growing demand from hybrid shoppers who are now expecting an integrated, multichannel shopping experience when purchasing books.

In addition, 2022 saw the continued success of Bookshop.org, an e-commerce platform and B-corp created to support independent bookstores. To date, Bookshop.org has raised $25,386,426 for independent bookstores through a bookstore distribution pool to independent bookstores and through independent bookstore affiliate pages. Bookshop.org also hosts a store finder to help readers find their local independent bookstore. ABA was a founding investor in Bookshop.org and currently owns three and one-half percent of the company. There are two seats on the Bookshop.org board reserved for ABA bookstore members.

Freedom of Expression

The wave of book banning and challenges escalated in 2022, putting the right to read at risk. American Booksellers for Free Expression (ABFE), the free speech initiative of ABA, launched a petition drive that garnered the signatures of more than 1,600 consumers and booksellers in opposition to the book bans and challenges popping up all over the country. ABFE provided member stores faced with local school and library book-banning challenges with resources and assistance. ABFE partnered to produce and promote Banned Books Week to educate people about the dangers of book banning and partnered with other coalitions to speak out against the violations of the First and Fourteenth Amendments that the current bans represent. ABA hosted a Banned Books Drag Bingo for members, and as part of the Kids' Right to Read Project, it wrote more than 30 letters to school districts around the country to oppose the suggested removal of books from school libraries and public libraries without following the proper protocol dictated by their policies.

Publisher Advocacy

In 2022 ABA continued to meet regularly with publishers to convey the value of the independent bookstore channel and advocate for better terms and support for its members. ABA conducted its second annual survey of members about publishers' performance in categories such as damages, diversity initiatives, and business-to-business terms. Results were analyzed for best practices to then share with publishers. These conversations and initiatives resulted in several programs and changes that helped bookstores.

Antiracism, Equity, Access, and Representation

In 2022 ABA continued its commitment to antiracism, equity, access, and representation with several new initiatives: an Advance Access program for underrepresented voices to introduce booksellers to diverse authors; the first full year with a diversity, equity, inclusion, and access (DEIA) member relations manager position (created in November 2021) to better support diverse members; advocacy in support of more representation among publisher sales forces; monthly affinity groups for BIPOC, LGBTQIA2S+, Neurodiverse, and members of the Disability Community; forums for BIPOC and LGBTQIA2S+ community members to meet with ABA staff to share their needs and concerns; an expanded ABA Diversity, Equity & Inclusion Council to ensure more representation and support of historically marginalized members; an updated ABA Code of Conduct; the addition of closed-captioning for virtual events; institutional changes in programming to ensure significant representation among authors; an institutionalized land acknowledgment that included a community donation and action to support Indigenous peoples in areas where ABA events occur; waived fees for new BIPOC members; and the addition of DEIA Guides in support of members attending in-person conferences. ABA also created a member dashboard to increase access to ABA's offerings and collect optional demographic information to better inform programming and support all members.

Marketing

In addition to these 2022 priorities, ABA continued to support members and create consumer awareness for the indies through events, including Independent Bookstore Day and Indies First; collaborations with Oprah's Book Club and *Good Morning America*; indie-branded book promotions, such as Indies Next List, Kids' Indie Next List, and the Indies Introduce debut author program; holiday shopping and seasonal marketing campaigns; and financial benchmarking. ABA also commissions a study through Civic Economics on the impact of shopping with Amazon for communities. The result is the yearly report, "Unfulfilled: Amazon and the American Retail Landscape," which highlights Amazon's detrimental impact on communities and the economic value of independent bookstores to communities. Approximately 29 percent of all revenue at independent bookstores immediately recirculates in the local economy. This translates to a local impact advantage of 109 percent over that of chain competitor Barnes & Noble and a massive 405 percent local impact advantage over Amazon.

Statistics

In 2022 194 new independent bookstores opened, 45 bookstores closed, and 16 stores changed ownership.

Members

Post-pandemic member trends have included more fluidity with store formats (brick-and-mortar stores adding a book bus, pop-ups evolving into brick-and-mortar locations, brick-and-mortar stores switching to online or pop-ups at the end of their lease, etc.), more bookstores focusing on an identity or a specialty, an adjustment of store hours that reflects both changes in consumer buying habits as well as the labor shortage, and more. The "pandemic pivot" continued among the bookselling community and could be seen in many ways.

Board and Staff

ABA has 39 full-time employees. ABA's CEO, Allison K. Hill, started her tenure on March 2, 2020, just as the COVID-19 pandemic began. Hill is the first woman to serve as CEO of the association. As of January 2022 ABA's executive team consisted of COO Joy Dallanegra-Sanger, chief communications officer Ray Daniels, and CFO PK Sindwani. ABA also has a volunteer board of 13 booksellers and bookstore owner members. These officers are elected or appointed on a rolling basis, so there was overlap last year, with some terms ending and the election of new officers. ABA's 2022 board of directors comprised ABA president Christine Onarati of WORD Bookstores in Brooklyn, New York, and Jersey City, New Jersey; co-vice-president/secretary Kelly Estep of Carmichael's Bookstore in Louisville, Kentucky; co-vice-president Angela María Spring of Duende District Books in Washington, D.C., and Albuquerque, New Mexico; Danny Caine of The Raven Book Store in Lawrence, Kansas; Diane Capriola of Little Shop of Stories in Decatur, Georgia; Jenny Cohen of Waucoma Bookstore in Hood River, Oregon; Cynthia Compton of 4 Kids Books & Toys in Zionsville, Indiana, and MacArthur Books in Carmel, Indiana; Jake Cumsky-Whitlock of Solid State Books in Washington, D.C.; Jeff Deutsch of Seminary Co-op and 57th St. Books in Chicago, Illinois; Michael Hermann of Gibson's Bookstore in Concord, New Hampshire; Melanie Knight of Books, Inc. in San Francisco, California; Michelle Malonzo of Changing Hands in Tempe and Phoenix, Arizona; Raquel Roque of Book and Books in Miami, Florida; and Tegan Tigani of Queen Anne Book Company in Seattle, Washington.

The Future

Booksellers remain optimistic and energized. Despite book bans that impede the right to read, lingering operational challenges related to the pandemic, an unlevel playing field, and barriers to small businesses, independent bookstores continue to grow and multiply. There are more than 323 stores in the pipeline to open in the next one to two years, and the existing stores continue to be integral to their communities. Contrary to the perception that bookstores are on the decline, the future of the independent bookstore is bright!

Association of Research Libraries

21 Dupont Circle NW, Washington, DC 20036
202-296-2296, email webmgr@arl.org,
http://www.arl.org

Jessica Aiwuyor
Senior Director of Communications

The Association of Research Libraries (ARL) is a nonprofit organization of research libraries in Canada and the United States whose vision is to create a trusted, equitable, and inclusive research and learning ecosystem and prepare library leaders to advance this work in strategic partnership with member libraries and other organizations worldwide. ARL's mission is to empower and advocate for research libraries and archives to shape, influence, and implement institutional, national, and international policy. ARL develops the next generation of leaders and enables strategic cooperation among partner institutions to benefit scholarship and society.

ARL's 2022 Year in Review

In 2022 ARL accomplished our 2021–2022 Action Plan goals and fulfilled our Core Commitments for ARL member representatives and the research library enterprise. In a time of significant change in member representation, we took this historic moment to refine our vision and mission and to launch our 2023–2026 Action Plan to achieve our aspirations, given our shared purpose.

Our first Core Commitment is "Engender a member experience in which all members feel welcome and can participate in and benefit from the Association." Our 2023–2026 Action Plan reflects our member institution priorities emerging from the pandemic, economic challenges, and sociopolitical instability.

We are dedicated to centering and uplifting structural equity and inclusion within our member experience and in the research and learning ecosystem. The ARL Learning Network and our diversity, equity, and inclusion programs cultivate diversity among leadership in the research library community, including providing scholarships to ensure equitable access to ARL programs. Our public policy and scholarship work centers on structural equity and inclusion, and the values accountability framework for research libraries that is underway will further reflect this commitment.

Our second Core Commitment is "Deepen and expand the understanding of the research library's value and brand identity, particularly in terms of its impact in the research enterprise and more broadly." ARL actively engages with our partners in research and learning to achieve our goals. Collaborations include project work and publications with the Association of American Universities, the Association of Public and Land-grant Universities, the Association of University Presses, the Council on Governmental Relations, the Library Copyright Alliance, the National Academies Board on Research Data and Information, and the National Academies U.S. National Committee for CODATA. This past year, ARL and the Canadian Association of Research Libraries (CARL) commissioned Ithaka S+R to consult with university leaders in Canada and the United States to identify their strategic priorities, to gauge their expectations of research libraries in achieving them, and, together with our members, to determine what more research libraries can do to advance those priorities. In April 2022 ARL and CARL shared the final report, "Aligning the Research Library to Organizational Strategy," with the members, the associations' leaders and their stakeholders who participated in the interviews and focus groups, and the public. Case studies on redressing relationships with the historically marginalized and more intensive discussions with seven institutions in Canada and the United States are underway on growth strategies and STEM.

ARL's staff served on national and international committees in research and learning as well as partnered with colleagues in the International Alliance of Research Library Associations (IARLA) to further advance shared goals. ARL worked with the U.S. Office of Science and Technology Policy (OSTP) and the U.S. National Institutes of Health (NIH) on their new guidelines for facilitating public access to the results of federally funded research.

ARL Board of Directors 2022

Jon E. Cawthorne (Wayne State University), Past President John Culshaw (University of Iowa), President K. Matthew Dames (University of Notre Dame), Trevor A. Dawes (University of Delaware), Treasurer Bob Fox (University of Louisville), Lorraine Haricombe (University of Texas–Austin), Melissa Just (University of Saskatchewan), Executive Director Mary Lee Kennedy (ARL), Joe Lucia (Temple University), Robert McDonald (University of Colorado–Boulder), Lisa O'Hara (University of Manitoba), Vice-President/President-Elect Susan Parker (University of British Columbia), Sarah Pritchard (Northwestern University), and Lorelei Tanji (University of California–Irvine).

ARL Staff 2022

Mary Lee Kennedy, Executive Director
Jessica Aiwuyor, Senior Director of Communications
Jessica Andrade, Associate Director of Board and Member Relations
Kevin Borden, Senior Director of Research and Analytics
Ryan Brennan, Accounting Manager
Jaymey Butler, Director of Events
DeLa Dos, Senior Director of Learning + DEI
Tony Ellis, Communications Coordinator
Deborah R. Grayson, Leadership and Organizational Development
Holly Gross, Senior Applications Developer
Kaylyn Groves, Senior Writer and Editor
Cynthia Hudson Vitale, Director of Scholars & Scholarship
Pat Kent, Accounting Coordinator
Katherine Klosek, Director of Information Policy
Anam Mian, Research Analyst
Samantha Musser, Program Manager

Angela Pappalardo, Program Manager
Gary Roebuck, Deputy Executive Director
Judy Ruttenberg, Senior Director of Scholarship and Policy
Mira Swearer, Senior Program Manager
Shawna Taylor, Project Manager for Realities of Academic Data Sharing
Amy Yeager, Communications Manager

Key 2021–2022 Action Plan Priority Outcomes

ARL achieved our Action Plan priorities. The outcomes have covered ground in advocacy and public policy; advancing research and scholarship; data and analytics; diversity, equity, and inclusion; and leadership.

In fulfilling our priority "Advocate for Public Policies in Support of Our Mission and Shared Objective":

- ARL partnered with the Social Science Research Council's (SSRC) #Media Well project to interview experts reflecting on the question of how fair use supports research, journalism, and truth.
- The Library Copyright Alliance (LCA)—which consists of the American Library Association (ALA), the Association of College and Research Libraries (ACRL), and ARL—successfully negotiated language that would carve libraries and higher education out of the "SMART" Copyright Act (S. 3880).
- Since OSTP released the August 2022 memo "Ensuring Free, Immediate, and Equitable Access to Federally Funded Research," ARL has produced a number of resources to help its members and the community navigate the guidance and communicate with campus stakeholders about the expected changes. ARL also helped its members and the library community prepare for the new NIH Data Management and Sharing Policy, which took effect January 2023.
- ARL updated Know Your Copyrights. This is a resource that supports library leaders and includes:

  - Conversations around copyrights and fair use
  - Maximizing the use of library rights
  - Not ceding rights due to restrictive license terms, shifts in technology and business models, or outdated practices rooted in risk aversion

In fulfilling our priority "Advocate for and Equip Research Library and Archives Leaders as Partners in Advancing Research and Scholarship That Is Increasingly Open and Equitable":

- The five-year pilot of Toward an Open Monograph Ecosystem (TOME) concluded with 143 books and an additional 20–30 in the pipeline.
- ARL published a survey report of member expenses on open access expenditures, which was subsequently cited in an OSTP report to Congress.

- ARL published the first report of Accelerating the Social Impact of Research (ASIR). The pilot engaged small teams from eight ARL member libraries who shared strategies to accelerate the adoption and implementation of open science principles for social-impact research and scholarship.
- ARL's Realities of Academic Data Sharing (RADS) initiative is conducting research, developing models, and collecting costing information for public access to research data across five disciplinary areas in the sciences. The RADS initiative outcomes are the following:

  – Partnerships—Council on Governmental Relations, the Data Curation Network, the Federal Demonstration Partnership
  – Cross-campus Collaborations—Identified teams and units within the institution that support data-sharing
  – Expenses for Public Access to Research Data—Collected expense information for public access to data services, infrastructure, and staffing
  – Metadata Analysis—Understanding where faculty are sharing their research data and the quality of the metadata
  – Public Access DMS Activities—Mapped activities across campus that support public data-sharing

In fulfilling our priority "Provide Data and Analytics on Research Library Practices, Effectiveness, and Impact":

- ARL published the ARL Annual Salary Survey 2020, ARL Statistics 2020, ARL Academic Law Library Statistics 2020, and ARL Academic Health Sciences Library Statistics 2020.
- ARL hosted its 2022 Library Assessment Conference virtually, November 1–4. The theme of the conference was Building Effective, Sustainable, Practical Assessment. There were 551 virtual attendees.
- Research Library Impact Framework Pilot Program projects are complete, and ARL has published all 18 practice briefs and reports.
- ARL developed a Research and Assessment Cycle Toolkit that covers five modules and 23 training videos and supporting materials. The Assessment Cycle includes Choosing a Focus and Setting Goals, Gathering and Analyzing Data, Making Decisions, Sharing Results, and Revising Goals.

In fulfilling our priority "Create Diverse, Equitable, Inclusive, and Accessible Work Environments, Services, and Collections":

- ARL's Diversity, Equity, and Inclusion Institute Task Force launched a community input survey. Responses will be used to inform the development of recommendations for a curriculum, success metrics, and benchmarks for the Diversity, Equity, and Inclusion (DEI) Institute.
- ARL's Kaleidoscope Program, with 160 participants in 2022, currently has two ongoing cohorts: 2021–2023 and 2022–2024. The goal of the program is to attract M.L.I.S. students from historically underrepresented racial and ethnic groups to careers in research libraries and archives.

- ARL's Leadership and Career Development Program (LCDP), with 95 participants, currently has one cohort for 2022–2023. The program continues to prepare mid-career librarians from historically underrepresented racial and ethnic groups to take on leadership roles in their careers and in the profession at large.
- ARL partnered with ALA, ACRL, and the Public Library Association (PLA) to develop and release Cultural Proficiencies for Racial Equity: A Framework.

In fulfilling our priority "Shape and Inform Leadership Practice throughout Research Libraries":

- ARL's 2021–2022 Leadership Fellows cohort met in Toronto during the Spring Association Meeting in April and visited Georgia Institute of Technology in May. This was ARL's most diverse cohort ever. Additionally, the Leadership Fellows curriculum was redesigned to center diversity, equity, and inclusion. The 2021–2022 program concluded during the Coalition for Networked Information (CNI) Membership Meeting in December.
- With the board's approval in February 2022, the ARL Academy was renamed the ARL Learning Network, which was formally launched over the following months. The ARL Learning Network focuses on:

  - Leadership
  - Skills development
  - Diversity, equity, and inclusion
  - Advancing professional development
  - Resources, tools, and networking

ARL's 2022 By the Numbers

ARL's programs, initiatives, and events included various partners and hundreds of attendees and participants:

- Convening—1,279 ARL event attendees at member meetings, forums, and conferences
- Informing—32 briefings and reports
- Shaping—$506,076 invested in fellows and scholars programs
- Influencing—45 amicus briefs, partner/coalition letters, statements, and public comments

The Scholarly Publishing and Academic Resources Coalition

Heather Joseph

Executive Director

1201 Connecticut Ave. NW, #608, Washington, DC 20036
202-630-5090, sparc@sparcopen.org
https://www.sparcopen.org

Background and Mission

The Scholarly Publishing and Academic Resources Coalition (SPARC) is a nonprofit advocacy organization that supports systems for research and education that are open by default and equitable by design. SPARC believes everyone should be able to access and contribute to knowledge that shapes our world.

As a catalyst for action, SPARC's programmatic agenda focuses on driving policy change, supporting member action, and cultivating communities that advance a vision of knowledge as a public good. From the local to the global level, SPARC works to address the ways in which knowledge systems exclude people due to racism, colonialism, and other legacies of injustice.

SPARC's membership includes about 250 libraries and academic organizations across North America. This membership is complemented by affiliated SPARC coalitions in Africa, Europe, and Japan, as well as individual member organizations in Australia, Hong Kong, and Saudi Arabia. Founded in 1998, SPARC operates as an independent project of the New Venture Fund, a 501(c)(3) nonprofit organization.

Strategy

To promote the changes in infrastructure, new norms, practices, and policies required to make open the default in research and education, SPARC's strategy is to:

- Advocate for policies that enable open practices throughout research and education
- Educate interested parties on opportunities to change the scholarly communication system
- Incubate projects that promote new models for sharing research outputs and develop educational materials that support the needs of scholars and society

SPARC works to identify shared values and opportunities for action between its library members and interested parties in the global research and education environment, including faculty and administration, public and private research funders, and the public. SPARC places a premium on empowering students and early career professionals and actively incorporates collaboration with them across all program areas.

Priorities

SPARC's work focuses on open access, open data, open education, open infrastructure, and realigning incentives to support open research. Additionally, to maximize progress, SPARC supports efforts that champion intellectual freedom, a free and open Internet, privacy, confidentiality, and equitable copyright and intellectual property policies.

The following were key priorities in 2022:

Drive Policy Change

SPARC continued to advance policies that enable open and equitable systems for research and education. SPARC works closely with decision-makers at the local, national, and international levels to align policy and incentive structures to support its vision. SPARC has advanced this priority by:

- Advocating for policies that enable and reward the open sharing of research outputs and educational materials, including the enactment of a zero-embargo national open access policy
- Educating key policymakers (including the U.S. Congress, the U.S. executive branch, the Canadian administration, state and provincial governments, and global public and private funders) on policies that advance openness and equity in research and education
- Advocating for improvements to existing public access policies to reflect emerging global norms, including immediate access; full reuse rights; FAIR data principles; harmonization of article and data-sharing requirements; and inclusion of code, software, algorithms, etc.
- Clearly communicating the potential social equity impacts of proposed policies
- Advocating for state and federal policies that incentivize the adoption of open educational resources, including continued funds for the federal Open Textbook Pilot Program
- Advocating for state and federal policies that ensure transparency, student consent, and privacy for textbook billing models such as Inclusive Access
- Leveraging leadership of and participation in coalitions to speed policy progress

Promote Incentives to Support Open Sharing of Research Outputs and Educational Materials

- Supporting the work of the Open Research Funders Group (ORFG)/ National Academies of Science, Engineering and Medicine (NASEM) Roundtable on Aligning Incentives for Open Science
- Supporting ORFG members to serve as peer influencers to promote incentive realignment
- Partnering with historically marginalized researchers and philanthropies to develop a model program to make both the process of grant making and the resulting research outputs more transparent, equitable, and inclusive

Support Member Action

SPARC's members are the core of its organization and a powerful force in advancing systems for research and education that are open by default and equitable by design. It provided timely resources, targeted briefings, and in-depth analyses to enhance the community's ability to take informed action. That work included:

- Providing a comprehensive landscape analysis of the academic publishing market, implications for libraries/academic institutions, and proposed strategic responses
- Delivering regular financial updates on key companies
- Educating members and policymakers on anti-competitive practices and antitrust concerns, as well as crafting proactive strategies
- Educating SPARC members about Environmental, Social, and Governance (ESG) Ratings and how they can help advance values alignment with vendors
- Leading research/development efforts on models for the collective provisioning of community-controlled infrastructure, including support for targeted new investment strategies that coordinate development, and operating funding instruments
- Partnering with funders, scholarly societies, and other nonprofit publishers to expand and accelerate adoption of inclusive open practices and explore shifts in business models for sustainable scholarship
- Increasing understanding and acceptance of Subscribe to Open and other non-author-processing charge (APC) open models
- Continuing to offer the highly successful SPARC Open Education Leadership Program
- Providing new professional development opportunities for advancing knowledge equity
- Providing up-to-the-moment updates and analyses of key policy and scholarly communications-related trends and developments
- Issuing action alerts and other opportunities for timely member library participation in advocacy, education, and partnership initiatives
- Delivering tools and resources to support campus advocacy and education activities

Cultivate Communities

SPARC seeks to cultivate communities that actively support the people doing the work of opening up research and education. SPARC organizes topic-specific communities of practice as well as broader efforts to build networks across SPARC's program areas:

- Convening an active Negotiations Community of Practice to provide data, resources, and support for libraries to improve their negotiating position with vendors

- Building an initiative to equip campus decision-makers to reexamine and renegotiate automatic textbook billing programs around InclusiveAccess.org
- Providing continued operational support for the Open Education Conference to the extent agreed upon with its newly founded community leadership
- Advancing a network of repositories in the United States, leveraging relevant international developments
- Developing a Privacy Community of Practice to educate SPARC members about growing privacy and surveillance threats facing libraries
- Leading the work of the International Open Access Week Advisory Committee to develop the annual theme and supporting events
- Continuing to support the OpenCon community and integrate leadership from the next generation throughout SPARC's work

Ensure Equitable and Sustainable Organizational Operations

Recognizing that centering equity is an iterative and continual process, SPARC regularly examined its organizational structures to ensure that they reflect its community's values:

- Reviewing and adjusting membership structure through a lens of anti-racism, equity, diversity, and inclusion (REDI)
- Creating deliberate, equitable relationships with and avenues to directly support Indigenous communities where SPARC operates as well as groups working to research, acknowledge, and atone for the legacy of slavery and global colonialism within a broader social justice lens
- Finalizing and adopting an executive succession plan
- Finalizing and adopting new compensation philosophy and structure guidelines
- Reviewing financial reporting practices to ensure appropriate levels of transparency and accountability
- Deploying flexible employment arrangements (Visiting Program Officers, etc.) that extend its organizational capacity while providing equitable compensation and professional development opportunities
- Annually evaluating new operational arrangements with New Venture Fund and modifying them as needed to ensure maximum operational efficiency
- Updating website and communications materials to better reflect our commitment to centering equity throughout SPARC's work

Ongoing Efforts
Global Collaboration

SPARC continued to reflect and support the global nature of scholarly communications by:

- Advocating for better global representation in the leadership of open and scholarly communications-related initiatives
- Drawing attention to the need for more globally inclusive business models for the communication of research results
- Coordinating and promoting International Open Access Week as a catalyst for action across the community
- Identifying new opportunities and establishing partnerships with key interested parties in other global regions

Supporting Students and Early Career Researchers

SPARC promoted the inclusion of students and early career academic professionals in all areas of open access by:

- Supporting the OpenCon community for students and early career academic professionals
- Continuing joint advocacy efforts to leverage community presence on open access, open data, and open education, and for related issues
- Maintaining relationships with key national and international organizations representing students and early career academic professionals

Program Activities and Outcomes 2022

Driving Policy Change

- Secured a landmark national policy making all research resulting from the annual $80 billion U.S. taxpayer investment openly and equitably available to all
- Led efforts to secure $11 million in federal funding for the U.S. Open Textbook Pilot grant program in fiscal year 2022
- Secured the re-introduction of the Affordable College Textbook Act to authorize a grant program, similar to the Open Textbook Pilot, which would expand funding for the creation and use of open textbooks at colleges and universities
- Received a four-year, $4 million grant from the Arcadia Fund to work in partnership with Creative Commons and Electronic Information for Libraries to develop a global campaign to embed open access policies and practices into the global climate change community
- Supported the open agenda for private funders via ORFG, which now includes 26 foundations that invest more than $12 billion in research funding annually
- Coordinated SPARC library community input on the UNESCO Recommendation on Open Science, the first-ever global framework for international open science policies and practices

Equipping Members for Successful Publisher Negotiations

- Conducted an "inflation watch" survey to identify current resource pricing trends

- Provided resources (member briefings, contract libraries, pricing information, guidance on data analysis for negotiation) to support libraries in preparing for negotiation
- Convened vendor-specific negotiation discussions for members to share strategies and learn from one another's experiences
- Hosted regular professional development opportunities related to negotiations, including staffing/expertise requirements, strategy development, reinvestment strategies, and more
- Supported the launch of the IMLS-funded Open Negotiation Education for Academic Libraries (ONEAL) project, which expands professional development opportunities for negotiations available to librarians

Centering Anti-Racism, Diversity, Equity, and Inclusivity (REDI)

- Regularly examined and revised its operations, finances, communications, and strategies to center REDI
- Resourced initiatives that promote REDI throughout the research communication system
- Convened a Knowledge Equity Discussion Series that provided an introduction to broad concepts and considerations of epistemic injustice and knowledge equity in the areas of academic libraries and archives
- Partnered with the Knowledge Equity Lab to produce the third season of the *Unsettling Knowledge Inequities* podcast series and sponsored a spring seminar learning opportunity for library and information studies (LIS) students that was focused on critical issues in epistemic justice relevant to LIS
- Developed the Open & Equitable Model Funding Program through ORFG and engaged 11 funders to test specific interventions designed to make both the process of grant making and the resulting research outputs more transparent, equitable, and inclusive

Realigning Research Incentives

- Along with ORFG, launched the Higher Education Leadership Initiative for Open Science, which includes university leaders from 85 institutions and is aimed at making open scholarship easier for individual researchers, aligning incentive structures, stimulating scalable infrastructure, and coordinating with like-minded sectors to promote a more transparent, inclusive, and trustworthy research ecosystem
- Partnered with NASEM to convene the Roundtable on Aligning Research Incentives for Open Science to reform research incentives to support open science
- Launched the Alliance for Open Scholarship—in collaboration with the NASEM Roundtable on Aligning Research Incentives for Open Science and ORFG—a group of 10 professional societies and associations committed to operationalizing open scholarship principles
- Worked with 18 philanthropies to develop and implement open science language in their grant-making policies, via an ORFG community of practice

Empowering Librarians through Online Resources and Development

- Released Gold Open Access 2016–2021: Articles in Journals, the seventh in a series of studies of business models supporting open access journals
- Conducted the Open Education Leadership Program, an intensive online professional development course, now with more than 100 graduates
- Played a key role in organizing the 2022 Open Education Conference
- Collaborated with the United Nations Library to organize the 2nd UN Open Science Conference
- Created opportunities for libraries to promote openness on campus by organizing the 2022 Open Access Week, with the theme Open for Climate Justice
- Expanded InclusiveAccess.org and offered more than two dozen presentations, workshops, and webinars to raise awareness of the downsides of automatic textbook billing

Encouraging Competition/Guarding against Antitrust

- Released an analysis of Elsevier's acquisition of Interfolio, outlining the increasing concentration in the nascent market for faculty information system products and the risks it may create in other markets
- Worked with antitrust and legal experts to challenge Clarivate's acquisition of ProQuest
- Proactively worked with regulators and legislators to educate them on issues in the scholarly publishing market and to initiate interventions where necessary

Supporting Community-Controlled and Open Infrastructure

- Catalyzed the creation of the U.S. Repository Network in partnership with COAR to develop a strategic vision for repositories as a critical component of national research infrastructure
- Created a new Privacy & Surveillance Community of Practice to explore library approaches to address privacy and surveillance concerns with vendors
- Created a new Community of Practice to increase library understanding of funding models that provide equitable open access to both readers and authors without relying on APCs, with specific focus on collective models such as Subscribe to Open
- Provided education to members on data privacy and surveillance issues in critical library infrastructure
- Supported the development of the global BOAI 20 recommendations on the 20th anniversary of the Budapest Open Access Initiative

Communication and Media

SPARC is regularly consulted and quoted as an expert source on topics relating to scholarly communications. Its programs have been featured in both the national

and trade press by such outlets as *Forbes,* the BBC, *The Chronicle of Higher Education, Nature, Inside Higher Ed, New York Times, Science,* and *Business Wire.*
Through its website, news stories about model policies, emerging trends, initiatives, and impact stories demonstrate how operating in the open is making a difference in advancing knowledge discovery.

SPARC-ACRL Forums

A major component of SPARC's community outreach occurs at meetings of the American Library Association (ALA), where SPARC works with the Association of College and Research Libraries (ACRL) and its scholarly communication committee to bring current issues to the attention of the community. In August 2022 SPARC and ACRL held a joint virtual forum on inclusive access.

Governance

SPARC is guided by a steering committee. The committee members are Jennifer Beamer (The Claremont Colleges), Gwen Bird (Simon Fraser University), Chris Bourg (Massachusetts Institute of Technology), Jonathan Cain (Columbia University), Vicki Coleman (North Carolina A&T State University), Karen Estlund (Colorado State University), Scarlet Galvan (Grand Valley State University), Harriett Green (Washington University), Lorraine Haricombe (University of Texas–Austin), April Hathcock (New York University), Mary Lee Kennedy (Association of Research Libraries), Yuan Li (Princeton University), Lisa Macklin (Emory University), Vince Mussehl (Chippewa Valley Technical College), Torsten Reimer (University of Chicago), Ariana Santiago (University of Houston), Yasmeen Shorish (James Madison University), Virginia Steel (University of California–Los Angeles), and Catherine Steeves (Western University).

Council on Library and Information Resources

1800 Diagonal Rd., Suite 600, Alexandria, VA 22314
https://www.clir.org
Twitter @CLIRNews

Kathlin Smith
Senior Director of Communications

The Council on Library and Information Resources (CLIR) is an independent, nonprofit organization that forges strategies to enhance research, teaching, and learning environments in collaboration with academic and cultural institutions, scholars, specialists, and practitioners. CLIR president Charles Henry leads the 21-member staff and works in close liaison with three CLIR Distinguished Presidential Fellows.

CLIR is supported by fees from sponsoring institutions, grants from public and private foundations, contracts with federal agencies, and donations from individuals. A list of current sponsors, members, and funders is available at https://www.clir.org/about/current-sponsors-and-funders.

CLIR's board establishes policy, oversees the investment of funds, sets goals, and approves strategies for their achievement. A full listing of CLIR board members is available at https://www.clir.org/about/governance.

Fellowships and Grants

Digitizing Hidden Special Collections and Archives: Amplifying Unheard Voices

In 2022 CLIR awarded its first grants in the Digitizing Hidden Special Collections and Archives: Amplifying Unheard Voices (DHC:AUV) program, a new iteration of the former Digitizing Hidden Special Collections and Archives program, which started in 2015. Supported by the Mellon Foundation, DHC:AUV focuses on the histories of marginalized peoples and communities whose work, experiences, and perspectives have been overlooked. In April 2022 CLIR awarded 15 projects a total of just more than $4 million. Forty-nine organizations located in 21 U.S. states and four Canadian provinces are involved in the projects. A list of projects and summaries is available at https://www.clir.org/hiddencollections/funded-projects.

Since 2015 Digitizing Hidden Special Collections and Archives has awarded $28 million to institutions for the purpose of digitizing collections of high value for research, teaching, and learning. A review panel, comprising experts from a range of scholarly and technical disciplines, evaluates proposals and recommends award recipients. Awards range from $50,000 to $250,000 for single-institution projects and $50,000 to $500,000 for collaborative projects.

In October 2022 CLIR shared for public comment a draft assessment of the DHC:AUV initiative. Conducted by Jesse A. Johnston and Ricardo L. Punzalan, the assessment's primary goal was to help CLIR's program staff, reviewers, and other stakeholders understand what is working in the revised program and to consider areas of program improvement. The report will be formally published early in 2023.

More information about the Digitizing Hidden Special Collections and Archives program, including a list of funded projects, is available at https://www.clir.org/hiddencollections.

Recordings at Risk

Launched in 2017 with funding from the Mellon Foundation, Recordings at Risk is a national regranting program to support the digital preservation of rare and unique audio, audiovisual, and other time-based media of high scholarly value. It is intended to encourage professionals who may be constrained by limited resources or technical expertise to act against the threats of media degradation and obsolescence. The program also helps institutions identify priorities and develop practical strategies for digital reformatting, build relationships with partners, and raise awareness of best practices.

In April 2022 CLIR awarded $570,595 to 20 projects that document 20th-century Native life in America, music history, labor and social justice activism, animal life, and the perspectives and creativity of people from California to Puerto Rico.

In December 2022 the Mellon Foundation awarded CLIR $4 million to continue the regranting program for three competitions between 2023 and 2025 that will award a total of $2.25 million. To date, the program has awarded more than $4.5 million for 147 projects.

More information about the program, including a list of funded projects, is available at https://www.clir.org/recordings-at-risk.

Postdoctoral Fellowship Program

CLIR's Postdoctoral Fellowship Program creates opportunities for recent Ph.D. graduates to develop research tools, resources, and services while exploring new career opportunities. Fellows work on projects that forge and strengthen connections among collections, technologies, and current research. Partner organizations benefit from fellows' field-specific expertise by gaining insights into their collections' potential uses and users, scholarly information behaviors, and current teaching and learning practices. Since its creation in 2004, the program has supported 221 fellows at 93 partner institutions across the United States, Canada, and overseas. Fellowships are typically for two or three years.

In 2022 CLIR launched the new Community Data fellowships—fellowships tied to projects that ethically capture and share data relevant to historically under-represented or misrepresented people, communities, and populations. Community data encompasses digital or digitized records of researchers and community members, materials from community archives, information captured from the web and social media, and records of individuals or organizations. Four organizations are hosting a total of six fellows in the 2022 cohort.

Early in 2022 CLIR published "Curated Futures Project: The Third Library Is Possible," in which fellows and alumni explore the possibility of a space that challenges the conception of a traditional library. The project encompasses podcasts, essays, and a visualization.

Additional information about the Postdoctoral Fellowship Program, including a list of current and former fellows, is available at https://www.postdoc.clir.org.

Mellon Fellowships for Dissertation Research in Original Sources

In May 2022 CLIR hosted a capstone symposium for program alumni to share lessons learned over 20 years and 18 cohorts of fellows. The symposium focused on the evolution of original source research since the program's inception and considered what the future may hold for archives and researchers. Fellows discussed how global changes have affected original source research and the risks facing researchers and collections today. They also considered the role that archives and archival research will play in addressing the social, political, and environmental challenges of the coming decades. A report of the symposium will be published in 2023.

Funded by the Mellon Foundation since 2002, the program issued its last grants in 2019. It has supported 258 fellows, representing 59 U.S. universities. Fellows have conducted research at more than 1,700 sites in 86 countries worldwide, working with original materials of every sort.

More information on the fellowship program, including a list of fellowship recipients, is available at https://www.clir.org/fellowships/mellon/fellowshiprecipients.

Programs and Partnerships

Digital Library Federation

A program of CLIR, the Digital Library Federation (DLF) is a community of practitioners who advance research, learning, social justice, and the public good through the creative design and wise application of digital library technologies. DLF connects CLIR's vision and research agenda to a network of practitioners working in digital libraries, archives, labs, museums, and elsewhere.

DLF Forum

DLF's annual signature event, the Forum, is open to digital library practitioners from member institutions and the broader community. The Forum provides an opportunity for DLF's working groups and community members to conduct business and present their work. It also enables community members to share experiences and practices with one another and support a broader level of information-sharing among professional staff. The Forum allows DLF to continually review and assess its progress with input from the community at large.

CLIR held the 2022 DLF Forum and affiliated events in Baltimore, Maryland, October 9–13. It was the first in-person Forum since the onset of the pandemic. The Forum, along with the National Digital Stewardship Alliance's Digital Preservation 2022: Preserving Legacy, Learn@DLF, and Digitizing Hidden Collections Symposium, encompassed presentations, panels, lightning talks, and workshops that drew nearly 600 attendees.

The 2023 DLF Forum and affiliated events will take place November 12–16 in St. Louis, Missouri.

Working Groups

DLF's 12 working groups represent a community of practitioners who collaborate year-round to solve problems in a variety of digital library subfields, from project management and assessment to labor and accessibility. Working groups are organized across institutional and geographical boundaries, and participation is open to anyone, regardless of institutional affiliation.

Two new groups formed in 2022: the Climate Justice Group and the Technology Strategy for Archives Group (TS4A). The Working Group on Privacy and Ethics in Technology became inactive in October 2022.

Working groups produced the following reports and resources in 2022:

Digital Library Pedagogy Group: *#DLFteach Toolkit, Volume 2*
Digital Accessibility Working Group: *Guide to Zotero Accessibility*
Born-Digital Access Working Group:

- Legal and Ethical Considerations for Born-Digital Access
- Description of Born Digital Materials in Finding Aids Portal
- An Exploration of Access Systems Framework (Version 3)
- Using Cloud Storage for Access to Digital Archives

Working groups are open to all interested professionals. A full list of DLF groups is available at https://www.diglib.org/groups.

National Digital Stewardship Alliance

CLIR serves as the host institution for the National Digital Stewardship Alliance (NDSA), a consortium of organizations, including universities, professional associations, businesses, government agencies, and nonprofit organizations, committed to the long-term preservation of digital information. NDSA activities are organized by three interest groups (Content, Infrastructure, and Standards and Practices), out of which smaller working groups often emerge. NDSA hosts the annual Digital Preservation Conference, which, since 2016, has followed the DLF Forum and—like the Forum—was held in person in 2022. More information about NDSA is available at https://ndsa.org.

HBCU Library Alliance Partnership

In July 2019 CLIR and the HBCU Library Alliance announced a long-term partnership to foster awareness of and access to collections held by Historically Black Colleges and Universities (HBCUs). In late 2020 the two organizations received a grant from the Mellon Foundation for a project to identify common values, priorities, and needs for describing and managing special and archival collections for HBCU Library Alliance members. The following year, three researchers conducted interviews and focus groups to help the HBCU Library Alliance envision how its member institutions can work together to preserve, describe, and digitize their unique collections. A public report of their findings, published in March 2022, is available at https://www.clir.org/pubs/reports/creating-access-to-hbcu-library-alliance-archives-needs-capacity-and-technical-planning.

In March 2022 CLIR launched season three of its podcast, *Material Memory*, in close collaboration with the HBCU Library Alliance. The eight-episode season, titled "HBCU Library Alliance Tour," spotlights people and collections in libraries at six HBCUs and offers insights on these cornerstones of culture and historical knowledge.

In May 2022 the partners announced that ten fellows had been selected for the final year of the Authenticity Project, a mentoring and leadership program for early- to mid-career library, archive, and museum staff from HBCUs. Throughout the year, fellows are mentored by 20 experienced library professionals from the HBCU Library Alliance or DLF communities. Both fellows and mentors gathered at the 2022 DLF Forum, where several fellows presented their work on a panel.

Throughout the year, the HBCU Library Alliance also worked with CLIR to plan an emerging Hidden Collections Africa initiative, described next.

More information about the HBCU Library Alliance and CLIR partnership is available at https://www.clir.org/initiatives-partnerships/hbcu-library-alliance.

Hidden Collections for Africa

Hidden Collections for Africa (HCA) is currently in an exploratory phase. Envisioned as a regranting program to digitize and describe African collections that are inaccessible or at risk of being lost forever, it draws inspiration from CLIR's large-scale grant programs, including Digitizing Hidden Special Collections and Archives. Its goals include digital preservation, equitable access, visibility, capacity building, and decolonizing knowledge spaces. HCA would directly support institutions and staff across the African continent, promoting resource-sharing and long-term sustainability.

The project was initially proposed by Buhle Mbambo-Thata, CLIR's board chair. CLIR is currently pursuing this initiative in partnership with the following:

- The Association of African Universities (AAU), based in Accra, Ghana
- The HBCU Library Alliance, based in Atlanta, Georgia
- UbuntuNet Alliance, the Regional Research and Education Network for Eastern and Southern Africa, based in Lilongwe, Malawi
- Réseau Francophone Numérique (RFN)-AISBL, a network of francophone libraries based in Brussels, Belgium

In November 2022 CLIR announced that it had signed memorandums of understanding with each of these partners and anticipates that additional partnerships will be announced in 2023. The program is currently pursuing funding for its core work and is open to aligned partnerships.

Digital Library of the Middle East

The Digital Library of the Middle East (DLME) is a public, open platform that aggregates digital records of published materials, documents, maps, artifacts, audiovisual recordings, and more from the Middle East and North Africa (MENA) region. The site, developed by CLIR and Stanford University Libraries in collaboration with Qatar National Library, is fully navigable in Arabic and English and is available at https://dlmenetwork.org/library.

In 2022 improvements were made to the user interface relating to searching capability, system performance, IIIF viewing, metadata processing, and site translation. There was also a focus on system automation for both indexing and reporting.

Since its launch in July 2020, DLME has grown to more than 150,000 objects in more than 100 collections from 35 institutions from around the world. It also provides an array of applications, tools, and descriptions that enrich the content and facilitate browsing, searching, and interpretation.

Leading Change Institute

The Leading Change Institute (LCI), cosponsored with EDUCAUSE, brings together information sector leaders, including deans, librarians, and information technologists, who seek to advocate for and advance change in today's rapidly evolving higher education environment. Each summer, a weeklong residential institute is held for a new cohort of participants who learn from and discuss current developments with colleagues from academia, associations, grant-making agencies, industry, and government. After attending the institute, participants join other alumni in monthly chats.

The 2022 LCI was held July 11–15 in Washington D.C., with Joanne Kossuth and Elliott Shore as deans for a class of 26 fellows. In October CLIR and EDUCAUSE announced that LCI will take a hiatus in 2023 to substantively evaluate the program. As in 2010, when an earlier program refresh saw the Frye Leadership Institute evolve into LCI, CLIR and EDUCAUSE will extensively consult with program alumni and leaders in the field of higher education throughout the process.

Chief Information Officers Group

Since 2002 CLIR has facilitated a semiannual forum of directors of organizations that have merged their library and information technology units on the campuses of liberal arts colleges and small universities. At their meetings and through a listserv, members discuss library and computing issues as an integrated whole. They have explored such topics as organizational models for optimizing success; governance structures; fostering diversity, equity, and inclusion in merged organizations; data security and privacy; and digital scholarship. A list of current members is available at https://www.clir.org/initiatives-partnerships/cios.

Affiliates

CLIR establishes collaborative relationships and cross-institutional initiatives with organizations that have similar missions in the pursuit of common goals. The affiliates program allows CLIR to serve as a fiscal or administrative home for mission-aligned organizations that may not need to be independent legal entities. Affiliates have their own governance and mission, while CLIR provides integrated services and access to tools, platforms, research, and expertise to reduce costs, create greater efficiencies, and enable affiliates to better serve their constituencies.

In 2022 CLIR welcomed its ninth affiliate, LD4 Community, which focuses on linking and using data on the web to advance the mission, goals, and objectives of libraries and archives. CLIR's other affiliates are code4lib, the Institute for Liberal Arts Digital Scholarship, the International Image Interoperability Framework, the International Internet Preservation Consortium, NDSA, Open Repositories, the Scholastic Commentaries and Texts Archive, and *Weave: Journal of Library User Experience.*

Publications

CLIR published four reports in 2022:

"Supporting Software Preservation Services in Research and Memory Organizations" (November 2022). This white paper from the Software Preservation Network's Research-in-Practice Working Group presents findings from a survey- and interview-based study of software preservation service providers, including archivists, librarians, preservation specialists, technologists, and other information professionals. It identifies concepts, skill sets, barriers, and future directions related to software preservation work.

"Accelerated Aging of Polyester-Based Legacy Audio Magnetic Tape Stock" (August 2022). This study, conducted by the Library of Congress Preservation Research and Testing Division in partnership with the FUJIFILM Recording Media Products Division, reports on new research into the longevity of polyester-based magnetic audio tapes.

"Creating Access to HBCU Library Alliance Archives: Needs, Capacity, and Technical Planning" (March 2022). This study explores the common barriers and shared visions for creating access to archival collections held by libraries at HBCUs. One of few reports that document the needs of HBCU libraries as they relate to archives and special collections, it is based on a series of online focus groups that author Sharon Ferguson Freeman facilitated with HBCU library directors and deans in 2021. The study provides insight into the significance of special and archival collections for HBCU libraries and their communities; the management and capacity of archives and special collections; and these libraries' values, priorities, needs, and aspirations.

"Curated Futures Project: A Third Library Is Possible" (February 2022). This compilation is a guide for professionals in galleries, libraries, archives, and museums to navigate beyond discussions of decolonizing collecting institutions to begin taking practical steps to enact change. CLIR fellows and alumni explore aligning libraries with social impact and provide examples in various mediums, including podcast conversations and visualizations.

Pocket Burgundy series. In May 2022 for the second year, CLIR invited proposals for its Pocket Burgundy series. The series is modeled on its "burgundy reports," so named for their cover color, but are shorter, and submissions are reviewed by an editorial committee. Four proposals were selected and announced in December 2022 at https://www.clir.org/2022/12/clir-announces-pocket-burgundy-awards. Reports funded in 2021 will be publicly available in 2023; reports funded in the second year will be published in 2024.

***Material Memory* podcast.** Season three of *Material Memory*, titled "HBCU Library Alliance Tour," spotlights people and collections at six HBCU libraries and explores how we tell the story of Black history from the archives. In eight episodes, host Sharon M. Burney, program officer at CLIR, talks with guests about the roles of cultural heritage institutions in preserving Black culture, the challenges these institutions face, and where we go from here. Episodes are available through major podcast apps, as well as at https://material-memory.clir.org.

CLIR News. In January 2022 the bimonthly newsletter CLIR Issues was renamed CLIR News; issues 145–150 were produced. CLIR News is available at https://www.clir.org/pubs/issues.

Association for Library and Information Science Education

ALISE Headquarters, 4 Lan Drive, Suite 100; Westford, MA 01886
978-674-6190, e-mail office@alise.org
http://www.alise.org

Rong Tang
President 2022–2023

The Association for Library and Information Science Education (ALISE) is an independent, nonprofit professional association founded in 1915 as the Association of American Library Schools (AALS). It changed to its current name in 1983 to more accurately reflect the mission, goals, and membership of the association. With its vision as "the global leader in education for the information professions," ALISE's mission is to promote innovative, high-quality education for the information professions internationally through engagement, advocacy, and research. With four strategic directions, ALISE's current strategic plan covers the years 2021–2025.

Membership

Membership is open to individuals and institutions. Personal members can include anyone interested in the objectives of the association, with categories such as full-time (faculty member, administrator, librarian, researcher, or other interested individual), emerging professional (doctoral students as they transition to faculty member status, maximum of three years), part-time/retired (part-time or adjunct faculty or retired professionals), and student (doctoral or other students, maximum of six years). Institutional members include schools with programs that offer a graduate degree in library and information science or a cognate field. International affiliate institutional membership is open to any school outside the United States or Canada that offers an educational program in library and information science at the professional level as defined or accepted by the country in which the school is located. Associate institutional membership status is accorded to libraries and organizations other than schools of library and information science.

In 2021 ALISE's board of directors and its membership approved a proposal presented by the membership committee to create a tiered dues structure based on World Bank Gross National Income (GNI) data. The tiered fee structure for personal memberships came into effect on January 1, 2022.

Structure and Governance

ALISE is constituted of operational groups, including the board of directors; committees; the Council of Deans, Directors, and Program Chairs; school representatives; and special interest groups (SIGs). The association was managed by McKenna Management, Inc. beginning in October 2018, with Cambria Happ as executive director. In May 2022 Barcami Lane, Inc. acquired McKenna Management, Inc.; since then, ALISE has been managed by Barcami Lane, Inc. in

Westford, Massachusetts, with Michaela Sawicki as executive director. The board of directors is composed of seven elected officers serving three-year terms. Officers for 2022–2023 are Rong Tang (Simmons University), president; Lucilia Santos Green (University of Iowa), president-elect; Lisa O'Connor (University of North Carolina–Greensboro), past president; Shimelis Assefa (University of Denver), secretary/treasurer; Daniella Smith (University of North Texas), director for membership; Monica Colon-Aguirre (University of South Carolina), director for community building; and Mega Subramaniam (University of Maryland), director for programming. At the end of the annual conference in October 2023, O'Connor and Subramaniam will conclude their terms of service, and two newly elected officers will join the board: a new vice-president/president-elect and a new director for programming.

The board establishes policy, sets goals and strategic direction, and provides oversight for the management of the association. Face-to-face meetings are held in conjunction with the annual conference to focus on policy, planning, programming, and other matters. For the remainder of the year, business is conducted through teleconferences, an online collaborative work platform, and e-mail.

Committees play a vital role in carrying out the work of the association. Since fall 2008 an open call for volunteers to serve on committees has been used to ensure broader participation in committee service, with members for the coming year appointed by the president-elect for most committees. Principal areas of activity include awards, conference program planning, governance, nominations, research competitions, advancement, programming, community building, and membership. (See https://www.alise.org/alise-committees for a full list.) Each committee is given an ongoing term of reference to guide its work as well as the specific charges for the year. Task forces can be charged to carry out tasks outside the scope of the existing standing committees.

The ALISE Council of Deans, Directors, and Program Chairs consists of the chief executive officers of each ALISE institutional member school. The group convenes at the annual conference and discusses issues via e-mail in the interim. Anthony Chow (San Jose State University), Sanda Erdelez (Simmons University), and Natalie Taylor (University of South Florida) serve as the 2022–2023 co-chairs.

Within each institutional member school, a school representative is named to serve as a direct link between the membership and the ALISE board. These individuals communicate to the faculty of their school about ALISE and the association's events and initiatives and provide input on membership issues to the ALISE board.

SIGs enable members with shared interests to communicate and collaborate, with a particular emphasis on programs at the annual conference. New SIGs are established as areas of interest emerge. Ongoing SIGs, grouped by thematic clusters, are:

- Roles and Responsibilities: Doctoral Students, Part-Time and Adjunct Faculty
- Teaching and Learning: Curriculum, Innovative Pedagogies
- Topics and Courses: Archival/Preservation Education, Disabilities in LIS, Equity and Social Justice, Gender Issues, Health, Historical Perspectives,

Information Ethics, Information Policy, International Library Education, School Library Media, Technical Services Education, Youth Services

In December 2022 the board of directors approved the establishment of the ALISE Accessibility Task Force (2022–2023). The charge of the task force is to perform relevant research and provide recommendations to the ALISE board on inclusive and cost-effective ways of accessible participation in the ALISE ongoing professional development events and the annual conference. The task force members are Keren Dali (University of Denver), Andrew J. Smith (Emporia State University), LaTesha Velez (University of North Carolina–Greensboro), Jesselyn Dreeszen Bowman (University of South Carolina), and Mega Subramaniam (University of Maryland; board liaison).

Communication

Announcements, notifications, and membership updates are posted to the ALISE membership listserv. News and events are published on ALISE's official website (http://www.alise.org). The organization has been actively using its social media accounts, including Twitter (@alisehq) and Facebook (https://www.facebook .com/ALISEHQ), to connect with its members and communities, as well as to post announcements and ALISE-related events in a timely manner.

Publications

The ALISE publications program has four components:

- The *Journal of Education for Library and Information Science* (*JELIS*) is a peer-reviewed quarterly journal edited by John Budd and Denice Adkins. It is a scholarly forum for discussion and presentation of research and issues within the field of library and information science (LIS) education. The University of Toronto Press began to serve as the publisher of *JELIS* in 2018. The journal is open access at a green level. It is indexed in Elsevier's Scopus, among other indexing sources.
- The *ALISE Library and Information Science Education Statistical Report* publishes data collected annually from its institutional members on their curriculum, faculty, students, and income and expenditures. Members can gain free access to existing reports by logging in to the members-only area of the ALISE website.
- The ALISE Book Series, published by Rowman & Littlefield, addresses issues critical to LIS education and research through the publication of epistemologically grounded scholarly texts that are inclusive of regional and national contexts around the world. The series editors are Jaya Raju (University of Cape Town) and Dietmar Wolfram (University of Wisconsin–Milwaukee). The first two books in this series were published in 2020: *The Information Literacy Framework: Case Studies of Successful Implementation* and *E.J. Josey: Transformational Leader of the Modern Library Profession.*

- The ALISE website is the public face of the association and provides information about the association and news of activities and opportunities of interest to members. It provides login access to the MemberClicks system, where members can access members-only benefits (reports, a member directory, etc.), renew membership, register for the conference and webinars, and access other services.

Annual Conference

The 2023 annual conference will be held in Milwaukee, Wisconsin, on October 2–5, 2023. The conference theme is Bridge the Gap: Teaching, Learning, Practice, and Competencies. Program co-chairs Denice Adkins (University of Missouri–Columbia) and Sean Burns (University of Kentucky), along with president Tang, are planning the conference. The event will offer presentations, poster sessions, and networking and placement opportunities, along with the unCommons—a gathering place to share, debate, brainstorm, and network.

Regarding the conference proceedings, in 2018 ALISE began to publish electronic proceedings housed by the IDEALS repository at the University of Illinois (https://www.ideals.illinois.edu/handle/2142/98929/browse?type=title). In 2022 ALISE transitioned to using the Open Journal Systems (OJS) provided by the University of Illinois. This platform offers the ability to assign DOIs to entries to ensure reliable sourcing. Past events and proceedings can be located at https://www.alise.org/past-events-proceedings.

Professional Development

ALISE offers regular, free webinars to members to facilitate virtual engagement with research and other membership interests during the year between conferences. Recent webinar offerings have included the ALISE Leadership Academy's "Career Development Dialogue: Job and Salary Negotiations" and "Career Tracks in LIS." Those who are interested in offering a webinar may submit a proposal through the webinar submission webpage (http://www.alise.org/webinar-proposals).

ALISE is redesigning its Leadership Academy (https://www.alise.org/leadership-academy) in 2023 through the work of its programming committee. In 2019 ALISE initiated the Leadership Academy to create communities within library and information science for the exploration of leadership roles such as chairs, directors, and deans. It aims to build interest in leadership and to build the confidence of prospective leaders. The academy also provides prior attendees with a forum to reconvene, to reflect on their learnings from the past year, and to gain new insights to deploy in the future.

Grants and Awards

ALISE supports research and recognizes accomplishments through its grants and awards programs. Research competitions include the ALISE Research Grant Competition, the ALISE/Bohdan S. Wynar Research Paper Competition, the

ALISE/ProQuest Methodology Paper Competition, the ALISE/Eugene Garfield Doctoral Dissertation Competition, and the ALISE Community conn@CT Mini-Grants. Support for conference participation is provided by the University of Washington Information School Youth Services Graduate Student Travel Award, the Doctoral Student to ALISE Award, the ALISE/Jean Tague Sutcliffe Doctoral Student Research Poster Competition, and the ALISE Diversity Travel Award to the ALISE Annual Conference. This last award was created in collaboration with the ALA Office for Diversity Spectrum Scholarship Program, which created a parallel award, the ALA/ALISE Spectrum Travel Award, partially funded by ALISE.

Awards recognizing outstanding accomplishments include the ALISE/Norman Horrocks Leadership Award (for early-career leadership), the ALISE/Pratt-Severn Faculty Innovation Award, the ALISE Service Award, the ALISE Award for Professional Contribution, the ALISE/Connie Van Fleet Award for Research Excellence in Public Library Services to Adults, and the ALISE Excellence in Teaching Award. Winners are recognized at an awards luncheon at the annual conference. For a list of award winners, see http://www.alise.org/awards-grants.

Collaboration with Other Organizations

ALISE seeks to collaborate with other organizations on activities of mutual interest. ALISE members also serve on committees for various national organizations, including American Library Association (ALA) committees.

ALISE continues to build its international connections, with members serving on International Federation of Library Associations and Institutions (IFLA) standing committees that address education and research. ALISE has been expanding its collaborations with peer organizations, including the Association for Information Science and Technology (ASIS&T) and the iSchools Organization; the partnership of these three organizations is called the iFederation.

Conclusion

ALISE is guided by its strategic plan. In 2020 the 2017–2020 strategic plan was closed out, and the association underwent a significant strategic process that resulted in a completely updated strategic plan for 2021–2025 (https://www.alise .org/history-strategic-direction). ALISE looks forward to continuing its leading role in LIS education and research.

International Reports

International Federation of Library Associations and Institutions

Postal Address: P.O. Box 95312, 2509 CH Den Haag, Netherlands
Visiting Address: Prins Willem-Alexanderhof 5, 2595 BE The Hague (Den Haag), Netherlands
Tel. +31 70 3140884, fax +31 70 3834827, e-mail ifla@ifla.org
http://www.ifla.org

The International Federation of Library Associations and Institutions (IFLA) is the preeminent international organization representing librarians, other information professionals, and library users. Its core values are:

- The endorsement of the principles of freedom of access to information, ideas, and works of imagination and freedom of expression embodied in Article 19 of the Universal Declaration of Human Rights
- The belief that people, communities, and organizations need universal and equitable access to information, ideas, and works of imagination for their social, educational, cultural, democratic, and economic well-being
- The conviction that delivery of high-quality library and information services helps guarantee that access
- The commitment to enable all members of the federation to engage in, and benefit from, its activities without regard to citizenship, disability, ethnic origin, gender, geographical location, language, political philosophy, race, or religion

IFLA Global Vision and IFLA Strategy 2019–2024

To provide direction and inspiration for all of its activities, IFLA in 2018 adopted a global vision of "A strong and united global library field powering literate, informed and participatory societies." The IFLA Strategy 2019–2024 was developed from the IFLA Global Vision. Glòria Pérez-Salmerón, president of IFLA from 2017 to 2019, and Gerald Leitner, secretary general from June 2016 to March 2022, unveiled the IFLA Strategy 2019–2024 at the World Library and Information Congress (WLIC) 2019. The IFLA Strategy presents four strategic directions: strengthen the global voice of libraries, inspire and enhance professional practice, connect and empower the field, and optimize the organization. Each strategic direction is supported by four key initiatives, forming a call to action for all libraries to inspire, engage, enable, and connect with their societies.

After working intensively since December 2019 to reexamine IFLA's organization and governance, IFLA now operates with a streamlined and more participatory governance structure. Pledging "no decisions about you without you," the governing board and IFLA headquarters staff issued an initial draft in June 2020, followed by a member survey and virtual workshops seeking feedback from individuals. A final proposal for a new governance structure and revised IFLA Statutes was accepted by the General Assembly in November 2020, and the governing board approved it in February 2021. The new governance structure and IFLA Statutes took effect on August 26, 2021.

The highest governance level of IFLA is its General Assembly of all members, meeting annually during WLIC and voting in person or electronically. The General Assembly determines the purposes and values of IFLA, approves amendments to the IFLA Statutes, determines the conditions of membership, and receives and approves the annual financial statements.

The new, streamlined governing board has only 11 members, eliminating the need for the former executive committee. The governing board members are the president, president-elect, and treasurer of IFLA; the chairs of the Professional and Regional councils; the chair of the Management of Library Associations Section, and five elected members-at-large.

A new Regional Council guides, supports, and sets priorities for IFLA's advocacy work in each of six regions of the world. Six new regional divisions report to the Regional Council: Asia and Oceania, including Australia and New Zealand; Middle East and North Africa; Latin America and the Caribbean; Sub-Saharan Africa; Europe, including Turkey; and North America. Because the six regional divisions follow the United Nations pattern of political divisions, the North America regional division includes only Canada and the United States (50 states and the District of Columbia), with Mexico and Puerto Rico assigned to Latin America and the Caribbean. The establishment of regional divisions, which prior to 2021 were a single division, will provide greater visibility to IFLA's regional advocacy work and foster greater participation in countries with developing economies.

Forty-two sections continue as professional units, organized in eight divisions, reporting to the Professional Council. The chair of each professional unit's standing committee is authorized to appoint five additional members to ensure that each region of the world is represented on the standing committee. The four IFLA strategic programs have been replaced by four advisory committees reporting to the governing board: Standards, Cultural Heritage, Copyright and Other Legal Matters, and Freedom of Access to Information and Free Expression. In contrast to the previous structure, the advisory committees report to the governing board but do not automatically have seats on the Professional Council. The new structure allows sections or divisions to sponsor special interest groups that may exist for two four-year terms before either disbanding or becoming full-fledged sections.

Reports

In 2022 IFLA released several reports, including "How Well Did Copyright Laws Serve Libraries during COVID-19?" which found that 83% of library professionals who responded to the report's survey said they had copyright-related challenges with providing materials during pandemic-related facility closures. These intersected with ongoing challenges that occurred before the pandemic, such as budget pressures, external financial crises, difficult negotiations with publishers, and demand for e-books that outpaced publisher offerings. "Impacts of Public Access to Computers and the Internet in Libraries," released in conjunction with Electronic Information for Libraries, provides libraries and other stakeholders with an easy-to-use overview of recent evidence, good practices, and methodologies for public access impact assessment.

Statements

In 2022 IFLA issued several statements, including the IFLA Statement on Cybersecurity. It details the following:

- What cybersecurity means for libraries—and the information system components this encompasses
- Key areas for library engagement and advocacy
- The relationship between cybersecurity and privacy
- The actions libraries can take if they have full or partial control over their information systems—and if they are a part of a wider institution or rely on third-party vendors
- What library associations and governments can do to support a safer digital environment

IFLA's Statement on Open Library Data calls on all governments to collect—or support the collection of—data about libraries and their use. It highlights that any such collection should not lead to a reduction of library budgets and that data should be collected in a way that allows for disaggregation. The statement also calls for questions about libraries to be integrated into household surveys in order to build a better understanding of how individuals use them.

IFLA's 10 Years of the IFLA Open Access Statement: A Call to Action updates IFLA's 2011 open access statement. It affirms the value of open access and related initiatives while outlining IFLA's ongoing work in the area. In addition, the statement reviews the steps taken toward the vision articulated by IFLA in 2011 and identifies new areas in need of urgent action. Libraries provide critical support for the development of open access as a societal good and are uniquely positioned to support the equitable and inclusive development of publishing opportunities, including serving as infrastructure for publishing initiatives and educating authors about pathways for publishing their works open access.

At WLIC 2022 in Dublin, Ireland, IFLA and UNESCO released the updated IFLA-UNESCO Public Library Manifesto. The manifesto was created in 1949 and has been updated over the decades as the role of libraries in society evolves. The most recent version, published in 1994, has long been a cornerstone of IFLA's public library advocacy. The goal of the update was to consider changes in technology and society and ensure that the manifesto continues to reflect the realities and mission of public libraries today. The updated manifesto upholds libraries as agents of sustainable development through their position as publicly accessible spaces for the exchange of information, the sharing of culture, and the promotion of civic engagement. This includes highlighting inclusion, access, and cultural participation for marginalized communities, Indigenous peoples, and users with special needs. It reflects the public library's role in helping all members of society access, produce, create, and share knowledge. This includes an increased focus on remote and digital access to information and materials, as well as access to the competencies and connectivity required to bridge the digital divide. The update stresses the development of media and information literacy and digital skills in the spirit of equipping informed, democratic societies. The updated text further states that libraries underpin healthy knowledge societies through providing access to and enabling the creation and sharing of knowledge of all sorts, including scientific and local knowledge without commercial, technological, or legal barriers. It further states that, in the digital era, copyright and intellectual property legislation must ensure public libraries the same capacity to procure and give access to digital content on reasonable terms as is the case with physical resources.

Milestones

In 2022 IFLA celebrated its 95th anniversary. Since its establishment in 1927, IFLA has provided a framework for international collaboration. This framework now consists of more than 50 committees working to boost knowledge within the library and information sector and support the goal of the best possible libraries for all.

In addition, in 2022 IFLA and UNESCO celebrated 75 years of partnership. The goal of this collaboration was to find ways for libraries to participate in UNESCO's mission. Throughout the years the two organizations have worked to establish libraries in the developing world. UNESCO has worked on issues relating to the provision of bibliographic services, development of learning tools and resources, and promotion of international cooperation. Cooperation with IFLA has included promoting thought leadership on technical library issues and the establishment and promotion of best professional practices.

Library and Archives Canada

An inspiring wind of change is blowing through Library and Archives Canada (LAC), the fourth-largest library in the world. In 2020 LAC, which plays the roles of both national library and national archives for Canada, embarked on a major transition to improve its services to Canadians and to more effectively fulfill its mandate of acquiring, preserving, processing, making accessible, and sharing Canada's documentary heritage, specifically through a significant technological shift. To focus its efforts, LAC developed a new strategic plan in consultation with its staff, partners, and clients. Unveiled in 2022, Vision 2030 now guides decision making, sets objectives to be reached by 2030, prioritizes activities to be performed, and influences the organizational culture. At the heart of LAC's priorities is access to the collections in its care and the harmonization of services while taking users' needs into account. For LAC, access is key to understanding.

The Vision 2030 statement "Discover. Understand. Connect." shows what motivates LAC in this great endeavor and is intended to challenge and inspire staff and users alike:

- **Discover.** This is about setting out in search of ourselves, the people who have inhabited this land since time immemorial and those who came to Canada recently or long ago. Thanks to the staff, the collections assist in this discovery.
- **Understand.** Delving into the past through LAC's resources helps Canadians to know themselves more fully as individuals and as a society, to better understand where they came from and where they are going, and how society came to be what it is and why.
- **Connect.** The collections at LAC are meeting places for people. They bring together the present and the past, the public and the staff, the users and the data, and citizens with each other. Connecting is about sharing, storytelling, reconciling, and uniting.

Access to Collections

In 2022 LAC continued to improve public access to the histories and stories preserved in the collections. The millions of documents and works contained there reflect the diversity of our past experiences and provide keys to deciphering our present-day ones.

LAC takes its users' feedback very seriously. Over the years, it became clear that the LAC website was not meeting the needs of the public. The work of several teams within the institution led to the launch of a brand-new website, library-archives.canada.ca, on August 30, 2022. Easy to use, intuitive, and accessible, the new site facilitates searching, navigating, and reading. It was designed based on users' expectations and Internet best practices. As a result, LAC hopes to exceed the 2.8 million unique visitors who accessed its website and online applications last year. The redesigned site includes the addition of the new My Account platform, which aims to customize the user experience. Users can now search, save, and review records in the Collection Search tool, access Co-Lab (a crowdsourcing tool that allows Canadians to transcribe, translate, and describe digitized collection materials), and track their registrations for LAC's public events.

LAC also focused on improving its access to information and privacy (ATIP) services to better respond to Canadians' requests. This was a significant undertaking, given that LAC holds and preserves the equivalent of more than 200 linear kilometers of historical records from more than 300 active or former federal departments and agencies, dating back to the 19th century. In response to the recommendations from the Office of the Information Commissioner of Canada released in spring 2022, which identified challenges with ATIP, LAC published an action plan, created a branch dedicated entirely to ATIP, and hired new staff to address the backlog of requests.

In line with the strategic priorities established for 2021–2022, LAC kept working on a fundamental transformation of its services to the public, both at its various service points and remotely. LAC continued to serve Canadians and to provide access to documentary heritage through its reference, genealogy, orientation, copying, and consultation services. LAC's points of service in Ottawa, Halifax, Winnipeg, and Vancouver completed 50,517 transactions, an increase of 38 percent over the previous year.

Despite the inherent challenges of the pandemic, LAC continued to offer public programming activities on its various virtual platforms and adapted its services to enable access to the collections. More than 177,000 people attended exhibitions and events organized by LAC or in collaboration with other organizations.

Unique Infrastructure

LAC has also set out to remain a world leader. Over the past few years, the federal institution has been working on two major construction projects: one to increase its preservation capacity and the other to revolutionize its services to the public.

In 2022 LAC opened its Preservation Storage Facility. This building expands LAC's storage capacity; more than 590,000 containers of published documents and analog archives, microfilms, and motion-picture films will be moved there. The design ensures the preservation conditions needed to retain documents for 500 years. It is also a true technological and environmental gem:

- The first net-zero-carbon archival center in the Americas
- The first federal special-purpose facility built in accordance with Canada's Greening Government Strategy
- The world's largest automated archive facility for the secure removal and return of archival containers

The other major project, Ādisōke, began to take shape in 2022, with the laying of the foundation for the joint facility to be shared by LAC and Ottawa Public Library. This is an unprecedented partnership between federal and municipal governments. Construction work will continue until the scheduled opening of the building in 2026. Ādisōke is located on the unceded traditional territory of the Algonquin Anishinābe Nation, which has inhabited the area since time immemorial. Elders and members of the host Nation were key partners in the design of the building and the selection of the name Ādisōke, which refers to storytelling in the Anishinābemowin language. With 1.7 million visitors expected annually, the new facility will allow LAC to increase its ability tenfold to share the collections in its care with the general public. Ādisōke will also provide a dynamic experience for LAC's users. Its programs, services, exhibitions, and events will showcase Indigenous histories and stories, as well as Canada's rich heritage, making Ādisōke a truly unique Canadian destination. Finally, this is LAC's second major sustainable infrastructure project, as it will be built to a net-zero-carbon standard.

Optimizing Digital Capacity

The quality of the user experience is now a critical success factor. Accustomed to working with search engines and social media, Canadians are eager for digital content and expect to find information quickly, easily, and intuitively, wherever it is located. To this end, LAC is expanding its initiatives to provide the public with faster and greater access to the rich collections that it holds.

In 2021–2022 LAC modernized elements of its infrastructure and processes. Its new Digital Asset Management System (DAMS), a set of automated and semi-automated digital tools, supports the acquisition, evaluation, description, integration, preservation, and discovery of the digital collections in LAC's care. These include materials from federal departments and agencies and from private donors, published heritage from Canadian publishers, and theses deposited by Canadian universities. DAMS provides secure access to the collections and monitors data integrity, which ensures long-term preservation.

Another significant improvement is that Canadian publishers and producers of cultural content can now submit their digital titles in batches using a brand-new web form. LAC has received more than 89,000 digital titles from more than 5,000 publishers and cultural-content producers, almost double the number from the previous year.

LAC has continued its mission to preserve Canada's digital heritage. For 2020–2022 alone, the numbers are impressive:

- The addition of 1,153 terabytes (TB) of digital content, or approximately 92 million files; the size of the preserved digital collection is now more than 9,000 TB
- The addition of more than 450 million digital items related to COVID-19
- The addition of more than 13 TB of webpages reflecting the evolution of Canadian society: media and federal government sites, Canadian political sites, and Indigenous resource sites
- The migration of more than 730,000 hours of audiovisual recordings (films, audio, and video recordings)

On the Road to Reconciliation

Thanks to its Indigenous initiatives, programs, and services, LAC supports the government's commitment to building a renewed relationship based on respect, recognition of rights, and cooperation and partnership with First Nations, Inuit, and the Métis Nation. As a memory institution, LAC places great importance on providing increased accessibility to Indigenous documentary heritage so that communities can reclaim their histories and stories.

In 2022 LAC continued its initiatives to preserve Indigenous heritage and languages. It processed ATIP requests related to the Federal Indian Day Schools class action, which seeks compensation for damages and abuse suffered by all students who were forced to attend these institutions.

Through LAC's Listen, Hear Our Voices initiative, Indigenous institutions (First Nations, Inuit, and the Métis Nation) across Canada have shared $1.7 million to digitize, preserve, and build capacity in their communities for their languages and cultures.

Since the start of its We Are Here: Sharing Stories initiative, LAC has digitized and described more than 600,000 items related to Indigenous peoples in the collections. These include textual records, photographs, works of art, maps, and publications about First Nations, Inuit, and the Métis Nation from private donors, as well as government documents and publications. This content is available to everyone through LAC's website, social media, and other online tools.

LAC has continued to build invaluable relationships with Indigenous publishers. It added 382 titles to the collections, in addition to acquiring several Indigenous newspapers.

Diversity, Inclusion, Equity, and Accessibility

LAC participates in the government of Canada's efforts to promote the values of equity, diversity, and inclusion in Canadian society. To ensure that the collections accurately reflect the diversity of communities in Canada, LAC has begun to revise its acquisition guidelines to include the documentary heritage of marginalized individuals and groups in its strategy. In the same vein, LAC has also implemented strategies to hire people from all walks of life to create a skilled and diversified workforce.

In December 2022 LAC released its first-ever accessibility plan, which includes a range of recommendations and actions to achieve its goal of being barrier-free for all staff and users by 2040. Since it serves the public, LAC has always made access to its facilities, programs, services, and collections a priority. This plan confirms that it will continue to improve accessibility. The next step for LAC in 2023–2024 will be the creation of a center of excellence for diversity and inclusion.

International Board on Books for Young People

Nonnenweg 12, 4055 Basel, Switzerland
E-mail ibby@ibby.org
http://www.ibby.org

Sylvia Vardell
President, 2022–2024

Carolina Ballester
Executive Director

The founding of the International Board on Books for Young People (IBBY) was the result of the visionary commitment of Jella Lepman (1891–1970). Born in Stuttgart, Germany, she became a politically active journalist. In 1936 she emigrated with her son and daughter from Nazi Germany to London and became a British citizen, working for the British Foreign Office and the BBC during World War II and, from 1941, for the American Broadcasting Station in Europe.

When the war ended, Lepman was engaged at the American headquarters in Germany as an adviser for questions relating to children and young people. Despite a lack of funds, she organized an exhibition of children's illustrations and children's books from 20 countries in Munich in 1946. Three years later, with initial funding from the Rockefeller Foundation, she established the International Youth Library in Munich and was its director until 1957.

In the postwar years, individuals actively engaged in the field of children's literature in many countries became aware of the importance of children's books as a means for promoting international understanding and peace. They realized that children everywhere should have access to books with high literary and artistic standards and thus become enthusiastic and informed readers.

With this vision in mind, in November 1951 Lepman organized a meeting in Munich under the title International Understanding Through Children's Books. The goal of the meeting was the foundation of an international organization to promote children's literature. The speeches and discussions at the event were covered by news media worldwide. The meeting resulted in the establishment of a committee to form the International Board on Books for Young People (IBBY).

The committee met in Munich in 1952 and made a formal declaration of intent. The meeting was chaired by Swiss publisher Hans Sauerländer, and the effort was international in character from the beginning, as the meeting included representatives from Austria, Germany, the Netherlands, Norway, Sweden, and Switzerland.

The success of this preparatory work resulted in the establishment of IBBY, which was registered as a nonprofit organization in Switzerland when the new organization's first General Assembly and Congress were held at the Swiss Federal Institute for Technology (ETHZ) in Zurich in October 1953. The congress brought together the organization's founding members, including authors Erich Kästner, Lisa Tetzner, Astrid Lindgren, Jo Tenfjord, Fritz Brunner, and Pamela Travers; Swiss illustrators Alois Carigiet and Hans Fischer; publishers Sauerländer and Bettina Hürlimann; and specialists in reading research, such as Richard Bamberger.

The initial capital for the founding of IBBY was donated by the Swiss foundation Pro Juventute, and its secretary general, Otto Binder, was elected as IBBY's first president. In the early years, IBBY also received support from the International Youth Library. However, the dues from the ten national sections that had joined IBBY by 1956 were not sufficient to establish a permanent office, and IBBY's activities were mainly carried out through donations and voluntary work. The organization of the administration was the task of the acting presidents who served for two-year terms during the first decade. Succeeding Binder were Swedish publisher Hans Rabén (1956–1958), Italian professor of education Enzo Petrini (1958–1960), and Lepman (1960–1962).

A notable professionalization of IBBY and an extension of membership were achieved during the presidency of Bamberger (1962–1966). In addition, the publication of IBBY's quarterly journal, *Bookbird*, edited by Lepman, Bamberger, and Lucia Binder, became a permanent activity at this time. During the presidencies of Slovenian publisher Zorka Persic (1966–1970) and Finnish school principal Niilo Visapää (1970–1974), IBBY grew so large that it was no longer possible to rely entirely on voluntary work. In 1974 a permanent office, the IBBY Secretariat, was established in Basel. Leena Maissen was appointed its director and remained in that post until her retirement in 2003. Liz Page, who had joined Maissen at the Secretariat in 1997, served as IBBY executive director from 2009 to 2022. Carolina Ballester was appointed to succeed her in September 2022.

IBBY is a nonprofit organization that represents an international network of people who are committed to bringing books and children together. The annual dues from the national sections are IBBY's only source of regular income; projects are supported by sponsors. IBBY cooperates with many international organizations and children's book institutions around the world and exhibits at the International Children's Book Fair in Bologna and other international book fairs.

The biennial IBBY World Congresses, which have taken place in 28 countries, have become increasingly important meeting points for the worldwide membership, now comprising 81 national sections, to share information and experiences.

Mission and Programs

IBBY's mission is:

- To promote international understanding through children's books
- To give children everywhere the opportunity to have access to books with high literary and artistic standards
- To encourage the publication and distribution of quality children's books, especially in developing countries
- To provide support and training for those involved with children and children's literature
- To stimulate research and scholarly works in the field of children's literature
- To protect and uphold children's rights as outlined in the United Nations Convention on the Rights of the Child

As part of its mission, IBBY administers three major international awards: the Hans Christian Andersen Award, which is presented to an author and illustrator whose body of work has made lasting contributions to children's literature; the IBBY-Asahi Reading Promotion Award, which is given to a group or an institution whose activities are judged to be making a lasting contribution to reading promotion programs for children and young people; and the IBBY-iRead Outstanding Reading Promoter Award, which recognizes outstanding individuals who are working to promote the expansion and development of children's reading. All three awards are given biennially and presented at the IBBY congresses; the next awards will be presented at the 39th IBBY Congress in Trieste, Italy, in 2024.

The IBBY Honour List is a biennial selection of outstanding recently published books, honoring writers, illustrators, and translators from IBBY member countries. An annotated catalog is published for each Honour List selection.

The IBBY Collection for Young People with Disabilities offers information and documentation services for organizations, research workers, teachers, students, librarians, publishers, authors, illustrators, policymakers, and the media who work with young people with special needs. The IBBY Selection of Outstanding Books for Young People with Disabilities is prepared biennially and presented in an annotated catalog. The collection is based at the North York Central Library Branch of the Toronto Public Library in Canada.

Traveling exhibitions of the IBBY Honour List and the Outstanding Books for Young People with Disabilities selections can be booked from IBBY. Detailed information can be found on the IBBY website (http://www.ibby.org).

IBBY established International Children's Book Day in 1967 to inspire a love of reading and to call attention to children's books. Each year the day is sponsored by an IBBY national section and is celebrated on or around Hans Christian Andersen's birthday, April 2.

The IBBY Yamada workshop and project program relies on its international network to help produce and develop book cultures for children within regions that have special needs and lack support.

IBBY established its Children in Crisis program to provide support for children whose lives have been disrupted by war, civil disorder, or natural disaster. The two main activities supported are the therapeutic use of books and storytelling in the form of bibliotherapy and the creation or replacement of collections of selected books that are appropriate to the situation. The Sharjah/IBBY Fund for Children in Crisis was active from 2012 to 2016. The fund supported projects in Afghanistan, Iran, Lebanon, Palestine, Pakistan, and Tunisia.

In response to the waves of refugees from Africa and the Middle East arriving on the Italian island of Lampedusa, IBBY launched the project Silent Books, from the World to Lampedusa and Back in 2012. The project involved creating the first library on Lampedusa to be used by local and immigrant children. It also developed a collection of silent books (wordless picture books) that could be understood and enjoyed by children regardless of language. These books were collected from IBBY National Sections. The books are deposited at the documentation and research archive in Rome (Palazzo della Esposizioni), while a second set is deposited at the library in Lampedusa, and a third makes a traveling exhibition for the IBBY network.

Congresses

IBBY's biennial World Congresses, hosted by different national sections, bring together IBBY members and other people involved in children's books and reading development from all over the world. In addition to lectures, panel discussions, seminars, and book exhibitions, the IBBY Membership Assembly takes place. The presentation of the Hans Christian Andersen Award, the IBBY-Asahi Reading Promotion Award, the IBBY-iRead Outstanding Reading Promoter Award, and the IBBY Honour List are highlights of the biennial congresses. The 38th IBBY Congress was held in Putrajaya, Malaysia, in 2022. The next one will take place in Trieste, Italy, from August 30 to September 1, 2024.

IBBY national sections also organize regional conferences to improve communication, networking, and professional exchange and to strengthen ties of friendship and cooperation among the sections in the region.

Bookbird: A Journal of International Children's Literature is a refereed quarterly journal published by IBBY and is open to any topic in the field of international children's literature. *Bookbird* also has occasional themed issues. Calls for manuscripts are posted on the IBBY website. Regular features include coverage of children's literature studies, IBBY activities, and children's literature awards around the world. *Bookbird* also pays special attention to reading promotion projects worldwide. Its editor works in cooperation with an international editorial review board, guest reviewers, and correspondents who are nominated by IBBY national sections.

IBBY cooperates with several international organizations, including the International Federation of Library Associations and Institutions (IFLA), the International Publishers Association (IPA), and the International Literacy Association (ILA).

IBBY's U.S. National Section

The United States Board on Books for Young People (USBBY) is the U.S. national section of IBBY. It is a nonprofit organization devoted to building bridges of international understanding through children's and young adult books. The Friends of IBBY in the United States was founded in 1976 and became a national section of IBBY in 1984. Membership in USBBY is open to individuals and organizations interested in its mission.

A volunteer board includes USBBY's president, president-elect, past president, recording secretary, treasurer, and 12 directors, four elected and eight appointed, representing the membership as well as the patron organizations that support USBBY, such as ILA, the Children's Book Council (CBC), the American Library Association (ALA), and the National Council of Teachers of English (NCTE).

USBBY offers a forum for those interested in national and international activities relating to children's literature. It publishes a semiannual newsletter for its members, creates an annual list of the most outstanding international literature published or distributed in the United States for children and young adults, maintains an active website, sponsors a biennial regional conference that features speakers of international interest, and cosponsors sessions held at annual conferences of ALA, ILA, and NCTE.

USBBY sponsors the publication of a series of annotated bibliographies of outstanding international literature for young people, the Bridges to Understanding series, published by Scarecrow Press. It also sponsors the creation of an annual USBBY Outstanding International Books (OIB) list, published yearly in *School Library Journal*, and a bookmark listing the selected titles is distributed via the USBBY website (https://www.usbby.org/outstanding-international-books-list. html) and at meetings and conferences throughout the year. [Find the 2022 list on page 356 of this volume—*Ed.*]

The OIB committee selects international books that are deemed most outstanding of those published during the calendar year. Books selected for the list represent the best of children's literature from other countries, introduce American readers to outstanding authors and illustrators from other countries, help American children see the world from other points of view, provide a perspective or address a topic otherwise missing from children's literature in the United States, exhibit a distinct cultural flavor, and are accessible to American readers. Committee members judge the books based on artistic and literary merit, originality or creativity of approach, distinctiveness of topic, uniqueness of origin, and qualities that engage and appeal to children.

USBBY also submits nominations for the Hans Christian Andersen Award and prepares a biennial selection of outstanding recently published books for the IBBY Honour List, the Silent Books project, and the IBBY list of Outstanding Books for Young People with Disabilities. In addition, it nominates programs for the IBBY-Asahi Reading Promotion Award and the IBBY-iRead Outstanding Reading Promoter Award.

USBBY's Bridge to Understanding Award formally acknowledges the work of adults who use books to promote international understanding among children. The award was established in memory of Arlene Pillar, an educator who served USBBY as newsletter editor from 1984 until her death in 1990. Organizations eligible for this award include schools, libraries, Scout troops, clubs, and bookstores. The winning program may be a one-time event or an ongoing series that serves children ranging in age from kindergarten through tenth grade. The award carries a prize of $1,000 and a certificate. Recent winners include Promoting Global Awareness in Second Graders, a project in the Madeira City School District in Cincinnati that involved four second-grade teachers as well as the elementary art, music, library, gym, and computer teachers. The project was described as helping students to "make personal connections to the characters of the books, develop empathy, and relate to other children of the world through literature."

Other USBBY activities include support of IBBY's Hands across the Sea Fund, which gives assistance to underfunded IBBY sections.

USBBY has an active twinning relationship with four other IBBY national sections, allowing USBBY members to know and work closely with specific countries and to internationalize USBBY perspectives. Specific initiatives within the twinning program may include payment of IBBY dues for underfunded national sections; provision of funding to purchase books or other needed resources for classrooms and libraries; providing funding or training for writers, illustrators, editors, librarians, and publishers; facilitating fellowships for writers, illustrators, editors, librarians, publishers, or those who want to study children's literature; supporting cultural exchange and visits between members of USBBY and twinning national sections; developing reciprocal website postings of newsletters, information about projects, lists of children's books published in each country, and relevant websites; and including news about twinning partners in Global Partnerships, a regular column in the USBBY newsletter, Bridges. Current USBBY twinning partners are Haiti, Lebanon, Palestine, and El Salvador.

The USBBY Secretariat is at the Center for Teaching through Children's Books at National Louis University, 1000 Capitol Drive, Wheeling, IL 60090. It can be reached by telephone at 224-233-2798, and its e-mail address is secretariat@usbby.org. Its website is http://www.usbby.org. USBBY's executive director is Junko Yokota, e-mail: executive.director@usbby.org.

Part 2
Legislation, Funding, and Grants

Legislation

Legislation and Regulations
Affecting Libraries in 2022

Anthony Aycock

After once-in-a-generation funding of America's libraries in 2021 through legislation such as the American Rescue Plan Act (ARPA) and the Infrastructure Investment and Jobs Act, Congress offered more modest support in 2022 with the Consolidated Appropriations Act. This spending bill authorized the following increases for federal agencies:

- National Endowment for the Humanities: $12.5 million
- Institute of Museum and Library Services: $11 million
- National Archives and Records Administration: $11 million
- National Historical Publications and Records Commission: $500,000

One program that ARPA established was the Coronavirus Capital Projects Fund, which made $10 billion available to states to fund three types of projects: construction and deployment of broadband infrastructure; purchase or installation of computers and/or public wifi equipment to facilitate broadband internet access; and construction or improvement of community buildings for the purpose of enabling work, education, and health monitoring (these are called "Multi-Purpose Community Facility Projects").

The U.S. Department of the Treasury began distributing Coronavirus Capital Projects Fund money in 2022. Most of the awards were for statewide broadband infrastructure projects, but one state, Delaware, was approved for $40.3 million in multipurpose community facility funds. The state intends to use these funds to create a competitive grants program for libraries. According to the Delaware Office of Management and Budget, libraries funded through the program will provide increased access to resources and programming for community members, including students, job-seekers, children, and parents.

A number of other bills were introduced in Congress that could benefit libraries, such as the Right to Read Act. The aim of this bill was to ensure that all students have access to a well-staffed, well-resourced school library by authorizing Comprehensive Literacy State Development Grants ($500 million), as well as

Anthony Aycock is the author of *The Accidental Law Librarian* (Information Today, Inc., 2013). He is a freelance writer (www.anthonyaycock.com) as well as the director of the North Carolina Legislative Library.

increasing the authorization for the Innovative Approaches to Literacy program ($100 million). However, none of these bills became law.

Following comments and recommendations by the American Library Association as well as the Association of Tribal Archives, Libraries, and Museums, the Federal Communications Commission proposed a final rule change to 47 CFR Part 54. The new rule clarified the eligibility of tribal libraries for E-rate—a program that provides discounts for telecommunications, Internet access, and related services to eligible schools and libraries—by updating the definition of "library" in the program rules to include them. The new rule became effective March 16, 2022.

If it was a quiet year for libraries at the federal level, the opposite was true in state legislatures across the country, as lawmakers challenged the ability of public and school libraries to manage their collections, serve their patrons, and be good stewards of public dollars. Florida became the bellwether in this regard with a pair of laws. The first requires school districts to be "transparent" in the selection of instructional material, encouraging parents to weigh in on curriculum decisions and library collections. The second is the Parental Rights in Education Act. Known as the "Don't Say Gay" Bill, the law bans public school employees, which could include librarians, from instructing students in sexual orientation or gender identity.

Other states passed bills that (1) prohibit the teaching of critical race theory, (2) give legislatures greater authority over local school boards, and (3) expand the definition of "obscene" materials. Included in this last category of bills is a worry that is new to most librarians: criminal liability. In Missouri, for instance, a 2022 law makes it illegal to provide access to books deemed "sexually explicit." Violators can be charged with a class A misdemeanor, which could lead to a year in jail and a $2,000 fine. Similarly, an Oklahoma law singles out employees of schools and public libraries as eligible for criminal prosecution for exposing students to indecent material.

Despite these developments, it wasn't all dire for libraries at the state level. Some legislation was far more encouraging. Kentucky, for example, passed the Read to Succeed Act, which strengthened the quality of reading instruction for K–3 students while streamlining the statewide systems for reading and literacy to better connect parents, teachers, and educators. Tennessee created a new position of state library coordinator to assist, train, and consult with school librarians on literacy and digital citizenship initiatives, as well as to be a statewide advocate for school libraries. Delaware passed the Digital Citizenship Education Act, which tapped the state Department of Education to develop and maintain evidence-based media literacy standards for use by school districts and charter schools serving students in grades K–12. A Hawaii law created a similar program.

Two judicial actions initiated in 2022 have deep implications for libraries. The first is President Joe Biden's Student Loan Debt Relief Plan, which, in addition to making the existing Public Service Loan Forgiveness program easier to navigate, promised to forgive up to $20,000 in student loan debt for individuals earning less than $125,000 per year (or couples earning less than $250,000). Many librarians would be eligible for such relief. Several groups sued the Biden administration over the program, claiming that the president lacks the authority to wipe out such debt. A federal court blocked the plan, and the Supreme Court agreed to issue a definitive ruling, which it will do in 2023.

In the second judicial action, the Supreme Court accepted and consolidated appeals in two cases, *Gonzalez v. Google* and *Twitter v. Taamneh*, in which private citizens are challenging the behavior of social media companies. In *Gonzalez v. Google*, the family of Nohemi Gonzalez claims that YouTube, owned by Google, allowed ISIS to recruit and radicalize members whose 2015 attack in Paris killed 130 people, including Ms. Gonzalez. In *Twitter v. Taamneh*, relatives of Nawras Alassaf, who was killed in a 2017 ISIS attack in Istanbul, Turkey, allege that by allowing the distribution of ISIS material without editorial supervision, companies like Twitter aided and abetted ISIS.

At the heart of these cases is Section 230 of the 1996 Communications Decency Act. Section 230 immunizes Internet companies from liability for the statements and activities of their users. Whether this protection applies in these cases could forever change how business—and culture—are conducted online.

Funding Programs and Grant-Making Agencies

National Endowment for the Humanities

400 7th St. S.W., Washington, DC 20506
202-606-8400, 800-634-1121
TDD (hearing impaired) 202-606-8282 or 866-372-2930 (toll free)
E-mail info@neh.gov, World Wide Web http://neh.gov

The National Endowment for the Humanities (NEH) is an independent federal agency created in 1965. It is one of the largest funders of humanities programs in the United States.

Because democracy demands wisdom, NEH serves and strengthens our republic by promoting excellence in the humanities and conveying the lessons of history to all Americans. It accomplishes this mission by awarding grants for top-rated proposals examined by panels of independent, external reviewers.

NEH grants typically go to cultural institutions, such as museums, archives, libraries, colleges, universities, public television, and radio stations, as well as to individual scholars. The grants do the following:

- Strengthen teaching and learning in schools and colleges
- Facilitate research and original scholarship
- Provide opportunities for lifelong learning
- Preserve and provide access to cultural and educational resources
- Strengthen the institutional base of the humanities

Since 1965 NEH has opened new worlds of learning for the American public with noteworthy projects such as the following:

- Seven thousand books, 16 of which have won Pulitzer Prizes and 20 of which have received the Bancroft Prize
- *The Civil War*, the landmark documentary by Ken Burns viewed by 38 million Americans
- The Library of America editions of novels, essays, and poems celebrating America's literary heritage
- The United States Newspaper Project, which cataloged and microfilmed 63.3 million pages of historic newspapers and paved the way for the National Digital Newspaper Program and its digital repository, Chronicling America

• Annual support for 56 states and territories to help support some 56,000 lectures, discussions, exhibitions, and other programs each year

For more than a half century, NEH has reached millions of people with projects and programs that preserve and study the nation's culture and history while providing a foundation for the future.

The endowment's mission is to enrich cultural life by promoting the study of the humanities. According to the National Foundation on the Arts and the Humanities Act, "The term 'humanities' includes, but is not limited to, the study of the following: language, both modern and classical; linguistics; literature; history; jurisprudence; philosophy; archaeology; comparative religion; ethics; the history, criticism, and theory of the arts; those aspects of social sciences which have humanistic content and employ humanistic methods; and the study and application of the humanities to the human environment with particular attention to reflecting our diverse heritage, traditions, and history and to the relevance of the humanities to the current conditions of national life."

The act, adopted by Congress in 1965, provided for the establishment of the National Foundation on the Arts and the Humanities in order to promote progress and scholarship in the humanities and the arts in the United States. The act included the following findings:

• The arts and the humanities belong to all the people of the United States.

• The encouragement and support of national progress and scholarship in the humanities and the arts, while primarily matters for private and local initiative, are also appropriate matters of concern to the federal government.

• An advanced civilization must not limit its efforts to science and technology alone but must give full value and support to the other great branches of scholarly and cultural activity in order to achieve a better understanding of the past, a better analysis of the present, and a better view of the future.

• Democracy demands wisdom and vision in its citizens. It must therefore foster and support a form of education, and access to the arts and the humanities, designed to make people of all backgrounds, and wherever located, masters of technology and not its unthinking servants.

• It is necessary and appropriate for the federal government to complement, assist, and add to programs for the advancement of the humanities and the arts by local, state, regional, and private agencies and their organizations. In doing so, the government must be sensitive to the nature of public sponsorship. Public funding of the arts and humanities is subject to the conditions that traditionally govern the use of public money. Such funding should contribute to public support and confidence in the use of taxpayer funds. Public funds provided by the federal government ultimately must serve public purposes the Congress defines.

• The arts and the humanities reflect the high place accorded by the American people to the nation's rich culture and history and to the fostering of mutual respect for the diverse beliefs and values of all persons and groups.

What NEH Grants Accomplish

Since its founding, NEH has awarded more than $5.6 billion for humanities projects through more than 64,000 grants.

Interpretive Exhibitions

Interpretive exhibitions provide opportunities for lifelong learning in the humanities for millions of Americans. Since 1967 NEH has awarded approximately $310 million in grants for interpretive exhibitions, catalogs, and public programs, which are among the most highly visible activities supported by the endowment. NEH support finances exhibitions; reading, viewing, and discussion programs; web-based programs; and other public education programs at venues across the country.

Renewing Teaching

Over NEH's history, more than 100,000 high school and college teachers have deepened their knowledge of the humanities through intensive summer study supported by the endowment; tens of thousands of students benefit from these better-educated teachers every year.

Reading and Discussion Programs

Since 1982 NEH has supported reading and discussion programs in the nation's libraries, bringing people together to discuss works of literature and history. Scholars in the humanities provide thematic direction for the discussion programs. Using selected texts and such themes as "Work," "Family," "Diversity," and "Not for Children Only," these programs have attracted more than 2 million Americans to read and talk about what they've read. Funded programs have included veterans' reading groups focused on classic Greek and Roman texts about the experience of war, community reading and discussion programs examining 200 years of Maine state history, and humanities-focused reading and discussion programs for at-risk youth. Most recently, NEH supported a national "Lift Every Voice" reading and discussion program on African American poetic traditions based around the Library of America anthology *African American Poetry: 250 Years of Struggle & Song*.

Chronicling America

NEH's National Digital Newspaper Program is supporting projects to convert microfilm of historically important U.S. newspapers into fully searchable digital files. Developed in partnership with the Library of Congress, this long-term project ultimately will make more than 30 million pages of newspapers accessible online. For more on this project, visit http://chroniclingamerica.loc.gov.

Stimulating Private Support

About $2 billion in humanities support has been generated by NEH challenge grants, which require grant recipients to match federal funds. NEH Infrastructure and Capacity Building Challenge grants leverage federal funding to spur private investment in capital projects and infrastructure upgrades to ensure the long-term health of our cultural institutions.

Presidential Papers

Ten presidential papers projects, from Washington to Eisenhower, have received support from NEH. Matching grants for the ten projects have leveraged millions of dollars in nonfederal contributions.

New Scholarship

NEH grants enable scholars to do in-depth study. Jack Rakove explored the making of the Constitution in his book *Original Meanings*, and James McPherson chronicled the Civil War in his book *Battle Cry of Freedom*.

History on Screen

Since 1967 NEH has awarded approximately $310 million to support the production of films for broad public distribution, including the Emmy Award-winning series *The Civil War*; the Oscar-nominated films *Brooklyn Bridge, The Restless Conscience,* and *Freedom on My Mind;* and film biographies of John and Abigail Adams, Eugene O'Neill, and Ernest Hemingway. Over seven successive nights on PBS, more than 33 million people watched Ken Burns's *The Roosevelts* (2014), which chronicles the lives of Teddy, Eleanor, and Franklin. The NEH-funded series *The Vietnam War* (2018), by Ken Burns and Lynn Novick, was seen by 39 million viewers. Other recent NEH-supported films include *The Vote*, on the women's suffrage movement; *Chasing the Moon*, on the U.S. Space Race; Stanley Nelson's *Freedom Riders* and *Freedom Summer* documentaries; and *Worlds of Ursula K. Le Guin*.

American Voices

NEH support for scholarly editions makes the writings of prominent and influential Americans accessible. Ten presidents are included, along with such key figures as Martin Luther King, Jr., George C. Marshall, and Eleanor Roosevelt. Papers of prominent writers—among them Emily Dickinson, Walt Whitman, Mark Twain, and Robert Frost—are also available.

Library of America

Millions of books have been sold as part of the Library of America series, a collection of the riches of the nation's literature. Begun with NEH seed money, the 303 volumes published to date include the works of such figures as Henry Adams, Edith Wharton, William James, Eudora Welty, and W.E.B. Du Bois.

The Library of America also received a $150,000 grant for the publication of *American Poetry: The Seventeenth and Eighteenth Centuries* (two volumes) and an expanded volume of selected works by Captain John Smith—a key figure in the establishment of the first permanent English settlement in North America, at Jamestown, Virginia—and other early exploration narratives.

Technical Innovation

NEH support for the digital humanities is fueling innovation and new tools for research in the humanities. Modern 3D technology allows students to visit sites ranging from ancient Egypt to the 1964–1965 New York World's Fair. Spectral imaging was used to create an online critical edition of explorer David Livingstone's previously unreadable field diary of 1871.

Science and the Humanities

The scientific past is being preserved with NEH-supported editions of the letters of Charles Darwin, the works of Albert Einstein, and the 14-volume papers of Thomas Edison. Additionally, NEH and the National Science Foundation have joined forces in Documenting Endangered Languages (DEL), a multiyear effort to preserve records of key languages that are in danger of becoming extinct.

EDSITEment

EDSITEment (http://edsitement.neh.gov) assembles the best humanities resources on the web, drawing more than 400,000 visitors each month. Incorporating these Internet resources, particularly primary documents, from more than 350 peer-reviewed websites, EDSITEment features more than 500 online lesson plans in all areas of the humanities. Teachers use EDSITEment's resources to enhance lessons and to engage students through interactive technology tools that hone critical-thinking skills.

Federal-State Partnership

The Office of Federal-State Partnership links NEH with the nationwide network of 56 humanities councils, which are located in each state, the District of Columbia, Puerto Rico, the U.S. Virgin Islands, the Northern Mariana Islands, American Samoa, and Guam. Each council funds humanities programs in its own jurisdiction.

Directory of State and Jurisdictional Humanities Councils

Alabama

Alabama Humanities Foundation
1100 Ireland Way, Suite 202
Birmingham, AL 35205
205-558-3980
http://www.alabamahumanities.org

Alaska

Alaska Humanities Forum
421 W. 1st Ave., Suite 200
Anchorage, AK 99501
907-272-5341
http://www.akhf.org

American Samoa

Amerika Samoa Humanities Council
P.O. Box 5800
Pago Pago, AS 96799
684-633-4870, fax 684-633-4873
http://ashcouncil.org

Arizona

Arizona Humanities Council
Ellis-Shackelford House
1242 N. Central Ave.
Phoenix, AZ 85004
602-257-0335, fax 602-257-0392
http://www.azhumanities.org

Arkansas

Arkansas Humanities Council
1400 W. Markham Street, Suite 400
Little Rock, AR 72201
501-353-0349
http://www.arkansashumanitiescouncil.org

California

California Humanities
538 9th St., #210
Oakland, CA 94607
415-391-1474
http://www.calhum.org

Colorado

Colorado Humanities
7935 E. Prentice Ave., Suite 450
Greenwood Village, CO 80111
303-894-7951, fax 303-864-9361
http://www.coloradohumanities.org

Connecticut

Connecticut Humanities
100 Riverview Center, Suite 290
Middletown, CT 06457
860-785-9640
http://cthumanities.org

Delaware

Delaware Humanities
100 W. Tenth St., Suite 509
Wilmington, DE 19801
302-657-0650
http://dehumanities.org

District of Columbia

Humanities DC
1804 T Street NW
Washington, DC 20009
240-266-8453
http://humanitiesdc.org

Florida

Florida Humanities
599 Second St. S.
St. Petersburg, FL 33701-5005
727-873-2000, fax 727-873-2014
http://www.floridahumanities.org

Georgia

Georgia Humanities
50 Hurt Plaza S.E., Suite 595
Atlanta, GA 30303-2915
404-523-6220, fax 404-523-5702
http://www.georgiahumanities.org

Guam

Humanities Guahan
Reflection Center
222 Chalan Santo Papa, Suite 106
Hagåtña, Guam 96910
671-472-4460, fax 671-472-4465
http://www.humanitiesguahan.org

Hawaii

Hawai'i Council for the Humanities
3599 Waialae Ave., Room 25
Honolulu, HI 96816
808-732-5402, fax 808-732-5432
http://www.hihumanities.org

Idaho

Idaho Humanities Council
217 West State St.
Boise, ID 83702
208-345-5346, fax 208-345-5347
http://www.idahohumanities.org

Illinois

Illinois Humanities
125 S. Clark St., Suite 650
Chicago, IL 60603
312-422-5580, fax 312-422-5588
http://www.ilhumanities.org

Indiana

Indiana Humanities
1500 N. Delaware St.
Indianapolis, IN 46202
317-638-1500, fax 800-675-8897
http://www.indianahumanities.org

Iowa

Iowa Department of Cultural Affairs
State Historical Building
600 E. Locust Street

Des Moines, IA 50319
515-281-5111
www.Iowaculture.gov

Kansas

Humanities Kansas
112 S.W. 6th Ave., Suite 210
Topeka, KS 66603
785-357-0359, fax 785-357-1723
https://www.humanitieskansas.org

Kentucky

Kentucky Humanities
206 E. Maxwell St.
Lexington, KY 40508
859-257-5932, fax 859-257-5933
http://www.kyhumanities.org

Louisiana

Louisiana Endowment for the Humanities
938 Lafayette St., Suite 300
New Orleans, LA 70113
504-523-4352
http://www.leh.org

Maine

Maine Humanities Council
674 Brighton Ave.
Portland, ME 04102-1012
207-773-5051, fax 207-773-2416
http://www.mainehumanities.org

Maryland

Maryland Humanities Council
108 W. Centre St.
Baltimore, MD 21201-4565
410-685-0095, fax 410-685-0795
http://www.mdhumanities.org

Massachusetts

Mass Humanities
66 Bridge St.
Northampton, MA 01060
413-584-8440, fax 413-584-8454
http://www.masshumanities.org

Michigan

Michigan Humanities

2364 Woodlake Drive, Suite 100
Okemos, MI 48864
517-372-7770
http://michiganhumanities.org

Minnesota

Minnesota Humanities Center
987 East Ivy Ave
St. Paul, MN 55106
651-774-0105
http://www.mnhum.org

Mississippi

Mississippi Humanities Council
3825 Ridgewood Rd., Room 311
Jackson, MS 39211
601-432-6752, fax 601-432-6750
http://www.mshumanities.org

Missouri

Missouri Humanities
105 N Main, Suite 108
St. Louis, MO 63301
314-781-9660
http://www.mohumanities.org

Montana

Humanities Montana
311 Brantly
Missoula, MT 59812-7848
406-243-6022
http://www.humanitiesmontana.org

Nebraska

Humanities Nebraska
215 Centennial Mall South, Suite 330
Lincoln, NE 68508
402-474-2131
http://www.humanitiesnebraska.org

Nevada

Nevada Humanities
1670-200 N. Virginia St.
P.O. Box 8029
Reno, NV 89507-8029
775-784-6587, fax 775-784-6527
http://www.nevadahumanities.org

New Hampshire

New Hampshire Humanities
117 Pleasant St.
Concord, NH 03301
603-224-4071, fax 603-224-4072
http://www.nhhumanities.org

New Jersey

New Jersey Council for the Humanities
336 Friends Street
Camden, NJ 08102
609-695-4838
http://www.njhumanities.org

New Mexico

New Mexico Humanities Council
4115 Silver Ave. S.E.
Albuquerque, NM 87108
505-633-7370, fax 505-633-7377
http://www.nmhum.org

New York

Humanities New York
150 Broadway, Suite 1700
New York, NY 10038
212-233-1131, fax 212-233-4607
http://www.humanitiesny.org

North Carolina

North Carolina Humanities
320 East 9th St., Suite 414
Charlotte, NC 28202
704-687-1520
http://www.nchumanities.org

North Dakota

Humanities North Dakota
418 E. Broadway, Suite 8
P.O. Box 2191
Bismarck, ND 58502
701-255-3360, fax 701-223-8724
http://www.humanitiesnd.org

Northern Marianas Islands

Northern Marianas Humanities Council
Springs Plaza
Chalan Pale Arnold Rd. + Gualo Rai Rd.
Saipan, MP 96950

670-235-4785
http://www.nmhcouncil.org/

Ohio

Ohio Humanities
541 West Rich Street
Columbus, OH 43215
614-461-7802
http://www.ohiohumanities.org

Oklahoma

Oklahoma Humanities
424 Concord Dr., Suite E
Oklahoma City, OK 73102
405-235-0280
http://www.okhumanities.org

Oregon

Oregon Humanities
619 SW Alder Street
Suite 1111
Portland, OR 97205
503-241-0543
http://www.oregonhumanities.org

Pennsylvania

Pennsylvania Humanities Council
230 South Broad Street
Suite 403
Philadelphia, PA 19102
215-925-1005, fax 215-925-3054
http://www.pahumanities.org

Puerto Rico

Fundación Puertorriqueña de las Humanidades
Ballaja Barracks, Norzagaray Street
Old San Juan
PO Box 9023920
San Juan, PR 00902-3920
787-721-2087, fax 787-721-2684
http://www.fphpr.org

Rhode Island

Rhode Island Council for the Humanities
131 Washington St., Suite 210
Providence, RI 02903
401-273-2250, fax 401-454-4872
http://www.rihumanities.org

South Carolina

South Carolina Humanities
2711 Middleburg Drive, Suite 203
Columbia, SC 29254
803-771-2477, fax 803-771-2487
http://www.schumanities.org

South Dakota

South Dakota Humanities Council
1215 Trail Ridge Rd., Suite A
Brookings, SD 57006
605-688-6113
http://www.sdhumanities.org

Tennessee

Humanities Tennessee
807 Main Street, Suite B
Nashville, TN 37206
615-770-0006, fax 615-770-0007
http://www.humanitiestennessee.org

Texas

Humanities Texas
1410 Rio Grande St.
Austin, TX 78701
512-440-1991, fax 512-440-0115
http://www.humanitiestexas.org

Utah

Utah Humanities
202 W. 300 North
Salt Lake City, UT 84103
801-359-9670
http://www.utahhumanities.org

Vermont

Vermont Humanities Council
11 Loomis St.
Montpelier, VT 05602
802-262-2626
http://www.vermonthumanities.org

U.S. Virginia Islands

Community Foundation of the Virginia Islands
PO Box 380
St. Thomas, VI 00804
340-774-6031, fax 340-774-3852
http://www.cfvi.net

Virginia

Virginia Humanities
946 Grady Ave., Suite 100
Charlottesville, VA 22903
434-924-3296
http://www.virginiahumanities.org

Washington

Humanities Washington
130 Nickerson Street, Suite 304
Seattle, WA 98109
206-682-1770
http://www.humanities.org

West Virginia

West Virginia Humanities Council
1310 Kanawha Blvd. East
Charleston, WV 25301
304-346-8500, fax 304-346-8504
http://wvhumanities.org/

Wisconsin

Wisconsin Humanities Council
3801 Regent St., Suite 201
Madison, WI 53705
608-262-0706
http://www.wisconsinhumanities.org

Wyoming

Wyoming Humanities
1315 E. Lewis St.
Laramie, WY 82072-3459
307-721-9243
http://www.thinkwy.org

NEH Overview

Division of Education Programs

The Division of Education Programs supports humanities education through programs aimed primarily at program and curriculum development and through professional development opportunities for K–12 and higher education faculty. Intensive reading and discussion programs featuring recognized scholars bring together small communities of teachers at both the higher education and K–12 levels to investigate new themes and innovative approaches to humanities subjects. Largely residential and held during the summer, these programs encourage the study of common texts and other resources, include visits to collections in libraries and museums, and help faculty integrate what has been learned back into their classrooms. The division has several grant programs to support broad institutional endeavors. Community colleges, historically Black colleges and universities, tribal colleges and universities, and Hispanic-serving institutions receive grants to enhance the humanities content of existing programs, develop new programs, or lay the foundation for more extensive endeavors. The division also supports creative, integrative, collaborative curricular projects at two- and four-year postsecondary institutions between the humanities and STEM, pre-professional and professional programs in law, the health sciences, etc. Finally, the division's veterans-centered program supports institutions interested in designing and implementing discussions programs that explore the experiences of war and military service through the examination of humanities texts and other resources.

Contact: 202-606-8500, e-mail education@neh.gov.

Division of Preservation and Access

Grants are made for projects that will create, preserve, and increase the availability of resources important for research, education, and public programming in the humanities.

Support may be sought to preserve the intellectual content and aid bibliographic control of collections; to compile bibliographies, descriptive catalogs, and guides to cultural holdings; and to create dictionaries, encyclopedias, databases, and electronic archives. Applications also may be submitted for education and training projects dealing with issues of preservation or access; for research and development leading to improved preservation and access standards, practices, and tools; and for projects to digitize historic U.S. newspapers and to document endangered languages. Grants are also made to help smaller cultural repositories preserve and care for their humanities collections. Proposals may combine preservation and access activities within a single project.

Contact: 202-606-8570, e-mail preservation@neh.gov.

Division of Public Programs

Public humanities projects enable millions of Americans to explore significant humanities works, ideas, and events. They offer new insights into familiar subjects and invite reflection upon important questions about human life. The division supports a wide range of public humanities programming that reaches large and diverse public audiences and makes use of a variety of formats—interpretation at historic sites, television and radio productions, museum exhibitions, podcasts, short videos, digital games, websites, mobile apps, and other digital media. Examples of funded projects include Ken Burns's *Civil War* documentary, which increased public understanding of a pivotal point in American history; the Walters Art Museum exhibition The Book of Kings: Art, War; the Morgan Library's

Medieval Picture Bible, which gave visitors insights into the role of religion in the Middle Ages; the reinterpretation of Historic Hudson Valley's Phillipsburg Manor, an 18th-century New York mill site, through which visitors learn about the contributions of enslaved African Americans in the North; and Walden, a free-to-educators digital game that allows players to spend a year at Walden Pond as Henry David Thoreau.

Program officers are prepared to answer a wide variety of questions from prospective applicants. They can provide information about the division's application guidelines and the eligibility or competitiveness of potential project ideas and provide tips about common proposal-writing mistakes to avoid. They will supply samples of successful application narratives in each grant category and even offer feedback for a preliminary draft of a proposal if it is submitted well before the deadline. All potential applicants are encouraged to contact a program officer early in their project conceptualization process.

Contact: 202-606-8269, e-mail publicpgms@neh.gov.

Division of Research Programs

The Division of Research Programs supports scholarly research that advances knowledge and understanding of the humanities. Through 12 annual funding opportunities, awards are made to scholars—individuals, collaborative teams, or institutions—working on research projects of significance to specific humanities fields and to the humanities as a whole. The projects that the division supports are as diverse as America itself: editions of the Dead Sea Scrolls, the history of "The Star Spangled Banner," and the autobiography of Mark Twain.

NEH's Fellowships program was established more than 50 years ago and was the first award offered by the endowment. Since then, approximately 7,000 books have been written by NEH fellows. In the academic world, "getting an NEH" is shorthand for receiving an NEH Fellowship, which indicates the award's widely respected reputation and prestige. Recognizing the specific needs of certain scholars, Awards for Faculty offer more flexible fellowships to those employed at historically Black colleges and universities, Hispanic-serving institutions, and tribal colleges and universities. Summer Stipends offer two-month awards to allow scholars to take a shorter break to pursue focused research. Public Scholar Awards encourage writing books for a wide readership. Placing NEH at the forefront of innovative methods in the humanities, NEH-Mellon Fellowships for Digital Publication support projects that require digital expression and digital publication. Books resulting from all of these grants regularly earn awards and recognition. NEH-funded work has been honored with Pulitzer Prizes and Bancroft Prizes, as well as awards from academic associations across the country and accolades from reviewers in major newspapers and literature journals.

While Research Programs is the only NEH division to make awards to individuals, institutional grants are also available. Collaborative Research supports projects by teams of scholars. Scholarly Editions and Scholarly Translations provides funding for time-intensive editing projects such as the Papers of George Washington, and Fellowship Programs at Independent Research Institutions provides American scholars with access to unique collections at American centers for humanities research around the world.

Teachers, too, make use of NEH-supported research in their classrooms—often with the aid of the web resources and books resulting from many projects. For example, the papers of William F. Cody (Buffalo Bill) and the Freedmen and Southern Society Project on the history of Emancipation are used in U.S. history classes, the papers of Albert Einstein in physics, and the literary works and letters of writers such as Willa Cather, Ernest Hemingway, and Samuel Beckett in English classes. Archaeology projects unearth artifacts used by museum curators in mounting exhibitions that teach us about life in ancient civilizations. Translations of materials in other languages bring little-known foreign works such as ancient Roman graffiti in Pompeii, the letters of the Dakota people, and contemporary Ukrainian literature to American readers. Documentarians, artists, and producers of all sorts of fiction and nonfiction media rely on new research findings in many fields—American history, literature, music, and the history of science and technology—to inform and inspire their audiences. Projects like these add to the existing store of knowledge and reach every area of the humanities.

Contact: 202-606-8200, e-mail research@neh.gov.

Office of Challenge Grants

Challenge Grants programs strengthen institutional and organizational capacity for work in the humanities. Institutions and organizations in the United States support the humanities by preserving and providing access to collections, conducting scholarship and research, and developing educational programs for various audiences. Challenge Grants projects may involve building and renovating structures such as museums and libraries and updating the infrastructure that undergirds humanities work in its many forms.

Successful applicants will be awarded matching funds intended to stimulate additional private, state, and local support for humanities infrastructure. Recipients must raise cash contributions from nonfederal third parties and have them certified by NEH before matching funds are released.

NEH offers two Challenge Grants funding opportunities. Their purpose is to strengthen the institutional base of the humanities with grants that support infrastructure development and capacity-building or that support work to maintain, modernize, and sustain digital infrastructure. Both approaches should help institutions secure and sustain their core activities for the long term.

Contact: 202-606-8309, e-mail challenge@neh.gov.

Office of Digital Humanities

The Office of Digital Humanities (ODH) offers grant programs that fund project teams experimenting with digital technologies to develop new methodologies for humanities research, teaching and learning, public engagement, and scholarly communications. ODH funds those studying digital culture from a humanistic perspective and humanists seeking to create digital publications. Another major goal of ODH is to increase capacity of the humanities in applying digital methods.

To best tackle the broad, interdisciplinary questions that arise when studying digital technology, ODH works closely with the scholarly community and other funding agencies in the United States and abroad to encourage collaboration across national and disciplinary boundaries.

Funded digital projects contribute to humanities scholarship that serve carefully identified audiences, address issues of accessibility and usability, and are designed to be open, replicable, and sustainable. All projects funded in this division analyze their workflows and publish their results in white papers that are shared widely. This body of work contributes to the bibliography of digital humanities.

ODH staff members participate in conferences and workshops with the scholarly community to help foster understanding of issues in the digital humanities and to ensure they are meeting the needs of the field.

Contact: 202-606-8401, e-mail odh@neh.gov.

A full list of NEH grants programs and deadlines is available on the endowment's website at http://www.neh.gov/grants.

Institute of Museum and Library Services

955 L'Enfant Plaza North, S.W., Suite 4000, Washington, DC 20024-2135
202-653-4657, fax 202-653-4600
http://www.imls.gov

Crosby Kemper III
Director

The Institute of Museum and Library Services (IMLS) is an independent grant-making agency and the primary source of federal support for the nation's libraries and museums. The mission of IMLS is to advance, support, and empower America's museums, libraries, and related organizations through grant making, research, and policy development. Its vision is a nation where museums and libraries work together to transform the lives of individuals and communities.

IMLS was created with the passage of the Museum and Library Services Act of 1996, which was reauthorized on December 31, 2018. The agency has statutory authority to award financial assistance, collect data, form strategic partnerships, and advise policymakers and other federal agencies on museum, library, and information services.

The agency consolidates federal library programs dating back to 1956 with museum programs dating back to 1976.

IMLS helps to ensure that all Americans have access to museum, library, and information services. The agency invests in new and exploratory approaches, as well as proven and tested methods. IMLS funds work that advances collective knowledge, lifelong learning, and cultural and civic engagement. And the agency builds capacity within the museum and library fields to enable better service to communities and to enhance community decision making by sharing trends and data.

IMLS has an expansive reach. The agency is the largest source of federal funding for libraries in the nation, directing population-based funding to all 50 states, the District of Columbia, the U.S. territories, and Freely Associated States through its Grants to States program. The agency's discretionary grants are selected through a highly respected and competitive peer-review process, drawing on professionals located across the nation. This work enables museums and libraries located in geographically and economically diverse areas to deliver essential services that make it possible for individuals and communities to flourish.

Strategic Goals and Objectives

When IMLS was established, lawmakers recognized that libraries and museums are powerful national assets. They saw "great potential in an Institute that is focused on the combined roles that libraries and museums play in our community life." The law charges IMLS with advising policymakers on library, museum, and information services and supporting a wide range of programs that improve the lives of millions.

IMLS carries out this charge as it adapts to meet the changing needs of our nation's museums and libraries and their communities. IMLS's role—to advance, support, and empower America's museums and libraries through its grant making, research, data collection, and policy development—is essential to helping these institutions navigate change and continue to improve their services.

With input from its stakeholders, IMLS developed a new strategic plan for 2022–2026 that was published in February 2022. The plan frames how the agency envisions meeting the essential information, education, research, economic, cultural, and civic needs of the American public over the next five years.

IMLS's goals and objectives are the following:

- Champion lifelong learning—IMLS seeks to champion lifelong learning by supporting library and museum projects that foster literacy, support cross-disciplinary and inquiry-based methods of learning, focus on lifelong learning for diverse families and individuals, and leverage the role of museums and libraries as trusted sources of information. In fiscal year (FY) 2022 this support was leveraged by museums and libraries to move from surviving toward thriving as the nation continues to heal from the peak of the pandemic. For the nation's museums, momentum shifted to investments in rebuilding and upskilling of staff to continue collection and preservation of artifacts from underrepresented communities and community-focused services. Library awards focused on expanding and diversifying learning opportunities for new Americans, individuals with disabilities, families, and rural communities. By providing access to learning and skill building, libraries contribute to improve outcomes for all communities. IMLS awarded 210 discretionary grants totaling $30 million, with awardee match of $27.1 million, in support of this goal.

- Strengthen community engagement—IMLS seeks to build field capacity by supporting the development of library and museum staff, adopting best practices and innovations, and strengthening museums' and libraries' capacity to serve as trusted spaces for community engagement and dialogue. In FY 2022 awards in this area to museums focused on strengthening institutions' relevance and service to the public, with a focus on investments in co-curation of content with community members and lowering barriers to access to museum services. Libraries strive to center communities, and 2022 library awards focused on collaboration, extensive partnerships, and co-creation to advance literacy, expand access to library resources, and amplify community memories and narratives. IMLS awarded 109 discretionary grants totaling $17.4 million, with awardee match of $12.8 million, in support of this goal.

- Advance collections stewardship and access—IMLS works to increase public access to museums and libraries by supporting library and museum stewardship, investing in tools and technology that enable people of all backgrounds and abilities to use museums and libraries, investing in policies and partnerships that address barriers to access, and engaging in effective communications. FY 2022 grants in this area supported museums in marrying traditional collections preservation with digitization strategies and engaging community members for preservation of all American histories. Additional focuses for FY 2022 awards included a renewed emphasis on improving foundational infrastructure and skills for preserving physical artifacts. Community archives are integral to shaping local and national narratives; library awards reflect efforts to empower communities and individuals to develop and preserve community memory. IMLS awarded 186 discretionary grants totaling $25.7 million, with awardee cost share of $17.5 million, in support of this goal.

- Demonstrate excellence in public service—This goal addresses IMLS's focus on achieving excellence by strategically aligning its resources and relationships to support libraries and museums nationwide. The goal's objectives reflect both inward to processes and activities that support IMLS's mission and other agency priority areas and outward to leveraging partnerships with other agencies and outside organizations.

Recent Statutory Authorities and Administration Priorities

Over the past two years the White House and Congress have provided IMLS with new statutory authority to carry out programs of financial support for American Latino museums, engage with other federal agencies to support digital access and inclusion, prepare for our nation's 250th anniversary, and develop information literacy strategies and resources. The Consolidated Appropriations Act of 2021 (enacted in December 2020) authorized the National Museum of the American Latino Act (NMALA) as well as the Advancing Critical Connectivity Expands Service, Small Business Resources, Opportunities, Access, and Data Based on Assessed Need and Demand Act, commonly referred to as the ACCESS Broadband Act. In addition to establishing a new museum at the Smithsonian Institution, NMALA directs IMLS to establish new grant and fellowship programs for American Latino museums and scholars throughout the nation. The ACCESS Broadband Act and the Infrastructure Investment and Jobs Act of 2021 recognize IMLS's role in supporting connectivity and digital inclusion and advancing access to broadband, working in coordination with other agencies. New authority under the U.S. Semiquincentennial Commission Amendments Act identifies the director of IMLS as an ex officio member of the commission. The Consolidated Appropriations Act of 2022 authorized the creation of an information literacy task force charged with developing guidance, instructional materials, and national strategies on information literacy, including a website to disseminate best practices on information literacy and toolkits. These new legislative authorities align with the White House's priorities for racial equity, COVID-19 response, economic recovery, and infrastructure.

IMLS Response to COVID-19

CARES Act Grants

On March 27, 2020, the president signed the Coronavirus Aid, Relief, and Economic Security (CARES) Act, Pub. L. 116-136, which authorized funding for IMLS to assist states, tribes, museums, and libraries to "prevent, prepare for, and respond to [the] coronavirus, ... expand digital network access, purchase internet accessible devices, and provide technical support services" for the benefit of communities impacted by the public health emergency.

In FY 2020, using a population-based formula, the Grants to States program awarded $30 million in CARES Act funds to the 59 State Library Administrative

Agencies (SLAAs) in the 50 states, the District of Columbia, the U.S. territories, and the Freely Associated States. IMLS distributed these awards on April 21, 2020, with funds remaining available until September 30, 2021. IMLS directed the SLAAs to prioritize (1) digital inclusion and related technical support, (2) other efforts that prevent, prepare for, and respond to COVID-19, and (3) reaching museum and tribal partners, in addition to traditionally eligible library entities, where appropriate.

SLAAs submitted reports in FY 2022 for the $30 million in CARES Act funds disseminated in 2020 through the Grants to States program, evidencing the reach of the funds during the pandemic. States reported reaching at least 13,600 libraries of all types (but primarily public libraries), as well as 113 museums and 28 tribes. Forty states made more than 3,000 sub-awards to directly reach communities in need, and of the 476 CARES Act projects reported through the program, 398 (84 percent) involved sub-awards. The majority of funded projects were related to connectivity and the digital divide, and among the funded areas, SLAAs reported purchasing at least 7,800 hotspots and another 7,700 devices such as laptops or tablets.

American Rescue Plan Act

The American Rescue Plan (ARP) Act of 2021 designated $200 million in pandemic response funding for IMLS "to carry out museum and library services" for the benefit of communities impacted by the COVID-19 public health emergency. The ARP Act enabled the agency to efficiently provide critical funding to SLAAs, located in every state and territory and with reach into local communities across the United States.

In addition to the $178 million allocated to SLAAs in FY 2021, IMLS also offered $15 million in grants in FY 2022 to museums, libraries, and Native American and Native Hawaiian communities to provide direct support to address community needs created or exacerbated by the COVID-19 pandemic and to assist with recovery. Projects could continue, enhance, or expand existing programs and services, or they could launch new ones to address emergent needs and unexpected hardships. IMLS received 572 applications for its ARP Act grant program, requesting more than $22.8 million. In October 2021 IMLS announced $15,255,733 in 390 ARP Act grants to institutions across 49 states, the District of Columbia, and Puerto Rico. Organizations receiving awards are matching them with $20,155,341 in non-federal funds.

Although not yet fully reported, IMLS gathered evidence of ARP Act spending by SLAAs through news media and informal updates, evidencing the reach of the $178 million during the pandemic. In keeping with ARP Act priorities around digital inclusion efforts and rapid emergency relief to libraries, publicized awards included an emphasis on connectivity as well as helping libraries safely reopen their physical spaces. In the first five months after the April 2021 ARP Act awards to SLAAs, they had already disseminated more than 2,600 sub-awards, reached at least 3,900 libraries, and anticipated reaching another 10,000 libraries of all types. Within those first five months, SLAAs and their sub-recipients had already announced the purchase of more than 5,300 devices, such as hotspots, laptops, and tablets, as well as 28 library vehicles to reach remote users, including bookmobiles and book bikes outfitted with hotspots.

Communities for Immunity

In FY 2022 IMLS partnered with the Centers for Disease Control and Prevention (CDC) to boost COVID-19 vaccine confidence in communities across the United States. With support from CDC and IMLS, the Association of Science and Technology Centers (ASTC), in collaboration with the American Alliance of Museums (AAM), launched Communities for Immunity to provide funding to museums and libraries to enhance vaccine confidence at the local level. Building on the many ways the organizations have supported their communities during the pandemic, the partnership helped museums and libraries create and deliver evidence-driven materials and develop resources, programs, and approaches specifically designed to help museums and libraries engage diverse audiences in building trust in the COVID-19 vaccine.

The American Library Association (ALA), the Association of African American Museums (AAAM), the Association of Children's Museums (ACM), the Association for Rural and Small Libraries (ARSL), the Association of Tribal Archives, Libraries, and Museums (ATALM), the Network of the National Library of Medicine (NLM), and the Urban Libraries Council (ULC) were partners in the initiative, which was designed to engage a broad and diverse set of communities and inform community health/resilience. During 2022 IMLS and ASTC supported an assessment of the program carried out by SRI International and convened a capstone event in October 2022 to explore the tools and techniques that museums and libraries used to address community health through the initiative and explore how promising practices and lessons learned might inform future efforts by cultural organizations in their communities.

Library Services

The Museum and Library Services Act (20 U.S.C. § 9171) authorizes IMLS's Office of Library Services to do the following:

- Enhance coordination among federal programs that relate to library, education, and information services
- Promote continuous improvement in library services in all types of libraries in order to better serve the people of the United States
- Facilitate access to resources in all types of libraries for the purpose of cultivating an educated and informed citizenry
- Encourage resource sharing among all types of libraries for the purpose of achieving economical and efficient delivery of library services to the public
- Promote literacy, education, and lifelong learning, such as by building learning partnerships with school libraries in the nation's schools, including tribal schools, and developing resources, capabilities, and programs in support of state, tribal, and local efforts to offer a well-rounded educational experience to all students
- Enable libraries to develop services that meet the needs of communities throughout the nation, including people of diverse geographic, cultural, and socioeconomic backgrounds; individuals with disabilities; residents of

rural and urban areas; Native Americans; military families; veterans; and caregivers

- Enable libraries to serve as anchor institutions to support community revitalization through enhancing and expanding the services and resources provided by libraries, including those services and resources relating to workforce development, economic and business development, critical-thinking skills, health information, digital literacy skills, financial literacy and other types of literacy skills, and new and emerging technology
- Enhance the skills of the current library workforce and recruit future professionals, including those from diverse and underrepresented backgrounds, to the field of library and information services
- Ensure the preservation of knowledge and library collections in all formats, and enable libraries to serve their communities during disasters
- Enhance the role of libraries within the information infrastructure of the United States in order to support research, education, and innovation
- Promote library services that provide users with access to information through national, state, local, regional, and international collaborations and networks
- Encourage, support, and disseminate model programs of library and museum collaboration

Grants to States

The library Grants to States program awards population-based formula grants to each SLAA in the 50 states; the District of Columbia; the U.S. territories of the Commonwealth of Puerto Rico, the U.S. Virgin Islands, American Samoa, Guam, the Commonwealth of the Northern Mariana Islands, and the Freely Associated States of the Federated States of Micronesia; the Republic of the Marshall Islands; and the Republic of Palau (20 U.S.C. § 9131).

The formula consists of a minimum allotment set by law plus a supplemental amount based on population (dependent on annual appropriations). Population data is based on the information available from the U.S. Census Bureau.

The Museum and Library Services Act of 2018 increased minimum allotments for states from $680,000 to $1,000,000 and for Pacific territories and Freely Associated States from $60,000 to $100,000. Increases to the minimum allotments depend on increases to the program's overall budget, which remained level-funded in FY 2022. Increases to date have not fully enacted the new statutory minimum allotments, but did raise the base to $833,845 for states, with $60,000 for other entities. The act limits administrative costs at the state level to 4 percent and requires a 34 percent match from non-federal state or local funds.

Programs and services delivered by each SLAA support the purposes and priorities set forth in the Library Services and Technology Act (LSTA). SLAAs must complete five-year plans, conduct a five-year evaluation based on these plans, and report annually to IMLS on their progress in strengthening library services, which helps improve practice and inform policy. SLAAs set goals and objectives for their states regarding the use of Grants to States funds within the statutorily required five-year plan approved by IMLS. These goals and objectives are determined through a planning process that includes statewide needs assessments.

Site visits allow Grants to States staff to monitor program administration at both the SLAA and sub-recipient levels and to assist SLAAs in the sound management of the program. By the end of FY 2022 staff had completed visits with all 59 SLAAs during the 2018–2022 five-year cycle. With pandemic adaptations beginning in 2020, program staff completed 32 in-person visits, 21 virtual visits, and six desk visits with outlying Pacific SLAAs at the 2022 biennial workshop.

Discretionary Grants

The Office of Library Services offered five funding opportunities in FY 2022:

- National Leadership Grants for Libraries invest in projects that address challenges faced by the library and archives fields and generate results such as new tools, research findings, or models that can be widely used.
- Native American Library Services: Basic Grants, which are awarded non-competitively, are available to eligible Native American and Native Alaskan organizations and may support existing library operations and/or maintain core library services.
- Native American Library Services: Enhancement Grants, which are awarded competitively, can be used to enhance existing library services or to implement new services.
- Native Hawaiian Library Services Grants may be used for existing library services or to implement new library services.
- The Laura Bush 21st Century Librarian Program supports professional development and training projects for libraries and archives.

Museum Services

The Museum and Library Services Act (20 U.S.C. § 9171) authorizes IMLS's Office of Museum Services to do the following;

- Encourage and support museums in carrying out their educational role as core providers of learning and in conjunction with schools, families, and communities
- Encourage and support museums in carrying out their public service role of connecting the whole of society to the cultural, artistic, historical, natural, and scientific understandings that constitute our diverse heritage
- Encourage leadership, innovation, and applications of the most current technologies and practices to enhance museum services through international, national, regional, state, and local networks and partnership
- Assist, encourage, and support museums in carrying out their stewardship responsibilities to achieve the highest standards in conservation and care of the diverse cultural, historic, natural, and scientific heritage of the United States to benefit future generations

- Assist, encourage, and support museums in achieving the highest standards of management and service to the public and to ease the financial burden borne by museums as they serve their communities in new and different ways
- Support resource sharing and partnerships among museums, libraries, schools, and other community organizations
- Encourage and support museums as a part of economic development and revitalization in communities
- Ensure museums of various types and sizes in diverse geographic regions of the United States are afforded attention and support
- Support efforts at the state and regional levels to leverage museum resources and maximize museum services
- Assist museums in their civic engagement efforts to ensure that every person in the United States has access to high-quality museum services

IMLS also conducts a grant program with the purpose of improving operations, care of collections, and development of professional management at African American museums, pursuant to the National Museum of African American History and Culture Act (20 U.S.C. § 80r-5).

Discretionary Grants

The Office of Museum Services offered six competitive funding opportunities in FY 2022: Museums for America (MFA), Inspire! Grants for Small Museums, Museums Empowered, National Leadership Grants for Museums, Native American/Native Hawaiian Museum Services, and Museum Grants for African American History and Culture.

Policy Research, Analysis, Data Collection, and Dissemination

The Museum and Library Services Act authorizes IMLS to support and conduct policy research, data collection, analysis and modeling, evaluation, and dissemination of information to extend and improve the nation's museum, library, and information services (20 U.S.C. § 9108). The act identifies the following objectives:

- To enhance and expand the capacity of museums, libraries, and information services to anticipate, respond to, and meet the evolving needs of communities and the public, including by identifying trends and developments that may impact the need for and delivery of services
- To provide information and data on the role, value, and impact of museum, library, and information resources, including the identification of trends and the potential gaps in the availability and use of museum and library services by their communities and the public
- To measure the effectiveness of museums, libraries, and information services throughout the United States, including the impact of federal programs authorized under the act

- To identify indicators and outcomes that can be used to create enhancements to the efficiency and efficacy of museum, library, and information services
- To promote advancement and growth in museum, library, and information services through the sharing of best practices and effective strategies in order to better serve the people of the United States
- To facilitate planning for, and the building of, institutional capacity in order to improve museum, library, and information services at the national, state, local, and regional levels and international communications and cooperative networks

In carrying out these objectives, IMLS engages with the SLAAs and networks of museums and libraries, as well as with national, state, tribal, and regional museum and library organizations.

Surveys

IMLS produces evaluations and performs data collection and analysis to inform policy decisions and support the museum and library fields of practice. These efforts identify trends, make important comparisons, and enable objective policy making at the national and state levels. The primary data products maintained by IMLS are the Public Libraries Survey (PLS) and the State Library Administrative Agency (SLAA) Survey.

The PLS has been conducted annually since 1988 and is a definitive source on the state of public libraries in the United States. PLS data provide key information on more than 9,000 public library systems and 17,000 public library outlets nationwide.

The SLAA Survey has been collected annually since 1994 and biennially after 2010. It is a definitive source on the state of state library agencies in the United States and provides key information on the state library agencies in all 50 states and the District of Columbia.

For IMLS surveys and data, visit https://www.imls.gov/research-tools/data-collection, and see the report "Highlights of IMLS Public Library Surveys" in Part 4 of this volume.

EveryLibrary

P.O. Box 406, Riverside, IL 60546
312-574-0316, e-mail info@everylibrary.org
World Wide Web http://www.everylibrary.org | action.everylibrary.org | SaveSchoolLibrarians.org |
http://everylibraryinstitute.org

John Chrastka
Executive Director

Founded in December 2012 as a political action committee for libraries, Every-Library focuses on building political power for libraries at all levels of government across all types of libraries. EveryLibrary is the first and only nationwide political action committee for libraries. Its mission statement is "Building voter support for libraries." Its vision statement, and the inspiration for its name, is "Any library funding issue anywhere should matter to every library everywhere." It is chartered in the state of Illinois as a nonprofit and is designated as a 501(c)4 social welfare organization by the IRS, enabling it to raise and expend funds on political engagement, legislative and regulatory matters, and direct and indirect lobbying of elected or appointed officials.

Board and Advisors

EveryLibrary is administered by a board of directors and is run by staff. It has no members. Its 2022 board of directors were John Chrastka, president and executive director; Erica Findley, treasurer; Patrick "PC" Sweeney, board secretary and political director; and Brian D. Hart, Harmony V. Faust, Peter Bromberg, Jeannie Allen, Lori Ayers, Roberto Delgadillo, Gary Kirk, and Kathleen McEvoy, directors.

Organizational History

As a 501(c)4 organization, EveryLibrary works to support the funding formula for libraries at the local, state, and national levels along with focusing on policies and legislation that support and extend the future of library work. For library Election Days, EveryLibrary works with library boards and staff on informational communications campaigns and with local citizen ballot committees as they conduct "Get Out the Vote" and "Vote Yes" campaigns for local library ballot measures. Through 2022 EveryLibrary has helped take 130 libraries to their Election Days, winning 85 percent and securing more than $402 million (aggregated per annum) in stable funding for those libraries. For school libraries, EveryLibrary supports direct action and outreach across local districts on its SaveSchoolLibrarans.org platform. During state or federal policy campaigns, EveryLibrary's national network of more than 400,000 library activists are engaged and empowered via the action.everylibrary.org platform.

EveryLibrary is funded by individual donors, both monthly and annually, and corporate (vendor) donors. Being able to provide its services at no cost to libraries and committees allows EveryLibrary to focus on best practices for campaigns rather than revenue generation from direct consulting.

Library Ballot Measures

In 2022 EveryLibrary supported seven public library campaigns to establish, renew, or expand funding for operations, collections, programs, services, and staffing or to issue a bond for the construction or remodeling of library facilities. It also supported one statewide General Obligation bond campaign. In addition, there was one opposition campaign that focused on a ballot measure to defund the library.

Direct Political Actions for Public Libraries

EveryLibrary has worked to amplify the agendas of local library stakeholders for more than 10 years. Whether it is on the ballot, at the statehouse, or fighting for the First Amendment with boards and commissions, its aim is to create a future in which libraries thrive in every community and school. EveryLibrary was founded on the principle that providing aid, support, and assistance is additive to the cause.

Fighting for the First Amendment

In 2022 EveryLibrary was deeply engaged in the fight to protect the First Amendment in libraries. It was at the forefront of national organizations fighting politicized and performative book bans and censorship efforts in local libraries and schools. Through the generous support of the Long Ridge Action Fund, EveryLibrary has provided digital organizing tools and campaign advice to dozens of local library alliances. Its First Amendment work is rooted in partnerships and coalitions with national allies and cosponsors such as PEN America, Red Wine and Blue, PFLAG, We Need Diverse Books, BookRiot, and the National Student Rights Coalition.

The Future of School Libraries

EveryLibrary's focus on school libraries extends beyond budgets and collections to support the rights and dignity of every student to read and learn. Over the prior five years, Follett Learning Solutions has been its lead donor on Save School Librarians, the only national advocacy platform dedicated solely to school library campaigns. In 2022 EveryLibrary's digital and field work focused on fighting anti-access legislation that would limit school libraries, improving budgets to hire more school librarians, supporting state library association legislative agendas, and countering book bans and censorship in school districts from coast to coast.

EveryLibrary collaborated with and supported several state school library association partners, including helping the New Jersey Association of School Librarians and the Delaware Library Association advance new information literacy and media literacy curriculum bills. Its ongoing support for Washington, D.C., school library stakeholders helped ensure another round of funding for a librarian in every school.

Reaching Americans about Libraries

EveryLibrary is the only national library organization that spends money every day on social media ads. Through its public-facing magazine on Medium, it has published and syndicated more than 150 stories to inform, engage, and activate people about libraries and librarians. EveryLibrary reached a milestone in 2022 with more than 400,000 people following the organization on Facebook, Twitter, LinkedIn, and Instagram. This social media reach means that it can support national, statewide, and local advocacy campaigns down to a single school district or ZIP code.

EveryLibrary Institute Public Policy Think Tank

EveryLibrary Institute is the 501(c)3 nonprofit companion organization to EveryLibrary. It is chartered to work on public policy, tax policy, and education policy issues affecting libraries in the United States and abroad. This includes conducting research and providing training and technical assistance to partner organizations.

In 2022 EveryLibrary Institute's key initiatives were to conduct polling about book bans; conduct emergency fundraising for libraries in crisis; publish seven white papers that explored topics like post-COVID school and public libraries, emerging issues in health and literacy services, and the tax code; and host the biennial Library Advocacy and Funding Conference (LAFCON), which offered sessions on political action, organizing, and fundraising from noted industry experts.

Research and Public Policy

Throughout 2022 EveryLibrary Institute supported the development and dissemination of a robust open access Book Challenge Database curated by Dr. Tasslyn Magnusson. Her independent research has focused on attempts to challenge books in school and public libraries and tracks successful banning efforts in particular. The dataset includes insights into the groups that are pushing anti-access and censorship agendas as well as local library alliances that are fighting for the First Amendment and the integrity of libraries.

EveryLibrary collaborated with Georgetown University Law Center's Intellectual Property & Information Policy Clinic ("iPIP") to write the School Library Database Procurement Act, new model legislation to help safeguard state library database contracts and student access to information and preempt legislation by grassroots anti-access activists.

Organizational Agenda

EveryLibrary will continue to work in 2023 to fulfill its core mission of building voter support for libraries of all types. EveryLibrary's six strategic priorities in 2023 continue to be:

- To deepen its efforts to support local library communities that go on the ballot to renew or extend their basic taxpayer-approved funding and cultivate opportunities for libraries that want to enhance services and facilities through municipal budgets or voter-approved measures
- To join and support coalitions that align with the mission of libraries as institutions; that promote and extend the rights and prosperity of the people

whom libraries serve; and that protect the rights, employment, and pensions of the people who work in all types of libraries
- To continue to build a unique and extensive network of Americans who believe in the power of libraries to change lives and build communities and who are ready to become advocates and activists for libraries
- To support the role of library boards and commissions in governing libraries, making policy, and setting budgets that are responsive to diverse local priorities and create inclusive, prosperous, and vibrant communities
- To focus its support of school library programs as effective solutions for some of the biggest problems facing schools and districts around the country
- To be a leader and a listener in a national discussion about the role that public, academic, and school libraries have in people's lives and to work within the profession and across civil society to find the best ways to preserve, protect, and extend everyone's right to use libraries.

Budget, Donor Transparency, and Reporting

EveryLibrary puts its donor funding to work in three ways: directly on local library campaigns—for both public libraries and school libraries; on building its national reach as an advocacy organization for libraries; and on staff and projects that run the organization. As the only national 501(c)4 for libraries, it "bundles" small donations from around the country and sends them to local Vote Yes committees where needed.

EveryLibrary is entirely supported by individual donors and library vendor donors. It does not ask for or receive any funding from grant-making, philanthropic, or charitable organizations. As an independent 501(c)4, EveryLibrary is ineligible for government grants (federal or state). EveryLibrary's operating budget allocates one-third to direct campaign expenditures, one-third to salaries and operations, and one-third to growing its organizational reach.

EveryLibrary provides a high level of transparency about its donations and is one of only a few national political action groups that encourage donors to self-disclose. EveryLibrary voluntarily provides annual financial disclosure information to GuideStar, a large national nonprofit clearinghouse and rating service, where it currently holds a Gold Rate certification.

Part 3
Library/Information Science Education and Career Resources

Career Resources, Podcasts, and Job Sites for Library and Information Professionals

Susanne Markgren

Job satisfaction can mean wildly different things to different people, and finding the right job and right fit can be a long and winding journey. When developing your personalized job-search strategy, it is important to research the existing job market, to take note of changes and trends in job postings and job titles, to identify your strengths and limitations, to reflect on your wants and expectations, and to incorporate creativity and self-kindness along the way. Remember that each job you take, each skill you acquire, and each connection you make contributes to your career pathway/trajectory and becomes a building block of your professional practice.

Coverage from *Library Journal*'s "Placements and Salaries 2022" shows a much-improved outlook for 2021 graduates, as compared to the 2020 (COVID-19) cohort. Salaries increased by nearly 8 percent, more graduates were hired in full-time permanent positions than in the previous years, and unemployment decreased. Another positive is a notable uptick in job satisfaction. When asked about the most important thing they look for in an employer (related to job satisfaction), the majority of responses cited a positive, healthy, supportive workplace culture; salary level; a good work-life balance; positive leadership traits around mentoring, vision, communication, and management; and finding the right fit/match for their skills and interests. Other responses included growth potential, location, job security, and the importance of diversity, equity, and inclusion (DEI) in the work environment.

San José State University's annual "MLIS Skills at Work" report (listed in the Career Advice Sites and Resources section) offers an overview of trends seen within the job postings themselves in the past year. The highest in-demand general skills were communication, being able to discuss DEI, managerial-related, and research/reference. The highest in-demand LIS skills were research/reference, instruction, computer technology, and supervisory-related. The report also found that job-specific experience (research, cataloging, data analysis, instruction, etc.) was required or preferred in 96 percent of job announcements. Based on the findings, the report provides some excellent recommendations for LIS job seekers and current students, such as networking, developing new skills, pursuing leadership opportunities early on, practicing adaptability, using social media professionally, thinking about your impact, and personalizing your job search strategy.

This article, which focuses on career resources and job listings, identifies a variety of relevant, current (at the time of publication), and potentially interesting online resources and tools to assist students, recent graduates, and experienced library professionals alike in their journeys to a new or enhanced position. The resources have been selected based on currency, popularity, and influence. All are freely available online, and as with every online information source, users should employ critical analysis and judgment to determine currency, accuracy, and bias.

Susanne Markgren is co-author of the career guidance books *How to Thrive as a Library Professional: Achieving Success and Satisfaction* (Libraries Unlimited, 2019), with Linda Miles, and *Career Q&A: A Librarian's Real-Life, Practical Guide to Managing a Successful Career* (Information Today, Inc., 2013), with Tiffany Eatman Allen.

The Directory of Library and Related Organizations in Part 6 of this volume may also prove useful for job seekers. Many of these organizations, institutions, libraries, consortia, and associations maintain their own job sites and social media accounts where active job listings can be found.

Organization of the Resources

The resources that follow are organized into three sections. The first, Career Advice Sites and Resources, lists informational websites that provide tips and strategies to assist those seeking advice on specific areas of librarianship and archive work. Many of these are association sites, and some offer materials and guidance on resume and cover letter writing and interviewing.

The second section, Podcasts, lists podcasts that provide listeners with current news, hot topics, interviews, and reviews, as well as real-world examples and narratives from library and informational professionals working in a variety of roles and settings. As a bonus, podcasts offer up an entertaining and insightful way to consume information and are a popular platform to increase awareness about trends and issues in librarianship.

The third section is for the active job seeker and offers a two-part section of job listings resources—the first grouping is specific to librarians, archivists, and information professionals; the second covers a broader range of resources that are not specific to library or information-related positions. The selected sites primarily post jobs in the United States, but some also list international opportunities. It is good practice to search a variety of job sites, systematically and routinely, to get the most comprehensive and current snapshot of available positions. It is also a good idea to seek out specific libraries, companies, institutions, and associations on their own websites and on social media. When available, Twitter handles have been included at the end of each listing.

Career Advice Sites and Resources

American Association of Law Libraries (AALL)—Career Center

https://www.aallnet.org/careers/career-center
Offers information on careers in law libraries, advice on how to find a job, and access to the AALL Salary Survey.   @aallnet

American Association of School Librarians (AASL)—Education and Careers

http://www.ala.org/aasl/about/ed
Career and education resources for those seeking to enter or advance in the school library field. Job listings are found at ALA JobLIST.   @aasl

American Library Association (ALA) JobLIST—Career Development Resources

http://www.ala.org/educationcareers/employment/career-resources
A wealth of resources from ALA to help with the job search as well as enhance career development efforts.   @ALA_JobLIST and @alaplacement

BCALA (Black Caucus of the American Library Association) Career Center

https://jobs.bcala.org/career-advice
Tools and resources to make your resume stand out, to ace the interview, and to advance your career.　@BC_ALA

Bureau of Labor Statistics, U.S. Department of Labor, Occupational Outlook Handbook, Librarians and Library Media Specialists

https://www.bls.gov/ooh/education-training-and-library/librarians.htm
Provides information on librarian jobs and salaries and insight into the growth and outlook of the profession.　@BLA_gov

HigherEdJobs

https://www.higheredjobs.com/career/resumes.cfm
Advice on writing cover letters, resumes, and CVs, as well as interviewing and developing job search strategies for landing a job in academe.　@HigherEdJobs

Hiring Librarians

https://hiringlibrarians.com
Posts interviews generated through online surveys and feature articles highlighting different LIS hiring and career-related resources. It also maintains a spreadsheet of questions asked in LIS interviews going back more than a decade.　@HiringLib

INALJ

https://inalj.com
Includes bios, interviews, book reviews, and original articles by information professionals, as well as an extensive list of job postings for information professionals.　@INALJNaomi

Library Worklife—HR E-News for Today's Leaders

http://ala-apa.org/newsletter
Informs readers on issues such as career advancement, certification, human resources practice, pay equity, recruitment, research, and work-life balance.　@alaapa

Medical Library Association (MLA) Career Center

http://www.mlanet.org/p/cm/ld/fid=352
Includes information, resources, and connections for students and job seekers alike.　@MedLibAssn

MLIS SKILLS AT WORK—A Snapshot of Job Postings Spring 2022

https://ischool.sjsu.edu/sites/main/files/file-attachments/career_trends.pdf
Prepared annually by the M.L.I.S. online degree program at the San José State University School of Information.　@SJSUiSchool

Public Library Association (PLA)—Careers in Public Librarianship

http://www.ala.org/pla/tools/careers
Information and career advice about public librarianship from a leading ALA division. Job listings are found at ALA JobLIST. @ALA_PLA

RBMS (Rare Books and Manuscripts Section of ACRL)—Careers FAQ

http://rbms.info/careers-faq
Advice and resources for those interested in careers in special collections. @RBMSinfo

SAA (Society of American Archivists) Career Learning Center

https://careers.archivists.org/jobseekers/resources/blueskyLMS
Encourages an integrative career and professional development process that enhances your skill set. @archivists_org

Your Library Career: Career Q&A for Library People

http://yourlibrarycareer.com
A Q&A forum and career development archive of professional guidance and advice for librarians, library staff, and those thinking of entering the profession. Includes "How I Got My First Job" interviews.

Podcasts

Against the Grain–The Podcast

https://atgthepodcast.libsyn.com/podcast
Reports on the issues, literature, and people that impact the world of books and journals

Call Number with American Libraries Podcast

https://soundcloud.com/dewey-decibel-703453552
Each month, host and *American Libraries* associate editor Diana Panuncial is the guide to conversations with librarians, authors, thinkers, and scholars about topics from the library world and beyond.

Circulating Ideas: The Librarian Interview Podcast

https://circulatingideas.com
Circulating Ideas facilitates conversations about the innovative people and ideas that are allowing libraries to thrive in the 21st century.

Leading from the Library

https://leading-through-the-library.simplecast.com
Offers stories and ideas from teacher librarians on collection development, diversity, virtual and school spaces, collaboration, empowering students, remote learning, and more

Library Pros

https://www.thelibrarypros.com
A librarian and information technology pro talking libraries, library tech, and everything in between

LibVoices

https://podcasts.apple.com/us/podcast/libvoices/id1502263387
Librarians of color speak to the fullness of their careers, including successes, challenges, and achievements.

Linking Our Libraries

https://linkingourlibraries.libsyn.com
The hosts share information with all types of libraries, archives, and other nonprofit staff and leaders working to build their skills.

Lost in the Stacks: The Research Library Rock'n'Roll Radio Show

https://lostinthestacks.libsyn.com
Each show features an hour of music, interviews, and library talk united by a common theme.

The Public Libraries Podcast

http://publiclibrariesonline.org/category/media/podcast
Covers current programs and initiatives in public libraries, such as serving the homeless, DEI, imposter syndrome, embedded librarianship, early literacy, social services, marketing, and much more

School Librarians United

https://schoollibrariansunited.libsyn.com
A podcast dedicated to the nuts and bolts of running a successful school library

T Is for Training

https://tisfortraining.wordpress.com
A podcast dedicated to improvement through learning. It also covers training, presenting, learning, teaching, understanding, and compassion.

Job Listings for Librarians, Archivists, and Information Professionals
ALA JobLIST

http://joblist.ala.org | @ALA_JobLIST

American Association of Law Libraries (AALL)—Career Center

https://careers.aallnet.org/jobs | @aallnet

Archives Gig

https://archivesgig.wordpress.com | @archivesgig

ARLIS/NA JobList

https://www.arlisna.org/professional-resources/arlis-na-joblist | @ARLIS_NA

Association for Information Science and Technology (ASIS&T) Careers

https://asist-jobs.careerwebsite.com | @asist_org

Association of Research Libraries (ARL)—Job/Residency/Internship Listings

http://www.arl.org/leadership-recruitment/job-listings | @ARLnews

American Theological Library Association (ATLA) Job Board

https://www.atla.com/jobs | @YourAtla

BCALA Jobs

https://jobs.bcala.org/jobs | @BC_ALA

INALJ Jobs

https://inalj.com/?p=1441

LibGig

https://www.libgig.com/careers/job-search | @libgig

LYRASIS Job Bank

https://www.lyrasis.org/about/Pages/Job-Bank.aspx | @LYRASIS

Metropolitan New York Library Council (METRO) Jobs

https://metro.org/jobs | @mnylc

Music Library Association Job Search

https://www.musiclibraryassoc.org/networking/opening_search.asp |
@musiclibassoc

NASIG Jobs

http://nasigjobs.wordpress.com | @NASIG

The Partnership Job Board (The Provincial and Territorial Library Associations of Canada)

https://partnershipjobs.ca/jobs

Special Library Association (SLA) Jobs

https://careers.sla.org | @SLAhq

Job Listings Not Specific to Librarians, Archivists, and Information Professionals

Higher Education

Chronicle of Higher Education: Jobs

https://jobs.chronicle.com | @chronicle

EDUCAUSE Career Center

https://jobs.educause.edu/jobs | @educause

HigherEdJobs.com

http://www.higheredjobs.com | @insidehighered

Government

USAJobs.gov

https://www.usajobs.gov | @USAJOBS

Interdisciplinary (mega job sites)

FlexJobs

https://www.flexjobs.com | @flexjobs

Indeed

https://www.indeed.com | @indeed

LinkedIn Jobs

https://www.linkedin.com/jobs | @LinkedIn

Monster

https://www.monster.com | @Monster

SimplyHired

https://www.simplyhired.com | @SimplyHired

Zip Recruiter

https://www.ziprecruiter.com | @ZipRecruiter

Accredited Master's Programs in Library and Information Studies

This list of graduate programs accredited by the American Library Association is issued by the ALA Office for Accreditation. Regular updates and additional details appear on the Office for Accreditation's website at http://www.ala.org/CFApps/ lisdir/index.cfm. A total of 128 U.S. and Canadian institutions offering both accredited and nonaccredited programs in librarianship are included in the 76th edition (2023–2024) of *American Library Directory* (Information Today, Inc.).

Northeast: Conn., D.C., Md., Mass., N.J., N.Y., Pa., R.I.

Catholic University of America, School of Arts and Sciences, Dept. of Lib. and Info. Science, 620 Michigan Ave. N.E., Washington, DC 20064. Young Choi. Tel. 202-319-5085, fax 319-5574, e-mail cua-lis@cua.edu, World Wide Web http://lis.cua.edu. Admissions contact: Louise Gray. Tel. 202-319-5085, fax 319-5574, e-mail cua-lis@cua.edu.

Drexel University, College of Computing and Informatics, Dept. of Info. Science, 3141 Chestnut St., Philadelphia, PA 19104-2875. Andrea Forte, dept. head. Tel. 215-895-2474, fax 215-895-2494, e-mail istinfo@ drexel.edu, World Wide Web http://drexel. edu/cci/academics/graduate-programs/ ms-In-information. Admissions contact: Matthew Lechtenburg. Tel. 215-895-1951, e-mail ml333@drexel.edu.

Long Island University, College of Education, Info. and Technology, Palmer School of Lib. and Info. Science, 720 Northern Blvd., Brookville, NY 11548-1300. Bea Baaden, dir. Tel. 516-299-3818, fax 516-299-4168, e-mail post-palmer@liu.edu, World Wide Web https://www.liu.edu/ post/Academics/College-of-Education-Information-and-Technology/Palmer-School-of-Library-Information-Science/ Academic-Programs/MS-Library-Informa tion-Science. Admissions contact: Heather Ranieri. Tel. 516-299-4110, e-mail heather. ranieri@liu.edu.

Pennsylvania Western University–Clarion, College of Education and Human Services, School of Info. Sciences, 210 Carlson Lib. Bldg., Clarion, PA 16214. Linda L. Lillard, chair. Tel. 866-272-5612, fax 814-393-2150, e-mail libsci@clarion.edu, World Wide Web http://www.clarion.edu/libsci. Admissions contact: Michelle Ritzler. Tel. 866-393-2337, e-mail gradstudies@clarion.edu.

Pratt Institute, School of Info. and Lib. Science, 144 W. 14 St., 6th Fl., New York, NY 10011. Anthony Cocciolo, dean. Tel. 212-647-7682, fax 212-367-2492, e-mail si@ pratt.edu, World Wide Web https://www. pratt.edu/academics/information/degrees/ library-and-information-science-mslis. Admissions contact: Quinn Lai. Tel. 212-647-7701, e-mail qlai@pratt.edu.

Queens College, Grad. School of Lib. and Info. Studies, Rm. 254, Rosenthal Lib., 65-30 Kissena Blvd., Flushing, NY 11367-1597. Dr. James Lowry, dir. Tel. 718-997-3790, fax 718-997-3797, e-mail qc_gslis@qc.cuny. edu, World Wide Web http://sites.google. com/a/qc.cuny.edu/gslis. Admissions contact: Dr. Shuheng Wu. Tel. 718-997-3790, e-mail shuheng.wu@qc.cuny.edu.

Rutgers University, School of Communication and Info., Dept. of Lib. and Info. Science, New Brunswick, NJ 08901-1071. Marie Radford, chair. Tel. 848-932-7602, e-mail: mi@comminfo.rutgers.edu, World Wide Web http://comminfo.rutgers.edu. Admissions contact: Lilia Pavlovsky. Tel. 732-932-7576.

Saint John's University, College of Liberal Arts and Sciences, Div. of Library and Information Science, 8000 Utopia Parkway, Queens, NY 11439. James Vorbach, dir. Tel. 718-990-1834, fax 718-990-2071, e-mail vorbach@stjohns.edu, World Wide Web http:// www.stjohns.edu/academics/programs/ library-and-information-science-master-sci ence. Admissions contact: Michael Crossfox. Tel. 718-990-6200, e-mail dlis@stjohns.edu.

Simmons University, School of Lib. and Info. Science, College of Organizational,

Computational and Info. Sci., 300 The Fenway, Boston, MA 02115. Laura Saunders. Tel. 617-521-2868, e-mail slisadm@simmons.edu, World Wide Web http://simmons.edu/slis. Admissions contact: Kate Benson. Tel. 617-521-2868, e-mail slisadm@simmons.edu.

Southern Connecticut State University, College of Education, Dept. of Info. and Lib. Sci., 501 Crescent St., New Haven, CT 06515. Hak Joon Kim. Tel. 203-392-5781, fax 203-392-5780, e-mail slis@southernct.edu, World Wide Web http://inside.southernct.edu/information-and-library-science. Admissions contact: Dr. Arlene Bielefield. Tel. 203-392-5708, e-mail bielefielda1@southernct.edu.

Syracuse University, School of Info. Studies, 343 Hinds Hall, Syracuse, NY 13244. Megan Oakleaf, MLIS program dir. Tel. 315-443-2911, fax 315-443-6886, e-mail ischool@syr.edu, World Wide Web http://ischool.syr.edu/academics/graduate/masters-degrees/ms-library-and-information-science. Admissions contact: Enrollment Management. Tel. 315-443-2911, e-mail iGrad@syr.edu.

University at Albany, State Univ. of New York, College of Emergency Preparedness, Homeland Security and Cybersecurity, Draper 015, Albany, NY 12222. Jennifer Goodall, vice dean. Tel. 518-442-5258, fax 518-442-5632, e-mail infosci@albany.edu, World Wide Web http://www.albany.edu/cehc/programs/ms-information-science. Admissions contact: Graduate Admissions. Tel. 518-442-3980, e-mail graduate@albany.edu.

University at Buffalo, State Univ. of New York, Graduate School of Educ., Dept. of Info. Sci, 534 Baldy Hall, Buffalo, NY 14260-1020. Dan Albertson, chair. Tel. 716-645-2412, fax 716-645-3775, e-mail ub-lis@buffalo.edu, World Wide Web http://ed.buffalo.edu/information/about.html. Admissions contact: Ryan Taughrin. Tel. 716-645-2110, e-mail gse-info@buffalo.edu.

University of Maryland, College of Info. Studies, 4121 Hornbake Bldg., College Park, MD 20742. Ursula Gorham, MLIS program dir. Tel. 301-405-2039, fax 301-314-9145, e-mail ischooladmission@umd.edu, World Wide Web http://ischool.umd.edu/academics/master-of-library-and-information-science.

Admissions contact: John Sherrin. Tel. 301-405-2039, e-mail mlisprogram@umd.edu.

University of Pittsburgh, School of Computing and Info., Info. Culture and Data Stewardship, 135 N. Bellefield Ave., Pittsburgh, PA 15260. Mary K. Biagini, chair. Tel. 412-624-5230, fax 412-648-7001, e-mail sciadmit@pitt.edu, World Wide Web http://www.sci.pitt.edu/academics/masters/mlis. Admissions contact: Prof. Elizabeth Mahoney, assoc. chair, Dept. of Info. Culture and Data Stewardship. Tel. 412-624-4704, e-mail etm@pitt.edu.

University of Rhode Island, Grad. School of Lib. and Info. Studies, Rodman Hall, 94 W. Alumni Ave., Kingston, RI 02881. Valerie Karno, dir. Tel. 401-874-2878, fax 401-874-4964, e-mail vkarno@uri.edu, World Wide Web http://www.uri.edu/artsci/lsc.

Southeast: Ala., Fla., Ga., Ky., La., Miss., N.C., S.C., Tenn., Va., P.R.

East Carolina University, College of Educ., Lib. Science Degree Program, Mailstop 172, ECU, Greenville, NC 27858. Lindsay Mattock, MLIS program coord. Tel. 252-737-2486, e-mail mattockl22@ecu.edu, World Wide Web http://bit.ly/ECUML. Admissions contact: Camilla King. Tel. 252-328-6012, e-mail gradschool@ecu.edu.

Florida State University, College of Communication and Info., School of Info., 142 Collegiate Loop, P.O. Box 3062100, Tallahassee, FL 32306-2100. Kathleen Burnett, dir. Tel. 850-644-5775, fax 850-644-9763, e-mail jb.mitchell@cci.fsu.edu, World Wide Web http://ischool.cci.fsu.edu. Admissions tel. 850-645-3280, e-mail ischooladvising@admin.fsu.edu.

Louisiana State University, College of Human Sciences and Education, School of Lib. and Info. Science, 267 Coates Hall, Baton Rouge, LA 70803. Carol Barry, dir. Tel. 225-578-3158, fax 225-578-4581, e-mail slis@lsu.edu, World Wide Web http://slis.lsu.edu. Admissions contact: LaToya Coleman Joseph. Tel. 225-578-3150, e-mail lcjoseph@lsu.edu.

North Carolina Central University, School of Lib. and Info. Sciences, P.O. Box 19586, Durham, NC 27707. Jon P. Gant, dean. Tel.

919-530-7585, fax 919-530-6402, e-mail slisadmissions@nccu.edu, World Wide Web http://www.nccuslis.org. Admissions contact: Nina Clayton. Tel. 919-530-5184.

Old Dominion University, Darden College of Educ. and Prof. Studies, Lib. and Info. Studies Program, STEM Educ. and Prof. Studies, 4301 Hampton Blvd., Norfolk, VA 23529. Dr. Sue C. Kimmel, contact. Tel. 757 683 4305, e-mail libraryscience@odu.edu, World Wide Web http://www.odu.edu/stemps/academics/library-science.

University of Alabama, College of Communication and Info. Sciences, School of Lib. and Info. Studies, Box 870252, Tuscaloosa, AL 35487-0252. Jamie Naidoo, interim dir. Tel. 205-348-4610, fax 205-348-3746, e-mail info@slis.ua.edu, World Wide Web http://www.slis.ua.edu. Admissions contact: Joi Mahand. Tel. 205-348-1527, e-mail wwmahand@ua.edu.

University of Kentucky, College of Communication and Info., School of Info. Science, 320 Little Library, Lexington, KY 40506-0224. Jeffrey T. Huber, dir. Tel. 859-218-2290, fax 859-257-4205, e-mail sis@uky.edu, World Wide Web http://www.uky.edu/cis/slis. Admissions contact: Will Buntin. Tel. 859-257-3317, e-mail wjbunt0@uky.edu.

University of North Carolina–Chapel Hill, School of Info. and Lib. Science, CB 3360, 100 Manning Hall, Chapel Hill, NC 27599-3360. Gary Marchionini, dean. Tel. 919-962-8366, fax 919-962-8071, e-mail info@ils.unc.edu, World Wide Web http://sils.unc.edu/programs/graduate/msls. Admissions contact: Lara Bailey.

University of North Carolina–Greensboro, School of Educ., Dept. of Lib. and Info. Studies, 446 School of Educ. Bldg., P.O. Box 26170, Greensboro, NC 27402-6170. Lisa O'Connor, chair. Tel. 336-334-3477, fax 336-334-4120, e-mail lis@uncg.edu, World Wide Web http://soe.uncg.edu/academics/departments/lis. Admissions contact: Nora Bird. Tel. 336-256-1313, e-mail njbird@uncg.edu.

University of Puerto Rico, Info. Sciences and Technologies, P.O. Box 21906, San Juan, PR 00931-1906. Noraida Dominguez-Flores, acting dir. Tel. 787-763-6199, fax 787-764-2311, e-mail egcti@uprrp.edu, World Wide Web http://egcti.upr.edu.

Admissions contact: Migdalia Dávila-Pérez. Tel. 787-764-0000 ext. 3530, e-mail migdalia.davila@upr.edu.

University of South Carolina, College of Info. and Communications, School of Lib. and Info. Science, 1501 Greene St., Columbia, SC 29208. Karen Gavigan, interim dir. Tel. 803-777-3858, fax 803-777-7938, e-mail kgavigan@sc.edu, World Wide Web http://www.libsci.sc.edu. Tel. 803-777-3887, e-mail slisss@mailbox.sc.edu.

University of South Florida, College of Arts and Sciences, School of Info., 4202 E. Fowler Ave., CIS 1040, Tampa, FL 33620. Randy Borum, dir. Tel. 813-974-3520, fax 813-974-6840, e-mail si@usf.edu, World Wide Web https://www.usf.edu/arts-sciences/departments/information/programs/graduate-programs/ma-in-library-and-information-sciences/index.aspx. Admissions contact: Alexis Shinawongse. Tel. 813-974-8022.

University of Southern Mississippi, College of Educ. and Health Sciences, School of Lib. and Info. Science, 118 College Dr., No. 5146, Hattiesburg, MS 39406-0001. Stacy Creel, interim dir. Tel. 601-266-4228, fax 601-266-5774, e-mail slis@usm.edu, World Wide Web http://www.usm.edu/slis. Admissions tel. 601-266-5137, e-mail graduatestudies@usm.edu.

University of Tennessee, College of Communication and Info., School of Info. Sciences, 451 Communication Bldg., Knoxville, TN 37996. Abebe Rorissa, interim dir. Tel. 865-974-2148, fax 865-974-4967, e-mail sis@utk.edu, World Wide Web http://www.sis.utk.edu, Admissions tel. 865-974-2148.

Valdosta State Univ., College of Education and Human Services, Dept. of Lib. and Info. Studies, 1500 N. Patterson St., Odum 4600, Valdosta, GA 31698-0133. Lenese Colson, interim dir. Tel. 229-333-5966, fax 229-259-5055, e-mail mlis@valdosta.edu, World Wide Web http://www.valdosta.edu/mlis. Admissions contact: Sheila Peacock.

Midwest: Ill., Ind., Iowa, Kan., Mich., Minn., Mo., Ohio, Wis.

Chicago State University, College of Arts & Sciences, Dept. of Computing, Information,

Mathematical Sciences and Technology, 9501 S. King Dr., Education Bldg., Room 208, Chicago, IL 60628-1598. Rae-Anne Montague, LIS program coordinator. Tel. 773-995-5016, e-mail montague@csu.edu, World Wide Web http://www.csu.edu/cimst/infostudies/lib_info_science_ms.htm. Admissions contact: Gloria Adams. Tel. 773-995-2404, e-mail graduateprograms@csu.edu.

Dominican University, School of Info. Studies, 7900 W. Division St., River Forest, IL 60305. Don Hamerly, dir. Tel. 708-524-6983, fax 708-524-6657, e-mail sois@dom.edu, World Wide Web http://www.dom.edu/academics/majors-programs/master-library-and-information-science. Admissions contact: Emma Schmidt-Swartz. Tel. 708-524-6571, e-mail eschmidtswartz@dom.edu.

Emporia State University, School of Lib. and Info. Management, Campus Box 4025, 1 Kellogg Circle, Emporia, KS 66801-5415. Wooseob Jeong, dean. Tel. 620-341-5203, fax 620-341-5233, e-mail sliminfo@emporia.edu, World Wide Web http://www.emporia.edu/school-library-and-information-management/programs-certificates-licensures/master-library-science. Admissions contact: Kathie Buckman. Tel. 620-341-5065.

Indiana University, School of Informatics, Computing and Engineering, Info. and Lib. Science, Luddy Hall, Suite 2999C, 700 N. Woodlawn Ave., Bloomington, IN 47408. Noriko Hara, chair. Tel. 812-855-2018, fax 812-855-6166, e-mail ilsmain@indiana.edu, World Wide Web http://www.ils.indiana.edu/about/accreditation.html. Admissions contact: Michelle Dunbar-Sims. Tel. 812-855-2018, e-mail ilsmain@indiana.edu.

Indiana University–Purdue University Indianapolis, School of Informatics and Computing, Dept. of Lib. and Info. Science, 535 W. Michigan St., IT 475, Indianapolis, IN 46202. Andrea Copeland, chair. Tel. 317-278-4636, fax 317-278-7669, e-mail soicindy@iupui.edu, World Wide Web http://soic.iupui.edu/lis. Admissions e-mail soicapps@iupui.edu.

Kent State University, School of Info., P.O. Box 5190, Kent, OH 44242-0001. Meghan Harper, dir. Tel. 330-672-2782, fax 330-672-7965, e-mail ischool@kent.edu, World Wide Web http://www.kent.edu/iSchool/

master-library-information-science. Admissions contact: Janna Korzenko.

Saint Catherine University, Graduate College, School of Humanities, Arts, and Sciences, MLIS Program/Information Management Department, 2004 Randolph Ave. No. 4125, St. Paul, MN 55105. Joyce Yakawa, interim dir. Tel. 651-690-6802, fax 651-690-8724, e-mail imdept@stkate.edu, World Wide Web https://www.stkate.edu/academics/academic-programs/gc-library-and-information-science. Admissions contact: Ashley Wells. Tel. 612-214-0741, e-mail aewells@stkate.edu.

University of Illinois–Urbana-Champaign, School of Info. Science, 501 E. Daniel St., Champaign, IL 61820-6211. Ted Underwood, assoc. dean for acad. affairs. Tel. 217-333-3280, fax 217-244-3302, e-mail ischool@illinois.edu, World Wide Web http://ischool.illinois.edu. Admissions contact: Katrina Hagler. Tel. 217-244-3432, e-mail kkappes2@illinois.edu.

University of Iowa, Graduate College, School of Lib. and Info. Science, 3087 Main Lib., Iowa City, IA 52242-1420. Lucy Santos Green, dir. Tel. 319-335-5707, fax 319-335-5374, e-mail slis@uiowa.edu, World Wide Web http://slis.grad.uiowa.edu. Admissions contact: Katie McCullough. Tel. 319-384-1538, e-mail katie-mccullough@uiowa.edu.

University of Michigan, School of Info., 4322 North Quad, 105 S. State St., Ann Arbor, MI 48109-1285. Cliff Lampe, assoc. dean for acad. affairs. Tel. 734-763-2285, fax 734-764-2475, e-mail umsi.admissions@umich.edu, World Wide Web http://si.umich.edu. Admissions contact: Laura Elgas. Tel. 734-763-2285, e-mail umsi.admissions@umich.edu.

University of Missouri, College of Educ., Info. Science and Learning Technologies, 303 Townsend Hall, Columbia, MO 65211. Cynthia Dudenhoffer, LIS program coord. Tel. 877-747-5868, fax 573-884-0122, e-mail sislt@missouri.edu, World Wide Web http://lis.missouri.edu. Admissions tel. 573-882-4546.

University of Wisconsin–Madison, College of Letters and Sciences, Info. School, 600 N. Park St., Madison, WI 53706. Alan Rubel, dir. Tel. 608-263-2900, fax 608-263-4849, e-mail info@ischool.wisc.edu, World Wide

Web http://ischool.wisc.edu. Admissions contact: Tanya Hendricks Cobb. Tel. 608-263-2909, e-mail student-services@slis.wisc.edu.

University of Wisconsin–Milwaukee, School of Info. Studies, P.O. Box 413, Milwaukee, WI 53201. Dietmar Wolfram, senior assoc. dean. Tel. 414-229-4707, fax 414-229-6699, e-mail soisinfo@uwm.edu, World Wide Web http://uwm.edu/informationstudies.

Wayne State University, School of Info. Science, 106 Kresge Lib., Detroit, MI 48202. Thomas D. Walker, assoc. dean. Tel. 313-577-1825, fax 313-577-7563, e-mail ask lis@wayne.edu, World Wide Web http://sis.wayne.edu/mlis/index.php. Admissions contact: Matthew Fredericks. Tel. 313-577-2446, e-mail mfredericks@wayne.edu.

Southwest: Ariz., Okla., Texas

Texas Woman's University, School of Lib. and Info. Studies, P.O. Box 425769, Denton, TX 76204-5438. Ling Hwey Jeng, dir. Tel. 940-898-2602, fax 940-898-2611, e-mail slis@twu.edu, World Wide Web http://www.twu.edu/slis. Admissions contact: Mary Honard. E-mail slis@twu.edu.

University of Arizona, College of Social and Behavioral Sciences, School of Info., 1103 E. Second St., Tucson, AZ 85721. Catherine Brooks, dir. Tel. 520-621-3565, fax 520-621-3279, e-mail si-info@email.arizona.edu, World Wide Web http://ischool.arizona.edu/master-arts-library-and-information-science. Admissions contact: Holly Brown. Tel. 520-621-3567, e-mail brownhb@email.arizona.edu.

University of North Texas, College of Info., Dept. of Info. Science, 1155 Union Circle, No. 311068, Denton, TX 76203-5017. Jiangping Chen, chair. Tel. 940-565-2445, fax 940-369-7600, e-mail lis-chair@unt.edu, World Wide Web http://informationscience.unt.edu./master-science. Admissions contact: Caley Barnhart. Tel. 940-891-6861, e-mail ci-admissions@unt.edu.

University of Oklahoma, School of Lib. and Info. Studies, College of Arts and Sciences, 401 W. Brooks, Norman, OK 73019-6032. Dr. June Abbas, acting dir. Tel. 405-325-3921, e-mail slisinfo@ou.edu, World Wide

Web http://slis.ou.edu. Admissions contact: Stacy Smith.

University of Texas–Austin, School of Info., Suite 5.202, 1616 Guadalupe St., Austin, TX 78701-1213. Eric T. Meyer, dean. Tel. 512-471-3821, fax 512-471-3971, e-mail info@ischool.utexas.edu, World Wide Web http://www.ischool.utexas.edu. Admissions contact: Carla Criner. Tel. 512-471-5654, e-mail criner@ischool.utexas.edu.

West: Calif., Colo., Hawaii, Wash.

San José State University, School of Info., College of Professional and Global Education, One Washington Sq., San Jose, CA 95192-0029. Anthony Chow, dir. Tel. 408-924-2490, fax 408-924-2476, e-mail sjsuischool@gmail.com, World Wide Web http://ischool.sjsu.edu/master-library-and-information-science. Admissions contact: Linda Main. Tel. 408-924-2494, e-mail linda.main@sjsu.edu.

University of California–Los Angeles, Graduate School of Educ. and Info. Studies, Dept. of Info. Studies, Box 951520, Los Angeles, CA 90095-1520. Todd Franke, chair. Tel. 310-825-8799, fax 310-206-3076, e-mail info@gseis.ucla.edu, World Wide Web http://is.gseis.ucla.edu. Admissions contact: Michelle Maye. Tel. 310-825-5269, e-mail maye@gseis.ucla.edu.

University of Denver, Morgridge College of Educ., Research Methods and Info. Science, 1999 E. Evans Ave., Denver, CO 80208-1700. Krystyna Matusiak, chair. Tel. 303-871-3587, fax 303-871-4456, e-mail mce@du.edu, World Wide Web http://www.du.edu/education. Admissions contact: Rachel Riley. Tel. 303-871-2508, e-mail rachel.riley@du.edu.

University of Hawaii, College of Natural Sciences, Lib. and Info. Science Program, 2550 McCarthy Mall, Honolulu, HI 96822. Rich Gazan, chair. Tel. 808-956-7321, fax 808-956-5835, e-mail slis@hawaii.edu, World Wide Web http://www.hawaii.edu/lis.

University of Southern California, Marshall School of Business, 3550 Trousdale Parkway, DML 312, Los Angeles, CA 90089-0183. Caroline Muglia, interim dir. Tel.

213-764-4593, e-mail mmlis.admissions@ marshall.usc.edu, World Wide Web http:// librarysciencedegree.usc.edu. Admissions contact: Tel. 213-740-2741, e-mail mmlis. admissions@marshall.usc.edu.

University of Washington, The Information School, 370 Mary Gates Hall, Seattle, WA 98195-2840. Anind Dey, dean. Tel. 206-685-9937, fax 206-616-3152, e-mail ischool@uw.edu, World Wide Web http:// ischool.uw.edu. Admissions contact: Tel. 206-543-1794, e-mail mlis@uw.edu.

Canada

Dalhousie University, School of Info. Management, Kenneth C. Rowe Management Bldg., Halifax, NS B3H 4R2. Sandra Toze, dir. Tel. 902-494-3656, fax 902-494-2451, e-mail sim@dal.ca, World Wide Web http://www. sim.management.dal.ca. Admissions contact: Janet Music. Tel. 902-494-2471, e-mail jlmusic@dal.ca.

McGill University, School of Info. Studies, 3661 Peel St., Montreal, QC H3A 1X1. Kimiz Dalkir, dir. Tel. 514-398-4204, fax 514-398-7193, e-mail sis@mcgill.ca, World Wide Web http://www.mcgill.ca/sis. Admissions contact: Kathryn Hubbard. Tel. 514-398-4204 ext. 0742, e-mail sis@mcgill.ca.

University of Alberta, School of Library and Information Studies, Faculty of Education, 7-104 Education North, Edmonton, AB T6G 2G5. Kenneth Gariepy, dir. Tel. 780-492-3932, fax 780-492-2024, e-mail slis@ ualberta.ca, World Wide Web http://www. ualberta.ca/school-of-library-and-informa tion-studies/programs. Admissions contact: Joan White. Tel. 780-492-3679, e-mail slis@ualberta.ca.

University of British Columbia, School of Information, Irving K. Barber Learning Centre, Suite 470, 1961 East Mall, Vancouver, BC V6T 1Z1. Erik Kwakkel, dir. Tel. 604-822-2404, fax 604-822-6006, e-mail ischool.info@ubc.ca, World Wide Web http://www.slais.ubc.ca. Admissions contact: Sandra Abah. Tel. 604-822-3459, e-mail ischool.program@ubc.ca.

Université de Montréal, École de bibliothéconomie et des sciences de l'information, C.P. 6128, Succursale Centre-Ville, Montreal, QC H3C 3J7. Lyne Da Sylva, dir. Tel. 514-343-6044, fax 514-343-5753, e-mail ebsiinfo@ebsi.umontreal.ca, World Wide Web http://www.ebsi.umontreal.ca. Admissions contact: Alain Tremblay. Tel. 514-343-6044, e-mail alain.tremblay.1@ umontreal.ca.

University of Ottawa, School of Info. Studies, Desmarais Bldg., Ottawa, ON K1N 6N5. Mary Cavanagh, dir. Tel. 613-562-5130, fax 613-562-5854, e-mail esis@uOttawa.ca, World Wide Web http://arts.uottawa.ca/sis. Admissions contact: Catherine Bernard. Tel. 613-562-5800 ext. 1324, e-mail artsgrad@ uottawa.ca.

University of Toronto, Faculty of Info., 140 George St., Toronto, ON M5S 3G6. Wendy Duff, dean. Tel. 416-978-3202, fax 416-978-5762, e-mail inquire.ischool@utoronto. ca, World Wide Web http://www.ischool. utoronto.ca. Admissions contact: Barbara Brown. Tel. 416-978-8589, e-mail barb. brown@utoronto.ca.

University of Western Ontario, Grad. Programs in Lib. and Info. Science, Faculty of Info. and Media Studies, Room 240, North Campus Bldg., London, ON N6A 5B7. Pam McKenzie, associate dean of graduate and postdoctoral programs (acting). Tel. 519-661-4017, fax 519-661-3506, e-mail mlisinfo@uwo.ca, World Wide Web http:// www.fims.uwo.ca. Admissions contact: Shelley Long.

Library Scholarship Sources

For a more complete list of scholarships, fellowships, and assistantships offered for library study, see Financial Assistance for Library and Information Studies, published annually by the American Library Association (ALA). The document is also available on the ALA website at https://www.ala.org/educationcareers/educa tion/financialassistance.

American Association of Law Libraries (AALL). (1) Degree Candidates Scholarships are available for individuals studying to become law librarians as either a library or law school student or to library school graduates seeking an advanced degree in a related field. Preference is given to AALL members, but scholarships are not restricted to members. Applicants with law library experience are also given preference, but it is not required. Evidence of financial need must be submitted. (2) The AALL Scholarship is awarded annually to individuals seeking a degree from an accredited library or law school and who intend to have a career in legal information or to a library school graduate seeking an advanced degree in a related field. (3) The LexisNexis John R. Johnson Memorial Scholarship is awarded annually to individuals seeking a degree from an accredited library or law school and who intend to have a career in legal information or to a library school graduate seeking an advanced degree in a related field. (4) The George A. Strait Minority Scholarship & Fellowship is awarded annually to students enrolled in an ALA-accredited library graduate school or a law school and who are members of a minority group as defined by current U.S. guidelines and are degree candidates in an accredited library or law school and intend to have a career in law librarianship. (5) The Marcia J. Koslov Scholarship supports AALL members who work in a government law library by providing funding to attend continuing education programs. For information, write to AALL Scholarship Committee, 230 W. Monroe St., Suite 2650, Chicago, IL 60606.

American Library Association (ALA). (1) The ALA Century Scholarship of $2,500 funds services or accommodation for a library school student(s) with disabilities admitted to an ALA-accredited library school. (2) The

David A. Clift Scholarship of $3,000 goes to a U.S./Canadian citizen or permanent resident who is pursuing an M.L.S. in an ALA-accredited program. (3) The Tom and Roberta Drewes Scholarship of $3,000 goes to a library support-staff member who is a U.S./Canadian citizen or permanent resident and is pursuing an M.L.S. in an ALA-accredited program. (4) The deg farrelly Memorial/Alexander Street Press AMIA/FMRT Media Librarian Scholarship is given once a year to a master's degree candidate in library science who intends to work professionally with media collections in libraries. (5) The Federal Librarians Cicely Phippen Marks Scholarship of $1,500 goes to a library school student who has an interest in working in a federal library. (6) The Mary V. Gaver Scholarship of $3,000 goes to a U.S./Canadian citizen or permanent resident who is pursuing an M.L.S. specializing in youth services in an ALA-accredited program. (7) The Miriam L. Hornback Scholarship of $3,000 goes to an ALA or library support staffer who is a U.S./Canadian citizen or permanent resident who is pursuing an M.L.S. in an ALA-accredited program. (8) The Christopher Hoy/ERT Scholarship of $5,000 goes to a U.S./Canadian citizen or permanent resident who is pursuing an M.L.S. in an ALA-accredited program. (9) The Julia J. Brody Public Librarian Scholarship of $4,000 goes to a U.S./Canadian citizen or permanent resident who is pursuing an M.L.S. specializing in public library services in an ALA-accredited program. (10) The Tony B. Leisner Scholarship of $3,000 goes to a library support-staff member who is a U.S./Canadian citizen or permanent resident pursuing an M.L.S. in an ALA-accredited program. (11) The Peter Lyman Memorial/SAGE Scholarship in New Media supports a student in an ALA-accredited master's program in library and information studies pursuing a specialty in new media. (12) The Regina U. Minudri Young Adult Scholarship of $3,000 is given once a year to a master's degree candidate in library science who intends to work professionally with young adults in public libraries. (13) The W. David Rozkuszka Scholarship of $3,000 goes to an individual who is currently working with government documents in a library and is working toward a master's degree in library science. (14) The Spectrum Scholarship Program is ALA's national diversity and recruitment effort designed to address the specific issue of underrepresentation of critically needed ethnic librarians within the profession while serving as a model for ways to bring attention to larger diversity issues in the future. For information, write to ALA Scholarship Clearinghouse, ALA Scholarship Clearinghouse, 225 N. Michigan Ave., Suite 1300, Chicago, IL 60601, or see http://www.ala.org/scholarships.

ALA/Association for Library Service to Children. (1) The Bound to Stay Bound Books Scholarship provides financial assistance for the education of individuals who intend to pursue an M.L.S. or advanced degree and who plan to work in the area of library service to children. (2) The Frederic G. Melcher Scholarship provides financial assistance for individuals who intend to pursue an M.L.S. degree and who plan to work in children's librarianship. For information, write to ALA Scholarship Clearinghouse, 225 N. Michigan Ave., Suite 1300, Chicago, IL 60611, or see http://www.ala.org/scholarships.

ALA/Association of College and Research Libraries. The ESS De Gruyter European Librarianship Study Grant supports research in European studies with an emphasis on librarianship, the book trade, resource documentation, and similar information-science-related topics. An award of €2,500 is given to cover travel to and from Europe and transportation, room, and board in Europe, for up to 30 consecutive days. The application is electronic only. Note: The 2023 grant is temporarily on hold due to funding suspension from the sponsor, and submissions are not currently being accepted.

ALA/CORE. (1) The CORE/Christian (Chris) Larew Memorial Scholarship of $3,000 is for study in an ALA-accredited M.L.S. program to encourage the entry of qualified persons into the library and information technology field. (2) The CORE/OCLC Spectrum Scholarship of $5,000 goes to a U.S. or Canadian citizen who is a qualified member of a principal minority group (American Indian or Alaskan native, Asian or Pacific Islander, African American, or Hispanic) for study in an ALA-accredited M.L.S. program, has a strong commitment to the use of automated systems in libraries, and plans to follow a career in the library and automation field. For information, write to ALA Scholarship Clearinghouse, 225 N. Michigan Ave., Suite 1300, Chicago, IL 60611, or see http://www.ala.org/scholarships.

ALA International Relations Committee. The Bogle Pratt International Library Travel Fund of $1,000 is given to an ALA personal member to attend their first international conference. Applications should be submitted via e-mail to the ALA International Relations Office, intl@ala.org.

American-Scandinavian Foundation. Fellowships (up to $23,000) and grants (up to $5,000) are available to pursue research, study, or creative arts projects in Denmark, Finland, Iceland, Norway, or Sweden. For information, write to Fellowships and Grants, American-Scandinavian Foundation, 58 Park Ave., New York, NY 10026, or see http://www.amscan.org/fellowships-and-grants.

Association for Library and Information Science Education (ALISE). (1) ALISE Community conn@CT mini-grants of $750 for ALISE members are given to address a library and information need of a social justice organization through community engagement (in a collaborative manner). (2) A varying number of research grants totaling $5,000 are awarded to members of ALISE. For information, write to ALISE, 4 Lan Drive, Suite 310, Westford, MA 01886.

Association of Bookmobile and Outreach Services (ABOS). (1) The Bernard Vavrek Scholarship of $1,000 goes to a student who is currently enrolled and has completed at least one semester in a library and/or information science graduate degree program and who is interested in becoming an outreach/bookmobile librarian. (2) The John Philip

Excellence in Outreach Award recognizes outstanding contributions and leadership by an individual in bookmobile and outreach services. (3) The Carol Hole Conference Attendance Award consists of ten awards of free conference registration and $500 stipends for the winners' travel expenses and/or accommodations for a conference. For information, write to Chair, ABOS Awards Committee, at awards@abos-outreach.com.

Association of Jewish Libraries. (1) One academic scholarship of $1,000 is given to a student who is enrolled or accepted in a graduate school of library and information science. Additionally, free, full conference registration is included and encouraged. (2) A conference subvention award is given to attend the Association of Jewish Libraries annual conference. Free, full conference registration; travel; and (shared) room are included. For information, see https://jew ishlibraries.org/student-scholarship-award.

Association of Seventh-Day Adventist Librarians. The D. Glenn Hilts Scholarship is awarded to a member of the Seventh-Day Adventist Church in an ALA-accredited graduate library program or, if attending outside the United States or Canada, a program recognized by the International Federation of Library Associations (IFLA). The recipient must be enrolled as a full-time student and use the scholarship only for tuition and books. For information, write to ASDAL Scholarship and Awards Committee, McKee Library, Southern Adventist University, P.O. Box 629, Collegedale, TN 37315.

Beta Phi Mu. (1) The Sarah Rebecca Reed Scholarship consists of two $2,250 awards for individuals beginning LIS studies at an ALA-accredited school. Note: Due to budgetary constraints, the Reed Scholarship will not be awarded in 2023. (2) The Frank B. Sessa Scholarship provides ten $150 awards for Beta Phi Mu members' continuing education. (3) The Harold Lancour Scholarship of $1,750 goes to a librarian who is conducting foreign research. (4) The Blanche E. Woolls Scholarship for School Library Media Service of $2,250 goes to an individual who is beginning LIS studies with a concentration in school library media. (5) The Eugene Garfield Doctoral Dissertation Scholarship of up to six $3,000 awards is for doctoral students who are working on their dissertations in LIS and related fields. For information, write to Beta Phi Mu Honor Society, P.O. Box 42139, Philadelphia, PA 19101, or see https://www.betaphimu.org/scholarships_overview.html.

Canadian Association of Law Libraries (CALL). (1) The Diana M. Priestly Scholarship of $2,500 is for a student enrolled in an approved Canadian law school or accredited Canadian library school. (2) The CALL/ACBD Research Grant of up to $3,000 is for research in areas of interest to members and to the association. (3) The CALL/ACBD Education Reserve Fund Grants for CALL go to members to further their education in pursuits that do not fit the guidelines of already established scholarships. (4) The James D. Lang Memorial Scholarship supports attendance at a continuing education program. (5) The Eunice Beeson Memorial Travel Fund assists members of the association who wish to attend the annual meeting but, for financial reasons, are unable to do so. (6) The Northern Exposure to Leadership Grant identifies individuals who demonstrate an aspiration to lead libraries or information service organizations or programs in the 21st century and motivates them to develop their leadership potential. (7) The Janine Miller Fellowship of $2,500 goes to one CALL member to attend the Law via the Internet Conference. For information, see https://www.callacbd.ca/Awards.

Canadian Federation of University Women (CFUW). (1) The Aboriginal Women's Award of $10,000–$25,000 is for studies in specific programs of law, medicine, or nurse practitioners or a master of Aboriginal studies. (2) The Ruth Binnie Fellowship of $6,000 is for a student in master's studies that focus on one or more aspect(s) of the field of human ecology/home economics/family and consumer sciences. (3) The Canadian Home Economics Association Fellowship of $6,000 is for a student enrolled in a postgraduate program in the field of human ecology/home economics/family and consumer sciences in Canada. (4) The CFUW Memorial Fellowship of $8,000 is for a student who is currently enrolled in a master's program in science, mathematics, or engineering in Canada or abroad. (5) The Bourse

Georgette LeMoyne Award of $5,000 is for graduate study in any field at a Canadian university (the candidate must be studying in French). (6) The Elizabeth and Rachel Massey Award of $5,000 is for postgraduate studies in the visual arts or in music. (7) The Margaret McWilliams Pre-Doctoral Fellowship of $11,000 is for a female student who has completed at least one full year as a full-time student in doctoral-level studies. (8) The 1989 Ecole Polytechnique Commemorative Award of $7,000 is for graduate studies in any field at the doctoral level, and there is one award of $5,000 for master's study. The applicant must justify the relevance of her work to women. (9) The Linda Souter Humanities Award of $6,000 is for a master's or doctoral student studying in the area of the humanities. (10) The Dr. Alice E. Wilson Award of $5,000 each is for four mature students returning to graduate studies in any field after at least three years. (11) The CFUW 100th Anniversary Legacy Fellowship of one $5,000 award goes to a woman who has completed one calendar year of a doctoral program. For information, write to Fellowships Program Manager, Canadian Federation of University Women, fellowships@cfuw-fcfdu.ca.

Chinese American Librarians Association (CALA). (1) The Sheila Suen Lai Scholarship of $500 goes to a Chinese descendant who has been accepted in an ALA-accredited program. (2) The CALA Scholarship of Library and Information Science of $1,000 is for a Chinese descendant who has been accepted in an ALA-accredited program. (3) The Huang Tso-ping and Wu Yao-yu Research and Scholarship awards faculty and students at Wuhan University in China; one award is for a library school faculty member ($400), and two awards go to library school students ($200 each). For information, write to Jen Woo at jennifer.woo@sfpl.org.

Massachusetts Black Librarians' Network. $500 for students of African descent entering an ALA-accredited master's program in library science. For information, write to Massachusetts Black Librarians' Network, P.O. Box 400504, Cambridge, MA 02140.

Medical Library Association (MLA). (1) The Cunningham Memorial International Fellowship is for health sciences librarians from countries other than the United States and Canada. (2) A scholarship of up to $5,000 goes to a person entering an ALA-accredited library program, with no more than one-half of the program yet to be completed. (3) A scholarship of up to $5,000 goes to a minority student studying health sciences librarianship. (4) A varying number of Research, Development, and Demonstration Project Grants of $100–$1,000 go to U.S. or Canadian citizens, preferably MLA members. (5) The MLA Doctoral Fellowship of $2,000 is for doctoral work in medical librarianship or information science. (6) The Librarians without Borders Ursula Poland International Scholarship of $1,000 funds an international project by a U.S. or Canadian health sciences librarian. For information, write to MLA Grants and Scholarships Coordinator, awards@mlahq.org, or see http://www.mlanet.org/page/awards.

Mountain Plains Library Association (MPLA). A varying number of grants of up to $600 are for applicants who are members of the association and have been for the preceding two years. For information, write to Judy Zelenski, Executive Secretary, MPLA, 14293 W. Center Drive, Lakewood, SD 80228, or see https://mpla.us/about/professional-development-grants.html.

Society of American Archivists (SAA). (1) The F. Gerald Ham and Elsie Ham Scholarship of $10,000 is for graduate students in archival education at a U.S. university that meets the society's criteria for graduate education. (2) The Mosaic Scholarship of $5,000 is for up to two U.S. or Canadian minority students enrolled in a graduate program in archival administration. (3) The Josephine Foreman Scholarship of $10,000 is for a U.S. citizen or permanent resident who is a minority graduate student enrolled in a program in archival administration. (4) The Oliver Wendell Holmes Travel Award of $1,000 enables foreign students involved in archival training in the United States or Canada to attend the SAA Annual Meeting. (5) The Donald Peterson Student Travel Award of up to $1,500 enables graduate students or recent graduates to attend the SAA Annual Meeting. (6) The Harold T. Pinkett Student of Color Awards enable minority students or graduate students to attend the SAA Annual

Meeting. (7) The Brenda S. Banks Travel Award recognizes and acknowledges individuals of color who have demonstrated professional archival experience and who manifest an interest in becoming active members of SAA. For details, write to Society of American Archivists, 17 N. State St., Suite 1425, Chicago, IL 60607, or see https://www2.archivists.org/governance/handbook/section12-ham.

Special Libraries Association (SLA). The Leadership Symposium Scholarship of $1,000 is for travel expenses and registration at the symposium (value $395) for members who demonstrate a desire and commitment to advance their leadership skills and abilities within SLA units. For information, write to Special Libraries Association, 7918 Jones Branch Dr., Suite 300, McLean, Virginia 22102.

Library Scholarship and Award Recipients, 2022

Compiled by the staff of *Library and Book Trade Almanac*

Scholarships and awards are listed by organization.

American Association of Law Libraries (AALL)

AALL Educational Scholarships. To assist individuals studying to become law librarians with their educational expenses. *Winners:* (law school graduate seeking library degree) Stephanie Falcon, Anjelica Violi; (library school graduate seeking law degree) Shelby M. Nivitanont.

AALL Grants. To enable law librarians to participate in professional educational opportunities at the AALL Annual Meeting or to engage in original research on topics important to law librarianship. *Winners:* (annual meeting grants) Thomas Baer, Sara Mauldin, Amy Small, Kaden Taylor; (Equal Justice Conference grant) Kristen Matteucci.

AALL Hall of Fame Award. Recognizes significant, substantial, and long-standing contributions to the profession and service to the association. *Winners:* Camille Broussard, Steven Antonio Lastres, Anne C. Matthewman, Kent C. Olson.

AALL New Product Award. For new commercial information products that enhance or improve existing law library services or procedures or innovative products that improve access to legal information, the legal research process, or procedures for technical processing of library materials. Not awarded in 2022.

AALL Spectrum Article of the Year Award. *Winners:* Pablo D. Arredondo and Javed Qadrud-Din for "From Vellum to Vectors" (May/June 2021).

AALL George A. Strait Minority Scholarship & Fellowship. *Winners:* (scholarship and fellowship) Margo Nguyen, Jeanine Xochitl Vasquez; (scholarship) Diona Eberhart Layden, Janisha Musco, Christian A. Wilson.

Joseph L. Andrews Legal Literature Award. *Winners:* Zanada Joyner and Cas Laskowski (editors) for *Introduction to Law Librarianship*; Emily S. Bremer, Kathryn E. Kovacs, and Charlotte D. Schneider (editors) for *Bremer-Kovacs Collection: Historic Documents Related to the Administrative Procedure Act of 1946.*

Emerging Leader Award. To recognize newer members who have made significant contributions to AALL and/or to the profession and have demonstrated the potential for leadership and continuing service. *Winners:* Sabrina Davis, Alyson Drake, Taryn Marks.

Excellence in Community Engagement Award. For outstanding achievement in public relations activities. *Winners:* Minnesota State Law Library, St. Paul, Minnesota, for "Appeals Self-Help Videos"; Greater Philadelphia Law Library Association (GPLLA), Law Library Association of Maryland (LLAM), and Law Librarians' Society of Washington, DC, Inc. (LLSDC) for "Project 20/20: From Transition to Transformation."

Marian Gould Gallagher Distinguished Service Award. To recognize extended and sustained service to law librarianship. *Winners:* Steven P. Anderson, Barbara A. Bintliff, Carol Bredemeyer, Michael G. Chiorazzi.

Innovations in Technology Award. To recognize an AALL member, special interest section, chapter, or library for innovative use of technology in the development and creation of an application or resource for law librarians or legal professionals. *Winners:* Avi Bauer, Mary Sarah Bilder, Laurel Davis, and Nick Szydlowski for *Robert Morris: Civil Rights Lawyer & Antislavery Activist.*

Law Library Journal Article of the Year. *Winner:* Rebecca Chapman for "Protecting Our Spaces of Memory: Rediscovering the Seneca Nation Settlement Act Through Archives" (2021).

LexisNexis Call for Papers Awards. To promote the scholarship of AALL members and of students on any subject relevant to law librarianship. *Winners:* (new member) Olivia R. Smith for "Ok, Zoomer: Teaching Legal Research to Gen Z"; (open) Kathleen

Darvil for "Increasing Access to Justice by Improving Usability of Statutory Code Websites."

LexisNexis/John R. Johnson Memorial Scholarships. *Winners:* (college graduate seeking library degree) Mia McGee; (law school graduate seeking library degree) Genesis M. Agosto, Julia Elina, Rachel M. Shields; (library school graduate seeking law degree) Kelsey Renz.

LexisNexis Research Fund Grants. *Winners:* Trezlen Drake for "FCIL Collections in U.S. Academic Law Libraries"; T.J. Striepe and Savanna Nolan for "Effectiveness of Research Plans: A Case Study."

Minority Leadership Development Award. *Winner:* Ana Rosa Ramirez Toft-Nielsen, professional development innovation manager for Greenberg Traurig in Miami, Florida.

Robert L. Oakley Advocacy Award. To recognize an AALL member who has been an outstanding advocate and has contributed significantly to the AALL policy agenda at the federal, state, local, or international level. *Winner:* Lewis M. Giles, assistant director of library services at UNT Dallas College of Law in Dallas, Texas.

Public Access to Government Information Award. Recognizes individuals or organizations that have made significant contributions to protect and promote greater access to government information. *Winner:* Deborah Hamilton, strategic services librarian for the law collection at Pikes Peak Library District in Colorado Springs, Colorado.

Volunteer Service Award. Honors volunteers who have made significant contributions to the work of AALL. *Winner:* Joseph D. Lawson, director of Harris County Robert W. Hainsworth Law Library in Houston, Texas.

American Library Association (ALA)

ALA Excellence in Library Programming Award ($5,000). For a cultural/thematic library program or program series that engages the community in planning, sponsorship, and/or active participation; addresses an identified community need; and has a measurable impact. *Donor:* ALA

Cultural Communities Fund. Not awarded in 2022.

ALA Honorary Membership. To recognize outstanding contributions of lasting importance to libraries and librarianship. *Honorees:* Jim Neal and Maureen Sullivan.

ALA/Information Today, Inc. Library of the Future Award ($1,500). For a library, consortium, group of librarians, or support organization for innovative planning for, applications of, or development of patron training programs about information technology in a library setting. *Donors:* Information Today, Inc. and IIDA. *Winner:* Las Vegas-Clark County Library District (LVCCLD) in Nevada for the Bringing the Library to Transit Riders program, enabling transit riders to instantly sign up for access to LVCCLD materials online using free onboard wifi on 400 city buses.

ALA Medal of Excellence. For creative leadership professional achievement in library management, training, cataloging, and classification and the tools and techniques of librarianship. *Donor:* OCLC. *Winner:* Judith Cannan.

Hugh C. Atkinson Memorial Award. For outstanding achievement (including risk taking) by academic librarians that has contributed significantly to improvements in library automation, management, and/or development or research. *Offered by:* ACRL, ALCTS, and Core. Not awarded in 2022.

Beta Phi Mu Award ($1,000). For distinguished service in library education. *Donor:* Beta Phi Mu International Library and Information Science Honorary Society. Not awarded in 2022.

Bogle-Pratt International Library Travel Fund Award ($1,000). To ALA members to attend their first international conference. *Donors:* Bogle Memorial Fund and Pratt Institute School of Information and Library Science. Not awarded in 2022.

W.Y. Boyd Literary Award for Excellence in Military Fiction. See "Literary Prizes, 2022" in Part 5.

Julia J. Brody Public Librarian Scholarship ($4,000). To a U.S. or Canadian citizen or permanent resident who is pursuing an M.L.S. specializing public library services in an ALA-accredited program. *Winner:* Adele Chase.

David H. Clift Scholarship ($3,000). To worthy U.S. or Canadian citizens enrolled in an ALA-accredited program toward an M.L.S. degree. *Winner:* Jennifer Bernal.

Tom and Roberta Drewes Scholarship ($3,000). To a library support staff member pursuing a master's degree in an ALA-accredited program. *Donor:* Quality Books. *Winner:* Patricia Martone.

EBSCO/ALA Conference Sponsorship Award ($1,000). To enable librarians to attend the ALA Annual Conference. *Donor:* EBSCO. *Winners:* Ashley Ehmig, Nathaniel Robert Harris, Amanda Lorge, Ashley R Hawkins, Jessica Regitano, Rukmal Ryder, Jennifer Washburn, Lindsey West.

EBSCO Information Services Library Staff Development Award ($3,500). To a library organization for a program to further its staff development goals and objectives. *Donor:* EBSCO. *Winner:* Arab Federation for Libraries and Information (AFLI), Cairo, Egypt.

Equality Award ($1,000). To an individual or group for an outstanding contribution that promotes equality in the library profession. *Donor:* Rowman & Littlefield. *Winner:* Fulton County (Pennsylvania) Library along with Emily Best and Sarah Cutchall.

Elizabeth Futas Catalyst for Change Award ($1,000). A biennial award to recognize a librarian who invests time and talent to make positive change in the profession of librarianship. *Donor:* Elizabeth Futas Memorial Fund. *Winner (2022):* Lessa Kanani'opua Pelayo-Lozada.

Gale, a Cengage Company, Financial Development Award ($2,500). To a library organization for a financial development project to secure new funding resources for a public or academic library. *Donor:* Gale, a Cengage Company. Not awarded in 2022.

Mary V. Gaver Scholarship ($3,000). To a student pursuing an M.L.S. degree and specializing in youth services. *Winner:* Nadine Said.

Ken Haycock Award for Promoting Librarianship ($1,000). For significant contribution to public recognition and appreciation of librarianship through professional performance, teaching, or writing. Not awarded in 2022.

Miriam L. Hornback Scholarship ($3,000). To an ALA or library support staff person pursuing a master's degree in library science. *Winner:* Mariam Jalalifard.

Paul Howard Award for Courage ($1,000). A biennial award to a librarian, library board, library group, or individual for exhibiting unusual courage for the benefit of library programs or services. *Donor:* Paul Howard Memorial Fund. Not awarded in 2022.

John Ames Humphry/OCLC/Forest Press Award ($1,000). To one or more individuals for significant contributions to international librarianship. *Donor:* OCLC/Forest Press. Not awarded in 2022.

Tony B. Leisner Scholarship ($3,000). To a library support staff member pursuing a master's degree. *Donor:* Tony B. Leisner. *Winner:* Araceli Argueta.

Joseph W. Lippincott Award ($1,500). For distinguished service to the library profession. *Donor:* Joseph W. Lippincott III. *Winner:* Dr. Kenneth A. Yamashita.

Peter Lyman Memorial/Sage Scholarship in New Media. To support a student seeking an M.L.S. degree in an ALA-accredited program and pursuing a specialty in new media. *Donor:* Sage Publications. *Winner:* Marco Lanier.

James Madison Award. To recognize efforts to promote government openness. Not awarded in 2022.

Schneider Family Book Awards. See "Literary Prizes, 2022" in Part 5.

Scholastic Library Publishing Award ($1,000). To a librarian whose "unusual contributions to the stimulation and guidance of reading by children and young people exemplifies achievement in the profession." *Sponsor:* Scholastic Library Publishing. *Winner:* Jillian Rudes.

Lemony Snicket Prize for Noble Librarians Faced with Adversity ($3,000 plus a $1,000 travel stipend to enable attendance at the ALA Annual Conference). To honor a librarian who has faced adversity with integrity and dignity intact. *Sponsor:* Lemony Snicket (author Daniel Handler). *Winner:* Martha Hickson of North Hunterdon High School in Annandale, New Jersey.

Spectrum Scholarships ($5,000). To minority students admitted to ALA-accredited library schools. *Donors:* ALA and the Institute of Museum and Library Services. *Winners:* Caitlin Abadir-Mullally, Marissa Arterberry,

Megha Bamola, Réna Leticia Barlow, Elise Bernal, Anjali Bhat, Jennifer Bartell Boykin, Carrieann Cahall, Marian Toledo Candelaria, Pamela Rodriguez Cervantes, Sanobar Chagani, Michelle Cheng, Carol Choi, Melissa Aslo De La Torre, Joseph Dellosa, Estefania Eiquihua, Rebeca Escamilla, Janin Escobedo-Garcia, Aliya Estes, Madison Evans, Mei'lani Eyre, Liliana Garcia, Danielle Galvan Gomez, Nancy Gonzalez Lopez, Zhaneille Green, Nestor Guerrero, Shauna-Kay Harrison, Cinthya Hernandez, Jessica Hom, Tamia Jackson, Kathrina Johnson, Kayla D. Johnson, Jenny Le, Maria Lee, Mare Lodu, Alejandra Lopez, Denise Mantey, Inbar Michael, Wardah Mohammed, Fiona Brown Ordway Mosser, Cristopher Vázquez Muñoz, Michelle Noriega, Wilsinia C. Ocasio, Hayley Park, Bianca Phipps, Danielle Pitter, Marycruz Flores Reynoso, Daynali Flores Rodriguez, Erica N. Rodriguez, Khahlia Sanders, Vilma A. Sandoval-Sall, Jack Schmitt, Wing Tang, Abraham Venegas, Makayla Walker, Dev, Aaron M. Wilson, Michelle Wolfson, Risell Yuen, Faria Zafer.

Sullivan Award for Public Library Administrators Supporting Services to Children. To a library supervisor/administrator who has shown exceptional understanding and support of public library services to children. *Donor:* Peggy Sullivan. *Winner:* Marie Jarry, director of public services for Hartford (Connecticut) Public Library.

American Association of School Librarians (AASL)

AASL/ABC-CLIO Leadership Grant (up to $1,750). To AASL affiliates for planning and implementing leadership programs at state, regional, or local levels. *Donor:* ABC-CLIO. *Winner:* Louisiana Association of School Librarians (LASL).

AASL Chapter of the Year ($1,000). In recognition of the AASL chapter most active and dynamic in achieving the goals of AASL at the state and local level. *Winner:* South Carolina Association of School Librarians (SCASL).

AASL Collaborative School Library Award ($2,500). For expanding the role of the library in elementary and/or secondary

school education. *Donor:* Scholastic Book Fairs. *Winners:* Michael Giller and David Gerhard from South Carolina Governor's School in Greenville, South Carolina.

AASL Distinguished School Administrator Award ($2,000). For expanding the role of the library in elementary and/or secondary school education. *Donor:* ProQuest. *Winner:* Tim Salem from Scotts Ridge Middle School in Ridgefield, Connecticut.

AASL/Frances Henne Award ($1,250). To a school library media specialist with five or fewer years in the profession to attend an AASL regional conference or ALA Annual Conference for the first time. *Donor:* Libraries Unlimited. *Winner:* Ashley Long from Talley Street Upper Elementary School in Decatur, Georgia.

AASL Innovative Reading Grant ($2,500). To support the planning and implementation of an innovative program for children that motivates and encourages reading, especially for struggling readers. *Sponsor:* Capstone. *Winner:* Samantha Archibald Mora from Wood River Middle School in Hailey, Idaho.

AASL President's Crystal Apple Award. To an individual, individuals, or group for a significant impact on school libraries and students. Not awarded in 2022.

Distinguished Service Award & Scholarship Fund. For outstanding contributions to librarianship and school library development. *Donor:* Rosen Publishing Group. Not awarded in 2022.

Intellectual Freedom Award ($2,000 plus $1,000 to the media center of the recipient's choice). To a school library media specialist and AASL member who has upheld the principles of intellectual freedom. *Donor:* ProQuest. *Winners:* FReadom Fighters (Becky Calzada, Carolyn Foote, Nancy Jo Lambert).

National School Library of the Year Award ($10,000). Honors school libraries exemplifying implementation of AASL's National School Library Standards for Learners, School Librarians, and School Libraries. *Donor:* Follett Library Resources. Not awarded in 2022.

Association for Library Service to Children (ALSC)

ALSC/Baker & Taylor Summer Reading Program Grant ($3,000). For implementation of an outstanding public library summer reading program for children. *Donor:* Baker & Taylor. *Winner:* Chicago Heights (Illinois) Public Library.

ALSC/Booklist/YALSA Odyssey Award for Excellence in Audiobook Production. To the producer of the best audiobook for children and/or young adults available in English in the United States. See Odyssey Award in "Literary Prizes, 2022" in Part 5.

ALSC/Candlewick Press "Light the Way" Grant ($3,000). To a library conducting exemplary outreach to underserved populations. *Donor:* Candlewick Press. *Winner:* Swanton (Vermont) Public Library.

ALSC Spectrum Scholarships. To a Spectrum applicant who expresses an interest in library service to children. *Winners:* Joseph Dellosa, Florida State University (in honor of Ellen Fader); Hayley Park, University of Washington; Danielle Pitter, Rutgers University; Erica N. Rodriguez, University of Illinois.

May Hill Arbuthnot Honor Lectureship. To an author, critic, librarian, historian, or teacher of children's literature who prepares a paper considered to be a significant contribution to the field of children's literature. Not awarded in 2022.

Mildred L. Batchelder Award. See "Literary Prizes, 2022" in Part 5.

Louise Seaman Bechtel Fellowship ($7,500). To allow qualified children's librarians to spend up to four weeks reading and studying at the Baldwin Library of Historical Children's Literature, a part of the George A. Smathers Libraries at the University of Florida. *Donor:* Bechtel Fund. *Winner:* J. Joseph Prince.

Pura Belpré Awards. See "Literary Prizes, 2022" in Part 5.

Bound to Stay Bound Books Scholarships ($7,000). For men and women who intend to pursue an M.L.S. or other advanced degree and who plan to work in the area of library service to children. *Donor:* Bound to Stay Bound Books. Not awarded in 2022.

Randolph Caldecott Medal. See "Literary Prizes, 2022" in Part 5.

Carnegie-Whitney Awards (up to $5,000). For the preparation of print or electronic reading lists, indexes, or other guides to library resources that promote reading or the use of library resources at any type of library. *Donors:* James Lyman Whitney and Andrew Carnegie Funds. *Winners:* Carol Choi for "Black-Built Environment: Race and Architecture in America"; Christine Shelek for "The Rainbow Connection: An Annotated Bibliography of LGBTQIA+ Books and Resources for Children"; Amanda Boczar for "Eco-Literacies for Climate Action in Florida: Teaching and Learning Resources Portal"; Erin Owens for "Parenting with a Disability or Chronic Illness: An Essential Bibliography"; Hannah Park for "Antiracist Praxis: A Guide to Theory and Instructional Practice"; Hayley Johnson and Sarah Simms for "Blood and Thunder: The Idealized American West and Its Place Today"; Michael Rodriguez and Rebecca Parmer for "What's the IDEA? Advancing Inclusion, Diversity, Equity, and Accessibility (IDEA) in Academic Library and Archival Collections: An Annotated Bibliography"; Nicole Cooke and Cearra Harris for "Equity, Social Justice, and Critical Race Theory in Librarianship: A Bibliography and Toolkit"; Shamella Cromartie and Heidi Buchanan for "Affrilachia: A Guide to Exploring African American Life in Appalachia"; Yolanda Bergstrom-Lynch for "Lady Plays the Blues Project: A Digital Bibliography and Multimedia Archive of Black Women Country Blues Guitarists."

Century Scholarship ($2,500). For a library school student or students with disabilities admitted to an ALA-accredited library school. *Winner:* Bishop Clarke.

Children's Literature Legacy Award. See "Literary Prizes, 2022" in Part 5.

Distinguished Service Award ($1,000). To recognize significant contributions to, and an impact on, library services to children and/or ALSC. *Winner:* Betsy Diamant-Cohen.

Theodor Seuss Geisel Award. See "Literary Prizes, 2022" in Part 5.

Maureen Hayes Author/Illustrator Visit Award (up to $4,000). For an honorarium and travel expenses to make possible a library talk to children by a nationally known author/illustrator. *Sponsor:* Simon & Schuster Children's Publishing. *Winner:* Roselle (Illinois) Public Library District.

Frederic G. Melcher Scholarships ($6,000). To two students entering the field of library service to children for graduate work in an ALA-accredited program. *Winners:* Ramona Edwards, University of South Carolina, and Roxanna Sanchez, University of Texas–Austin.

John Newbery Medal. See "Literary Prizes, 2022" in Part 5.

Penguin Random House Young Readers Group Awards ($600). To children's librarians in school or public libraries with ten or fewer years of experience to attend the ALA Annual Conference. *Donor:* Penguin Young Readers Group and Random House Children's Books. Not awarded in 2022.

Robert F. Sibert Medal. See "Literary Prizes, 2022" in Part 5.

Association of College and Research Libraries (ACRL)

ACRL Academic or Research Librarian of the Year Award ($5,000). For outstanding contribution to academic and research librarianship and library development. *Donor:* YBP Library Services. Not awarded in 2022.

ACRL/CLS Innovation in College Librarianship Award ($3,000). To academic librarians who show a capacity for innovation in the areas of programs, services, and operations or creating innovations for library colleagues that facilitate their ability to better serve the library's community. Not awarded in 2022.

ACRL/Routledge Distance Learning Librarian Conference Sponsorship Award ($1,200). To an ACRL member working in distance-learning librarianship in higher education. *Sponsor:* Routledge/Taylor & Francis. Not awarded in 2022.

ACRL/EBSS Distinguished Education and Behavioral Sciences Librarian Award. To an academic librarian who has made an outstanding contribution as an education and/or behavioral sciences librarian through accomplishments and service to the profession. *Donor:* John Wiley & Sons. Not awarded in 2022.

ACRL/STS Oberly Award for Bibliography in the Agricultural or Natural Sciences. Awarded biennially for the best English-language bibliography in the field of agriculture or a related science in the preceding two-year period. *Donor:* Eunice Rockwood Oberly. *Winners (2021):* Jen Kirk, government information librarian at Utah State University, and Helen F. Smith, agricultural sciences librarian at Pennsylvania State University, for An Inventory of Published Soil Surveys of the United States.

ACRL/WGSS Award for Career Achievement in Women and Gender Studies Librarianship ($750). To a distinguished academic librarian who has made outstanding contributions to women and gender studies through accomplishments and service to the profession. *Donor:* Duke University Press. Not awarded in 2022.

ACRL/WGSS Award for Significant Achievement in Women and Gender Studies Librarianship ($750). To a distinguished academic librarian who has made outstanding contributions to women and gender studies through accomplishments and service to the profession. *Donor:* Duke University Press. Not awarded in 2022.

Hugh C. Atkinson Memorial Award. *See under:* American Library Association.

CJCLS/EBSCO Community College Learning Resources Leadership Award ($750). Recognizes significant achievement in community college programs. *Donor:* EBSCO. Not awarded in 2022.

CJCL/EBSCO Community College Learning Resources Program Award ($750). Recognizes significant achievement in community college programs. *Donor:* EBSCO. Not awarded in 2022.

Miriam Dudley Instruction Librarian Award ($1,000). For a contribution to the advancement of bibliographic instruction in a college or research institution. Not awarded in 2022.

ESS De Gruyter European Librarianship Study Grant (€2,500). Supports research pertaining to European studies, librarianship, or the book trade. *Sponsor:* Walter de Gruyter Foundation for Scholarship and Research. Not awarded in 2022.

Excellence in Academic Libraries Awards ($3,000). To recognize outstanding college and university libraries. *Donor:* YBP Library Services. Not awarded in 2022.

Instruction Section Innovation Award ($3,000). To librarians or project teams in recognition of a project that demonstrates creative, innovative, or unique approaches to information literacy instruction or programming. *Donor:* ProQuest. Not awarded in 2022.

Marta Lange/Sage-CQ Press Award. To recognize an academic or law librarian for contributions to bibliography and information service in law or political science. *Donor:* Sage-CQ Press. Not awarded in 2022.

Katharine Kyes Leab and Daniel J. Leab American Book Prices Current Exhibition Catalog Awards (citations). For the best catalogs published by American or Canadian institutions in conjunction with exhibitions of books and/or manuscripts. *Sponsor:* Leab Endowment. Not awarded in 2022.

Ilene F. Rockman Instruction Publication of the Year Award ($3,000). To recognize an outstanding publication relating to instruction in a library environment. *Sponsor:* Emerald Group. Not awarded in 2022.

Black Caucus of the American Library Association (BCALA)

Baker & Taylor Support Staff Award. For dedicated and outstanding performance by a library support staff member. Not awarded in 2022.

BCALA Book Literary Award. *Winners:* (first novelist) Honorée Fanonne Jeffers for *The Love Songs of W.E.B. Du Bois* (HarperCollins); (fiction) S.A. Cosby for *Razorblade Tears* (Flatiron Books); (nonfiction) Cicely Tyson with Michelle Burford for *Just as I Am: A Memoir* (HarperCollins); (poetry) Jasmine Mans for *Black Girl, Call Home* (Berkley, an imprint of Penguin Random House); (Outstanding Contribution to Publishing Citation Award) Ibram X. Kendi and Keisha N. Blain (editors) for *Four Hundred Souls: A Community History of African America, 1619–2019* (One World, an imprint of Random House).

BCALA Trailblazers Award. Presented once every five years in recognition of outstanding and unique contributions to librarianship. *Winners (2021):* Shirley A. Coaston.

DEMCO/BCALA Excellence in Librarianship Award. To a librarian who has made significant contributions to promoting the status of African Americans in the library profession. Not awarded in 2022.

E.J. Josey Scholarship Award ($2,000). To African American students enrolled in or accepted by ALA-accredited programs who submit a three-to-five-page essay on social justice, voting rights and civic engagement, immigration, or diversity and inclusion, designing a program for your local community and including objectives and desired outcomes. *Winners:* Danette Jasper, University of Washington; Katrina Gardner, San Jose State University; Maleeha Killian, University of Wisconsin–Milwaukee; Devyn Wilder, University of Washington.

Core: Leadership, Infrastructure, Futures

ALA/AIA Library Building Awards. Cosponsored by the American Library Association (ALA) and the American Institute of Architects (AIA), the annual competition recognizes excellence in the architectural design and planning of libraries. The program is managed by the Core Library Buildings Awards Committee. *Winners:* Adams Street Library, Brooklyn, New York, Work Architecture Company (WORKac); Asante Library, Surprise, Arizona, Richard Kennedy Architects; Cruzen-Murray Library, Caldwell, Idaho, Richard Kennedy Architects; Indian Creek Library, Olathe, Kansas, Gould Evans; Martin Luther King Jr. Memorial Library, Washington, D.C., OTJ Architects (executive architect), Mecanoo (design architect).

Hugh C. Atkinson Memorial Award. *See under:* American Library Association.

John Cotton Dana Library Public Relations Awards ($10,000). To libraries or library organizations of all types for public relations programs or special projects ended during the preceding year. *Donors:* H.W. Wilson Foundation and EBSCO. *Winners:* Chattanooga (Tennessee) Public Library for the Here We Grow campaign to inform existing and potential customers of library services and materials through a series of TV commercials, online video ads, and billboards; Enoch Pratt Free Library in Baltimore, Maryland, for its Summer in a Box summer reading program modeled after popular subscription box services using a coordinated marketing effort that included targeted radio ads, social media, and television commercials combined with traditional media relations and digital strategies; Los Angeles County (California) Library for Laptop & Hotspot Loans, repurposing in-stock laptops and wireless hotspots during the pandemic to reach customers most in need; Niles-Maine District Library in Niles, Illinois, for its Not So Haunted Open House event to attract new patrons, re-engage lapsed patrons, and welcome patrons back to the library post-pandemic; Rochester (New York) Institute of Technology Library for an integrated campaign to increase the community's awareness of the library's temporary move to the campus hockey rink with a naming contest that resulted in "Wallace on Ice" as well as raising awareness of the benefits of the new space and an increased number of users; Tacoma (Washington) Public Library for a fundraising campaign to provide new services and broaden awareness of the library's Digital Media Labs—studios at the library utilized by filmmakers, musicians, audio engineers, students, podcasters, and other creatives in the arts community; Watertown (Massachusetts) Free Public Library for the Copy and Resist! marketing campaign to introduce young people to the library and empower the community to tell stories through zines; Wilmington (Delaware) Institute Free Library for a campaign to generate new library users and revitalize the downtown area, where the library is located.

Frederick G. Kilgour Award for Research in Library and Information Technology ($2,000 and expense-paid attendance at the ALA Annual Conference). To bring attention to research relevant to the development of information technologies. *Donor:* OCLC. Not awarded in 2022.

Christian Larew Memorial Scholarship in Library and Information Technology ($3,000). Provides tuition help for library school students to follow a career in the library and information technology field. *Winner:* Christoforos Sassaris.

Margaret Mann Citation (includes $2,000 scholarship award to the U.S. or Canadian library school of the winner's choice). To a cataloger or classifier for achievement in the areas of cataloging or classification. *Donor:* OCLC. *Winner:* Judith P. Cannan.

Ethnic and Multicultural Information and Exchange Round Table (EMIERT)

David Cohen/EMIERT Multicultural Award ($300). A biennial award to recognize articles of significant research and publication that increase understanding and promote multiculturalism in North American libraries. *Donor:* Routledge. *Winner (2022):* Dr. LaTesha Velez, University of North Carolina–Greensboro.

EMIERT Distinguished Librarian Award. Given biennially to recognize significant accomplishments in library services that are national or international in scope and that include improving, spreading, and promoting multicultural librarianship. *Winner (2021):* K.C. Boyd.

Coretta Scott King Book Awards. See "Literary Prizes, 2022" in Part 5.

Exhibits Round Table (ERT)

Christopher J. Hoy/ERT Scholarship ($5,000). To an individual or individuals who will work toward an M.L.S. degree in an ALA-accredited program. *Donor:* Family of Christopher Hoy. *Winner:* Maria Partida.

Freedom to Read Foundation

Freedom to Read Foundation Gordon M. Conable Conference Scholarship. To enable a library school student or new professional to attend the ALA Annual Conference. *Winner (2021):* Marisol Moreno Ortiz.

Freedom to Read Foundation Roll of Honor (citation): To recognize individuals who have contributed substantially to the foundation. *Winner:* Eldon Ray James.

Judith Krug Fund Banned Books Week Event Grants ($1,000–$2,500). To support activities that raise awareness of intellectual freedom and censorship issues during the annual Banned Books Week celebration. *Winners:* Athens-Clarke County (Georgia) Library for the permanent exhibit "Imagination Squared: Pathways to Resilience," featuring nearly 2,000 5" x 5" block squares decorated by community members on the theme What Resilience Means to You; Friends of the Chesapeake (Virginia) Public Library for making banned books the focus of its third annual Black Ink festival, which celebrates local authors of color; Kean University (Sayre, Pennsylvania) for its Common Read Program, which champions the idea that a single book can join a diverse community together and expand critical thinking habits for the institution at large; Mary Lou Johnson Hardin County (Ohio) Library for Books Unite Us: Expanding Our Cultural Horizons with a "world fair" of stations where patrons learn about banned books in diverse cultures and societies; Medina County (Ohio) District Library, collaborating with Medina County Juvenile Detention Center, Access the Arts, and all six district library locations to provide programming to children and teens ages 10–18 focused on Books Unite Us: Censorship Divides Us; Sidney Silverman Library at Bergen Community College in Paramus, New Jersey, for turning a selection of readings from banned books into scripts that will be read by students and faculty before a live audience in the student center and/or an outdoor classroom.

Gay, Lesbian, Bisexual, and Transgender Round Table (GLBTRT)

Larry Romans Mentorship Award ($1,000). To recognize librarians who, through their sustained mentoring efforts, have made a difference in our profession. Not awarded in 2022.

Stonewall Book Awards. See "Literary Prizes, 2022" in Part 5.

Government Documents Round Table (GODORT)

James Bennett Childs Award. To a librarian or other individual for distinguished lifetime contributions to documents librarianship. *Winner:* Dan Barkley, TRAIL processing coordinator at the University of Arizona Libraries in Tucson, Arizona.

GODORT-Sponsored ALA Emerging Leader Award. A leadership development program that enables newer library workers from across the country to participate in problem-solving work groups, network with peers, gain an inside look into ALA structure, and have an opportunity to serve the profession in a leadership capacity. *Winner:* Lauren Hall.

Bernadine Abbott Hoduski Founders Award. To recognize documents librarians who may not be known at the national level but who have made significant contributions to the field of local, state, federal, or international documents. *Winner:* Blaine Redemer from Illinois State Library in Springfield, Illinois.

Margaret T. Lane/Virginia F. Saunders Memorial Research Award. Not awarded in 2022.

NewsBank/Readex/GODORT/ALA Catharine J. Reynolds Research Grant. To documents librarians for travel and/or study in the field of documents librarianship or an area of study benefiting their performance. *Donor:* NewsBank and Readex Corporation. Not awarded in 2022.

ProQuest/GODORT/ALA Documents to the People Award. To an individual, library, organization, or noncommercial group that most effectively encourages or enhances the use of government documents in library services. *Winner:* Bobby Griffith from the University of North Texas Libraries in Denton, Texas.

Larry Romans Mentorship Award ($1,000). To recognize librarians who, through their sustained mentoring efforts, have made a difference in our profession. Not awarded in 2022.

W. David Rozkuszka Scholarship ($3,000). To provide financial assistance to individuals currently working with government documents in a library while completing a master's program in library science. Not awarded in 2022.

Intellectual Freedom Round Table (IFRT)

Gerald Hodges Intellectual Freedom Chapter Relations Award. *Winners:* Tennessee Library Association and Tennessee Association of School Librarians.

John Phillip Immroth Memorial Award for Intellectual Freedom ($500). For notable contribution to intellectual freedom fueled by personal courage. *Winner:* Terri Lesley from Campbell County Public Library in Gillette, Wyoming.

Eli M. Oboler Memorial Award. See "Literary Prizes, 2022" in Part 5.

Library History Round Table (LHRT)

Phyllis Dain Library History Dissertation Award. Given irregularly in odd-numbered years to the author of a dissertation treating the history of books, libraries, librarianship, or information science. *Winner (2021):* Dr. Cindy Anh Nguyen for "Reading and Misreading: The Social Life of Libraries and Colonial Control in Vietnam, 1865–1958."

Donald G. Davis Article Award (certificate). Awarded biennially for the best article written in English in the field of U.S. and Canadian library history. *Winner (2022):* Alex H. Poole for "'Tearing the Shroud of Invisibility': Communities of Protest Information Practices and the Fight for LGBTQ Rights in U.S. Librarianship" in *Library Quarterly* (Vol. 90, No. 4, 2020).

Eliza Atkins Gleason Book Award. Presented every third year to the author of a book in English in the field of library history. *Winner (2022):* Rebecka Taves Sheffield for *Documenting Rebellions: A Study of Four Lesbian and Gay Archives in Queer Times* (Litwin Books).

Justin Winsor Library History Essay Award ($500). To the author of an outstanding essay embodying original historical research on a significant subject of library history. Not awarded in 2022.

Library Research Round Table (LRRT)

Jesse H. Shera Award for Excellence in Published Research. For a research article on library and information studies published in English during the calendar year. *Winners:* Maria Cahill, Erin Ingram, and Soohyung Joo for "Storying Programs as Mirrors, Windows, and Sliding Glass Doors? Addressing Children's Need through Diverse Book Selection" in *Library Quarterly* (Vol. 91, No. 3, 2021).

Jesse H. Shera Award for Support of Dissertation Research. To recognize and support dissertation research employing exemplary research design and methods. *Winner:* Amber Matthews for "Advancing Anti-Racism in Public Libraries for Black Youth in Canada."

Map and Geospatial Information Round Table (MAGIRT)

MAGIRT Honors Award. To recognize outstanding achievement and major contributions to map and geospatial librarianship. Not awarded in 2022.

New Members Round Table (NMRT)

NMRT ALA Student Chapter of the Year Award. To an ALA student chapter for outstanding contributions to the association. *Winner:* San Jose State University.

NMRT Annual Conference Professional Development Attendance Award (formerly the Marshall Cavendish Award) (tickets to the ALA Annual Conference event of the winners' choice). *Winners:* Addie R. Holloman and Kristy Browning.

NMRT Professional Development Grant. To new NMRT members to encourage professional development and participation in national ALA and NMRT activities. Not awarded in 2022.

Shirley Olofson Memorial Award ($1,000). To an individual to help defray costs of attending the ALA Annual Conference. Not awarded in 2022.

Office for Diversity

Achievement in Library Diversity Research Honor. To an ALA member who has made significant contributions to diversity research in the profession. Not awarded in 2022.

Diversity Research Grants ($2,500). To the authors of research proposals that address critical gaps in the knowledge of diversity issues within library and information science. Not awarded in 2022.

Office for Information Technology Policy

L. Ray Patterson Copyright Award. To recognize an individual who supports the constitutional purpose of U.S. copyright law, fair use, and the public domain. *Sponsor:* Freedom to Read Foundation. *Winner:* James G. Neal, University Librarian Emeritus, Columbia University, New York, New York.

Office for Literacy and Outreach Services (OLOS)

Jean E. Coleman Library Outreach Lecture. *Sponsor:* OLOS Advisory Committee. *Lecturer:* Dr. Jeanie Austin.

Public Library Association (PLA)

Baker & Taylor Entertainment Audio Music/ Video Product Grant ($2,500 worth of audio music or video products). To help a public library to build or expand a collection of either or both formats. *Donor:* Baker & Taylor. Not awarded in 2022.

Gordon M. Conable Award ($1,500). To a public library staff member, library trustee, or public library for demonstrating a commitment to intellectual freedom and the Library Bill of Rights. *Sponsor:* LSSI. Not awarded in 2022.

EBSCO Excellence in Rural Library Service Award ($1,000). Honors a library serving a population of 10,000 or fewer that demonstrates excellence of service to its community as exemplified by an overall service program or a special program of significant accomplishment. *Donor:* EBSCO. Not awarded in 2022.

Helping Communities Come Together Award. Recognizes a public library's ability to identify community needs specifically in times of crisis and division and respond in creative and exemplary ways. *Donor:* The Singer Group. Not awarded in 2022.

John Iliff Award ($1,000). To a library worker, librarian, or library for the use of technology and innovative thinking as a tool to improve services to public library users. *Sponsor:* Innovative. Not awarded in 2022.

Allie Beth Martin Award ($3,000). To honor a public librarian who has demonstrated extraordinary range and depth of knowledge about books or other library materials and has distinguished ability to share that knowledge. *Donor:* Baker & Taylor. Not awarded in 2022.

New Leaders Travel Grants (up to $1,500). To PLA members who have not attended a major PLA continuing education event in the past five years. Not awarded in 2022.

PLA Library Innovation Award ($2,000). To recognize a public library's innovative achievement in planning and implementing a creative community service program. Not awarded in 2022.

Charlie Robinson Award ($1,000). To honor a public library director who, over a period of seven years, has been a risk-taker, an innovator, and/or a change agent in a public library. *Donor:* Baker & Taylor. Not awarded in 2022.

Romance Writers of America Library Grant ($4,500). To a library to build or expand a fiction collection and/or host romance fiction programming. *Donor:* Romance Writers of America. Not awarded in 2022.

Public Programs Office

Sara Jaffarian School Library Program Award for Exemplary Humanities Programming ($5,000). To honor a K–8 school library that has conducted an outstanding humanities program or series. *Donors:* Sara Jaffarian and ALA Cultural Communities Fund. *Winner:* Saint Marys (Pennsylvania) Area Middle School for Empathizing with Teens in Trauma: Terezín/Theresienstadt Museum Project.

Reference and User Services Association (RUSA)

Award for Excellence in Reference and Adult Library Services ($1,500). To recognize a library or library system for developing an imaginative and unique library resource to meet patrons' reference needs. *Donor:* Data Axle. *Winner:* Marie Concannon from the Government Information & Data Archives at the University of Missouri Library.

BRASS Academic Business Librarianship Travel Award ($1,250). To recognize a librarian who's new to the field of academic business librarianship and support his or her attendance at the ALA Annual Conference. *Donor:* Global Financial Data. *Winner:* Alison Messier from the W.E.B. Du Bois Library at the University of Massachusetts–Amherst.

BRASS Excellence in Business Librarianship Award ($4,000). For distinguished activities in the field of business librarianship *Donor:* Mergent by FTSE Russell. *Winner:* Wendy G. Pothier, University of New Hampshire.

BRASS Public Librarian Support Award ($1,250). To support attendance at the ALA Annual Conference of a public librarian who has performed outstanding business reference service. *Donor:* Morningstar. Not awarded in 2022.

BRASS Research Grant Award ($2,500). To an ALA member seeking support to conduct research in business librarianship. *Donor:* Emerald Publishing. Not awarded in 2022.

BRASS Student Travel Award ($1,250). To enable a student enrolled in an ALA-accredited master's program to attend the ALA Annual Conference. *Donor:* Simply Analytics. *Winner:* Jennifer Nelson from Neuse Regional Libraries in Kinston, North Carolina.

Sophie Brody Medal. See "Literary Prizes, 2022" in Part 5.

Federal Rising Stars Initiative. To a member who's new to the profession in a federal or armed forces library or government information management setting. Not awarded in 2022.

Francis Joseph Campbell Award. For a contribution of recognized importance to library service for the blind and physically handicapped. Not awarded in 2022.

CODES Zora Neale Hurston Award. To recognize the efforts of RUSA members in promoting African American literature. *Donor:* HarperCollins. Not awarded in 2022.

CODES Louis Shores Award (citation). To an individual, team, or organization in recognition of excellence in reviewing of books and other materials for libraries. Not awarded in 2022.

ETS Achievement Award. To recognize excellence in service to RUSA's Emerging Technologies Section (ETS). *Winner:* Courtney Renee McDonald from University Libraries at the University of Colorado–Boulder.

Federal Achievement Award. For achievement in the promotion of library and information service and the information profession in the federal community. *Winner:* Lee Lipscomb of the Federal Judicial Center in Washington, D.C.

HS Genealogy/History Achievement Award ($1,500). To encourage and commend professional achievement in historical reference and research librarianship. *Donor:* ProQuest. *Winner:* Marie Concannon from the Government Information & Data Archives at the University of Missouri Library.

HS History Research and Innovation Award ($2,500). To an M.L.S.-degreed librarian from an ALA-accredited school to facilitate and further research relating to history and history librarianship. *Donor:* Gale Cengage. *Winner:* Lara Nicosia, humanities librarian at the University of Rochester.

Margaret E. Monroe Library Adult Services Award ($1,250). To a librarian for his or her impact on library service to adults. *Donor:* NoveList. *Winner:* Timothy J. Dickey, Columbus (Ohio) Metropolitan Library.

Isadore Gilbert Mudge Award ($5,000). For distinguished contributions to reference librarianship. *Donor:* EBSCO. *Winner:* Melissa A. Wong from the University of Illinois–Urbana-Champaign.

RSS Service Achievement Award. To an RSS member who has made either a sustained contribution toward attaining the goals of the Reference Services Section or a single significant contribution that has resulted in a positive impact upon the work of the section. Not awarded in 2022.

RUSA Exceptional Service Award. To recognize exceptional service to patients, to the homebound, to people of all ages who live in group homes or residences, and to inmates, and to recognize professional leadership, effective interpretation of programs, pioneering activity, and significant research of experimental projects. Not awarded in 2022.

RUSA/Keystone Library Automation System (KLAS) & National Organization on Disability (NOD) Award ($1,000). To a library organization to recognize an innovative project to benefit people with disabilities. *Donor:* Keystone Systems. Not awarded in 2022.

John Sessions Memorial Award (plaque). To a library or library system in recognition of work with the labor community. *Donor:* Department for Professional Employees, AFL/CIO. *Winner:* Nash Photo Collection of the Manuscripts, Archives, and Special Collections department at Washington State University Libraries in Pullman, Washington.

STARS Mentoring Award ($1,250). To a library practitioner new to the field of interlibrary loan, resource sharing, or electronic reserves, to attend the ALA Annual Conference.

Donor: Atlas Systems. *Winner:* Jose F. Rodriguez, University of Miami.

STARS Virginia Boucher Distinguished ILL Librarian Award ($2,000). To a librarian for outstanding professional achievement, leadership, and contributions to interlibrary loan and document delivery. *Winner:* Miriam Wnuk, Northwest Interlibrary Loan and Resource Sharing Conference.

United for Libraries

Trustee Citation. To recognize public library trustees for individual service to library development on the local, state, regional, or national level. *Winner:* Susan McDermott.

United for Libraries/Baker & Taylor Awards. To recognize library friends groups for outstanding efforts to support their libraries. *Donor:* Baker & Taylor. Not awarded in 2022.

United for Libraries Major Benefactors Citation. To individuals, families, or corporate bodies that have made major benefactions to public libraries. Not awarded in 2022.

United for Libraries Public Service Award. To a legislator who has been especially supportive of libraries. Not awarded in 2022.

United for Libraries/Thrift Books Friends Grant ($850 plus free conference registration). Enables one member of a Friends of the Library group at a public library to attend the ALA Annual Conference. *Donor:* Thrift Books. Not awarded in 2022.

Young Adult Library Services Association (YALSA)

Baker & Taylor/YALSA Collection Development Grants ($1,000). To YALSA members who represent a public library and work directly with young adults for collection development materials for young adults. *Donor:* Book Wholesalers, Inc. *Winner:* Montrose (Colorado) Regional Library.

Baker & Taylor/YALSA Conference Scholarship Grants ($1,000). To young adult librarians in public or school libraries to attend the ALA Annual Conference for the first time. *Donor:* Baker & Taylor. Not awarded in 2022.

Dorothy Broderick Student Scholarship ($1,000). To enable a graduate student to attend the ALA Annual Conference for the first time. *Sponsor:* YALSA Leadership Endowment. Not awarded in 2022.

Margaret A. Edwards Award. See "Literary Prizes, 2022" in Part 5.

Great Books Giveaway (approximately 3,000 books, videos, CDs, and audiocassettes). Not awarded in 2022.

Frances Henne/YALSA Research Grant ($1,000). To provide seed money to an individual, institution, or group for a project to encourage research on library service to young adults. *Donor:* Greenwood Publishing Group. Not awarded in 2022.

William C. Morris YA Debut Award. See "Literary Prizes, 2022" in Part 5.

Michael L. Printz Award. See "Literary Prizes, 2022" in Part 5.

YALSA/MAE Award for Best Literature Program for Teens ($500 for the recipient plus $500 for his or her library). For an exemplary young adult reading or literature program. *Sponsor:* Margaret A. Edwards Trust. Not awarded in 2022.

YALSA Service to Young Adults Outstanding Achievement Award ($2,000). Biennial award to a YALSA member who has demonstrated unique and sustained devotion to young adult services. Not awarded in 2022. *Winner (2020):* Mega Subramaniam from the College of Information Studies (iSchool) at the University of Maryland.

Art Libraries Society of North America (ARLIS/NA)

ARLIS/NA Distinguished Service Award. To honor an individual whose exemplary service in art librarianship, visual resources curatorship, or a related field has made an outstanding national or international contribution to art information. *Winner:* Louis Adrean.

ARLIS/NA Wolfgang M. Freitag Internship Award ($3,000). To provide financial support for students preparing for a career in art librarianship or visual resource librarianship. *Winner:* Joana Stillwell.

Melva J. Dwyer Award. To the creators of exceptional reference or research tools relating to Canadian art and architecture. *Winner:* Dana Claxton and Timothy Long (editors) for The Sioux Project—Tatanka

Oyate (Information Office/MacKenzie Art Gallery).

Gerd Muehsam Award. To one or more graduate students in library science programs to recognize excellence in a graduate paper or project. *Winner:* Sam Regal.

H.W. Wilson Foundation Research Award ($3,000). For research activities by ARLIS/NA individual members in the fields of librarianship, visual resources curatorship, and the arts. *Winners:* Sandra Cowan for "The Research Methods of Artists"; Lelland Reed for "Curating the B-Roll: Scoping Practice of Unedited and Raw Audiovisual Materials in Memory Institutions."

George Wittenborn Memorial Book Awards. See "Literary Prizes, 2022" in Part 5.

Asian/Pacific Americans Libraries Association (APALA)

APALA Scholarship ($1,000). For a student of Asian or Pacific background who is enrolled in, or has been accepted into, a master's or doctoral degree program in library and/or information science at an ALA-accredited school. *Winner:* Hayley Park.

APALA Travel Grant ($500). To a U.S. or Canadian citizen or permanent resident enrolled in a master's or doctoral degree program in library and/or information science at an ALA-accredited school, or a professional possessing a master's degree or doctoral degree in library and/or information science, to enable attendance at the ALA Annual Conference. *Winner:* Kristine Techavanich.

Emerging Leaders Sponsorship. To enable newer library workers to participate in problem-solving work groups, network with peers, gain an inside look into ALA structure, and have an opportunity to serve the profession. *Winner:* Noelle Cruz.

Association for Information Science and Technology (ASIS&T)

ASIS&T Award of Merit. For an outstanding contribution to the field of information science. *Winner:* Harry Bruce.

ASIS&T Best Information Science Book. *Winner:* Kate Crawford for *Atlas of AI: Power, Politics, and the Planetary Costs of Artificial Intelligence* (Yale University Press).

ASIS&T Doctoral Dissertation Proposal Scholarship ($2,000). *Winner:* Nilavra Bhattacharya for "A Longitudinal Study to Understand University Students' Searching as a Learning Process."

ASIS&T Outstanding Information Science Teacher Award ($1,500). To recognize the unique teaching contribution of an individual as a teacher of information science. *Winner:* Kathleen (Kate) McDowell from the School of Information Sciences at the University of Illinois–Urbana-Champaign.

ASIS&T ProQuest Doctoral Dissertation Award ($1,000 plus expense-paid attendance at the ASIS&T Annual Meeting). *Winner:* Jelina Haines for "Researching the Knowledge Journey Practices of Indigenous Elders Relevant to the Younger Generation: A Community-Based Participatory Study."

ASIS&T Research in Information Science Award. For a systematic program of research in a single area at a level beyond the single study, recognizing contributions in the field of information science. *Winner:* Heather O'Brien, University of British Columbia iSchool.

James M. Cretsos Leadership Award. To recognize new ASIS&T members who have demonstrated outstanding leadership qualities in professional ASIS&T activities. *Winner:* Bhakti Gala from the School of Library and Information Science at Central University of Gujarat.

Watson Davis Award for Service. For outstanding continuous contributions and dedicated service to the society. *Winner:* Soo Young Rieh, University of Texas–Austin.

Louise Lunin Award. To recognize individuals who have made noteworthy contributions to the practice of information science and technology through leadership, mentoring, and innovation. *Winner:* Zhe He from Florida State University in Tallahassee, Florida.

Pratt Severn Best Student Research Paper Award. To encourage student research and writing in the field of information science. *Winner:* Jesse Ludington for "Social Media as Archival Practice and Paradigm Shifter in United States Death Care."

John Wiley Best *JASIST* Paper Award. *Winners:* Mikael Laakso, Lisa Matthias, and Najko Jahn for "Open Is Not Forever: A Study of Vanished Open Access Journals" (*Journal of the Association for Information Science & Technology*, Vol. 72, Issue 9).

Bob Williams Research Grant Award. Not awarded in 2022.

Bob Williams Research Paper Award. Not awarded in 2022.

Association for Library and Information Science Education (ALISE)

ALISE Award for Professional Contribution. *Winner:* Karen Snow, River Forest, Illinois.

ALISE Best Conference Paper Award. *Winners:* Beth Patin and Tyler Youngman, Syracuse University, for "The Sankofa Intervention: Combatting the Epistemicide of Parasitic Omission through Civil Rights Literacy in Community Information Contexts."

ALISE Community conn@CT Mini-Grants. Not awarded in 2022.

ALISE Diversity Travel Award ($750 for travel expenses, complimentary registration to the ALISE annual conference, and a one-year student membership). To increase diversity in LIS education/research for an individual who wishes to address issues of diversity through doctoral study or teaching. *Winner:* Diogenes da Silva Santos from the University of Missouri in Columbia, Missouri.

ALISE Excellence in Teaching Award. *Winner:* Lisa Hussey from Simmons University in Boston, Massachusetts.

ALISE/Eugene Garfield Doctoral Dissertation Competition. *Winner:* Deborah Garwood from Drexel University in Philadelphia, Pennsylvania, for "To Our Health: A Case Study of Archivists' Information Work and Information Practices at History of Medicine Collections in Philadelphia."

ALISE/Norman Horrocks Leadership Award. To recognize a new ALISE member who has demonstrated outstanding leadership qualities in professional ALISE activities. Not awarded in 2022.

ALISE/Pratt-Severn Faculty Innovation Award. To recognize innovation by full-time faculty members in incorporating evolving information technologies in the curricula of accredited master's degree programs in library and information studies. *Winner:* Jenna Hartel, University of Toronto, for the INFIDEOS series.

ALISE/ProQuest Methodology Paper Competition. *Winner:* Nitzan Koren, David Weintrop, and Mega Subramaniam from the University of Maryland in College Park, Maryland, for "Using Design Based Implementation Research Method to Create Computational Thinking Assessment Tools for Youth Programs in Public Libraries."

ALISE Research Grant Competition (one or more grants totaling $5,000). *Winner:* Lynne Bowker, University of Ottawa, for Promoting Multilingual Scholarly Communication: Using Plain Language and Machine Translation as Stepping Stone.

ALISE Service Award. *Winner:* Stephen Bajjaly from Wayne State University in Detroit, Michigan.

ALISE/Jean Tague Sutcliffe Doctoral Student Research Poster Competition. *Winners:* (first place) Philips Ayeni from McGill University in Montreal, Quebec, Canada; (second place) Li-Min Huang from the University of Tennessee in Knoxville, Tennessee; (third place) Ting Wang from Emporia State University in Emporia, Kansas.

ALISE/University of Washington Information School Youth Services Graduate Student Travel Award. To support the costs associated with travel to and participation in the ALISE Annual Conference. *Winner:* Julia Burns Petrella, University of Illinois–Urbana-Champaign.

ALIS/Connie Van Fleet Award for Research Excellence in Public Library Services to Adults. To recognize LIS research concerning services to adults in public libraries. *Winner:* Jenny Bossaller from the University of Missouri in Columbia, Missouri.

ALISE/Bohdan S. Wynar Research Paper Competition. *Winners:* Xiaofeng Li, Clarion University of Pennsylvania, and Shelly Mathis, Grand County (Colorado) Library District, for "My Mom Recommended It to Me."

Doctoral Students to ALISE Grant. To support the attendance of one or more promising LIS doctoral students at the ALISE Annual Conference. *Sponsor:* Libraries Unlimited/

Linworth. *Winner:* Kaeli Nieves-Whitmore, University of Alabama.

Association of Jewish Libraries (AJL)

AJL Scholarships ($1,000). For students enrolled in accredited library schools who plan to work as Judaica librarians. Not awarded in 2022.

Fanny Goldstein Merit Award. To honor loyal and ongoing contributions to the association and to the profession of Jewish librarianship. *Winner:* Lisa Silverman.

Life Membership Award. To recognize outstanding leadership and professional contributions to the association and to the profession of Jewish librarianship. Not awarded in 2022.

Association of Research Libraries (ARL)

ARL Diversity Scholarships (stipend of up to $10,000). To a varying number of M.L.S. students from underrepresented groups who are interested in careers in research libraries. *Sponsors:* ARL member libraries and the Institute of Museum and Library Services. *Winners:* Arianna Alcaraz, University of Alberta; Melissa Aslo De La Torre, University of Texas–Austin; Imani Benjamin-Wharton, Valdosta State University; Jennifer Nguyen Bernal, University of California–Los Angeles; David Castro, San Jose State University; Amanda Chaplin, University at Albany, SUNY; Ariana Cook, Syracuse University; Kesheena Doctor, San Jose State University; Blanca Garcia-Barron, San Jose State University; Zahra Garrett, Simmons University; sourav guha, San Jose State University; Vita Kurland, New York University and Long Island University; Amina Malik, University of Illinois–Urbana-Champaign; Christiana McClain, University of Maryland; Ezekiel Amari McGee, Syracuse University; Inbar Michael, University of Illinois–Urbana-Champaign; Alona Norwood, University of North Carolina–Chapel Hill; Vivian Poon, University of Alberta; Ruth Xing, Syracuse University.

Association of Seventh-Day Adventist Librarians

D. Glenn Hilts Scholarship ($1,500) for a member or members of the Seventh-Day Adventist Church who are enrolled in a graduate library program. Not awarded in 2022.

Beta Phi Mu

Beta Phi Mu Award. *See under:* American Library Association.

Eugene Garfield Doctoral Dissertation Fellowships ($3,000). *Winners:* Qiuyan Guo, University of Illinois, for "Exploring Chinese Celebrity Fans' Online Information Behaviors and Understandings of Their Fandom"; Carina Guzman, University of Toronto, for "Stor(y)ing mi Desmadre: Trans-Feminist and Queer Community Archival and Digital Custodial Praxes in Latin America"; Kaeli Nieves-Whitmore, University of Alabama, for "Students' Experiences of Library Anxiety in Physical Academic Library Space"; Cynthia Orozco, University of California–Los Angeles, for "Community College Archives as Activism: A Case Study of a Faculty-Library Oral History Partnership Assignment"; Grace Seo, University of Missouri, for "Sustaining Open Educational Resources Initiatives in Higher Education: Case Studies and Analysis"; Paul Thomas, Emporia State University, for "The Information Behavior of Wikipedia Fan Editors: A Digital Autoethnography."

Harold Lancour Scholarship for Foreign Study ($1,750). For graduate study in a country related to the applicant's work or schooling. Not awarded in 2022.

Sarah Rebecca Reed Scholarship ($2,250). For study at an ALA-accredited library school. Not awarded in 2022.

Frank B. Sessa Scholarship for Continuing Professional Education ($1,500). For continuing education for a Beta Phi Mu member. *Winners:* Melinda Berg, University of South Florida, Beta Phi Chapter; Molly Brown, Simmons College, Beta Beta Chapter; Diane Dias De Fazio, Pratt Institute, Theta Chapter; Livia Garza, University of Illinois–Urbana-Champaign, Alpha Chapter; Hazlett Henderson, Emporia State

University, Beta Epsilon Chapter; Kevin Kelley, University of Illinois–Urbana-Champaign, Alpha Chapter; Gail Kuroda, University of Hawaii–Manoa, Xi Chapter; Sarah Cruz Mendoza, University of South Florida, Beta Phi Chapter; Chrissy O'Grady, University of Illinois–Urbana-Champaign, Alpha Chapter; Caterina Reed, University at Buffalo, Beta Delta Chapter.

Blanche E. Woolls Scholarship ($2,250). For a beginning student in school library media services. Not awarded in 2022.

Bibliographical Society of America (BSA)

BSA Fellowships ($1,500–$6,000). For scholars involved in bibliographical inquiry and research in the history of the book trades and in publishing history. *Winners:* (Fredson Bowers Award) Charles Johanningsmeier for "American Literature Goes Global: Tauchnitz's Collection of British & American Authors"; (BSA-ASECS Fellowship for Bibliographical Studies in the Eighteenth Century) Tom Hillard for "Sally Sayward Wood: A Bibliographical Study and Critical Edition"; (BSA Peck-Stacpoole Fellowship for Early Career Collections Professionals) Saeko Suzuki for "The Representation of a Woman in Woodblock-Print Illustrated Books: A Political Device in Mid-Nineteenth Century Japan"; Krystle Trevisan, Anna Scala, and Marco Palma, for "Incunabula in Malta"; (BSA-Pine Tree Foundation Fellowship in Culinary Bibliography) Rose Byfleet for "'Libri Profumati': Caterina Sforza and the Origin of Perfume at the Medici Fonderia"; (BSA-Pine Tree Foundation Fellowship in Hispanic Bibliography) Matilde Malaspina for "Escritos de mano, de muy mala letra': A Study of the Rough Copy of Hernando Colón's Libro de los Epítomes"; (BSA-St. Louis Mercantile Library Fellowship for Research in North American Bibliography) Sarah Heying for "Jewelle Gomez's Speculative Archive of Queer Afro-Indigenous Vampire Mythology"; (BSA Short Term Fellowships) Laura Helton for "Black Lyric Bibliography: Catherine Latimer's Poetry and Songs Index"; Renske Hoff for "Between Making

and Using: The Performativity and Functionality of Dutch 'Hybrid Books' Around the Turn of the Sixteenth Century"; Vaibhav Singh for "Lithography in Nineteenth Century Marathi Printing and Publishing"; Maria Beliaeva Solomon for "Recovering the Revue des Colonies (1834–1842): The First French Periodical for and by People of Color"; (Caxton Club Fellowship for Midwestern Bibliographers) Charles Johanningsmeier for "American Literature Goes Global: Tauchnitz's 'Collection of British and American Authors'"; (The Katharine Pantzer Junior Fellowship in the British Book Trades) Lindsey Eckert for "Odious! In Boards': Byron, John Murray, and Binding Poetry"; (Katharine F. Pantzer Senior Fellow in the British Book Trades) Sandro Jung for "Eighteenth-Century British Regional Book Illustrations of Literature: Models, Production, and Commercial Use in the North of England"; (Reese Fellowship for American Bibliography and the History of the Book in the Americas) Emily Floyd for "Jesuits, Saints, and Regional Exchange: Eighteenth-Century Printing in Quito"; (Charles J. Tanenbaum Fellowship in Cartographical Bibliography) Roberto Chauca Tapia for "A River of Names"; (Dorothy Porter Wesley Fellowship) Sara Johnson for "Moreau de Saint-Méry: A Slaveholding Bibliophile."

William L. Mitchell Prize for Research on Early British Serials ($1,000). Awarded triennially for the best single work published in the previous three years. *Winner (2021):* Dr. Megan Peiser for "William Lane and the Minerva Press in the Review Periodical, 1790–1820" in *Romantic Textualities* (Summer 2020).

New Scholars Program. To promote the work of scholars who are new to the field of bibliography. *Winners:* (Pantzer New Scholar) Eve Houghton for "'I Am Always Sorry to Antagonize Collectors': Henrietta Bartlett and the 1916 Census of Shakespeare Quartos"; (Malkin New Scholar) Christopher Adams for "'Could You Make It Rather More of a He and She Picture?': The Queer Dust-Jacket and Postwar British Fiction"; (BSA New Scholar) Liza Mardoyan for "Decorative Bird Initials in the Medieval Armenian Manuscript Culture."

St. Louis Mercantile Library Prize ($2,000). Awarded triennially for outstanding scholarship in the bibliography of American history and literature. *Sponsor:* St. Louis Mercantile Library, University of Missouri, St. Louis. *Winners (2020):* Dr. Lindsay DiCuirci for *Colonial Revivals: The Nineteenth-Century Lives of Early American Books* (University of Pennsylvania Press); Dr. Derrick R. Spires for *The Practice of Citizenship: Black Politics and Print Culture in the Early United States* (University of Pennsylvania Press).

Justin G. Schiller Prize for Bibliographical Work on Pre-20th Century Children's Books ($2,000). A triennial award to encourage scholarship in the bibliography of historical children's books. *Winner (2022):* Hannah Field for *Playing with the Book: Victorian Movable Picture Books and the Child Reader* (University of Minnesota Press).

Catholic Library Association

Regina Medal. For continued, distinguished contribution to the field of children's literature. *Winner:* Sophie de Mullenheim.

Chinese American Librarians Association (CALA)

CALA Conference Travel Grant. Not awarded in 2022.

CALA Distinguished Service Award. To a librarian who has been a mentor, role model, and leader in the fields of library and information science. *Winner:* Weiling Liu.

CALA Outstanding Library Leadership Award in Memory of Dr. Margaret Chang Fung. *Winner:* Dr. Lian Ruan.

CALA President's Recognition Award. *Winners:* (individuals) Crystal Chen, Feng-Ru Sheu, Jianye He, Lei Jin, Leping He, Lijuan Xu, Jennifer Woo, Min Tong, Sai Deng, Ying Liao, Yuan Li, Zeng Yang; (teams) Newsletter Subcommittee, Web Committee, *International Journal of Librarianship* (*IJOL*) Editorial Team, CALASYS Team CALA 50th Anniversary Taskforce.

CALA Scholarship of Library and Information Science ($1,000). Not awarded in 2022.

Sheila Suen Lai Scholarship ($500). Not awarded in 2022.

Lisa Zhao Scholarship ($500). Not awarded in 2022.

Coalition for Networked Information (CNI)

Paul Evan Peters Award. Awarded biennially to recognize notable and lasting international achievements relating to high-performance networks and the creation and use of information resources and services that advance scholarship and intellectual productivity. *Sponsors:* Association of Research Libraries, CNI, EDUCAUSE. *Winner (2022):* Paul Courant, University of Michigan.

Paul Evan Peters Fellowship ($5,000 a year for two years). Awarded biennially to a student or students pursuing a graduate degree in librarianship or the information sciences. *Sponsors:* Association of Research Libraries, CNI, EDUCAUSE. *Winners (2020):* Hugh Paterson III and Jamie Flood.

Council on Library and Information Resources (CLIR)

CLIR Postdoctoral Fellowships in Scholarly Information Resources. *Current fellows (2022):* Jason M. Chernesky, Rachel Corbman, Taiwo Lasisi, Katie Mackinnon, Heidi Nicholls, Erin Yunes.

Digitizing Hidden Special Collections and Archives Awards. *Sponsor:* Andrew W. Mellon Foundation. *Winners (2022):* Mid-Atlantic Regional Moving Image Archive (MARMIA) for "Broadcasting Baltimore: Digitizing Hidden Histories in the WJZ-TV Collection"; National Museum of African American History and Culture, Clark Atlanta University, Florida A&M University, Jackson State University, Tuskegee University, and Texas Southern University for "History and Culture Access Consortium for HBCU Museums and Archives: Lifting Every Voice"; Japanese American National Museum for "Unboxed: Revealing Untold Stories of Japanese Americans During World War II"; University of California–Irvine for "Prison Pandemic: Digitizing Incarcerated

People's Experiences during COVID-19"; Office of the Treaty Commissioner for "Amplifying Indigenous Oral Histories of Treaties in Canada"; Christiansburg Institute and Virginia Polytechnic Institute and State University for "Changing the Narrative: Modeling Equitable Stewardship of African American Storytelling & History"; College of the Holy Cross for "Digitizing the Deaf Catholic Archives: A Project to Open and Provide Access to a Collection of Print and (Audio)Visual Materials, Which Document the History, Culture and Religious Education of Deaf Catholics in the United States and Beyond"; Sealaska Heritage Institute for "The Indigenous Eye–Digitizing the Cyril George Photograph Collection"; Creative Growth Art Center for "Fifty Years of Creative Growth: How a Grassroots Art Center in Oakland, California, Amplified the Voices of People with Developmental Disabilities and Changed the Contemporary Art World"; Haida Gwaii Museum for "Digitizing Haida Narratives and Oral History"; Northeastern University; the American Antiquarian Society; The ArQuives; The Lesbian, Gay, Bisexual, and Transgender Community Center; Louise Lawrence Transgender Archives; ONE Archives at the University of Southern California Libraries; the Tretter Collection of the University of Minnesota; Harry Ransom Center of the University of Texas–Austin; Transgender Archives of the University of Victoria; OUTWORDS; and the University of Winnipeg for "'Y'all Better Quiet Down': Trans BIPOC Digitization Initiative"; Iowa State University, the African American Museum of Iowa, Des Moines Public Library, Grout Museum District, State Historical Museum of Iowa, Nodaway Valley Historical Museum, Grinnell College, and Fort Des Moines Museum & Education Center for "Amplifying Black Voices in Iowa"; Washington State University, American Philosophical Society, and the University of Washington in partnership with Coeur d'Alene Tribe, Confederated Tribes of the Colville Reservation, Confederated Salish and Kootenai Tribes, Spokane Tribe of Indians, Confederated Tribes of Warm Spring, Nimíipuu (Nez Perce) Tribe, Quinault Indian Nation, Snoqualmie Indian Tribe, and the Yakama Nation for "Native

Northwest Online: Connecting Communities and Collections through Collaborative Curation"; Juan Antonio Corretjer Puerto Rican Cultural Center for "Digitizing the Barrio: Documenting and Disseminating the Puerto Rican Experience in Chicago through Community-Based Inquiry"; Beck Cultural Exchange Center for "Cherished Institutions Project: Digitizing the History of Education of the Black Community in Knoxville, Tennessee."

EDUCAUSE

EDUCAUSE Community Leadership Award. *Winner:* Lisa A. Stephens, assistant dean at the School of Engineering and Applied Sciences at the University at Buffalo and senior strategist for academic innovation at SUNY.

EDUCAUSE DEI Leadership Award. To acknowledge and celebrate exemplary leadership in advancing equity, diversity, and inclusion. *Winner:* Keith W. "Mac" McIntosh, vice-president and chief information officer for the University of Richmond.

EDUCAUSE Leadership Award. To acknowledge leadership in higher education information technology. *Winners:* Michael Berman, former chief information officer for California State University, and Sue B. Workman, former vice-president and chief information officer for Case Western Reserve University.

EDUCAUSE Rising Star Award. To recognize early-career information technology professionals who demonstrate exceptional achievement in the area of information technology in higher education. *Winner:* Joseph Licata, product management consultant and former associate chief information officer for Maricopa County Community Colleges District.

Friends of the National Library of Medicine

Michael E. DeBakey Librarian Outreach and Community Collaboration Award. To recognize outstanding service and contributions to rural and underserved communities by a practicing health sciences librarian. *Winner:* Steve Wilson, web architect and outreach librarian at the Charles S. and Donna H. Bryan School of Medicine Library, University of South Carolina.

Institute of Museum and Library Services

National Medal for Museum and Library Service. For extraordinary civic, educational, economic, environmental, and social contributions ($5,000). *Winners:* (libraries) Amistad Research Center in New Orleans, Louisiana; St. Louis County (Missouri) Library; Wilmington (Delaware) Institute Free Library; (museums) Asheville (North Carolina) Art Museum; Burke Museum of Natural History and Culture in Seattle, Washington; Oakland (California) Museum of California.

International Association of School Librarians (IASL)

Ken Haycock Leadership Development Grant ($1,000). Awarded in odd-numbered years to enable applicants from any nation to attend their first IASL Annual Conference. Not awarded in 2021.

Jean Lowrie Leadership Development Grant ($1,000). Awarded in even-numbered years to enable applicants from developing nations to attend their first IASL Annual Conference. *Winner (2022):* Poonam Gola, India.

Takeshi Murofushi Research Award ($500). For funding a research project, preferably of international interest. *Winners:* Dr. Rashmi Kumbar, Dr. Pradeepa Wijetunge, Sagender Singh Parmar, Dr. Ruwan Gamage, and Uditha Alahakoon.

Diljit Singh Leadership Development Grant ($1,000). To enable applicants from developing nations to attend their first IASL conference. *Winner:* L.H.W.R. Silva, Sri Lanka.

International Board on Books for Young People (IBBY)

IBBY-Asahi Reading Promotion Award ($10,000). Awarded biennially to projects that are making a lasting contribution to reading promotion for young people. *Offered by:* International Board on Books for Young People. *Sponsor:* Asahi Shimbun. *Winner (2022):* Ilitaqsinniq–Pinnguaqta, a community-based early childhood education program designed and centered on Inuit societal values, Rankin Inlet, Nunavut, Canada.

International Federation of Library Associations and Institutions (IFLA)

International Federation of Library Associations and Institutions (IFLA) Honorary Fellow. For distinguished service to IFLA. Not awarded in 2022.

IFLA Medal. To a person or organization for a distinguished contribution either to IFLA or to international librarianship. *Winners:* Lorcan Dempsey and Filiberto Felipe Martínez Arellano.

Jay Jordan IFLA/OCLC Early Career Development Fellowships. To library and information science professionals from countries with developing economies who are in the early stages of their careers. Not awarded in 2022.

Dr. Shawky Salem Conference Grant (up to $1,900). To enable an expert in library and information science who is a national of an Arab country to attend the IFLA Conference for the first time. Not awarded in 2022.

Library Journal

Gale/*Library Journal* Library of the Year. *Sponsor:* Gale Cengage Learning. Not awarded in 2022.

Library Journal Best Small Library in America ($20,000). To honor a public library that profoundly demonstrates outstanding service to populations of 25,000 or fewer. *Cosponsors: Library Journal* and the Bill and Melinda Gates Foundation. Not awarded in 2022.

Library Journal Librarian of the Year. *Winners:* All Library Staff for their work throughout the pandemic.

Library Journal Paralibrarian of the Year Award. Not awarded in 2022.

Library of Congress

Kluge Fellowships in Digital Studies. To promote examination of the impact of the digital revolution on society, culture, and international relations using the library's collections and resources. Not awarded in 2022.

Library of Congress Literacy Awards. *Sponsor:* David M. Rubenstein. *Winners:* (David M. Rubenstein Prize, $150,000, for a groundbreaking or sustained record of advancement of literacy by any individual or entity) Street Child, London, U.K., and Washington, D.C., for outstanding and measurable contribution to increasing literacy levels in multiple parts of the world; (American Prize, $50,000, for a project developed and implemented successfully during the past decade for combating illiteracy and/or aliteracy) Make Way for Books, Tucson, Arizona; (International Prize, $50,000, for the work of an individual, nation, or nongovernmental organization working in a specific country or region) Young African Refugees for Integral Development (YARID), Kampala, Uganda.

Library of Congress Prize for American Fiction. See "Literary Prizes, 2022" in Part 5.

Medical Library Association (MLA)

Virginia L. and William K. Beatty MLA Volunteer Service Award. To recognize a medical librarian who has demonstrated outstanding, sustained service to the Medical Library Association and the health sciences library profession. *Winner:* Ryan Harris.

Estelle Brodman Award for the Academic Medical Librarian of the Year. To honor significant achievement, potential for leadership, and continuing excellence at midcareer in the area of academic health sciences librarianship. Not awarded in 2022.

Lois Ann Colaianni Award for Excellence and Achievement in Hospital Librarianship. To a member of MLA who has made significant contributions to the profession in the area of overall distinction or leadership in hospital librarianship. *Winner:* Lisa Huang.

Consumer Health Librarian of the Year Award. To recognize those who demonstrate excellence in consumer health information services, promote innovation and collaboration, and provide examples to follow for other consumer health librarians. Not awarded in 2022.

Cunningham Memorial International Fellowships. For health sciences librarians from countries outside the United States and Canada to provide for attendance at the MLA Annual Meeting and observation and supervised work in one or more medical libraries. *Winner:* Kubra Zayum Gedik.

Louise Darling Medal. For distinguished achievement in collection development in the health sciences. *Winner:* Sarah McClung.

Janet Doe Lectureship. *Winner:* Michael R. Kronenfeld for "Health Science Libraries in the Emerging Digital Information Era: Charting the Course."

EBSCO/MLA Annual Meeting Grants (up to $1,000). To enable four health sciences librarians to attend the MLA Annual Meeting. *Winners:* Kelsa Bartley, Becca Billings, Valerie Lookingbill, Tenley Sablatzky.

Ida and George Eliot Prize. To recognize a work published in the preceding calendar year that has been judged most effective in furthering medical librarianship. *Winners:* Laura Menard, Amy Blevins, Daniel J. Trujillo, and Kenneth H. Lazarus for "Integrating Evidence-Based Medicine Skills into a Medical School Curriculum: A Quantitative Outcomes Assessment."

Carla J. Funk Governmental Relations Award ($500). To recognize a medical librarian who has demonstrated outstanding leadership in the area of governmental relations at the federal, state, or local level and who has furthered the goal of providing quality information for improved health. *Sponsor:* Kent A. Smith. *Winner:* Sandra L. Bandy.

T. Mark Hodges International Service Award. To honor outstanding achievement in promoting, enabling, or delivering improved health information internationally. *Winner:* Erin RB Eldermire.

David A. Kronick and Charles W. Sargent Visiting Fellowship ($1,000). *Sponsor:* Bowden-Massey Foundation. Not awarded in 2022.

Joseph Leiter NLM/MLA Lectureship. *Winner:* Amanda Rinehart for "Data Management, Sharing and Re-use."

Donald A.B. Lindberg Research Fellowship ($10,000). To fund research aimed at expanding the research knowledge base, linking the information services provided by librarians to improved health care and advances in biomedical research. *Winner:* Jonathan Eldredge for "Evidence Based Practice: A Practical Guide for Health Information Professionals."

Lucretia W. McClure Excellence in Education Award. To an outstanding educator in the field of health sciences librarianship and informatics. *Winner:* Andrew S. Hamilton.

John P. McGovern Award Lectureship. *Winner:* Mona Hanna-Attisha, M.D. for "What the Eyes Don't See: A Story of Crisis, Resistance, and Hope in an American City."

Medical Informatics Section Career Development Grant ($1,500). To support a career development activity that will contribute to advancement in the field of medical informatics. Not awarded in 2022.

Erich Meyerhoff Prize. For the best unpublished essay on the history of medicine and allied sciences written by a health sciences librarian. *Sponsor:* MLA History of the Health Sciences Section. Not awarded in 2022.

MLA Award for Distinguished Public Service. *Winner:* Francis S. Collins, M.D., Ph.D., director of National Institutes of Health.

MLA Chapter Project of the Year Award. *Winner:* Midcontinental Chapter of the Medical Library Association for its project to publish the chapter Annual Meeting Proceedings.

MLA Continuing Education Grant ($100–$500). *Winner:* Shannon Compton, Ph.D.

MLA Scholarship (up to $5,000). For graduate study at an ALA-accredited library school. *Winner:* Kristen Burroughs.

MLA Scholarship for Under-Represented Students (up to $5,000). For graduate study at an ALA-accredited library school. *Winner:* Jasmine Goodman.

Marcia C. Noyes Award. For an outstanding contribution to medical librarianship. *Winner:* Jane Blumenthal.

President's Award. To an MLA member for a notable or important contribution made during the past association year. *Winners:* Hospital Library Advocacy Team (Ellen M. Aaronson, Heidi Sue Adams, Brian Lee Baker, Helen-Ann Brown Epstein, Julia Esparza, Michelle Kraft, Elizabeth Laera, Heather J. Martin, Angela Spencer, and Jill M. Tarabula) for their work developing the "Partner with Hospital Librarians to Improve Patient Care" statement.

Rittenhouse Award. For the best unpublished paper on medical librarianship submitted by a student enrolled in, or having been enrolled in, a course for credit in an ALA-accredited library school or a trainee in an internship program in medical librarianship. *Donor:* Rittenhouse Book Distributors. Not awarded in 2022.

Frank Bradway Rogers Information Advancement Award. To recognize outstanding contributions to the application of technology to the delivery of health science information, to the science of information, or to the facilitation of the delivery of health science information. Not awarded in 2022.

Music Library Association (MLA)

Vincent H. Duckles Award. For the best book-length bibliography or other tool in music. *Winner:* Alexander Sanchez-Behar for *John Adams: A Research and Information Guide* (Routledge).

Dena Epstein Award for Archival and Library Research in American Music. To support research in archives or libraries internationally on any aspect of American music. *Winners:* Michael Cooper for his book-length biography project about Margaret Allison Bonds; Michael Kramer for his book project, "This Machine Kills Fascists: What the Folk Music Revival Can Teach Us About the Digital Age"; David Rugger for his book project, "Simple Man: Klaus Nomi's Life and Art"; Emmalouise St. Amand for her dissertation on semi-professional and amateur Black girl groups in New York City between 1950 and 1965.

Kevin Freeman Travel Grants. To colleagues who are new to the profession to enable them to attend the MLA Annual Meeting. *Winners:* Margot Cuddihy, Geo Flores, Jackson Harmeyer, Mia Watts.

Walter Gerboth Award. To members of the association who are in the first five years of their professional library careers to assist research in progress in music or music librarianship. Not awarded in 2022.

Richard S. Hill Award. For the best article on music librarianship or article of a music-bibliographic nature. *Winners:* Elizabeth Berndt-Morris and Sandi-Jo Malmon for "Surveying Composers: Methods of Distribution, Discoverability, and Accessibility of Their Works and the Corresponding Impact on Library Collections" in *Fontes Artis Musicae* 67, no. 2 (2020): 81–98.

MLA Citation. Awarded in recognition of contributions to the profession over a career. *Winner:* Randye Jones.

MLA Diversity Scholarship ($3,000). Provides candidates from underrepresented groups with the opportunity to pursue a master's degree in library and information science. *Winners:* Michelle Rivera and Jade Vaughan.

Eva Judd O'Meara Award. For the best review published in *Notes. Winner:* K. Dawn Grapes for a review of *The Norton Guide to Teaching Music History* in *Notes* 77, no. 2 (2020): 310–312.

A. Ralph Papakhian Special Achievement Award. To recognize extraordinary service to the profession of music librarianship over a relatively short period of time. Not awarded in 2022.

National Library Service for the Blind and Print Disabled, Library of Congress

Library of the Year Awards ($1,000). *Winner:* (Regional Library of the Year) Washington Talking Book and Braille Library in Seattle, Washington; (Subregional Library/Advisory and Outreach Center of the Year) Pinellas Talking Book Library in Clearwater, Florida.

REFORMA (National Association to Promote Library and Information Services to Latinos and the Spanish-Speaking)

Elizabeth A. Martinez Lifetime Achievement Award. To recognize those who have achieved excellence in librarianship over an extended period of service and who have made significant and lasting contributions to REFORMA and the Latino community. *Winner:* Oralia Garza de Cortés.

REFORMA scholarships (up to $1,500). To students who qualify for graduate study in library science and who are citizens or permanent residents of the United States. (Rose Trevino Memorial Scholarship) Not awarded in 2022. (REFORMA Scholarship) Not awarded in 2022.

Arnulfo D. Trejo Librarian of the Year Award. To recognize a librarian who has promoted and advocated services to the Spanish-speaking and Latino communities and made outstanding contributions to REFORMA. *Winner:* Alicia K. Long from Manatee-Sarasota Libraries at the State College of Florida.

Society of American Archivists (SAA)

Brenda S. Banks Travel Award. For individuals of color (such as those of African, Asian, Latinx, Middle Eastern/North African, Native American, Alaska Native, or Pacific Islander descent) who have demonstrated professional archival experience and manifest an interest in becoming active members of the Society of American Archivists. *Winner:* Polly Peralta.

C.F.W. Coker Award for Description. To recognize creators of tools that enable archivists to produce more effective finding aids. *Winner:* Philadelphia Area Consortium of Special Collections Libraries, Inc. (PACSCL) for In Her Own Right.

Distinguished Service Award. To recognize an archival institution, education program, nonprofit organization, or governmental organization that has given outstanding service to its public and has made an exemplary contribution to the archives profession. *Winner:* ChromaDiverse, Inc.

Diversity Award. To an individual, group, or institution for outstanding contributions to advancing diversity within the archives profession, SAA, or the archival record. *Winner:* Julie Varee, community outreach archivist at the Anchorage (Alaska) Museum.

Fellows' Ernst Posner Award. For an outstanding essay dealing with a facet of archival administration, history, theory, or methodology published in *American Archivist. Winner:* Eliot Wilczek for "Archival

Engagements with Wicked Problems" (Fall/Winter 2021, Vol. 84.2).

Josephine Forman Scholarship ($10,000). *Sponsor:* General Commission on Archives and History of the United Methodist Church. *Winner:* Elias Larralde, University of Arizona.

Mark A. Greene Emerging Leader Award. To recognize early-career archivists who have completed archival work of broad merit, demonstrated significant promise of leadership, performed commendable service to the archives profession, or accomplished a combination of these requirements. *Winner:* Sara Davis, Wyoming State Archives.

F. Gerald Ham and Elsie Ham Scholarship ($7,500). To recognize an individual's past performance in a graduate archival studies program and his or her potential in the field. *Winner:* Sarah Shepherd, Simmons University.

Philip M. Hamer and Elizabeth Hamer Kegan Award. For individuals and/or institutions that have increased public awareness of a specific body of documents. Not awarded in 2021.

Oliver Wendell Holmes Travel Award. To enable overseas archivists already in the United States or Canada for training to attend the SAA Annual Meeting. *Winner:* Chaeyeon Kim.

J. Franklin Jameson Archival Advocacy Award. For individuals and/or organizations that promote greater public awareness of archival activities and programs. Not awarded in 2022.

Sister M. Claude Lane, O.P., Memorial Award. For a significant contribution to the field of religious archives. *Winner:* Carol W. Smith from Christ Church Preservation Trust in Philadelphia, Pennnsylvania.

Waldo Gifford Leland Award. To encourage and reward writing of superior excellence and usefulness in the field of archival history, theory, or practice. *Winner:* Jason Lustig for *A Time to Gather* (Oxford University Press).

Theodore Calvin Pease Award. For the best student paper ($100 and publication in *American Archivist*). Not awarded in 2022.

Donald Peterson Student Travel Award (up to $1,000). To enable a student or recent graduate to attend the SAA Annual Meeting. *Winner:* Katherine Schlesinger from the Library and Information Science Program at the University of Arizona.

Harold T. Pinkett Student of Color Award. To encourage minority students to consider careers in the archival profession and to promote minority participation in SAA. *Winner:* Erin Castillo from the Library and Information Science Program at San Jose State University.

Preservation Publication Award. To recognize an outstanding work published in North America that advances the theory or the practice of preservation in archival institutions. *Winners:* Monique Lassere and Jess Whyte for "Balancing Care and Authenticity in Digital Collections: A Radical Empathy Approach to Working with Disk Images" in *Journal of Critical Library and Information Studies* (Volume 3, 2021).

SAA Archival Innovator Award. To an archivist, group of archivists, repository, or organization that demonstrates the greatest overall current impact on the profession or their communities. *Winners:* Arizona State University Library and Center for Michigan Jewish Heritage.

SAA Fellows. To a limited number of members for their outstanding contribution to the archival profession. *Honored:* Steven Booth, Getty Research Institute; L. Rebecca Johnson Melvin, University of Delaware; Emilie Leumas, EGL Consultants; Elizabeth Myers, Smith College Libraries; Kathryn Neal, University of California–Berkeley; Edward Ryan, Ford Motor Company Archives.

SAA Mosaic Scholarship ($5,000). To minority students pursuing graduate education in archival science. *Winner:* Sean Payne, Syracuse University.

SAA Spotlight Award. To recognize the contributions of individuals who work for the good of the profession and of archival collection and whose work would not typically receive public recognition. *Winner:* Georgina Tom, archivist at 'Iolani School in Honolulu, Hawaii.

Special Libraries Association (SLA)

SLA James M. Matarazzo Rising Star Award. To SLA members in the first five years of membership who demonstrate exceptional promise of leadership. *Winners:* Julia

Bhojoo, Samuel Hansen, Valerie Moore, Wei Zakharov.

SLA Fellows. *Honored*: Eugene Giudice, Lateka Grays, Nabi Hasan, Barbara Kern, Shelly Ray.

SLA Hall of Fame Award. For outstanding performance and distinguished service to SLA. *Winners:* Ruth Kneale and Tony Stankus.

Rose L. Vormelker Award. To SLA members for exceptional service through the education and mentoring of students and working professionals. *Winner:* Lynn Weinstein.

Theatre Library Association (TLA)

Brooks McNamara Performing Arts Librarian Scholarship ($500 and a one-year TLA membership). A biennial award acknowledging the outstanding professional accomplishments of a promising student currently enrolled in an M.L.I.S. or archival training program specializing in performing arts librarianship. Not awarded in 2022.

Louis Rachow Distinguished Service in Performing Arts Librarianship Award. For extraordinary contributions to performing arts. Not awarded in 2022.

George Freedley Memorial Award. *Winner:* Katrina M. Phillips for *Staging Indigeneity: Salvage Tourism and the Performance of Native American History* (University of North Carolina Press).

Richard Wall Memorial Award. See "Literary Prizes, 2022" in Part 5.

Other Awards of Distinction

Robert B. Downs Intellectual Freedom Award. To recognize individuals or groups who have furthered the cause of intellectual freedom, particularly as it affects libraries and information centers and the dissemination of ideas. *Offered by:* Graduate School of Library and Information Science at the University of Illinois–Urbana-Champaign.

Sponsor: Sage Publications. *Winner (2022):* To be announced. *Winner (2021):* #FReadom Fighters and the ALA Office for Intellectual Freedom staff for their contributions in the defense of intellectual freedom.

I Love My Librarian Awards ($5,000, a plaque, and a $500 travel stipend to attend the awards ceremony). To recognize librarians for service to their communities, schools, and campuses. Winners are nominated by library patrons. *Sponsors:* Carnegie Corporation of New York and the *New York Times*. *Winners:* Yuliana Aceves, Arlington (Texas) Public Library; Shamella Cromartie, Western Carolina University in Cullowhee, North Carolina; William Gibbons, City College of New York in New York, New York; Renee Greenlee, Marion (Iowa) Public Library; Shannon Horton, Decorah (Iowa) Middle School and High School; John Paul Mahofski, Eastern Correctional Institution in Westover, Maryland; Tammi Moe, Octavia Fellin Public Library in Gallup, New Mexico; George Oberle, George Mason University in Fairfax, Virginia; Melissa Pillot, Forsyth School in St. Louis, Missouri; Arnulfo Talamantes, Sul Ross Middle School in San Antonio, Texas.

RWA Cathie Linz Librarian of the Year. To a librarian who demonstrates outstanding support of romance authors and the romance genre. *Offered by:* Romance Writers of America. Not awarded in 2022.

USBBY Bridge to Understanding Award ($1,000). To acknowledge the work of adults who use books to promote international understanding among children. *Offered by:* United States Board on Books for Young People. *Winner (2022):* To be announced.

Women's National Book Association Award. Awarded biennially to a living American woman who derives part or all of her income from books and allied arts and who has done meritorious work in the world of books. *Offered by:* Women's National Book Association (WNBA). *Winner (2021):* Hannah Oliver Depp from Loyalty Bookstores in Washington, D.C., and Silver Spring, Maryland.

Part 4
Research and Statistics

Library Research and Statistics

Number of Libraries in the United States and Canada

Statistics are from the *American Library Directory* (*ALD*) 2023–2024 (Information Today, Inc., 2023). Data are exclusive of elementary and secondary school libraries.

Libraries in the United States

Public Libraries	16,974*
Public libraries, excluding branches	9,634
Main public libraries that have branches	1,444
Public library branches	7,340
Academic Libraries	3,493*
Community college	1,089
Departmental	275
Medical	6
Religious	5
University and college	2,404
Departmental	1,135
Law	188
Medical	236
Religious	245
Armed Forces Libraries	224*
Air Force	62
Medical	3
Army	103
Medical	21
Marine Corps	12
Navy	47
Law	1
Medical	8
Government Libraries	786*
Law	346
Medical	104

Special Libraries (excluding public, academic, armed forces, and government)	4,325*
Law	608
Medical	746
Religious	348
Total Special Libraries (including public, academic, armed forces, and government)	5,488
Total law	1,143
Total medical	1,124
Total religious	758
Total Libraries Counted (*)	25,802

Libraries in Regions Administered by the United States

Public Libraries	18*
Public libraries, excluding branches	9
Main public libraries that have branches	3
Public library branches	9
Academic Libraries	38*
Community college	3
Departmental	1
University and college	35
Departmental	18
Law	3
Medical	3
Religious	1
Armed Forces Libraries	2*
Air Force	1
Army	1
Government Libraries	3*
Law	1
Medical	1
Special Libraries (excluding public, academic, armed forces, and government)	4*
Law	3
Religious	1
Total Special Libraries (including public, academic, armed forces, and government)	13
Total law	7
Total medical	4
Total religious	2
Total Libraries Counted (*)	65

Libraries in Canada

Public Libraries	2,224*
Public libraries, excluding branches	798
Main public libraries that have branches	159
Public library branches	1,426
Academic Libraries	316*
Community college	75
Departmental	14
Religious	1
University and college	241
Departmental	178
Law	16
Medical	11
Religious	32
Government Libraries	152*
Law	25
Medical	4
Special Libraries (excluding public, academic, armed forces, and government)	495*
Law	85
Medical	114
Religious	20
Total Special Libraries (including public, academic, armed forces, and government)	584
Total law	126
Total medical	129
Total religious	67
Total Libraries Counted (*)	3,187

Summary

Total U.S. Libraries	25,802
Total Libraries Administered by the United States	65
Total Canadian Libraries	3,187
Grand Total of Libraries Listed	29,054

Note: Numbers followed by an asterisk are added to find "Total Libraries Counted" for each of the three geographic areas (United States, U.S.-administered regions, and Canada). The sum of the three totals is the "Grand Total of Libraries Listed" in *ALD*. For details on the count of libraries, see the preface to the 76th edition of *ALD.—Ed.*

School Librarian Employment in the United States, 2020–2021 to 2021–2022

Debra E. Kachel and Keith Curry Lance
The School Librarian Investigation—Decline or Evolution?
The SLIDE Project

The status of school librarianship is the subject of a three-year research project funded by a Laura Bush 21st Century Librarian grant from the Institute of Museum and Library Services (IMLS) to Antioch University Seattle. The School Librarian Investigation—Decline or Evolution? (SLIDE) began in September 2020. Debra E. Kachel (dkachel@antioch.edu) is the project director, and Keith Curry Lance, Ph.D. (keithlance@comcast.net), is the principal investigator. For the latest information about the SLIDE study, visit its website—https://libSLIDE.org—which provides access to its reports and infographics, videos and PowerPoint files for conference and workshop presentations, external links to news articles and editorials citing the study, and a powerful set of interactive data tools delivering on-demand access to user-selected data about school librarian employment from 2009 to 2010 to the present. Embedded, step-by-step tutorials make it possible to use these tools quickly and easily.

For this year's update, a comparison of data for the 2020–2021 and 2021–2022 school years provides some indications of how the status of school librarians is continuing to change. Three findings stand out: 1) for the first time in many years, the year-to-year change in the number of school librarians has not been a substantial decrease, 2) also for the first time in years, a substantial group of states experienced increases in school librarian employment, and 3) due to the combination of state-level increases and decreases, state-to-state inequality in student and teacher access to school librarians continues to increase dramatically.

Change from 2020–2021 to 2021–2022

Between the 2020–2021 and 2021–2022 school years—the two most recent for which data are available—27 states experienced net gains of school librarians in full-time equivalents (FTEs), while 20 states experienced net librarian losses (see Table 1). Only one state, Alabama, reported no change in the number of librarians during the latest one-year interval. The status of three states is unknown. Nevada did not report its number of school librarians for 2021–2022, and Illinois and Utah did not report that figure for 2020–2021. (For those three states, the reported figure is repeated for the missing year.)

Between those two latest school years, 14 of the 27 states gaining school librarians experienced double-digit numerical increases. New York reported 88.27 more librarian FTEs for 2021–2022 than 2020–2021—by far the largest numerical increase for a single state. Six other states reported net gains in their numbers of school librarians of 25 FTEs or more: Massachusetts, 56.07; Arizona, 49.34; Tennessee, 39.7; Michigan, 36.62; Wisconsin, 29.37; and Washington, 27.59. Six states and the District of Columbia reported net gains of ten librarian FTEs or

Table 1 / Number of School Librarians in Full-Time Equivalents by State, 2020–2021 to 2021–2022 *(continued on next page)*

State	State Name	Librarians 2021–2022	Librarians 2020–2021	Number Change	Percent Change
AL	ALABAMA	1,305.34	1,305.34	0.00	0.0%
AK	ALASKA	130.89	132.35	-1.46	-1.1%
AZ	ARIZONA	464.80	415.46	49.34	11.9%
AR	ARKANSAS	898.60	894.33	4.27	0.5%
CA	CALIFORNIA	591.35	620.94	-29.59	-4.8%
CO	COLORADO	474.49	468.60	5.89	1.3%
CT	CONNECTICUT	681.50	668.10	13.40	2.0%
DE	DELAWARE	107.80	105.30	2.50	2.4%
DC	DISTRICT OF COLUMBIA	100.34	88.00	12.34	14.0%
FL	FLORIDA	1,911.18	1,923.52	-12.34	-0.6%
GA	GEORGIA	2,040.00	2,033.30	6.70	0.3%
HI	HAWAII	87.50	114.00	-26.50	-23.2%
ID	IDAHO	34.15	41.67	-7.52	-18.0%
IL*	ILLINOIS	1,496.14	1,496.14	0.00	0.0%
IN	INDIANA	458.00	522.54	-64.54	-12.4%
IA	IOWA	384.82	376.73	8.09	2.1%
KS	KANSAS	600.32	602.99	-2.67	-0.4%
KY	KENTUCKY	1,026.80	1,010.54	16.26	1.6%
LA	LOUISIANA	922.78	926.54	-3.76	-0.4%
ME	MAINE	183.80	181.70	2.10	1.2%
MD	MARYLAND	1,132.63	1,132.73	-0.10	-0.0%
MA	MASSACHUSETTS	611.52	555.45	56.07	10.1%
MI	MICHIGAN	516.58	479.96	36.62	7.6%
MN	MINNESOTA	400.27	433.52	-33.25	-7.7%
MS	MISSISSIPPI	740.65	725.03	15.62	2.2%
MO	MISSOURI	1,278.58	1,302.60	-24.02	-1.8%
MT	MONTANA	370.52	362.42	8.10	2.2%
NE	NEBRASKA	519.20	532.99	-13.79	-2.6%
NV*	NEVADA	258.00	258.00	0.00	0.0%
NH	NEW HAMPSHIRE	327.30	325.80	1.50	0.5%
NJ	NEW JERSEY	1,206.18	1,216.14	-9.96	-0.8%
NM	NEW MEXICO	207.64	190.57	17.07	9.0%
NY	NEW YORK	1,043.85	955.58	88.27	9.2%
NC	NORTH CAROLINA	2,018.78	2,023.42	-4.64	-0.2%
ND	NORTH DAKOTA	179.29	174.58	4.71	2.7%
OH	OHIO	701.86	722.72	-20.86	-2.9%
OK	OKLAHOMA	883.39	879.82	3.57	0.4%
OR	OREGON	158.35	146.70	11.65	7.9%
PA	PENNSYLVANIA	1,494.61	1,521.78	-27.17	-1.8%
RI	RHODE ISLAND	169.96	176.16	-6.20	-3.5%
SC	SOUTH CAROLINA	1,091.55	1,086.40	5.15	0.5%
SD	SOUTH DAKOTA	64.50	66.38	-1.88	-2.8%
TN	TENNESSEE	1,372.89	1,333.19	39.70	3.0%
TX	TEXAS	4,384.81	4,485.48	-100.67	-2.2%
UT*	UTAH	233.80	233.80	0.00	0.0%

Table 1 / Number of School Librarians in Full-Time Equivalents by State, 2020–2021 to 2021–2022 (continued)

State	State Name	Librarians 2021–2022	Librarians 2020–2021	Number Change	Percent Change
VT	VERMONT	205.48	202.80	2.68	1.3%
VA	VIRGINIA	1,799.00	1,779.53	19.47	1.1%
WA	WASHINGTON	820.18	792.59	27.59	3.5%
WV	WEST VIRGINIA	185.14	200.59	-15.45	-7.7%
WI	WISCONSIN	928.04	898.67	29.37	3.3%
WY	WYOMING	80.08	77.11	2.97	3.9%
50 STATES and DC		**39,285.23**	**39,200.60**	**84.63**	**0.2%**
BI	BUREAU OF INDIAN EDUCATION	41.50	44.00	-2.50	-5.7%
GU	GUAM	39.00	39.00	0.00	0.0%
PR	PUERTO RICO	773.00	774.00	-1.00	-0.1%
VI	U.S. VIRGIN ISLANDS	11.00	13.00	-2.00	-15.4%

* For Ilinois, Nevada, and Utah, italicized data are repeated from the other school year, owing to non-reports.

more: Virginia, 19.47; New Mexico, 17.07; Kentucky, 16.26; Mississippi, 15.62; Connecticut, 13.4; the District of Columbia, 12.34; and Oregon, 11.65.

During the same interval, 11 of the 20 states losing librarians experienced double-digit numerical decreases in their numbers of school librarians. Texas reported a loss of 100.67 FTEs—by far the largest numerical loss for a single state. Five other states reported net librarian losses of 25 FTEs or more: Indiana, 64.54; Minnesota, 33.25; California, 29.59; Pennsylvania, 27.17; and Hawaii, 26.5. Four additional states reported losses of ten FTEs or more: Missouri, 24.02; Ohio, 20.86; Nebraska, 13.79; and Florida, 12.34.

Between those two most recent school years, two states and the District of Columbia experienced double-digit percentage gains in their numbers of school librarian FTEs. The District of Columbia gained 14 percent; Arizona, 11.9 percent; and Massachusetts, 10.1 percent.

During the same interval, three states experienced double-digit percentage losses of school librarian FTEs. Hawaii lost 23.2 percent; Idaho, 18 percent; and Indiana, 12.4 percent.

Ratio of Librarians to Schools, 2021–2022

Because the FTE of school librarians is reported at the district level and not at the school level, assessing the level of librarian staffing at the school level can only be approximated by calculating the ratio of librarians to schools (see Table 2). The result may be interpreted in two ways, suggesting either the percentage of schools with a full-time librarian or the FTE per schools, if school librarians were equally distributed among a district's schools (notably, something that is rarely the case).

Table 2 / Ratio of Librarians to Schools and Ratios of Students and Teachers Per Librarian by State, 2021–2022 *(continued on next page)*

tate	State Name	Librarians	Schools	Ratio of Librarians to Schools	Students	Students Per Librarian	Teachers	Teachers Per Librarian
L	ALABAMA	1,305.34	1,507	0.87	748,274	573.24	38,835	29.75
K	ALASKA	130.89	500	0.26	129,944	992.77	7,246	55.36
Z	ARIZONA	464.80	2,418	0.19	1,133,284	2,438.22	51,093	109.93
R	ARKANSAS	898.60	1,084	0.83	489,565	544.81	38,846	43.23
A	CALIFORNIA	591.35	10,327	0.06	5,892,073	9,963.77	267,759	452.79
O	COLORADO	474.49	1,941	0.24	880,597	1,855.88	53,903	113.60
T	CONNECTICUT	681.50	1,000	0.68	509,748	747.98	41,686	61.17
E	DELAWARE	107.80	229	0.47	139,935	1,298.10	9,965	92.44
C	DISTRICT OF COLUMBIA	100.34	240	0.42	88,908	886.07	7,828	78.02
L	FLORIDA	1,911.18	4,191	0.46	2,833,186	1,482.43	159,866	83.65
A	GEORGIA	2,040.00	2,314	0.88	1,740,875	853.37	119,831	58.74
I	HAWAII	87.50	294	0.30	173,178	1,979.18	12,026	137.44
)	IDAHO	34.15	784	0.04	314,258	9,202.28	17,935	525.18
N	ILLINOIS	1,496.14	4,386	0.34	1,868,482	1,248.87	139,378	93.16
	INDIANA	458.00	1,915	0.24	1,036,625	2,263.37	66,414	145.01
A	IOWA	384.82	1,325	0.29	510,661	1,327.01	36,059	93.70
S	KANSAS	600.32	1,355	0.44	485,424	808.61	38,353	63.89
Y	KENTUCKY	1,026.80	1,535	0.67	654,239	637.16	43,380	42.25
A	LOUISIANA	922.78	1,367	0.68	683,216	740.39	38,773	42.02
E	MAINE	183.80	598	0.31	173,215	942.41	15,418	83.88
D	MARYLAND	1,132.63	1,417	0.80	881,461	778.24	62,443	55.13
A	MASSACHU- SETTS	611.52	1,847	0.33	921,180	1,506.38	76,329	124.82
I	MICHIGAN	516.58	3,538	0.15	1,440,090	2,787.74	86,258	166.98
N	MINNESOTA	400.27	2,661	0.15	870,506	2,174.80	55,662	139.06
S	MISSISSIPPI	740.65	1,040	0.71	442,000	596.77	31,686	42.78
O	MISSOURI	1,278.58	2,453	0.52	888,823	695.16	69,569	54.41
T	MONTANA	370.52	827	0.45	150,195	405.36	11,042	29.80
E	NEBRASKA	519.20	1,083	0.48	327,564	630.90	24,230	46.67
V *	NEVADA	*258.00*	746	0.35	486,648	1,886.23	23,746	92.04
H	NEW HAMPSHIRE	327.30	494	0.66	170,005	519.42	14,626	44.69
J	NEW JERSEY	1,206.18	2,558	0.47	1,372,381	1,137.79	117,127	97.11
M	NEW MEXICO	207.64	890	0.23	316,785	1,525.65	21,475	103.42
Y	NEW YORK	1,043.85	4,802	0.22	2,548,490	2,441.43	215,092	206.06
C	NORTH CAROLINA	2,018.78	2,719	0.74	1,525,223	755.52	102,034	50.54
D	NORTH DAKOTA	179.29	513	0.35	116,864	651.82	9,531	53.16
H	OHIO	701.86	3,659	0.19	1,683,612	2,398.79	99,442	141.68
K	OKLAHOMA	883.39	1,792	0.49	698,696	790.93	43,090	48.78
R	OREGON	158.35	1,285	0.12	553,012	3,492.34	31,629	199.74
A	PENNSYLVANIA	1,494.61	2,941	0.51	1,695,092	1,134.14	126,345	84.53
I	RHODE ISLAND	169.96	315	0.54	138,566	815.29	10,774	63.39
C	SOUTH CAROLINA	1,091.55	1,267	0.86	780,878	715.38	55,489	50.83
D	SOUTH DAKOTA	64.50	721	0.09	141,307	2,190.81	10,216	158.39
N	TENNESSEE	1,372.89	1,906	0.72	996,709	725.99	64,747	47.16
X	TEXAS	4,384.81	9,105	0.48	5,428,613	1,238.05	371,002	84.61
T	UTAH	233.80	1,106	0.21	690,934	2,955.24	30,860	132.00

Table 2 / Ratio of Librarians to Schools and Ratios of Students and
Teachers Per Librarian by State, 2021–2022 (continued)

State	State Name	Librarians	Schools	Ratio of Librarians to Schools	Students	Students Per Librarian	Teachers	Teache Per Libraria
VT	VERMONT	205.48	305	0.67	83,975	408.68	7,965	38.
VA	VIRGINIA	1,799.00	2,129	0.84	1,249,815	694.73	86,917	48
WA	WASHINGTON	820.18	2,546	0.32	1,081,835	1,319.02	60,147	73
WV	WEST VIRGINIA	185.14	694	0.27	252,720	1,365.02	18,724	101
WI	WISCONSIN	928.04	2,243	0.41	829,359	893.67	60,337	65
WY	WYOMING	80.08	359	0.22	93,093	1,162.50	7,308	91.
50 STATES and DC		**39,285.23**	**99,271**	**0.40**	**49,342,118**	**1,256.00**	**3,210,437**	**81.**
BI	BUREAU OF INDIAN EDUCATION	41.50	174	0.24	32,457	782.10	4,638	111.
GU	GUAM	39.00	44	0.89	28,402	728.26	1,767	45.
PR	PUERTO RICO	773.00	851	0.91	259,535	335.75	23,348	30.
VI	U.S. VIRGIN ISLANDS	11.00	21	0.52	10,234	930.36	916	83

* For 2021–2022, Nevada did not report school librarian FTE. Its reported figure for 2020–2021 was used to fill t‖ gap.

The reality in many districts is that some schools have librarians, while others do not. In some cases, district administrators have chosen to concentrate librarians at either the elementary or secondary level, while in others, the decision is made by each principal.

For the 2021–2022 school year, only six states—notably, all in the South— had a ratio of librarians to schools of .75 or greater: Georgia, .88; Alabama, .87; South Carolina, .86; Virginia, .84; Arkansas, .83; and Maryland, .80. These ratios suggest either that the vast majority of schools have full-time librarians or that the average FTE per school is close to full time.

Eleven states had a ratio of librarians to schools greater than .50 and less than .75: North Carolina, .74; Tennessee, .72; Mississippi, .71; Connecticut, .68; Louisiana, .68; Vermont, .67; Kentucky, .67; New Hampshire, .66; Rhode Island, .54; Missouri, .52; and Pennsylvania, .51. These ratios suggest that between half and three-quarters of schools have full-time librarians or that the average FTE per school represents a presence of a librarian during at least half of the school week, although fewer than four days per week. Notably, ten of these 11 states are east of the Mississippi River.

Twenty states had a ratio of librarians to schools greater than .25 and less than .50: Oklahoma, .49; Texas, .48; Nebraska, .48; New Jersey, .47; Delaware, 47; Florida, .46; Montana, .45; Kansas, 44; the District of Columbia, .42; Wisconsin, .41; North Dakota, .35; Nevada, .35; Illinois, .34; Massachusetts, .33; Washington, .32; Maine, .31; Hawaii, .30; Iowa, .29; West Virginia, .27; and Alaska, .26. These ratios suggest that between a quarter and half of schools in these states have full-time librarians or that the average FTE per school represents a presence of a librarian for as little as one or two days per week. Notably, these 20 states are almost equally divided between the nation's four major geographical regions: six

Table 3 / States with 50 Percent or More of Local Districts Reporting Zero Librarian FTEs, 2021–2022

State	State Name	Districts Reporting Zero Librarian FTEs	
		Number	Percent
CA	CALIFORNIA	772	77.9%
AK	ALASKA	41	75.9%
ID	IDAHO	85	73.9%
SD	SOUTH DAKOTA	105	70.5%
OR	OREGON	123	70.3%
MI	MICHIGAN	360	66.8%
MN	MINNESOTA	216	65.7%
AZ	ARIZONA	146	64.6%
CO	COLORADO	106	59.6%
WA	WASHINGTON	177	59.2%
NM	NEW MEXICO	52	58.4%
ME	MAINE	138	53.9%
IL	ILLINOIS	432	50.4%

in the Midwest, five (including the District of Columbia) in the South, five in the West, and four in the Northeast.

Eleven states had a ratio of librarians to schools greater than .10 and less than .25: Colorado, .24; Indiana, .24; New Mexico, .23; Wyoming, .22; New York, .22; Utah, .21; Arizona, .19; Ohio, .19; Minnesota, .15; Michigan, .15; and Oregon, .12. These ratios suggest that between one in ten and one in four schools in these states have a full-time librarian or that the average FTE per school represents a librarian presence for as little as half a day per week or, at best, a little more than one day per week. Notably, six of these 11 states are in the West, and four are in the Midwest.

Three states have a ratio of librarians to schools less than .10: South Dakota, .09; California, .06; and Idaho, .04. These ratios suggest that fewer than one school in every ten in these states has a full-time librarian or that the average FTE per school represents a librarian presence of two or three hours per week.

Students Per Librarian and Teachers Per Librarian

Ratios of students and teachers per librarian are most meaningful at the district or school level; however, even at the state level, they indicate something of the adequacy or inadequacy of library staffing levels (see Table 2).

Nationwide, during the 2021–2022 school year, there were more than 1,200 students and more than 80 teachers for every full-time librarian. Ideally, school librarians are supposed to promote a love of reading and teach information literacy skills to students and collaborate with classroom teacher colleagues to facilitate instruction more generally. Ratios such as these, however, suggest that school librarians face daunting challenges. The underlying realities are quite different though. Inequitable access to school librarians means that a privileged few

Table 4 / States with 10 Percent or More of Local
Districts Missing Data for Librarian FTEs, 2021–2022

State	State Name	Districts Missing Data for Librarian FTEs	
		Number	Percent
NV	NEVADA	18	100.0%
KS	KANSAS	66	49.0%
WV	WEST VIRGINIA	26	47.3%
NJ	NEW JERSEY	138	24.6%
MA	MASSACHUSETTS	66	20.5%
VT	VERMONT	17	13.4%
CT	CONNECTICUT	20	11.8%
NH	NEW HAMPSHIRE	18	10.0%

students and teachers experience the contributions of librarians, while many students and teachers have no experience of them at all.

Thus, these two ratios are most meaningful as measures of inequality. Consider the extremes for students per librarian: Montana and Vermont each have approximately 400 students for each librarian FTE, while Idaho and California each have more than 9,000 students per librarian. There are similar extremes for teachers per librarian: Alabama and Montana each have fewer than 30 teachers per librarian, while California has more than 450 teachers per librarian and Idaho has more than 500 teachers per librarian.

States with a Majority of Local Districts Reporting Zero Librarian FTEs

A more concrete measure of the extent of inequities in access to school librarians is the percentage of a state's local districts that report no librarians. These are not districts that declined to report about librarian FTEs; rather, they are ones that actually reported zero librarians in FTEs (see Table 3).

In five states—California, Alaska, Idaho, South Dakota, and Oregon—seven out of ten districts reported no librarians for 2021–2022. In the same school year, in four states—Michigan, Minnesota, Arizona, and Colorado—at least six out of ten local districts were without any librarians. And, in four additional states—Washington, New Mexico, Maine, and Illinois—more than half of local districts reported no librarians. Given that 2021–2022 was the first school year for many years when a substantial number of states gained librarian FTEs compared to the previous year, it is a noteworthy sign of educational inequality that school librarians are entirely absent from a majority of districts in more than a quarter of U.S. states.

Ongoing Data Issues

The only source of detailed data about school librarian employment is the National Center for Education Statistics's (NCES) Common Core of Data (CCD). Only NCES has the fiscal and personnel wherewithal to annually collect and report educational statistics at national, state, and district levels.

There are three critical problems with the CCD effort that seriously compromise the completeness and accuracy of school librarian data. First and foremost is the variable response rate from state to state. While the majority of states have very high response rates from their local districts, a few states—too many of them large states—have very low response rates. The problem for low-response-rate states is that when school librarian FTEs are being totaled at the state level, there is no difference between a reported zero and a non-response; a non-response is implicitly treated as a zero.

Eight states failed to report school librarian FTEs for 10 percent or more of their local districts (see Table 4). For 2021–2022, Nevada did not report this figure for any district. In Kansas and West Virginia, the number of librarian FTEs was unreported for almost half of local districts. This figure was also missing for a quarter of New Jersey districts and one-fifth of Massachusetts districts. And librarian FTEs went unreported for more than one in ten districts in Vermont, Connecticut, and New Hampshire. Because NCES does not impute missing data, these missing-data districts are treated as if they reported zero librarian FTEs. This might be accurate … and it might not.

The second data-quality issue is NCES's failure to impute missing data before calculating state totals. Generally, it is undesirable to treat reported zeroes and non-responses the same. When a district fails to report its school librarian FTEs, the missing data ought to be imputed on some reasonable basis. This is precisely what IMLS does when local public library jurisdictions omit data from the annual Public Library Survey. If a local district reported its librarian FTEs for a previous year, that value could be imputed for the year in which it is missing, or, if there has been significant change for similar districts, the previous year's value could be increased or decreased accordingly. In the absence of previous data for a district, a missing figure could be imputed based on the average for a peer district (that is, one that's similar in enrollment, locale, per-pupil expenditures, and/or other characteristics). In reality, unfortunately, data remain missing for some districts in some states, and it may or may not be accurate for those missing data to become implied zeroes.

The third data-quality issue is NCES's failure to adjust its state-level data for district-level non-response. Historically, there was never missing data for librarian FTEs at the state level. In recent years, NCES has reported no data for librarian FTEs for some states, making it impossible to calculate national totals from the official data.

Clearly, at both federal and state levels, the agencies that are responsible for data about public education have failed to follow up when districts and even states have failed to report required data. This lack of follow-up has profound consequences for the completeness and accuracy of the only data about school librarian employment. Whether it is a matter of agency funding, staffing, or priorities, necessary steps should be taken to close these gaps that compromise data quality.

Library Acquisition Expenditures, 2022–2023 U.S. Public, Academic, Special, and Government Libraries

The information in these tables is taken from the 2022–2023 edition of *American Library Directory* (*ALD*) (Information Today, Inc.). The tables report acquisition expenditures by public, academic, special, and government libraries.

Understanding the Tables

"Number of Libraries" includes only those U.S. libraries in *ALD* that reported annual acquisition expenditures. Libraries that reported annual income but not expenditures are not included in the count. Academic libraries include university, college, and community college libraries. Special academic libraries, such as law and medical libraries, that reported acquisition expenditures separately from the institution's main library are counted as independent libraries.

The amount in the "Total Acquisition Expenditures" column for a given state is generally greater than the sum of the categories of expenditures. This is because the total acquisition expenditures amount also includes the expenditures of libraries that did not itemize by category.

Figures in "Categories of Expenditures" columns represent only those libraries that itemized expenditures. Libraries that reported a total acquisition expenditure amount but did not itemize are only represented in the total acquisition expenditures column.

Table 1 / Public Library Acquisition Expenditures

State	Number of Libraries	Total Acquisition Expenditures	Books	Other Print Materials	Periodicals/ Serials	Manuscripts & Archives	AV Equipment	AV Materials	Microforms	Electronic Reference	Preservation
Alabama	8	22,22,123	4,55,038	11,091	6,087	0	4,700	15,004	0	1,13,541	20,000
Alaska	5	1,74,412	77,820	44	8,414	43,021	1,500	26,489	0	8,949	175
Arizona	10	75,27,368	9,68,098	89,424	23,674	0	0	9,06,322	0	2,37,429	0
Arkansas	7	1,47,17,446	2,57,433	250	20,874	500	0	39,307	0	42,186	0
California	25	4,03,27,258	1,32,51,724	78,307	10,38,973	2,500	34,987	58,29,538	31,422	1,56,60,671	16,698
Colorado	8	88,80,371	38,17,846	4,34,162	3,51,090	0	15,000	19,25,661	0	23,36,612	0
Connecticut	23	1,45,17,826	18,03,573	4,549	5,87,538	4,705	4,918	4,51,280	1,080	10,13,859	39,362
Delaware	2	4,30,391	46,238	2,011	10,308	0	0	7,642	0	6,410	0
District of Columbia	0	0	0	0	0	0	0	0	0	0	0
Florida	19	1,47,76,272	57,62,859	7,86,484	3,49,486	0	52,514	13,88,539	35,350	39,31,134	0
Georgia	3	10,99,797	5,93,006	42,253	55,893	0	0	1,99,737	1,750	2,07,158	0
Hawaii	1	42,42,675	24,91,491	43,698	1,20,461	0	0	0	43,895	11,20,394	0
Idaho	4	5,20,585	1,01,668	1,236	82	0	0	5,411	0	11,360	0
Illinois	52	8,25,38,972	54,22,532	1,43,628	2,72,191	0	10,900	20,10,317	8,299	43,35,811	2,500
Indiana	27	2,03,78,777	75,58,000	1,800	7,97,799	0	1,11,925	29,75,831	0	49,76,198	0
Iowa	29	60,57,901	11,54,635	55,504	1,42,361	4,000	1,840	3,06,858	850	5,08,464	0
Kansas	17	48,18,892	9,16,028	0	1,00,282	0	4,300	2,83,581	5,000	63,577	3,600
Kentucky	16	1,03,15,081	12,75,697	16,668	2,86,557	0	20,071	6,12,958	0	16,89,477	40,776
Louisiana	7	1,16,39,584	33,40,178	89,614	4,76,463	0	1,75,561	14,77,182	0	36,43,907	0
Maine	11	4,36,309	1,93,108	700	9,384	500	0	51,832	0	6,135	0
Maryland	2	77,61,058	0	0	0	0	0	0	0	0	0
Massachusetts	31	94,69,127	14,49,153	26,314	1,76,153	5,000	5,000	4,95,194	11,484	4,09,096	5,500
Michigan	28	1,60,23,809	14,38,156	4,711	1,37,671	0	450	5,46,822	800	6,93,740	0
Minnesota	14	7,69,34,574	15,97,669	0	6,750	0	83	3,40,233	0	3,40,979	0
Mississippi	2	1,60,660	92,177	0	130	0	0	5,178	26,000	2,500	2,162
Missouri	15	1,65,96,866	38,21,811	1,05,000	2,62,063	0	10,045	20,12,949	26,414	27,89,135	0
Montana	9	2,77,641	1,51,844	26,432	6,882	0	4,373	44,531	0	23,409	6,302

Category of Expenditures (in U.S. dollars)

Table 1 / Public Library Acquisition Expenditures (cont.)

State	Number of Libraries	Total Acquisition Expenditures	Books	Other Print Materials	Periodicals/ Serials	Manuscripts & Archives	AV Equipment	AV Materials	Microforms	Electronic Reference	Preservation
Nebraska	13	1,13,44,544	1,87,373	1,19,000	16,261	0	0	42,550	440	7,56,484	0
Nevada	3	3,74,744	1,27,003	0	9,621	0	0	33,388	0	20,000	894
New Hampshire	20	6,40,886	3,83,365	900	22,839	0	0	90,295	2,980	56,445	400
New Jersey	24	1,65,75,070	68,16,103	34,614	5,24,905	500	500	11,07,054	13,000	9,27,836	5,456
New Mexico	10	33,93,577	8,15,673	7,084	46,938	0	1,000	1,43,070	9,013	2,08,441	0
New York	55	2,55,61,980	60,70,039	1,67,465	4,58,862	0	7,661	8,23,347	24,459	7,17,600	2,775
North Carolina	4	6,32,254	3,32,412	0	18,162	0	0	59,333	3,707	57,922	0
North Dakota	7	31,81,510	2,38,710	300	26,700	0	0	60,925	0	16,354	0
Ohio	30	4,15,78,785	80,85,838	1,18,587	8,14,580	133	41,960	35,63,510	3,777	76,54,313	6,013
Oklahoma	10	71,85,651	27,50,043	12,007	2,24,633	0	0	18,08,498	1,695	16,59,188	1,000
Oregon	9	26,90,752	4,12,760	1,33,530	43,952	0	500	1,81,502	150	12,56,853	0
Pennsylvania	28	1,56,46,111	29,00,293	8,48,370	6,09,177	1,56,260	1,686	19,43,944	1,54,309	13,44,735	38,551
Rhode Island	4	5,33,104	2,77,219	0	12,654	0	0	1,10,200	0	1,28,669	650
South Carolina	4	2,78,33,240	12,81,495	15,327	0	0	0	45,27,350	0	5,81,719	0
South Dakota	5	12,04,979	5,68,484	0	6,000	0	16,846	1,45,475	0	4,64,174	12,107
Tennessee	9	46,95,24,942	2,36,64,925	2,76,606	7,27,506	1,000	24,33,770	86,30,677	0	1,83,99,536	29,000
Texas	42	1,36,67,692	48,68,885	98,582	2,41,088	27,500	3,000	8,52,464	8,700	52,50,680	29,000
Utah	4	1,65,701	92,675	0	0	0	0	16,091	0	6,935	0
Vermont	9	1,99,193	1,09,087	90	8,403	215	0	30,500	0	28,202	0
Virginia	16	79,35,112	32,53,223	4,700	1,96,243	0	22,043	10,26,890	8,056	19,97,243	0
Washington	9	29,06,214	7,30,943	66,526	50,918	0	1,975	1,78,605	0	2,94,643	400
West Virginia	3	4,01,403	2,25,058	1,000	7,500	0	0	58,625	0	67,356	0
Wisconsin	30	26,37,928	13,11,004	71,389	55,259	0	2,000	4,40,522	2,746	2,27,620	0
Wyoming	3	70,72,378	0	0	0	0	0	0	0	0	0
Puerto Rico	0	0	0	0	0	0	0	0	0	0	0
Total	726	1,03,57,33,525	12,35,40,392	39,39,957	93,69,767	2,45,834	29,91,108	4,78,33,211	4,25,376	8,62,95,079	2,34,321
Estimated % of Acquisition			44.94	1.43	3.41	0.09	1.09	17.40	0.15	31.40	0.09

Category of Expenditures (in U.S. dollars)

Table 2 / Academic Library Acquisition Expenditures

State	Number of Libraries	Total Acquisition Expenditures	Books	Other Print Materials	Periodicals/ Serials	Manuscripts & Archives	AV Equipment	AV Materials	Microforms	Electronic Reference	Preservation
					Category of Expenditures (in U.S. dollars)						
Alabama	6	27,81,049	1,17,482	1,200	13,83,276	0	0	12,026	0	2,06,900	1,600
Alaska	0	0	0	0	0	0	0	0	0	0	0
Arizona	2	17,91,124	37,897	0	31,902	0	0	60	0	2,04,245	0
Arkansas	5	93,56,113	9,15,103	4,19,834	54,80,911	34,264	2,000	6,098	4,02,861	2,12,800	0
California	16	2,27,39,075	14,24,907	3,06,859	11,04,695	1,00,000	2,772	83,496	10,169	58,60,943	60,113
Colorado	8	64,22,564	10,92,926	25,081	3,81,366	0	100	1,19,339	0	49,78,403	25,547
Connecticut	7	81,91,519	6,78,867	15,690	24,50,379	0	80,000	21,684	0	3,95,197	18,429
Delaware	2	1,28,39,012	0	0	0	0	0	0	0	0	0
District of Columbia	0	0	0	0	0	0	0	0	0	0	0
Florida	7	1,85,66,828	15,56,315	3,559	72,53,434	0	0	90,966	0	59,49,070	42,781
Georgia	9	1,53,12,925	4,91,793	0	77,733	0	98	26,300	0	17,45,558	300
Hawaii	0	0	0	0	0	0	0	0	0	0	0
Idaho	1	43,18,101	0	0	0	0	0	0	0	0	0
Illinois	20	4,88,88,221	11,47,622	7,000	18,72,182	0	0	48,774	17,741	16,34,288	67,721
Indiana	10	1,58,94,750	12,28,122	20,385	44,82,788	0	0	44,306	4,496	27,45,794	21,033
Iowa	10	1,78,57,578	21,01,741	1,42,660	36,42,665	0	6,000	53,222	5,201	17,95,907	34,211
Kansas	8	64,05,265	2,10,131	800	56,31,138	3,000	0	4,681	0	4,00,128	16,150
Kentucky	6	2,05,07,580	1,38,841	17,945	13,41,620	0	2,886	1,562	14,722	3,85,628	4,969
Louisiana	5	31,78,158	1,99,118	0	5,73,235	500	0	2,000	36,508	21,43,615	23,182
Maine	2	19,21,046	4,67,431	0	12,50,225	0	0	0	0	0	0
Maryland	9	16,53,95,353	12,58,971	34,648	79,96,527	11,934	0	37,469	6,549	10,23,014	44,412
Massachusetts	8	1,65,35,708	5,88,437	0	21,25,228	36,000	19,011	4,875	0	12,67,585	48,341
Michigan	12	43,22,471	6,71,086	6,821	12,86,414	0	0	29,157	0	22,97,605	5,669
Minnesota	5	25,86,581	2,86,343	0	9,70,663	8,200	5,000	14,508	0	7,66,205	3,910
Mississippi	1	96,040	10,000	0	2,700	0	0	0	0	83,340	0
Missouri	9	34,44,552	1,35,698	0	6,40,368	0	4,120	22,611	40,000	10,41,135	5,148
Montana	1	83,000	30,000	0	53,000	0	0	0	0	0	0

Table 2 / Academic Library Acquisition Expenditures *(cont.)*

State	Number of Libraries	Total Acquisition Expenditures	Books	Other Print Materials	Periodicals/ Serials	Manuscripts & Archives	AV Equipment	AV Materials	Microforms	Electronic Reference	Preservation
Nebraska	5	1,23,28,286	1,64,514	3,620	16,42,199	0	0	41,578	34,226	15,07,639	12,312
Nevada	0	0	0	0	0	0	0	0	0	0	0
New Hampshire	0	0	0	0	0	0	0	0	0	0	0
New Jersey	6	5,74,19,116	4,20,509	0	20,77,930	1,000	0	10,800	0	9,73,239	2,574
New Mexico	0	0	0	0	0				0	0	0
New York	23	3,12,72,104	53,01,498	1,26,882	71,66,446	22,914	25,249	2,19,365	23,727	79,00,927	1,81,237
North Carolina	11	1,10,94,746	1,20,422	82,542	4,63,505	0	2,000	41,236	0	1,70,728	13,000
North Dakota	1	3,07,078	77,357	0	1,43,943	0	0	12,892	684	72,202	0
Ohio	14	1,50,80,341	13,54,756	0	27,70,601	1,605	150	88,171	10,000	3,86,749	8,492
Oklahoma	6	49,05,242	2,04,141	575	28,36,564	1,000	0	17,378	0	9,70,780	4,431
Oregon	2	1,69,20,728	0	0	0	0	0	0	0	0	0
Pennsylvania	11	45,85,492	7,53,314	2,614	16,75,395	1,688	0	27,523	13,800	18,43,036	12,894
Rhode Island	1	2,70,098	1,26,351	0	40,197	0	0	16,168	0	80,708	6,674
South Carolina	6	77,83,936	9,16,653	0	6,01,565	0	0	89,483	37,624	15,50,460	47,030
South Dakota	1	5,00,854	37,161	0	2,40,618	0	718	18,515	2,816	1,06,460	737
Tennessee	5	55,93,792	1,37,945	0	4,53,231	0	0	27,812	0	5,81,219	425
Texas	17	2,77,34,828	31,91,355	2,63,714	1,24,78,011	0	4,800	69,004	3,500	36,94,004	46,332
Utah	2	71,42,967	1,59,582	0	6,188	0	0	5,458	0	1,82,205	21,249
Vermont	2	7,73,460	1,61,235	0	5,50,487	0	0	22,323	0	35,202	4,213
Virginia	7	1,38,97,281	29,86,538	0	54,07,631	0	0	2,12,306	11,903	42,44,379	50,658
Washington	5	1,69,73,879	11,19,151	0	69,85,017	0	27,400	30,442	0	88,11,869	0
West Virginia	3	18,50,366	10,170	57	13,345	0	0	1,493	0	72,801	7,500
Wisconsin	6	95,02,713	2,26,133	238	8,10,373	0	0	65,917	24,505	12,80,651	140
Wyoming	0	0	0	0	0	0	0	0	0	0	0
Puerto Rico	2	7,02,713	17,673	1,000	2,22,751	0	0	24,796	0	4,36,493	0
Total		65,60,74,633	3,22,75,289	14,83,724	9,66,18,446	2,22,105	1,82,304	16,65,794	7,01,032	7,00,39,111	8,43,414
Estimated % of Acquisition			15.82	0.73	47.35	0.11	0.09	0.82	0.34	34.33	0.41

Category of Expenditures (in U.S. dollars)

Table 3 / Special Library Acquisition Expenditures

State	Number of Libraries	Total Acquisition Expenditures	Books	Other Print Materials	Periodicals/ Serials	Manuscripts & Archives	AV Equipment	AV Materials	Microforms	Electronic Reference	Preservation
Alabama	0	0	0	0	0	0	0	0	0	0	0
Alaska	0	0	0	0	0	0	0	0	0	0	0
Arizona	1	78,000	52,000	0	26,000	0	0	0	0	0	0
Arkansas	0	0	0	0	0	0	0	0	0	0	0
California	5	2,78,964	1,17,834	0	49,122	600	0	24,090	0	86,588	730
Colorado	0	0	0	0	0	0	0	0	0	0	0
Connecticut	1	45,000	5,000	0	40,000	0	0	0	0	0	0
Delaware	0	0	0	0	0	0	0	0	0	0	0
District of Columbia	2	71,000	48,000	0	20,000	0	0	0	2,000	0	1,000
Florida	0	0	0	0	0	0	0	0	0	0	0
Georgia	0	0	0	0	0	0	0	0	0	0	0
Hawaii	0	0	0	0	0	0	0	0	0	0	0
Idaho	0	0	0	0	0	0	0	0	0	0	0
Illinois	3	46,02,300	52,000	0	55,300	4,000	0	0	0	49,000	5,000
Indiana	1	95,000	0	0	0	0	0	0	0	0	0
Iowa	0	0	0	0	0	0	0	0	0	0	0
Kansas	1	6,000	3,000	0	3,000	0	0	0	0	0	0
Kentucky	0	0	0	0	0	0	0	0	0	0	0
Louisiana	1	18,000	5,000	0	13,000	0	0	0	0	0	0
Maine	0	0	0	0	0	0	0	0	0	0	0
Maryland	1	1,000	500	0	300	100	0	0	0	0	100
Massachusetts	0	0	0	0	0	0	0	0	0	0	0
Michigan	0	0	0	0	0	0	0	0	0	0	0
Minnesota	0	0	0	0	0	0	0	0	0	0	0
Mississippi	0	0	0	0	0	0	0	0	0	0	0
Missouri	0	0	0	0	0	0	0	0	0	0	0

Category of Expenditures (in U.S. dollars)

Table 3 / Special Library Acquisition Expenditures (cont.)

State	Number of Libraries	Total Acquisition Expenditures	Books	Other Print Materials	Periodicals/ Serials	Manuscripts & Archives	AV Equipment	AV Materials	Microforms	Electronic Reference	Preservation
								Category of Expenditures (in U.S. dollars)			
Montana	0	0	0	0	0	0	0	0	0	0	0
Nebraska	0	0	0	0	0	0	0	0	0	0	0
Nevada	0	0	0	0	0	0	0	0	0	0	0
New Hampshire	0	0	0	0	0	0	0	0	0	0	0
New Jersey	2	4,200	1,000	0	0	0	0	0	0	0	200
New Mexico	0	0	0	0	0	0	0	0	0	0	0
New York	7	4,95,948	2,51,900	0	43,300	0	4,000	0	0	38,350	1,52,500
North Carolina	0	0	0	0	0	0	0	0	0	0	0
North Dakota	1	8,098	2,660	0	3,975	0	0	0	0	0	1,463
Ohio	1	5,71,876	10,166	0	557	1,066	0	0	0	5,832	0
Oklahoma	1	1,60,000	8,000	0	45,000	0	0	0	0	0	0
Oregon	0	0	0	0	0	0	0	0	0	0	0
Pennsylvania	0	0	0	0	0	0	0	0	0	0	0
Rhode Island	0	0	0	0	0	0	0	0	0	0	0
South Carolina	0	0	0	0	0	0	0	0	0	0	0
South Dakota	1	1,05,000	0	0	0	0	0	0	0	0	0
Tennessee	0	0	0	0	0	0	0	0	0	0	0
Texas	2	5,65,011	14,810	0	17	0	54	130	0	50,000	0
Utah	1	75,000	5,000	5,000	10,000	0	5,000	0	0	0	0
Vermont	0	0	0	0	0	0	0	0	0	0	0
Virginia	2	58,923	17,026	0	2,050	3,000	0	0	0	30,000	6,900
Washington	1	19,800	7,000	0	10,200	0	0	0	0	0	2,600
West Virginia	0	0	0	0	0	0	0	0	0	0	0
Wisconsin	2	85,500	4,000	0	20,000	0	0	0	0	60,000	0
Wyoming	0	0	0	0	0	0	0	0	0	0	0
Puerto Rico	0	0	0	0	0	0	0	0	0	0	0
Total		73,44,620	6,04,896	5,000	3,41,821	8,766	9,054	24,220	2,000	3,19,770	1,70,493

Table 4 / Government Library Acquisition Expenditures

State	Number of Libraries	Total Acquisition Expenditures	Books	Other Print Materials	Periodicals/ Serials	Manuscripts & Archives	AV Equipment	AV Materials	Microforms	Electronic Reference	Preservation
										Category of Expenditures (in U.S. dollars)	
Alabama	0	0	0	0	0	0	0	0	0	0	0
Alaska	0	0	0	0	0	0	0	0	0	0	0
Arizona	1	2,012	2,000	0	12	0	0	0	0	0	0
Arkansas	0	0	0	0	0	0	0	0	0	0	0
California	4	5,50,755	2,33,514	0	1,442	0	0	0	0	1,58,082	0
Colorado	0	0	0	0	0	0	0	0	0	0	0
Connecticut	0	0	0	0	0	0	0	0	0	0	0
Delaware	0	0	0	0	0	0	0	0	0	0	0
District of Columbia	0	0	0	0	0	0	0	0	0	0	0
Florida	0	0	0	0	0	0	0	0	0	0	0
Georgia	0	0	0	0	0	0	0	0	0	0	0
Hawaii	0	0	0	0	0	0	0	0	0	0	0
Idaho	0	0	0	0	0	0	0	0	0	0	0
Illinois	0	0	0	0	0	0	0	0	0	0	0
Indiana	0	0	0	0	0	0	0	0	0	0	0
Iowa	0	0	0	0	0	0	0	0	0	0	0
Kansas	1	5,15,260	26,852	0	3,96,491	0	0	0	0	85,690	6,227
Kentucky	0	0	0	0	0	0	0	0	0	0	0
Louisiana	1	16,27,826	5,24,121	0	11,796	0	0	0	887	2,21,858	8,034
Maine	1	3,80,116	0	0	0	0	0	0	0	0	0
Maryland	1	37,000	5,000	0	32,000	0	0	0	0	0	0
Massachusetts	0	0	0	0	0	0	0	0	0	0	0
Michigan	0	0	0	0	0	0	0	0	0	0	0
Minnesota	1	74,500	10,000	0	45,500	0	0	0	0	19,000	0
Mississippi	0	0	0	0	0	0	0	0	0	0	0
Missouri	0	0	0	0	0	0	0	0	0	0	0
Montana	0	0	0	0	0	0	0	0	0	0	0

Table 4 / Government Library Acquisition Expenditures (cont.)

State	Number of Libraries	Total Acquisition Expenditures	Category of Expenditures (in U.S. dollars)								
			Books	Other Print Materials	Periodicals/ Serials	Manuscripts & Archives	AV Equipment	AV Materials	Microforms	Electronic Reference	Preservation
Nebraska	0	0	0	0	0	0	0	0	0	0	0
Nevada	0	0	0	0	0	0	0	0	0	0	0
New Hampshire	0	0	0	0	0	0	0	0	0	0	0
New Jersey	0	0	0	0	0	0	0	0	0	0	0
New Mexico	0	0	0	0	0	0	0	0	0	0	0
New York	0	0	0	0	0	0	0	0	0	0	0
North Carolina	0	0	0	0	0	0	0	0	0	0	0
North Dakota	0	0	0	0	0	0	0	0	0	0	0
Ohio	0	0	0	0	0	0	0	0	0	0	0
Oklahoma	0	0	0	0	0	0	0	0	0	0	0
Oregon	0	0	0	0	0	0	0	0	0	0	0
Pennsylvania	1	1,25,000	0	0	0	0	0	0	0	0	0
Rhode Island	0	0	0	0	0	0	0	0	0	0	0
South Carolina	0	0	0	0	0	0	0	0	0	0	0
South Dakota	0	0	0	0	0	0	0	0	0	0	0
Tennessee	0	0	0	0	0	0	0	0	0	0	0
Texas	0	0	0	0	0	0	0	0	0	0	0
Utah	0	0	0	0	0	0	0	0	0	0	0
Vermont	0	0	0	0	0	0	0	0	0	0	0
Virginia	0	0	0	0	0	0	0	0	0	0	0
Washington	0	0	0	0	0	0	0	0	0	0	0
West Virginia	0	0	0	0	0	0	0	0	0	0	0
Wisconsin	1	10,000	0	0	0	0	0	0	0	0	0
Wyoming	0	0	0	0	0	0	0	0	0	0	0
Puerto Rico	0	0	0	0	0	0	0	0	0	0	0
Total		33,22,469	8,01,487	0	4,87,241	0	0	0	887	4,84,630	14,261
Estimated % of Acquisition Expenditures			44.81	0.00	27.24	0.00	0.00	0.00	0.05	27.10	0.80

Public Library State Rankings, 2020

State	Library Visits Per Capita	Registered Users Per Capita	Total Circulation Per Capita	Children's Material Circulation Percentage
Alabama	39	25	44	40
Alaska	8	27	19	17
American Samoa	53	54	53	2
Arizona	26	43	18	46
Arkansas	44	9	46	53
California	25	14	34	9
Colorado	41	8	7	42
Connecticut	4	43	21	25
Delaware	19	53	35	39
District of Columbia	22	13	22	49
Florida	42	27	41	43
Georgia	40	49	50	4
Guam	54	47	54	1
Hawaii	37	4	45	8
Idaho	17	27	5	11
Illinois	2	50	6	16
Indiana	32	40	13	38
Iowa	7	9	17	24
Kansas	31	1	12	18
Kentucky	23	16	25	44
Louisiana	45	34	47	55
Maine	13	27	32	14
Maryland	18	34	8	19
Massachusetts	5	22	14	20
Michigan	12	42	9	34
Minnesota	46	9	26	31
Mississippi	51	27	51	29
Missouri	10	12	3	33
Montana	15	46	31	32
Nebraska	27	6	20	3
Nevada	28	43	33	47
New Hampshire	24	34	29	37
New Jersey	43	39	40	28
New Mexico	14	3	30	21
New York	34	27	43	51
North Carolina	33	20	37	5
North Dakota	48	51	42	22
Northern Mariana Islands	52	2	52	50
Ohio	8	5	2	45
Oklahoma	16	16	15	23
Oregon	1	6	1	54
Pennsylvania	47	47	38	48
Rhode Island	11	51	27	30
South Carolina	29	22	36	35
South Dakota	36	40	28	13

State	Library Visits Per Capita	Registered Users Per Capita	Total Circulation Per Capita	Children's Material Circulation Percentage
Tennessee	34	38	39	26
Texas	48	22	48	6
Utah	21	16	4	7
Vermont	3	25	16	15
Virgin Islands (U.S.)	55	55	55	27
Virginia	20	16	24	12
Washington	50	27	11	52
West Virginia	38	20	49	41
Wisconsin	29	37	23	36
Wyoming	6	14	10	10

State	Number of Public Access Internet Computers	Number of Public Access Internet Computers Per 5,000 Population	Average Number of Public Access Internet Computers Per Stationary Outlet	Public Access Internet Computer User Sessions Per Capita
Alabama	27	35	30	29
Alaska	47	6	42	8
American Samoa	54	53	44	52
Arizona	23	46	8	28
Arkansas	32	22	35	51
California	1	47	10	25
Colorado	30	49	38	40
Connecticut	26	9	15	3
Delaware	45	20	3	30
District of Columbia	52	54	52	4
Florida	4	40	2	32
Georgia	7	31	5	7
Guam	48	1	1	54
Hawaii	51	52	40	1
Idaho	37	14	36	22
Illinois	5	7	12	5
Indiana	13	15	22	36
Iowa	8	2	23	17
Kansas	29	10	47	32
Kentucky	22	19	6	13
Louisiana	21	17	24	37
Maine	36	5	49	32
Maryland	19	33	4	12
Massachusetts	14	23	25	9
Michigan	6	12	17	17
Minnesota	20	27	26	48
Mississippi	33	34	39	40
Missouri	24	39	34	11
Montana	44	18	46	23
Nebraska	34	4	43	24
Nevada	39	51	20	14
New Hampshire	41	25	54	42

State	Number of Public Access Internet Computers	Number of Public Access Internet Computers Per 5,000 Population	Average Number of Public Access Internet Computers Per Stationary Outlet	Public Access Internet Computer User Sessions Per Capita
New Jersey	11	36	19	44
New Mexico	38	16	28	2
New York	3	30	21	38
North Carolina	12	44	16	35
North Dakota	50	25	48	44
Northern Mariana Islands	53	42	32	52
Ohio	9	41	37	30
Oklahoma	28	24	27	9
Oregon	31	32	31	16
Pennsylvania	15	50	41	50
Rhode Island	40	8	14	20
South Carolina	25	28	9	19
South Dakota	46	13	53	27
Tennessee	18	37	13	25
Texas	2	45	11	44
Utah	35	48	29	38
Vermont	43	3	51	14
Virgin Islands (U.S.)	55	55	55	55
Virginia	10	28	7	20
Washington	16	38	18	47
West Virginia	42	43	49	42
Wisconsin	17	21	32	48
Wyoming	49	11	45	6

State	Number of Print Materials In Thousands	Number of Print Materials Per Capita	Number of E-Books In Thousands	Number of E-Books Per Capita
Alabama	27	35	23	29
Alaska	49	15	44	24
American Samoa	55	54	52	50
Arizona	30	53	20	30
Arkansas	34	30	29	28
California	2	48	6	37
Colorado	24	41	28	33
Connecticut	18	6	39	40
Delaware	50	46	49	45
District of Columbia	52	55	51	53
Florida	9	51	16	46
Georgia	16	49	38	48
Guam	51	40	54	54
Hawaii	42	29	50	51
Idaho	39	21	45	39
Illinois	3	13	5	12
Indiana	11	8	15	20
Iowa	20	5	7	4
Kansas	28	11	2	1

State	Number of Print Materials In Thousands	Number of Print Materials Per Capita	Number of E-Books In Thousands	Number of E-Books Per Capita
Kentucky	25	31	13	8
Louisiana	21	27	26	31
Maine	32	1	35	9
Maryland	22	39	36	42
Massachusetts	6	3	10	14
Michigan	7	23	11	23
Minnesota	17	28	33	38
Mississippi	36	34	47	47
Missouri	13	20	24	32
Montana	46	26	37	17
Nebraska	35	8	30	15
Nevada	41	52	48	49
New Hampshire	37	4	22	5
New Jersey	8	19	8	18
New Mexico	40	24	46	41
New York	1	12	4	21
North Carolina	14	47	21	35
North Dakota	48	17	43	25
Northern Mariana Islands	54	43	53	52
Ohio	4	13	1	2
Oklahoma	33	36	25	26
Oregon	26	22	18	13
Pennsylvania	10	33	17	36
Rhode Island	43	18	32	7
South Carolina	29	37	31	34
South Dakota	45	10	40	19
Tennessee	23	44	9	10
Texas	5	50	14	44
Utah	31	32	27	27
Vermont	44	2	42	16
Virgin Islands (U.S.)	53	41	54	54
Virginia	15	37	12	22
Washington	19	44	34	43
West Virginia	38	25	19	6
Wisconsin	12	16	3	3
Wyoming	47	7	41	11

State	Number of Audio Physical Materials Per Capita	Number of Audio Downloadable Materials Per Capita	Number of Video Physical Materials Per Capita	Number of Video Downloadable Materials Per Capita
Alabama	32	34	42	20
Alaska	16	23	2	18
American Samoa	51	52	54	48
Arizona	43	23	40	26
Arkansas	39	20	30	23
California	43	37	46	19
Colorado	25	28	24	9

State	Number of Audio Physical Materials Per Capita	Number of Audio Downloadable Materials Per Capita	Number of Video Physical Materials Per Capita	Number of Video Downloadable Materials Per Capita
Connecticut	6	40	11	42
Delaware	29	44	34	38
District of Columbia	54	51	53	48
Florida	43	16	42	31
Georgia	50	48	49	35
Guam	54	52	55	48
Hawaii	40	50	46	48
Idaho	20	41	22	42
Illinois	5	14	12	10
Indiana	10	31	9	20
Iowa	10	5	6	38
Kansas	16	1	6	1
Kentucky	32	21	26	23
Louisiana	35	33	15	10
Maine	8	10	10	6
Maryland	25	39	35	26
Massachusetts	8	25	13	26
Michigan	14	19	16	8
Minnesota	20	43	31	42
Mississippi	47	49	44	42
Missouri	16	35	20	20
Montana	29	12	24	17
Nebraska	19	9	20	42
Nevada	40	45	35	37
New Hampshire	10	3	6	2
New Jersey	1	11	18	4
New Mexico	29	42	22	35
New York	20	32	16	31
North Carolina	47	47	50	38
North Dakota	25	26	28	13
Northern Mariana Islands	52	52	50	48
Ohio	2	2	1	3
Oklahoma	35	29	33	29
Oregon	13	15	13	7
Pennsylvania	25	36	35	15
Rhode Island	20	18	18	29
South Carolina	40	30	35	23
South Dakota	20	22	28	42
Tennessee	43	13	46	19
Texas	47	45	45	38
Utah	14	6	26	15
Vermont	6	8	4	48
Virgin Islands (U.S.)	52	52	52	48
Virginia	35	17	40	14
Washington	32	38	35	31
West Virginia	35	7	31	4
Wisconsin	4	4	5	31
Wyoming	3	27	3	12

State	Number of Public Libraries	Total Paid Staff	Total Librarians	Percentage of Total Librarians with ALA-MLS
Alabama	15	30	25	39
Alaska	38	50	49	30
American Samoa	50	55	53	1
Arizona	31	24	28	16
Arkansas	42	33	38	36
California	18	2	2	7
Colorado	26	14	20	22
Connecticut	19	22	16	23
Delaware	49	48	50	31
District of Columbia	50	43	51	1
Florida	35	6	7	12
Georgia	40	19	32	1
Guam	50	53	55	55
Hawaii	50	44	47	5
Idaho	28	34	41	35
Illinois	2	4	3	21
Indiana	12	9	9	24
Iowa	4	29	18	45
Kansas	9	28	26	41
Kentucky	24	21	13	47
Louisiana	39	20	15	42
Maine	14	39	37	37
Maryland	46	16	10	32
Massachusetts	8	13	6	26
Michigan	6	7	8	20
Minnesota	22	23	22	27
Mississippi	43	37	30	54
Missouri	21	15	21	43
Montana	33	46	43	46
Nebraska	13	38	35	51
Nevada	48	36	44	18
New Hampshire	16	35	31	38
New Jersey	10	8	11	6
New Mexico	31	40	39	33
New York	1	1	1	15
North Carolina	33	17	23	8
North Dakota	36	51	48	40
Northern Mariana Islands	50	53	52	52
Ohio	11	3	4	19
Oklahoma	25	31	19	50
Oregon	23	26	33	14
Pennsylvania	5	11	12	17
Rhode Island	44	42	40	9
South Carolina	45	25	29	13
South Dakota	27	49	45	49
Tennessee	17	27	27	34
Texas	3	5	5	25
Utah	37	32	34	29

State	Number of Public Libraries	Total Paid Staff	Total Librarians	Percentage of Total Librarians with ALA-MLS
Vermont	20	47	42	44
Virgin Islands (U.S.)	50	52	53	1
Virginia	30	10	17	11
Washington	41	12	24	10
West Virginia	29	41	36	53
Wisconsin	7	18	14	28
Wyoming	47	45	46	48

State	Total Revenue Per Capita	State Revenue Per Capita	Local Revenue Per Capita	Other Revenue Per Capita
Alabama	46	29	45	37
Alaska	9	26	7	31
American Samoa	55	7	53	52
Arizona	42	45	40	47
Arkansas	38	20	38	24
California	26	36	19	27
Colorado	6	41	3	12
Connecticut	10	43	13	4
Delaware	37	11	41	34
District of Columbia	1	50	1	22
Florida	41	31	37	48
Georgia	50	13	49	42
Guam	54	50	51	53
Hawaii	44	2	53	41
Idaho	25	25	21	20
Illinois	4	12	4	14
Indiana	8	10	8	16
Iowa	27	34	20	23
Kansas	11	22	11	7
Kentucky	21	23	18	33
Louisiana	12	32	9	36
Maine	28	42	34	1
Maryland	17	3	29	8
Massachusetts	18	21	16	15
Michigan	20	28	17	17
Minnesota	24	23	25	18
Mississippi	51	16	50	40
Missouri	15	33	14	21
Montana	39	30	35	29
Nebraska	31	40	26	30
Nevada	35	5	42	42
New Hampshire	19	48	15	19
New Jersey	13	39	10	35
New Mexico	34	14	36	25
New York	5	15	6	2
North Carolina	45	26	43	37
North Dakota	40	18	39	39
Northern Mariana Islands	53	50	52	54

State	Total Revenue Per Capita	State Revenue Per Capita	Local Revenue Per Capita	Other Revenue Per Capita
Ohio	3	1	27	6
Oklahoma	29	37	24	28
Oregon	2	44	2	13
Pennsylvania	43	9	47	10
Rhode Island	16	4	30	3
South Carolina	33	17	33	45
South Dakota	36	50	32	44
Tennessee	49	47	46	49
Texas	48	50	44	50
Utah	30	38	22	45
Vermont	23	50	28	5
Virgin Islands (U.S.)	52	6	53	54
Virginia	32	19	31	51
Washington	7	46	5	32
West Virginia	47	8	48	26
Wisconsin	22	35	23	11
Wyoming	14	49	12	9

State	Total Operating Expenditures Per Capita	Staff Expenditures Per Capita	Collection Expenditures Per Capita	Other Operating Expenditures Per Capita
Alabama	46	46	47	45
Alaska	9	9	18	7
American Samoa	54	55	53	53
Arizona	42	45	23	28
Arkansas	44	41	40	38
California	24	24	36	14
Colorado	8	12	3	11
Connecticut	5	4	13	15
Delaware	38	39	48	21
District of Columbia	1	1	1	3
Florida	43	43	39	30
Georgia	50	49	50	51
Guam	55	54	55	55
Hawaii	41	42	41	26
Idaho	27	30	24	17
Illinois	4	5	8	2
Indiana	11	17	4	5
Iowa	22	20	15	31
Kansas	10	16	10	4
Kentucky	31	32	19	27
Louisiana	18	19	9	9
Maine	23	21	38	22
Maryland	14	10	11	40
Massachusetts	15	14	12	29
Michigan	21	25	22	12
Minnesota	26	28	28	16
Mississippi	51	51	51	50
Missouri	17	22	5	6

Montana	39	38	42	44
Nebraska	30	31	21	32
Nevada	37	35	29	42
New Hampshire	19	15	27	34
New Jersey	13	11	25	18
New Mexico	35	36	17	36
New York	3	2	16	10
North Carolina	45	44	44	48
North Dakota	36	37	35	33
Northern Mariana Islands	53	52	54	54
Ohio	6	8	2	8
Oklahoma	28	27	14	35
Oregon	2	3	6	1
Pennsylvania	40	40	45	37
Rhode Island	16	13	33	20
South Carolina	33	33	26	41
South Dakota	34	34	34	39
Tennessee	49	48	49	46
Texas	47	47	46	49
Utah	29	29	19	25
Vermont	20	18	30	22
Virgin Islands (U.S.)	52	53	52	52
Virginia	32	26	37	43
Washington	7	6	7	13
West Virginia	48	50	43	47
Wisconsin	25	23	32	24
Wyoming	12	7	31	19

Book Trade Research and Statistics

Prices of U.S. and Foreign Published Materials

Sylvia Orner

Editor, ALA Core Library Materials Price Index Editorial Board

The Library Materials Price Index (LMPI) Editorial Board of Core, a division of the American Library Association, continues to monitor prices for a range of library materials from sources within North America and other key publishing centers worldwide.

The U.S. Consumer Price Index (CPI) increased by 6.5 percent in 2022. CPI figures are obtained from the Bureau of Labor Statistics at http://www.bls.gov.

In 2017 all tables that utilized a base index price increase reset their base year to 2010. All indexes continue to utilize the 2010 base year. Percent changes in average prices from 2019 to 2023 are conveniently noted in the chart below.

	Average Price Percent Change				
Index	2019	2020	2021	2022	2023
U.S. Consumer Price Index	2.3	1.4	7.0	6.5	n.a.
U.S. Periodicals (Table 1)	6.7	6.7*	2.3	5.6	5.4
Legal Serials Services (Table 2)	10.9	21.4	20.4	21.7	26.1
Hardcover Books (Table 3)	-1.7*	-0.2*	0.3*	2.2	n.a.
Academic Books (Table 4)	-0.9	8.3	-0.9	5.3	n.a.
Academic E-Books (Table 4A)	0.3	4.9	-1.8	5.0	n.a.
Academic Textbooks (Table 4B)	2.0	2.8	6.8	-2.8	n.a.
U.S. College books (Table 5)	1.3	13.5	6.1	-3.7	n.a.
U.S. Mass Market Paperbacks (Table 6)	2.4*	1.5*	2.1*	1.3	n.a.
U.S. Paperbacks (Table 7)	-8.5*	-3.5*	4.3*	-3.1	n.a.
U.S. Audiobooks (Table 7A)	1.6	0.2	-23.3*	56.8	n.a.
U.S. E-Books (Table 7B)	1.5	6.5	-13.2	9.27	n.a.
+Serials (Table 8)	6.1	6.0*	3.6	3.7*	5.2
+Online Serials (Table 8A)	6.5*	6.1*	3.7*	3.3	5.7
British Academic Books (Table 9)	-1.8	-1.4	16.2*	-1.9	n.a.

*= figures revised from previous editions based on new data
+Dataset changes each year.

U.S. Published Materials

Tables 1 through 7B indicate average prices and price indexes for library materials published primarily in the United States. These indexes are U.S. Periodicals (Table 1),

Legal Serials Services (Table 2), U.S. Hardcover Books (Table 3), North American Academic Books (Table 4), North American Academic E-Books (Table 4A), North American Academic Textbooks (Table 4B), U.S. College Books (Table 5), U.S. Mass Market Paperback Books (Table 6), U.S. Paperbacks (Excluding Mass Market) (Table 7), U.S. Audiobooks (Table 7A), and U.S. E-Books (Table 7B).

Periodical and Serials Prices

The U.S. Periodical Price Index (USPPI) (Table 1) was reestablished in 2014 by Stephen Bosch of the University of Arizona and is now being compiled by Cynthia Elliott in consultation with him. The index is updated here for 2023 using data supplied by EBSCO Information Services. This report includes 2019–2023 data indexed to the base year of 2010. Table 1 is derived from a selected set of titles that, as much as possible, will remain as the sample base for the index for future comparisons. The data in Table 1 are from a print preferred data pull, but more than 71 percent of the titles in the index are based on online pricing, and only 29 percent are print only. The data provide a strong mix of both print and online pricing, characteristic of a current academic library's serials collection. The subscription prices used are publishers' list prices, excluding publisher discount or vendor service charges. The pricing data for 2010–2014, the base years for the new USPPI, published in 2014, were created from one single report that pulled pricing information for a static set of titles for the five-year period. The pricing data for 2019–2023 are based on that same sampling of titles but are not an exact match due to changes that occur with serial titles. Some titles fell off the list due to pricing not being available, while other titles on the list for which pricing had not been available in 2014 now have pricing available.

The new USPPI works from a title list of more than 7,400 titles and is run for both print preferred data and online preferred data in order to get both sets of pricing. The original title list covered only about 3,700 titles. The previous versions of USPPI treated Russian translations as a separate category. Russian translations are no longer a focus of this index and are not tracked as a category. These were once seen as a major cost factor, but this is no longer the case, and, therefore, their inclusion in or exclusion from the index no longer makes sense. There are Russian translation titles in the index, but they are not reported separately.

The main barrier to creating this index is the difficulty of maintaining the title list and obtaining standard retail pricing for titles on the list. Changes in serials titles due to ceased publication, movement to open access, mergers, combining titles in packages, moving to direct orders, and publication delays are a few of the situations that can affect compilers' ability to obtain current pricing information. The new index retained that part of the title list from the previous index that remained viable and added new titles to that list based on data from EBSCO Information Services on the most frequently ordered serials in its system. From that list of serials, titles were selected for the new index to ensure that the distribution by subject was similar to the distribution in the original index. There are more titles in the selected title set than the number of titles that produced prices over the past six years. This should allow the current index to be sustainable into the future as titles fall off the list and pricing becomes available for titles that may have been delayed or are no longer in memberships.

The first five years of data, published in 2014, showed consistent price changes across subject areas due to the fact that the pricing data was a historical look at the prices of the same set of journals. The data for 2019–2023 are based on the same sample list but are not the exact same list of titles as the data for 2010–2014 due to the previously mentioned issues that can impact pricing availability. Across subject areas, the changes in price were basically flat this year, showing an overall 5.4 percent increase compared to the 5.6 percent increase in 2022. This is comparable to price changes seen in other pricing studies (see Table 8), which showed a 5.7 percent increase. The impact of current increases in the CPI may have contributed to part of this increase. At the subject level, the sample sizes are smaller, so a few changes can cause a large swing in the overall price for that area. In 2023 there was a variation from 2.3 to 11.4 percent. The outliers in 2023 were subjects with small numbers of titles, so the changes in price in a small number of titles can drop or raise the average price from the norm.

Direct comparisons between Table 1 and Table 8 should be avoided, especially at the subject level. Both tables show the overall rate of increase in serial prices to be around 5 percent; however, beyond that point, there is little that makes a statistically valid comparison. Table 8 has a slightly lower overall average price and price increase in most subject areas. This is due to Table 8's larger set of data coming from a broad mix of sources, including a much larger set of journals from foreign sources and a higher mix of non-STM titles. Table 1 is a mix of journals that attempts to reflect the journal collections in an average U.S. library, so the mix of journals contains fewer trade and popular titles than would be found in Table 8, but Table 8 has more foreign titles, and prices for those can be impacted by the strength of the U.S. dollar. Differences in the two datasets yield different results.

The most important trend seen in this data (Table 1) is that the consistent increase in prices that had averaged around 6 percent prior to 2020 and had been subdued due to the impact of the pandemic on library budgets has now rebounded. In 2023 prices increased at a higher rate, 5.4 percent, which is closer to the years prior to 2020. This year titles in a broad mix of social science and STM subjects dominate the list of areas with larger price increases. Average prices for journals in the science and technology area are still far higher than in other areas, and that trend continues, with the average cost of chemistry journals being $6,617 and physics journals being $4,982.

The Legal Serials Services Index is compiled by Ajaye Bloomstone of the Louisiana State University Law Center Library, using data collected from various legal serials vendors. The base year for this index is 2010. This index presents price data covering the years 2010–2023.

As in past years, vendors and publishers were asked to provide cost data on particular titles with the assumption that the title or set has been held as an active subscription over a period of time by a large academic research law library. The cost recorded in the index is intended to be based on the upkeep cost of a particular title, not necessarily the cost incurred in purchasing a new set, although sometimes the cost is the same, and often, the cost of updates can be more expensive than purchasing a new set. A nuance of legal publishing is that for some of the larger legal publishers, hard prices for a calendar year are not set at the beginning of that calendar

(text continues on page 274)

Table 1 / U.S. Periodicals: Average Prices and Price Indexes 2019–2023

Index Base 2010 = 100

Subject	LC Class	Titles	2010 Average Price	2019 Average Price	2020 Average Price	2021 Average Price	2022 Average Price	2023 Average Price	Percent Change 2022–2023	Index
Agriculture	S	292	$579.48	$1,331.73	$1,401.91	$1,461.75	$1,526.07	$1,618.98	6.1%	279.4
Anthropology	GN	70	373.64	767.46	798.91	835.35	879.96	914.94	4.0	244.9
Arts and Architecture	N	124	112.39	344.92	363.84	375.33	388.90	411.09	5.7	365.8
Astronomy	QB	40	1,793.08	3,005.82	3,210.45	3,065.84	3,236.80	3,310.72	2.3	184.6
Biology	QH	595	2,053.06	3,303.40	3,444.26	3,528.89	3,697.61	3,918.99	6.0	190.9
Botany	QK	99	1,361.09	2,180.88	2,264.88	2,317.03	2,406.84	2,545.13	5.7	187.0
Business and Economics	HA-HJ	621	351.29	778.36	825.87	846.96	880.82	920.46	4.5	262.0
Chemistry	QD	232	3,396.26	5,546.65	5,896.99	6,006.17	6,346.83	6,616.88	4.3	194.8
Education	L	356	354.92	760.29	812.66	851.70	899.20	957.70	6.5	269.8
Engineering	T	824	1,244.39	2,483.03	2,655.72	2,735.11	2,905.01	3,087.62	6.3	248.1
Food Science	TX	50	356.17	1,250.20	1,340.44	1,395.10	1,471.44	1,584.50	7.7	444.9
General Science	Q	150	998.51	1,876.29	1,974.97	2,042.83	2,141.99	2,293.93	7.1	229.7
General Works	A	114	85.84	162.37	170.91	184.81	197.44	206.07	4.4	240.1
Geography	G-GF	137	670.60	1,372.06	1,469.70	1,526.02	1,596.47	1,708.12	7.0	254.7
Geology	QE	123	1,368.79	2,255.52	2,370.74	2,449.56	2,532.54	2,638.04	4.2	192.7
Heath Sciences	R	1,308	1,009.55	1,824.40	1,951.68	2,016.63	2,138.88	2,247.12	5.1	222.6

History	C,D,E,F	458	202.39	444.19	468.41	485.82	507.38	528.90	4.2	261.3
Language and Literature	P	425	168.12	311.67	329.42	333.89	344.36	364.45	5.8	216.8
Law	K	270	214.01	457.78	480.06	493.75	525.13	551.75	5.1	257.8
Library Science	Z	106	290.02	652.10	696.24	710.07	750.83	769.47	2.5	265.3
Math and Computer Science	QA	612	1,242.13	1,999.55	2,149.81	2,204.41	2,327.80	2,457.19	5.6	197.8
Military and Naval Science	U,V	42	239.90	453.64	476.88	487.46	501.25	521.38	4.0	217.3
Music	M	64	82.18	284.90	300.61	310.07	320.48	329.87	2.9	401.4
Philosophy and Religion	B-BD, BH-BX	360	232.37	449.89	470.41	476.95	503.49	519.71	3.2	223.7
Physics	QC	266	2,845.54	4,321.42	4,555.14	4,664.33	4,808.51	4,982.03	3.6	175.1
Political Science	J	152	312.76	838.89	914.51	954.87	986.31	1,038.40	5.3	332.0
Psychology	BF	203	648.21	1,224.24	1,321.11	1,358.98	1,430.25	1,522.37	6.4	234.9
Recreation	GV	64	69.79	304.25	317.79	329.02	347.11	370.04	6.6	530.2
Social Sciences	H	75	351.40	935.53	990.39	993.40	1,040.35	1,097.06	5.5	312.2
Sociology	HM-HX	403	482.59	1,002.02	1,067.11	1,101.86	1,156.78	1,228.04	6.2	254.5
Technology	TA-TT	169	535.73	1,376.46	1,482.17	1,545.15	1,632.55	1,818.43	11.4	339.4
Zoology	QL	174	1,454.26	2,601.40	2,713.10	2,687.98	2,778.43	2,866.19	3.2	197.1
Total		8,978	$843.46	$1,642.22	$1,742.91	$1,789.88	$1,881.76	$1,982.73	5.4%	235.1

Compiled by Cynthia Elliott in consultation with Stephen Bosch of the University of Arizona, based on subscription information supplied by EBSCO Information Services

(continued from page 271)

year, but halfway through, so only gross price estimates may be available in time for publication of this article. In addition to titles issued on a "regular" basis (e.g., journals and law reviews published monthly, quarterly, etc.), legal serials may also be updated throughout the year with both regular and/or irregular updates or releases, new editions, and new or revised volumes. If a title is updated irregularly, the price for its renewal may increase or decrease from one year to the next, depending on the supplier's plans for keeping the title current. It is noteworthy that although legal serials in print format are still produced, titles continue migrating to an electronic-only format, which is reflected strongly in this 2023 survey.

Some prices were provided to the compiler with the caveat "no longer available for new sales," meaning that a print subscription can continue to be ordered in that format if it is currently an existing subscription of the purchaser. There is also a trend for titles purchased in print to now come with an electronic component. For such titles, the purchasing library may have no choice but to accept both formats, even if the print title is preferred. If one could purchase the print format without the electronic component, the cost might conceivably change. This leads one to believe that if the publication is not to be phased out immediately, then the title might, at some point soon, no longer be available in print, and this process will serve to "wean" the print subscriber to an electronic format if the publication doesn't entirely cease. More than 20 titles used to compile Table 2 ceased publication in 2019. To compensate for the loss of titles, new titles were added. The new titles were added with the intent to match the previous year's cost of the ceased publications plus the average percentage of an increase for the remainder of the titles from 2018 to 2019. Further substitutions occurred between 2019 and 2020 due to titles discontinuing print and migrating to an electronic format or ceasing

Table 2 / Legal Serials Services:
Average Prices and Price Indexes, 2010–2023
Index Base: 2010 = 100

Year	Titles	Average Price	Percent Change	Index
2010	217	$1,714.96	3.5%	100.0
2011	217	1,904.69	11.1	111.1
2012	219	2,058.66	8.1	120.0
2013	218	2,241.42	8.9	130.7
2014	219	2,473.44	10.4	144.2
2015	218	2,818.02	13.9	164.3
2016	217	3,085.34	9.5	179.9
2017	218	3,446.12	11.7	200.9
2018	185	4,195.99	21.8	244.7
2019	191	4,653.97	10.9	271.4
2020	187	5,648.39	21.4	329.4
2021	186	6,802.39	20.4	396.6
2022	183	8,277.79	21.7	482.7
2023	163	10,437.24	26.1	608.6

Compiled by Ajaye Bloomstone, Louisiana State University Law Center Library altogether, although, in terms of the titles tracked in this list over time, the number that have ceased seems to have been curtailed, at least temporarily, through 2022. With the 2022 survey, it was decided that there would be no substitutions made for the two titles indicated as ceased or discontinued by the supplier; it is assumed that there would be little or no variance in the three ultimate determinants for the annual survey: average cost per title, percent of change, and index.

With the 2023 price collection, however, it was found that one major publisher made a deliberate decision to discontinue the print format for a number of titles that had been tracked for this table, and the one title that has remained in print is supposed to cease in that format by the end of this calendar year. The publisher willingly shared reasons for the decision and subsequent demise of its print products: production costs, shipping, and with subscriber numbers dwindling, it becomes more expensive for those subscribers that choose to keep purchasing a particular title in print format. When deciding which titles to discontinue in print, those with low subscriber numbers were preferred.

Book Prices

Tables 3 (U.S. Hardcover Books), 6 (U.S. Mass Market Paperback Books), 7 (U.S. Paperbacks, Excluding Mass Market), 7A (U.S. Audiobooks), and 7B (U.S. E-Books) were prepared by Narda Tafuri, retired, from the University of Scranton. They were derived from data provided by book wholesaler Baker & Taylor. Figures for 2020 have been revised again in order to reflect additional late updates to the Baker & Taylor database. Data for 2019 should now be considered finalized. The 2021 figures given here may be similarly revised in next year's tables and should be considered preliminary, as are the 2022 figures. The figures for this edition of the *Library and Book Trade Almanac* were provided by Baker & Taylor and are based on the Book Industry Study Group's BISAC categories. The BISAC juvenile category (fiction and nonfiction) has been divided into children and young adult. For more information on the BISAC categories, visit http://www.bisg.org.

Once again, average book prices overall saw both increases and decreases in 2022. List prices for hardcover books (Table 3) and mass market paperback books (Table 6) showed slight increases of 2.18 percent and 1.27 percent, respectively. E-books (Table 7B) exhibited a substantial increase of 9.27 percent. Trade paperbacks (Table 7) exhibited a slight decrease of -3.07 percent. Audiobooks (Table 7A) saw the greatest increase, at 56.79 percent.

The North American Academic Books Price Indexes (Tables 4, 4A, and 4B) were prepared by Cynthia Elliott, in consultation with Stephen Bosch. The current version of North American Academic Books: Average Prices and Price Indexes, 2019–2022 (Table 4) has been stable for the past several years, so it is a good summary of change in the academic book market since 2010. Direct comparisons with earlier versions published before 2014 show variations since the number of titles treated and their average prices have changed. This is especially true for those versions published before 2009. Data for the current indexes are supplied by ProQuest Books (formerly Ingram Content Group-Coutts Information Services) and by GOBI Library Solutions from EBSCO (formerly YBP Library Services). Prior to ProQuest/Coutts supplying data, the book pricing data was obtained from Blackwell Book Services and YBP.

(text continues on page 284)

Table 3 / Hardcover Books: Average Prices and Price Indexes, 2019–2022

Index Base: 2010 = 100

BISAC Category	2010 Average Price	2019 Final Average Price	Volumes	Index	2020 Final Average Price	Volumes	Index	2021 Preliminary Average Price	Volumes	Index	2022 Preliminary Average Price	Volumes	Index
Antiques and Collectibles	$51.44	$66.07	101	128.4	$78.00	94	151.6	$76.55	80	148.8	$75.34	85	146.5
Architecture	85.52	94.78	928	110.8	96.79	896	113.2	94.45	832	110.4	102.87	814	120.3
Art	71.53	74.24	2,247	103.8	83.75	2,028	117.1	84.73	1,815	118.5	75.89	2,039	106.1
Bibles	37.50	57.63	188	153.7	54.01	221	144.0	64.03	215	170.7	57.01	375	152.0
Biography and Autobiography	53.41	41.72	1,575	78.1	43.35	1,525	81.2	41.35	1,786	77.4	41.22	1,954	77.2
Body, Mind and Spirit	36.91	25.78	291	69.9	22.98	308	62.3	29.55	307	80.1	30.42	371	82.4
Business and Economics	134.61	142.57	4,346	105.9	142.97	4,154	106.2	138.90	4,392	103.2	140.92	4,553	104.7
Children	24.63	25.42	16,335	103.2	26.92	15,551	109.3	26.80	14,637	108.8	25.36	14,015	103.0
Comics and Graphic Novels	31.51	48.59	689	154.2	46.62	650	147.9	48.90	634	155.2	52.64	789	167.1
Computers	138.53	162.78	1,118	117.5	160.72	1,035	116.0	187.45	1,054	135.3	207.76	1,247	150.0
Cooking	30.91	30.26	1,110	97.9	31.71	933	102.6	33.41	954	108.1	33.73	972	109.1
Crafts and Hobbies	33.28	32.38	158	97.3	32.59	147	97.9	31.55	138	94.8	32.24	126	96.9
Design	76.59	68.60	365	89.6	70.80	307	92.4	70.02	263	91.4	74.19	324	96.9
Drama	42.91	111.60	84	260.1	107.60	77	250.7	94.42	81	220.0	94.63	92	220.5
Education	117.59	168.75	2,556	143.5	160.99	2,307	136.9	146.17	2,323	124.3	149.71	2,413	127.3
Family and Relationships	32.24	46.85	225	145.3	51.63	224	160.1	68.00	243	210.9	46.27	241	143.5
Fiction	32.20	29.73	5,055	92.3	29.93	4,539	92.9	29.21	5,112	90.7	30.36	4,688	94.3
Foreign Language Study	132.47	121.91	216	92.0	122.30	239	92.3	117.98	243	89.1	129.11	242	97.5
Games and Activities	52.07	38.50	145	73.9	40.78	141	78.3	57.38	121	110.2	47.16	149	90.6
Gardening	36.42	39.28	121	107.9	38.61	110	106.0	35.98	120	98.8	34.93	128	95.9
Health and Fitness	48.51	83.96	393	173.1	87.06	350	179.5	76.67	375	158.0	100.80	426	207.8
History	82.65	103.28	6,222	125.0	111.18	5,665	134.5	103.62	5,657	125.4	95.81	5,508	115.9

Law	114.46	2,212	175.77	100.7	2,274	169.16	106.4	2,363	176.92	101.4	2,369	173.49	100.6
Literary Collections	83.49	272	135.18	161.9	254	109.44	131.1	255	83.19	99.6	240	92.28	110.5
Literary Criticism	117.63	2,649	125.12	106.4	2,572	130.27	110.7	2,665	130.29	110.8	2,673	126.97	107.9
Mathematics	133.23	994	148.16	111.2	841	148.02	111.1	824	145.93	109.5	821	136.11	102.2
Medical	171.13	3,547	175.16	102.4	2,857	185.73	108.5	2,571	193.02	112.8	3,047	204.99	119.8
Music	87.84	675	96.38	109.7	650	100.32	114.2	587	99.57	113.4	601	108.54	123.6
Nature	74.89	466	94.56	126.3	457	86.37	115.3	527	87.26	116.5	505	91.84	122.6
Performing Arts	76.27	775	121.13	158.8	789	105.52	138.3	843	104.36	136.8	830	101.72	133.4
Pets	24.66	56	27.34	110.9	60	22.71	92.1	51	26.52	107.5	69	26.06	105.7
Philosophy	108.93	1,899	115.44	106.0	1,753	123.54	113.4	1,700	114.66	105.3	1,724	113.91	104.6
Photography	107.99	825	69.86	64.7	786	60.17	55.7	598	123.52	114.4	610	68.35	63.3
Poetry	40.76	320	36.98	90.7	261	35.10	86.1	357	33.22	81.5	339	45.40	111.4
Political Science	110.32	5,551	127.46	115.5	3,635	116.14	105.3	3,409	122.21	110.8	3,378	124.27	112.6
Psychology	109.85	2,736	144.60	131.6	1,172	151.80	138.2	1,138	158.66	144.4	1,217	158.75	144.5
Reference	302.69	311	280.56	92.7	243	364.86	120.5	221	317.43	104.9	208	462.67	152.9
Religion	80.88	2,746	87.44	108.1	2,840	86.01	106.3	2,939	85.75	106.0	2,661	85.99	106.3
Science	192.20	4,144	189.21	98.4	3,547	193.58	100.7	3,432	193.43	100.6	3,945	189.56	98.6
Self-Help	27.11	438	24.20	89.2	424	23.66	87.3	467	24.51	90.4	446	25.62	94.5
Social Science	100.47	5,354	128.55	127.9	3,969	129.22	128.6	4,020	130.86	130.2	4,283	127.00	126.4
Sports and Recreation	41.23	541	52.27	126.8	498	56.49	137.0	516	61.85	150.0	565	65.94	159.9
Study Aids	101.54	9	177.87	175.2	30	126.20	124.3	13	145.30	143.1	13	159.61	157.2
Technology and Engineering	164.66	3,007	185.86	112.9	3,170	188.64	114.6	3,368	199.11	120.9	3,828	188.80	114.7
Transportation	84.28	301	86.46	102.6	218	89.49	106.2	236	93.58	111.0	234	88.81	105.4
Travel	41.32	238	41.78	101.1	216	37.33	90.4	174	43.12	104.4	197	36.60	88.6
True Crime	34.83	107	37.37	107.3	82	63.97	183.7	101	42.96	123.3	111	30.55	87.7
Young Adult	35.99	1,995	37.65	104.6	1,481	32.76	91.0	1,254	28.79	80.0	1,161	26.65	74.0
Totals and Averages	$89.54	88,601	$99.74	111.4	78,262	$99.57	111.2	77,703	$99.82	111.5	79,248	$102.00	113.9

Compiled by Narda Tafuri, retired, University of Scranton, from data supplied by Baker & Taylor

Table 4 / North American Academic Books: Average Prices and Price Indexes, 2019–2022

(Index Base: 2010 = 100)

Subject Area	LC Class	2010		2019		2020		2021		2022			
		Titles	Average Price	Titles	Average Price	Titles	Average Price	Titles	Average Price	Titles	Average Price	Percent Change 2021–2022	Index
Agriculture	S	1,139	$107.44	1,915	$115.92	1,969	$127.89	2,035	$129.89	2,079	$132.14	1.7%	123.0
Anthropology	GN	609	91.96	857	94.56	918	103.45	882	100.17	722	110.26	10.1	119.9
Botany	QK	260	125.84	456	136.82	525	156.64	561	149.49	483	153.15	2.5	121.7
Business and Economics	H	10,916	97.31	14,431	107.54	15,110	113.58	15,341	107.22	14,156	118.54	10.6	121.8
Chemistry	QD	667	223.03	918	191.15	926	215.75	883	240.41	805	239.01	-0.6	107.2
Education	L	4,688	86.47	7,122	93.01	7,488	102.26	7,279	97.83	6,886	112.65	15.1	130.3
Engineering and Technology	T	6,913	133.45	11,202	153.75	12,737	155.18	12,835	158.54	12,627	162.13	2.3	121.5
Fine and Applied Arts	M-N	5,535	57.17	7,694	74.66	7,456	82.74	8,186	81.83	7,571	82.83	1.2	144.9
General Works	A	80	75.60	290	98.42	295	103.92	295	99.47	299	104.88	5.4	138.7
Geography	G	1,144	104.98	1,900	123.05	2,005	123.77	2,064	113.49	1,842	124.41	9.6	118.5
Geology	QE	276	114.34	429	133.49	404	119.64	427	131.35	391	118.23	-10.0	103.4
History	C-D-E-F	10,079	65.29	15,105	73.36	14,357	85.45	15,103	79.78	12,965	84.17	5.5	128.9
Home Economics	TX	812	44.35	1,170	63.04	901	72.68	774	67.31	872	78.63	16.8	177.3
Industrial Arts	TT	265	52.60	297	57.59	207	77.94	169	71.96	290	66.51	-7.6	126.4

Subject	LC	Titles	Avg Price	Titles	Avg Price	Titles	Avg Price	Titles	Avg Price	Titles	Avg Price	% Change	Index
Law	K	4,596	125.35	6,728	128.39	7,039	134.26	7,859	139.91	6,168	144.13	3.0	115.0
Library and Information Science	Z	636	90.18	921	99.72	912	101.49	889	96.59	732	108.48	12.3	120.3
Literature and Language	P	19,364	57.31	30,452	58.25	30,316	66.40	30,006	67.07	27,685	68.62	2.3	119.7
Mathematics and Computer Science	QA	3,965	103.85	5,318	116.20	6,724	120.42	6,757	121.38	6,111	126.66	4.4	122.0
Medicine	R	8,679	112.66	12,452	137.62	12,982	135.98	12,447	137.47	11,504	144.51	5.1	128.3
Military and Naval Science	U-V	773	79.99	1,391	78.80	1,429	78.83	1,412	75.78	1,219	81.36	7.4	101.7
Philosophy and Religion	B	7,386	81.75	12,153	80.10	12,020	85.98	12,830	88.07	11,154	92.09	4.6	112.7
Physical Education and Recreation	GV	1,788	56.03	2,983	71.12	3,028	76.19	2,957	71.82	2,744	81.05	12.8	144.7
Physics and Astronomy	QB	1,627	128.36	2,342	127.36	2,297	131.51	2,444	130.20	2,138	140.77	8.1	109.7
Political Science	J	3,549	99.70	5,991	96.67	5,919	103.36	5,639	102.67	4,839	110.01	7.1	110.3
Psychology	BF	1,730	76.65	2,944	82.11	2,965	94.77	2,898	94.85	2,873	94.75	-0.1	123.6
Science (general)	Q	631	108.40	1,175	112.86	1,696	134.16	1,717	133.26	1,608	144.73	8.6	133.5
Sociology	HM	6,666	88.75	11,518	89.35	11,870	100.38	11,471	97.02	10,760	102.35	5.5	115.3
Zoology	QH, L,P,R	3,029	140.26	3,916	133.28	3,843	137.87	3,794	134.61	3,539	138.96	3.2	99.1
Totals and Averages		107,802	$89.15	164,070	$95.87	168,338	$103.87	169,954	$102.98	155,062	$108.47	5.3%	121.7

Compiled by Cynthia Elliott in consultation with Stephen Bosch from the University of Arizona from electronic data provided by ProQuest (formerly Ingram Content Group-Coutts Information Services) and GOBI Library Solutions from EBSCO (formerly YBP Library Services). The data represent all titles (includes e-books, hardcover, trade, and paperback books, as well as annuals) treated for all approval plan customers serviced by the vendors. This table covers titles published or distributed in the United States and Canada during the calendar years listed.

This index does not include paperback editions and electronic books. The inclusion of these items does impact pricing in the index.

Table 4 A / North American Academic E-Books: Average Prices and Price Indexes, 2019–2022

(Index Base: 2010 = 100)

Subject Area	LC Class	2010 Titles	2010 Average Price	2019 Titles	2019 Average Price	2020 Titles	2020 Average Price	2021 Titles	2021 Average Price	2022 Titles	2022 Average Price	2022 Percent Change 2021–2022	2022 Index
Agriculture	S	697	$168.73	874	$132.96	961	$146.83	971	$147.63	1008	$148.61	0.7%	88.1
Anthropology	GN	385	109.96	393	103.92	435	114.52	429	107.84	339	121.63	12.8	110.6
Botany	QK	190	175.23	193	159.51	257	168.72	261	165.04	219	166.23	0.7	94.9
Business and Economics	H	8,481	102.87	6797	118.09	7625	123.43	7931	115.69	7125	130.75	13.0	127.1
Chemistry	QD	521	232.57	446	186.38	499	228.23	453	267.56	417	259.57	-3.0	111.6
Education	L	2,852	99.96	3231	101.52	3660	114.12	3627	106.42	3422	121.58	14.2	121.6
Engineering and Technology	T	4,976	152.33	5281	165.33	6404	165.47	6471	170.13	6366	175.80	3.3	115.4
Fine and Applied Arts	M,N	1,493	83.35	2338	96.52	2822	106.81	3047	104.18	2773	108.10	3.8	129.7
General Works	A	53	89.13	132	97.67	148	108.32	139	112.94	146	118.82	5.2	133.3
Geography	G	829	117.83	828	141.23	993	135.83	1045	123.54	898	138.45	12.1	117.5
Geology	QE	178	146.85	186	152.31	171	133.30	197	151.11	167	140.43	-7.1	95.6
History	C,D, E,F	5,189	89.42	6233	87.41	6582	94.95	7126	90.81	6195	97.96	7.9	109.5
Home Economics	TX	211	78.08	435	81.29	407	92.92	323	84.86	394	102.96	21.3	131.9

Subject	LC Class	No.	Price	No.	Price	No.	Price	No.	Price	No.	Price	%	Index
Industrial Arts	TT	23	46.11	77	66.08	77	109.80	67	93.09	128	80.74	-13.3	175.1
Law	K	2,433	147.66	2650	147.22	3256	146.01	3911	154.66	2979	166.53	7.7	112.8
Library and Information Science	Z	387	89.43	378	111.23	383	113.09	377	108.73	309	130.26	19.8	145.7
Literature and Language	P	7,664	103.12	10276	81.88	11922	92.77	12413	89.81	11565	92.39	2.9	89.6
Mathematics and Computer Science	QA	3,000	112.65	2231	128.80	3376	131.14	3422	133.85	3067	142.33	6.3	126.3
Medicine	R	6,404	134.60	5741	164.83	6297	153.95	6154	154.54	5608	165.86	7.3	123.2
Military and Naval Science	U,V	487	105.07	598	93.88	663	89.29	634	89.45	582	96.22	7.6	91.6
Philosophy and Religion	B	4,262	110.31	5189	94.03	5983	96.13	6599	97.18	5805	105.27	8.3	95.4
Physical Education and Recreation	GV	791	76.57	1257	89.00	1437	91.84	1433	82.64	1347	94.83	14.7	123.8
Physics and Astronomy	QB	1,288	147.50	1078	145.53	1154	148.24	1171	157.26	1025	168.50	7.2	114.2
Political Science	J	2,638	110.10	2738	110.76	2944	114.09	2938	111.17	2426	122.00	9.7	110.8
Psychology	BF	1,062	91.35	1342	95.97	1460	110.12	1466	108.17	1407	111.62	3.2	122.2
Science (general)	Q	462	122.51	495	125.52	874	140.77	893	139.98	818	153.22	9.5	125.1
Sociology	HM	4,520	103.73	5140	103.29	5803	113.97	5838	107.97	5363	115.59	7.1	111.4
Zoology	QH,L, P,R	2,336	164.82	1655	152.48	1803	160.50	1707	153.42	1646	155.46	1.3	94.3
Totals and Averages		63,812	$116.25	63670	$114.61	68212	$114.95	78396	$120.64	73544	$126.70	5.0%	109.0

Compiled by Cynthia Elliott in consultation with Stephen Bosch from the University of Arizona from electronic data provided by ProQuest (formerly Ingram Content Group-Coutts Information Services) and GOBI Library Solutions from EBSCO (formerly YBP Library Services). The data represent all e-book titles treated for all approval plan customers serviced by the vendors. This table covers titles published or distributed in the United States and Canada during the calendar years listed. It is important to note that e-books that were released in a given year may have been published in print much earlier.

Table 4B / North American Academic Textbooks: Average Prices and Price Indexes 2019–2022

(Index Base: 2010 = 100)

Subject Area	LC Class	2010		2019		2020		2021		2022			
		Titles	Average Price	Titles	Average Price	Titles	Average Price	Titles	Average Price	Titles	Average Price	Percent Change 2021–2022	Index
Agriculture	S	49	$115.80	65	$133.22	98	$138.63	59	$132.09	87	$143.06	8.3%	123.5
Anthropology	GN	35	90.65	54	103.15	47	99.66	39	92.46	28	94.58	2.3	104.3
Botany	QK	11	109.52	8	119.10	21	143.66	18	144.38	11	126.76	-12.2	115.7
Business and Economics	H	694	121.36	1058	121.32	1073	117.37	972	130.19	794	128.15	-1.6	105.6
Chemistry	QD	94	134.59	109	130.15	131	157.96	92	174.76	87	124.66	-28.7	92.6
Education	L	271	87.75	525	83.92	419	95.97	334	101.64	301	88.21	-13.2	100.5
Engineering and Technology	T	744	116.38	1142	141.11	1229	146.31	936	143.21	921	130.93	-8.6	112.5
Fine and Applied Arts	M,N	73	93.33	171	104.39	142	96.90	112	115.12	101	105.60	-8.3	113.1
General Works	A	0	0.00	6	114.52	7	109.84	7	85.84	2	120.00	39.8	N/A
Geography	G	78	105.21	127	121.51	101	128.18	109	117.91	78	127.06	7.8	120.8
Geology	QE	36	117.97	46	165.25	36	152.19	37	165.20	26	116.98	-29.2	99.2
History	C,D, E,F	81	81.49	158	91.78	133	96.79	145	103.14	102	85.98	-16.6	105.5
Home Economics	TX	39	89.52	39	145.85	35	146.18	20	178.06	23	180.78	1.53	202.0
Industrial Arts	TT	14	84.72	6	99.87	8	87.86	7	36.82	6	121.46	229.9	143.4

Law	K	242	102.09	464	120.14	393	123.34	352	129.18	315	111.30	-13.8	109.0
Library and Information Science	Z	19	70.30	33	70.01	26	85.31	31	77.47	21	77.86	0.5	110.7
Literature and Language	P	309	77.71	559	89.22	561	103.08	425	103.43	395	97.09	-6.1	124.9
Mathematics and Computer Science	QA	683	96.11	997	117.72	1073	119.49	914	128.81	939	120.10	-6.8	125.0
Medicine	R	1512	126.75	2153	138.65	1832	138.27	1620	157.76	1618	164.47	4.3	129.8
Military and Naval Science	U,V	3	122.65	27	138.42	25	154.76	14	115.39	29	131.71	14.1	107.4
Philosophy and Religion	B	101	72.13	179	70.29	141	69.93	149	81.22	82	73.06	-10.1	101.3
Physical Education and Recreation	GV	51	79.39	129	96.87	98	110.60	110	112.72	102	105.83	-6.1	133.3
Physics and Astronomy	QB	243	107.38	402	131.64	390	130.44	392	129.12	352	126.43	-2.1	117.7
Political Science	J	110	80.09	267	92.27	216	93.41	205	116.91	157	95.36	-18.4	119.1
Psychology	BF	138	95.95	210	120.23	167	109.64	150	143.00	191	121.40	-15.1	126.5
Science (general)	Q	33	97.14	79	95.33	100	111.17	74	126.97	87	108.67	-14.4	111.9
Sociology	HM	353	86.97	674	102.18	507	104.30	427	112.75	380	112.61	-0.1	129.5
Zoology	QH,L; P,R	227	109.82	354	139.56	335	138.44	267	136.79	244	147.46	7.8	134.3
Totals and Averages		6243	$107.94	9373	$117.79	10041	$123.49	8017	$131.87	7479	$128.25	-2.8%	118.8

Compiled by Cynthia Elliott in consultation with Stephen Bosch from the University of Arizona from electronic data provided by ProQuest (formerly Ingram Content Group–Coutts Information Services) and GOBI Library Solutions from EBSCO (formerly YBP Library Services). The data represent all textbook titles treated for all approval plan customers serviced by the vendors. This table covers titles published or distributed in the United States and Canada during the calendar years listed.

(continued from page 275)

Over time, the data and the data suppliers have changed due to changes in the industry. When compared with earlier versions, the North American Academic Books Price Index now contains many more titles in the source data, which has affected the index considerably. ProQuest Books treats far more titles in its approval programs than the former Blackwell Book Services. For indexes published before 2009, Blackwell was a supplier of data for the index. Blackwell was purchased in 2009 by YBP, and the vendor data used to create the index changed at that time. After 2009 the data came from Ingram (Coutts) and YBP. Prior to 2009 the data came from Blackwell and YBP. With recent changes at both ProQuest and GOBI, there have been changes to how the annual price data are pulled for books. Starting in 2016 each vendor supplied data in separate files for print, e-books, and textbooks. Prior to 2016 this was not the case, and this change caused large variations in the numbers of titles in the tables and the average prices. The data for 2014 were normalized in 2016 to conform to the current sets of data, so the numbers of titles and prices have changed from those published in 2015 and previous years. This approach to gathering the data—separate data files for print, electronic, and texts—improves the consistency of the data, especially for e-books. Another major change was made in 2017, when the base index year was moved to 2010 to provide consistency across the various indexes published by the Library Materials Price Index Committee.

The overall average price for books in the North American Academic Books Price Index (Table 4) saw an increase in 2022 by 5.3 percent over 2021. In 2021 data showed a small increase, by 1 percent, and in 2020, a spike in the average price occurred after several years of relatively flat increases, mainly due to the growth in the number of e-books in the index. In 2022 there were no large swings in the number of print books or e-books, and the price changes were fairly consistent across the entire dataset. The overall number of titles has been fairly consistent since 2018. In 2022 the number of titles was 155,062. The overall growth in available titles, as well as increasing prices, are pressure points for library budgets. The increase in price for 2022 was due to increases in the number of the most expensive books. Overall, the ratio of print to electronic has been fairly consistent for the last three years: 47 percent in 2020, 48 percent in 2021, and 47 percent in 2022.

Since 2008 two additional indexes have been available, one for e-books only (Table 4A) and another for textbooks (Table 4B). Based on users' high interest, the indexes continue to be published. In 2017 the base index was set to 2010. In the academic market, it has always been assumed that e-books are more expensive than their print counterparts. The cheaper versions of e-books available to consumers through such channels as Amazon and Google Books are not available to libraries at similar prices if they are available at all in the library market. At best, the academic pricing will match the print price for single-user license models, with multiuser models being far more expensive than print. The e-book index points out this difference in price: The average price of an e-book in 2022 was $126.70, while the average price for all books was $108.47. The average price of a print book drops to $88.07 if the e-books are removed from the overall index. The high price for e-books is not that surprising, as most pricing models for academic e-books generally charge a higher price than the list print price for access to the e-books. Another factor is that STEM publishing migrated more quickly to electronic formats for books, with social science and humanities slower to adopt digital publishing. STEM books have always been more expensive than those of other subjects, so this contributes to the higher cost for e-books.

Over the past two years it is becoming common practice for single-user licenses to be priced at the same price as print. Multiuser licenses are still significantly more expensive than print. Responding to customer demands, publishers and vendors offer e-books on multiple platforms with multiple pricing models; consequently, there can be multiple prices for the same title. For these indexes, only the first license level (normally single-user) is included in the data. Where multiple prices are available for different use models, the lowest price is included in the index. Because electronic access is a major market trend, it is appropriate to have e-books as a separate index. It is important to note that the e-book market is rapidly changing. It is also important to note that by using the lowest price available for e-books, this approach may be artificially keeping the average price of e-books low for libraries that generally buy multiuser licenses. As with the overall market, prices increased for e-books in 2022, 5.0 percent, driven by an increase in the number of titles in the high end of the price range.

The cost of course materials continues to be an important topic on many college campuses. The index for textbooks (Table 4B) documents price changes in this area. The data show that textbooks tend to be more expensive than other types of books, with an average price of $128.25 in 2022. This represents a 2.7 percent decrease. This is not great news for students, as textbooks remain more expensive than regular print or e-books, and the prices have only slightly moderated. Note that this index does not measure the impact of new programs like inclusive access for textbooks. Only changes in the publisher's retail price are measured. The flat increases in previous years seemed to be a positive trend, as it seemed textbook publishers were responding to market pressure and scaled back large price increases. Textbooks are expensive, and the prices are not dropping significantly to make required reading less expensive for students. Pressure on the textbook market from alternative sources like rental services for either print or electronic versions or resales of used copies may have slowed price increases but has not resulted in an overall significant price drop. Electronic versions are included in the textbook index, so migration to the electronic format does not seem to be lowering costs. This is not much consolation for cash-strapped students.

The average price of North American academic books in 2022 (Table 4) increased by 5.3 percent as compared with the 2021 average price. This is mainly due to changes in the number of titles treated in the upper part of the price bands (below $120) and decreases in numbers for all other price bands (see Figure 1). The increase in titles costing more than $120 and the decrease in the number of titles costing less than $120 helped drive prices up in 2022.

One thing that stands out when looking at the data by price band is that the highest end of the price bands ($120 and up) continues to have a huge impact on the costs for books. The impact on pricing from the titles in the $120-and-up price band is confirmed if you look at the actual dollar values in groups (sum of all prices for titles in the group). The increase in the top end of the index was the main component in the overall changes in the index for 2019–2022, and the minimal growth led to a decrease in 2021. In 2022 the impact of the highest range offset the decrease in the lower ranges. Again, changes in the number of titles available are a significant driver in the increase or decrease in costs, as within the price bands, the average price remains constant. Unlike serials, where inflation in price drives higher costs, this data show that changes in the number of titles were the primary driver in escalating costs, not inflationary increases in price. (See Figures 2 and 3.)

The data used for this index are derived from all titles treated by ProQuest Books (formerly Ingram Content Group-Coutts Information Services) and GOBI Library Solutions in their approval plans during the calendar years listed. The index includes e-books as well as paperback editions as supplied by these vendors, and this inclusion of paperbacks and e-books as distributed as part of the approval plans has influenced the prices reflected in the index figures. The index is inclusive of the broadest categories of materials, as that is the marketplace in which academic libraries operate, and the index attempts to chart price changes that impact that market.

Price changes vary, as always, among subject areas. This year there were multiple double-digit increases in subject areas. The 2022 data indicate that those areas with the largest increases were not concentrated in one area but included all broad subject areas. Overall, prices for books in the STM subjects are still more expensive than the humanities. STM publishers have tended to be early adopters of e-books and have been publishing them for a while. The high average prices in the sciences reflect the availability and higher pricing of e-books as well as the overall high cost of STM books.

It is good to remember that price indexes become less accurate at describing price changes the smaller the sample becomes. Home economics is a small sample (872 titles) and showed a very large price increase of 16.8 percent in 2022, but to conclude that all books in that area increased at like amounts is not correct. In small

(text continues on page 288)

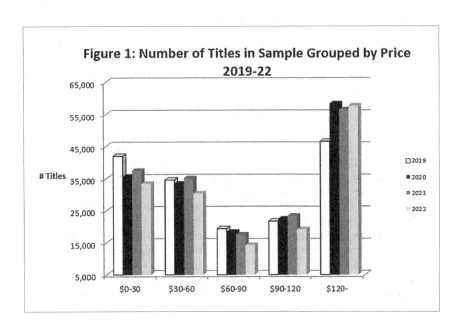

Figure 1: Number of Titles in Sample Grouped by Price 2019-22

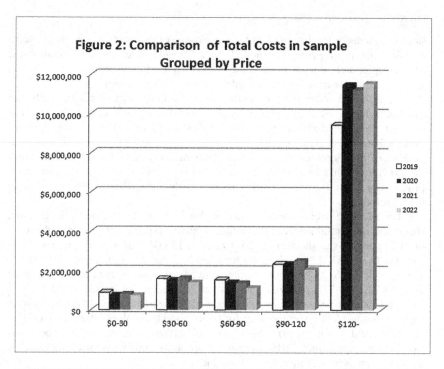

Figure 2: Comparison of Total Costs in Sample Grouped by Price

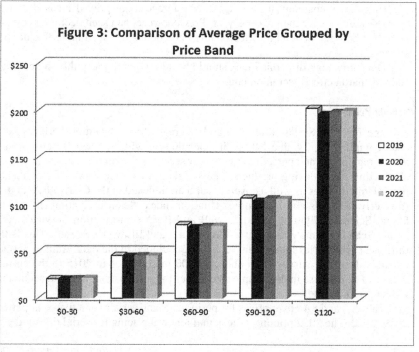

Figure 3: Comparison of Average Price Grouped by Price Band

(continued from page 286)

samples, inclusion/exclusion of just a few expensive or low-priced items can have a major impact on prices for the category. The increases in home economics, for example, were due to an increase in expensive titles. Because the sample is small, more-expensive books caused the overall price to increase.

Data for the index were compiled from 3,663 reviews of books published in *Choice* during 2022. An additional seven print titles reviewed in *Choice* were omitted from the analysis due to price ($500 or more). These books were removed from the analysis so that the average prices were not skewed. The total number of books reviewed for this analysis has increased by 1.1 percent from the previous year's total of 3,623 books. This index includes some paperback prices; as a result, the average price of books is less than if only hardcover books were included.

For 2022 the overall average price for books in the humanities, sciences, and social and behavioral sciences (including reference books) was $84.75, a decrease of -3.74 percent over the average 2021 price of $88.04. The average price of reference books was $124.93, a slight decrease of -0.83 percent from the previous year's average price of $125.97. Excluding reference books, the average 2022 book price was $83.74, or a -3.58 percent decrease over the average 2021 price of $86.85.

The average 2022 price for humanities titles decreased by -2.46 percent over the previous year. The average price for science and technology titles decreased by -11.22 percent, while the price for social and behavioral sciences titles decreased by -2.89 percent. Since 2010 there has been an overall book price increase of 27.89 percent when reference books are included.

Calculated separately, the average 2022 reference book price decreased slightly by -0.83 percent over the previous year. Previous years had seen declining costs of reference books. The overall price of reference books has seen large fluctuations over the past several years.

Questions regarding this index should be addressed to the author at her email address: narda.tafuri@scranton.edu.

Serials Prices

Average Price of Serials (Table 8) and Average Price of Online Serials (Table 8A), compiled by Cynthia Elliott, in consultation with Stephen Bosch, provide the average prices and percent increases for serials based on titles in select serials' abstracting and indexing products. The serials in this price survey are published in the United States as well as overseas and are indexed in the Clarivate Analytics (formerly ISI) Arts and Humanities Citation Index, Science Citation Index, and Social Sciences Citation Index, as well as EBSCO Information Service's Academic Search Ultimate and Masterfile Premier and Elsevier's Scopus. This is the third year when titles indexed in Scopus are included in the data. Adding Scopus expands this price survey from about 11,000 priced titles in 2015 to the current 30,160. The increase in the sample size makes the results more likely to accurately reflect pricing trends.

Tables 8 and 8A cover prices for periodicals and serials for a five-year period, 2019–2022. The 2022 pricing is the actual renewal pricing for serial titles indexed

(text continues on page 300)

Table 5 / U.S. College Books : Average Prices and Price Indexes, 2020–2022

Index Base: 2010 = 100

Subject	2010		2020				2021				2022				% Change 2021–2022
	Titles	Average Price	Titles	Average Price	Indexed to 2010	Indexed to 2019	Titles	Average Price	Indexed to 2010	Indexed to 2020	Titles	Average Price	Indexed to 2010	Indexed to 2021	
HUMANITIES															
Art and Architecture	91	$58.99	43	$72.40	122.73	88.73	41	$89.23	151.26	123.25	35	$78.55	133.16	88.03	-11.97%
Fine Arts	149	61.69	90	67.44	109.32	95.56	73	77.62	125.82	115.09	95	70.25	113.88	90.51	-9.49
Architecture	92	67.13	51	59.71	88.95	97.50	41	58.23	86.74	97.52	45	75.06	111.81	128.90	28.90
Photography	48	61.53	20	76.47	124.28	101.29	26	80.99	131.63	105.91	37	60.00	97.51	74.08	-25.92
Communication	28	53.02	15	58.98	111.24	80.43	13	60.52	114.15	102.61	13	57.99	109.37	95.82	-4.18
Language and Literature	112	59.97	48	78.05	130.15	107.01	63	95.56	159.35	122.43	75	84.00	140.07	87.90	-12.10
African and Middle Eastern	94	68.66	58	84.00	122.34	101.69	69	82.56	120.24	98.29	84	78.15	113.82	94.66	-5.34
Asian and Oceanian	24	62.28	8	80.49	129.24	125.43	9	84.88	136.29	105.45	11	103.24	165.77	121.63	21.63
Classical	24	71.99	12	70.08	97.35	89.24	10	91.40	126.96	130.42	23	99.03	137.56	108.35	8.35
	24	78.76	19	72.96	92.64	81.60	26	108.41	137.65	148.59	23	78.62	99.82	72.52	-27.48
English and American	394	61.96	167	80.17	129.39	99.37	181	80.65	130.16	100.60	169	83.44	134.67	103.46	3.46
Germanic	22	70.36	13	84.28	119.78	96.26	23	85.47	121.48	101.41	14	91.21	129.63	106.72	6.72
Romance	70	59.00	25	74.03	125.47	92.61	26	78.61	133.24	106.19	26	86.63	146.83	110.20	10.20
Slavic	32	35.95	14	62.91	174.99	77.10	13	84.22	234.27	133.87	23	82.56	229.65	98.03	-1.97
Performing Arts	30	61.97	8	83.74	147.14	99.16	13	76.83	123.98	91.75	7	88.00	142.00	114.54	14.54
Film	130	64.13	73	91.18	123.34	101.84	69	85.17	132.81	93.41	85	99.36	154.94	116.66	16.66
Music	123	61.01	61	79.10	153.01	103.89	108	79.95	131.04	101.07	92	80.76	132.37	101.01	1.01
Theater and Dance	45	62.38	21	93.35	146.55	116.67	26	104.41	167.38	111.85	26	87.28	139.92	83.59	-16.41
Philosophy	198	63.45	119	91.42	122.47	123.32	167	92.74	146.16	101.44	140	90.52	142.66	97.61	-2.39
Religion	272	57.18	150	77.71	137.83	111.03	149	82.72	144.67	106.45	134	76.64	134.03	92.65	-7.35
TOTAL HUMANITIES	2,002	$61.60	1,015	$78.81	127.94	102.48	1,146	$84.26	136.79	106.92	1,157	$82.19	133.43	97.54	-2.46%

(table continued on next page)

Table 5 / U.S. College Books : Average Prices and Price Indexes, 2020–2022 (continued)

Index Base: 2010 = 100

Subject	2010 Titles	2010 Average Price	2020 Titles	2020 Average Price	2020 Indexed to 2010	2020 Indexed to 2019	2021 Titles	2021 Average Price	2021 Indexed to 2010	2021 Indexed to 2020	2022 Titles	2022 Average Price	2022 Indexed to 2010	2022 Indexed to 2021	% Change 2021–2022
SCIENCE AND TECHNOLOGY	110	$58.09	35	$65.26	112.34	107.97	28	$85.68	147.50	131.29	49	$80.50	138.58	93.95	-6.05%
History of Science and Technology	78	54.10	42	74.00	136.78	128.90	25	67.12	124.07	90.70	57	81.29	150.26	121.11	21.11
Astronautics and Astronomy	63	55.58	21	69.65	125.31	128.98	14	63.52	114.29	91.20	25	66.92	120.40	105.35	5.35
Biology	151	72.74	60	98.09	134.85	136.22	49	78.80	108.33	80.33	57	96.30	132.39	122.21	22.21
Botany	85	85.09	20	94.43	110.98	166.28	7	139.41	163.84	147.63	16	61.11	71.82	43.83	-56.17
Zoology	121	64.33	43	84.71	131.68	135.73	39	91.09	141.60	107.53	47	77.23	120.05	84.78	-15.22
Chemistry	42	115.42	12	141.21	122.34	137.44	17	152.56	132.18	108.04	11	140.00	121.30	91.77	-8.23
Earth Science	102	63.33	36	78.65	124.19	105.63	34	118.49	187.10	150.65	88	83.68	132.13	70.62	-29.38
Engineering	103	88.38	56	136.71	154.68	170.29	35	143.04	161.85	104.63	67	122.78	138.92	85.84	-14.16
Health Sciences	146	56.14	129	98.85	176.08	141.66	99	98.24	174.99	99.38	164	87.48	155.82	89.05	-10.95
Information and Computer Science	83	73.50	45	92.86	126.34	120.04	44	120.23	163.58	129.47	53	112.31	152.80	93.41	-6.59
Mathematics	108	61.97	51	94.45	152.41	116.60	56	110.54	178.38	117.04	29	91.13	147.06	82.44	-17.56
Physics	50	54.74	34	127.39	232.72	200.65	38	94.96	173.47	74.54	36	84.23	153.87	88.70	-11.30
Sports and Physical Education	67	54.06	43	71.78	132.78	115.03	27	76.63	141.75	106.76	49	78.08	144.43	101.89	1.89
TOTAL SCIENCE	1,309	$67.13	627	$95.09	141.65	140.19	512	$101.31	150.92	106.54	748	$89.94	133.98	88.78	-11.22%
SOCIAL AND BEHAVIORAL SCIENCES	129	$66.32	118	$83.26	125.54	118.60	115	$82.53	124.44	99.12	112	$82.15	123.87	99.54	-0.46%
Anthropology	139	63.60	117	93.06	146.32	103.78	113	96.14	151.16	103.31	110	88.80	139.62	92.37	-7.63
Business Management and Labor	150	58.00	68	68.31	117.78	127.63	84	85.98	148.24	125.87	107	84.16	145.10	97.88	-2.12
Economics	270	61.16	70	69.38	113.44	113.76	41	82.80	135.38	119.34	54	81.49	133.24	98.42	-1.58
Education	158	62.56	123	82.02	131.11	112.76	144	88.41	141.32	107.79	124	84.68	135.36	95.78	-4.22
History, Geography and Area Studies	154	58.16	89	84.21	144.79	143.83	115	76.84	132.12	91.25	81	75.65	130.07	98.45	-1.55

				135.45	151.69	81.83	91.83	150.84	108.16					
Central and Eastern Europe	56	66.53	38	80.53	121.04	119.82	56	91.64	137.74	113.80	45	81.90	134.53	89.19	-10.81
Latin America and Caribbean	54	59.31	44	80.26	135.32	104.83	44	90.58	152.72	112.86	47	76.22	114.56	83.17	-16.83
Middle East and North Africa	43	65.57	69	81.47	124.25	123.22	56	91.08	138.90	112.86	52	76.05	128.22	83.96	-16.04
North America	444	45.50	184	58.60	128.79	119.69	201	55.86	122.77	95.32	49	90.08	137.38	98.90	-1.10
United Kingdom	80	69.56	46	75.65	108.76	134.04	52	71.82	103.25	94.94	161	53.77	118.18	96.26	-3.74
Western Europe	138	59.14	65	78.91	133.43	127.52	74	80.57	136.24	102.10	45	75.39	108.38	104.97	4.97
Political Science	4	84.36	26	81.20	96.25	109.55	59	96.39	114.26	118.71	57	74.65	126.23	92.65	-7.35
Comparative Politics	183	66.34	38	89.07	134.26	125.34	26	97.31	146.68	109.25	44	85.25	101.06	88.44	-11.56
International Relations	213	65.64	67	98.19	149.59	171.66	90	100.15	152.57	102.00	31	82.17	123.86	84.44	-15.56
Political Theory	73	56.74	45	79.02	139.27	109.26	48	95.42	168.17	120.75	68	96.15	146.48	96.01	-3.99
U.S. Politics	253	53.03	122	61.61	116.18	101.63	82	65.84	124.16	106.87	34	89.67	158.04	93.97	-6.03
Psychology	126	60.55	82	77.96	128.75	95.84	90	86.19	142.35	110.56	74	70.10	132.19	106.47	6.47
Sociology	226	60.71	181	83.50	137.54	117.41	212	93.78	154.47	112.31	123	93.41	154.27	108.38	8.38
TOTAL BEHAVIORAL SCIENCES	3,052	$59.09	1,741	$78.56	132.95	117.73	1,855	$84.47	142.95	107.52	1,668	$82.03	138.82	97.11	-2.89%
TOTAL GENERAL, HUMANITIES, SCIENCE AND SOCIAL SCIENCE (without Reference)	6,363	$61.53	3,383	$81.70	132.78	116.12	3,513	$86.85	141.15	106.30	3,573	$83.74	136.10	96.42	-3.58%
REFERENCE															
General	29	$61.17	13	$131.30	214.65	110.78	4	$52.74	86.22	40.17	10	$84.90	138.79	160.98	60.98%
Humanities	128	117.12	32	107.96	92.18	102.89	23	125.43	107.10	116.18	24	158.95	135.72	126.72	26.72
Library and Information Sciences	n.a.	n.a.	21	75.32	n.a.	n.a.	25	68.14	n.a.	90.47	22	76.54	n.a.	112.33	12.33
Science and Technology	76	133.19	7	186.00	139.65	132.81	8	98.11	73.66	52.75	10	129.59	97.30	132.09	32.09
Social and Behavioral Sciences	216	152.91	46	134.35	87.86	85.68	50	165.44	108.19	123.14	24	150.00	98.10	90.67	-9.33
TOTAL REFERENCE	449	$133.44	119	$119.54	89.58	92.82	110	$125.97	94.40	105.38	90	$124.93	93.62	99.17	-0.83%
GRAND TOTAL	6,812	$66.27	3,502	$82.98	125.22	113.50	3,623	$88.04	132.85	106.10	3,663	$84.75	127.89	96.26	-3.74%

Compiled by Narda Tafuri, retired, University of Scranton

n.a. = not available

Table 6 / U.S. Mass Market Paperback Books: Average Prices and Price Indexes, 2019–2022

Index Base: 2010 = 100

BISAC Category	2010 Average Price	2019 Final Volumes	2019 Final Average Price	2019 Final Index	2020 Final Volumes	2020 Final Average Price	2020 Final Index	2021 Preliminary Volumes	2021 Preliminary Average Price	2021 Preliminary Index	2022 Preliminary Volumes	2022 Preliminary Average Price	2022 Preliminary Index
Antiques and Collectibles	$8.77	n.a.	n.a.	n.a.	n.a.	n.a.	n.a.	n.a.	n.a.	n.a.	n.a.	n.a.	n.a.
Architecture	n.a.	n.a.	n.a.	n.a.	n.a.	n.a.	n.a.	n.a.	n.a.	n.a.	n.a.	n.a.	n.a.
Art	n.a.	n.a.	n.a.	n.a.	n.a.	n.a.	n.a.	n.a.	n.a.	n.a.	n.a.	n.a.	n.a.
Bibles	n.a.	n.a.	n.a.	n.a.	n.a.	n.a.	n.a.	n.a.	n.a.	n.a.	n.a.	n.a.	n.a.
Biography and Autobiography	7.51	3	$9.99	133.0	3	$9.32	124.1	4	$8.74	116.4	2	$8.49	113.0
Body, Mind and Spirit	7.99	n.a.	n.a.	n.a.	n.a.	n.a.	n.a.	n.a.	n.a.	n.a.	n.a.	n.a.	n.a.
Business and Economics	9.32	n.a.	n.a.	n.a.	n.a.	n.a.	n.a.	n.a.	n.a.	n.a.	1	9.99	107.2
Children	6.22	187	8.58	137.9	221	8.02	128.9	211	8.10	130.2	204	8.13	130.7
Comics and Graphic Novels	n.a.	n.a.	n.a.	n.a.	n.a.	n.a.	n.a.	n.a.	n.a.	n.a.	n.a.	n.a.	n.a.
Computers	n.a.	n.a.	n.a.	n.a.	n.a.	n.a.	n.a.	n.a.	n.a.	n.a.	n.a.	n.a.	n.a.
Cooking	n.a.	n.a.	n.a.	n.a.	n.a.	n.a.	n.a.	n.a.	n.a.	n.a.	n.a.	n.a.	n.a.
Crafts and Hobbies	n.a.	n.a.	n.a.	n.a.	n.a.	n.a.	n.a.	n.a.	n.a.	n.a.	n.a.	n.a.	n.a.
Design	n.a.	n.a.	n.a.	n.a.	n.a.	n.a.	n.a.	n.a.	n.a.	n.a.	n.a.	n.a.	n.a.
Drama	6.30	n.a.	n.a.	n.a.	n.a.	n.a.	n.a.	n.a.	n.a.	n.a.	n.a.	n.a.	n.a.
Education	n.a.	n.a.	n.a.	n.a.	n.a.	n.a.	n.a.	n.a.	n.a.	n.a.	n.a.	n.a.	n.a.
Family and Relationships	7.99	n.a.	n.a.	n.a.	2	9.49	118.8	n.a.	n.a.	n.a.	n.a.	n.a.	n.a.
Fiction	6.80	2,468	7.45	109.6	2,252	7.59	111.6	2,228	7.78	114.4	2,017	7.86	115.6
Foreign Language Study	7.08	n.a.	n.a.	n.a.	n.a.	n.a.	n.a.	n.a.	n.a.	n.a.	n.a.	n.a.	n.a.
Games and Activities	n.a.	n.a.	n.a.	n.a.	n.a.	n.a.	n.a.	n.a.	n.a.	n.a.	n.a.	n.a.	n.a.
Gardening	n.a.	n.a.	n.a.	n.a.	n.a.	n.a.	n.a.	n.a.	n.a.	n.a.	n.a.	n.a.	n.a.
Health and Fitness	7.92	1	13.99	176.6	1	8.99	113.5	2	8.99	113.5	n.a.	n.a.	n.a.
History	9.95	4	8.99	90.4	4	9.99	100.4	2	9.99	100.4	2	9.99	100.4
House and Home	n.a.	n.a.	n.a.	n.a.	n.a.	n.a.	n.a.	n.a.	n.a.	n.a.	n.a.	n.a.	n.a.
Humor	n.a.	n.a.	n.a.	n.a.	n.a.	n.a.	n.a.	n.a.	n.a.	n.a.	n.a.	n.a.	n.a.
Language Arts and Disciplines	12.95	1	7.99	60.2	n.a.	n.a.	n.a.	n.a.	n.a.	n.a.	n.a.	n.a.	n.a.

Subject												
Law	n.a.	n.a.	n.a.	n.a.	n.a.	n.a.	n.a.	n.a.	n.a.	n.a.	n.a.	n.a.
Literary Collections	5.95	n.a.	n.a.	n.a.	n.a.	n.a.	n.a.	n.a.	n.a.	n.a.	n.a.	n.a.
Literary Criticism	7.99	n.a.	n.a.	n.a.	n.a.	n.a.	n.a.	n.a.	n.a.	n.a.	n.a.	n.a.
Mathematics	n.a.	n.a.	n.a.	n.a.	n.a.	n.a.	n.a.	n.a.	n.a.	n.a.	n.a.	n.a.
Medical	8.99	n.a.	n.a.	n.a.	n.a.	n.a.	n.a.	n.a.	n.a.	n.a.	n.a.	n.a.
Music	n.a.	n.a.	n.a.	n.a.	n.a.	n.a.	n.a.	n.a.	n.a.	n.a.	n.a.	n.a.
Nature	n.a.	n.a.	n.a.	n.a.	n.a.	n.a.	n.a.	n.a.	n.a.	n.a.	n.a.	n.a.
Performing Arts	9.99	1	8.99	90.0	n.a.	n.a.	n.a.	n.a.	n.a.	n.a.	n.a.	n.a.
Pets	7.99	n.a.	n.a.	n.a.	n.a.	n.a.	n.a.	n.a.	n.a.	n.a.	n.a.	n.a.
Philosophy	6.47	n.a.	2	3.99	n.a.	3.99	61.7	1	3.99	61.7	n.a.	n.a.
Photography	n.a.	n.a.	n.a.	n.a.	n.a.	n.a.	n.a.	n.a.	n.a.	n.a.	n.a.	n.a.
Poetry	7.95	n.a.	n.a.	n.a.	n.a.	n.a.	1	3.99	50.2	1	3.99	n.a.
Political Science	7.97	1	9.99	125.3	n.a.	n.a.	n.a.	n.a.	n.a.	n.a.	n.a.	n.a.
Psychology	n.a.	n.a.	n.a.	n.a.	n.a.	n.a.	n.a.	n.a.	n.a.	n.a.	n.a.	n.a.
Reference	7.99	1	8.99	112.5	1	8.99	112.5	3	7.83	98.0	1	8.99	112.5
Religion	7.99	n.a.	n.a.	n.a.	n.a.	n.a.	n.a.	n.a.	n.a.	n.a.	n.a.	n.a.
Science	n.a.	n.a.	n.a.	n.a.	n.a.	n.a.	n.a.	n.a.	n.a.	n.a.	n.a.	n.a.
Self-Help	7.99	4	12.74	159.4	n.a.	n.a.	n.a.	3	7.99	100.0	3	7.99	100.0
Social Science	n.a.	n.a.	n.a.	n.a.	n.a.	n.a.	n.a.	n.a.	n.a.	n.a.	n.a.	n.a.
Sports and Recreation	7.99	n.a.	n.a.	n.a.	n.a.	n.a.	n.a.	1	9.99	125.0	n.a.	n.a.
Study Aids	n.a.	n.a.	n.a.	n.a.	n.a.	n.a.	n.a.	n.a.	n.a.	n.a.	n.a.	n.a.
Technology and Engineering	n.a.	n.a.	n.a.	n.a.	n.a.	n.a.	n.a.	n.a.	n.a.	n.a.	n.a.	n.a.
Transportation	n.a.	n.a.	n.a.	n.a.	n.a.	n.a.	n.a.	n.a.	n.a.	n.a.	n.a.	n.a.
Travel	n.a.	n.a.	n.a.	n.a.	n.a.	n.a.	n.a.	n.a.	n.a.	n.a.	n.a.	n.a.
True Crime	7.64	6	8.82	115.4	5	8.99	117.7	4	9.74	127.5	6	9.66	126.4
Young Adult	8.13	36	9.71	119.4	45	10.72	131.9	34	10.90	134.1	34	12.11	149.0
Totals and Averages	$6.83	2,713	$7.58	111.0	2,536	$7.69	112.6	2,494	$7.85	114.9	2,267	$7.95	116.4

Compiled by Narda Tafuri, retired, University of Scranton, from data supplied by Baker & Taylor

n.a. = not available

Table 7 / U.S. Paperback Books (Excluding Mass Market): Average Prices and Price Indexes, 2019–2022

Index Base: 2010 = 100

BISAC Category	2010 Average Price	2019 Final			2020 Final			2021 Preliminary			2022 Preliminary		
		Volumes	Average Price	Index	Volumes	Average Price	Index	Volumes	Average Price	Index	Volumes	Average Price	Index
Antiques and Collectibles	$25.53	87	$41.73	163.5	79	$45.16	176.9	76	$41.31	161.8	90	$46.20	181.0
Architecture	45.31	914	50.45	111.3	892	50.29	111.0	808	55.74	123.0	738	53.21	117.4
Art	38.25	1,759	39.55	103.4	1,578	40.82	106.7	1,453	41.46	108.4	1,503	41.93	109.6
Bibles	38.66	630	48.55	125.6	467	56.76	146.8	502	61.37	158.8	492	64.95	168.0
Biography and Autobiography	20.35	2,424	20.81	102.3	2,299	21.39	105.1	2,451	21.60	106.1	2,426	22.06	108.4
Body, Mind and Spirit	18.03	826	19.05	105.7	820	19.09	105.9	849	19.98	110.8	830	20.04	111.1
Business and Economics	69.30	6,730	73.39	105.9	6,178	71.80	103.6	5,981	76.26	110.0	5,793	74.88	108.0
Children	10.42	12,027	12.86	123.4	10,741	12.50	120.0	10,298	12.88	123.6	10,512	12.73	122.2
Comics and Graphic Novels	16.11	2,196	20.64	128.1	1,832	19.11	118.7	2,162	18.94	117.6	2,513	19.01	118.0
Computers	70.42	3,387	102.85	146.0	2,988	85.79	121.8	2,695	88.18	125.2	2,654	86.73	123.2
Cooking	19.95	832	22.13	110.9	809	21.42	107.4	759	21.78	109.2	606	23.36	117.1
Crafts and Hobbies	19.34	577	22.39	115.8	572	21.71	112.3	501	22.11	114.3	501	21.92	113.3
Design	63.98	253	46.01	71.9	210	37.28	58.3	217	39.83	62.2	196	42.79	66.9
Drama	18.95	463	23.02	121.5	391	22.27	117.5	405	19.94	105.2	384	21.89	115.5
Education	42.98	4,852	131.68	306.4	3,810	107.06	249.1	3,467	60.21	140.1	3,402	56.34	131.1
Family and Relationships	18.72	635	21.97	117.4	613	21.53	115.0	625	21.59	115.3	590	21.85	116.7
Fiction	17.99	10,014	17.59	97.8	9,296	17.70	98.4	10,867	17.77	98.8	9,832	18.18	101.1
Foreign Language Study	31.33	1,012	42.09	134.3	928	46.03	146.9	515	48.57	155.0	794	39.74	126.8
Games and Activities	16.57	635	18.04	108.9	681	18.06	109.0	690	18.24	110.1	719	18.26	110.2
Gardening	23.45	126	22.45	95.7	99	23.46	100.0	114	25.29	107.8	140	26.08	111.2
Health and Fitness	26.95	968	32.89	122.0	929	32.67	121.2	936	34.12	126.6	740	35.41	131.4
History	35.79	6,654	40.45	113.0	6,535	41.61	116.3	5,978	41.41	115.7	5,954	39.41	110.1
House and Home	21.19	109	24.31	114.7	65	23.03	108.7	74	26.03	122.9	68	24.92	117.6

Subject												
Law	72.07	3,146	86.04	119.4	3,209	89.16	123.7	3,426	87.20	93.3	1,344	59.68	92.6
Literary Collections	36.42	464	24.92	68.4	435	29.01	79.7	459	30.59	121.0	2,818	84.41	117.1
Literary Criticism	36.57	2,352	44.69	122.2	2,231	43.57	119.1	2,247	47.48	84.0	446	28.70	78.8
Mathematics	86.13	1,373	76.41	88.7	1,156	74.38	86.4	1,113	84.76	129.8	2,009	46.67	127.6
Medical	90.22	4,470	87.02	96.4	3,602	82.72	91.7	3,983	89.86	98.4	908	87.41	101.5
Music	22.83	2,056	30.41	133.2	3,724	27.64	121.1	1,768	29.87	99.6	3,413	92.58	102.6
Nature	37.28	668	42.20	113.2	697	36.11	96.9	752	46.79	130.8	3,598	27.99	122.6
Performing Arts	33.53	972	38.50	114.8	834	39.80	118.7	901	45.67	125.5	608	39.28	105.4
Pets	17.34	123	20.37	117.5	99	18.46	106.5	95	20.19	136.2	925	41.35	123.3
Philosophy	52.66	1,947	42.39	80.5	1,815	44.59	84.7	1,821	51.56	116.4	91	21.70	125.2
Photography	31.30	319	40.11	128.1	295	36.80	117.6	220	47.65	97.9	1,742	49.89	94.7
Poetry	16.73	2,062	17.35	103.7	1,922	17.47	104.4	1,926	17.81	152.2	209	34.77	111.1
Political Science	41.00	4,398	50.66	123.6	4,840	48.54	118.4	4,484	52.78	106.4	1,746	18.58	111.1
Psychology	47.98	2,130	51.87	108.1	1,805	57.35	119.5	1,721	55.92	128.7	3,728	52.40	127.8
Reference	84.85	399	128.42	151.3	264	205.07	241.7	221	227.71	116.6	1,677	58.13	121.2
Religion	22.08	6,867	28.09	127.2	5,840	27.65	125.2	5,292	30.36	268.4	181	235.88	278.0
Science	116.37	4,172	94.71	81.4	3,385	99.02	85.1	3,903	114.50	137.5	4,658	28.33	128.3
Self-Help	17.84	1,310	17.90	100.4	1,229	17.97	100.8	1,244	17.94	98.4	3,154	115.46	99.2
Social Science	45.05	5,640	49.65	110.2	5,894	49.34	109.5	4,801	52.55	100.6	1,220	18.54	103.9
Sports and Recreation	22.30	996	26.95	120.9	837	27.43	123.0	811	27.86	116.7	4,403	51.91	115.2
Study aids	49.24	2,593	43.61	88.6	2,421	43.60	88.5	804	46.87	124.9	750	30.11	135.0
Technology and engineering	111.20	3,099	118.63	106.7	2,985	131.58	118.3	3,405	151.23	95.2	438	44.32	90.0
Transportation	36.26	388	37.99	104.8	340	35.99	99.2	259	35.09	136.0	3,463	159.98	143.9
Travel	20.93	1,545	21.50	102.7	918	20.84	99.6	748	21.59	96.8	327	34.56	95.3
True Crime	20.94	248	20.01	95.6	212	20.45	97.7	246	21.19	101.2	1,025	22.15	105.8
Young Adult	14.86	2,889	18.70	125.8	2,303	16.97	114.2	2,122	16.10	108.3	2,211	16.28	109.6
Totals and Averages	$42.06	116,708	$48.30	114.8	107,755	$46.59	110.8	102,883	$48.57	115.5	98,938	$47.08	111.9

Compiled by Narda Tafuri, retired, University of Scranton, from data supplied by Baker & Taylor

Table 7A / U.S. Audiobooks: Average Prices and Price Indexes, 2019–2022

Index Base: 2010 = 100

BISAC Category	2010 Average Price	2019 Final Volumes	Average Price	Index	2020 Final Volumes	Average Price	Index	2021 Preliminary Volumes	Average Price	Index	2022 Preliminary Volumes	Average Price	Index
Antiques and Collectibles	$36.66	n.a.	n.a.	n.a.	3	$40.99	111.8	9	$19.66	53.6	3	$53.66	146.4
Architecture	41.24	8	$33.12	80.3	5	41.99	101.8	12	25.82	62.6	8	47.74	115.8
Art	58.21	8	31.05	53.3	13	33.37	57.3	47	22.20	38.1	30	49.91	85.7
Bibles	43.28	3	76.31	176.3	12	32.17	74.3	8	52.15	120.5	7	50.83	117.5
Biography and Autobiography	50.79	1,376	43.63	85.9	1,244	43.40	85.5	3,115	30.34	59.7	1,720	50.64	99.7
Body, Mind and Spirit	32.98	180	35.17	106.6	167	36.07	109.4	403	25.48	77.3	262	46.31	140.4
Business and Economics	49.70	656	36.87	74.2	717	41.41	83.3	1,174	27.98	56.3	1,113	48.82	98.2
Children	37.80	1,555	37.14	98.2	1,943	34.53	91.3	1,533	35.11	92.9	1,528	40.78	107.9
Comics and Graphic Novels	n.a.	66	37.57	n.a.	37	32.77	n.a.	4	29.49	n.a.	18	27.14	n.a.
Computers	45.00	33	38.05	84.6	12	34.73	77.2	108	27.50	61.1	56	56.43	125.4
Cooking	44.97	16	37.30	82.9	34	38.92	86.6	144	26.55	59.0	41	49.38	109.8
Crafts and Hobbies	24.98	5	39.79	159.3	3	39.99	160.1	13	17.02	68.1	n.a.	n.a.	n.a.
Design	n.a.	1	39.99	n.a.	4	41.24	n.a.	6	21.49	n.a.	16	51.05	n.a.
Drama	33.21	98	22.32	67.2	38	26.67	80.3	124	29.18	87.9	14	34.34	103.4
Education	45.71	39	38.20	83.6	32	40.36	88.3	181	24.71	54.1	131	51.24	112.1
Family and relationships	41.17	185	37.01	89.9	162	37.52	91.1	625	22.53	54.7	239	44.04	107.0
Fiction	50.38	11,455	40.16	79.7	14,035	39.85	79.1	20,035	32.50	64.5	14,285	49.00	97.3
Foreign Language Study	45.11	147	86.40	191.5	39	53.37	118.3	3	33.64	74.6	1	41.95	93.0
Games	n.a.	2	22.49	n.a.	7	47.85	n.a.	23	26.21	n.a.	5	58.19	n.a.
Gardening	47.82	1	14.99	31.3	9	37.55	78.5	10	26.39	55.2	8	40.74	85.2
Health and Fitness	43.09	242	40.17	93.2	226	43.52	101.0	515	29.18	67.7	210	49.00	113.7
History	58.07	811	46.40	79.9	783	48.09	82.8	2,203	28.90	49.8	1,007	55.55	95.7
...and Home	n.a.	13	34.45	n.a.	17	39.52	n.a.	28	23.31	n.a.	13	35.14	n.a.

Law	64.49	25	31.15	48.3	31	39.50	61.3	111	24.09	37.4	68	51.19	79.4
Literary Collections	52.07	66	42.00	80.7	34	39.40	75.7	101	31.27	60.1	88	48.80	93.7
Literary Criticism	42.53	27	32.61	76.7	39	35.86	84.3	118	25.94	61.0	65	41.88	98.5
Mathematics	n.a.	7	46.70	n.a.	8	34.99	n.a.	27	27.51	n.a.	6	54.99	n.a.
Medical	40.13	31	32.70	81.5	50	43.67	108.8	170	27.15	67.6	86	50.05	124.7
Music	35.67	64	41.50	116.4	51	36.94	103.6	204	26.66	74.7	89	60.35	169.2
Nature	41.20	93	41.92	101.8	122	43.62	105.9	240	26.36	64.0	123	50.54	122.7
Performing Arts	40.60	116	41.09	101.2	180	42.98	105.9	376	32.59	80.3	158	35.03	86.3
Pets	38.33	18	42.77	111.6	18	37.82	98.7	107	21.80	56.9	30	45.28	118.1
Philosophy	53.05	74	34.24	64.5	59	39.58	74.6	256	25.19	47.5	109	46.37	87.4
Photography	n.a.	n.a.	n.a.	n.a.	1	29.99	n.a.	7	18.99	n.a.	7	36.56	n.a.
Poetry	33.59	106	28.89	86.0	139	30.56	91.0	123	19.07	56.8	55	32.20	95.9
Political Science	48.04	368	43.14	89.8	409	45.68	95.1	877	29.24	60.9	617	51.38	106.9
Psychology	45.42	99	35.16	77.4	200	48.97	107.8	469	28.04	61.7	250	50.55	111.3
Reference	59.99	7	30.70	51.2	13	50.53	84.2	34	31.15	51.9	7	41.56	69.3
Religion	33.94	930	35.14	103.5	831	38.07	112.2	1,174	27.31	80.5	1,315	40.37	119.0
Science	51.89	168	41.25	79.5	238	41.14	79.3	624	30.63	59.0	237	51.71	99.7
Self-Help	39.43	517	35.41	89.8	521	38.17	96.8	829	28.58	72.5	469	44.11	111.9
Social Science	48.07	265	41.89	87.1	295	40.73	84.7	789	27.00	56.2	454	50.16	104.3
Sports and Recreation	48.48	142	42.11	86.9	153	39.28	81.0	354	25.92	53.5	109	49.06	101.2
Study Aids	19.41	2	63.00	324.5	3	38.66	199.2	6	24.73	127.4	n.a.	n.a.	n.a.
Technology and Engineering	53.33	13	39.29	73.7	19	40.78	76.5	112	27.54	51.6	26	57.17	107.2
Transportation	46.28	2	49.99	108.0	3	46.66	100.8	43	18.81	40.6	6	48.66	105.1
Travel	50.96	49	42.42	83.2	35	40.99	80.4	144	27.84	54.6	44	50.07	98.3
True Crime	52.58	193	43.11	82.0	159	46.75	88.9	454	28.47	54.2	234	48.39	92.0
Young Adult	44.81	1,224	43.81	97.8	1,233	43.98	98.1	1,297	37.62	84.0	1,274	51.36	114.6
Totals and Averages	$48.00	21,627	$40.32	84.0	24,506	$40.24	83.8	39,794	$30.87	64.3	26,755	$48.40	100.8

Compiled by Narda Tafuri, retired, University of Scranton, from data supplied by Baker & Taylor

Table 7B / U.S. E-Books: Average Prices and Price Indexes, 2019–2022

Index Base: 2010 = 100

BISAC Category	2010 Average Price	2019 Final Volumes	2019 Final Average Price	2019 Final Index	2020 Final Volumes	2020 Final Average Price	2020 Final Index	2021 Preliminary Volumes	2021 Preliminary Average Price	2021 Preliminary Index	2022 Preliminary Volumes	2022 Preliminary Average Price	2022 Preliminary Index
Antiques and Collectibles	$30.24	147	$11.97	39.6	168	$22.89	75.7	189	$15.54	51.4	149	$18.58	61.4
Architecture	66.57	498	50.78	76.3	513	49.40	74.2	506	47.58	71.5	296	48.62	73.0
Art	41.56	1,724	36.27	87.3	1,380	42.03	101.1	1,275	36.02	86.7	970	36.01	86.6
Bibles	6.11	300	14.33	234.5	415	17.31	283.4	408	14.98	245.2	549	12.57	205.7
Biography and Autobiography	15.47	7,127	23.27	150.4	8,891	27.45	177.5	11,684	27.81	179.8	9,329	30.87	199.5
Body, Mind and Spirit	13.95	3,575	13.22	94.7	4,729	15.28	109.6	5,691	15.93	114.2	4,799	19.07	136.7
Business and Economics	44.82	24,398	68.27	152.3	22,716	56.95	127.1	14,844	38.73	86.4	8,753	42.03	93.8
Children	13.82	28,490	19.62	141.9	29,175	20.49	148.3	33,452	19.79	143.2	27,204	20.73	150.0
Comics and Graphic Novels	11.39	1,062	11.85	104.0	2,636	9.04	79.3	1,997	12.80	112.4	1,458	23.32	204.7
Computers	62.09	2,448	63.22	101.8	2,558	55.63	89.6	2,251	52.66	84.8	1,530	63.51	102.3
Cooking	16.79	2,935	14.17	84.4	4,416	14.28	85.1	4,101	18.15	108.1	2,238	24.47	145.7
Crafts and hobbies	17.63	563	15.66	88.8	930	16.35	92.7	1,201	16.37	92.9	700	19.98	113.3
Design	37.03	139	43.68	118.0	196	30.75	83.1	215	25.35	68.5	143	29.70	80.2
Drama	4.86	989	15.09	310.6	952	21.38	440.0	733	16.44	338.3	825	13.17	271.0
Education	45.95	5,349	42.81	93.2	4,406	47.70	103.8	4,435	39.88	86.8	2,885	43.79	95.3
Family and Relationships	14.79	2,304	15.37	103.9	3,563	16.60	112.2	4,121	16.63	112.4	3,082	20.98	141.8
Fiction	7.06	85,303	13.64	193.1	107,411	19.70	279.1	108,884	16.54	234.3	82,310	21.37	302.7
Foreign Language Study	46.68	1,560	34.05	72.9	5,340	18.93	40.6	1,617	28.48	61.0	620	21.94	47.0
Games and Activities	12.85	342	20.13	156.6	539	25.27	196.7	699	17.72	137.9	342	19.98	155.5
Gardening	17.41	290	18.83	108.2	465	19.02	109.2	710	18.20	104.6	376	27.05	155.4
Health and Fitness	18.78	3,002	17.12	91.1	4,872	17.08	91.0	5,409	18.50	98.5	3,398	24.11	128.4
History	48.20	9,283	56.72	117.7	14,597	45.26	93.9	9,939	51.19	106.2	7,495	47.52	98.6
House and Home	21.57	245	19.92	92.3	332	18.84	87.3	390	19.59	90.8	297	25.19	116.8

Law	112.19	2,804	139.87	124.7	3,013	141.07	125.7	2,443	135.43	120.7	818	91.57	81.6
Literary Collections	20.27	6,169	5.18	25.6	1,915	19.35	95.5	1,747	19.54	96.4	1,563	22.13	109.2
Literary Criticism	87.17	3,266	97.71	112.1	3,548	167.44	192.1	2,814	120.84	138.6	1,717	142.01	162.9
Mathematics	112.32	910	97.07	86.4	766	97.74	87.0	440	95.09	84.7	286	75.97	67.6
Medical	135.71	2,739	128.56	94.7	2,750	91.87	67.7	2,428	77.86	57.4	1,447	86.11	63.5
Music	32.65	1,785	30.06	92.1	2,800	26.89	82.4	2,852	24.84	76.1	1,368	27.75	85.0
Nature	59.48	784	30.04	50.5	910	30.05	50.5	1,318	28.28	47.5	953	33.67	56.6
Performing Arts	32.17	2,000	28.86	89.7	2,057	28.32	88.0	1,989	34.34	106.8	1,012	45.85	142.5
Pets	14.50	438	14.41	99.4	467	16.39	113.0	590	17.79	122.7	485	15.69	108.2
Philosophy	71.43	2,847	52.54	73.6	4,055	50.30	70.4	2,540	65.39	91.5	1,839	52.38	73.3
Photography	27.23	259	22.67	83.3	444	21.52	79.0	383	20.92	76.8	189	29.00	106.5
Poetry	9.54	4,621	9.84	103.2	5,720	9.39	98.4	7,439	9.02	94.6	3,955	11.86	124.4
Political Science	59.74	3,882	54.40	91.1	4,313	49.80	83.4	4,180	45.80	76.7	3,015	53.14	88.9
Psychology	56.42	1,883	50.01	88.6	3,034	36.25	64.3	2,834	33.55	59.5	2,079	33.62	59.6
Reference	22.92	871	74.31	324.2	1,007	64.06	279.5	1,111	74.12	323.4	624	94.17	410.9
Religion	27.81	11,169	30.63	110.1	15,244	30.92	111.2	15,641	23.07	82.9	11,741	24.62	88.5
Science	155.80	3,715	105.24	67.5	3,446	110.15	70.7	3,023	86.92	55.8	1,850	88.82	57.0
Self-Help	14.06	6,550	13.05	92.8	10,046	14.17	100.8	13,019	14.32	101.9	6,937	21.46	152.6
Social Science	56.83	4,445	58.86	103.6	4,604	73.25	128.9	4,976	59.36	104.4	3,623	57.72	101.6
Sports and Recreation	19.22	1,437	21.84	113.6	1,612	23.45	122.0	1,769	23.18	120.6	1,305	28.61	148.9
Study Aids	13.94	3,206	31.77	227.9	1,598	14.41	103.3	1,396	15.44	110.8	948	22.01	157.9
Technology and Engineering	158.44	2,588	123.84	78.2	1,741	97.16	61.3	1,531	103.25	65.2	1,009	108.01	68.2
Transportation	33.12	294	30.43	91.9	627	29.48	89.0	376	25.21	76.1	345	32.12	97.0
Travel	15.84	2,785	12.64	79.8	2,319	17.07	107.8	1,760	21.31	134.5	1,385	26.92	169.9
True Crime	10.37	559	25.87	249.5	852	23.52	226.8	1,429	16.58	159.9	688	34.55	333.2
Young Adult	11.96	6,672	19.83	165.8	7,531	21.14	176.7	8,420	21.14	176.7	7,097	28.52	238.4
Totals and Averages	$41.61	264,737	$33.25	79.9	311,163	$32.59	78.3	306,163	$26.75	64.3	220,239	$29.23	70.3

Compiled by Narda Tafuri, retired, University of Scranton, from data supplied by Baker & Taylor

(continued from page 288)

in the selected products. These tables were derived from pricing data supplied by EBSCO Information Services and reflect broad pricing changes aggregated from serials that are indexed in the six major products previously mentioned. USPPI (Table 1) is based on price changes seen in a static set of approximately 6,000 serial titles. Average Price of Serials (Table 8) is based on a much broader set of titles, approximately 30,160; however, the indexed titles are not static year to year, so this pricing study does not rise to the level of a price index. This study is still useful in showing price changes for periodicals. The indexes selected for this price survey were deemed to be representative of serials that are frequently purchased in academic and public libraries. There are some foreign titles in the indexes, so the scope is broader, and this may give a better picture of the overall price pressures experienced in libraries. Table 8 contains both print and online serials pricing. Table 8A is a subset of the titles treated in Table 8 and contains only online serials pricing.

The most important trend seen in the data in Table 8 is that increases in serial prices are trending back toward the 6 percent increase common in the past 10 years prior to the impact of the pandemic. In previous years, the 6 percent price increases had remained constant since 2010. There is a difference between the average prices for print serials and online serials, so, at least for this set of data, print formats do cost less than their online counterparts. Several large publishers have made online pricing only available through custom quotes, so there is not a standard retail price for those titles, and those publishers' pricing data are not available for this survey. Consequently, the number of titles covered in the online survey (Table 8A) is less than the number of titles in Table 8, but titles with print-only pricing are now 35 percent of the overall data set.

Another interesting trend is that the science areas do not dominate the list of subjects with the largest price increases. The subject areas that displayed large increases were quite varied. Engineering, education, food sciences, sociology, general science, technology, and recreation saw higher increases than most areas. Most of these same areas showed the highest increases in the online table (Table 8A) as well. Average prices of journals in the science and technology areas are by far higher than average prices in other areas, and that trend continues, with the average cost of chemistry and physics journals being $5,739 and $4,412, respectively. Online journals (Table 8A) showed similar average prices for chemistry $5,928 and physics $4,650.

In this price study, as in similar price surveys, the data become less accurate at describing price changes as the sample size becomes smaller. For that reason, drawing conclusions about price changes in subject areas with a limited number of titles will be less accurate than for large areas or the broader price survey. Price changes are far more volatile where smaller datasets are used. For example, recreation (136 titles) showed a price change of 7.2 percent in 2023, which was higher than most other areas. Librarians are encouraged to look at an average price change over a period of years or the overall number for the price study (5.2 percent) to calculate inflation in the recreation area or any area with a small number of titles in the sample size. Year-to-year price changes in small subject areas are too unstable to be reliable indicators of future prices for budgeting purposes.

Foreign Prices

As shown in the chart below, in 2022 the U.S. dollar retained parity with the Canadian dollar (5.5 percent), British pound sterling (12.2 percent), and euro (6.8 percent). The U.S. dollar strengthened against the Japanese yen (14.6 percent).

	12/31/2018	12/31/2019	12/31/2020	12/31/2021	12/31/2022
Canada	1.36	1.30	1.28	1.28	1.35
Euro	0.87	0.89	0.82	0.88	0.94
U.K.	0.78	0.76	0.73	0.74	0.83
Japan	109.85	108.53	103.08	115.04	131.83

Data from the Bureau of Fiscal Services. U.S. Treasury Department (https://fiscaldata.treasury.gov/datasets/treasury-reporting-rates-exchange/treasury-reporting-rates-of-exchange)

Foreign Book Prices

British Academic Books (Table 9), compiled by Sylvia Orner of the University of Scranton, indicates the average prices and price indexes from 2019 through 2022. The percent change in titles and the average price are calculated for 2021–2022, and the index price shows the percent change between 2022 and the base year of 2010. This index is compiled using data from GOBI Library Solutions and utilizes prices from cloth editions except when not available. The data also draw from select titles from continental Europe and Africa. The index does not separate more expensive reference titles. Small numbers of titles that include higher-priced reference sets may not be reliable indicators of price changes. This table does not include e-book prices.

Data in the Totals and Averages row include the total of the LC Classes profiled in this table, not the total of all books profiled by GOBI Library Solutions. In 2022 total British academic books profiled by GOBI Library Solutions decreased to 17,830, a drop of approximately 3.6 percent from the previous year.

In 2022 British academic books experienced a minor decrease of approximately -1.9 percent, with the overall average price being £81.49. Based on new data from GOBI Library Solutions, the 2021 average was recalculated at £83.12, which represents an approximately 16.2 percent increase from 2020.

The 2022 price decrease comes when the United Kingdom's Consumer Price Index saw high inflation of 9.2 percent as of December 2022 (http://www.ons.gov.uk).

Table 9 shows how average prices have increased or decreased compared to the 2010 base year. For 2021 the overall index price for all LC subjects profiled in this table is 153.3 percent. All LC classes listed are currently above their 2010 base prices. The highest increases in comparison with the 2010 base prices are home economics (242.1 percent), sports and recreation (228.5 percent), industrial arts (211.6 percent), and psychology (209.8 percent). There are currently no known reliable indicators for a 2023 industry forecast.

(text continues on page 308)

Table 8 / Changes in the Average Price of Serials 2019–2023, Based on Titles in Select Serial Indexes

Subject	LC Class	Titles	2019 Average Price	2020 Average Price	Percent Change 2019–2020	2021 Average Price	Percent Change 2020–2021	2022 Average Price	Percent Change 2021–2022	2023 Average Price	Percent Change 2022–2023
Agriculture	S	545	$1,324.34	$1,400.77	5.8%	$1,462.44	4.4%	$1,519.11	3.9%	$1,602.04	2.7%
Anthropology	GN	175	699.78	734.31	4.9	764.47	4.1	795.23	4.0	834.40	3.1
Arts and Architecture	N	275	566.57	608.72	7.4	630.68	3.6	659.62	4.6	698.38	3.9
Astronomy	QB	82	2,238.82	2,373.43	6.0	2,316.53	-2.4	2,413.03	4.2	2,477.99	4.1
Biology	QH	1,320	2,763.37	2,896.89	4.8	2,984.03	3.0	3,102.16	4.0	3,244.90	4.2
Botany	QK	197	1,694.51	1,773.41	4.7	1,823.41	2.8	1,886.08	3.4	1,965.11	4.2
Business and Economics	HA-HJ	1,924	1,630.54	1,717.17	5.3	1,783.64	3.9	1,768.30	-0.9	1,852.22	4.4
Chemistry	QD	494	4,866.97	5,123.40	5.3	5,248.56	2.4	5,497.36	4.7	5,738.62	4.6
Education	L	693	1,040.22	1,108.28	6.5	1,162.53	4.9	1,193.87	2.7	1,267.62	4.7
Engineering	T	2,438	2,159.63	2,304.58	6.7	2,396.08	4.0	2,507.19	4.6	2,660.99	4.7
Food Science	TX	96	2,312.08	2,439.50	5.5	2,554.36	4.7	2,481.28	-2.9	2,637.55	4.7
General Science	Q	304	1,556.30	1,629.18	4.7	1,688.36	3.6	1,753.12	3.8	1,872.43	4.8
General Works	A	118	508.90	532.31	4.6	550.70	3.5	565.95	2.8	596.78	4.9
Geography	G-GF	374	1,279.06	1,366.02	6.8	1,418.61	3.8	1,486.07	4.8	1,565.32	5.1
Geology	QE	273	1,935.71	2,053.81	6.1	2,136.28	4.0	2,221.81	4.0	2,326.00	5.2
Health Sciences	R	4,605	1,491.60	1,593.64	6.8	1,661.61	4.3	1,739.94	4.7	1,830.08	5.2
History	C,D,E,F	990	489.83	516.31	5.4	541.26	4.8	562.25	3.9	589.26	5.2

Subject	LC Class	Titles									
Language and Literature	P	1,190	456.30	481.72	5.6	501.62	4.1	522.85	4.2	551.27	5.3
Law	K	424	608.29	639.46	5.1	669.75	4.7	750.89	12.1	786.49	5.4
Library Science	Z	195	1,284.13	1,357.55	5.7	1,407.86	3.7	1,340.27	-4.8	1,416.11	5.4
Math and Computer Science	QA	1,351	1,617.96	1,726.34	6.7	1,786.25	3.5	1,875.37	5.0	1,972.90	5.5
Military and Naval Science	U,V	103	803.82	855.17	6.4	895.54	4.7	937.48	4.7	985.68	5.7
Music	M	137	373.99	393.46	5.2	407.32	3.5	419.16	2.9	436.39	5.9
Philosophy and Religion	B-BD, BH-BX	659	466.22	487.96	4.7	504.63	3.4	530.71	5.2	552.84	5.9
Physics	QC	588	3,806.21	4,009.88	5.4	4,117.68	2.7	4,246.02	3.1	4,411.94	6.0
Political Science	J	382	869.30	932.85	7.3	971.16	4.1	1,003.33	3.3	1,063.00	6.1
Psychology	BF	427	986.72	1,060.39	7.5	1,094.14	3.2	1,149.41	5.1	1,218.83	6.2
Recreation	GV	136	871.03	926.42	6.4	983.07	6.1	1,037.53	5.5	1,112.70	6.3
Social Sciences	H	171	982.56	1,039.03	5.7	1,047.43	0.8	1,102.17	5.2	1,158.97	6.8
Sociology	HM-HX	1,047	996.15	1,061.08	6.5	1,102.53	3.9	1,140.44	3.4	1,217.50	6.8
Technology	TA-TT	493	1,953.67	2,068.80	5.9	2,150.94	4.0	2,140.78	-0.5	2,288.75	6.9
Zoology	QL	346	1,823.40	1,908.40	4.7	1,912.02	0.2	1,973.73	3.2	2,035.64	7.2
Totals and Averages		22,552	$1,569.78	$1,664.11	6.0%	$1,724.31	3.6%	$1,787.50	3.7%	$1,880.44	5.2%

Compiled by Cynthia Elliott in consultation with Stephen Bosch from the University of Arizona, based on data on serial pricing supplied by EBSCO information Services and based on titles indexed in EBSCO Academic Search Ultimate, EBSCO Masterfile Complete, Clarivate Analytics (formerly ISI) Arts and Humanities Citation Index, Clarivate Analytics Science Citation Index, Clarivate Analytics Social Sciences Citation Index, and Elsevier's Scopus

Table 8A / Changes in the Average Price of Online Serials 2019–2023, Based on Titles in Select Serial Indexes

Subject	LC Class	Titles	2019 Average Price	2020 Average Price	Percent Change 2019–2020	2021 Average Price	Percent Change 2020–2021	2022 Average Price	Percent Change 2021–2022	2023 Average Price	Percent Change 2022–2023
Agriculture	S	343	$1,358.55	$1,434.66	5.6%	$1,505.71	5.0%	$1,555.57	3.3%	$1,654.64	6.4%
Anthropology	GN	134	778.51	818.24	5.1	852.89	4.2	890.58	4.4	941.37	5.7
Arts and Architecture	N	190	643.93	687.14	6.7	714.83	4.0	744.91	4.2	797.59	7.1
Astronomy	QB	59	2,496.35	2,657.83	6.5	2,563.54	-3.5	2,679.74	4.5	2,745.09	2.4
Biology	QH	855	2,644.28	2,761.10	4.4	2,844.58	3.0	2,968.46	4.4	3,149.93	6.1
Botany	QK	138	1,793.24	1,868.15	4.2	1,919.26	2.7	1,993.59	3.9	2,118.47	6.3
Business and Economics	HA-HJ	1,429	1,831.30	1,925.91	5.2	2,004.03	4.1	1,964.04	-2.0	2,059.14	4.8
Chemistry	QD	330	4,950.91	5,229.10	5.6	5,369.57	2.7	5,645.19	5.1	5,927.59	5.0
Education	L	605	1,099.85	1,172.39	6.6	1,231.33	5.0	1,260.52	2.4	1,342.36	6.5
Engineering	T	1,567	2,245.71	2,401.61	6.9	2,504.46	4.3	2,611.00	4.3	2,778.18	6.4
Food Science	TX	80	2,280.16	2,399.91	5.3	2,517.28	4.9	2,387.85	-5.1	2,541.16	6.4
General Science	Q	222	1,785.25	1,865.25	4.5	1,936.90	3.8	2,011.22	3.8	2,150.63	6.9
General Works	A	52	804.00	847.66	5.4	882.71	4.1	910.02	3.1	973.58	7.0
Geography	G-GF	282	1,202.89	1,289.18	7.2	1,344.37	4.3	1,410.25	4.9	1,505.85	6.8
Geology	QE	184	1,877.54	1,987.97	5.9	2,061.08	3.7	2,139.80	3.8	2,251.35	5.2
Health Sciences	R	2,700	1,561.39	1,671.95	7.1	1,736.90	3.9	1,815.26	4.5	1,915.94	5.5
History	C,D,E,F	723	554.90	586.00	5.6	617.13	5.3	641.05	3.9	672.90	5.0

Subject	LC Class	Titles	Price	Price	%	Price	%	Price	%	Price	%
Language and Literature	P	807	536.94	568.46	5.9	593.97	4.5	620.09	4.4	656.43	5.9
Law	K	272	669.40	703.59	5.1	735.89	4.6	794.83	8.0	831.35	4.6
Library Science	Z	157	1,401.86	1,476.77	5.3	1,539.57	4.3	1,447.95	-6.0	1,519.39	4.9
Math and Computer Science	QA	1,046	1,661.89	1,783.91	7.3	1,852.38	3.8	1,951.42	5.3	2,065.91	5.9
Military and Naval Science	U,V	85	815.09	866.93	6.4	911.13	5.1	956.95	5.0	1,009.42	5.5
Music	M	104	417.10	438.61	5.2	453.94	3.5	467.23	2.9	487.21	4.3
Philosophy and Religion	B-BD, BH-BX	448	541.63	569.45	5.1	588.68	3.4	620.26	5.4	647.73	4.4
Physics	QC	440	3,967.60	4,194.95	5.7	4,323.81	3.1	4,462.76	3.2	4,649.69	4.2
Political Science	J	311	936.38	1,004.86	7.3	1,048.38	4.3	1,081.70	3.2	1,145.28	5.9
Psychology	BF	309	1,021.54	1,104.89	8.2	1,135.76	2.8	1,193.28	5.1	1,271.83	6.6
Recreation	GV	108	953.76	1,013.57	6.3	1,075.25	6.1	1,134.66	5.5	1,217.86	7.3
Social Sciences	H	124	1,020.26	1,084.57	6.3	1,098.23	1.3	1,157.66	5.4	1,232.44	6.5
Sociology	HM-HX	850	1,076.20	1,148.20	6.7	1,191.91	3.8	1,233.46	3.5	1,318.42	6.9
Technology	TA-TT	320	2,391.19	2,531.77	5.9	2,634.81	4.1	2,597.20	-1.4	2,787.64	7.3
Zoology	QL	224	1,914.38	2,023.48	5.7	2,022.96	0.0	2,085.91	3.1	2,175.78	4.3
Totals and Averages		15,498	$1,634.12	$1,734.47	6.1%	$1,798.93	3.7%	$1,858.61	3.3%	$1,964.65	5.7%

Compiled by Cynthia Elliott in consultation with Stephen Bosch from the University of Arizona, based on data on serial pricing supplied by EBSCO information Services and based on titles indexed in EBSCO Academic Search Ultimate, EBSCO Masterfile Complete, Clarivate Analytics (formerly ISI) Arts and Humanities Citation Index, Clarivate Analytics Science Citation Index, Clarivate Analytics Social Sciences Citation Index, and Elsevier's Scopus

Table 9 / British Academic Books: Average Prices and Price Indexes, 2019–2022

Index Base: 2010 = 100

Subject	LC Class	2010		2019		2020		2021*		2022			
		Titles	Average Price (£)	Titles	Average Price (£)	Titles	Average Price (£)	Titles	Average Price (£)	Titles	Average Price (£)	Percent Change 2021–2022	Index
Agriculture	S	154	£63.97	154	£84.11	613	£87.95	150	£97.25	145	£97.68	0.4%	152.7
Anthropology	GN	154	50.85	173	74.65	294	70.16	188	76.85	154	71.79	-6.6	141.2
Botany	QK	45	66.08	36	89.13	162	115.45	30	95.38	33	97.04	1.7	146.9
Business and Economics	H-HJ	1,913	60.54	2,185	80.42	4,409	78.68	2,089	85.41	2,012	89.38	4.6	147.6
Chemistry	QD	96	105.68	61	121.99	309	130.53	64	164.2	45	141.39	-13.9	133.8
Education	L	558	52.21	731	78.83	2,315	69.15	698	85.45	679	89.51	4.8	171.4
Engineering and Technology	T-TS	742	61.84	693	90.24	3,845	109.15	612	100.06	623	89.08	-11.0	144.1
Fine and Applied Arts	M, N	1,037	35.95	989	60.88	3,601	50.02	1,006	64.03	970	62.95	-1.7	175.1
General Works	A	30	60.03	37	85.11	90	91.85	40	121.47	43	112.74	-7.2	187.8
Geography	G-GF, GR-GT	276	65.69	342	81.01	798	82.65	362	85.57	318	84.51	-1.2	128.6
Geology	QE	33	52.28	51	58.66	123	106.49	39	51.83	45	55.18	6.5	105.6
History	C,D,E,F	1,822	42.55	2,215	57.95	4,813	62.73	1,986	65.96	1,953	69.54	5.4	163.4
Home Economics	TX	46	30.48	37	91.70	333	46.16	46	92.17	41	73.79	-19.9	242.1
Industrial Arts	TT	41	28.47	23	51.59	105	55.50	23	58.04	24	60.25	3.8	211.6

Subject	LC Class	Titles	Avg. Price	Titles	Avg. Price	Titles	Avg. Price	Titles	Avg. Price	Titles	Avg. Price	% Change	
Language and Literature	P	3,987	31.58	3,219	55.93	7,444	47.93	3,006	63.72	3,020	63.11	-1.0	199.9
Law	K	1,153	83.10	1,313	99.48	2,050	89.98	1,268	104.46	1,292	107.64	3.0	129.5
Library and Information Science	Z	100	53.58	85	79.97	269	73.66	91	75.71	67	71.17	-6.0	132.8
Mathematics and Computer Science	QA	207	48.29	222	78.73	2,189	77.88	202	80.22	217	73.36	-8.6	151.9
Medicine	R	1,182	55.12	1,081	76.98	3,880	94.36	1,113	83.35	987	82.32	-1.2	149.3
Military and Naval Sciences	U, V	184	40.95	165	57.91	520	55.82	188	66.73	155	54.81	-17.9	133.8
Philosophy and Religion	B-BD, BH-BX	1,336	48.17	1,505	69.70	3,998	53.46	1,479	72.81	1,378	71.50	-1.8	148.4
Physics and Astronomy	QB, QC	214	64.83	200	75.70	751	93.42	195	65.4	222	73.56	12.5	113.5
Political Science	J	737	71.88	1,107	77.96	1,670	73.37	996	84.97	989	88.37	4.0	122.9
Psychology	BF	265	39.69	414	80.74	854	63.66	350	84.44	359	83.29	-1.4	209.8
Science (general)	Q	60	40.70	99	71.83	521	85.30	97	71.31	99	74.56	4.6	183.2
Sociology	HM-HX	1,169	58.24	1,685	73.91	3,367	66.26	1,661	72.8	1,513	76.91	5.6	132.1
Sports and Recreation	GV	192	36.76	216	80.04	645	51.38	182	87.03	184	83.97	-3.5	228.5
Zoology	QH, QL-QR	382	65.79	321	85.51	1,203	101.95	341	84.74	263	98.57	16.3	149.8
Totals and Averages		18,115	£50.50	19,350	£72.61	51,171	£71.56	18,502	£83.12	17,830	£81.49	-1.9%	162.5

Compiled by Sylvia Orner from the University of Scranton, based on information provided by GOBI Library Solutions

*2021 titles and prices have been updated to reflect new information from GOBI Library Solutions.

(continued from page 301)

Using the Price Indexes

Librarians are encouraged to monitor publishing industry trends and changes in economic conditions when preparing budget forecasts and projections. The LMPI Editorial Board endeavors to make information on publishing trends readily available by sponsoring the annual compilation and publication of price data contained in our published tables. The indexes cover newly published library materials and document prices and rates of percent changes at the national and international levels. They are useful benchmarks to compare against local costs. Still, because they reflect retail prices in the aggregate, they are not a substitute for cost data that reflect the collecting patterns of individual libraries. They are not a substitute for specific cost studies.

Differences between local prices and those found in national indexes arise partially because these indexes exclude discounts, service charges, shipping and handling fees, and other discounts or costs that a library might see. Discrepancies may also relate to a library's subject coverage, its mix of titles purchased—including both current and backfiles—and the proportion of the library's budget expended on domestic or foreign materials. These variables can affect the average price paid by an individual library, although the individual library's rate of increase may not differ greatly from the national indexes.

Closing Note

The LMPI Editorial Board is interested in pursuing studies that correlate a particular library's costs with the national prices. The group consists of compilers Ajaye Bloomstone, Stephen Bosch, Cynthia Elliott, Sylvia Orner, and Narda Tafuri. Sylvia Orner serves as editor. While it will not be meeting at the American Library Association's Annual Conference, the group welcomes interested parties to contact Sylvia Orner (sylvia.orner@scranton.edu).

Book Title Output and Average Prices: 2020–2022

Constance Harbison

Baker & Taylor

The figures appearing in this report were provided for publication in *Library and Book Trade Almanac* by book wholesaler Baker & Taylor and are based on the Book Industry Study Group's BISAC Subject Headings. Figures for 2020 and 2021 have been revised since the previous edition was published, reflecting updates to the Baker & Taylor database. Figures for 2022 are considered preliminary at the time of this report.

Annual book title output in the United States took a slight downturn from 2021 to 2022, decreasing by only 1.56 percent; however, a more significant drop of 4.5 percent occurred from 2020 to 2022 (see Table 1). This drop in output has been continuous since the country entered quarantine in March 2020 due to the COVID-19 pandemic. The 2022 title output is the lowest it has been in over a decade. This output may show some growth when the 2022 numbers are restated in next year's edition, but the 2020 and 2021 outputs should stay relatively the same and are also quite low in comparison to those of 2013–2019. Publishers continue to face post-pandemic challenges and are taking a conservative approach to the acquisition of new content as they determine where new growth opportunities are and what readers want.

The popular subject category of Fiction trended upward for 2021, but looks to have slowed for 2022, which is currently 9.3 percent below the output of 2021. Children and Young Adults also continue to trend downward from 2019. This decline may be attributed to lackluster sales of these genres during the shutdown of bookstores, libraries, and book fairs in the early days of the pandemic, leading to disruption in the discovery process. Declining sales to these two audiences are resulting in a decrease in the output of books marketed to them.

Those categories showing the highest percentage increase from 2021 to 2022 are Bibles (21 percent), Foreign Language Study (36.5 percent), Music (78 percent), and Travel (32.5 percent). This suggests where the interests of post-pandemic consumers are headed. The increase in title output of Foreign Language Study and Travel books indicates that people are anxious to travel again, and not just domestically. The category with the most significant drop is Study Aids, which saw a 44 percent decrease in output. This makes sense, as more and more colleges are making standardized tests optional. Students are also turning to more interactive online resources for studying for standardized tests, many of which are available at no cost.

Typically, preliminary figures are revised upward as late-arriving materials are added to the database, suggesting that the final "total" 2022 output shown in Table 1 may increase and show less dramatic changes between 2021 and 2022.

Output and Prices by Format and Category

The average pricing for titles published in 2020 and 2021 was relatively flat (2021 shows a .25 percent average price increase); however, the average price in 2022 is 2.2 percent higher than that of 2021. This is somewhat expected, as there has been significant inflation over the past few years; because of increases in both production and shipping costs, publishers have likely found it necessary to increase prices in order to remain profitable.

While it was Bibles, Photography, and Games & Activities that saw the biggest average price increase between 2020 and 2021, it is Health & Fitness, Poetry, and Reference that are seeing an increase from 2021 to 2022. It could be that publishers are seeing growth in these areas and thus raising prices. Significant drops in average pricing are seen in Family & Relationships and Photography. The latter showed a dramatic increase in average pricing from 2020 to 2021, but that average has come back down in 2022, dropping by almost 45 percent.

The average price of hardcover titles remained consistent from 2020 to 2022, although output dropped within that period (see Tables 2 and 3). The period from 2020 to 2022 shows only a 1.9 percent increase in average price. The average price of hardcover Fiction had been trending downward since 2019, down almost 3 percent from 2019 to 2021, but jumped 2.7 percent from 2021 to 2022. In terms of output, Children's titles and Fiction showed the most significant drops in output since 2021, with the former dropping by 4 percent and the latter by 8.5 percent.

The two categories showing the most significant price increases from 2021 to 2022 are Drama and Study Aids, but the title counts are very low for each (fewer than 35 titles), so one high-priced or low-priced book can greatly skew the average in either direction. The Architecture category remained the most consistent, showing the same average price of $52.61 in both 2021 and 2022. From 2020 to 2022, 15 categories had an average price increase of less than 2 percent, and five of these (Bibles, Family & Relationships, Fiction, Performing Arts, and Social Science) showed an increase of less than 1 percent over 2020. Since 2020, Games & Activities and Humor have increased the most, but, again, neither of these categories has had more than 225 titles output during the period covered. Seven categories had a steady drop in average price of their hardcover titles since 2020, including Gardening, Psychology, and Young Adult.

Mass market titles had a slight average price increase from 2020 to 2021, and the preliminary 2022 average price is moving in the same direction, with an increase of 1.21 percent over 2021; however, the preliminary 2022 figures show mass market output dropping 9.1 percent from 2021 and 10.6 percent from 2020 (see Table 4). In addition to the drop in output of mass market titles, there was also a drop in categories having mass market titles. In 2021 mass market titles were published in 12 categories, but in only eight in 2022. In fact, for 2020, 2021, and 2022, more than 99 percent of title output comprised Fiction, Children's books, and Young Adult books. This suggests that publishers are concentrating the focus of mass market titles into only specific, more consumer-focused categories. As with most years, mass market titles were dominated by the Fiction category, making up 89 percent of the output (the same percentage for 2020, 2021, and 2022). The average price of these Fiction titles has

(text continues on page 317)

Table 1 / American Book Production 2020–2022

BISAC Category	2020	2021	2022
Antiques and Collectibles	173	156	175
Architecture	1,788	1,641	1,555
Art	3,611	3,274	3,543
Bibles	690	717	866
Biography and Autobiography	3,827	4,238	4,366
Body, Mind and Spirit	1,128	1,156	1,201
Business and Economics	10,517	10,497	10,410
Children	26,558	25,171	24,744
Comics and Graphic Novels	2,482	2,796	3,302
Computers	4,085	3,771	3,916
Cooking	1,740	1,713	1,577
Crafts and Hobbies	737	665	636
Design	517	480	520
Drama	468	486	476
Education	6,195	5,820	5,831
Family and Relationships	840	869	830
Fiction	16,089	18,207	16,512
Foreign Language Study	1,196	760	1,037
Games and Activities	823	811	869
Gardening	209	234	267
Health and Fitness	1,294	1,322	1,169
History	12,242	11,671	11,474
House and Home	181	196	215
Humor	461	437	358
Language Arts and Disciplines	2,814	2,853	2,681
Law	5,570	5,838	5,245
Literary Collections	692	714	684
Literary Criticism	4,804	4,912	4,678
Mathematics	2,086	1,977	1,739
Medical	6,491	6,608	6,508
Music	4,387	2,359	4,193
Nature	1,156	1,283	1,112
Performing Arts	1,624	1,748	1,757
Pets	0	146	160
Philosophy	3,581	3,534	3,475
Photography	1,081	818	819
Poetry	2,182	2,283	2,082
Political Science	8,486	7,908	7,109
Psychology	3,022	2,909	2,971
Reference	511	447	390
Religion	8,687	8,229	7,311
Science	7,054	7,422	7,194
Self-Help	1,655	1,714	1,652
Social Science	9,921	8,859	8,741
Sports and Recreation	1,338	1,330	1,311
Study Aids	2,452	817	451
Technology and Engineering	6,199	6,793	7,309
Transportation	558	495	560
Travel	1,134	922	1,222
True Crime	299	351	295
Young Adult	3,826	3,408	3,395
Totals	189,461	183,765	180,893

Table 2 / Hardcover Output and Average Per-Volume Prices, 2020–2022

BISAC Category	2020 Vols.	2020 $ Total	2020 Avg.	2021 Vols.	2021 $ Total	2021 Avg.	2022 Vols.	2022 $ Total	2022 Avg.
Antiques and Collectibles	94	$7,332.19	$78.00	80	$6,124.34	$76.55	85	$6,403.94	$75.34
Architecture	896	$86,720.72	$96.79	832	$78,583.12	$94.45	814	$83,736.83	$102.87
Art	2,028	$169,852.14	$83.75	1,815	$153,790.08	$84.73	2,039	$154,738.45	$75.89
Bibles	221	$11,936.63	$54.01	215	$13,766.66	$64.03	375	$21,377.92	$57.01
Biography and Autobiography	1,525	$66,109.08	$43.35	1,786	$73,853.96	$41.35	1,954	$80,536.70	$41.22
Body, Mind and Spirit	308	$7,078.56	$22.98	307	$9,073.04	$29.55	371	$11,286.42	$30.42
Business and Economics	4,154	$593,887.08	$142.97	4,392	$610,029.55	$138.90	4,553	$641,620.21	$140.92
Children	15,551	$418,582.70	$26.92	14,637	$392,252.43	$26.80	14,015	$355,399.43	$25.36
Comics and Graphic Novels	650	$30,301.73	$46.62	634	$31,003.24	$48.90	789	$41,532.90	$52.64
Computers	1,035	$166,344.46	$160.72	1,054	$197,574.23	$187.45	1,247	$259,078.09	$207.76
Cooking	933	$29,589.00	$31.71	954	$31,874.76	$33.41	972	$32,784.23	$33.73
Crafts and Hobbies	147	$4,790.16	$32.59	138	$4,353.63	$31.55	126	$4,062.21	$32.24
Design	307	$21,736.85	$70.80	263	$18,414.46	$70.02	324	$24,036.88	$74.19
Drama	77	$8,284.95	$107.60	81	$7,647.69	$94.42	92	$8,705.99	$94.63
Education	2,307	$371,406.59	$160.99	2,323	$339,548.35	$146.17	2,413	$361,258.39	$149.71
Family and Relationships	224	$11,564.77	$51.63	243	$16,524.60	$68.00	241	$11,150.36	$46.27
Fiction	4,539	$135,840.68	$29.93	5,112	$149,322.42	$29.21	4,688	$142,323.01	$30.36
Foreign Language Study	239	$29,229.61	$122.30	243	$28,668.30	$117.98	242	$31,245.27	$129.11
Games and Activities	141	$5,749.99	$40.78	121	$6,943.45	$57.38	149	$7,026.83	$47.16
Gardening	110	$4,247.39	$38.61	120	$4,317.42	$35.98	128	$4,470.66	$34.93
Health and Fitness	350	$30,469.95	$87.06	375	$28,750.14	$76.67	426	$42,940.49	$100.80
History	5,665	$629,825.96	$111.18	5,657	$586,184.68	$103.62	5,508	$527,719.34	$95.81
House and Home	116	$4,591.43	$39.58	122	$5,350.72	$43.86	147	$6,684.51	$45.47
Humor	249	$5,169.34	$20.76	228	$5,369.92	$23.55	171	$4,639.40	$27.13

Law	2,274	$430,201.69	$189.18	2,363	$418,072.31	$176.92	2,369	$415,738.61	$175.49
Literary Collections	254	$27,797.13	$109.44	255	$21,214.15	$83.19	240	$22,146.07	$92.28
Literary Criticism	2,572	$335,047.42	$130.27	2,665	$347,215.00	$130.29	2,673	$339,378.16	$126.97
Mathematics	841	$124,482.89	$148.02	824	$120,247.77	$145.93	821	$111,749.77	$136.11
Medical	2,857	$530,634.70	$185.73	2,571	$496,262.99	$193.02	3,047	$624,591.83	$204.99
Music	650	$65,210.59	$100.32	587	$58,447.92	$99.57	601	$65,233.56	$108.54
Nature	457	$39,471.89	$86.37	527	$45,984.46	$87.26	505	$46,380.35	$91.84
Performing Arts	789	$83,253.08	$105.52	843	$87,974.52	$104.36	830	$84,428.12	$101.72
Pets	60	$1,362.43	$22.71	51	$1,352.52	$26.52	69	$1,798.21	$26.06
Philosophy	1,753	$216,574.08	$123.54	1,700	$194,919.03	$114.66	1,724	$196,387.46	$113.91
Photography	786	$47,296.47	$60.17	598	$73,863.61	$123.52	610	$41,692.17	$68.35
Poetry	261	$9,162.11	$35.10	357	$11,860.23	$33.22	339	$15,390.43	$45.40
Political Science	3,635	$422,169.67	$116.14	3,409	$416,630.62	$122.21	3,378	$419,798.18	$124.27
Psychology	1,172	$177,903.83	$151.80	1,138	$180,550.98	$158.66	1,217	$193,200.99	$158.75
Reference	243	$88,662.14	$364.86	221	$70,151.05	$317.43	208	$96,234.64	$462.67
Religion	2,840	$244,276.98	$86.01	2,939	$252,025.70	$85.75	2,661	$228,824.67	$85.99
Science	3,547	$686,620.90	$193.58	3,432	$663,863.59	$193.43	3,945	$747,816.09	$189.56
Self-Help	424	$10,030.35	$23.66	467	$11,444.78	$24.51	446	$11,425.94	$25.62
Social Science	3,969	$512,873.84	$129.22	4,020	$526,062.74	$130.86	4,283	$543,919.94	$127.00
Sports and Recreation	498	$28,130.81	$56.49	516	$31,914.35	$61.85	565	$37,257.79	$65.94
Study Aids	30	$3,786.13	$126.20	13	$1,888.89	$145.30	13	$2,074.91	$159.61
Technology and Engineering	3,170	$597,977.40	$188.64	3,368	$670,593.07	$199.11	3,828	$722,716.95	$188.80
Transportation	218	$19,509.73	$89.49	236	$22,085.48	$93.58	234	$20,781.69	$88.81
Travel	216	$8,063.90	$37.33	174	$7,503.21	$43.12	197	$7,210.08	$36.60
True Crime	82	$5,245.72	$63.97	101	$4,339.23	$42.96	111	$3,391.57	$30.55
Young Adult	1,481	$48,520.75	$32.76	1,254	$36,100.36	$28.79	1,161	$30,937.26	$26.65
Totals	78,262	$7,792,730.65	$99.57	77,703	$7,756,666.51	$99.82	79,248	$8,088,074.51	$102.06

Table 3 / Hardcover Output and Average Per-Volume Prices, Less than $81, 2020–2022

BISAC Category	2020 Vols.	2020 $ Total	2020 Avg.	2021 Vols.	2021 $ Total	2021 Avg.	2022 Vols.	2022 $ Total	2022 Avg.
Antiques and Collectibles	64	$2,792.20	$43.63	57	$2,853.35	$50.06	59	$2,394.00	$40.58
Architecture	529	$27,147.91	$51.32	484	$25,462.49	$52.61	432	$22,729.49	$52.61
Art	1,406	$65,985.71	$46.93	1,242	$58,733.20	$47.29	1,460	$69,485.09	$47.59
Bibles	193	$8,480.91	$43.94	174	$7,103.06	$40.82	332	$14,670.21	$44.19
Biography and Autobiography	1,395	$43,116.45	$30.91	1,631	$51,337.79	$31.48	1,795	$57,488.33	$32.03
Body, Mind and Spirit	299	$5,861.57	$19.60	292	$6,727.19	$23.04	347	$7,641.59	$22.02
Business and Economics	1,432	$60,818.65	$42.47	1,528	$63,296.48	$41.42	1,415	$57,488.51	$40.63
Children	15,192	$326,051.17	$21.46	14,281	$293,811.60	$20.57	13,711	$290,675.49	$21.20
Comics and Graphic Novels	555	$18,381.97	$33.12	525	$17,883.45	$34.06	626	$21,489.16	$34.33
Computers	177	$10,583.02	$59.79	200	$11,971.47	$59.86	225	$13,926.24	$61.89
Cooking	906	$25,107.38	$27.71	926	$27,420.84	$29.61	951	$29,005.33	$30.50
Crafts and Hobbies	145	$4,530.16	$31.24	135	$3,928.63	$29.10	125	$3,955.71	$31.65
Design	212	$9,485.96	$44.75	186	$8,326.57	$44.77	233	$11,706.09	$50.24
Drama	21	$909.05	$43.29	26	$922.45	$35.48	33	$1,364.22	$41.34
Education	478	$25,986.79	$54.37	416	$23,397.10	$56.24	363	$20,108.82	$55.40
Family and Relationships	187	$4,794.68	$25.64	200	$5,179.77	$25.90	208	$5,349.09	$25.72
Fiction	4,493	$130,242.85	$28.99	5,065	$143,641.56	$28.36	4,633	$134,833.07	$29.10
Foreign Language Study	70	$4,130.14	$59.00	77	$4,508.94	$58.56	78	$4,689.60	$60.12
Games and Activities	130	$4,141.04	$31.85	100	$3,467.46	$34.67	136	$5,137.12	$37.77
Gardening	104	$3,356.49	$32.27	113	$3,644.47	$32.25	123	$3,880.66	$31.55
Health and Fitness	224	$6,279.42	$28.03	267	$7,772.69	$29.11	244	$7,862.68	$32.22
History	2,565	$112,468.82	$43.85	2,438	$106,894.10	$43.84	2,327	$103,739.52	$44.58
House and Home	109	$3,920.44	$35.97	114	$4,395.77	$38.56	138	$5,646.51	$40.92
Humor	246	$4,744.34	$19.29	222	$4,484.97	$20.20	164	$3,724.40	$22.71
Language Arts and Disciplines	201	$11,667.97	$58.05	224	$12,654.35	$56.49	187	$10,150.08	$54.28

Category	Qty	Amount	Avg	Qty	Amount	Avg	Qty	Amount	Avg
Law	241	$13,571.63	$56.31	268	$14,699.54	$54.85	315	$19,127.60	$60.72
Literary Collections	120	$4,699.33	$39.16	146	$4,678.69	$32.05	135	$4,736.76	$35.09
Literary Criticism	574	$32,309.95	$56.29	572	$32,449.16	$56.73	596	$34,060.94	$57.15
Mathematics	124	$7,400.76	$59.68	138	$8,284.99	$60.04	138	$8,558.10	$62.02
Medical	263	$14,402.17	$54.76	287	$15,688.92	$54.67	290	$16,160.75	$55.73
Music	278	$12,113.18	$43.57	255	$11,053.36	$43.35	260	$11,774.36	$45.29
Nature	269	$8,935.50	$33.22	315	$10,236.25	$32.50	277	$8,943.52	$32.29
Performing Arts	242	$10,180.91	$42.07	279	$12,108.02	$43.40	283	$11,979.92	$42.33
Pets	59	$1,254.48	$21.26	50	$1,152.52	$23.05	68	$1,678.21	$24.68
Philosophy	453	$22,543.33	$49.76	432	$22,709.83	$52.57	451	$22,842.93	$50.65
Photography	700	$32,848.67	$46.93	520	$24,803.26	$47.70	525	$26,012.53	$49.55
Poetry	239	$6,604.26	$27.63	327	$8,995.43	$27.51	284	$8,502.61	$29.94
Political Science	1,075	$47,162.86	$43.87	912	$43,044.39	$47.20	851	$38,650.90	$45.42
Psychology	216	$9,987.15	$46.24	235	$10,845.65	$46.15	221	$9,923.86	$44.90
Reference	96	$2,717.42	$28.31	82	$2,042.65	$24.91	62	$1,680.80	$27.11
Religion	1,576	$55,490.85	$35.21	1,610	$56,119.19	$34.86	1,392	$48,899.06	$35.13
Science	538	$24,254.18	$45.08	564	$24,692.82	$43.78	556	$25,641.76	$46.12
Self-Help	421	$9,610.35	$22.83	464	$11,079.84	$23.88	442	$10,882.37	$24.62
Social Science	1,010	$49,279.07	$48.79	921	$44,920.71	$48.77	957	$46,917.79	$49.03
Sports and Recreation	403	$13,350.09	$33.13	400	$13,087.07	$32.72	421	$14,339.17	$34.06
Study Aids	23	$1,281.76	$55.73	6	$259.91	$43.32	4	$227.94	$56.99
Technology and Engineering	219	$12,331.47	$56.31	222	$12,169.96	$54.82	186	$10,589.66	$56.93
Transportation	162	$7,710.34	$47.59	166	$7,887.83	$47.52	177	$9,218.83	$52.08
Travel	200	$6,330.05	$31.65	158	$5,129.01	$32.46	189	$6,295.08	$33.31
True Crime	79	$2,366.72	$29.96	95	$3,195.23	$33.63	111	$3,391.57	$30.55
Young Adult	1,445	$36,559.88	$25.30	1,232	$30,007.42	$24.36	1,147	$27,562.61	$24.03
Totals	42,358	$1,366,281.45	$32.26	41,579	$1,331,161.40	$32.02	40,683	$1,337,740.64	$32.88

Table 4 / Mass Market Paperbacks Output and Average Per-Volume Prices, 2020–2022

BISAC Category	2020 Vols.	2020 $ Total	2020 Avg.	2021 Vols.	2021 $ Total	2021 Avg.	2022 Vols.	2022 $ Total	2022 Avg.
Biography and Autobiography	3	$27.97	$9.32	4	$34.96	$8.74	2	$16.98	$8.49
Business and Economics							1	$9.99	$9.99
Children	221	$1,771.76	$8.02	211	$1,709.89	$8.10	204	$1,658.96	$8.13
Family and Relationships	2	$18.98	$9.49						
Fiction	2,252	$17,090.20	$7.59	2,228	$17,330.14	$7.78	2,017	$15,844.79	$7.86
Health and Fitness	1	$8.99	$8.99	2	$17.98	$8.99			
History	4	$39.96	$9.99	2	$19.98	$9.99	2	$19.98	$9.99
Philosophy	2	$7.98	$3.99	1	$3.99	$3.99			
Poetry				1	$3.99	$3.99			
Reference	1	$8.99	$8.99	3	$23.50	$7.83	1	$8.99	$8.99
Self-Help				3	$23.97	$7.99			
Sports and Recreation				1	$9.99	$9.99			
True Crime	5	$44.95	$8.99	4	$38.96	$9.74	6	$57.94	$9.66
Young Adult	45	$482.55	$10.72	34	$370.66	$10.90	34	$411.66	$12.11
Totals	2,536	$19,502.33	$7.69	2,494	$19,588.01	$7.85	2,267	$18,029.29	$7.95

(continued from page 310)

increased by only 3.5 percent, suggesting that publishers are trying to continue making mass market affordable to all consumers. Many of the STEM titles, as categorized by such subjects as Mathematics, Science, and Technology & Engineering, do not have any titles published as mass market.

The preliminary 2022 counts show a decrease in output from 2020 to 2022 for trade paperbacks of 8.2 percent less (see Table 5). The average price of trade paperbacks has fluctuated between 2020 and 2022: The average price increased 4.25 percent from 2020 to 2021, but then decreased 3 percent from 2021 to 2022. The category of Music saw the greatest increase in output for 2022; after showing a 46 percent drop in output between 2020 and 2021, the category grew by 103 percent in 2022, bringing it to only 3.4 percent less than the 2020 output. Less significant growth was noticed in Comics & Graphic Novels and Foreign Language Study, the former growing by 16.2 percent and the latter by 54.2 percent. In the previous edition of *Library and Book Trade Almanac*, the categories Foreign Language Study and Travel showed the most dramatic drops in output from 2020 to 2021, with the former dropping 111.72 percent and the latter dropping 106 percent. In that edition, it was remarked that it will be interesting to see if these categories trend upward once there is a demand for them as people start traveling again, and, indeed, output is trending upward for both from 2021 to 2022.

The output figures of physically packaged audiobooks for 2021 (see Table 6) show a spike in output and then a drop back to the 20,000 range for 2022. Judging by reports of the skyrocketing sales of audiobooks, an increase in the 2022 preliminary numbers will probably be seen in the next edition. Pre-pandemic, audiobooks enjoyed popularity with commuters, as people would pass the time sitting in traffic listening to a book. In early 2020 when most of the country began spending more time in their homes than in their cars, it was expected that audiobooks would become less popular. But with the growth of downloadable audio and options for subscription services for audiobooks, they have become less expensive, easier to obtain, and more portable. The audiobook is now a convenient substitute for radio or television. The average pricing of audiobooks looks to be trending upward in 2022, as the preliminary numbers show the average price to be 20.3 percent above the 2020 average. More than 50 percent of audiobooks output in 2022 was in the Fiction category, as it was in 2020 and 2021. In 2021 and 2022 this was followed by Biography & Autobiography, which contributed to 7.83 percent and 6.43 percent of total output, respectively.

Average e-book pricing continues to fluctuate: 2021 was down from both 2019 and then 2020, but 2022 shows an average price increase of 9.3 percent (see Table 7). E-book output has steadily decreased since 2019, dropping 1.6 percent from 2020 to 2021 (less than originally projected) and then again dropping 28 percent from 2021 to 2022. Late additions of 2021 records narrowed the margin between 2020 output and 2021 output, so perhaps the margin between 2021 and 2022 will be shown to narrow as well in next year's edition. A few categories had a significant drop in e-book output, most notably Fiction, which dropped 24.4 percent. There were only three categories in e-books that showed an increase in output: Bibles (+34.4 percent), Drama (+12.5 percent), and Humor (+.70 percent).

(text continues on page 324)

Table 5 / Trade Paperbacks Output and Average Per-Volume Prices, 2020–2022

BISAC Category	2020 Vols.	2020 $ Total	2020 Avg.	2021 Vols.	2021 $ Total	2021 Avg.	2022 Vols.	2022 $ Total	2022 Avg.
Antiques and Collectibles	79	$3,567.39	$45.16	76	$3,139.48	$41.31	90	$4,157.69	$46.20
Architecture	892	$44,860.31	$50.29	808	$45,041.84	$55.74	738	$39,267.69	$53.21
Art	1,578	$64,407.07	$40.82	1,453	$60,245.29	$41.46	1,503	$63,026.46	$41.93
Bibles	467	$26,505.78	$56.76	502	$30,809.94	$61.37	492	$31,955.63	$64.95
Biography and Autobiography	2,299	$49,174.35	$21.39	2,451	$52,934.40	$21.60	2,426	$53,508.17	$22.06
Body, Mind and Spirit	820	$15,654.06	$19.09	849	$16,959.12	$19.98	830	$16,629.35	$20.04
Business and Economics	6,178	$443,569.63	$71.80	5,981	$456,119.63	$76.26	5,793	$433,769.16	$74.88
Children	10,741	$134,251.84	$12.50	10,298	$132,666.65	$12.88	10,512	$133,856.50	$12.73
Comics and Graphic Novels	1,832	$35,018.57	$19.11	2,162	$40,957.87	$18.94	2,513	$47,775.23	$19.01
Computers	2,988	$256,337.47	$85.79	2,695	$237,656.20	$88.18	2,654	$230,171.57	$86.73
Cooking	809	$17,327.76	$21.42	759	$16,532.57	$21.78	606	$14,158.62	$23.36
Crafts and Hobbies	572	$12,419.01	$21.71	501	$11,076.38	$22.11	501	$10,980.72	$21.92
Design	210	$7,828.93	$37.28	217	$8,642.51	$39.83	196	$8,387.56	$42.79
Drama	391	$8,707.80	$22.27	405	$8,075.07	$19.94	384	$8,404.00	$21.89
Education	3,810	$407,914.80	$107.06	3,467	$208,747.23	$60.21	3,402	$191,671.73	$56.34
Family and Relationships	613	$13,196.86	$21.53	625	$13,493.92	$21.59	590	$12,893.03	$21.85
Fiction	9,296	$164,503.79	$17.70	10,867	$193,109.13	$17.77	9,832	$178,785.72	$18.18
Foreign Language Study	928	$42,715.87	$46.03	515	$25,014.90	$48.57	794	$31,552.25	$39.74
Games and Activities	681	$12,300.80	$18.06	690	$12,582.60	$18.24	719	$13,127.57	$18.26
Gardening	99	$2,322.26	$23.46	114	$2,883.01	$25.29	140	$3,650.54	$26.08
Health and Fitness	929	$30,349.50	$32.67	936	$31,936.37	$34.12	740	$26,204.31	$35.41
History	6,535	$271,928.96	$41.61	5,978	$247,545.36	$41.41	5,954	$234,675.91	$39.41
House and Home	65	$1,496.70	$23.03	74	$1,926.37	$26.03	68	$1,694.71	$24.92
Humor	212	$3,560.95	$16.80	209	$3,518.20	$16.83	188	$3,279.19	$17.44
Language Arts and Disciplines	1,439	$83,763.66	$58.21	1,479	$88,959.43	$60.15	1,344	$80,206.28	$59.68

Category	Count	Amount	Avg	Count	Amount	Avg	Count	Amount	Avg
Law	3,209	$286,124.72	$89.16	3,426	$298,747.19	$87.20	2,818	$237,871.41	$84.41
Literary Collections	435	$12,620.53	$29.01	459	$14,040.90	$30.59	446	$12,798.33	$28.70
Literary Criticism	2,231	$97,193.53	$43.57	2,247	$106,697.18	$47.48	2,009	$93,756.47	$46.67
Mathematics	1,156	$85,984.39	$74.38	1,113	$94,332.35	$84.76	908	$79,367.77	$87.41
Medical	3,602	$297,951.74	$82.72	3,983	$357,924.11	$89.86	3,413	$315,984.57	$92.58
Music	3,724	$102,934.29	$27.64	1,768	$52,810.02	$29.87	3,598	$100,710.78	$27.99
Nature	697	$25,168.90	$36.11	752	$35,189.63	$46.79	608	$23,882.47	$39.28
Performing Arts	834	$33,191.68	$39.80	901	$41,145.08	$45.67	925	$38,249.34	$41.35
Pets	99	$1,827.86	$18.46	95	$1,917.69	$20.19	91	$1,975.02	$21.70
Philosophy	1,815	$80,925.21	$44.59	1,821	$93,887.50	$51.56	1,742	$86,914.92	$49.89
Photography	295	$10,854.80	$36.80	220	$10,482.43	$47.65	209	$7,266.04	$34.77
Poetry	1,922	$33,580.09	$17.47	1,926	$34,297.84	$17.81	1,746	$32,444.89	$18.58
Political Science	4,840	$234,915.31	$48.54	4,484	$236,655.49	$52.78	3,728	$195,331.31	$52.40
Psychology	1,805	$103,519.58	$57.35	1,721	$96,246.25	$55.92	1,677	$97,487.69	$58.13
Reference	264	$54,138.72	$205.07	221	$50,324.74	$227.71	181	$42,693.60	$235.88
Religion	5,840	$161,465.07	$27.65	5,292	$160,650.64	$30.36	4,658	$131,954.54	$28.33
Science	3,385	$335,172.85	$99.02	3,903	$446,892.12	$114.50	3,154	$364,165.19	$115.46
Self-Help	1,229	$22,090.80	$17.97	1,244	$22,318.84	$17.94	1,220	$22,619.22	$18.54
Social Science	5,894	$290,801.18	$49.34	4,801	$252,304.46	$52.55	4,403	$228,576.15	$51.91
Sports & Recreation	837	$22,962.16	$27.43	811	$22,593.57	$27.86	750	$22,579.59	$30.11
Study Aids	2,421	$105,552.17	$43.60	804	$37,683.38	$46.87	438	$19,413.84	$44.32
Technology and Engineering	2,985	$392,777.45	$131.58	3,405	$514,954.49	$151.23	3,463	$554,018.10	$159.98
Transportation	340	$12,235.30	$35.99	259	$9,087.51	$35.09	327	$11,301.83	$34.56
Travel	918	$19,133.08	$20.84	748	$16,146.04	$21.59	1,025	$22,702.05	$22.15
True Crime	212	$4,335.97	$20.45	246	$5,212.95	$21.19	181	$3,816.11	$21.08
Young Adult	2,303	$39,083.02	$16.97	2,122	$34,158.93	$16.10	2,211	$35,995.36	$16.28
Totals	107,755	$5,020,224.52	$46.59	102,883	$4,997,274.80	$48.57	98,938	$4,657,666.18	$47.08

Table 6 / Audiobook Output and Average Per-Volume Prices, 2020–2022

BISAC Category	2020 Vols.	2020 $ Total	2020 Avg.	2021 Vols.	2021 $ Total	2021 Avg.	2022 Vols.	2022 $ Total	2022 Avg.
Antiques and Collectibles	3	$122.97	$40.99	9	$176.91	$19.66	3	$160.97	$53.66
Architecture	5	$209.95	$41.99	12	$309.81	$25.82	8	$381.92	$47.74
Art	13	$433.87	$33.37	47	$1,043.49	$22.20	30	$1,497.28	$49.91
Bibles	12	$386.00	$32.17	8	$417.23	$52.15	7	$355.83	$50.83
Biography and Autobiography	1,244	$53,992.41	$43.40	3,115	$94,523.69	$30.34	1,720	$87,104.70	$50.64
Body, Mind and Spirit	167	$6,024.51	$36.07	403	$10,269.87	$25.48	262	$12,133.73	$46.31
Business and Economics	717	$29,688.25	$41.41	1,174	$32,852.86	$27.98	1,113	$54,338.72	$48.82
Children	1,943	$67,086.36	$34.53	1,533	$53,830.38	$35.11	1,528	$62,317.16	$40.78
Comics and Graphic Novels	37	$1,212.63	$32.77	4	$117.96	$29.49	18	$488.47	$27.14
Computers	12	$416.74	$34.73	108	$2,970.45	$27.50	56	$3,160.17	$56.43
Cooking	34	$1,323.43	$38.92	144	$3,822.90	$26.55	41	$2,024.45	$49.38
Crafts and Hobbies	3	$119.97	$39.99	13	$221.25	$17.02	16	$816.77	$51.05
Design	4	$164.96	$41.24	6	$128.94	$21.49	14	$480.72	$34.34
Drama	38	$1,013.47	$26.67	124	$3,618.24	$29.18	131	$6,712.22	$51.24
Education	32	$1,291.58	$40.36	181	$4,472.33	$24.71	239	$10,524.55	$44.04
Family and Relationships	162	$6,078.84	$37.52	625	$14,081.74	$22.53			
Fiction	14,035	$559,262.03	$39.85	20,035	$651,206.90	$32.50	14,285	$699,944.77	$49.00
Foreign Language Study	39	$2,081.24	$53.37	3	$100.93	$33.64	1	$41.95	$41.95
Games and Activities	7	$334.93	$47.85	23	$602.74	$26.21	5	$290.95	$58.19
Gardening	9	$337.91	$37.55	10	$263.86	$26.39	8	$325.92	$40.74
Health and Fitness	226	$9,835.67	$43.52	515	$15,029.95	$29.18	210	$10,290.56	$49.00
History	783	$37,655.17	$48.09	2,203	$63,667.85	$28.90	1,007	$55,935.88	$55.55
House and Home	17	$671.82	$39.52	28	$652.73	$23.31	13	$456.87	$35.14
Humor	90	$3,690.70	$41.01	316	$6,427.10	$20.34	72	$3,079.95	$42.78
…	…	$1,???.??	$44.00	1??	$?,???.??	$27.01	42	$1,???.??	$42.65

Law	31	$1,224.56	$39.50	111	$2,674.39	$24.09	68	$3,480.90	$51.19
Literary Collections	34	$1,339.45	$39.40	101	$3,158.52	$31.27	88	$4,294.00	$48.80
Literary Criticism	39	$1,398.47	$35.86	118	$3,061.44	$25.94	65	$2,722.28	$41.88
Mathematics	8	$279.92	$34.99	27	$742.74	$27.51	6	$329.95	$54.99
Medical	50	$2,183.29	$43.67	170	$4,615.15	$27.15	86	$4,303.88	$50.05
Music	51	$1,883.92	$36.94	204	$5,438.90	$26.66	89	$5,370.95	$60.35
Nature	122	$5,322.00	$43.62	240	$6,325.80	$26.36	123	$6,215.92	$50.54
Performing Arts	180	$7,736.26	$42.98	376	$12,255.22	$32.59	158	$5,534.79	$35.03
Pets	18	$680.83	$37.82	107	$2,332.77	$21.80	30	$1,358.50	$45.28
Philosophy	59	$2,335.30	$39.58	256	$6,448.26	$25.19	109	$5,054.76	$46.37
Photography	1	$29.99	$29.99	7	$132.93	$18.99	7	$255.93	$36.56
Poetry	139	$4,248.05	$30.56	123	$2,345.34	$19.07	55	$1,771.13	$32.20
Political Science	409	$18,682.15	$45.68	877	$25,639.57	$29.24	617	$31,699.41	$51.38
Psychology	200	$9,793.55	$48.97	469	$13,149.95	$28.04	250	$12,636.93	$50.55
Reference	13	$656.88	$50.53	34	$1,059.03	$31.15	7	$290.93	$41.56
Religion	831	$31,633.53	$38.07	1,174	$32,058.59	$27.31	1,315	$53,091.70	$40.37
Science	238	$9,791.80	$41.14	624	$19,110.56	$30.63	237	$12,255.32	$51.71
Self-Help	521	$19,885.73	$38.17	829	$23,691.60	$28.58	469	$20,686.73	$44.11
Social Science	295	$12,013.94	$40.73	789	$21,302.54	$27.00	454	$22,772.70	$50.16
Sports and Recreation	153	$6,009.39	$39.28	354	$9,176.23	$25.92	109	$5,347.32	$49.06
Study Aids	3	$115.97	$38.66	6	$148.38	$24.73			
Technology and Engineering	19	$774.74	$40.78	112	$3,084.51	$27.54	26	$1,486.39	$57.17
Transportation	3	$139.97	$46.66	43	$808.85	$18.81	6	$291.94	$48.66
Travel	35	$1,434.59	$40.99	144	$4,009.47	$27.84	44	$2,203.21	$50.07
True Crime	159	$7,432.65	$46.75	454	$12,926.57	$28.47	234	$11,323.48	$48.39
Young Adult	1,233	$54,228.48	$43.98	1,297	$48,796.95	$37.62	1,274	$65,427.92	$51.36
Totals	24,506	$986,011.48	$40.24	39,794	$1,228,248.16	$30.87	26,755	$1,294,904.71	$48.40

Table 7 / E-Book Output and Average Per-Volume Prices, 2020–2022

BISAC Category	2020 Vols.	2020 $ Total	2020 Avg.	2021 Vols.	2021 $ Total	2021 Avg.	2022 Vols.	2022 $ Total	2022 Avg.
Antiques and Collectibles	168	$3,845.14	$22.89	189	$2,937.42	$15.54	149	$2,767.78	$18.58
Architecture	513	$25,342.43	$49.40	506	$24,073.84	$47.58	296	$14,390.87	$48.62
Art	1,380	$58,003.42	$42.03	1,275	$45,929.64	$36.02	970	$34,928.42	$36.01
Bibles	415	$7,184.77	$17.31	408	$6,111.56	$14.98	549	$6,900.02	$12.57
Biography and Autobiography	8,891	$244,097.73	$27.45	11,684	$324,940.44	$27.81	9,329	$287,952.64	$30.87
Body, Mind and Spirit	4,729	$72,279.47	$15.28	5,691	$90,649.81	$15.93	4,799	$91,504.38	$19.07
Business and Economics	22,716	$1,293,773.97	$56.95	14,844	$574,952.59	$38.73	8,753	$367,873.62	$42.03
Children	29,175	$597,793.63	$20.49	33,452	$661,959.65	$19.79	27,204	$564,072.43	$20.73
Comics and Graphic Novels	2,636	$23,820.57	$9.04	1,997	$25,565.32	$12.80	1,458	$33,999.15	$23.32
Computers	2,558	$142,289.97	$55.63	2,251	$118,528.12	$52.66	1,530	$97,166.82	$63.51
Cooking	4,416	$63,068.56	$14.28	4,101	$74,424.79	$18.15	2,238	$54,765.43	$24.47
Crafts and Hobbies	930	$15,205.92	$16.35	1,201	$19,664.66	$16.37	700	$13,984.25	$19.98
Design	196	$6,027.81	$30.75	215	$5,451.04	$25.35	143	$4,247.61	$29.70
Drama	952	$20,356.70	$21.38	733	$12,051.64	$16.44	825	$10,865.97	$13.17
Education	4,406	$210,159.34	$47.70	4,435	$176,884.32	$39.88	2,885	$126,346.83	$43.79
Family and Relationships	3,563	$59,139.17	$16.60	4,121	$68,522.05	$16.63	3,082	$64,652.59	$20.98
Fiction	107,411	$2,116,446.55	$19.70	108,884	$1,800,933.82	$16.54	82,310	$1,758,951.60	$21.37
Foreign Language Study	5,340	$101,102.20	$18.93	1,617	$46,055.63	$28.48	620	$13,605.86	$21.94
Games and Activities	539	$13,620.80	$25.27	699	$12,384.34	$17.72	342	$6,831.79	$19.98
Gardening	465	$8,844.39	$19.02	710	$12,924.95	$18.20	376	$10,169.53	$27.05
Health and Fitness	4,872	$83,217.68	$17.08	5,409	$100,078.98	$18.50	3,398	$81,929.77	$24.11
History	14,597	$660,641.61	$45.26	9,939	$508,779.91	$51.19	7,495	$356,189.60	$47.52
House and Home	332	$6,254.61	$18.84	390	$7,641.74	$19.59	297	$7,480.38	$25.19
Humor	931	$15,408.06	$16.55	1,005	$18,304.45	$18.21	1,012	$22,337.25	$22.07
Language Arts and Disciplines	2,613	$287,390.73	$109.98	1,959	$142,815.80	$72.90	1,201	$90,200.79	$75.10

Law	3,013	$425,044.58	$141.07	2,443	$330,866.30	$135.43	818	$74,907.57	$91.57
Literary Collections	1,915	$37,051.91	$19.35	1,747	$34,137.05	$19.54	1,563	$34,584.67	$22.13
Literary Criticism	3,548	$594,076.57	$167.44	2,814	$340,033.01	$120.84	1,717	$243,822.86	$142.01
Mathematics	766	$74,868.32	$97.74	440	$41,838.59	$95.09	286	$21,726.04	$75.97
Medical	2,750	$252,649.32	$91.87	2,428	$189,044.41	$77.86	1,447	$124,606.35	$86.11
Music	2,800	$75,292.84	$26.89	2,852	$70,843.61	$24.84	1,368	$37,957.33	$27.75
Nature	910	$27,342.15	$30.05	1,318	$37,269.12	$28.28	953	$32,088.70	$33.67
Performing Arts	2,057	$58,262.49	$28.32	1,989	$68,306.54	$34.34	1,012	$46,404.28	$45.85
Pets	467	$7,654.75	$16.39	590	$10,494.78	$17.79	485	$7,610.52	$15.69
Philosophy	4,055	$203,975.91	$50.30	2,540	$166,078.18	$65.39	1,839	$96,317.78	$52.38
Photography	444	$9,556.89	$21.52	383	$8,010.72	$20.92	189	$5,480.36	$29.00
Poetry	5,720	$53,695.17	$9.39	7,439	$67,115.66	$9.02	3,955	$46,925.43	$11.86
Political Science	4,313	$214,803.40	$49.80	4,180	$191,464.39	$45.80	3,015	$160,207.20	$53.14
Psychology	3,034	$109,995.93	$36.25	2,834	$95,088.47	$33.55	2,079	$69,890.04	$33.62
Reference	1,007	$64,510.97	$64.06	1,111	$82,343.46	$74.12	624	$58,760.69	$94.17
Religion	15,244	$471,401.84	$30.92	15,641	$360,768.83	$23.07	11,741	$289,114.19	$24.62
Science	3,446	$379,568.86	$110.15	3,023	$262,748.00	$86.92	1,850	$164,316.13	$88.82
Self-Help	10,046	$142,366.60	$14.17	13,019	$186,472.39	$14.32	6,937	$148,848.68	$21.46
Social Science	4,604	$337,254.11	$73.25	4,976	$295,357.72	$59.36	3,623	$209,122.75	$57.72
Sports and Recreation	1,612	$37,794.33	$23.45	1,769	$41,011.59	$23.18	1,305	$37,336.23	$28.61
Study Aids	1,598	$23,020.50	$14.41	1,396	$21,556.55	$15.44	948	$20,866.34	$22.01
Technology and Engineering	1,741	$169,156.86	$97.16	1,531	$158,071.89	$103.25	1,009	$108,977.55	$108.01
Transportation	627	$18,484.66	$29.48	376	$9,477.81	$25.21	345	$11,082.68	$32.12
Travel	2,319	$39,588.26	$17.07	1,760	$37,501.86	$21.31	1,385	$37,280.49	$26.92
True Crime	852	$20,036.40	$23.52	1,429	$23,694.38	$16.58	688	$23,771.02	$34.55
Young Adult	7,531	$159,181.65	$21.14	8,420	$177,961.82	$21.14	7,097	$202,391.26	$28.52
Totals	311,163	$10,141,950.50	$32.59	306,163	$8,190,123.64	$26.75	220,239	$6,438,512.52	$29.23

(continued from page 317)

As with most years, Children's books was the dominant category represented in Table 1, making up 13.68 percent of 2022's preliminary output and having 4.55 percent more output in 2022 than the next highest category, Fiction. Although this category ranks highly in most of the individual publication formats, it is the highest ranked among hardcovers, overtaking Fiction by 33.8 percent more titles in 2022. The average price of Children's titles is consistent across all formats, varying by plus or minus $1, with the only outlier being audiobooks, with an increase of more than $5 between 2021 and 2022. The Young Adult category appears stable in both output and pricing for most publication formats, although it is worth noting that there are very few mass market titles published for the Young Adult market. The Young Adult market exploded around 2008, when *Twilight* was released; more recently, the total output of Young Adult titles has been decreasing slightly each year, as from 2020 to 2021 when it decreased 10.9 percent. This trend may change, as we are only seeing a .38 percent drop so far between 2021 and preliminary 2022.

Fiction, consistently a major category across all publication formats, dropped in output for 2020 and did make a comeback in 2021. However, the 2022 output looks to have dropped for all formats, bringing the output number for 2022 more in line with that of 2020. For example, in overall output, Fiction increased by 13.2 percent from 2020 to 2021, but then decreased by 9.3 percent from 2021 to 2022. The mass market format in general has had declining output over the past few years overall, although the average price for mass market Fiction has only increased by 3.5 percent between 2020 and 2022. Fiction prices remained stable in most formats, although an increase was seen in all. However, audiobooks and e-books, which saw dramatic drops in average prices from 2020 to 2021, had dramatic increases in average prices for Fiction from 2021 to 2022. The two topics most often in the spotlight for the three-year period looked at—Health & Fitness and Political Science—did not show the rise in output one might expect, but rather a drop for the period from 2021 to 2022 of 11.6 percent and 10.10 percent, respectively.

There were not really any trends noticed across formats in terms of output. Comics & Graphic Novels does have traction in some formats, such as hardcover and trade paperback; the output for Comics & Graphic Novels may continue to move upward, as the North American market for manga is currently booming.

Number of Book Outlets in the United States and Canada

The *American Book Trade Directory* (Information Today, Inc.) has been published since 1915. Revised annually, it features lists of booksellers, wholesalers, periodicals, reference tools, and other information about the U.S. and Canadian book markets. The data shown in Table 1, the most current available, are from the 2023–2024 edition of the directory.

The 10,026 stores of various types shown are located throughout the United States, Canada, and regions administered by the United States. "General" bookstores stock trade books and children's books in a general variety of subjects. "College" stores (both general and specified) carry college-level textbooks. "Educational" outlets handle school textbooks up to and including the high school level. "Mail order" outlets (both general and specified) sell general trade books by mail and are not book clubs; all others operating by mail are classified according to the kinds of books carried.

"Antiquarian" dealers sell old and rare books. Stores handling secondhand books are classified as "used." "Paperback" stores have more than 80 percent of their stock in paperbound books. Stores with paperback departments are listed under the appropriate major classification ("general," "department store," "stationer," and so forth). Bookstores with at least 50 percent of their stock on a particular subject are classified by subject.

Table 1 / Bookstores in the United States and Canada, 2022

Category	United States	Canada
Antiquarian General	341	34
Antiquarian Mail Order	105	5
Antiquarian Specialized	66	1
Art Supply Store	11	1
College General	15,490	104
College Specialized	75	5
Comics	179	24
Computer Software	2	0
Cooking	170	7
Department Store	182	18
Educational	103	5
Federal Sites	296	1
Foreign Language	9	2
General	1,939	393
Gift Shop	74	6
Juvenile	40	11
Mail Order General	32	3
Mail Order Specialized	127	6

Table 1 / Bookstores in the United States and Canada, 2022
(cont.)

Category	United States	Canada
Metaphysics, New Age and Occult	89	12
Museum Store and Art Gallery	365	26
Nature and Natural History	27	5
Newsdealer	7	1
Office Supply	5	1
Other	2,054	276
Paperback	13	1
Religious	721	61
Self Help/Development	11	2
Stationer	3	2
Toy Store	44	71
Used	319	43
Totals	8,899	1,127

Part 5
Reference Information

Ready Reference

How to Obtain an ISBN

Beat Barblan

United States ISBN/SAN Agency

The International Standard Book Numbering (ISBN) system was introduced into the United Kingdom by J. Whitaker & Sons Ltd. in 1967 and into the United States in 1968 by R. R. Bowker. The Technical Committee on Documentation of the International Organization for Standardization (ISO TC 46) is responsible for the international standard.

The purpose of this standard is to "establish the specifications for the International Standard Book Number (ISBN) as a unique international identification system for each product form or edition of a monographic publication published or produced by a specific publisher." The standard specifies the construction of an ISBN, the rules for assignment and use of an ISBN, and all metadata associated with the allocation of an ISBN.

Types of monographic publications to which an ISBN may be assigned include printed books and pamphlets (in various product formats); electronic publications (either on the Internet or on physical carriers such as CD-ROMs or diskettes); educational/instructional films, videos, and transparencies; educational/instructional software; audiobooks on cassette or CD or DVD; braille publications; and microform publications.

Serial publications, printed music, and musical sound recordings are excluded from the ISBN standard as they are covered by other identification systems.

The ISBN is used by publishers, distributors, wholesalers, bookstores, and libraries, among others, in more than 200 countries and territories as an ordering and inventory system. It expedites the collection of data on new and forthcoming editions of monographic publications for print and electronic directories used by the book trade. Its use also facilitates rights management and the monitoring of sales data for the publishing industry.

As of January 1, 2007, a revision to the ISBN standard substantially increased the numbering capacity of the system. The 10-digit ISBN identifier (ISBN-10) was replaced by the ISBN 13-digit identifier (ISBN-13). All facets of book publishing are now expected to use the ISBN-13, and the ISBN agencies throughout the world are now issuing only ISBN-13s to publishers. Publishers with existing ISBN-10s need to convert their ISBNs to ISBN-13s by the addition of the EAN prefix 978 and recalculation of the new check digit:

ISBN-10: 0-8352-8235-X
ISBN-13: 978-0-8352-8235-2

As the inventory of 978 prefixes has started to exhaust, ISBN agencies have begun assigning ISBN-13s with the "979" prefix. There is no 10-digit equivalent for 979 ISBNs.

Construction of an ISBN

An ISBN currently consists of 13 digits separated into the following parts:

1   A prefix of "978" for an ISBN-10 converted to an ISBN-13 and a prefix of "979" for ISBN-13s without a 10-digit equivalent
2   Group or country identifier, which identifies a national or geographic grouping of publishers
3   Publisher identifier, which identifies a particular publisher within a group
4   Title identifier, which identifies a particular title or edition of a title
5   Check digit, the single digit at the end of the ISBN that validates the ISBN-13

For more information regarding ISBN-13 conversion services provided by the U.S. ISBN Agency at R. R. Bowker, LLC, visit the ISBN Agency website at http://www.isbn.org, or contact the U.S. ISBN Agency at isbn-san@bowker.com.

Publishers requiring their ISBNs to be converted from the ISBN-10 to ISBN-13 format can use the U.S. ISBN Agency's free ISBN-13 online converter at http://isbn.org/converterpub.asp. Publishers can also view their ISBNs online by accessing their personal account at http://www.myidentifiers.com.

Displaying the ISBN on a Product or Publication

When an ISBN is written or printed, it should be preceded by the letters ISBN, and each part should be separated by a space or hyphen. In the United States, the hyphen is used for separation, as in the following example: ISBN 978-0-8352-8235-2. In this example, 978 is the prefix that precedes the ISBN-13, 0 is the group identifier, 8352 is the publisher identifier, 8235 is the title identifier, and 2 is the check digit. The group of English-speaking countries, which includes the United States, Australia, Canada, New Zealand, and the United Kingdom, uses the group identifiers 0 and 1. The 979 assignments by the United States ISBN Agency will start with 979-8. The 8 will be unique to the United States. Of course, as with the 978-0 and 978-1, an ISBN starting with 979-8 will allow U.S. publishers and self-publishers to market their books anywhere in the world.

The ISBN Organization

The administration of the ISBN system is carried out at three levels—through the International ISBN Agency in the United Kingdom, through the national agencies, and through the publishing houses themselves. The International ISBN Agency, which is responsible for assigning country prefixes and for coordinating the worldwide implementation of the system, has an advisory panel that represents the

International Organization for Standardization (ISO), publishers, and libraries. The International ISBN Agency publishes the *Publishers International ISBN Directory*, which is a listing of all national agencies' publishers with their assigned ISBN publisher prefixes. R. R. Bowker, as the publisher of *Books in Print*, with its extensive and varied database of publishers' addresses, was the obvious place to initiate the ISBN system and to provide the service to the U.S. publishing industry. To date, the U.S. ISBN Agency has entered more than 450,000 publishers into the system.

ISBN Assignment Procedure

Assignment of ISBNs is a shared endeavor between the U.S. ISBN Agency and the publisher. Publishers can apply online through the ISBN Agency's website www.myidentifiers.com. Once the order is processed, an e-mail confirmation will be sent with instructions for managing the account. The publisher then has the responsibility of assigning an ISBN to each title, keeping an accurate record of each number assigned, and registering each title in the *Books in Print* database at www.myidentifiers.com. It is the responsibility of the ISBN Agency to validate assigned ISBNs and keep a record of all ISBN publisher prefixes in circulation.

ISBN implementation is very much market-driven. Major distributors, wholesalers, retailers, and so forth recognize the necessity of the ISBN system and request that publishers register with the ISBN Agency. Also, the ISBN is a mandatory bibliographic element in the International Standard Bibliographical Description (ISBD). The Library of Congress Cataloging in Publication (CIP) Division directs publishers to the agency to obtain their ISBN prefixes.

Location and Display of the ISBN

On books, pamphlets, and other printed material, the ISBN shall be printed on the verso of the title leaf or, if this is not possible, at the foot of the title leaf itself. It should also appear on the outside back cover or on the back of the jacket if the book has one (the lower right-hand corner is recommended). The ISBN shall also appear on any accompanying promotional materials following the provisions for location according to the format of the material.

On other monographic publications, the ISBN shall appear on the title or credit frames and any labels permanently affixed to the publication. If the publication is issued in a container that is an integral part of the publication, the ISBN shall be displayed on the label. If it is not possible to place the ISBN on the item or its label, then the number should be displayed on the bottom or the back of the container, box, sleeve, or frame. It should also appear on any accompanying material, including each component of a multitype publication.

Printing of ISBN in Machine-Readable Coding

All books should carry ISBNs in the EAN-13 bar code machine-readable format. All ISBN EAN-13 bar codes start with the EAN prefixes 978 and 979 for books. As of January 1, 2007, all EAN bar codes should have the ISBN-13 appearing immediately above the bar code in eye-readable format, preceded by the acronym

"ISBN." The recommended location of the EAN-13 bar code for books is in the lower right-hand corner of the back cover (see Figure 1).

Figure 1 / Printing the ISBN in Bookland/EAN Symbology

Five-Digit Add-On Code

In the United States, a five-digit add-on code is used for additional information. In the publishing industry, this code is used for price information. The lead digit of the five-digit add-on has been designated a currency identifier, when the add-on is used for price. Number 5 is the code for the U.S. dollar, while 6 denotes the Canadian dollar. Publishers that do not want to indicate price in the add-on should print the code 90000 (see Figure 2).

Figure 2 / Printing the ISBN Bookland/EAN Number in Bar Code with the Five-Digit Add-On Code

978 = ISBN Bookland/EAN prefix   90000 means no information
5 = Code for U.S. $ in the add-on code
2499 = $24.99

Reporting the Title and the ISBN

After the publisher reports a title to the ISBN Agency, the number is validated and the title is listed in the many R. R. Bowker hard-copy and electronic publications, including *Books in Print*; *Forthcoming Books*; *Paperbound Books in Print*; *Books in Print Supplement*; *Books Out of Print*; *Books in Print Online*; *Books in Print Plus-CD ROM*; *Children's Books in Print*; *Subject Guide to Children's Books in*

Print; *Books Out Loud: Bowker's Guide to AudioBooks*; *Bowker's Complete Video Directory*; *Software Encyclopedia*; *Software for Schools*; and other specialized publications.

For an ISBN application and information, visit the ISBN Agency website at www.myidentifiers.com, call 856-399-7495, fax 908-623-8508, or write to the United States ISBN Agency, 26 Main Street, Suite 102, Chatham, NJ 07928.

The ISSN, and How to Obtain One

U.S. ISSN Center
Library of Congress

In the early 1970s the rapid increase in the production and dissemination of information and an intensified desire to exchange information about serials in computerized form among different systems and organizations made it increasingly clear that a means to identify serial publications at an international level was needed. The International Standard Serial Number (ISSN) was developed and became the internationally accepted code for identifying serial publications.

The ISSN is an international standard. ISO 3297:2022, the seventh edition of the standard, published in 2022, is a minor revision of the sixth edition, which expanded on the role of the ISSN for digital resources, provided detailed information on implementing the standard in various technical environments, and explained the concept of "cluster ISSNs."

The scope of the ISSN is "continuing resources," a concept that was introduced with the 2007 edition. Continuing resources include not only serials such as journals, magazines, open-ended series, and blogs but also open-ended publications such as updating databases, updating loose-leaf services, and certain types of updating websites.

The number itself has no significance other than as a brief, unique, and unambiguous identifier. The ISSN consists of eight digits in the Arabic numerals 0 to 9, except for the last ("check") digit, which is calculated using Modulus 11 and uses an "X" in place of the numeral 10 to maintain the ISSN at 8 digits. The numbers appear as two groups of four digits separated by a hyphen and preceded by the letters ISSN—for example, ISSN 1234-5679.

The ISSN is not self-assigned by publishers. Administration of the ISSN is coordinated through the ISSN Network, an intergovernmental organization within the UNESCO/UNISIST program. The ISSN Network consists of more than 90 national ISSN centers, coordinated by the ISSN International Centre, located in Paris. National ISSN Centers are responsible for registering serials published in their respective countries. Responsibility for the assignment of ISSNs to titles from multinational publishers is allocated among the ISSN Centers in which the publisher has offices. A list of these publishers and the corresponding ISSN centers is located on the ISSN International Centre's website, http://www.issn.org.

The ISSN International Centre handles ISSN assignments for international organizations and for countries that do not have a national center. It also maintains and distributes the ISSN Register and makes it available in a variety of products, most commonly via the ISSN Portal, an online subscription database containing full metadata records for each ISSN as well as other features and functionality. In January 2018 a new ISSN Portal was released that includes free look-up and access to a subset of ISSN metadata. The ISSN Register is also available via Z39.50 access and as a data file. Selected ISSN data can also be obtained in customized files or database extracts that can be used, for example, to check the accuracy or completeness of a requestor's list of titles and ISSN. Another available ISSN service is OAI-PMH, a customizable "harvesting" protocol through which external applications can automatically and regularly gather new and updated metadata on a defined schedule. The ISSN Register contains bibliographic records corresponding to each ISSN assignment as reported by national ISSN centers. The database contains records for more than 2.5 million ISSNs.

The ISSN is used all over the world by serials publishers to identify their serials and to distinguish their titles from others that are the same or similar. It is used by subscription services and libraries to manage files for orders, claims, and back issues. It is used in automated check-in systems by libraries that wish to process receipts more quickly. Copyright centers use the ISSN as a means to collect and disseminate royalties. It is also used as an identification code by postal services and legal deposit services. The ISSN is included as a verification element in interlibrary lending activities and for union catalogs as a collocating device. The ISSN is also incorporated into bar codes for optical recognition of serial publication identification and metadata and into the standards for the identification of issues and articles in serial publications. A key use of the ISSN is as an identifier in online systems, where it can serve to connect catalog records or citations in abstracting and indexing databases with full-text journal content via OpenURL resolvers or reference linking services, and as an identifier and link in archives of electronic and print serials.

Because serials are generally known and cited by title, assignment of the ISSN is inseparably linked to the key title, a standardized form of the title derived from information in the serial issue. Only one ISSN can be assigned to a title in a particular medium. For titles issued in multiple media—e.g., print, online, CD-ROM—a separate ISSN is assigned to each medium version. If a major title change occurs or the medium changes, a new ISSN must be assigned. Centers responsible for assigning ISSNs also construct the key title and create an associated bibliographic record.

A significant new feature of the 2007 ISSN standard was the Linking ISSN (ISSN-L), a mechanism that enables collocation or linking among different media versions of a continuing resource. The Linking ISSN allows a unique designation (one of the existing ISSNs) to be applied to all media versions of a continuing resource while retaining the separate ISSN that pertains to each version. When an ISSN is functioning as a Linking ISSN, the eight digits of the base ISSN are prefixed with the designation "ISSN-L." The Linking ISSN facilitates search, retrieval, and delivery across all medium versions of a serial or other continuing resource for improved ISSN functionality in OpenURL linking, search engines, library catalogs, and knowledge bases.

The ISSN standard also supports interoperability by specifying the use of ISSN and ISSN-L with other systems such as DOI, OpenURL, URN, and EAN bar codes. ISSN-L was implemented in the ISSN Register in 2008. To help ISSN users implement the ISSN-L in their databases, two free tables are available from the ISSN International Centre: one lists each ISSN and its corresponding ISSN-L; the other lists each ISSN-L and its corresponding ISSNs. The Linking ISSN is the first example of a cluster ISSN; in 2020 the sixth edition of the standard introduced the potential for additional cluster ISSNs.

In the United States, the U.S. ISSN Center at the Library of Congress is responsible for assigning and maintaining the ISSNs for all U.S. serial and other continuing resource publications. Publishers wishing to have an ISSN assigned should follow the instructions on the U.S. ISSN Center's website to apply using an online system, ISSN Uplink. Although some of the more than 90 ISSN centers worldwide charge for ISSNs, ISSN assignment by the U.S. ISSN Center is free.

To obtain an ISSN for a U.S. publication by using the new application system, ISSN Uplink, or for more information about ISSNs in the United States, libraries, publishers, and other ISSN users should visit the U.S. ISSN Center's website, http://www.loc.gov/issn, or contact the U.S. ISSN Center, U.S. Programs, Law, and Literature Division, Library of Congress, 101 Independence Ave. S.E., Washington, DC 20540-4284; e-mail issn@loc.gov.

For information about ISSN products and services, and for application procedures that non-U.S. parties should use to apply for an ISSN, visit the ISSN International Centre's website, http://www.issn.org, or contact the International Centre at 45 rue de Turbigo, 75003 Paris, France (telephone 33-1-44-88-22-20, e-mail issnic@issn.org).

How to Obtain an SAN

Beat Barblan

United States ISBN/SAN Agency

SAN stands for Standard Address Number. The SAN system, an American National Standards Institute (ANSI) standard, assigns a unique identification number that is used to positively identify specific addresses of organizations in order to facilitate buying and selling transactions within the industry. It is recognized as the identification code for electronic communication within the industry.

For purposes of this standard, the book industry includes book publishers, book wholesalers, book distributors, book retailers, college bookstores, libraries, library binders, and serial vendors. Schools, school systems, technical institutes, and colleges and universities are not members of this industry, but are served by it and therefore included in the SAN system.

The purpose of the SAN is to ease communications among these organizations, of which there are several hundreds of thousands that engage in a large volume of separate transactions with one another. These transactions include purchases of books by book dealers, wholesalers, schools, colleges, and libraries from publishers and wholesalers; payments for all such purchases; and other communications between participants. The objective of this standard is to establish an identification code system by assigning each address within the industry a unique code to be used for positive identification for all book and serial buying and selling transactions.

Many organizations have similar names and multiple addresses, making identification of the correct contact point difficult and subject to error. In many cases, the physical movement of materials takes place between addresses that differ from the addresses to be used for the financial transactions. In such instances, there is ample opportunity for confusion and errors. Without identification by SAN, a complex record-keeping system would have to be instituted to avoid introducing errors. In addition, problems with the current numbering system—such as errors in billing, shipping, payments, and returns—are significantly reduced by using the SAN system. The SAN also eliminates one step in the order fulfillment process: the "look-up procedure" used to assign account numbers. Previously a store or library dealing with 50 different publishers was assigned a different account number by each of the suppliers. The SAN solved this problem. If a publisher prints its SAN on its stationery and ordering documents, vendors to whom it sends transactions do not have to look up the account number, but can proceed immediately to process orders by SAN.

Libraries are involved in many of the same transactions as book dealers, such as ordering and paying for books and charging and paying for various services to other libraries. Keeping records of transactions—whether these involve buying, selling, lending, or donations—entails operations suited to SAN use. SAN stationery speeds up order fulfillment and eliminate errors in shipping, billing, and crediting; this, in turn, means savings in both time and money.

History

Development of the Standard Address Number began in 1968, when Russell Reynolds, general manager of the National Association of College Stores (NACS), approached R. R. Bowker and suggested that a "Standard Account Number" system be implemented in the book industry. The first draft of a standard was prepared by an American National Standards Institute (ANSI) Committee Z39 subcommittee, which was co-chaired by Reynolds and Emery Koltay of Bowker. After Z39 members proposed changes, the current version of the standard was approved by NACS on December 17, 1979.

Format

The SAN consists of six digits plus a seventh *Modulus 11* check digit; a hyphen follows the third digit (XXX-XXXX) to facilitate transcription. The hyphen is to be used in print form, but need not be entered or retained in computer systems. Printed on documents, the Standard Address Number should be preceded by the identifier "SAN" to avoid confusion with other numerical codes (SAN XXXXXXX).

Check Digit Calculation

The check digit is based on *Modulus 11*, and can be derived as follows:

1. Write the digits of the basic number.   2 3 4 5 6 7
2. Write the constant weighting factors associated with
   each position by the basic number.   7 6 5 4 3 2
3. Multiply each digit by its associated weighting factor.   14 18 20 20 18 14
4. Add the products of the multiplications. $14 + 18 + 20 + 20 + 18 + 14 = 104$
5. Divide the sum by Modulus 11 to find the remainder. $104 \div 11 = 9$ plus a remainder of 5
6. Subtract the remainder from the Modulus 11 to generate the required check digit. If there is no remainder, generate a check digit of zero. If the check digit is 10, generate a check digit of X to represent 10, since the use of 10 would require an extra digit. $11 - 5 = 6$
7. Append the check digit to create the standard seven-digit Standard Address Number.   SAN 234-5676

SAN Assignment

R. R. Bowker accepted responsibility for being the central administrative agency for SAN, and in that capacity assigns SANs to identify uniquely the addresses of organizations. No SANs can be reassigned; in the event that an organization should cease to exist, for example, its SAN would cease to be in circulation entirely. If an organization using an SAN should move or change its name with no change in ownership, its SAN would remain the same, and only the name or address would be updated to reflect the change.

The SAN should be used in all transactions; it is recommended that the SAN be imprinted on stationery, letterheads, order and invoice forms, checks, and all other documents used in executing various book transactions. The SAN should always be printed on a separate line above the name and address of the organization, preferably in the upper left-hand corner of the stationery to avoid confusion with other numerical codes pertaining to the organization, such as telephone number, zip code, and the like.

SAN Functions

The SAN is strictly a Standard Address Number, becoming functional only in applications determined by the user; these may include activities such as purchasing, billing, shipping, receiving, paying, crediting, and refunding. It is the method used by Pubnet and PubEasy systems and is required in all electronic data interchange communications using the Book Industry Systems Advisory Committee (BISAC) EDI formats. Every department that has an independent function within an organization could have an SAN for its own identification.

For additional information or to make suggestions, write to ISBN/SAN Agency, R. R. Bowker, LLC, 26 Main Street, Suite 102, Chatham, NJ 07928, call 856-399-7495, or fax 908-623-8508. The e-mail address is san@bowker.com. An SAN can be ordered online through the website www.myidentifiers.com, or an application can be requested by e-mail through san@bowker.com.

Distinguished Books

The Year's Notable Books

The Notable Books Council of the Reference and User Services Association (RUSA), a division of the American Library Association, released its annual list of notable books on January 29, 2023. These titles were selected for their significant contributions to the expansion of knowledge or for the pleasure they can provide to adult readers.

Fiction

Elsewhere by Alexis Schaitkin (Celadon books, a division of Macmillan Publishers)

The Haunting of Hajji Hotak: And Other Stories by Jamil Jan Kochai (Viking, an imprint of Penguin Random House, LLC)

Horse by Geraldine Brooks (Viking, an imprint of Penguin Random House, LLC)

Seeking Fortune Elsewhere by Sindya Bhanoo (Catapult)

Stories from the Tenants Downstairs by Sidik Fofana (Scribner, an imprint of Simon & Schuster, Inc.)

The Furrows by Namwali Serpell (Hogarth, an imprint of Random House Publishing Group, a division of Penguin Random House, LLC)

The Rabbit Hutch by Tess Gunty (Alfred A. Knopf, a division of Penguin Random House, LLC)

The Swimmers by Julie Otsuka (Alfred A. Knopf, a division of Penguin Random House, LLC)

Trust by Hernan Diaz (Riverhead Books, an imprint of Penguin Random House, LLC)

Vagabonds! by Eloghosa Osunde (Riverhead Books, an imprint of Penguin Random House, LLC)

What We Fed to the Manticore by Talia Lakshmi Kolluri (Tin House)

Nonfiction

Also a Poet: Frank O'Hara, My Father, and Me by Ada Calhoun (Grove Press, an imprint of Grove Atlantic)

An Immense World: How Animal Senses Reveal the Hidden Realms Around Us by Ed Yong (Random House, an imprint and division of Penguin Random House, LLC)

Bitch: On The Female of the Species by Lucy Cooke (Basic books, an imprint of Perseus Books, LLC, a subsidiary of Hachette Book Group)

Easy Beauty by Chloe Cooper Jones (Avid Reader Press, an imprint of Simon & Schuster, Inc.)

The Escape Artist: The Man Who Broke Out of Auschwitz to Warn the World by Jonathan Freedland (Harper, an imprint of HarperCollins Publishers)

His Name Is George Floyd: One Man's Life and the Struggle for Racial Justice by Robert Samuels and Toluse Olorunnipa (Viking, an imprint of Penguin Random House, LLC)

The Song of the Cell: An Exploration of Medicine and the New Human by Siddhartha Mukherjee (Scribner, an imprint of Simon & Schuster, Inc.)

This Body I Wore: A Memoir by Diana Goetsch (Farrar, Straus and Giroux)

Under the Skin: The Hidden Toll of Racism on American Lives and the Health of Our Nation by Linda Villarosa (Doubleday, a division of Penguin Random House, LLC)

The Vortex: A True Story of History's Deadliest Storm, An Unspeakable War and Liberation by Scott Carney and Jason Miklian (Ecco, an imprint of HarperCollins Publishers)

We Are the Middle of Forever: Indigenous Voices from Turtle Island on the Changing Earth edited by Dahr Jamail and Stan Rushworth (The New Press)

Poetry

Alive at the End of the World by Saeed Jones (Coffee House Press)

Bless the Daughter Raised by a Voice in Her Head by Warsan Shire (Random House, an imprint and division of Penguin Random House, LLC)

The Rupture Tense by Jenny Xie (Graywolf Press)

Your Emergency Contact Has Experienced an Emergency by Chen Chen (BOA Editions Ltd.)

The Reading List

Established in 2007 by the CODES section of the Reference and User Services Association (RUSA), this list highlights outstanding genre fiction that merits special attention by general adult readers and the librarians who work with them.

The winners were selected by the Reading List Council, whose members include 12 librarians who are experts in readers' advisory and collection development. The eight genres currently included in the council's considerations are adrenaline titles (suspense, thrillers, and action adventure), fantasy, historical fiction, horror, mystery, romance, science fiction, and relationship fiction. The RUSA website provides additional details on each of the winning titles along with shortlists of "Readalikes" and runners-up.

Adrenaline

Killers of a Certain Age by Deanna Raybourn (Berkley, an imprint of Penguin Random House, LLC)

Fantasy

Nettle & Bone by T. Kingfisher (A Tor Book, published by Tom Doherty Associates)

Historical Fiction

By Her Own Design: A Novel of Ann Lowe, Fashion Designer to the Social Register by Piper Huguley (William Morrow, an imprint of HarperCollins Publishers)

Horror

Leech by Hiron Ennes (A Tordotcom Book, published by Tom Doherty Associates)

Mystery

The Binding Room: A Novel by Nadine Matheson (Hanover Square Press)

Relationship Fiction

Mika in Real Life: A Novel by Emiko Jean (William Morrow, an imprint of HarperCollins Publishers)

Romance

The Undertaking of Hart and Mercy by Megan Bannen (Orbit, a division of Hachette Book Group)

Science Fiction

Drunk On All Your Strange New Words by Eddie Robson (A Tordotcom Book, published by Tom Doherty Associates)

The Listen List

Established in 2010 by the CODES section of the Reference and User Services Association (RUSA), The Listen List: Outstanding Audiobook Narration seeks to highlight outstanding audiobook titles that merit special attention by general adult listeners and the librarians who work with them. The Listen List Council selects a list of 12 titles, including fiction, nonfiction, poetry, and plays. To be eligible, titles must be available for purchase and circulation by libraries. The council consists of seven librarians who are experts in readers' advisory and collection development.

An annotated version of the list on the RUSA website includes more information on each choice and lists additional audiobooks of interest.

The Angel of Rome: And Other Stories by Jess Walter, narrated by Edoardo Ballerini and Julia Whelan (HarperAudio)

The Bangalore Detectives Club by Harini Nagendra, narrated by Soneela Nankani (Blackstone Publishing)

Book Lovers by Emily Henry, narrated by Julia Whelan (Books on Tape)

The Diamond Eye by Kate Quinn, narrated by Saskia Maarleveld (HarperAudio)

An Immense World: How Animal Senses Reveal the Hidden Realms Around Us by Ed Yong, narrated by Ed Yong (Books on Tape)

Iona Iverson's Rules for Commuting by Clare Pooley, narrated by Clare Corbett (Books on Tape)

A Lady's Guide to Fortune-Hunting by Sophie Irwin, narrated by Eleanor Tomlinson (Books on Tape)

The Patron Saint of Second Chances by Christine Simon, narrated by Tim Francis (Simon & Schuster Audio)

Playing with Myself by Randy Rainbow, narrated by Randy Rainbow (Macmillan Audio)

River of the Gods: Genius, Courage, and Betrayal in the Search for the Source of the Nile by Candice Millard, narrated by Paul Michael (Books on Tape)

Stories from the Tenants Downstairs by Sidik Fofana, narrated by Joniece Abbott-Pratt, Nile Bullock, Sidik Fofana, Dominic Hoffman, DePre Owens, André Santana, Bahni Turpin, and Jade Wheeler (Simon & Schuster Audio)

Take My Hand by Dolen Perkins-Valdez, narrated by Lauren J. Daggett (Books on Tape)

Unlikely Animals by Annie Hartnett, narrated by Mark Bramhall and Kirby Heyborne (Books on Tape)

Best Fiction for Young Adults

Each year a committee of the Young Adult Library Services Association (YALSA), a division of the American Library Association, compiles a list of the best fiction appropriate for young adults ages 12–18. Selected on the basis of each book's proven or potential appeal and value to young adults, the titles span a variety of subjects as well as a broad range of reading levels. An asterisk denotes the title was selected as a top ten.

A Magic Steeped in Poison by Judy I. Lin (Feiwel & Friends/Macmillian). 978-1250767080.

A Scatter of Light by Malinda Lo (Dutton Books for Young Readers/Penguin Random House). 978-0525555285.

A Thousand Steps into Night by Traci Chee (Clarion Books/HarperCollins). 978-0358469988.

African Town by Irene Latham and Charles Waters (G.P. Putnam's Sons Books for Young Readers/Penguin Random House). 978-0593322888.

Ain't Burned All the Bright by Jason Reynolds (Atheneum/Caitlyn Dlouhy Books/Simon & Schuster). 978-1534439467.

*All My Rage by Sabaa Tahir (Razorbill/Penguin Random House). 978-0593202340.

All of Us Villains by Amanda Foody and C.L. Herman (Tor Teen/Macmillan). 978-1250789259.

All That's Left in the World by Erik J. Brown (Balzer + Bray/HarperCollins). 978-0063054974.

Alone Out Here by Riley Redgate (Disney-Hyperion). 978-1368064729.

Bitter by Akwaeke Emezi (Knopf Books for Young Readers/Penguin Random House). 978-0593309032.

Dark Room Etiquette by Robin Roe (Harper Teen/HarperCollins). 978-0063051737.

Foul Lady Fortune by Chloe Gong (Margaret K. McElderry Books/Simon & Schuster). 978-1665905589.

Four for the Road by K.J. Reilly (Atheneum Books for Young Readers/Simon & Schuster). 978-1665902281.

Gallant by V.E. Schwab (Greenwillow Books/HarperCollins). 978-0062835772.

*Gideon Green in Black and White by Katie Henry (Katherine Tegen Books/HarperCollins). 978-0062955739.

Hollow Fires by Samira Ahmed (Little, Brown Young Readers). 978-0316282642.

Home Field Advantage by Dahlia Adler (Wednesday Books/Macmillan). 978-1250765840.

Hopepunk by Preston Norton (Little, Brown Young Readers). 978-1368057851.

Hotel Magnifique by Emily J. Taylor (Razorbill/Penguin Random House). 978-0593404515.

How to Survive Your Murder by Danielle Valentine (Razorbill/Penguin Random House). 978-0593352014.

How You Grow Wings by Rimma Onoseta (Workman Publishing). 978-1643751917.

I Kissed Shara Wheeler by Casey McQuiston. (Wednesday Book/Macmillan). 978-1250244468.

*I Must Betray You by Ruta Sepetys (Philomel Books/Penguin Random House). 978-1984836038.

I'm the Girl by Courtney Summers (Wednesday Books/Macmillan). 978-1250808363.

Icebreaker by A.L. Graziadei (Holt/Macmillan). 978-1250777119.

If You Could See the Sun by Ann Liang (Inkyard Press/Harlequin). 978-1335915849.

In the Serpent's Wake by Rachel Hartman (Random House Books for Young Readers/Penguin Random House). 978-1101931325.

Into the Sublime by Kate A. Boorman (Holt/Macmillan). 978-1250191700.

Iron Widow by Xiran Jay Zhao (Penguin Teen Canada/Penguin Random House). 978-0735269934.

Iveliz Explains It All by Andrea Beatriz Arango. Illustrated by Alyssa Bermudez. (Random House Books for Young Readers/Penguin Random House). 978-0593563977.

Jumper by Melanie Crowder (Viking Books for Young Readers/Penguin Random House). 978-059332696.

Kiss & Tell by Adib Khorram (Dial Books/Penguin Teen). 978-0593325261.

Lakelore by Anna-Marie McLemore (Feiwel & Friends/Macmillan). 978-1250624147.

Live, Laugh, Kidnap by Gabby Noone (Razorbill/Penguin Random House). 978-05933 27296.

Love Radio by Ebony LaDelle (Simon & Schuster Books for Young Readers/Simon & Schuster). 978-1665908153.

Loveless by Alice Oseman (Scholastic). 978-1338751932.

*Man Made Monsters by Andrea L. Rogers (Levine Querido). 978-1646141791.

No One Is Alone by Rachel Vincent (Bloomsbury YA/Bloomsbury). 978-1547609192.

Nothing Burns as Bright as You by Ashley Woodfolk (Versify/HarperCollins). 978-0358655350.

Nothing More to Tell by Karen McManus (Delacorte Press/Penguin Random House). 978-0593175903.

One for All by Lillie Lainoff (Farrar, Straus and Giroux/Macmillan). 978-0374314613.

One True Loves by Elise Bryant (Balzer + Bray/HarperCollins). 978-0062982865.

Our Crooked Hearts by Melissa Albert (Flatiron Books/Macmillan). 978-1250826367.

Queen of the Tiles by Hanna Alkaf (Salaam Reads/Simon & Schuster Books for Young Readers). 978-1534494558.

Rust in the Root by Justina Ireland (Balzer + Bray/HarperCollins). 978-0063038226.

Scout's Honor by Lily Anderson (Holt/Macmillan). 978-1250246738.

Sunny G's Series of Rash Decisions by Navdeep Singh Dhillon (Dial Books/Penguin Random House). 978-0593109977.

The Agathas by Kathleen Glasgow and Liz Lawson (Delacorte/Penguin Random House). 978-0593431115.

*The Door of No Return by Kwame Alexander (Little, Brown Young Readers). 978-0316441865.

The Drowned Woods by Emily Lloyd-Jones (Little, Brown Young Readers). 978-0759556317.

*The Getaway by Lamar Giles (Scholastic). 978-1338752014.

*The Girl Who Fell Beneath the Sea by Axie Oh (Feiwel & Friends/Macmillan). 978-1250780867.

The Honeys by Ryan LaSala (Scholastic). 978-1338745313.

The Last Laugh by Mindy McGinnis (Katherine Tegen Books/HarperCollins). 978-0062982452.

The Last Mapmaker by Christina Soontornvat (Candlewick/Penguin Random House). 978-1536204957.

The Lesbiana's Guide to Catholic School by Sonora Reyes (Balzer + Bray/HarperCollins). 978-0063060234.

*The Life and Crimes of Hoodie Rosen by Isaac Blum (Philomel Books/Penguin Random House). 978-0593525821.

The Most Dazzling Girl in Berlin by Kip Wilson (Versify/HarperCollins). 978-0358448907.

The Name She Gave Me by Betty Culley (Harper Teen/HarperCollins). 978-0063157835.

The Ogress and the Orphans by Kelly Barnhill (Workman Publishing). 978-1643750743.

The Red Palace by June Hur (Feiwel & Friends/Macmillan). 978-1250800558.

*The Summer of Bitter and Sweet by Jen Ferguson (Heartdrum/HarperCollins). 978-0063086166.

*The Sunbearer Trials by Aiden Thomas (Feiwel & Friends/Macmillan). 978-1250822130.

The Weight of Blood by Tiffany D. Jackson (Katherine Tegen Books/HarperCollins). 978-0063029149.

The Year I Stopped Trying by Katie Heaney (Knopf Books for Young Readers/Penguin Random House). 978-1118283.

Thirst by Varsha Bajaj (Nancy Paulsen Books/Penguin Random House). 978-0593354391.

This Vicious Grace by Emily Thiede (Wednesday Books/Macmillan). 978-1250794055.

Undercover Latina by Aya de León (Candlewick/Penguin Random House). 978-1536223743.

Valiant Ladies by Melissa Grey (Feiwel & Friends/Macmillan). 978-1250622204.

Very Bad People by Kit Frick (Margaret K. McElderry Books/Simon & Schuster). 978-1534449732.

Vinyl Moon by Mahogany L. Browne (Crown Books for Young Readers/Penguin Random House). 978-0593176436.

We Weren't Looking to Be Found by Stephanie Kuehn (Disney-Hyperion). 978-1368064101.

What We Harvest by Ann Fraistat (Delacorte Press/Penguin Random House). 978-0593382165.

When You Get the Chance by Emma Lord (Wednesday Books/Macmillan). 978-1250783349.

You'd Be Home Now by Kathleen Glasgow (Delacorte Press/Penguin Random House). 978-0525708049.

Quick Picks for Reluctant Young Adult Readers

The Young Adult Library Services Association (YALSA), a division of the American Library Association, annually chooses a list of outstanding titles that may stimulate the interest of reluctant teen readers. The list is intended to attract teens who are not inclined to read, for whatever reason. This year's list includes 66 fiction, nonfiction, and graphic novel or illustrated text titles published from late 2021 through 2022. An asterisk denotes the title was selected as a top ten.

Fiction

The Agathas. By Kathleen Glasgow and Liz Lawson. 2022. 405p. Delacorte Press, $18.99 (9780593431115). Gr. 8–12. Classmates Alice and Iris team up to investigate the murder of a young girl who is found dead after a party. Using Agatha Christie as their guide, the two tenacious teens set out to uncover the truth about what happened while digging up dirty secrets about their small town.

Alone Out Here. By Riley Redgate. 2022. 392p. Hyperion, $18.99 (9781368064729). Gr. 9–12. Leigh Chen and a small group of teens escape a cataclysmic volcanic eruption on a starship. As isolation increases and food supplies decrease, it becomes clear that the crew faces danger both in the starship and in the vast outer space as they search for a habitable planet.

Arden Grey. By Ray Stoeve. 2022. 278p. Amulet Books, $18.99 (9781419746000). Gr. 9–12. Arden Grey is dealing with a lot—a toxic mother who abandoned her, a newly transitioned best friend, and questions about her own sexual identity. Finding solace in film photography and a new group of friends, Arden slowly discovers what it means to find herself.

At the End of Everything. By Marieke Nijkamp. 2022. 386p. Sourcebooks Fire, $18.99 (9781492673156). Gr. 8–11. Hope Juvenile Treatment Center is a last chance at rehabilitation for troubled teens until the adult staff deserts the facility. With the outside world on lockdown because of a deadly virus, the teens must learn how to survive on their own.

Bad Girls Never Say Die. By Jennifer Mathieu. 2021. 295p. Roaring Brook Press, $18.99 (9781250232588). Gr. 8–12. A feminist spin on S.E. Hinton's classic novel, *The Outsiders,* Evie Barnes and her fierce and loyal friends are considered "bad girls." After a traumatic experience, their bond becomes even tighter. These girls must put their trust in one another to prevent another tragedy.

Blaine for the Win. By Robbie Couch. 2022. 326p. Simon & Schuster Books for Young Readers, $19.99 (9781534497467). Gr. 9–12. Blaine is devastated when he gets dumped by his boyfriend because Blaine isn't "serious enough" about his future. To prove Joey wrong and win him back, Blaine decides to run for senior class president.

Break This House. By Candice Iloh. 2022. 205p. Dutton Books, $17.99 (9780525556237). Gr. 9–12. After relocating with her father to leave her tragic past behind, Yaminah learns of a family reunion that is also a celebration of life for her mother, whom she didn't know had passed away. What will deciding to go mean for her new life?

Cold. By Mariko Tamaki. 2022. 229p. Roaring Brook Press, $18.99 (9781626722736). Gr. 8–11. A mystery-homicide in which both the ghost and the girl are trying to determine what happened and how they are unknowingly connected

Counting Scars. By Melinda Di Lorenzo. 2022. 113p. Orca Book Publishers, $10.95 (9781459833555). Gr. 8–12. Busted for shoplifting, Adele is sent to Camp Happy instead of juvie. She quickly finds herself attracted to a quietly mysterious teen who just might be a stone cold killer capable of murdering his mother.

*Daughter. By Kate McLaughlin. 2022. 330p. Wednesday Books, $18.99 (9781250817440). Gr. 9–12. Scarlet has no idea that her boring life and her paranoid mother are protecting her from her true identity. She is the daughter of notorious

serial killer Jeff Lake, and he is willing to spill the secrets of his murder victims—but only to her.

Dead End Girls. By Wendy Heard. 2022. 324p. Christy Ottaviano Books, $17.99 (9780316310413). Gr. 9–12. Maude has decided to fake her death. She wants to escape her heartless family and start fresh. With meticulous planning, she's ready to fake her death while her entire family is on vacation in Hawaii. Maude's plans are upended when her step-cousin Frankie discovers the plan and wants in.

Diamond Park. By Phillippe Diederich. 2022. 275p. Dutton Books, $17.99 (9780593354254). Gr. 9–12. After a skipped day of school to retrieve an Impala goes awry, Flaco and his friends are left to either wait for the police to solve a murder in which their friend is implicated or try to prove her innocence on their own.

Dig Two Graves. By Gretchen McNeil. 2022. 342p. Hyperion, $17.99 (9781368072847). Gr. 9–12. When Neve meets Diane at summer camp, they instantly bond over the betrayals of people who had been close to them. Together, they make a fantasy pact to kill their betrayers, but when Neve's betrayer ends up dead, Neve realizes that Diane might be taking the pact seriously.

The Getaway. By Lamar Giles. 2022. 382p. Scholastic Press, $19.99 (9781338752014). Gr. 9–12. Four teenagers living and working in the world's best resort find themselves fighting for their lives when a global catastrophe reveals the park is an end-of-the-world vacation spot for the earth's most ruthless billionaires, who expect top-notch services from their new employee—or else.

Girl Overboard. By Sandra Block. 2022. 248p. Underlined, $9.99 (9780593483466). Gr. 9–12. Izzy is expecting a boring family vacation on a cruise to Bermuda until she meets Jade, who turns the trip into an edgy adventure. It's all fun and parties until Jade goes missing and Izzy discovers that there is something very sinister on board their ship.

A Girl's Guide to Love and Magic. By Debbie Rigaud. 2022. 270p. Scholastic Press, $18.99 (9781338681741). Gr. 8–12. Cicely's birthday plans devolve into a fast-paced scavenger hunt to reverse a spirit's possession of her aunt's body following a Vodou

reading that goes amok set against the backdrop of Brooklyn's West Indian Day Parade.

Gold Mountain. By Betty G. Yee. 2022. 280p. Carolrhoda Lab, $18.99 (9781728415826). Gr. 6–10. Tam Ling Fan disguises herself as her dead brother to work on the Central Pacific Railroad. Facing dangerous working conditions and railroad saboteurs, she struggles to keep her identity a secret while earning enough to pay for her father's release from a Chinese prison.

Happily Ever Island. By Crystal Cestari. 2022. 326p. Disney-Hyperion, $18.99 (9781368075473). Gr. 9–12. Best friends Madison and Lanie are selected for the trip of a lifetime on Disney's immersive experience resort, Happily Ever Island. Their island adventure is filled with romance, self-discovery, and a whole lot of Disney magic.

*Horror Hotel. By Victoria Fulton and Faith McClaren. 2022. 242p. Underlined, $9.99 (9780593483480). Gr. 8–12. No one loves a haunted place the night before Halloween more than a group of ghost hunters. The group of four thinks filming at the notorious Hearst Hotel in Los Angeles will be the secret to reaching one million subscribers to their YouTube channel, but soon discover unexpected secrets.

Hotel Magnifique. By Emily Taylor. 2022. 391p. Razorbill, $18.99 (9780593404515). Gr. 7–10. Sisters Jani and Zosa escape their mundane lives by entering the magical, enchanting world of the Hotel Magnifique, only to discover that danger and secrets lurk behind the beauty.

*Jumper. By Melanie Crowder. 2022. 327p. Viking, $18.99 (9780593326961). Gr. 10–12. Nineteen-year-old Blair Scott's dream of being accepted into the Forest Service's class of jumpers is complicated by a fierce fire season and a medical condition that endangers her life. Together with her best friend Jason, Blair treads the line between risk-taking and reckless and learns what it means to survive.

Kneel. By Candace Buford. 2022. 311p. Inkyard Press, $18.99 (9781335454355). Gr. 8–11. After his best friend is unfairly suspended from the varsity football team in their senior year, Russell must decide if he should stay under the radar in the hope of scoring a scholarship or use his voice to protest the racism in his small town.

Live, Laugh, Kidnap. By Gabby Noone. 2022. 330p. Razorbill, $17.99 (9780593327296). Gr. 8–12. Genesis (lives on a commune), Holly (staying for the summer), and Zoe (saving money to leave with her girlfriend) have one thing in common: distrust towards Hope Harvest Ministries. When an accidental encounter leads them to kidnap the teenage son of Hope's leaders, they see a way out of town.

Long Live the Pumpkin Queen. By Shea Ernshaw. 2022. 315p. Disney Press, $18.99 (9781368069601). Gr. 7–12. When the Pumpkin Queen, Sally Skellington, discovers a doorway to one of the ancient realms, she inadvertently unleashes the long-forgotten Sandman on the holiday and human worlds.

Love Radio. By Ebony LaDelle. 2022. 316p. Simon and Schuster BFYR, $19.99 (9781665908153). Gr. 9–12. Prince is a romantic, but he hasn't got time for love unless it's helping callers to his radio show. Dani is focused on her plan to move to New York and become a famous author. When these two meet, they agree to give each three dates to see where it leads.

Mirror Girls. By Kelly McWilliams. 2022. 308p. Little, Brown and Company, $17.99 (9780759553873). Gr. 9–12. After being separated at birth, two biracial twins, one presenting as black and the other passing as white, reunite in Jim Crow Georgia to break the curse on their family.

My Dearest Darkest. By Kayla Cottingham. 2022. 353p. Sourcebooks Fire, $10.99 (9781728236414). Gr. 10–12. Two students at an elite boarding school unwittingly summon a mysterious creature from beneath the school and must work together to banish it before it destroys everyone they love.

No One Is Alone. By Rachel Vincent. 2022. 420p. Bloomsbury, $17.99 (9781547609192). Gr. 8–11. When Michaela's mom suddenly dies, she moves in with her estranged father and his secret family. As Michaela tries to adjust, she inadvertently angers her new half-sister Emery by receiving the star role in the school play and drawing the attention of Emery's ex-boyfriend.

Nothing Burns as Bright as You. By Ashley Woodfolk. 2022. 277p. Versify, $18.99 (9780358655350). Gr. 9–12. This novel-in-verse burns with intensity and passion as a relationship quickly combusts from friendship to love and the two characters go to destructive lengths to be together.

Our Crooked Hearts. By Melissa Albert. 2022. 340p. Flatiron Books, $18.99 (9781250826367). Gr. 9–12. A dark fantasy of witchcraft, secrets, and lies. A mother and daughter play with supernatural fire, pushing the limits of darkness.

Out of the Fire. By Andrea Contos. 2021. 323p. Scholastic Press, $18.99 (9781338726169). Gr. 9–12. Cass is determined to track down her kidnapper and exact justice. A chance encounter with a sympathetic girl in the bathroom leads her to the realization that there are other teens who need closure to their own traumas. Together, four young women make a pact to make their abusers pay.

Practice Girl. By Estelle Laure. 2022. 307p. Viking, $18.99 (9780593350911). Gr. 9–12. Jo, a wrestling manager for her high school team, has a desire for a close relationship with a boy. She finds out she is considered a "practice girl" for boys to hook up with, but not to be in a relationship with. She must dig deep to find out what she wants and how to get it.

Queen of the Tiles. By Hannah Alkaf. 2022. 294p. Salaam Reads, $18.99 (9781534494558). Gr. 8–11. One year ago, Najwa Bakri's best friend, Trina Lowe, collapsed during a Scrabble Tournament. Now, Najwa has returned determined to win Trina's title and heal herself. All bets are off when Trina's inactive Instagram account begins posting cryptic messages suggesting that someone at the tournament murdered Trina.

Rain Rising. By Courtne Comrie. 2022. 327p. Harper, $16.99 (9780063159730). Gr. 5–8. Comparing herself to her best friend, eighth grader Rain Washington feels fat, ugly, and untalented. After a vicious attack on her older brother, Rain begins to discover a support system of classmates and school staff who want to help her see herself as they see her: beautiful, talented, and worthy.

Remember Me Gone. By Stacy Stokes. 2022. 362p. Viking, $17.99 (9780593327661). Gr. 8–12. Lucy and her father share the ability to erase other people's memories. As Lucy works to develop her ability, she discovers that her father holds memories of her mother that don't match the narrative Lucy's been given, as well as a malevolent hometown history.

The Rumor Game. By Dhonielle Clayton and Sona Charaipotra. 2022. 471p. Hyperion, $18.99 (9781368014144). Gr. 9–12. After a summer scandal, Bryn returns to Foxham Prep an outcast. Georgie returns after a summer at a weight loss camp to new popularity. Cora is Bryn's ex-best friend. When a rumor puts the three of them in the center of school and online gossip, reputations are at stake.

The Sea Knows My Name. By Laura Brooke Robson. 2022. 261p. Dial Books, $18.99 (9780525554066). Gr. 9–12. Among the volcanic ruins of Astoria, a mythical country ruled by pirates and nature, Thea must come to terms with the ruthlessness of her pirate queen mother and the betrayal of her first love.

Stinetinglers: All New Stories by the Master of Scary Tales. By R.L. Stine. 2022. 210p. Feiwel and Friends, $16.99 (978-1250836274). Gr. 3–6. These short stories vary from creepy bugs, haunted homes, grotesque body changes, and other spooky things that are unexplainable. Each offers what seems to be an average life of a tween before strange things occur. Included are Stine's personal notes to his past or what inspired each story.

Sunny G's Series of Rash Decisions. By Navdeep Singh Dhillon. 2022. 300p. Dial Books, $17.99 (9780593109977). Gr. 9–12. On the one-year anniversary of his brother's death, a stolen journal leads Sunny on an all-night adventure full of romantically wonderful and ridiculously reckless choices that irrevocably reshape his outlook on life.

Survive the Dome. By Kosoko Jackson. 2022. 326p. Sourcebooks Fire, $18.99 (9781728239088). Gr. 9–12. Teen journalist Jamal Lawson is catapulted into a living nightmare when he is covering protests of police brutality when the city of Baltimore is encased in an impenetrable dome by corrupt city officials.

These Deadly Games. By Diana Urban. 2022. 404p. Wednesday Books, $18.99 (9781250797193). Gr. 9–12. Crystal Donovan's laser focus on her team's upcoming *Mortal Dusk* tournament is shattered and she must choose between the tournament and completing tasks given by an anonymous stranger that have increasingly deadly consequences for her team and her family.

This Golden State. By Marit Weisenberg. 2022. 384p. Flatiron Books, $18.99 (9781250786272). Gr. 8–12. Poppy and her family have been living on the run and following a set of strict rules to keep them "safe" for as long as she can remember. When they move to California and Poppy takes a DNA test, she inadvertently discovers the truth about her family's paranoia.

This Might Get Awkward. By Kara McDowell. 2022. 319p. Scholastic Press, $17.99 (9781338746235). Gr. 7–10. Gemma Wells is prepared to spend a boring summer alone. All that changes when she rescues the super popular (and her secret crush) Beau Booker. As Beau lies comatose in the hospital, Gemma discovers that she may just be falling for his older brother, Griff.

TJ Powar Has Something to Prove. By Jesmeen Deo. 2022. 359p. Viking, $17.99 (9780593403396). Gr. 9–12. In response to an ugly meme targeting her cousin, debate star TJ Powar gives up hair removal to prove she can be hairy and beautiful.

Trigger. By N. Griffin. 2022. 244p. Atheneum, $18.99 (9781533487178). Gr. 10–12. Didi lives in isolation and off the grid with a demanding father who expects her to be perfect in chess competitions and in shocking games of survival in which she is pitted against older men.

Two Truths and a Lie. By April Henry. 2022. 273p. Little, Brown and Company, $17.99 (9780316323338). Gr. 9–12. When a high school acting group gets trapped in a creepy motel during a blizzard, what starts as a silly game of two truths and a lie quickly turns deadly.

Vinyl Moon. By Mahogany L. Browne. 2022. 166p. Crown, $18.99 (9780593176436). Gr. 9–12. Angel has just moved to Brooklyn to try to escape a violent event with her ex-boyfriend. Searching for a way forward, she finds solace in a group of young Black women who are willing to share their pains and dreams with her.

Well, That Was Unexpected. By Jesse Sutano. 2022. 406p. Delacorte Press, $18.99 (9780593433973). Gr. 9–12. In this hilarious rom-com set in Indonesia, Sharlot and George discover just how awkward it is to be catfished by their own parents, as they embark on a fake relationship that ultimately challenges their assumptions and causes them to question their own paths.

What We Harvest. By Ann Fraistat. 2022. 329p. Delacorte Press, $18.99 (9780593382165). Gr. 9–12. Wren must uncover her small town's secrets as a blight turns every living creature into rotting, mindless zombies—and she's infected.

When You Get the Chance. By Emma Lord. 2022. 320p. Wednesday Books, $18.99 (9781250783349). Gr. 8–12. Millie discovers an old online journal written by her single dad and realizes that three of the women he talks about might be her unknown mother. Millie sets out on a series of stunts and schemes to meet the women and find out which one is her mom.

White Smoke. By Tiffany D. Jackson. 2021. 373p. Katherine Tegen Books, $18.99 (9780063029095). Gr. 9–12. The move to Cedarville is supposed to get Mari away from the scandal of a drug overdose in California, but it turns out that the family's new home—while free—comes with some malevolent guests who want their home back.

Wrecked. By Heather Henson. 2022. 252p. Atheneum, $18.99 (9781442451056). Gr. 9–12. As the Wizard's daughter, Miri feels like she can never escape her meth-making father's shadow. Rebuilding motorcycles and her childhood friend, Clay, are the only things keeping Miri from running away—until Fen shows up.

You'd Be Home Now. By Kathleen Glasgow. 2021. 387p. Delacorte Press, $18.99 (9780525708049). Gr. 9–12. Emory survived a fatal car crash, but even as she is healing physically and emotionally, her parents make her responsible for her older brother's recovery from a heroin addiction.

*You'll Be the Death of Me. By Karen M. McManus. 2021. 326p. Delacorte Press, $19.99 (9780593175866). Gr. 8–12. Estranged friends, Ivy, Mateo, and Cal skip school to relive "the best day ever" from middle school. After finding a dead classmate, they become more than witnesses and realize their former friends have secrets of their own.

gnant and educational collection of poems that chronicle the Civil Rights Movement. Each chapter highlights major events and people from the time.

Code Name Badass: The True Story of Virginia Hall. By Heather Demetrios. 2021. 368p. Atheneum, $19.99 (9781534431874). Gr. 8–12. Heather Demetrios proves that Virginia "Dindy" Hall was far more than the daughter of wealth and privilege in this rollicking biography that recounts Hall's role in the French resistance during World War II and subsequent contributions to the United States intelligence community.

Hometown Victory: A Coach's Story of Football, Fate, and Coming Home. By Keanon Lowe. 2022. 223p. Flatiron Books, $28.99 (9781250807632). Drawn home to mourn a friend's death by overdose, Keanon Lowe takes a coaching position in his hometown of Portland, Oregon. This memoir tells how he inspired a team of young men to overcome their personal challenges to become a winning team in just two years.

In Harm's Way: The Sinking of the USS Indianapolis and the Story of Its Survivors. By Doug Stanton and Michael J. Tougias. 2022. 226p. Henry Holt & Company, $19.99 (9781250771322). Gr. 6–10. When the USS Indianapolis is torpedoed during World War II and sinks, nearly 1,000 sailors are stranded in the ocean facing unimaginable dangers. They have no supplies and get continual blisters from the sun, and then there are the sharks that feed on them while they await rescue.

*Punching Bag. By Rex Ogle. 2021. 207p. Norton Young Readers, $17.95 (9781324016236). Gr. 7–10. In this autobiographical follow up to his first book, *Free Lunch*, we follow Rex as he struggles through his teen years in a home full of domestic violence, mental illness, and substance abuse. Imagining his deceased sister as a guardian angel, Rex endeavors to shield his younger brother and survive.

Nonfiction

And We Rise: The Civil Rights Movement in Poems. By Erica Martin. 2022. 153p. Viking, $17.99 (9780593352526). Gr. 9–12. A poi-

Graphic Novel or Illustrated Text

Ain't Burned All the Bright. By Jason Reynolds. Art by Jason Griffin. 2022. 384p. Atheneum, $19.99 (9781534439467). Gr. 7–12. A mashup of art and text that explores what it means to breathe, to exist, and to move closer to those you love through the eyes of a young Black man.

Batter Royale. By Leisl Adams. Art by the Author. 2022. 234p. Amulet Books, $24.99 (9781419750755). Gr. 8–11. Seventeen-year-old Rose and her best friend Fred enter a baking competition that tests their relationship and baking skills. With a $500,000 prize at stake, Batter Royale will be no cake walk.

*Button Pusher. By Tyler Page. Art by the Author. 2022. 244p. First Second, $21.99 (9781250758347). Gr. 5–8. Through illustrations and humor, Page recounts his childhood from his ADHD diagnosis to high school graduation using the history and evolution of the neurodivergence to explain in detail this common experience.

Girl on Fire. By Alicia Keys. Art by Brittney Williams. 2022. 215p. HarperAlley, $19.99 (9780063029569). Gr. 8–12. Lolo Wright discovers she has unexpected superpowers when her brother is accosted and brutalized by a pair of cops in a case of mistaken identity. Her control over her powers grows as she must battle the local drug dealer who wants to recruit her for his own nefarious purposes.

Muhammad Ali. By Gabe Soria. Illustrated by Chris Brunner, Colors by Rico Renzi. 2022. 63p. Penguin Workshop, $7.99 (9780593224625). Gr. 3–6. Boxing fanatics would argue that the Thrilla in Manila was one of the greatest boxing matches of all time. This abbreviated biography of the fighters, the venue, and the fight's outcome is gorgeously written and illustrated.

Squire. By Sara Alfageeh & Nadia Shammas. Art by Sara Alfageeh. 2022. 302p. Quill Tree Books, $21.99 (9780062945853). Gr. 8–11. Looked down upon for her Ornu heritage, Aiza's opportunity for citizenship in the Bayt-Sajji Empire appears when she enlists for squire training. However, the cost of military honor is a dark reality that leaves Aiza calculating what morals are worth sacrificing in the name of duty.

*Swim Team. By Johnnie Christmas. Art by the Author. 2022. 245p. HarperAlley, $21.99 (9780063056770). Gr. 4–7. Bree's move to Florida introduces her not only to a group of new friends, but to an opportunity to overcome her fear of swimming in this beautifully written full-color graphic novel.

The Alex Awards

The Young Adult Library Services Association (YALSA), a division of the American Library Association, has selected ten adult books with special appeal to teen readers to receive the 2023 Alex Awards. The award is sponsored by the Margaret A. Edwards Trust. Edwards pioneered young adult library services and worked for many years at the Enoch Pratt Library in Baltimore, Maryland. Her work is described in her book *The Fair Garden and the Swarm of Beasts*, and over the years, she has served as an inspiration to many librarians who serve young adults. The Alex Awards are named after Edwards, who was called "Alex" by her friends.

A Lady's Guide to Fortune-Hunting by Sophie Irwin, published by Pamela Dorman Books, an imprint of Penguin Random House (9780593491348)

Babel, Or the Necessity of Violence: An Arcane History of the Oxford Translators' Revolution by R. F. Kuang, published by Harper Voyager, an imprint of HarperCollins (9780063021426)

Chef's Kiss by Jarrett Melendez, illustrated by Danica Brine, published by Oni Press, an imprint of Oni-Lion Forge Publishing Group (9781620109045)

Daughter of the Moon Goddess by Sue Lynn Tan, published by Harper Voyager, an imprint of HarperCollins (9780063031302)

I'm Glad My Mom Died by Jennette McCurdy, published by Simon & Schuster (9781982185824)

Solito: A Memoir by Javier Zamora, published by Hogarth, an imprint of Random House, a division of Penguin Random House (9780593498064)

The High Desert: Black. Punk. Nowhere. written and illustrated by James Spooner, published by Harper, an imprint of HarperCollins (9780358659112)

The Kaiju Preservation Society by John Scalzi, published by Tor Books, an imprint of Tom Doherty Associates, a division of Macmillan (9780765389121)

True Biz by Sara Nović, published by Random House, an imprint and division of Penguin Random House (9780593241509)

Wash Day Diaries by Jamila Rowser, illustrated by Robyn Smith, published by Chronicle Books (9781797205458)

Amazing Audiobooks for Young Adults

Each year, the Amazing Audiobooks Blogging Team of the Young Adult Library Services Association (YALSA), a division of the American Library Association, selects and annotates a list of notable audio recordings significant to young adults from among those released in the past two years. This year's list comprises 43 titles selected from among 51 nominations that were posted and discussed on YALSA's teen collection blog, The Hub. While the list as a whole addresses the interests and needs of young adults, individual titles need not appeal to this entire age range but rather to parts of it. An asterisk denotes the title was selected as a top ten.

The Agathas. By Kathleen Glasgow. Read by a full cast. 2022. 11hr. Listening Library, $69 (9780593585023).

*Ain't Burned All the Bright. By Jason Reynolds. Read by the author and a full cast. 2022. 40min. Simon & Schuster Audio, $19.99 (9781797137544).

*All My Rage. By Sabaa Tahir. Read by a full cast. 2022. 10.5hr. Listening Library, $69 (9780593502235).

Alma Presses Play. By Tina Cane. Read by Dana Wing Lau. 2021. 5.5hr. Listening Library, $34 (9780593216774).

Alone Out Here. By Riley Redgate. Read by the author. 2022. 11.5hr. Findaway/Disney Hyperion, $39.99 (9781368080651).

Anatomy: A Love Story. By Dana Schwartz. Read by Mhairi Morrison and Tim Campbell. 2022. 9.5hr. Macmillan Audio/Macmillan Young Listeners, $44.99 (9781250840578).

Answers in the Pages. By David Levithan. Read by a full cast. 2022. 4hr. Listening Library, $45 (9780593608258).

*Azar on Fire. By Olivia Abtahi. Read by Alex McKenna. 2022. 9hr. Listening Library, $63 (9780593610305).

Bitter. By Akwaeke Emezi. Read by Bahni Turpin. 2022. 7hr. Listening Library, $50 (9780593416662).

The Bone Spindle. By Leslie Vedder. Read by Lindsey Dorcus. 2022. 12hr. Listening Library, $75 (9780593503164).

Chasing After Knight. By Heather Buchta. Read by Kate Rudd. 2022. 9.5hr. Listening Library, $63 (9780593507926).

Daughter of the Moon Goddess. By Sue Lynn Tan. Read by Natalie Naudus. 2022. 15hr. HarperAudio, $82.37 (9780063031340).

Dead End Girls. By Wendy Heard. Read by Natalie Naudus and Taylor Meskimen.

2022. Hachette Audio/Christy Ottaviano Books, $65 (9781668613238).

*The Door of No Return. By Kwame Alexander. Read by Kobna Holdbrook-Smith. 2022. 3.5hr. Hachette Audio, $65 (9781668616437).

The Epic Story of Every Living Thing. By Deb Caletti. Read by Brittany Pressley. 2022. 12.5hr. Listening Library, $75 (9780593611661).

Gallant. By V.E. Schwab. Read by Julian Rhind-Tutt. 2022. 7.5hr. HarperCollins Publishers, Inc./Greenwillow Books, $64.35 (9780063220751).

The Getaway. By Lamar Giles. Read by a full cast. 2022. 10hr. Scholastic, Inc. (U.S.)/Scholastic Press, $83.99 (9781338752038).

Golden Boys. By Phil Stamper. Read by a full cast. 2022. 9hr. Listening Library, $64 (9780593347690).

Heat Wave. By T.J. Klune. Read by Michael Lesley. 2022. 13hr. Macmillan Audio/Macmillan Young Listeners, $59.99 (9781250856142).

*The Honeys. By Ryan La Sala. Read by Pete Cross. 2022. 11hr. Scholastic, Inc. Audiobooks, $83.99 (9781338853186).

Hunting by Stars. By Cherie Dimaline. Read by Meegwun Fairbrother and Michelle St. John. 2021. 12.5hr. Books on Tape/Tundra Books/Penguin Teen Canada, $43 (9780735269705).

Icebreaker. By A.L. Graziadei. Read by Tom Picasso. 2022. 8.5hr. Recorded Books, Inc., $79 (9781705051429).

Iron Widow. By Xiran Jay Zhao. Read by Rong Fu. 2021. 12hr. Books on Tape/Tundra Books/Penguin Teen Canada, $60 (9780735269972).

Jennifer Chan Is Not Alone. By Tae Keller. Read by a full cast. 2022. 7hr. Listening Library, $56 (9780593559994).

The Last Cuentista. By Donna Barba Higuera. Read by Frankie Corzo. 2021. 8.5hr. Recorded Books, Inc., $79 (9781705044308).

Little Thieves. By Margaret Owen. Read by Saskia Maarleveld. 2021. 14hr. Macmillan Audio/Macmillan Young Listeners, $59.99 (9781250795434).

Loveless. By Alice Oseman. Read by a full cast. 2022. 10.5hr. Scholastic, Inc., $89.99 (9781338780512).

The Peach Rebellion. By Wendelin Van Draanen. Read by Lauri Jo Daniels and Emily Ellet. 2022. 12hr. Listening Library, $75 (9780593585009).

Queer Ducks (and Other Animals). By Eliot Schrefer. Read by a full cast. 2022. 5.5hr. HarperCollins Publishers, Inc./Katherine Tegen Books, $56.62 (9780063069527).

The Silence That Binds Us. By Joanna Ho. Read by Raechel Wong. 2022. 11.5hr. HarperCollins Publishers, Inc. HarperTeen, $72.02 (9780063059375).

Skin of the Sea. By Natasha Bowen. Read by Yetide Badaki. 2022. 11.5 hr. Listening Library, $75 (9780593343692).

Soul of the Deep. By Natasha Bowen. Read by Yetide Badaki. 2022. 11hr. Listening Library, $69 (9780593609743).

A Spindle Splintered. By Alix E. Harrow. Read by Amy Landon. 2021. 3.5hr. Macmillan Audio, $24.99 (9781250824486).

The Sunbearer Trials. By Aiden Thomas. Read by André Santana. 2022. 13.5hr.

Macmillan Audio/Macmillan Young Listeners, $59.99 (9781250866189).

Sunny G's Series of Rash Decisions. By Navdeep Singh Dhillon. Read by Shahjehan Khan. 2022. 7.5hr. Listening Library, $56 (9780593411315).

Together We Burn. By Isabel Ibañez. Read by Ana Osorio. 2022. 13hr. Macmillan Audio/Macmillan Young Listeners, $59.99 (9781250855282).

Tumble. By Celia C. Pérez. Read by Victoria Villareal. 2022. 9hr. Listening Library, $63 (9780593590393).

Vespertine. By Margaret Rogerson. Read by Caitlin Davies. 2021. 12hr. Simon & Schuster Audio, $79.99 (9781797130415).

Vinyl Moon. By Mahogany L. Browne. Read by Bahni Turpin. 2022. 5hr. Listening Library, $38 (9780593506462).

The Weight of Blood. By Tiffany D. Jackson. Read by a full cast. 2022. 11hr. HarperCollins Publishers, Inc./Katherine Tegen Books, $72.07 (9780063029170).

What About Will. By Ellen Hopkins. Read by Michael Wetherbee. 2021. 5hr. Listening Library, $38 (9780593453797).

When We Make It. By Elisabet Velasquez. Read by the author. 2021. 4hr. Listening Library, $38 (9780593455937).

You've Reached Sam. By Dustin Thao. Read by Soneela Nankani. 2021. 9.5hr. Macmillan Audio/Macmillan Young Listeners, $49.99 (9781250820822).

Outstanding International Books for Young Readers

Since 2006, the United States Board on Books for Young People (USBBY) has selected an annual honor list of international books for young people. The 42 titles on this year's Outstanding International Books (OIB) list, all published or released in 2022, have been identified as significant for both their exceptional quality and globe-spanning origins.

Preschool to Grade 2

Howden, Sarah. *The Tunnel.* Illus. by Erika Rodriguez Medina. Owlkids. (Canada)

Jihyun, Kim. *The Depth of the Lake and the Height of the Sky.* Trans. from Korean by S.B. Rights Agency. Illus. by author. Floris Books. (South Korea)

Lee, Gee-Eun. *My GrandMom.* Trans. from Korean by Sophie Bowman. Illus. by author. Amazon Crossing Kids. (South Korea)

Mahiout, Anouk. *A Place for Pauline.* Trans. from French by Groundwood. Illus. by Marjolaine Perreten. Groundwood Books. (Canada)

Moahloli, Refiloe. *I Am You: A Book about Ubuntu.* Illus. by Zinelda McDonald. Amazon Crossing Kids. (South Africa)

Nainy, Mamta. *Rainbow Hands.* Illus. by Jo Loring-Fisher. Lantana. (India/United Kingdom)

Parappukkaran, Sandhya. *The Boy Who Tried to Shrink His Name.* Illus. by Michelle Pereira. Abrams Books for Young Readers. (Australia)

Ray, Achintyarup. *Jhupli's Honey Box.* Trans. from Bengali by author. Illus. by Shivam Choudhary. Tulika Publishers. (India)

Rodari, Gianni. *Telling Stories Wrong.* Trans. from Italian by Antony Shugaar. Illus. by Beatrice Alemagna. Enchanted Lion Books. (Italy)

Skomsvold, Kjersti Annesdatter. *Bedtime for Bo.* Trans. from Norwegian by Kari Dickson. Illus. by Mari Kanstad Johnsen. Enchanted Lion Books. (Norway)

Togo, Narisa. *When the Sakura Bloom.* Trans. from Japanese by Michael Sedunary. Berbay Publishing. (Japan)

Yage, Wang. *Playing with Lanterns.* Trans. from Simplified Chinese by Helen Wang. Illus. by Zhu Chengliang. Amazon Crossing Kids. (China)

Grades 3 to 5

Atinuke. *Too Small Tola and the Three Fine Girls.* Illus. by Onyinye Iwu. Candlewick. (Nigeria)

Ávila, Pilar López. *With a Butterfly's Wings.* Trans. from Spanish by Jon Brokenbrow. Illus. by Zuzanna Celej. Cuento de Luz. (Spain)

Dumas, William. *The Gift of the Little People.* Illus. by Rhian Brynjolson. HighWater Press. (Rocky Cree/Canada)

Earle, Phil. *When the Sky Falls.* Bloomsbury Children's Books. (England)

Guridi, Raúl Nieto. *it's so difficult.* Trans. from Spanish by Lawrence Schimel. Illus. by author. Eerdmans Books for Young Readers. (Spain)

Montañés, Mónica. *Different: A Story of the Spanish Civil War.* Trans. from Spanish by Lawrence Schimel. Illus. by Eva Sánchez Gómez. Eerdmans Books for Young Readers. (Spain)

Mountford, Karl James. *The Circles in the Sky.* Illus. by author. Candlewick Studio. (U.K.)

Oziewicz, Tina. *What Feelings Do When No One's Looking.* Trans. from Polish by Jennifer Croft. Illus. by Aleksandra Zając. elsewhere editions. (Poland)

Sardà, Júlia. *The Queen in the Cave.* Illus. by author. Candlewick Press. (United Kingdom)

Stridsberg, Sara. *The Summer of Diving.* Trans. from Swedish by B.J. Woodstein. Illus. by Sara Lundberg. Seven Stories Press/Triangle Square Books for Young Readers. (Sweden)

Sunar, Özge Bahar. *My Grandma's Photos.* Illus. by Senta Urgan. Trans. by Amy Marie Spangler. Amazon Crossing Kids. (Turkey)

Thompson, Sam. *Wolfstongue.* Illus. by Anna Tromop. Little Island Books. (Ireland)

White, Paula. *The Baker by the Sea.* Illus. by author. Templar Books. (England)

Widmark, Martin. *Dreams of Near and Far.* Trans. from Swedish by Polly Lawson. Illus. by Emilia Dziubak. Floris Books. (Sweden)

Wright, Felicity. *A Kunwinjku Counting Book.* Illus. by Gabriel Maralngurra. Enchanted Lion Books. (Bininj/Australia)

Spencer, Kim. *Weird Rules to Follow.* Orca Book Publishers. (Ts'msyen Nation/Canada)

Wolo, Mamle. *The Kaya Girl.* Little, Brown and Company. (Ghana)

Grades 6 to 8

Cley, Amanda. *The Pack.* Trans. from Italian by Eerdmans Books for Young Readers. Illus. by Cecilia Ferri. Eerdmans Books for Young Readers. (Italy)

Giménez, Regina. *Geo-graphics.* Trans. from Catalan by Alexis Romay and Valerie Block. Illus. by author. Levine Querido. (Spain)

Nannestad, Katrina. *We Are Wolves.* Illus. by Martina Heiduczek. Atheneum. (Prussia/Australia)

Neruda, Pablo. *Book of Questions: Selections/Libros de las preguntas: Selecciones.* Trans. from Spanish by Sara Lissa Paulson. Illus. by Paloma Valdivia. Enchanted Lion Books. (Chile)

Newman, Carey & Kirstie Hudson. *The Witness Blanket: Truth, Art and Reconciliation.* Orca Book Publishers. (Canada)

Richardson, Bill. *Last Week.* Illus. by Emilie Leduc. Groundwood Books. (Canada)

Grades 9 to 12

Canizales. *Amazona.* Trans. from Spanish by Sofía Huitrón Martínez. Illus. by author. Lerner/Graphic Universe. (Columbia)

Conyngham, Richard. *All Rise: Resistance and Rebellion in South Africa 1910–1948: A Graphic History.* Illus. by Saaid Rahbeeni, The Trantraal Brothers, Liz Clarke, Dada Khanyisa, Tumi Mamabolo, and Mark Modimola. Catalyst Press. (South Africa)

Martins, Vitor. *This Is Our Place.* Trans. from Brazilian Portuguese by Larissa Helena. Scholastic/PUSH. (Brazil)

Miyazaki, Hayao. *Shuna's Journey.* Trans. from Japanese by Alex Dudok de Wit. Illus. by the author. FirstSecond. (Japan)

Van Rijckeghem, Jean-Claude. *Ironhead or, Once a Young Lady.* Trans. from French by Kristen Gehrman. Levine Querido. (Belgium)

Notable Children's Books

Each year, a committee of the Association for Library Service to Children (ALSC) identifies the best of the best in children's books. According to the Notables Criteria, "notable" is defined as: Worthy of note or notice, important, distinguished, outstanding. As applied to children's books, notable should be thought to include books of especially commendable quality; books that exhibit venturesome creativity; and books of fiction, information, poetry, and pictures for all age levels (birth through age 14) that reflect and encourage children's interests in exemplary ways. [See "Literary Prizes, 2022" later in Part 5 for Caldecott, Newbery, and other award winners—*Ed.*]

Younger Readers

Also. By E.B. Goodale. Illus. by the author. Clarion.

Bathe the Cat. By Alice B. McGinty. Illus. by David Roberts. Chronicle.

Berry Song. By Michaela Goade. Illus. by the author. Little, Brown. (A 2023 Caldecott Honor Book)

The Coquíes Still Sing: A Story of Home, Hope, and Rebuilding. By Karina Nicole González. Illus. by Krystal Quiles. Roaring Brook. (A 2023 Pura Belpré Illustrator and Children's Author Honor Book)

Endlessly Ever After: Pick Your Path to Countless Fairy Tale Endings. By Laurel Snyder. Illus. by Dan Santat. Chronicle.

Every Dog in the Neighborhood. By Philip C. Stead. Illus. by Matthew Cordell. Holiday/Neal Porter.

Everything in Its Place: A Story of Books and Belonging. By Pauline David-Sax. Illus. by Charnelle Pinkney Barlow. Doubleday.

Farmhouse. By Sophie Blackall. Illus. by the author. Little, Brown.

Finding Fire. By Logan S. Kline. Illus. by the author. Candlewick.

Fire Chief Fran. By Linda Ashman. Illus. by Nancy Carpenter. Astra/Astra Young Readers.

Fish and Wave. By Sergio Ruzzier. Illus. by the author. HarperAlley. (A 2023 Geisel Honor Book)

The Flamingo. By Guojing. Art by the author. Random House Studio.

Gigi and Ojiji. By Melissa Iwai. Illus. by the author. Harper. (A 2023 Geisel Honor Book)

H Is for Harlem. By Dinah Johnson. Illus. by April Harrison. Little, Brown/Christy Ottaviano.

Hello, Puddle! By Anita Sanchez. Illus. by Luisa Uribe. Clarion.

A History of Me. By Adrea Theodore. Illus. by Erin K. Robinson. Holiday/Neal Porter.

Honeybee Rescue: A Backyard Drama. By Loree Griffin Burns. Illus. by Ellen Harasimowicz. Charlesbridge.

Hot Dog. By Doug Salati. Illus. by the author. Knopf. (The 2023 Caldecott Medal winner)

How to Say Hello to a Worm: A First Guide to the Outside. By Kari Percival. Illus. by the author. Penguin Workshop/RISE.

I Did It! By Michael Emberley. Illus. by the author. Holiday. (The 2023 Geisel Award Book)

João by a Thread. By Roger Mello. Illus. by the author. Trans. by Daniel Hahn. Elsewhere Editions (A 2023 Batchelder Honor Book)

John's Turn. By Mac Barnett. Illus. by Kate Berube. Candlewick.

Kitty. By Rebecca Jordan-Glum. Illus. by the author. Roaring Brook.

Knight Owl. By Christopher Denise. Illus. by the author. Little, Brown/Christy Ottaviano. (A 2023 Caldecott Honor Book)

A Land of Books: Dreams of Young Mexihcah Word Painters. By Duncan Tonatiuh. Illus. by the author. Abrams. (A 2023 Pura Belpré Illustrator Honor Book)

Listen: How Evelyn Glennie, a Deaf Girl, Changed Percussion. By Shannon Stocker. Illus. by Devon Holzwarth. Dial.

Lizzy and the Cloud. By Terry Fan and Eric Fan. Illus. by the authors. Simon & Schuster.

Luli and the Language of Tea. By Andrea Wang. Illus. by Hyewon Yum. Holiday/Neal Porter.

Magic: Once Upon a Faraway Land. By Mirelle Ortega. Illus. by the author. Cameron Kids. (A 2023 Pura Belpré Illustrator Honor Book)

Me and the Boss: A Story about Mending and Love. By Michelle Edwards. Illus. by April Harrison. Random/Anne Schwartz.

The Notebook Keeper: A Story of Kindness from the Border. By Stephen Briseño. Illus. by Magdalena Mora. Random House Studio. (A 2023 Pura Belpré Children's Author Honor Book)

Out of a Jar. By Deborah Marcero. Illus. by the author. Putnam.

Owl and Penguin. By Vikram Madan. Illus. by the author. Holiday. (A 2023 Geisel Honor Book)

Powwow Day. By Traci Sorell. Illus. by Madelyn Goodnight. Charlesbridge.

A Seed Grows. By Antoinette Portis. Illus. by the author. Holiday/Neal Porter. (A 2023 Geisel and Sibert Honor Book)

Still Dreaming/Seguimos soñando. By Claudia Guadalupe Martínez. Illus. by Magdalena Mora. Tr. by Luis Humberto Crosthwaite. Lee & Low/Children's Book. (A 2023 Pura Belpré Illustrator Honor Book)

Sweet Justice: Georgia Gilmore and the Montgomery Bus Boycott. By Mara Rockliff. Illus. by R. Gregory Christie. Random House Studio. (A 2023 Sibert Honor Book)

The Talk. By Alicia D. Williams. Illus. by Briana Mukodiri Uchendu. Atheneum/Caitlyn Dlouhy.

The Three Billy Goats Gruff. By Mac Barnett. Illus. by Jon Klassen. Scholastic/Orchard.

Too Early. By Nora Ericson. Illus. by Elly MacKay. Abrams.

The Tower of Life: How Yaffa Eliach Rebuilt Her Town in Stories and Photographs. By Chana Stiefel. Illus. by Susan Gal. Scholastic. (A 2023 Sibert Honor Book)

A Walk through the Rain Forest. By Martin Jenkins. Illus. by Vicky White. Candlewick.

Where Wonder Grows. By Xelena González. Illus. by Adriana M. Garcia. 2021. Cinco Puntos. (The 2023 Pura Belpré Illustrator Award winner)

The World Belonged to Us. By Jacqueline Woodson. Illus. by Leo Espinosa. Penguin/Nancy Paulsen.

Yellow Dog Blues. By Alice Faye Duncan. Illus. by Chris Raschka. Eerdmans.

Yes We Will: Asian Americans Who Shaped This Country. By Kelly Yang. Dial.

Yoshi and the Ocean: A Sea Turtle's Incredible Journey Home. By Lindsay Moore. Illus. by the author. Greenwillow.

Middle Readers

Aviva vs. the Dybbuk. By Mari Lowe. Levine Querido.

Black Bird, Blue Road. By Sofiya Pasternack. HarperCollins/Versify.

Choosing Brave: How Mamie Till-Mobley and Emmett Till Sparked the Civil Rights Movement. By Angela Joy. Illus. by Janelle Washington. Roaring Brook. (A 2023 Caldecott and Sibert Honor Book)

Concrete: From the Ground Up. By Larissa Theule. Illus. by Steve Light. Candlewick.

Different: A Story of the Spanish Civil War. By Mónica Montañés. Illus. by Eva Sánchez Gómez. Tr. by Lawrence Schimel. Eerdmans. (A 2023 Batchelder Honor Book)

Dragonfly Eyes. By Cao Wenxuan. Tr. by Helen Wang. Candlewick. (A 2023 Batchelder Honor Book)

Freewater. By Amina Luqman-Dawson. Little, Brown. (The 2023 Newbery Award winner)

Frizzy. By Claribel A. Ortega. Art by Rose Bousamra. First Second. (The 2023 Pura Belpré Children's Author Award winner)

Jennifer Chan Is Not Alone. By Tae Keller. Random.

Just a Girl: A True Story of World War II. By Lia Levi. Illus. by Jess Mason. Tr. by Sylvia Notini. Harper. (The 2023 Batchelder Award Book)

The Last Mapmaker. By Christina Soontornvat. Candlewick. (A 2023 Newbery Honor Book)

Little Monarchs. By Jonathan Case. Art by the author. Holiday/Margaret Ferguson.

Love in the Library. By Maggie Tokuda-Hall. Illus. by Yas Imamura. Candlewick.

Maizy Chen's Last Chance. By Lisa Yee. Random. (A 2023 Newbery Honor Book)

Odder. By Katherine Applegate. Illus. by Charles Santoso. Feiwel and Friends.

The Ogress and the Orphans. By Kelly Barnhill. Algonquin.

On the Move: Home Is Where You Find It. By Michael Rosen. Illus. by Quentin Blake. Candlewick.

Out of the Shadows: How Lotte Reiniger Made the First Animated Fairytale Movie. By Fiona Robinson. Illus. by the author. Abrams.

Phenomenal AOC: The Roots and Rise of Alexandria Ocasio-Cortez. By Anika Aldamuy Denise. Illus. by Loris Lora. Harper. (A 2023 Pura Belpré Illustrator Honor Book)

A River's Gifts: The Mighty Elwha River Reborn. By Patricia Newman. Illus. by Natasha Donovan.Lerner/Millbrook.

A Rover's Story. By Jasmine Warga. HarperCollins/Balzer + Bray.

The Secret Battle of Evan Pao. By Wendy Wan-Long Shang. Scholastic.

Seeking Freedom: The Untold Story of Fortress Monroe and the Ending of Slavery in America. By Selene Castrovilla. Illus. by E.B. Lewis. Astra/Calkins Creek.

Seen and Unseen: What Dorothea Lange, Toyo Miyatake, and Ansel Adams's Photographs Reveal about the Japanese American Incarceration. By Elizabeth Partridge. Illus. by Lauren Tamaki. Chronicle. (The 2023 Sibert Award winner)

Smaller Sister. By Maggie Edkins Willis. Art by the author. Roaring Brook.

Srta. Quinces. By Kat Fajardo. Art by the author. Scholastic/Graphix. (A 2023 Pura Belpré Illustrator Honor Book)

Swim Team. By Johnnie Christmas. Art by the author. HarperAlley.

Those Kids from Fawn Creek. By Erin Entrada Kelly. Greenwillow.

Tumble. By Celia C. Pérez. Penguin/Kokila. (A 2023 Pura Belpré Children's Author Honor Book)

The Universe in You. By Jason Chin. Illus. by the author. Holiday/Neal Porter.

Violet and Jobie in the Wild. By Lynne Rae Perkins. Illus. by the author. Greenwillow.

Older Readers

Ain't Burned All the Bright. By Jason Reynolds. Illus. by Jason Griffin. Atheneum/Caitlyn Dlouhy. (A 2023 Caldecott Honor Book)

American Murderer: The Parasite That Haunted the South. By Gail Jarrow. Astra/Calkins Creek.

The Bluest Sky. By Christina Diaz Gonzalez. Knopf.

Caprice. By Coe Booth. Scholastic.

The Door of No Return. By Kwame Alexander. Little, Brown.

How to Build a Human: In Seven Evolutionary Steps. By Pamela S. Turner. Illus. by John Gurche. Charlesbridge.

I Must Betray You. By Ruta Sepetys. Philomel.

In the Key of Us. By Mariama J. Lockington. Farrar.

Iveliz Explains It All. By Andrea Beatriz Arango. Illus. by Alyssa Bermudez. Random. (A 2023 Newbery Honor Book)

The Patron Thief of Bread. By Lindsay Eagar. Candlewick.

The Road to After. By Rebekah Lowell. Illus. by the author. Penguin/Nancy Paulsen.

Star Child: A Biographical Constellation of Octavia Estelle Butler. By Ibi Zoboi. Dutton.

Victory. Stand! Raising My Fist for Justice. By Tommie Smith and Derrick Barnes. Art by Dawud Anyabwile. Norton/Young Readers.

All Ages

Blue: A History of the Color as Deep as the Sea and as Wide as the Sky. By Nana Ekua Brew-Hammond. Illus. by Daniel Minter. Knopf.

Isla to Island. By Alexis Castellanos. Art by the author. Atheneum.

Killer Underwear Invasion! How to Spot Fake News, Disinformation & Conspiracy Theories. By Elise Gravel. Art by the author. Chronicle.

Marshmallow Clouds: Two Poets at Play among Figures of Speech. By Ted Kooser and Connie Wanek. Illus. by Richard Jones. Candlewick.

The Real Dada Mother Goose: A Treasury of Complete Nonsense. By Jon Scieszka. Illus. by Julia Rothman. Candlewick.

Standing in the Need of Prayer: A Modern Retelling of the Classic Spiritual. By Carole Boston Weatherford. Illus. by Frank Morrison. Crown.

Notable Recordings for Children

This annual listing of notable recordings for children 14 years and younger is produced by the Association for Library Service to Children (ALSC), a division of the American Library Association. Chosen by children's librarians and educators, the list includes recordings deemed to be of especially commendable quality that demonstrate respect for young people's intelligence and imagination, exhibit venturesome creativity, and reflect and encourage the interests of children and young adolescents in exemplary ways.

A Is for Oboe: The Orchestra's Alphabet. By Lera Auerbach, Marilyn Nelson. Read by Thomas Quasthoff. 2022. 1hr. Listening Library, DD (9780593346228). Gr. 1–5. A poet and a composer have creatively teamed up to present the orchestra's world through verse. This audio version of the picture book combines the deep, expressive voice of Thomas Quasthoff with musical accompaniments to illustrate the instruments and vocabulary for each verse. From the sound of a single instrument to the whole orchestra, the audio presents a much richer version of this book.

Ain't Burned All the Bright. By Jason Reynolds. Take One read by Jason Reynolds. Take Two read by a full cast. 2022. .5hr. Simon & Schuster Audio, DD (9781797137544). Gr. 6+. What does it really mean to breathe? In this poem told in three parts, Jason Reynolds explores what it means to be Black in America in 2022. Listeners get to experience this piece twice, read once by Reynolds and a second time by a full cast. Each retelling brings something different to the story, but both use the rhythm of spoken word to bring this poetry to life.

Boys Will Be Human. By Justin Baldoni. Read by the author. 2022. 7hr. HarperAudio, DD (9780063067233). Gr. 6+. Raw, vulnerable, and intimate, this nonfiction book, read by the author, about what it means to grow up, draws the listener into the conversation. Despite the sometimes-difficult topics presented, personal anecdotes and a willingness to be silly create a comfortable atmosphere, keeping the audiobook authentic and honest.

Coraline. By Neil Gaiman. Read by a full cast. 2022. 3.5hr. HarperAudio, DD (9780063243255). Gr. 4+. When Coraline ventures through a mysterious door to find an uncanny version of her own home, she must use all of her courage and cleverness to escape from this Other world. Gaiman's beloved text is given new life in this full-cast recording in which each narrator, perfectly cast, captures both the story's magic and its true horror.

Daughter of the White Rose. By Diane Zahler. Read by a full cast. 2022. 7hr. Live Oak Media, DD (9781430144823). Gr. 4–7. Set in medieval England during the reign of King Edward IV, this historical fiction narrative follows a common girl's friendship with the young prince born on the same day as her. The full-cast narration enhances the story, as the listener becomes immersed in the world of royalty, intrigue, and betrayal.

Drita, My Homegirl. By Jenny Lombard. Read by Carlotta Brentan and Jeanette Illidge. 2022. 3hr. Listening Library, DD (9780593587676). Gr. 4+. Drita and her family flee war-torn Kosovo for America with dreams as well as struggles to adapt and fit in. Two skilled narrators use authentic accents and respectful dialects to help listeners navigate between main and secondary characters in this novel of friendship, culture, and survival.

The First Helping (Lunch Lady Books 1 & 2). By Jarrett J. Krosoczka. Read by a full cast. 2022. 1hr. Listening Library, DD (9780593397145). K–Gr. 3. The first two books in Krosoczka's beloved Lunch Lady graphic novel series get a refresh in this hilarious and cleverly adapted audiobook. An immersive soundscape and a talented full cast of narrators capture the energy and spirit of the books readers already know and love. (2023 Odyssey Honor)

Gallant. By V.E. Schwab. Read by Julian Rhind-Tutt. 2022. 7.75hr. HarperAudio,

DD. (9780063220751). Gr. 6+. Reminiscent of a Vincent Price movie, the listener is drawn into this eerie tale through the effective and creative use of voice, pauses, and pace. The tone of the gripping story of a girl trying to solve the mysteries of her family's past comes through, capturing and holding the attention of the listener.

Inheritance: A Visual Poem. By Elizabeth Acevedo. Read by the author. 2022. 5m. HarperAudio, DD (9780063250390). Gr. 8+. With dynamic narration and exquisite emotional resonance, Acevedo's poetic performance celebrates the multidimensional subject of Black hair in the context of the author's Dominican identity. (2023 Odyssey Honor)

Isaiah Dunn Saves the Day. By Kelly J. Baptist. Read by Adam Lazarre-White. 2022. 5hr. Listening Library, DD (9780593560228). Gr. 4–7. This versatile, talented narrator brings Isaiah's start of middle school to life through culturally authentic use of tone, pace, and intonation. This sequel to *Isaiah Dunn Is My Hero* stands on its own.

Kapaemahu. By Hinaleimoana Wong-Kalu, Dean Hamer, and Joe Wilson. Read by Hinaleimoana Wong-Kalu. 2022. .5hr. Listening Library, DD (9780593605929). Gr. 2–6. This bilingual recording is an ode to a 15th-century Indigenous Hawaiian legend about healing and the Mahu people with dual male and female spirit. A rich soundscape and poignant narration enrich and extend the engaging text.

Listen: How Evelyn Glennie, A Deaf Girl, Changed Percussion. By Shannon Stocker. Narrated by Elle Newlands. 17m. Listening Library, DD (9780593508985). PreS–Gr. 2. This picture book biography of a deaf girl who made her life about percussion is beautifully presented. Supported by a dynamic soundscape, the narrator effectively uses her voice in both the storyline and the distinct vocables.

Max and the Midknights and the Tower of Time. By Lincoln Peirce. Read by a full cast. 3hr. Listening Library, DD (9780593505601). Gr. 3–7. The medieval tale of a knight-in-training continues with Book 3 of the Max and the Midknights series, as Max strives to find her twin. The full cast, with each reader distinct and talented, provides what feels like a cinematic experience, often inviting

listeners to participate with humor and interactivity.

Mel Fell. By Corey R. Tabor. Illustrated by the author. Read by Noah Wall. 2022. 5.5m. Weston Woods, CD and book (9781338837971). PreS–K. Upbeat background music complements Mel the kingfisher's leap of faith, bringing it to life. As the stakes rise, so does the tempo and intensity of the music. The narrator's outstanding vocals capture an excited bird's story.

Onyeka and the Academy of the Sun. By Tolá Okogwu. Read by Nneka Okoye. 2022. 7.5hr. Simon & Schuster Audio, DD (9781797148953). Gr. 4+. Onyeka's unruly afro hair has always made her feel different, but when she learns that it has psychokinetic superpowers, everything changes. Nneka Okoye deftly switches between British and Nigerian accents, even using Pidgin English, adding authentic flair for listeners that pulls them even further into this story of self-discovery and acceptance.

The Patron Thief of Bread. By Lindsay Eager. Read by Moira Quirk. 2022. 12.5hr. Listening Library, DD (9780593632291). Gr. 6+. Moira Quirk's nuanced performance brings to life a large cast of characters, including a group of street urchins, a young thief turned baker's apprentice, and a grumpy gargoyle who watches them all from a cathedral high above their medieval town.

The Peach Rebellion. By Wendelin Van Draanen. Narrated by Emily Ellet and Lauri Jo Daniels. 2022. 12h. Listening Library, DD (9780593584996). Gr. 8+. This story of childhood friends coming of age in the years following the Great Depression is brought to life by dual narrators who fully embody the young heroines. This recording captures issues of class, young love, and adolescence with the talents of two skilled performers.

The Rainbow Parade. By Emily Neilson. Read by the author. 2022. 7min. Listening Library, DD (9780593593486). PreS–Gr. 2. With perfect pacing, a rich soundscape, and lively narration, this joyful recording celebrates the LGBTQ+ community as a girl marches in a Pride parade with her two moms for the first time. Based on the author's lived experience.

Real Pigeons Eat Danger (Book 2). By Andrew McDonald. Read by Sean Kenin Elias-

Reyes. 2022. 2.75hr. Listening Library, DD (9780593560068). Gr. 2–6. Elias-Reyes presents a performance that immerses the listener in the adventures of a group of crime-fighting pigeons. Through effective vocal characterizations as well as balanced music and sound effects, the audio carries the story along as the pigeons work to solve cases in their park neighborhood.

The Road to After. By Rebekah Lowell. Read by Elena Rey. 2022. 2.5hr. Listening Library, DD (9780593590287). Gr. 6+. Rey's authentic narration chronicles 11-year-old Lacey as she, her sisters, and her mother flee their home after years living with domestic violence. With raw vulnerability, this nuanced performance sensitively captures a story of pain, trauma, and hope for renewal and recovery.

Rules for Vampires. By Alex Foulkes. Read by Kristin Atherton. 2021. 9hr. Simon & Schuster Audio, DD (9781797134499). Gr. 4–7. The narrator's vocal range captures Eleonora's Birthnight perfectly. With a wide range of accents, this recording expands and elevates the text. It is a tale of vampires that is not canned or overdone.

Standing in the Need of Prayer. By Carole Boston Weatherford. Read and sung by the author. 2022. 19min. Listening Library, DD (9780593613702). Gr. 1–4. This retelling of the classic spiritual incorporates struggles and triumphs of African American history and is presented in a careful, authentic, and dynamic way by the author. Accented throughout by deliberately selected background music, the text is elevated when the author sings at the conclusion of the book in a beautifully personal way.

Stuntboy, in the Meantime. By Jason Reynolds. Read by a full cast. 2021. 2hr 47min. Simon & Schuster Audio, DD. (9781508246237). Gr. 2–6. Portico's adventures in his apartment building are brought to life in a dynamic and playful way that transports the listener in this high-energy and thrilling chapter book. With a full cast and a soundscape that blends seamlessly with the narration, listeners will not be able to help being drawn into the fun. (2023 Odyssey Award for Children)

This Is Music: Drums. By Rekha S. Rajan. Read by the author. 2022. 7 minutes. Listening Library, DD (9780593634530). PreS–Gr. 1

This Is Music: Horns. By Rekha S. Rajan. Read by the author. 2022. 8 minutes. Listening Library, DD (9780593634554). PreS–Gr. 1. This introduction to a family of musical instruments for our youngest listeners is dynamic and engaging. Listeners hear the different types of instruments in the family during the introduction of the book. The sounds are then matched with the name and purpose and other facts for each specific instrument. Listeners are invited to "name that sound" at the end of the recording.

The Three Billy Goats Gruff. By Mac Barnett. Read by the author. 2022. 20min. Scholastic, Inc., DD (9781338897609). PreS–Gr. 2. Filled with music, forest sounds, and talented narration, Mac Barnett's ability to capture energy and humor coupled with the zestful soundscape brings this retelling of a classic folk tale to life. (2023 Odyssey Honor)

Three Strike Summer. By Skyler Schrempp. Read by the author. 2022. 7hr. Simon & Schuster Audio, DD (9781797148182). Gr. 5+. From dried-up farmland to the peach orchards of California, Gloria Mae and her family are barely surviving the Great Depression. This novel reveals challenges faced by 1930s crop pickers and the heart of a young girl set on playing baseball. A single narrator (the author) adeptly delivers multiple characters and emotional tension using no bells and whistles, just powerful pacing and believable Oklahoma accents.

Watercress. By Andrea Wang. Illustrated by Jason Chin. Read by Sunny Lu. 2022. 8m. Weston Woods, CD and book, (9781338811216). PreS–Gr. 2. A young girl is embarrassed when her family stops to gather watercress from a roadside ditch. She has a change of heart when her parents share their stories of life in China over dinner. The audio elevates the text authentically and gently. The background music is culturally respectful.

When Grandfather Flew. By Patricia MacLachlan. Illustrated by Chris Sheban. Read by Katie Schorr and George Guidall. 2022. 9m. Live Oak Media, CD and book (9781430144977). K–Gr. 3. This picture book recording offers listeners a full sensory experience. Bird calls, sound effects, and even pleasing contrasts between characters are presented by two skilled narrators who evoke this love story between a grandfather's awe and reverence for birds and his grandchildren's affection for the man who taught them to pay attention.

Wishes. By Mượn Thị Văn. Illustrated by Victo Ngai. Read by Mượn Thị Văn. Music by Ernest Troost. 2021. 17m. Weston Woods, CD and book, (9781338825992). PreS–Gr. 2. With subtle background music and sound effects, Văn narrates this emotional story of escape and starting over. The audio conveys the emotions of the journey and provides an immersive experience when paired with the text and illustrations.

Notable Children's Digital Media

The Association for Library Service to Children (ALSC), a division of the American Library Association, produces this annual list covering a diverse array of digital media for children 14 and younger. The Notable Children's Digital Media list recognizes real-time, dynamic, and interactive media content that enables and encourages active engagement and social interaction while informing, educating, and entertaining in exemplary ways. This list represents the titles selected by the committee for the first half of 2022 and titles added in January 2023.

Art Adventure. App: iOS and Google Play. Younger. Middle. Crafts & Hobbies. https://www.foxandsheep.com/apps-for-kids/artadventure. Art Adventure is an app designed to encourage children and their caregivers to be creative with various shapes, colors, and texts as they design their own masterpiece. The collage art style differentiates this app from many of the other coloring and drawing apps for children. Available in English, Dutch, French, German, Italian, Japanese, Korean, Portuguese, Russian, Simplified Chinese, Spanish, Swedish, and Turkish.

Audio Adventure. App: iOS and Google Play. Younger. Middle. Literature. https://www.foxandsheep.com/apps-for-kids/audio-adventure-sound-studio. Audio Adventure is an app that allows children to develop their own radio dramas using their own sound creations and a selection of various sound effects and background music. Controls are intuitive and easy to use, making this a fun, creative storytelling experience. Available in English, Dutch, French, German, Italian, Japanese, Korean, Portuguese, Russian, Simplified Chinese, Spanish, Swedish, and Turkish.

Daniel Tiger for Parents. App: iOS and Android. Younger. Parents/Caregivers. Songs, Music. https://pbskids.org/apps/daniel-tiger-for-parents.html. Daniel Tiger for Parents is a free app library of songs and videos from the PBS KIDS series *Daniel Tiger's Neighborhood*. The content is simple, educational, and entertaining, and it includes songs on social-emotional topics and skills such as feelings, self-control, and responsibility. Also included are video clips, conversation starters, and tips for parents that model and help with how to use these songs with their children in everyday life. Available in English and Spanish.

Labo Doodle. App: iOS and Google Play. Younger. Crafts & Hobbies. https://www.labolado.com. Labo Doodle is a step-by-step drawing education app for children that they can use to create their own characters and learn how to draw them. In addition to learning how to draw, they can use their imaginations and free-draw on the drawing board. Available in English, Arabic, Catalan, Croatian, Czech, Danish, Dutch, Finnish, French, German, Greek, Hebrew, Hindi, Hungarian, Indonesian, Italian, Japanese, Korean, Malay, Norwegian Bokmål, Polish, Portuguese, Romanian, Russian, Simplified Chinese, Slovak, Spanish, Swedish, Thai, Traditional Chinese, Turkish, Ukrainian, and Vietnamese.

Light and Color by Tinybop. App: iOS. Younger. Middle. Science, Nature, Environment. https://tinybop.com/apps/light-and-color. Light and Color, a paid app by Tinybop, teaches about color and light by allowing children to explore these topics in a variety of ways. Children can mix colors; hunt for colors in their world; line up blocks in order of shades, tints, and gradients; and play with color and light. They can use the "Understand" section to see the world through a dog's eye view or "Connect" to think about how colors and emotions interact. Interactive labels can toggle on and off. Available in 50+ different languages.

MathTango. App: iOS. Younger. Middle. Math. https://www.originatorkids.com/mathtango. With MathTango, earn monster badges, complete missions, build unique worlds, and practice valuable math skills. MathTango allows students in grades K–5 to practice and build their addition, subtraction, multiplication, and division skills through engaging puzzles and activities. Available in English.

National Museum of African American History and Culture Learning Lab. Website. Younger. Middle. American History, Civil Rights,

History, Social Sciences. https://learninglab. si.edu/org/nmaahc. This interactive website shares resources from the National Museum of African American History and Culture organized in curated collections for a variety of age groups. Utilizing objects, documents, imagery, and videos that enhance historical content knowledge as well as the guided activities and lessons provided, users can hone historical thinking skills and be inspired to see themselves as agents of change. Available in English.

Ology: Science for Kids. App: iPadOS. Younger. Middle. Natural History, Science. https:// www.amnh.org/explore/ology. Created by the educators at the American Museum of Natural History, the free Ology app allows school-age children to play fun interactive games, watch videos, and read articles about all kinds of science. The interface is bright and eye-catching, and content areas are well-organized while also creating plenty of opportunity for discovery. Available in English, with some videos also available in Spanish.

Rebel Girls. App: iOS. All Ages. Literature, History, Social Sciences. https://www.rebel girls.com/audio. Kids of all ages can listen to more than 150 engaging stories, soundscapes, and activities featuring a variety of amazing women. The Rebel Girls app features stories of present-day heroes and historical figures from the award-winning podcast "Good Night Stories for Rebel Girls." Listeners can browse based on interest or length of story. Each story is 10–20 minutes in length. Available in English.

Sago Mini First Words. App: iOS. Younger. Parents/Caregivers. Language. https://sago mini.com/first-words. This paid, subscription-model app, created in consultation with speech-language pathologists, provides learning games that offer opportunities for young children to practice speaking skills such as articulation and pronunciation. Activities, updated monthly, center around topics that children are naturally interested in, helping to build vocabulary and create curiosity. Available in English.

Sesame Street in Communities. Website. Younger. Parents/Caregivers. Crafts & Hobbies, Health & Medicine. https://sesamestreetin communities.org. A free website that provides activities, videos, and tips for parents in family interactions and conversations, from the everyday to the more difficult. Topics include grief, divorce, daily routine, eating well, family bonding, and more. Each video or activity is accompanied by a helpful list of opportunities and suggestions for conversation. Available in English and Spanish.

Spellie. Website. Middle. Language. https:// spelliegame.com. This free website is a simple spelling guessing game for kids that has been compared to Wordle. Spellie has three modes: easy (4 letters with one hint given), medium, and hard. You "unlock" an emoji for that word for your "collection" (in easy/medium), the website gives hints if needed, and there are some options in the settings (capitals or lowercase, keyboard layout or alphabetical, high contrast). Available in English.

Swift Playgrounds. App: iOS. Middle. Computer Science. https://www.apple.com/ swift/playgrounds. Swift Playgrounds is a free app created specifically for iPad and Mac that teaches users how to use Swift, a programming language created by Apple. Fun activities and interactive walkthroughs show beginners where to start, while advanced users can learn to create their own real-life apps. The interface is user-friendly and intuitive, creating a fun learning experience. Available in 14 different languages.

Teach Monster: Number Skills. App: iOS and Android. Younger. Science. https://www. teachyourmonster.org/numberskills. Teach Monster: Number Skills is a free app designed for children to practice number recognition, counting, and simple addition through various games. The focus is up to number 5. Participants have opportunities to revisit favorite games and build their skills. Available in English.

Thinkrolls Play & Code School. App: iOS. Younger. Middle. Computer Science. https://www.avokiddo.com. Thinkrolls Play & Code School is a paid, subscription-model app in which children can solve various logic puzzles, play memory games, create their own puzzles, play puzzles created by others, and more. The wide variety of activities are fun and help to build computational thinking skills. Available in English, Dutch, French, German, Japanese, Korean, Portuguese, Russian, Simplified Chinese, Spanish, and Swedish.

Top Ten Book Lists, 2022

Sources included in this roundup of 2022's bestselling and most popular books are *Publishers Weekly*, *USA Today*, Barnes & Noble, Amazon, and Goodreads for print titles and Amazon for Kindle. Library-centric lists include the top ten adult print book checkouts reported by two major U.S. public library systems—New York Public Library and San Diego County Library—and the ten most popular library e-books and audiobooks as reported by OverDrive. [Due to varying selection criteria among the sources, apples-to-apples comparisons are not practicable.—*Ed.*]

Print Bestsellers

Publishers Weekly

1. *Activities of Daily Living*, Lisa Hsiao Chen
2. *All the Lovers in the Night*, Mieko Kawakami, trans. from the Japanese by Sam Bett and David Boyd
3. *The Birdcatcher*, Gayl Jones
4. *Ducks: Two Years in the Oil Sands*, Kate Beaton
5. *The Furrows*, Namwali Serpell
6. *G-Man: J. Edgar Hoover and the Making of the American Century*, Beverly Gage
7. *The Grimkes: The Legacy of Slavery in an American Family*, Kerri K. Greenidge
8. *An Immense World: How Animal Senses Reveal the Hidden Realms Around Us*, Ed Yong
9. *The Invisible Kingdom: Reimagining Chronic Illness*, Meghan O'Rourke
10. *The Rabbit Hutch*, Tess Gunty

USA Today

1. *It Starts with Us*, Colleen Hoover
2. *The Choice*, Nora Roberts
3. *The Light We Carry*, Michelle Obama
4. *Diary of a Wimpy Kid: Diper Överlöde*, Jeff Kinney
5. *It Ends with Us*, Colleen Hoover
6. *Verity*, Colleen Hoover
7. *Ugly Love*, Colleen Hoover
8. *The Boys from Biloxi*, John Grisham
9. *Where the Crawdads Sing*, Delia Owens
10. *The Whittiers*, Danielle Steel

Barnes & Noble

1. *Lessons in Chemistry*, Bonnie Garmus
2. *The Light We Carry: Overcoming in Uncertain Times*, Michelle Obama
3. *I'm Glad My Mom Died*, Jennette McCurdy
4. *Our Missing Hearts*, Celeste Ng
5. *A World of Curiosities*, Louise Penny
6. *Babel: Or, The Necessity of Violence: An Arcane History of the Oxford Translators' Revolution*, R.F. Kuang
7. *The Song of the Cell: An Exploration of Medicine and the New Human*, Siddhartha Mukherjee
8. *The Rabbit Hutch*, Tess Gunty
9. *Prisoners of the Castle: An Epic Story of Survival and Escape from Colditz, the Nazis' Fortress Prison*, Ben Macintyre
10. *Skandar and the Unicorn Thief*, A.F. Steadman

Amazon

1. *It Ends with Us*, Colleen Hoover
2. *It Starts with Us*, Colleen Hoover
3. *Verity*, Colleen Hoover
4. *Where the Crawdads Sing*, Delia Owens
5. *Atomic Habits: An Easy & Proven Way to Build Good Habits & Break Bad Ones*, James Clear
6. *Reminders of Him*, Colleen Hoover
7. *Ugly Love*, Colleen Hoover
8. *The Seven Husbands of Evelyn Hugo*, Taylor Jenkins Reid
9. *The Body Keeps the Score: Brain, Mind, and Body in the Healing of Trauma*, Bessel van der Kolk, M.D.
10. *The Very Hungry Caterpillar*, Eric Carle

Goodreads Most Popular Books Added by Readers

1. *Reminders of Him*, Colleen Hoover
2. *It Starts with Us*, Colleen Hoover
3. *Book Lovers*, Emily Henry
4. *Things We Never Got Over*, Lucy Score
5. *Tomorrow, and Tomorrow, and Tomorrow*, Gabrielle Zevin
6. *Lessons in Chemistry*, Bonnie Garmus
7. *I'm Glad My Mom Died*, Jennette McCurdy
8. *The Paris Apartment*, Lucy Foley
9. *The Maid*, Nita Prose
10. *Every Summer After*, Carley Fortune

Digital Bestsellers

Amazon Kindle

1. *Reminders of Him*, Colleen Hoover
2. *Things We Never Got Over*, Lucy Score
3. *The Perfect Marriage*, Jeneva Rose
4. *The Housemaid*, Freida McFadden
5. *Verity*, Colleen Hoover
6. *My Evil Mother*, Margaret Atwood
7. *Where the Crawdads Sing*, Delia Owens
8. *Regretting You*, Colleen Hoover
9. *It Ends with Us*, Colleen Hoover
10. *The Locked Door*, Freida McFadden

Top Print, Digital, and Audiobook Titles from the Library

New York Public Library Top Ten Checkouts System-Wide†

1. *The Midnight Library*, Matt Haig
2. *Lessons in Chemistry*, Bonnie Garmus
3. *The Lincoln Highway*, Amor Towles
4. *Malibu Rising*, Taylor Jenkins Reid
5. *People We Meet on Vacation*, Emily Henry
6. *This Time Tomorrow*, Emma Straub
7. *The Seven Husbands of Evelyn Hugo*, Taylor Jenkins Reid
8. *Book Lovers*, Emily Henry
9. *Verity*, Colleen Hoover
10. *It Ends with Us*, Colleen Hoover

San Diego County Library Top Ten Checkouts System-Wide†

1. *The Last Thing He Told Me*, Laura Dave
2. *Apples Never Fall*, Lianne Moriarty
3. *Where the Crawdads Sing*, Delia Owens
4. *The Vanishing Half*, Brit Bennett
5. *The Paris Apartment*, Lucy Foley
6. *The Seven Husbands of Evelyn Hugo*, Taylor Jenkins Reid
7. *The Lincoln Highway*, Amor Towles
8. *The Four Winds*, Kristin Hannah
9. *The Invisible Life of Addie LaRue*, V.E. Schwab
10. *Book Lovers*, Emily Henry

† Lists include adult fiction and nonfiction checkouts only.

OverDrive's Top Ten Most Popular Library E-Books and Audiobooks

E-Books

1. *The Last Thing He Told Me*, Laura Dave
2. *Apples Never Fall*, Liane Moriarty
3. *The Four Winds*, Kristin Hannah
4. *Verity*, Colleen Hoover
5. *The Seven Husbands of Evelyn Hugo*, Taylor Jenkins Reid
6. *The Lincoln Highway*, Amor Towles
7. *It Ends with Us*, Colleen Hoover
8. *The Girl in His Shadow*, Audrey Blake
9. *The Judge's List*, John Grisham
10. *The Invisible Life of Addie LaRue*, V.E. Schwab

Audiobooks

1. *Where the Crawdads*, Delia Owens
2. *The Last Thing He Told Me*, Laura Dave
3. *The Four Winds*, Kristin Hannah
4. *Apples Never Fall*, Liane Moriarty
5. *The Guest List*, Lucy Foley
6. *Atomic Habits*, James Clear
7. *Dune*, Frank Herbert
8. *The Subtle Art of Not Giving a F*ck*, Mark Manson
9. *The Seven Husbands of Evelyn Hugo*, Taylor Jenkins Reid
10. *Pride and Prejudice*, Jane Austen

Literary Prizes, 2022

Compiled by the staff of *Library and Book Trade Almanac*

Academy of American Poets Fellowship ($25,000). For outstanding poetic achievement. *Offered by:* Academy of American Poets. *Winner:* Jericho Brown.

Academy of American Poets Laureate Fellowships ($50,000 each). Emanuelee Outspoken Bean, Poet Laureate Fellow, Houston, Texas; Cyrus Cassells, Poet Laureate Fellow, Texas; Andru Defeye, Poet Laureate Fellow, Sacramento, California; Ashanti Files, Poet Laureate Fellow, Urbana, Illinois; B.K. Fischer, Poet Laureate Fellow, Westchester County, New York; KaNikki Jakarta, Poet Laureate Fellow, Alexandria, Virginia; Ashley M. Jones, Poet Laureate Fellow, Alabama; Holly Karapetkova, Poet Laureate Fellow, Arlington, Virginia; Kealoha, Poet Laureate Fellow, Hawaii; J. Drew Lanham, Poet Laureate Fellow, Edgefield, South Carolina; Julia B. Levine, Poet Laureate Fellow, Davis, California; Matt Mason, Poet Laureate Fellow, Nebraska; Airea D. Matthews, Poet Laureate Fellow, Philadelphia, Pennsylvania; Ray McNiece, Poet Laureate Fellow, Cleveland Heights, Ohio; Huascar Medina, Poet Laureate Fellow, Kansas; Gailmarie Pahmeier, Poet Laureate Fellow, Nevada; Catherine Pierce, Poet Laureate Fellow, Mississippi; Rena Priest, Poet Laureate Fellow, Washington; Lynne Thompson, Poet Laureate Fellow, Los Angeles, California; Emma Trelles, Poet Laureate Fellow, Santa Barbara, California; Gwen Nell Westerman, Poet Laureate Fellow, Minnesota; Crystal Wilkinson, Poet Laureate Fellow, Kentucky.

Jane Addams Children's Book Awards. For children's books that effectively promote the cause of peace, social justice, world community, and equality. *Offered by:* Jane Addams Peace Association. *Winners:* (younger children) Alicia D. Williams (author) and April Harrison (illustrator) for *Shirley Chisholm Dared: The Story of the First Black Woman in Congress* (Anne Schwartz Books); (older children) Veera Hiranandani for *How to Find What You're Not Looking For* (Kokila, an imprint of Random House, LLC).

Aesop Prize. For outstanding illustrated children's publications utilizing folkloric themes. *Offered by:* American Folklore Society. *Winners:* Angela McAllister (author) and Anna Shepeta (illustrator) for *A Bedtime Full of Stories: 50 Folktales and Legends from Around the World* (Frances Lincoln Children's Books); Nadja Spiegelman (author) and Sergio Garcia Sanchez (illustrator) for *Blancaflor, The Hero with Secret Powers: A Folktale from Latin America* (TOON Graphics).

Agatha Awards. For mystery writing in the method exemplified by author Agatha Christie. *Offered by:* Malice Domestic Ltd. *Winners:* (contemporary novel) Ellen Byron for *Cajun Kiss of Death* (Crooked Lane Books); (first novel) Mia P. Manansala for *Arsenic and Adobo* (Berkley); (historical) Lori Rader-Day for *Death at Greenway* (HarperCollins); (young adult) Alan Orloff for *I Play One on TV* (Down & Out Books); (nonfiction) Lee Child and Laurie R. King (editors) for *How to Write a Mystery: A Handbook from Mystery Writers of America* (Simon & Schuster); (short story) Shawn Reilly Simmons for "Bay of Reckoning" in *Murder on the Beach* (Destination Murders).

Ambroggio Prize ($1,000 and publication by the University of Arizona Press). *Offered by:* Academy of American Poets. For a book-length poetry manuscript originally written in Spanish and with an English translation. *Winner:* Elizabeth Torres for *La Lotería: Sorteo Nocturno/The Lottery: Nocturnal Sweepstakes* (University of Arizona Press).

American Academy of Arts and Letters Award of Merit ($25,000). Given annually, in rotation, for a short story, sculpture, novel, poetry, drama, or painting. *Offered by:* American Academy of Arts and Letters. *Winner:* Stephen Dobyns (poetry).

American Academy of Arts and Letters Awards in Literature ($10,000 each). To honor eight writers for exceptional accomplishment in any genre. *Offered by:* American Academy of Arts and Letters. *Winners:* Catherine Barnett, Jo Ann Beard, Aleshea Harris, Sarah

Manguso, Joyelle McSweeney, Susan Brind Morrow, Doug Peacock, Adrian Nathan West.

American Academy of Arts and Letters Blake-Dodd Prize ($25,000). Triennial prize to a nonfiction writer. *Offered by:* American Academy of Arts and Letters. *Winner (2020):* Janine Di Giovanni.

American Academy of Arts and Letters Benjamin H. Danks Award ($20,000). Given annually, in rotation, to a composer of ensemble works, a playwright, and a writer. *Offered by:* American Academy of Arts and Letters. *Winner:* Martyna Majok (drama).

American Academy of Arts and Letters E.M. Forster Award ($20,000). To a young writer from the United Kingdom or Ireland for a stay in the United States. *Offered by:* American Academy of Arts and Letters. Not awarded in 2022.

American Academy of Arts and Letters Gold Medal in Drama. For distinguished achievement. *Offered by:* American Academy of Arts and Letters. *Winner:* Adrienne Kennedy.

American Academy of Arts and Letters Gold Medal in Graphic Arts. For distinguished achievement. *Offered by:* American Academy of Arts and Letters. *Winner:* Kara Walker.

American Academy of Arts and Letters William Dean Howells Medal. Given once every five years in recognition of the most distinguished American novel published during that period. *Offered by:* American Academy of Arts and Letters. *Winner (2020):* Richard Powers for *The Overstory* (W.W. Norton & Company).

American Academy of Arts and Letters Sue Kaufman Prize for First Fiction ($5,000). For a work of first fiction (novel or short stories). *Offered by:* American Academy of Arts and Letters. *Winner:* Jackie Polzin for *Brood* (Doubleday).

American Academy of Arts and Letters Addison M. Metcalf Award ($10,000). Given biennially to a young writer of fiction, nonfiction, drama, or poetry. *Offered by:* American Academy of Arts and Letters. *Winner (2021):* Kali Fajardo-Anstine.

American Academy of Arts and Letters Katherine Anne Porter Award ($20,000). Awarded biennially to a prose writer of demonstrated achievement. *Offered by:* American Academy of Arts and Letters. *Winner (2022):* Lynne Tillman.

American Academy of Arts and Letters Arthur Rense Poetry Prize ($20,000). Triennial prize to an exceptional poet. *Offered by:* American Academy of Arts and Letters. *Winner (2020):* Mary Ruefle.

American Academy of Arts and Letters Rosenthal Family Foundation Award ($10,000). To a young writer of considerable literary talent for a work of fiction. *Offered by:* American Academy of Arts and Letters. *Winner:* Kirstin Valdez Quade for *The Five Wounds* (W.W. Norton & Company).

American Academy of Arts and Letters John Updike Award ($10,000). Biennial prize to a writer in midcareer whose work has demonstrated consistent excellence. *Offered by:* American Academy of Arts and Letters. *Winners (2021):* Stephen Adly Guirgis and Diane Seuss.

American Academy of Arts and Letters Harold D. Vursell Memorial Award ($20,000). To a writer whose work merits recognition for the quality of its prose style. *Offered by:* American Academy of Arts and Letters. *Winner:* Joshua Cohen.

American Academy of Arts and Letters Christopher Lightfoot Walker Award ($100,000). Biennial award to a writer of fiction or nonfiction who has made a significant contribution to American literature. *Offered by:* American Academy of Arts and Letters. *Winner (2022):* Phillip Lopate.

American Academy of Arts and Letters E.B. White Award ($10,000). Biennial award to a writer for achievement in children's literature. *Offered by:* American Academy of Arts and Letters. *Winner (2021):* Kate DiCamillo.

American Book Awards. For literary achievement by people of various ethnic backgrounds. *Offered by:* Before Columbus Foundation. *Winners:* Spencer Ackerman for *Reign of Terror: How the 9/11 Era Destabilized America and Produced Trump* (Viking); Esther G. Belin, Jeff Burgland, Connie A. Jacobs, and Anthony K. Webster (editors) for *The Diné Reader: An Anthology of Navajo Literature* (University of Arizona Press); Emma Brodie for *Songs in Ursa Major* (Knopf); Daphne A. Brooks for

Liner Notes for the Revolution: The Intellectual Life of Black Feminist Sound (Harvard University Press); Myriam J.A. Chancy for *What Storm, What Thunder* (Tin House Books); Francisco Goldman for *Monkey Boy* (Grove Press); Zakiya Dalila Harris for *The Other Black Girl: A Novel* (Atria Books); Fatima Shaik for *Economy Hall: The Hidden History of a Free Black Brotherhood* (The Historic New Orleans Collection); Edwin Torres for *Quanundrum: [i will be your many angled thing]* (Roof Books); Truong Tran for *Book of the Other: Small in Comparison* (Kaya Press); Mai Der Vang for *Yellow Rain* (Graywolf Press); Phillip B. Williams for *Mutiny* (Penguin Books); Michelle Zauner for *Crying in H Mart: A Memoir* (Knopf); (lifetime achievement) Gayl Jones; (Walter & Lillian Lowenfels Criticism Award) Jessica E. Teague for *Sound Recording Technology and American Literature, from the Phonograph to the Remix* (Cambridge University Press); (anti-censorship award) Jeffrey St. Clair (editor) for *CounterPunch* (magazine); (editor/publisher award) Wave Books: Charlie Wright (publisher) and Joshua Beckman (editor in chief).

American Indian Youth Literature Awards. Offered biennially to recognize excellence in books by and about American Indians. *Offered by:* American Indian Library Association. *Winners (2022):* (picture book) Daniel W. Vandever (author) and Corey Begay (illustrator) for *Herizon* (South of Sunrise Creative); (middle school) Brian Young for *Healer of the Water Monster* (Heartdrum, an imprint of HarperCollins); (young adult) Eric Gansworth for *Apple Skin to the Core* (Levine Querido).

American Poetry Review/Honickman First Book Prize in Poetry ($3,000 and publication of the book). To encourage excellence in poetry and to provide a wide readership for a deserving first book of poems. *Winner:* Chelsea Harlan for *Bright Shade* (Copper Canyon Press).

Américas Book Award for Children's and Young Adult Literature. To recognize U.S. works of fiction, poetry, folklore, or selected nonfiction that authentically and engagingly portray Latin America, the Caribbean, or Latinos in the United States.

Sponsor: Consortium of Latin American Studies Programs (CLASP). *Winners:* Gloria Amescua (author) and Duncan Tonatiuh (illustrator) for *Child of the Flower-Song People* (Abrams ComicArts); David Bowles (author) and Erika Meza for *My Two Border Towns* (Kokila).

Hans Christian Andersen Literature Award (500,000 Danish kroner, about $73,000). Biennial prize to a writer whose work can be compared with that of Andersen. *Offered by:* Hans Christian Andersen Literary Committee. *Winner (2022):* Karl Ove Knausgård.

Anthony Awards. For superior mystery writing. *Offered by:* Bouchercon World Mystery Convention. *Winners:* (novel) S.A. Cosby for *Razorblade Tears* (Flatiron Books); (first novel) Mia P. Manansala for *Arsenic and Adobo* (Berkley); (paperback original/ebook/audiobook original novel) Jess Lourey for *Bloodline* (Thomas & Mercer); (short story) S.A. Cosby for "Not My Cross to Bear" in *Trouble No More: Crime Fiction Inspired by Southern Rock and the Blues* (Down & Out Books); (critical/nonfiction) Lee Child and Laurie R. King (editors) for *How to Write a Mystery: A Handbook from Mystery Writers of America* (Simon & Schuster); (juvenile/young adult) Alan Orloff for *I Play One on TV* (Down & Out Books); (anthology/collection) Hank Phillippi Ryan (editor) for *This Time for Sure: Bouchercon Anthology 2021* (Down & Out Books).

Asian/Pacific American Awards for Literature. For books that promote Asian/Pacific American culture and heritage. Sponsor: Asian/Pacific American Librarians Association (APALA). *Winners:* (adult fiction) Hiromi Goto (author) and Ann Xu (illustrator) for *Shadow Life* (First Second, an imprint of Macmillan Children's Publishing Group); (adult nonfiction) Grace M. Cho for *Tastes Like War: A Memoir* (Feminist Press); (young adult) Malinda Lo for *Last Night at the Telegraph Club* (Dutton Books for Young Readers, an imprint of Penguin Young Readers, a division of Penguin Random House); (children's) Hena Khan for *Amina's Song* (Salaam Reads/Simon & Schuster Books for Young Readers); (picture book) Andrea Wang (author) and Jason Chin (illustrator) for *Watercress* (Neal Porter Books).

Aspen Words Literary Prize ($35,000). For a work of fiction that illuminates a vital contemporary issue and demonstrates the transformative power of literature on thought and culture. *Winner:* Dawnie Walton for *The Final Revival of Opal and Nev* (37 Ink).

Astounding Award for Best New Writer (formerly the John W. Campbell Award for Best New Writer). For the best new science fiction or fantasy writer whose first work of science fiction or fantasy was published in a professional publication in the previous two years. *Offered by:* Dell Magazines. *Winner:* Shelley Parker-Chan for *She Who Became the Sun* (Tor Books).

Atwood Gibson Writers' Trust Prize for Fiction (C$60,000) (Canada). *Offered by:* Writers' Trust of Canada. *Winner:* Nicholas Herring for *Some Hellish* (Goose Lane Editions).

Audio Publishers Association Awards (Audies). To recognize excellence in audiobooks. *Winners:* (audiobook of the year) *Project Hail Mary* by Andy Weir, narrated by Ray Porter (Audible Studios); (drama) *Sherlock Holmes-The Seamstress of Peckham Rye* by Jonathan Barnes, performed by Nicholas Briggs, Richard Earl, Lucy Briggs-Owen, India Fisher, James Joyce, Anjella MacKintosh, Glen McCready, and Mark Elstob (Big Finish Productions); (autobiography/memoir) *Somebody's Daughter* by Ashley C. Ford, narrated by Ashley C. Ford (Macmillan Audio); (best female narrator) *The Parted Earth* by Anjali Enjeti, narrated by Deepti Gupta (Novel audio); (best male narrator) *Aristotle and Dante Dive into the Waters of the World* by Benjamin Alire Sáenz, narrated by Lin-Manuel Miranda (Simon & Schuster Audio); (business/personal development) *Machiavelli for Women* by Stacey Vanek Smith, narrated by Stacey Vanek Smith (Simon & Schuster Audio); (faith-based fiction or nonfiction) *The Gift of Black Folk* by W.E.B. Du Bois, narrated by Arnell Powell (Brilliance Publishing); (fantasy) *Rhythm of War* by Brandon Sanderson, narrated by Michael Kramer and Kate Reading (Macmillan Audio); (fiction) *The Final Revival of Opal & Nev* by Dawnie Walton, narrated by Janina Edwards, Bahni Turpin, James Langton, Gabra Zackman, Dennis Boutsikaris, Steve West, André De Shields, Matthew Lloyd Davies, David Sadzin, Fiona Hardingham,

George Newbern, Leon Nixon, Ines del Castillo, Jackie Sanders, Leon Nixon, Pete Simonelli, Priya Ayyar, and Robin Miles (Simon & Schuster Audio); (history/biography) *Clanlands: Whisky, Warefare, and a Scottish Adventure Like No Other* by Sam Heughan and Graham McTavish, narrated by Sam Heughan and Graham McTavish (Hodder & Stoughton); (humor) *How Y'all Doing?* by Leslie Jordan, narrated by Leslie Jordan (HarperAudio); (literary fiction and classics) *All Creatures Great and Small* by James Herriot, narrated by Nicholas Ralph (Macmillan Audio); (middle grade) *Playing the Cards You're Dealt* by Varian Johnson, narrated by Dion Graham (Scholastic Audio); (multivoiced performance) *Heresy* by Melissa Lenhardt, narrated by Barrie Kreinik, Bailey Carr, Ella Turenne, Nikki Massoud, Natalie Naudus, Imani Jade Powers, and James Fouhey (Hachette Audio); (mystery) *Later* by Stephen King, narrated by Seth Numrich (Simon & Schuster Audio); (narration by the author or authors) *A Promised Land* by Barack Obama, narrated by Barack Obama (Penguin Random House Audio); (nonfiction) *The Joy of Sweat* by Sarah Everts, narrated by Sophie Amoss (Penguin Random House Audio); (original work) *Heroine* by Mary Jane Wells, narrated by Mary Jane Wells (Author's Republic); (romance) *Reel: Hollywood Renaissance, Book 1* by Kennedy Ryan, narrated by Eboni Flowers, Jakobi Diem, Nicole Small, and April Christina (Scribechick Media, LLC, produced by Lyric Audiobooks); (science fiction) *Project Hail Mary* by Andy Weir, narrated by Ray Porter (Audible Studios); (short stories/collections) *Blackout* by Dhonielle Clayton, Tiffany D. Jackson, Nic Stone, Angie Thomas, Ashley Woodfolk, and Nicola Yoon, narrated by Joniece Abbott-Pratt, Dion Graham, Imani Parks, Jordan Cobb, Shayna Small, A.J. Beckles, and Bahni Turpin (HarperAudio); (Spanish language) *La Casa de Bernarda Alba* by Federico García Lorca, narrated by Gloria Muñoz, Elena González, Rebeca Hernando, Carmen Mayordomo, Marta Poveda, Sol de la Barreda, Beatriz Melgares, Cristina Arias, and Antonio Martínez Asensio (Penguin Random House Grupo Editorial México); (thriller/suspense) *Local Woman Missing* by

Mary Kubica, narrated by Brittany Press-ley, Jennifer Jill Araya, Gary Tiedemann, and Jesse Vilinsky (HarperAudio); (young adult) *Be Dazzled* by Ryan La Sala, narrated by Pete Cross (Dreamscape Media); (young listeners up to age eight) *I and I Bob Marley* by Tony Medina, narrated by Jaime Lincoln Smith and Tony Medina (Live Oak Media).

Authors Guild Distinguished Service to the Literary Community Award. *Sponsor:* Authors Guild Foundation. *Winner:* Tracie D. Hall.

Authors Guild Literature That Inspires Change Award. *Sponsor:* Authors Guild Foundation. *Winners:* (author) Amanda Gorman; (publisher) David and Michelle Baldacci.

Bad Sex in Fiction Award (United Kingdom). To "draw attention to the crude, badly written, often perfunctory use of redundant passages of sexual description in the modern novel, and to discourage it." *Sponsor: Literary Review.* Not awarded in 2022.

Bailey's Women's Prize for Fiction. See Women's Prize for Fiction.

Baillie Gifford Prize for Non-Fiction (£50,000, about $63,000). For a nonfiction work published in the United Kingdom in English. *Offered by:* Board of Directors of The Samuel Johnson Prize for Non-Fiction Limited. *Sponsor:* Baillie Gifford. *Winner:* Katherine Rundell for *Super-Infinite: The Transformations of John Donne* (Faber & Faber).

Bancroft Prizes ($10,000). For books of exceptional merit and distinction in American history, American diplomacy, and the international relations of the United States. *Offered by:* Columbia University. *Winners:* Mia Bay for *Traveling Black: A Story of Race and Resistance* (Belknap Press/Harvard University Press); Mae Ngai for *The Chinese Question: The Gold Rushes and Global Politics* (W.W. Norton & Company).

Barnes & Noble Book of the Year. To honor the book that Barnes & Noble booksellers nominate as the book they are most proud to sell. *Offered by:* Barnes & Noble. *Winner:* Bonnie Garmus for *Lessons in Chemistry* (Doubleday).

Barnes & Noble Children's & Young Adult Book Awards. For emerging talent in children's publishing. *Offered by:* Barnes & Noble. *Winners:* (picture book) Christopher Denise for *Knight Owl* (Little, Brown Books for Young Readers); (young reader) Míriam

Bonastre Tur for *Hooky* (HarperCollins); (young adult) Xiran Jay Zhao for *Iron Widow* (Penguin Teen).

Barnes & Noble Discover Prize. For a new author of fiction. *Offered by:* Barnes & Noble. *Winner:* Tess Gunty for *The Rabbit Hutch* (Alfred A. Knopf/Penguin Random House).

Mildred L. Batchelder Award. To the American publisher of a children's book originally published in a language other than English and subsequently published in English in the United States. *Offered by:* American Library Association's Association for Library Service to Children. *Winner:* Yonder: Restless Books for Young Readers for *Temple Alley Summer,* originally published in Japanese as *Kimyōji Yokochō no Natsu,* written by Sachiko Kashiwaba, illustrated by Miho Satake, and translated by Avery Fischer Udagawa.

BBC National Short Story Award (United Kingdom) (£15,000, about $18,500). *Winner:* Saba Sams for "Blue 4Eva."

James Beard Foundation Book Awards. *Offered by:* James Beard Foundation. *Winners:* (baking and desserts) Kristina Cho for *Mooncakes and Milk Bread: Sweet and Savory Recipes Inspired by Chinese Bakeries* (Harper Horizon); (beverage with recipes) Julia Momosé with Emma Janzen for *The Way of the Cocktail: Japanese Traditions, Techniques, and Recipes* (Penguin Random House); (beverage without recipes) Mallory O'Meara for *Girly Drinks: A World History of Women and Alcohol* (Hanover Square Press); (general) Gregory Gourdet with JJ Goode for *Everyone's Table: Global Recipes for Modern Health* (Harper Wave); (international) Hawa Hassan with Julia Turshen for *In Bibi's Kitchen: The Recipes and Stories of Grandmothers from the Eight African Countries That Touch the Indian Ocean* (Ten Speed Press); (reference, history, and scholarship) Adrian Miller for *Black Smoke: African Americans and the United States of Barbecue* (University of North Carolina Press); (restaurant and professional) Brandon Jew and Tienlon Ho for *Mister Jiu's in Chinatown: Recipes and Stories from the Birthplace of Chinese American Food* (Ten Speed Press); (single subject) Jesse Griffiths for *The Hog Book: A Chef's Guide to Hunting, Butchering and Cooking Wild Pigs*

(Wild Hog Project); (U.S. foodways) Melissa M. Martin for *Mosquito Supper Club: Cajun Recipes from a Disappearing Bayou* (Artisan Books); (vegetable-focused cooking) Joanne Lee Molinaro for *The Korean Vegan Cookbook: Reflections and Recipes from Omma's Kitchen* (Avery); (visuals) Rob Palmer and Daniel New for *Take One Fish: The New School of Scale-to-Tail Cooking and Eating* (Hardie Grant); (writing) Marcia Chatelain for *Franchise: The Golden Arches in Black America* (Liveright); (cookbook hall of fame) Judy Rodgers for *The Zuni Café Cookbook: A Compendium of Recipes and Cooking Lessons from San Francisco's Beloved Restaurant* (W.W. Norton & Company); (emerging voice) Kristina Cho for *Mooncakes and Milk Bread: Sweet and Savory Recipes Inspired by Chinese Bakeries* (Harper Horizon).

Pura Belpré Awards. To a Latino/Latina writer and illustrator whose work portrays, affirms, and celebrates the Latino cultural experience in an outstanding work of literature for children and youth. *Offered by:* American Library Association's Association for Library Service to Children. *Winners:* (children's narrative) Donna Barba Higuera for *The Last Cuentista* (Levine Querido); (youth illustration) Raúl Gonzalez for *¡Vamos! Let's Cross the Bridge* (Versify, an imprint of HarperCollins Publishers); (young adult narrative) Raquel Vasquez Gilliland for *How Moon Fuentez Fell in Love with the Universe* (Simon & Schuster Books for Young Readers, an imprint of Simon & Schuster Children's Publishing Division).

Helen B. Bernstein Book Award for Excellence in Journalism ($15,000). To a journalist who has written at book length about an issue of contemporary concern. *Offered by:* New York Public Library. *Winner:* Andrea Elliott for *Invisible Child: Poverty, Survival and Hope in an American City* (Penguin Random House).

BIO Award. Presented to an individual for contributions to advancing the art and craft of biography. *Offered by:* Biographers International Organization. *Winner:* Megan Marshall.

The Black Caucus of the American Library Association (BCALA) and BiblioLabs E-book Literary Awards. For the best self-published e-books in fiction and poetry by an African American author in the U.S. *Winners:* (fiction) Nikki Marsh for *The JuJu Girl* (independently published); (poetry) Marquise Jackson for *I Forget I'm Only Human* (independently published).

Black Caucus of the American Library Association (BCALA) and *School Library Journal* Children and Youth Literary Awards. Honoring works by Black authors highlighting the diversity of the Black experience. *Winners:* (first novelist) Kaija Langley for *When Langston Dances* (Simon & Schuster); (fiction) Brittney Morris for *The Cost of Knowing* (Simon & Schuster); (nonfiction) Traci N. Todd (author) and Christian Robinson (illustrator) for *Nina: A Story of Nina Simone* (Penguin Random House); (graphic novel) David F. Walker (author) and Marcus Kwame Anderson (illustrator) for *The Black Panther Party: A Graphic Novel History* (Ten Speed Press).

Black Caucus of the American Library Association (BCALA) Literary Awards. *Winners:* (first novelist) Honorée Fanonne Jeffers for *The Love Songs of W.E.B. Du Bois: A Novel* (HarperCollins); (poetry) Jasmine Mans for *Black Girl, Call Home* (Berkley, an imprint of Penguin Random House); (fiction) S.A. Cosby for *Razorblade Tears* (Flatiron Books); (nonfiction) Cicely Tyson with Michelle Burford for *Just as I Am: A Memoir* (HarperCollins); (outstanding contribution to publishing) Ibram X. Kendi and Keisha N. Blain (editors) for *Four Hundred Souls: A Community History of African America, 1619–2019* (One World, an imprint of Random House).

Irma Simonton Black and James H. Black Award for Excellence in Children's Literature. To a book for young children in which the text and illustrations work together to create an outstanding whole. *Offered by:* Bank Street College of Education. *Winner:* The Fan Brothers for *It Fell from the Sky* (Simon & Schuster).

James Tait Black Memorial Prize (United Kingdom) (£10,000). To recognize literary excellence in fiction and biography. *Offered by:* University of Edinburgh. *Winners:* (fiction) Keith Ridgway for *A Shock* (Picador); (biography) Amit Chaudhuri for *Finding the Raga: An Improvisation on Indian Music* (Faber & Faber).

James Tait Black Prizes (United Kingdom) (£10,000, about $12,500). *Offered by:* University of Edinburgh's School of Literatures, Languages, and Cultures. *Winners:* (fiction) Keith Ridgway for *A Shock* (Picador); (biography) Amit Chaudhuri for *Finding the Raga: An Improvisation on Indian Music* (Faber).

Blue Peter Book of the Year (United Kingdom). To recognize excellence in children's books. Winners are chosen by a jury of viewers, ages 8–12, of the BBC television children's program *Blue Peter.* *Winners:* (best story) Hannah Gold (author) and Levi Pinfold (illustrator) for *The Last Bear* (HarperCollins); (best book with facts) Christiane Dorian (author) and Gosia Herba (illustrator) for *Invented by Animals* (Wide Eyed Editions/The Quarto Group).

Rebekah Johnson Bobbitt National Prize for Poetry ($10,000). A biennial prize for the most distinguished book of poetry written by an American and published during the preceding two years. *Offered by:* Library of Congress. *Donor:* Family of Rebekah Johnson Bobbitt. *Winners (2022):* Heid E. Erdrich for *Little Big Bully* (Penguin Books); (lifetime achievement) Rita Dove.

Booker Prize for Fiction (United Kingdom) (£50,000, about $62,000). For the best English-language novel. *Offered by:* Crankstart. *Winner:* Shehan Karunatilaka for *The Seven Moons of Maali Almeida* (Sort of Books).

Bookseller/Diagram Prize for Oddest Title of the Year. *Sponsor: The Bookseller* magazine. *Winners:* Lindsay Bryde and Tommy Mayberry for *RuPedagogies of Realness: Essays on Teaching and Learning with RuPaul's Drag Race* (McFarland & Company).

Boston Globe/Horn Book Awards. For excellence in children's literature. *Winners:* (fiction and poetry) Sabaa Tahir for *All My Rage* (Razorbill/Penguin Random House); (nonfiction) Brandy Colbert for *Black Birds in the Sky: The Story and Legacy of the 1921 Tulsa Race Massacre* (Balzer + Bray/HarperCollins); (picture book) Jason Reynolds (author) and Jason Griffin (illustrator) for *Ain't Burned All the Bright* (Atheneum/Caitlyn Dlouhy Books).

W.Y. Boyd Literary Award for Excellence in Military Fiction ($5,000). For a military novel that honors the service of American veterans during a time of war. *Offered by:* American Library Association. *Donor:* W.Y. Boyd II. *Winner:* Jeff Shaara for *The Eagle's Claw: A Novel of the Battle of Midway* (Ballantine Books).

Bracken Brower Prize (£15,000, about $18,600). To encourage young authors to tackle emerging business themes. *Offered by: Financial Times* and McKinsey & Company. *Winner:* Âriel de Fauconberg for the book proposal *Before the Dawn: Racing to Net Zero on the Front Lines of Climate Innovation.*

Branford Boase Award (United Kingdom). To the author and editor of an outstanding novel for young readers by a first-time writer. *Winners:* Maisie Chan (author) and Georgia Murray (editor) for *Danny Chung Does Not Do Maths* (Piccadilly Press).

Bridport International Creative Writing Prizes (United Kingdom). For poetry and short stories. *Offered by:* Bridport Arts Centre. *Winners:* (poetry, £5,000, about $6,200) Chaun Ballard for "My Father and I Drive Back to St. Louis for His Mother's Funeral"; (short story, £5,000, about $6,200) Trent England for "This Is Going to Be Huge"; (flash fiction, 250-word maximum, £1,000, about $1,200) Hilary Taylor for "Some Creatures Trapped in Ice"; (memoir, £1,500, about $1,800) Joanne Briggs for *The Scientist Who Wasn't There*; (Peggy Chapman-Andrews Award for a First Novel, £1,500, about $1,800) Zad El Bacha for *I Want*; (Dorset Award) Paul Saville; (Young Writer Award) Nicole Adabunu for "Game" and Freya Bantiff for "Working Debenhams' Late Shift."

British Book Awards (aka the Nibbies) (United Kingdom). *Offered by: The Bookseller.* *Winners:* (book of the year) Marcus Rashford with Carl Anka for *You Are a Champion* (Macmillan Children's Books); (fiction) Meg Mason for *Sorrow and Bliss* (Orion/Weidenfeld & Nicolson); (debut) Caleb Azumah Nelson for *Open Water* (Viking); (crime and thriller) Ian Rankin and William McIlvanney for *The Dark Remains* (Canongate Books); (children's fiction) Phil Earle for *When the Sky Falls* (Andersen Press); (children's nonfiction and illustrated) Marcus Rashford with Carl Anka for *You Are a Champion* (Macmillan Children's Books);

(children's illustrated) Dapo Adeola and 18 illustrators for *Hey You!* (Puffin); (nonfiction narrative) Sathnam Sanghera for *Empireland: How Imperialism Has Shaped Modern Britain* (Viking); (nonfiction lifestyle) Paul McCartney (author) and Paul Muldoon (editor) for *The Lyrics: 1956 to the Present* (Allen Lane); (pageturner book of the year) Clare Chambers for *Small Pleasures* (Orion/ Weidenfeld & Nicolson); (audio fiction) *The Wizards of Once: Never and Forever* by Cressida Cowell, narrated by David Tennant (Hodder Children's Books); (audio nonfiction) Billy Connolly for *Windswept and Interesting* (John Murray Press).

British Fantasy Awards. *Offered by:* British Fantasy Society. *Winners:* (Karl Edward Wagner Award) Maureen Kincaid Speller; (Sydney J. Bounds Award for a newcomer) Shelley Parker-Chan for *She Who Became the Sun* (Tor); (magazine/periodical) *Apex Magazine*; (nonfiction) Dan Coxon and Richard V. Hirst (editors) for *Writing the Uncanny* (Dead Ink); (comic/graphic novel) Molly Knox Ostertag for *The Girl from the Sea* (Graphix); (independent press) Luna Press Publishing; (artist) Jenni Coutts; (anthology) Xueting C. Ni (editor) for *Sinopticon: A Celebration of Chinese Science Fiction* (Solaris); (collection) Isabel Yap for *Never Have I Ever* (Small Beer Press); (film/ television production) *Last Night in Soho* (Universal Pictures); (audio) H.R. Owen for *Monstrous Agonies* (podcast); (novella) Nino Cipri for *Defekt* (Tordotcom); (short fiction) Lorraine Wilson for "Bathymetry" in *Strange Horizons* (March 8, 2021); (August Derleth Award for horror novel) Catriona Ward for *The Last House on Needless Street* (Viper Books); (Robert Holdstock Award for fantasy novel) Shelley Parker-Chan for *She Who Became the Sun* (Tor).

Sophie Brody Medal. For the U.S. author of the most distinguished contribution to Jewish literature for adults, published in the preceding year. *Donors:* Sophie and Arthur Brody Foundation. *Offered by:* American Library Association's Reference and User Services Association. *Winner:* Jane Yolen for *Kaddish Before the Holocaust and After: Poems* (Holy Cow Press).

AKO Caine Prize for African Writing (£10,000, about $12,500). For a short story by an African writer, published in English. *Winner:* Idza Luhumyo for "Five Years Next Sunday" in *Disruption: New Short Fiction from Africa* (Catalyst Press).

Randolph Caldecott Medal. For the artist of the most distinguished picture book. *Offered by:* American Library Association's Association for Library Service to Children. *Winner:* Jason Chin for *Watercress*, written by Andrea Wang (Neal Porter Books/Holiday House).

California Book Awards. To California residents to honor books of fiction, nonfiction, and poetry published in the previous year. *Offered by:* Commonwealth Club of California. *Winners:* (fiction) Shruti Swamy for *The Archer* (Algonquin Books); (first fiction) Yoon Choi for *Skinship* (Alfred A. Knopf); (nonfiction) Lizzie Johnson for *Paradise: One Town's Struggle to Survive an American Wildfire* (Crown); (poetry) Will Alexander for *Refractive Africa* (New Directions); (juvenile) Mươn Thị Văn and Victo Ngai for *Wishes* (Orchard Books/Scholastic); (young adult) Safia Elhillo for *Home Is Not a Country* (Make Me a World); (contribution to publishing) Little Tokyo Historical Society for *A Rebel's Outcry* by Naomi Hirahara; (Californiana) Rosecrans Baldwin for *Everything Now: Lessons from the City-State of Los Angeles* (MCD/Farrer, Straus & Giroux).

Eleanor Cameron Notable Middle Grade Books List. See Core Excellence in Children's and Young Adult Science Fiction.

John W. Campbell Memorial Award. For science fiction writing. *Offered by:* Gunn Center for the Study of Science Fiction. Not awarded in 2022.

Andrew Carnegie Medal for Excellence in Fiction and Nonfiction. For adult books published during the previous year in the United States. *Sponsors:* Carnegie Corporation of New York, ALA/RUSA, and *Booklist*. *Winners:* (fiction) Tom Lin for *The Thousand Crimes of Ming Tsu* (Little, Brown and Company); (nonfiction) Hanif Abdurraqib for *A Little Devil in America: In Praise of Black Performance* (Random House).

Carnegie Medal (United Kingdom). See Yoto Carnegie Medal.

Robert and Ina Caro Research/Travel Fellowship. Open to BIO members with a work in progress to receive funding for research trips to archives or to important settings in their subjects' lives. *Offered by:* Biographers International Organization. *Winners:* Lauren Arrington for research on the sculptor Lenore Thomas Straus, and Bill Goldstein for research on the playwright Larry Kramer.

Center for Fiction First Novel Prize ($10,000). *Offered by:* Center for Fiction, Mercantile Library of New York. *Winner:* Noor Naga for *If an Egyptian Cannot Speak English* (Graywolf Press).

Chicago Folklore Prize. For the year's best folklore book. *Offered by:* American Folklore Society. *Winner:* Jerrilyn McGregory for *One Grand Noise: Boxing Day in the Anglicized Caribbean World* (University Press of Mississippi).

Chicago Tribune Nelson Algren Short Story Award ($3,500). For unpublished short fiction. *Offered by:* Chicago Tribune. Not awarded in 2022.

Chicago Tribune Heartland Prize for Fiction ($7,500). *Offered by:* Chicago Tribune. Not awarded in 2022.

Chicago Tribune Heartland Prize for Nonfiction ($7,500). *Offered by:* Chicago Tribune. Not awarded in 2022.

Chicago Tribune Literary Award. To recognize lifetime achievement of a prominent writer, usually someone with strong connections to the Midwest. *Offered by:* Chicago Tribune. Not awarded in 2022.

Chicago Tribune Young Adult Literary Prize. *Offered by:* Chicago Tribune. To recognize a distinguished literary career. Not awarded in 2022.

Children's Africana Book Awards. To recognize and encourage excellence in children's books about Africa. *Offered by:* Africa Access, African Studies Association. *Winners:* (young readers) Useni Eugene Perkins (author) and Laura Freeman (illustrator) for *Kwame Nkrumah's Midnight Speech for Independence* (Just Us Books); (older readers) Safia Elhillo for *Home Is Not a Country* (Make Me a World).

Children's Literature Legacy Award. Awarded to an author or illustrator whose books have made a substantial and lasting contribution to children's literature. *Offered by:* American Library Association's Association for Library Service to Children. *Winner:* Grace Lin.

Cholmondeley Awards for Poets (United Kingdom) (£1,680, about $2,000). For a poet's body of work and contribution to poetry. *Winners:* David Kinloch, Gerry Loose, Maggie O'Sullivan, Menna Elfyn, and Tiffany Atkinson.

CILIP Carnegie Medal (United Kingdom). See Yoto Carnegie Medal.

CILIP Kate Greenaway Medal and Colin Mears Award (United Kingdom). See Yoto Kate Greenaway Medal.

Arthur C. Clarke Award. For the best science fiction novel published in the United Kingdom. *Offered by:* British Science Fiction Association. *Winner:* Harry Josephine Giles for *Deep Wheel Orcadia* (Picador).

Hal Clement Notable Young Adult Books List. See Core Excellence in Children's and Young Adult Science Fiction.

David Cohen Prize for Literature (United Kingdom) (£40,000, about $50,000). Awarded biennially to a living British writer, novelist, poet, essayist, or dramatist in recognition of an entire body of work written in the English language. *Offered by:* David Cohen Family Charitable Trust. *Winner (2021):* Colm Tóibín.

Matt Cohen Award: In Celebration of a Writing Life (C$20,000). To a Canadian author whose life has been dedicated to writing as a primary pursuit, for a body of work. *Offered by:* Writers' Trust of Canada. *Sponsors:* Marla and David Lehberg. *Winner:* Candace Savage.

Commonwealth Short Story Prize (United Kingdom) (£5,000 for overall winner; £2,500 for each regional winner). To reward and encourage new short fiction by Commonwealth writers. *Offered by:* Commonwealth Institute. *Winners:* (regional winner, Africa, and overall winner) Ntsika Kota (Eswatini) for "and the earth drank deep"; (regional winner, Asia) Sofia Mariah Ma (Singapore) for "The Last Diver on Earth"; (regional winner, Canada and Europe) Cecil Browne (United Kingdom and St. Vincent and the Grenadines) for "'A Hat for Lemer"; (regional winner, Caribbean) Diana McCaulay (Jamaica) for "Bridge over the Yallahs River"; (regional winner, Pacific) Mary Rokonadravu (Fiji) for "The Nightwatch."

Core Excellence in Children's and Young Adult Science Fiction. *Sponsor:* Core division of the American Library Association. *Winners:* (Golden Duck Notable Picture Books List) James McGowan (author) and Graham Carter (illustrator) for *Good Night, Oppy!* (Astra Young Readers); Rachel Noble (author) and Zoey Abbott (illustrator) for *Marty* (Holiday House); Joy Keller (author) and Ashley Belote (illustrator) for *Frankenslime* (Feiwel & Friends); Jami Gigot for *Starboy: Inspired by the Life and Lyrics of David Bowie* (Henry Holt & Company); Sue Fliess (author) and Annabel Tempest (illustrator) for *Sadie Sprocket Builds a Rocket* (Two Lions); Heather Tekavec (author) and Guillaume Perreault (illustrator) for *Arnold the Superish Hero* (Kids Can Press); (Eleanor Cameron Notable Middle Grade Books List) Sarah Prineas for *Trouble in the Stars* (Philomel); Kwame Mbalia and Prince Joel Makonnen for *Last Gate of the Emperor* (Scholastic); Eve L. Ewing (author) and Christine Almeda (illustrator) for *Maya and the Robot* (Kokila); Jennifer L. Holm for *The Lion of Mars* (Random House Books for Young Readers); Irene Latham for *D-39:A Robodog's Journey* (Charlesbridge); Nicole Kornher-Stace for *Jillian vs. Parasite Planet* (Tachyon Publications); John David Anderson for *Stowaway* (Walden Pond Press); Christopher Swiedler for *The Orpheus Plot* (HarperCollins); Greg van Eekhout for *Weird Kid* (HarperCollins); Donna Barba Higuera for *The Last Cuentista* (Levine Querido); Daniel José Older for *Flood City* (Scholastic); (Hal Clement Notable Young Adult Books List) Heather Einhorn, Adam Staffaroni, and Janet Harvey for *The Curie Society* (MIT Press); E.K. Johnston for *Aetherbound* (Dutton Books); Joan He for *The Ones We're Meant to Find* (Roaring Brook Press); Xiran Jay Zhao for *Iron Widow* (Penguin Teen); Cherie Dimaline for *Hunting By Stars* (Amulet Books); Eliot Schrefer for *The Darkness Outside Us* (Tegen Books); David Arnold for *The Electric Kingdom* (Viking Books for Young Readers); Anna Carey for *This Is Not the Jess Show* (Quirk); Josh Swiller for *Bright Shining World* (Knopf Books for Young Readers); Mackenzi Lee for *Gamora and Nebula: Sisters in Arms* (Marvel Press).

Jeanne Córdova Prize for Lesbian/Queer Nonfiction. *Offered by:* Lambda Literary Foundation. *Winner:* Aisha Sabatini Sloan.

Costa Book Awards (United Kingdom) (£5,000 plus an additional £25,000 for Book of the Year). For literature of merit that is readable on a wide scale. *Offered by:* Booksellers Association of Great Britain and Costa Coffee. Award discontinued.

Costa Short Story Award (United Kingdom) (£3,500). Award discontinued.

Crime Writers' Association (CWA) Dagger Awards (United Kingdom). *Winners:* (diamond dagger, for significant contribution to crime writing) C.J. Sansom; (gold dagger, for best novel) Ray Celestin for *Sunset Swing* (Mantle); (gold dagger, for nonfiction) Julia Laite for *The Disappearance of Lydia Harvey: A True Story of Sex, Crime and the Meaning of Justice* (Profile Books); (Ian Fleming steel dagger, for best thriller) M.W. Craven for *Dead Ground* (Constable); (John Creasey dagger, for best debut crime novel) Janice Hallett for *The Appeal* (Viper Books); (CWA historical dagger, for the best historical crime novel) Ray Celestin for *Sunset Swing* (Mantle); (CWA short story dagger) Paul Magrs for "Flesh of a Fancy Woman in *Criminal Pursuits: Crime through Time*" (Telos Publishing); (crime fiction in translation dagger) Simone Buchholz for *Hotel Cartagena*, translated by Rachel Ward (Orenda Books); (CWA Dagger in the Library, for a body of work) Mark Billingham; (debut dagger, for a previously unpublished crime writer) Anna Maloney for Deception: "The 10:12."

Cundill History Prize ($75,000). For a book that embodies historical scholarship, originality, literary quality and broad appeal. *Administered by:* McGill University. *Winner:* Tiya Miles for *All That She Carried: The Journey of Ashley's Sack, a Black Family Keepsake* (Random House).

Benjamin H. Danks Award ($20,000). Given annually, in rotation, to a composer of ensemble works, a playwright, and a writer. *Offered by:* American Academy of Arts and Letters. *Winner:* Martyna Majok (drama).

Dartmouth Medal. For creating current reference works of outstanding quality and significance. *Donor:* Dartmouth College. *Offered by:* American Library Association's Reference and User Services Division. *Winner:* David Wondrich with Noah Rothbaum (editors) for *The Oxford Companion to Spirits and Cocktails* (Oxford University Press).

Dayton Literary Peace Prize ($10,000). For adult fiction and nonfiction published within the previous year that address the theme of peace on a variety of levels, such as between individuals; among families and communities; or between nations, religions, or ethnic groups. *Offered by:* Dayton Literary Peace Prize Foundation. *Winners:* (fiction) Honorée Fanonne Jeffers for *The Love Songs of W.E.B Du Bois* (HarperCollins); (nonfiction) Clint Smith for *How the Word Is Passed* (Little, Brown and Company).

Derringer Awards. To recognize excellence in short crime and mystery fiction. *Sponsor:* Short Mystery Fiction Society. *Winners:* (flash fiction, up to 1,000 words) John M. Floyd for "Tourist Trap" in *Pulp Modern Flash* (March 2021); (short story, 1,001–4,000 words) Trey Dowell for "Yelena Tried to Kill Me" in *Mystery Weekly Magazine* (August 2021); (long story, 4,001–8,000 words) Michael Bracken for "The Downeaster Alexa" in *Only the Good Die Young: Crime Fiction Inspired by the Songs of Billy Joel* (Untreed Reads Publishing); (novelette, 8,001–20,000 words) Stacy Woodson for "Two Tamales, One Tokarev, and a Lifetime of Broken Promises" in *Guns + Tacos: Season Three* (Down & Out Books).

Diagram Prize for Oddest Title of the Year. See Bookseller/Diagram Prize for Oddest Title of the Year.

Philip K. Dick Award. For a distinguished science fiction paperback published in the United States. *Sponsor:* Philadelphia Science Fiction Society and the Philip K. Dick Trust. *Winner:* Kali Wallace for Dead Space (Berkley Books).

Digital Book Awards. To recognize high-quality digital content available to readers as e-books and enhanced digital books. *Sponsor:* Digital Book World. Not awarded in 2022.

Donner Prize ($50,000). To a book that showcases excellence and innovation in public policy writing by Canadians. *Sponsor:* Donner Canadian Foundation. *Winner (2022):* To be announced. *Winner (2021):* Dan Breznitz for *Innovation in Real Places: Strategies for Prosperity in an Unforgiving World* (Oxford University Press).

DSC Prize for South Asian Literature ($25,000). To recognize outstanding literature from or about the South Asian region and raise awareness of South Asian culture around the world. *Sponsor:* DSC Limited. Not awarded in 2022.

Dublin Literary Award (Ireland) (€100,000, about $109,000). For a book of high literary merit, written in English or translated into English; if translated, the author receives €75,000 (about $82,000) and the translator €25,000 (about $27,000). *Offered by:* City of Dublin. *Winner:* Alice Zeniter for *The Art of Losing* (Picador).

Jim Duggins, PhD Outstanding Mid-Career Novelist Prize. *Offered by:* Lambda Literary Foundation. *Winners:* Vi Khi Nao and Silas House.

Dundee Picture Book Award (Scotland) (£1,000, about $1,200). To recognize excellence in storytelling for children. The winner is chosen by the schoolchildren of Dundee. Not awarded in 2022.

Edgar Awards. For outstanding mystery, suspense, and crime writing. *Offered by:* Mystery Writers of America. *Winners:* (novel) James Kestrel for *Five Decembers* (Hard Case Crime); (first novel by an American author) Erin Flanagan for *Deer Season* (University of Nebraska Press); (paperback original) Alan Parks for *Bobby March Will Live Forever* (Europa Editions/World Noir); (fact crime) Elon Green for *Last Call: A True Story of Love, Lust, and Murder in Queer New York* (Celadon); (critical/biographical) Edward White for *The Twelve Lives of Alfred Hitchcock: An Anatomy of the Master of Suspense* (W.W. Norton & Company); (short story) R.T. Lawton for "The Road to Hana" in *Alfred Hitchcock Mystery Magazine* (May/June 2021); (juvenile) Christina Diaz Gonzalez for *Concealed* (Scholastic); (young adult) Angeline Boulley for *Firekeeper's Daughter* (Henry Holt & Company Books for Young Readers); (television episode teleplay) Iturri Sosa for "Boots on the Ground" episode of *Narcos: Mexico* (Netflix); (Robert L. Fish Memorial Award) Rob Osler for "Analogue" in *Ellery Queen Mystery Magazine* (January/February 2021); (grand master) Laurie R. King; (Raven Award) Lesa Holstine; (Ellery Queen Award) Juliet Grames; (Simon & Schuster Mary Higgins Clark Award) Naomi Hirahara for *Clark and Division* (Soho Crime);

(G.P. Putnam's Sons Sue Grafton Memorial Award) Tracy Clark for *Runner* (Kensington).

Educational Writers' Award (United Kingdom) (£2,000, about $2,500). For noteworthy educational nonfiction for children. *Offered by:* Authors' Licensing and Collecting Society. *Winner:* Juno Dawson (author) and Soofiya (illustrator) for *What's the T?* (Wren & Rook).

Margaret A. Edwards Award ($2,000). To an author whose book or books have provided young adults with a window through which they can view their world and that will help them to grow and to understand themselves and their role in society. *Donor: School Library Journal. Winner:* A.S. King.

T.S. Eliot Prize for Poetry (United Kingdom) (£20,000, about $24,800). *Offered by:* Poetry Book Society. *Winner:* Anthony Joseph for *Sonnets for Albert* (Bloomsbury Poetry).

Encore Award (United Kingdom) (£10,000, about $12,500). Awarded for the best second novel. *Offered by:* Royal Society of Literature. *Winner:* Francis Spufford for *Light Perpetual* (Faber & Faber).

European Union Prize for Literature (€5,000, about $5,500). To recognize outstanding European writing. *Sponsor:* Creative Europe program of the European Union. *Winners:* Kjersti Anfinnsen (Norway), Jacobo Bergareche (Spain), Vladimir Jankovski (North Macedonia), Takis Kampylis (Greece), Peter Karoshi (Austria), Eugenia Kuznetsova (Ukraine), Tadhg Mac Dhonnagáin (Ireland), Daniele Mencarelli (Italy), Raluca Nagy (Romania), Slađana Nina Perković (Bosnia and Herzegovina), Iva Pezuashvili (Georgia), Richard Pupala (Slovakia), Gaea Schoeters (Belgium), Tomas Vaiseta (Lithuania).

FIL Literary Award in Romance Languages (formerly the Juan Rulfo International Latin American and Caribbean Prize) (Mexico) ($150,000). For lifetime achievement in any literary genre. *Offered by:* Juan Rulfo International Latin American and Caribbean Prize Committee. *Winner:* Mircea Cărtărescu.

Financial Times Business Book of the Year Award (£30,000). To recognize books that provide compelling and enjoyable insight into modern business issues. *Winner:* Chris Miller for *Chip War* (Simon & Schuster UK).

Sid Fleischman Humor Award. See Golden Kite Awards.

ForeWord Reviews Book of the Year Awards ($1,500). For independently published books. *Offered by: ForeWord Reviews* magazine. Not awarded in 2022.

E.M. Forster Award ($20,000). To a young writer from the United Kingdom or Ireland for a stay in the United States. *Offered by:* American Academy of Arts and Letters. Not awarded in 2022.

Forward Prizes (United Kingdom). For poetry. *Offered by: The Forward. Winners:* (best collection, £10,000, about $12,500) Kim Moore for *All the Men I Never Married* (Seren); (Felix Dennis Prize for best first collection, £5,000, about $6,200) Stephanie Sy-Quia for *Amnion* (Granta Poetry); (best single poem, £1,000, about $1,200) Nick Laird for "Up Late" (Granta).

Josette Frank Award. For a work of fiction in which children or young people deal in a positive and realistic way with difficulties in their world and grow emotionally and morally. *Offered by:* Bank Street College of Education and the Florence M. Miller Memorial Fund. *Winners:* (younger readers) Matt de la Peña (author) and Christian Robinson (illustrator) for *Milo Imagines the World* (G.P. Putnam's Sons); (older readers) Angeline Boulley for *Firekeeper's Daughter* (Henry Holt & Company Books for Young Readers).

George Freedley Memorial Award. For the best English-language work about live theater published in the United States. *Offered by:* Theatre Library Association. *Winner:* Katrina M. Phillips for *Staging Indigeneity: Salvage Tourism and the Performance of Native American History* (University of North Carolina Press).

French-American Foundation Translation Prize ($10,000). For a translation or translations from French into English of works of fiction and nonfiction. *Offered by:* French-American Foundation. *Donor:* Florence Gould Foundation. *Winners:* (fiction) Lara Vergnaud for her translation of *Life Sciences* by Joy Sorman (Restless Books); (nonfiction) Susan Emanuel for her translation of *The Belle Époque* by Dominique Kalifa (Columbia University Press).

Frost Medal. To recognize achievement in poetry over a lifetime. *Offered by:* Poetry Society of America. *Winner:* Sharon Olds.

Ernest J. Gaines Award for Literary Excellence ($15,000). To inspire and recognize rising African American fiction writers. *Offered by:* Baton Rouge Area Foundation. *Winner:* Jacinda Townsend for *Mother Country* (Graywolf Press).

Lewis Galantière Award. Awarded biennially for a literary translation into English from any language other than German. *Offered by:* American Translators Association. *Winner (2022):* Natasha Wimmer for her translation of *The Twilight Zone* by Nona Fernandez (Graywolf Press).

Theodor Seuss Geisel Award. For the best book for beginning readers. *Offered by:* American Library Association's Association for Library Service to Children. *Winner:* Corey R. Tabor for *Fox at Night* (Balzer + Bray, an imprint of HarperCollins Publishers).

Giller Prize (Canada). See Scotiabank Giller Prize.

Gival Press Novel Award ($3,000 and publication by Gival Press). Given biennially. *Winner (2022):* Khanh Ha for *Her: The Flame Tree.*

Gival Press Oscar Wilde Award ($500 and publication by Gival Press). Given annually to an original, unpublished poem that relates LGBTQ life by a poet who is 18 or older. *Winner:* Brad Fairchild for "Vowelish Palares."

Gival Press Poetry Award ($1,000 and publication by Gival Press). Given biennially. *Winner (2021):* Kate Monaghan for "Disputed Site."

Gival Press Short Story Award ($1,000 and publication by Gival Press). Given annually. *Winner:* Aaron Tillman for "Kennebunk Correction."

Giverny Award. For an outstanding children's science picture book. *Offered by:* 15 Degree Laboratory. *Winner:* Deb Pilutti for *Old Rock (is not boring)* (G.P. Putnam's Sons Books for Young Readers).

Alexander Gode Medal. To an individual or institution for outstanding service to the translation and interpreting professions. *Offered by:* American Translators Association. Not awarded in 2022.

Golden Duck Notable Picture Books List. See Core Excellence in Children's and Young Adult Science Fiction.

Golden Kite Awards ($2,500 plus an additional $1,000 to donate to a nonprofit organization of the winner's choice). For children's books. *Offered by:* Society of Children's Book Writers and Illustrators. *Winners:* (middle grade fiction) Michael Leali for *The Civil War of Amos Abernathy* (HarperCollins); (young adult fiction) Emily Inouye Huey for *Beneath the Wide Silk Sky* (Scholastic); (nonfiction text for younger readers) Stacy McAnulty for *Our Planet! There's No Place Like Earth,* illustrated by David Litchfield (Henry Holt & Company Books for Young Readers); (nonfiction text for older readers) Tara Lazar for *Absurd Words: A Kid's Fun and Hilarious Vocabulary Builder for Future Word Nerds* (Sourcebooks); (picture book illustration) Nathalie Dion for *Kumo the Bashful Cloud,* written by Kyo Maclear (Tundra Books/Penguin Random House Canada); (picture book text) Brittany J. Thurman for *Fly,* illustrated by Anna Cunha (Caitlyn Dlouhy Books/Atheneum); (illustrated book for older readers) Isabel Roxas for *The Adventures of Team Pom: Squid Happens* (Flying Eye Books); (Sid Fleischman Humor Award) Rachel Elliott for *The Real Riley Mayes* (Balzer + Bray).

Governor General's Literary Awards (Canada) (C$25,000, plus C$3,000 to the publisher). For works, in English and French, of fiction, nonfiction, poetry, and drama and for translation. *Offered by:* Canada Council for the Arts. *Winners:* (fiction, English) Sheila Heti for *Pure Colour* (Knopf Canada/Penguin Random House Canada); (nonfiction, English) Eli Baxter for *Aki-wayn-zih: A Person as Worthy as the Earth* (McGill-Queen's University Press); (poetry, English) Annick MacAskill for *Shadow Blight* (Gaspereau Press); (drama, English) Dorothy Dittrich for *The Piano Teacher: A Healing Key* (Talonbooks); (young people's literature—text, English) Jen Ferguson for *The Summer of Bitter and Sweet* (Heartdrum/HarperCollins Publishers); (young people's literature—illustrated) Naseem Hrab and Nahid Kazemi for *The Sour Cherry Tree* (Owlkids Books); (translation from French to English) Judith Weisz Woodsworth for *History of the Jews in Quebec,* translation of *Histoire des Juifs au Québec* by Pierre Anctil (University of Ottawa Press); (fiction, French) Alain Farah for *Mille secrets mille dangers* (Le Quartanier); (nonfiction, French) Sylveline Bourion for *La Voie romaine* (Les Éditions du Boréal); (poetry, French) Maya Cousineau Mollen for *Enfants du lichen* (Éditions Hannenorak); (drama, French) David Paquet for *Le poids des fourmis* (Leméac Éditeur); (young people's literature—text, French) Julie Champagne for *Cancer ascendant Autruche* (la courte échelle); (young people's literature—illustrated, French) Nadine Robert and Qin Leng for *Trèfle* (Comme des géants); (translation from English to French) Mélissa Verreault for *Partie de chasse au petit gibier entre lâches au club de tir du coin*, translation of *Small Game Hunting at the Local Coward Gun Club* by Megan Gail Coles (Éditions Québec Amérique).

Dolly Gray Children's Literature Awards. Presented biennially for fiction or biographical children's books with positive portrayals of individuals with developmental disabilities. *Offered by:* Council for Exceptional Children, Division on Autism and Developmental Disabilities. *Winners (2022):* (picture book) Anitra Rowe Schulte (author) and Ziyue Chen (illustrator) for *Dancing with Daddy* (Two Lions); (chapter book) Nicole Panteleakos for *Planet Earth Is Blue* (Yearling).

Graywolf Press Nonfiction Prize ($20,000 advance, $2,000 stipend to support completion of the project and publication by Graywolf Press). To the most promising and innovative literary nonfiction project by a writer not yet established in the genre. *Winner:* Jung Hae Chae for *Pojangmacha People.*

Kate Greenaway Medal and Colin Mears Award. See Yoto Kate Greenaway Medal.

Eric Gregory Awards (United Kingdom) (£4,000, about $5,000). For a published or unpublished collection by poets under the age of 30. *Winners:* Joe Carrick-Varty, Courtney Conrad, Jack Cooper, Daniella Fearon, Maisie Newman, Rhiya Pau, Stephanie Sy-Quia.

Griffin Poetry Prizes (Canada) (C$65,000). To a living Canadian poet or translator and a living poet or translator from any country, which may include Canada. *Offered by:* Griffin Trust. *Winners:* (international) Douglas Kearney for *Sho* (Wave Books); (Canadian) Tolu Oloruntoba for *The Junta of Happenstance* (Palimpsest Press).

Gryphon Award ($1,000). To recognize a noteworthy work of fiction or nonfiction for younger children. *Offered by:* The Center for Children's Books. Award discontinued.

Hadada Award. To a distinguished member of the writing community who has made a strong and unique contribution to literature. Offered by: *The Paris Review. Winner:* Jamaica Kincaid.

Dashiell Hammett Prize. For a work of literary excellence in the field of crime writing by a U.S. or Canadian writer. *Offered by:* North American Branch of the International Association of Crime Writers. *Winner (2022):* To be announced. *Winner (2021):* S.A. Cosby for *Razorblade Tears* (Flatiron Books).

R.R. Hawkins Award. For the outstanding professional/scholarly work of the year. *Offered by:* Association of American Publishers. *Winner:* Duke University Press for *Experiments in Skin: Race and Beauty in the Shadows of Vietnam* by Thuy Linh Nguyen Tu.

Hayek Book Prize ($50,000). Honors a book published in the previous two years that best reflects F.A. Hayek's vision of economic and individual liberty. *Offered by:* Manhattan Institute. *Winner:* Joseph Henrich for *The WEIRDest People in the World: How the West Became Psychologically Peculiar and Particularly Prosperous* (Farrar, Straus and Giroux).

Anthony Hecht Poetry Prize ($3,000 and publication by Waywiser Press). For an unpublished first or second book-length poetry collection. *Winner:* James D'Agostino for *The Goldfinch Caution Tapes* (Waywiser Press).

Drue Heinz Literature Prize ($15,000 and publication by University of Pittsburgh Press). For short fiction. *Winner:* Ramona Reeves for *It Falls Gently All Around and Other Stories* (University of Pittsburgh Press).

O. Henry Awards. See PEN/O. Henry Prize.

William Dean Howells Medal. Given once every five years in recognition of the most distinguished American novel published during that period. *Offered by:* American Academy of Arts and Letters. *Winner (2020):* Richard Powers for *The Overstory* (W.W. Norton & Company).

Hugo Awards. For outstanding science fiction writing. *Offered by:* World Science Fiction Convention. *Winners:* (novel) Arkady

Martine for *A Desolation Called Peace* (Tor); (novella) Becky Chambers for *A Psalm for the Wild-Built* (Tordotcom); (novelette) Suzanne Palmer for "Bots of the Lost Ark" (*Clarkesworld*, June 2021); (short story) Sarah Pinsker for "Where Oaken Hearts Do Gather" (*Uncanny Magazine*, March/April 2021); (series) Seanan McGuire for *Wayward Children* (Tordotcom); (related work) Charlie Jane Anders for *Never Say You Can't Survive* (Tordotcom); (graphic story or comic) N.K. Jemisin (author) and Jamal Campbell (illustrator) for *Far Sector* (DC); (dramatic presentation, long form) Jon Spaihts, Denis Villeneuve, and Eric Roth (screenplay) and Denis Villeneuve (director) for *Dune* (Warner Bros./Legendary Entertainment); (dramatic presentation, short form) Daniel Abraham, Ty Franck, and Naren Shankar (writers) and Breck Eisner (director) for *The Expanse: Nemesis Games* (Amazon Studios); (Lodestar Award for Best Young Adult Book) Naomi Novik for *The Last Graduate* (Del Rey Books); *As-tounding* Award for Best New Writer: Shelley Parker-Chan.

ILA Children's and Young Adults' Book Awards. For first or second books in any language published for children or young adults. *Offered by:* International Literacy Association. *Winners:* (primary fiction) Alexandra Alessandri for *Isabel and Her Colores Go to School* (Sleeping Bear Press); (primary nonfiction) Kristen Nordstrom for *Mimic Makers: Biomimicry Inventors Inspired by Nature* (Charlesbridge); (intermediate fiction) Lisa Fipps for *Starfish* (Penguin Young Readers); (intermediate nonfiction) Dr. Jennifer Gardy for *It Takes Guts: How Your Body Turns Food into Fuel (and Poop)* (Greystone Kids); (young adult fiction) Peyton Thomas for *Both Sides Now* (Penguin Young Readers); (young adult nonfiction) Lee Wind for *No Way, They Were Gay?: Hidden Lives and Secret Loves* (Lerner).

Independent Publisher Book Awards (IPPY). Created to recognize exemplary independent, university, and self-published titles across a wide spectrum of genres. *Sponsor:* Jenkins Group/Independent Publisher Online. *Winners:* (fine art) Martin Gayford and David Hockney for *Spring Cannot Be Canceled: David Hockney in Normandy* (Thames & Hudson); (performing arts) Kristin Juarez, Rebecca Peabody, and Glenn Phillips (editors) for *Blondell Cummings: Dance as Moving Pictures* (X Artists' Books); (photography) Jason Franz (editor) for *Manifest International Photography Annual 8* (Manifest Creative Research Gallery and Drawing Center); (architecture) Patrick F. Cannon and James Caulfield for *At Home in Chicago: A Living History of Domestic Architecture* (CityFiles Press); (coffee table books) Janice Sutton for *Winter Wild: A Feast of Dark Delights* (Janice Sutton Communications); (popular fiction) Susan Schoenberger for *The Liability of Love* (She Writes Press); (literary fiction) Jean McNeil for *Day for Night* (ECW Press); (short story fiction) Whitney Collins for *Big Bad* (Sarabande Books); (poetry–standard) (tie) Andrea Gibson for *You Better Be Lightning* (Button Poetry) and Quincy Scott Jones for *How to Kill Yourself Instead of Your Children* (C&R Press); (poetry–specialty) Renee Sarojini Saklikar for *Bramah and the Beggar Boy* (Nightwood Editions); (anthologies) Ayelet Tsabari, Eufemia Fantetti, and Leonarda Carranza (editors) for *Tongues: On Longing and Belonging through Language* (Book*hug Press); (juvenile fiction) Payal Doshi for *Rea and the Blood of the Nectar* (Mango and Marigold Press); (young adult fiction) E.J. Schwartz for *Before We Were Blue* (Flux); (young adult fantasy) Laura Rueckert for *Dragonbird in the Fern* (Flux); (fantasy) Iris Compiet for *Faeries of the Faultlines* (Eye of Newt Books); (science fiction) Susan Hasler for *KRILL: When the Good Choices Are Gone* (Bear Page Press); (LGBT+ fiction) Yang Huang for *My Good Son* (University of New Orleans Press); (erotica) Sara Wetmore for *The Golden Girl* (self-published); (historical fiction) C.F. Yetmen for *That Which Remains* (Ypsilon & Co Press); (military/wartime fiction) William Carpenter for *Silence* (Islandport Press); (horror) Preston Fassel for *The Despicable Fantasies of Quentin Sergenov* (Encyclopocalypse Publications); (multicultural fiction) Leah Ranada for *The Cine Star Salon* (NeWest Press); (multicultural fiction–juvenile/young adult) Gayatri Sethi for *Unbelonging* (Mango and Marigold Press); (mystery)

Joanna FitzPatrick for *The Artist Colony* (She Writes Press); (suspense/thriller) Helaine Mario for *Shadow Music* (Oceanview Publishing); (religious fiction) Kerry Chaput for *Daughter of the King* (Black Rose Writing); (romance) Katie Rose Guest Pryal for *Take Your Charming Somewhere Else* (Blue Crow Books); (visionary/new age fiction) Rea Nolan Martin for *Sunnyside Up* (Wia-Waka Press); (true crime) Adam Selzer for *Murder Maps USA: Crime Scenes Revisited. Bloodstains to Ballistics. 1865–1939* (Thames & Hudson); (graphic novel/drawn book) Myriam Steinberg (author) and Christache (illustrator) for *Catalogue Baby: A Memoir of (In)fertility* (Page Two Books); (humor) William Sibley for *Here We Go Loop de Loop* (Atmosphere Press); (children's picture book–age seven and under) Gabby Dawnay (author) and Ian Morris (illustrator) for *The Library Book* (Thames & Hudson); (children's picture book–all ages) Wafa' Tarnowska, (author) and Vali Mintzi (illustrator) for *Nour's Secret Library* (Barefoot Books); (children's interactive) Elias Barks for *Alien Baby!* (Hazy Dell Press); (juvenile/young adult nonfiction) (tie) Caris Snider for *Anxiety Elephants for Tween Girls* (End Game Press) and Caris Snider *Anxiety Elephants for Tween Boys* (End Game Press); (multicultural nonfiction juvenile/young adult) Rochelle Riley and Cristi Smith-Jones for *That They Lived* (Wayne State University Press).

International Booker Prize (United Kingdom) (£50,000, about $63,000). To the author and translator of a work translated into English. *Offered by:* Crankstart. *Winner:* Geetanjali Shree for *Tomb of Sand*, translated from Hindi by Daisy Rockwell (Tilted Axis Press).

International Prize for Arabic Fiction ($50,000 and publication in English). To reward excellence in contemporary Arabic creative writing. *Sponsors:* Booker Prize Foundation, Emirates Foundation for Philanthropy. *Winner:* Geetanjali Shree (India) for *Tomb of Sand*, translated by Daisy Rockwell (Tilted Access Press).

Jerusalem Prize (Israel). Awarded biennially to a writer whose works best express the theme of freedom of the individual in society. *Offered by:* Jerusalem International Book Fair. *Winner (2021):* Julian Barnes.

Jewish Book Council Awards. *Winners:* (Jewish Book of the Year) Michael W. Twitty for *Koshersoul: The Faith and Food Journey of an African American Jew* (Amistad); (American Jewish studies) Nomi M. Stolzenberg and David N. Myers for *American Shtetl: The Making of Kiryas Joel, a Hasidic Village in Upstate New York* (Princeton University Press); (autobiography and memoir) Stephen Mills for *Chosen: A Memoir of Stolen Boyhood* (Metropolitan Books); (biography) Jonathan Freedland for *The Escape Artist: The Man Who Broke Out of Auschwitz to Warn the World* (HarperCollins Publishers); (book club award) Miriam Ruth Black for *Shayna* (Kirk House Publishers); (children's picture book) Shoshana Nambi (author) and Moran Yogev (illustrator) for *The Very Best Sukkah: A Story from Uganda* (Kalaniot Books); (contemporary Jewish life and practice) Danya Ruttenberg for *On Repentance and Repair: Making Amends in an Unapologetic World* (Beacon Press); (debut fiction) Ashley Goldberg for *Abomination* (Vintage Australia); (education and Jewish identity) Sivan Zakai for *My Second-Favorite Country* (New York University Press); (fiction) Dani Shapiro for *Signal Fires* (Alfred A. Knopf); (food writing and cookbooks) Benedetta Jasmine Guetta for *Cooking alla Giudia: A Celebration of the Jewish Food of Italy* (Artisan); (history) Kenneth B. Moss for *An Unchosen People: Jewish Political Reckoning in Interwar Poland* (Harvard University Press); (Holocaust) Jonathan Freedland for *The Escape Artist: The Man Who Broke Out of Auschwitz to Warn the World* (HarperCollins Publishers); (Holocaust memoir) Michael Frank for *One Hundred Saturdays: Stella Levi and the Search for a Lost World* (Avid Reader Press/Simon & Schuster); (middle grade literature) Stacy Nockowitz for *The Prince of Steel Pier* (Kar-Ben); (modern Jewish thought and experience) Sidra DeKoven Ezrahi for *Figuring Jerusalem: Politics and Poetics in the Sacred Center* (University of Chicago Press); (poetry) Sean Singer for *Today in the Taxi* (Tupelo Press); (scholarship) Jay Michaelson for *The Heresy of Jacob Frank: From Jewish Messianism to Esoteric Myth* (Oxford University Press); (Sephardic culture) Michael Frank for *One Hundred Saturdays: Stella Levi and* the *Search for a Lost World* (Avid Reader Press/Simon & Schuster); (visual arts) Liana Finck for *Let There Be Light: The Real Story of Her Creation* (Penguin Random House); (women's studies) Elisheva Baumgarten for *Biblical Women and Jewish Daily Life in the Middle Ages* (University of Pennsylvania Press); (writing based on archival material) Laura Hobson Faure for "*A Jewish Marshall Plan*": *The American Jewish Presence in Post-Holocaust France* (Indiana University Press); (young adult literature) Susan Wider for *It's My Whole Life: Charlotte Salomon: An Artist in Hiding During World War II* (Norton Young Readers).

Sue Kaufman Prize for First Fiction ($5,000). For a work of first fiction (novel or short stories). *Offered by:* American Academy of Arts and Letters. *Winner:* Jackie Polzin for *Brood* (Doubleday).

Ezra Jack Keats Awards. For children's picture books. *Offered by:* New York Public Library and the Ezra Jack Keats Foundation. *Winners:* (writer award) Paul Harbridge for *Out into the Big Wide Lake,* illustrated by Josée Bisaillon (Tundra Books, an imprint of Penguin Random House); (illustrator award) Gracey Zhang (author and illustrator) for *Lala's Words* (Orchard Books, an imprint of Scholastic).

Randall Kenan Prize for Black LGBTQ Fiction. *Offered by:* Lambda Literary Foundation. *Winner:* Kalynn Bayron.

Kerlan Award. To recognize singular attainments in the creation of children's literature and in appreciation for generous donation of unique resources to the Kerlan Collection for the study of children's literature. *Offered by:* Kerlan Children's Literature Research Collections, University of Minnesota. *Winner:* Andrea Davis Pinkney.

Coretta Scott King Book Awards ($1,000). To an African American author and illustrator of outstanding books for children and young adults. *Offered by:* American Library Association's Ethnic and Multicultural Exchange Round Table (EMIERT). *Winners:* (author) Carole Boston Weatherford for *Unspeakable: The Tulsa Race Massacre,* illustrated by (Carolrhoda Books, an imprint of Lerner Publishing Group, Inc.); (illustrator) Floyd Cooper for *Unspeakable: The Tulsa Race Massacre,* written by Carole Boston Weath-

erford (Carolrhoda Books, an imprint of Lerner Publishing Group, Inc.).

Coretta Scott King/Virginia Hamilton Award for Lifetime Achievement. Given in even-numbered years to an African American author, illustrator, or author/illustrator for a body of books for children or young adults. In odd-numbered years, the award honors substantial contributions through active engagement with youth, using award-winning African American literature for children or young adults. *Winner:* Nikki Grimes.

Coretta Scott King/John Steptoe Award for New Talent. To offer visibility to a writer and illustrator at the beginning of their careers. *Sponsor:* Coretta Scott King Book Award Committee. *Winners:* (author) Amber McBride for *Me (Moth)* (Feiwell and Friends, an imprint of Macmillan Publishing Group); (illustrator) Regis and Kahran Bethencourt for *The Me I Choose to Be,* written by Natasha Anastasia Tarpley (Little, Brown and Company).

Kirkus Prize ($50,000). For outstanding fiction, nonfiction, and young readers literature. *Offered by:* Kirkus Reviews. *Winners:* (fiction) Hernan Diaz for *Trust* (Riverhead Books); (nonfiction) Tanaïs for *In Sensorium* (Harper, an imprint of HarperCollins Publishers); (young readers) Harmony Becker for *Himawari House* (First Second).

Lambda Literary Awards. To honor outstanding lesbian, gay, bisexual, transgender, and queer (LGBTQ) literature. *Offered by:* Lambda Literary Foundation. *Winners:* (lesbian fiction) Mia McKenzie for *Skye Falling* (Random House); (gay fiction) Brontez Purnell for *100 Boyfriends* (Farrar, Straus and Giroux); (bisexual fiction) Alix Ohlin for *We Want What We Want* (House of Anansi Press); (transgender fiction) Jeanne Thornton for *Summer Fun* (Soho Press); (bisexual nonfiction) Aisha Sabatini Sloan for *Borealis* (Coffee House Press); (transgender nonfiction) Da'Shaun L. Harrison for *Belly of the Beast: The Politics of Anti-Fatness as Anti-Blackness* (North Atlantic Books); (LGBTQ nonfiction) Sarah Schulman for *Let the Record Show: A Political History of Act Up New York, 1987–1993* (Farrar, Straus and Giroux); (lesbian poetry) Tamiko Beyer for *Last Days* (Alice James Books); (gay poetry) John Keene for *Punks: New and Selected Poems* (The Song Cave); (bisexual poetry) Aurielle Marie for *Gumbo Ya Ya* (University of Pittsburgh Press); (transgender poetry) Mason J. for *Crossbones on My Life* (Nomadic Press); (lesbian memoir/ biography) Sophie Santos for *The One You Want to Marry (And Other Identities I've Had): A Memoir* (Topple Books); (gay memoir/biography) Brian Broome for *Punch Me Up to the Gods* (Mariner Books); (lesbian romance) Milena McKay for *The Headmistress* (self-published); (gay romance) Larry Benjamin for *Excellent Sons: A Love Story in Three Acts* (Beaten Track Publishing); (LGBTQ anthology) Briona Simone Jones (editor) for *Mouths of Rain: An Anthology of Black Lesbian Thought* (New Press); (LGBTQ children's/middle grade) JR and Vanessa Ford (author) and Kayla Harren (illustrator) for *Calvin* (G.P. Putnam's Sons Books for Young Readers); (LGBTQ young adult) A.R. Capetta for *The Hearbreak Bakery* (Candlewick Press); (LGBTQ comics) Lee Lei for *Stone Fruit* (Fantagraphics); (LGBTQ drama) R. Eric Thomas for *Mrs. Harrison* (TRW Plays); (LGBTQ erotica) Samuel R. Delany for *Big Joe* (Inpatient Press); (LGBTQ mystery) John Copenhaver for *The Savage Kind* (Pegasus Books); (LGBTQ speculative fiction) Cadwell Turnbull for *No Gods, No Monsters* (Blackstone Publishing); (LGBTQ studies) Anna Lvovsky for *Vice Patrol: Cops, Courts, and the Struggle over Urban Gay Life before Stonewall* (University of Chicago Press).

Harold Morton Landon Translation Award ($1,000). For a book of verse translated into English. *Offered by:* Academy of American Poets. *Winner:* Adriana X. Jacobs for *The Truffle Eye* by Vaan Nguyen (Zephyr Press).

David J. Langum, Sr. Prize in American Historical Fiction ($1,000). To honor a book of historical fiction published in the previous year. *Offered by:* Langum Foundation. *Winner (2020):* Michael Punke for *Ridgeline* (Henry Holt & Company).

David J. Langum, Sr. Prize in American Legal History or Biography ($1,000). For a university press book that is accessible to the educated general public, rooted in sound scholarship, with themes that touch upon matters of general concern. *Offered by:* Langum Foundation. *Winner (2021):* Mia

Bay for *Traveling Black: A Story of Race and Resistance* (Belknap Press/Harvard University Press).

Latner Writers' Trust Poetry Prize (C$25,000) (Canada). To a writer with an exceptional body of work in the field of poetry. *Offered by:* Writers' Trust of Canada. *Sponsor:* Latner Family Foundation. *Winner:* Joseph Dandurand.

James Laughlin Award ($5,000). To commend and support a second book of poetry. *Offered by:* Academy of American Poets. *Winner:* Annelyse Gelman for *Vexations* (University of Chicago Press).

Library of Congress Prize for American Fiction. To an author for a body of extraordinary work. *Winner:* Jesmyn Ward.

Claudia Lewis Award. For the best poetry book. *Offered by:* Bank Street College of Education. *Winner:* Diana Whitney (editor) for *You Don't Have to Be Everything: Poems for Girls Becoming Themselves* (Workman).

Ruth Lilly and Dorothy Sargent Rosenberg Poetry Fellowships ($25,800). To emerging poets to support their continued study and writing of poetry. *Offered by:* The Poetry Foundation. *Winners:* Tarik Dobbs, Diamond Forde, Tariq Luthun, Troy Osaki, Alan Pelaez Lopez.

Ruth Lilly Poetry Prize ($100,000). To a U.S. poet in recognition of lifetime achievement. *Offered by:* The Poetry Foundation. *Winners (Note: 11 prizes were awarded in 2022):* Sandra Cisneros, CAConrad, Rita Dove, Nikki Giovanni, Juan Felipe Herrera, Angela Jackson, Haki Madhubuti, Sharon Olds, Sonia Sanchez, Patti Smith, and Arthur Sze.

Astrid Lindgren Memorial Award (Sweden) (5 million kroner, more than $575,000). In memory of children's author Astrid Lindgren, to honor outstanding children's literature and efforts to promote it. *Offered by:* Government of Sweden and the Swedish Arts Council. *Winner:* Eva Lindström.

LITA Excellence in Children's and Young Adult Science Fiction. See Core Excellence in Children's and Young Adult Science Fiction.

Locus Awards. For science fiction writing. *Offered by:* Locus Publications. *Winners:* (science fiction) Arkady Martine for *A Desolation Called Peace* (Tor); (fantasy) Fonda Lee for *Jade Legacy* (Orbit); (horror)

Stephen Graham Jones for *My Heart Is a Chainsaw* (Saga); (young adult) Charlie Jane Anders for *Victories Greater Than Death* (Tor Teen); (first novel) P. Djèlí Clark for *A Master of Djinn* (Tordotcom); (novella) Martha Wells for *Fugitive Telemetry* (Tordotcom); (novelette) John Wiswell for "That Story Isn't the Story" in *Uncanny* (November/December 2021); (short story) Sarah Pinsker for "Where Oaken Hearts Do Gather" in *Uncanny* (March/April 2021); (anthology) C.L. Clark and Charles Payseur (editors) for *We're Here: The Best Queer Speculative Fiction 2020* (Neon Hemlock); (collection) Charlie Jane Anders for *Even Greater Mistakes* (Tor); (nonfiction) Andrew Nette and Iain McIntyre (editors) for *Dangerous Visions and New Worlds: Radical Science Fiction, 1950–1985* (PM); (art book) Charles Vess for *The Art of Neil Gaiman and Charles Vess's Stardust* (Titan).

Elizabeth Longford Prize for Historical Biography (United Kingdom) (£5,000, about $6,200). *Sponsors:* Flora Fraser and Peter Soros. *Winner:* Andrew Roberts for *George III: The Life and Reign of Britain's Most Misunderstood Monarch* (Allen Lane).

Los Angeles Times Book Prizes. To honor literary excellence. *Offered by:* Los Angeles Times. *Winners:* (Art Seidenbaum Award for First Fiction) Jackie Polzin for *Brood* (Doubleday); (biography) Paul Auster for *Burning Boy: The Life and Work of Stephen Crane* (Henry Holt & Company); (Christopher Isherwood Prize for Autobiographical Prose) Deborah Levy for *Real Estate: A Living Autobiography* (Bloomsbury); (current interest) Adam Schiff for *Midnight in Washington: How We Almost Lost Our Democracy and Still Could* (Random House); (fiction) Véronique Tadjo for *In the Company of Men* (Other Press); (graphic novel/comics) R. Kikuo Johnson for *No One Else* (Fantagraphics); (history) Ada Ferrer for *Cuba: An American History* (Scribner); (mystery/thriller) Megan Abbott for *The Turnout* (G.P. Putnam's Sons); (poetry) Diane Seuss for *frank: sonnets* (Graywolf Press); (Ray Bradbury Prize for Science Fiction, Fantasy & Speculative Fiction) Zen Cho for *Spirits Abroad* (Small Beer Press); (science and technology) Chanda Prescod-Weinstein for *The Disordered Cosmos:*

A Journey into Dark Matter, Spacetime, and Dreams Deferred (Bold Type Books); (young adult literature) Rita Williams-Garcia for *A Sitting in St. James* (HarperCollins/Quill Tree Books).

Amy Lowell Poetry Traveling Scholarship. For one or two U.S. poets to spend one year outside North America in a country the recipients feel will most advance their work. *Offered by:* Amy Lowell Poetry Traveling Scholarship. *Winners:* Derrick Austin and Devon E. Walker Figueroa.

Walter & Lillian Lowenfels Criticism Award. *Offered by:* Before Columbus Foundation. *Winner:* Jessica E. Teague for *Sound Recording Technology and American Literature, from the Phonograph to the Remix* (Cambridge University Press).

J. Anthony Lukas Awards. For nonfiction writing that demonstrates literary grace, serious research, and concern for an important aspect of American social or political life. *Offered by:* Columbia University Graduate School of Journalism and the Nieman Foundation for Journalism at Harvard. *Winners:* (Lukas Book Prize, $10,000) Andrea Elliott for *Invisible Child: Poverty, Survival & Hope in an American City* (Random House); (Mark Lynton History Prize, $10,000) Jane Rogoyska for *Surviving Katyń: Stalin's Polish Massacre and the Search for Truth* (Oneworld Publications); (Work-in-Progress Award, two prizes of $25,000 each) Roxanna Asgarian for *We Were Once a Family: The Hart Murder-Suicide and the System Failing Our Kids* and May Jeong for *The Life: Sex, Work, and Love in America*.

Macavity Awards. For excellence in mystery writing. *Offered by:* Mystery Readers International. *Winners:* (mystery novel) S.A. Cosby for *Razorblade Tears* (Flatiron Books); (first mystery) Mia P. Manansala for *Arsenic and Adobo* (Berkley); (nonfiction/critical) Lee Child and Laurie R. King (editors) for *How to Write a Mystery: A Handbook from Mystery Writers of America* (Scribner); (short story) Richard Helms for "Sweeps Week" in *Ellery Queen Mystery Magazine* (July/August 2021); (Sue Feder Historical Mystery Award) Naomi Hirahara for *Clark and Division* (Soho Crime).

Judith A. Markowitz Award for Emerging LGBTQ Writers. *Offered by:* Lambda Literary

Foundation. *Winners:* Ching-In Chen and Morgan Thomas.

Lenore Marshall Poetry Prize ($25,000). For an outstanding book of poems published in the United States. *Offered by:* Academy of American Poets. *Winner:* Mai Der Vang for *Yellow Rain* (Graywolf Press).

Somerset Maugham Awards (United Kingdom) (£2,500, about $3,100). For works in any genre except drama by a writer younger than 35, to enable young writers to enrich their work by gaining experience of foreign countries. *Winners:* Caleb Azumah Nelson for *Open Water* (Penguin Books); Tice Cin for *Keeping the House* (And Other Stories)*; Maia Elsner for *Overrun by Wild Boars* (Flipped Eye Publishing); Lucia Osbourne-Crowley for *My Body Keeps Your Secrets* (The Indigo Press).

McKitterick Prize (United Kingdom) (£4,000, about $5,000). To an author older than 40 for a first novel, published or unpublished. *Winner:* David Annand for *Peterdown* (Little, Brown Book Group).

Medal for Editorial Excellence (formerly the Maxwell E. Perkins Award). To honor an editor, publisher, or agent who has discovered, nurtured, and championed writers of fiction in the United States. *Offered by:* Center for Fiction, Mercantile Library of New York. *Winner:* Sarah McGrath.

Addison M. Metcalf Award in Literature ($2,000). Awarded biennially to a writer of great promise. *Winner (2021):* Kali Fajardo-Anstine.

Vicky Metcalf Award for Literature for Young People (C$25,000) (Canada). To a Canadian writer of children's literature for a body of work. *Offered by:* Writers' Trust of Canada. *Sponsor:* Metcalf Foundation. *Winner:* Elise Gravel.

Midwest Booksellers Choice Awards. *Offered by:* Midwest Independent Publishers Association. *Winners:* (anthology nonfiction) Amy Zellmer and Dr. Shane Steadman for *Concussion Discussions: A Functional Approach to Recovery after Brain Injury* (Faces of TBI); (arts/photography/coffee table) Richard Bresnahan for *Kura: Prophetic Messenger* (Kura Book Publishing); (autobiography/memoir) Courtney Burnett for *Difficult Gifts: A Physician's Journey to Heal Body and Mind* (Wise Ink Creative

Publishing); (biography) Joseph Bruchac for *A Peacemaker for Warring Nations: The Founding of the Iroquois League* (Wisdom Tales Press/World Wisdom); (business) James D. Johnson for *Ready, Mindset, Grow!: Nuggets Mined from the Leadership Journeys* (Calumet Editions); (children's fiction) Samantha Edwards for *Tale as Tall as Jacob* (Andrews McMeel Universal); (children's and young adult nonfiction) Rochelle Riley and Cristi Smith-Jones for *That They Lived* (Wayne State University Press); (children's picture) Krista Betcher for *Breathe, Ollie!* (Beaver's Pond Press); (cookbooks/crafts/hobbies) Angie Asche, M.S., R.D., C.S.S.D., for *Fuel Your Body: How to Cook and Eat for Peak Performance: 77 Simple, Nutritious, Whole-Food Recipes for Every Athlete* (Agate); (education/learning) Monica H. Kang for *Rethink Creativity: How to Innovate, Inspire and Thrive at Work* (Publish Your Purpose Press); (family/parenting) Lizann Lightfoot for *Open When: Letters of Encouragement for Military Spouses* (Elva Resa Publishing); (fantasy/sci-fi/horror/paranormal fiction) E.D.E. Bell for *Just Bart* (Atthis Arts); (graphic novel) Hilary Campbell for *Murder Book* (Andrews McMeel Universal); (health) Hillary L. McBride, Ph.D., for *The Wisdom of Your Body: Finding Healing, Wholeness, and Connection through Embodied Living* (Brazos Press); (history) Dan Patterson and Clinton Terry for *Surveying in Early America: The Point of Beginning, An Illustrated History* (University of Cincinnati Library Publishing Services); (regional history) Ron Faiola for *The Wisconsin Supper Clubs Story: An Illustrated History, with Relish* (Agate); (humor nonfiction) Mike Lein for *Cabin Fever: Life Goes On in the Northwoods* (The Jackpine Writers Bloc); (inspiration) Prakash Mathew for *We Are Called . . . To Do the Right Thing: A Practical Guide for Leaders Based on Personal Reflections and Experiences from a Longtime Higher Education Leader* (North Dakota State University Press); (literary/contemporary/historical fiction) Jim Guhl for *South of Luck* (University of Wisconsin Press); (mystery/thriller fiction) Jerry McGinley for *A Driftless Murder* (University of Wisconsin Press); (nature) Heather Holm for *Wasps: Their Biology, Diversity,* and *Role as Beneficial Insects and Pollinators of Native Plants* (Pollination Press); (poetry) Laura Apol for *A Fine Yellow Dust* (Michigan State University Press); (poetry anthology) Christopher Nelson (editor) for *Essential Voices: Poetry of Iran and Its Diaspora* (Green Linden Press); (debut poetry) Daniel Lassell for *Spit* (Wheelbarrow Books, an imprint of Michigan State University Press); (regional poetry) Jim Daniels for *Gun/Shy* (Wayne State University Press); (recreation/sports/travel) Beverly L. Gillen for *The Gift of Green Time: 50 Ways for Families to Disconnect (and Reconnect) Outdoors–Door County* (self-published); (religion/philosophy) Frithjof Schuon for *The Eye of the Heart: A New Translation with Selected Letters* (World Wisdom); (romance fiction) Annmarie Boyle for *Don't Let the Music Die* (Dahlia Media); (short story/anthology fiction) Anthony Bukoski for *The Blondes of Wisconsin* (University of Wisconsin Press); (social science/political science/culture) Mariame Kaba for *We Do This 'Til We Free Us: Abolitionist Organizing and Transforming Justice* (Haymarket Books); (young adult fiction) Colby Smith for *Call Me Athena* (Andrews McMeel Universal).

William C. Morris YA Debut Award. To honor a debut book published by a first-time author writing for teens and celebrating impressive new voices in young adult literature. *Offered by:* American Library Association's Young Adult Library Services Association. *Donor:* William C. Morris Endowment. *Winner:* Angeline Boulley for *Firekeeper's Daughter* (Henry Holt & Company, an imprint of Macmillan Children's Publishing Group).

Mythopoeic Fantasy Awards. To recognize fantasy or mythic literature for children and adults that best exemplifies the spirit of the Inklings, a group of fantasy writers that includes J.R.R. Tolkien, C.S. Lewis, and Charles Williams. *Offered by:* Mythopoeic Society. *Winners:* (adult literature) Jo Walton for *Or What You Will* (Tor); (children's literature) (tie) Lori M. Lee for *Pahua and the Soul Stealer* (Rick Riordan Presents) and Eden Royce for *Root Magic* (Walden Pond Press); (Mythopoeic Scholarship Award in Inklings Studies) Holly Ordway for *Tolkien's Modern Reading: Middle-earth beyond* the Middle Ages (Word on Fire Academic); (Mythopoeic Scholarship Award in Myth and Fantasy Studies) Philip Ball for *The Modern Myths: Adventures in the Machinery of the Popular Imagination* (University of Chicago Press).

National Book Awards. To celebrate the best in American literature. *Offered by:* National Book Foundation. *Winners:* (fiction) Tess Gunty for *The Rabbit Hutch* (Alfred A. Knopf/Penguin Random House); (nonfiction) Imani Perry for *South to America: A Journey Below the Mason-Dixon to Understand the Soul of a Nation* (Ecco/HarperCollins Publishers); (poetry) John Keene for *Punks: New & Selected Poems* (The Song Cave); (translated literature) Samanta Schweblin for *Seven Empty Houses*, translated from the Spanish by Megan McDowell (Riverhead Books/Penguin Random House); (young people's literature) Sabaa Tahir for *All My Rage* (Razorbill/Penguin Random House).

National Book Critics Circle Awards. For literary excellence. *Offered by:* National Book Critics Circle. *Winners:* (fiction) Ling Ma for *Bliss Montage: Stories* (Farrar, Straus and Giroux); (nonfiction) Isaac Butler for *The Method: How the Twentieth Century Learned to Act* (Bloomsbury); (biography) Beverly Gage for *G-Man: J. Edgar Hoover and the Making of the American Century* (Viking); (autobiography) Hua Hsu for *Stay True: A Memoir* (Doubleday); (poetry) Cynthia Cruz for *Hotel Oblivion* (Four Way); (criticism) Timothy Bewes for *Free Indirect: The Novel in a Postfictional Age* (Columbia); (John Leonard Prize) Morgan Talty for *Night of the Living Rez* (Tin House); (Gregg Barrios Book in Translation) Boris Dralyuk for his translation of *Grey Bees* by Andrey Kurkov (Deep Vellum); (Nona Balakian Citation for Excellence in Reviewing) Jennifer Wilson; (Ivan Sandrof Lifetime Achievement Award) Joy Harjo; (Toni Morrison Achievement Award) City Lights; (NBCC Service Award) Barbara Hoffert.

National Book Foundation Literarian Award for Outstanding Service to the American Literary Community. *Offered by:* National Book Foundation. *Winner:* Tracie D. Hall.

National Book Foundation Medal for Distinguished Contribution to American Letters

($10,000). To a person who has enriched the nation's literary heritage over a life of service or corpus of work. *Offered by:* National Book Foundation. *Winner:* Art Spiegelman.

National Translation Awards ($5,000). To honor translators whose work has made a valuable contribution to literary translation into English. *Offered by:* American Literary Translators Association. *Winners:* (prose) Martin Aitken, translator from Norwegian, for *The Morning Star* by Karl Ove Knausgaard (Penguin Press); (poetry) D.M. Black, translator from Italian, for *Purgatorio* by Dante Alighieri (NYRB Classics).

Nebula Awards. For science fiction writing. *Offered by:* Science Fiction and Fantasy Writers of America (SFWA). *Winners:* (novel) P. Djèlí Clark for *A Master of Djinn* (Tordotcom); (novella) Premee Mohamed for "And What Can We Offer You Tonight" (Neon Hemlock); (novelette) Oghenechovwe Donald Ekpeki for "O2 Arena" (Galaxy's Edge); (short story) Sarah Pinsker for "Where Oaken Hearts Do Gather" (*Uncanny*); (Ray Bradbury Award for dramatic presentation) Peter Cameron, Mackenzie Dohr, Laura Donney, Bobak Esfarjani, Megan McDonnell, Jac Schaeffer, Cameron Squires, Gretchen Enders, and Chuck Hayward for *WandaVision*: Season 1 (Marvel Studios); (Andre Norton Award for young adult science fiction and fantasy) Darcie Little Badger for *A Snake Falls to Earth* (Levine Querido).

John Newbery Medal. For the most distinguished contribution to literature for children. *Offered by:* American Library Association's Association for Library Service to Children. *Winner:* Donna Barba Higuera for *The Last Cuentista* (Levine Querido).

Next Generation Indie Book Awards ($1,500). *Offered by:* Independent Book Publishing Professionals Group. *Winner:* (fiction) Sissel Waage (author) and Ana-Maria Cosma (illustrator) for *The ForestGirls, with the World Always* (Lulu Press); (nonfiction) Jane Marshall (author) and Harriet Sheffer (illustrator) for *The Naked Truth about Breast Cancer* (Publish Central).

Nibbies (United Kingdom). See British Book Awards.

Nimrod Literary Awards ($2,000 plus publication). *Offered by:* Nimrod International Journal of Prose and Poetry. *Winners:* (Pab-

lo Neruda Prize in Poetry) Lory Bedikian for "Ode to Their Leaving" and other poems; (Katherine Anne Porter Prize in Fiction) Treena Thibodeau for "My Mother Says Our House Is Haunted."

Nobel Prize in Literature (Sweden). For the total literary output of a distinguished career. *Offered by:* Swedish Academy. *Winner:* Annie Ernaux.

Eli M. Oboler Memorial Award. Given biennially to an author of a published work in English or in English translation dealing with issues, events, questions, or controversies in the area of intellectual freedom. *Offered by:* American Library Association's Intellectual Freedom Round Table. *Winner (2022):* Jamie M. Gregory for *Intellectual Freedom Blog* (American Library Association's Office for Intellectual Freedom).

Flannery O'Connor Award for Short Fiction. For collections of short fiction. *Offered by:* University of Georgia Press. *Winner:* Carol Roh Spaulding for *Waiting for Mr. Kim and Other Stories* (University of Georgia Press).

Oddest Book Title of the Year Award. See Bookseller/Diagram Prize for Oddest Title of the Year.

Scott O'Dell Award for Historical Fiction ($5,000). *Offered by: Bulletin of the Center for Children's Books,* University of Chicago. *Winner:* Justina Ireland for *Ophie's Ghosts* (Balzer + Bray).

Odyssey Award. To the producer of the best audiobook for children and/or young adults available in English in the United States. *Sponsors:* American Library Association ALSC/Booklist/YALSA. *Winners:* (children) HarperAudio/Katherine Tegen Books for *Boogie Boogie, Y'all*, written and narrated by C.G. Esperanza; (young adult) HarperAudio/Quill Tree Books for *When You Look Like Us*, written by Pamela N. Harris and narrated by Preston Butler III.

Seán Ó Faoláin Short Story Competition (€2,000, about $2,200, and publication in the literary journal *Southword). Offered by:* Munster Literature Centre, Cork, Ireland. *Winner:* E.M. Hughes for "Infestato."

Dayne Ogilvie Prize (C$4,000) (Canada). To an emerging Canadian writer from the LGBT community who demonstrates promise through a body of quality work. *Offered by:* Writers' Trust of Canada. *Winner:*

francesca ekwuyasi for *Butter Honey Pig Bread* (Arsenal Pulp Press).

Orbis Pictus Award for Outstanding Nonfiction for Children. *Offered by:* National Council of Teachers of English. *Winner:* Traci N. Todd (author) and Christian Robinson (illustrator) for *Nina: A Story of Nina Simone* (G.P. Putnam's Sons Books for Young Readers).

Oxford-Weidenfeld Translation Prize. *Winner:* Nancy Naomi Carlson for her translation from French of *Cargo Hold of Stars* by Khal Torabully (Seagull Books).

PEN Award for Poetry in Translation ($3,000). For a book-length translation of poetry from any language into English, published in the United States. *Offered by:* PEN American Center. *Winners:* Jennifer Grotz and Piotr Sommer for their translation from the Polish of *Everything I Don't Know* by Jerzy Ficowski (World Poetry Books).

PEN/Saul Bellow Award for Achievement in American Fiction ($25,000). Awarded biennially to a distinguished living American author of fiction. *Offered by:* PEN American Center. Not awarded in 2022.

PEN/Bellwether Prize for Socially Engaged Fiction ($25,000). Awarded biennially to the author of a previously unpublished novel that addresses issues of social justice and the impact of culture and politics on human relationships. *Founder:* Barbara Kingsolver. *Winner (2021):* Jamila Minnicks Gleason for *Hydrangeas of New Jessup.*

PEN/Robert W. Bingham Prize ($25,000). To a writer whose first novel or short story collection represents distinguished literary achievement and suggests great promise. *Offered by:* PEN American Center. *Winner:* Yoon Choi for *Skinship: Stories* (Alfred A. Knopf).

PEN/Robert J. Dau Short Story Prize for Emerging Writers ($2,000 to 12 writers). To recognize 12 emerging fiction writers for their debut short stories. *Offered by:* PEN American Center. *Winners:* Catherine Bai for "Writing with Blood" in *Flock*; R.Z. Baschir for "The Chicken" in *The White Review*; Erin Connal for "The Black Kite and the Wind" in *Virginia Quarterly Review*; C.K. Kane for "Them Bones" in Hobart; Patch Kirschenbaum for "For Future Reference: Notes on the 7-10 Split" in *Cincin-*

nati Review; Yasmin Adele Majeed for "A Wedding in Multan, 1978" in *Asian American Literary Review*; Oyedotun Damilola Muees for "All We Have Left Is Ourselves" in *Reckoning*; Edward Salem for "Sacrilege" in *BOMB Magazine*; Emma Shannon for "Beat by Beat" in *Barrelhouse Magazine*; Cal Shook for "Man, Man, Et Cetera" in *Virginia Quarterly Review*; Preeti Vangani for "Work Wives" in *Typehouse Literary Magazine*; Seth Wang for "The Cacophobe" in *Ploughshares.*

PEN/Diamonstein-Spielvogel Award for the Art of the Essay ($10,000). For a book of essays by a single author that best exemplifies the dignity and esteem of the essay form. *Winner:* Margaret Renkl for *Graceland, at Last: Notes on Hope and Heartache from the American South* (Milkweed Editions).

PEN/Faulkner Award for Fiction ($15,000). To honor the year's best work of fiction published by an American. *Winner:* Rabih Alameddine for *The Wrong End of the Telescope* (Grove Press).

PEN/John Kenneth Galbraith Award for Nonfiction ($10,000). Given for a distinguished book of general nonfiction. *Offered by:* PEN American Center. *Winner:* Tiya Miles for *All That She Carried: The Journey of Ashley's Sack, a Black Family's Keepsake* (Random House).

PEN Grant for the English Translation of Italian Literature ($5,000). *Winner:* Tim Cummins for his translation from the Italian of *We Will Take Our Revenge* by Paolo Nori.

PEN/Heim Translation Fund Grants ($2,000–$4,000). To support the translation of book-length works of fiction, creative nonfiction, poetry, or drama that have not previously appeared in English or have appeared only in an egregiously flawed translation. *Winners:* Bernard Capinpin, Rajnesh Chakrapani, Anca Roncea, Danielle Legros Georges, Ryan Greene, Bani May Huang, Mirgul Kali, Adam Mahler, Mui Poopoksakul, Jay Rubin, Yasmine Seale.

PEN/Ernest Hemingway Foundation Award. For a distinguished work of first fiction by an American. *Offered by:* PEN New England. *Winner:* Torrey Peters for *Detransition, Baby* (MCD/Farrar, Straus and Giroux).

PEN/O. Henry Prize. For short stories of exceptional merit, in English, published in U.S.

and Canadian magazines. *Winners:* Alejandro Zambra for "Screen Time," translated by Megan McDowell in *The New York Times Magazine*; Daniel Mason for "The Wolves of Circassia" in *Zoetrope*; Tere Dávila for "Mercedes's Special Talent," translated by Rebecca Hanssens-Reed in *The Offing*; Joseph O'Neill for "Rainbows" in *The New Yorker*; Shanteka Sigers for "A Way with Bea" in *The Paris Review*; Olga Tokarczuk for "Seams," translated by Jennifer Croft in *Freeman's*; Yohanca Delgado for "The Little Widow from the Capital" in *The Paris Review*; Eshkol Nevo for "Lemonade," translated by Sondra Silverston in *The Paris Review*; 'Pemi Aguda for "Breastmilk" in *One Story*; Amar Mitra for "The Old Man of Kusumpur," translated by Anish Gupta in *The Common*; Christos Ikonomou for "Where They Always Meet," translated by Karen Emmerich in *The Yale Review*; Janika Oza for "Fish Stories" in *The Kenyon Review*; Vladimir Sorokin for "Horse Soup," translated by Max Lawton in *n+1*; Francisco González for "Clean Teen" in *Gulf Coast*; Michel Nieva for "Dengue Boy," translated by Natasha Wimmer in *Granta*; Chimamanda Ngozi Adichie for "Zikora" (Amazon Original Stories); Gunnhild Øyehaug for "Apples," translated by Kari Dickson in *Freeman's*; David Ryan for "Warp and Weft" in *Harvard Review*; Lorrie Moore for "Face Time" in *The New Yorker*; Samanta Schweblin for "An Unlucky Man," translated by Megan McDowell in *McSweeney's Quarterly Concern*.

PEN/Nora Magid Award ($2,500). Awarded biennially to honor a magazine editor who has contributed significantly to the excellence of the publication he or she edits. *Winner (2021):* Kwame Dawes for *Prairie Schooner*.

PEN/Malamud Award. To recognize a body of work that demonstrates excellence in the art of short fiction. *Winner:* Yiyun Li.

PEN/Ralph Manheim Medal for Translation. Given triennially to a translator whose career has demonstrated a commitment to excellence. *Winner (2021):* Pierre Joris.

PEN/Nabokov Award for Achievement in International Literature ($50,000). To a writer of any genre and of any nationality for their exceptional body of work. *Winner:* Ngũgĩ wa Thiong'o.

PEN/Phyllis Naylor Grant for Children's and Young Adult Novelists ($5,000). To a published author of children's or young adult fiction to aid in completing a book-length work in progress. *Offered by:* PEN American Center. *Winner:* Joy Jones for *Walking the Boomerang* (work in progress).

PEN/Mike Nichols Writing for Performance Award ($25,000). To a writer whose work exemplifies excellence and influence in the world of theater, television, or film. *Winner:* Elaine May.

PEN Open Book Award (formerly PEN Beyond Margins Award) ($5,000). For book-length writings by authors of color, published in the United States during the current calendar year. *Offered by:* PEN American Center. *Winner:* Divya Victor for *Curb* (Nightboat Books).

PEN/Laura Pels International Foundation for Theater Award. To a playwright working at the highest level of achievement in mid-career. *Offered by:* PEN American Center. *Winner:* Jackie Sibblies Drury.

PEN/Jean Stein Book Award ($75,000). To recognize a book-length work of any genre for its originality, merit, and impact. *Winner:* Daisy Hernández for *The Kissing Bug: A True Story of a Family, an Insect, and a Nation's Neglect of a Deadly Disease* (Tin House Books).

PEN/Jean Stein Grant for Literary Oral History ($10,000 each). Two awards for literary works of nonfiction that use oral history to illuminate an event, individual, place, or movement. *Winners:* Simar Preet Kaur for *A Hyphenway in the Sky* (work in progress) and Deborah Jackson for *Taffa, Whiskey Tender* (work in progress).

PEN Translation Prize ($3,000). To promote the publication and reception of translated world literature in English. *Winner:* Julia Sanches for her translation from Spanish of *Migratory Birds* by Mariana Oliver (Transit Books).

PEN/Edward and Lily Tuck Award for Paraguayan Literature ($3,000 to author and $3,000 to translator). Given in even-numbered years to the living author of a major work of Paraguayan literature. Not awarded in 2022.

PEN/Voelcker Award for Poetry Collection. Given annually to a poet for a distinguished collection that represents a notable and accomplished literary presence, expanding the scope of American poetry. *Offered by:* PEN American Center. *Winner:* Diane Seuss for *frank: sonnets* (Graywolf Press).

PEN/Jacqueline Bograd Weld Award for Biography ($5,000). To the author of a distinguished biography published in the United States during the previous calendar year. *Offered by:* PEN American Center. *Winner:* Rebecca Donner for *All the Frequent Troubles of Our Days: The True Story of the American Woman at the Heart of the German Resistance to Hitler* (Little, Brown and Company).

PEN/E.O. Wilson Literary Science Writing Award ($10,000). For a book of literary nonfiction on the subject of the physical and biological sciences. *Winner:* Catherine Raven for *Fox & I: An Uncommon Friendship* (Spiegel & Grau).

Maxwell E. Perkins Award. See Medal for Editorial Excellence.

Aliki Perroti and Seth Frank Most Promising Young Poet Award ($1,000). For a student poet 23 years old or younger. *Offered by:* Academy of American Poets. *Winner:* Danielle Emerson for "shíma yazhí ahéhee' / thank you, auntie."

Phoenix Awards. To the authors of English-language children's books that failed to win a major award at the time of publication 20 years earlier. *Offered by:* Children's Literature Association. *Winner:* Julie Otsuka for *When the Emperor Was Divine* (Alfred A. Knopf).

Plimpton Prize for Fiction ($10,000). For an outstanding story published by an emerging writer in *The Paris Review* in the previous calendar year. *Offered by: The Paris Review. Winner:* Chetna Maroo.

Plutarch Award ($1,000). To the best biography of the year. *Offered by:* Biographers International Organization. *Winner:* Frances Wilson for *Burning Man: The Trials of D.H. Lawrence* (Farrar, Straus and Giroux).

Edgar Allan Poe Awards. See Edgar Awards.

Poets Out Loud Prize ($1,000 and publication by Fordham University Press). For a book-length poetry collection. *Sponsor:* Poetic Justice Institute at Fordham University. *Winners (2022):* To be announced. *Winners (2021):* Jennifer Atkinson for *A Gray Realm*

the Ocean (Fordham University Press); (editors prize) Alison Powell for *Boats in the Attic* (Fordham University Press).

Katherine Anne Porter Award. See American Academy of Arts and Letters Katherine Anne Porter Award.

Michael L. Printz Award. For excellence in literature for young adults. *Offered by:* American Library Association's Young Adult Library Services Association. *Winner:* Angeline Boulley for *Firekeeper's Daughter* (Henry Holt & Company, an imprint of Macmillan Children's Publishing Group).

V.S. Pritchett Short Story Prize (United Kingdom) (£1,000, about $1,200). For a previously unpublished short story. *Offered by:* Royal Society of Literature. *Winner (2022):* To be announced. *Winner (2021):* Leeor Ohayon for "Gahnun on Shabbat."

Pritzker Military Library Literature Award ($100,000). To recognize a living author for a body of work that has profoundly enriched the public understanding of American military history. *Sponsor:* Tawani Foundation. Not awarded in 2022.

Prix Aurora Awards (Canada). For science fiction. *Offered by:* Canadian SF & Fantasy Association. *Winners:* (novel) Fonda Lee for *Jade Legacy* (Orbit US); (young adult novel) Wab Kinew for *Walking in Two Worlds* (Penguin Teen); (novelette/novella) Premee Mohamed for *The Annual Migration of Clouds* (ECW); (short story) Phoebe Barton for "The Mathematics of Fairyland" in *Lightspeed* (March 2021); (related work) Kelly Robson for *Alias Space and Other Stories* (Subterranean); (graphic novel) Kari Maaren for *It Never Rains* (webcomic); (poem/song) Carolyn Clink for "Cat People Café" in *Polar Starlight* (October 2021); (artist) Samantha M. Beiko; (visual presentation) Denis Villeneuve (director) for *Dune* (NBCUniversal Syndication Studios/ Netflix).

Prix Goncourt (France). For "the best imaginary prose work of the year." *Offered by:* Société des Gens des Lettres. *Winner:* Brigitte Giraud for *Vivre Vite* (Flammarion).

PROSE Awards. For outstanding professional and scholarly works. Offered by: Association of American Publishers. *Winners:* (biological and life sciences) Harvard University Press for Global Health Security:

A Blueprint for the Future by Lawrence O. Gostin; (humanities) Duke University Press for *Experiments in Skin: Race and Beauty in the Shadows of Vietnam* by Thuy Linh Nguyen Tu; (physical sciences and mathematics) MIT Press for *Atlas of Forecasts: Modeling and Mapping Desirable Futures* by Katy Börner; (social sciences) Little, Brown and Company for *Halfway Home* by Reuben Miller.

Publishing Triangle Awards. For the best LGBTQ fiction, nonfiction, poetry, and trans literature. Offered by: Publishing Triangle. (Ferro-Grumley Award for LGBTQ Fiction) Anthony Veasna So for *Afterparties: Stories* (Ecco); (Edmund White Award for Debut Fiction) Robert Jones, Jr. for *The Prophets* (G.P. Putnam's Sons); (Thom Gunn Award for Gay Poetry) John Keene for *Punks: New and Selected Poems* (The Song Cave); (Audre Lorde Award for Lesbian Poetry) Cheryl Boyce Taylor for *Mama Phife Represents* (Haymarket Books); (Publishing Triangle Award for Trans and Gender-Variant Literature) Ari Banias for *A Symmetry* (W.W. Norton & Company); (Judy Grahn Award for Lesbian Nonfiction) Briona Simone Jones (editor) for *Mouths of Rain: An Anthology of Black Lesbian Thought* (New Press); (Randy Shilts Award for Gay Nonfiction) Brian Broome for *Punch Me Up to the Gods* (Mariner).

Pulitzer Prizes in Letters ($10,000). To honor distinguished work dealing preferably with American themes. *Offered by:* Columbia University Graduate School of Journalism. *Winners:* (fiction) Joshua Cohen for *The Netanyahus* (New York Review Books); (drama) James Ijames for *Fat Ham*; (history) Nicole Eustace for *Covered with Night: A Story of Murder and Indigenous Justice in Early America* (Liveright/W.W. Norton & Company) and Ada Ferrer for *Cuba: An American History* (Scribner); (biography/autobiography) Winfred Rembert, as told to Erin I. Kelly, for *Chasing Me to My Grave: An Artist's Memoir of the Jim Crow South* (Bloomsbury); (poetry) Dianne Seuss for *frank: sonnets* (Graywolf Press); (general nonfiction) Andrea Elliott for *Invisible Child: Poverty, Survival & Hope in an American City* (Random House).

Raiziss/De Palchi Translation Award ($10,000 book award and a $25,000 fellowship, awarded in alternate years). For a translation into English of a significant work of modern Italian poetry by a living translator. *Offered by:* Academy of American Poets. Not awarded in 2022.

RBC Bronwen Wallace Award for Emerging Writers (C$10,000) (Canada). For writers younger than 35 who are unpublished in book form. *Offered by:* Writers' Trust of Canada. *Sponsor:* Royal Bank of Canada. *Winner:* (short story) Teya Hollier for "Watching, Waiting"; (poetry) Patrick James Errington for "If Fire, Then Bird."

Arthur Rense Poetry Prize ($20,000). Awarded triennially to an exceptional poet. *Offered by:* American Academy of Arts and Letters. *Winner (2020):* Mary Ruefle.

Sami Rohr Prize for Jewish Literature ($100,000). For emerging writers of Jewish literature. *Offered by:* Family of Sami Rohr. *Winner:* (Inspiration Award for Fiction) Menachem Kaiser.

Frances "Frank" Rollin Fellowship ($2,000). To an author working on a biographical work about an African American figure or figures whose story provides a significant contribution to our understanding of the Black experience. *Offered by:* Biographers International Organization. *Winner:* Marion Orr for his proposed biography of former U.S. Congressman Charles Diggs, Jr.

Rosenthal Family Foundation Award ($10,000). To a young writer of considerable literary talent for a work of fiction. *Offered by:* American Academy of Arts and Letters. *Winner:* Kirstin Valdez Quade for *The Five Wounds* (W.W. Norton & Company).

Hazel Rowley Prize ($2,000). For the best proposal from a first-time biographer. *Offered by:* Biographers International Organization. *Winner:* Laura Michele Diener for her proposal for a biography of the Norwegian-Danish writer Sigrid Undset (1882–1949).

Royal Society of Literature Benson Medal (United Kingdom). To recognize meritorious works in poetry, fiction, history, and belles letters, honoring an entire career. The recipient may be someone who is not a writer but has done conspicuous service to literature. *Winner:* Sandra Agard.

Royal Society of Literature Giles St Aubyn Awards for Non-Fiction (United Kingdom). For first-time writers of nonfiction. *Offered by:* Royal Society of Literature. *Winners:* (£10,000, about $12,500) Nuzha Nuseibeh for *Namesake* (Canongate); (£5,000, about $6,200) Ellen Atlanta for *Pixel Flesh: Modern Beauty Culture and The Women It Harms* (Headline/Hachette); (£2,500, about $3,100) Malachi McIntosh for *A Revolutionary Consciousness: Black Britain, Black Power, and the Caribbean Artists Movement* (Faber).

Royal Society of Literature Ondaatje Prize (United Kingdom) (£10,000, about $12,500). For a distinguished work of fiction, nonfiction, or poetry evoking the spirit of a place. *Offered by:* Royal Society of Literature. *Winner:* Lea Ypi for *Free: Coming of Age at the End of History* (Allen Lane).

Saltire Society Scotland Literary Awards. To recognize noteworthy work by writers of Scottish descent or living in Scotland or by anyone who deals with the work or life of a Scot or with a Scottish problem, event, or situation. *Offered by:* Saltire Society. *Winners:* (history and book of the year) David Alston for *Slaves and Highlanders: Silenced Histories of Scotland and the Caribbean* (Edinburgh University Press); (fiction) Mara Menzies for *Blood & Gold: A Journey of Shadows* (Birlinn Ltd.); (debut) Will McPhail for *In: The Graphic Novel* (Sceptre/ Hodder & Stoughton); (nonfiction) Chitra Ramaswamy for *Homelands: The History of a Friendship* (Canongate Books); (poetry) Claire Askew for *How to Burn a Woman* (Bloodaxe Books); (research) Patricia Macdonald (editor) for *Surveying the Anthropocene: Environment and Photography Now* (Edinburgh University Press); (lifetime achievement) Alexander McCall Smith.

J. Michael Samuel Prize for Emerging Writers Over 50. *Offered by:* Lambda Literary Foundation. *Winner:* Jobert E. Abueva.

Carl Sandburg Literary Awards. *Sponsor:* Chicago Public Library Foundation. *Winner:* Tony Kushner; (21st Century Award, for an early career author with ties to Chicago) Shermann "Dilla" Thomas.

Schneider Family Book Awards ($5,000). To honor authors and illustrators for books that embody artistic expressions of the disability experience of children and adolescents. *Offered by:* American Library Association. *Donor:* Katherine Schneider. *Winners:* (young children) Darren Lebeuf (auth-

or) and Ashley Barron (illustrator) for *My City Speaks* (Kids Can Press Ltd.); (middle school) Alison Green Myers for *A Bird Will Soar* (Dutton Books for Young Readers, an imprint of Penguin Young Readers, a division of Penguin Random House); (teen) Asphyxia for *Words in My Hands* (Annick Press).

Scotiabank Giller Prize (Canada) (C$100,000 first place, C$10,000 to each of the finalists). For the best Canadian novel or short story collection written in English. *Offered by:* Giller Prize Foundation and Scotiabank. *Winner:* Suzette Mayr for *The Sleeping Car Porter* (Coach House Books); (finalists) Kim Fu for *Lesser-Known Monsters of the 21st Century* (Coach House Books); Rawi Hage for *Stray Dogs* (Knopf Canada); Tsering Yangzom Lama for *We Measure the Earth with Our Bodies* (McClelland & Stewart); Noor Naga for *If an Egyptian Cannot Speak English* (Graywolf Press).

Shamus Awards. To honor mysteries featuring independent private investigators. *Offered by:* Private Eye Writers of America. *Winners:* (hardcover novel) S.J. Rozan for *Family Business* (Pegasus); (original paperback) John McFetridge for *Every City Is Every Other City* (ECW Press); (short story) John M. Floyd for "Sweeps Week" in *Ellery Queen Mystery Magazine* (July/August 2021); (debut) Gregory Stout for *Lost Little Girl* (Level Best Books).

Shelley Memorial Award ($6,000–$9,000). To a poet or poets living in the United States, chosen on the basis of genius and need. *Offered by:* Poetry Society of America. *Winner:* Joyelle McSweeney.

Robert F. Sibert Medal. For the most distinguished informational book for children. *Offered by:* American Library Association's Association for Library Service to Children. *Winners:* Cynthia Levinson (author) and Evan Turk (illustrator) for *The People's Painter: How Ben Shahn Fought for Justice with Art* (Abrams Books for Young Readers).

Society of Authors Traveling Scholarships (United Kingdom) (£1,333 each, about $1,660). *Winners:* Alice Albinia, Maame Blue, Linda Brogan, Ben Judah, Ayisha Malik, Dylan Moore.

Spur Awards. *Offered by:* Western Writers of America. *Winners:* (contemporary novel) C.J. Box for *Dark Sky: A Joe Pickett Novel* (G.P.

Putnam's Sons); (historical novel) Michael Punke for *Ridgeline* (Henry Holt & Company); (traditional novel) Chase Pletts for *The Loving Wrath of Eldon Quint* (Inkshares); (historical nonfiction) Terry Mort for *Cheyenne Summer: The Battle of Beecher Island* (Pegasus Books); (contemporary nonfiction) Finis Dunaway for *Defending the Arctic Refuge: A Photographer, an Indigenous Nation, and a Fight for Environmental Justice* (University of North Carolina Press); (biography) Wynne Brown for *The Forgotten Botanist: Sara Plummer Lemmon's Life of Science and Art* (Bison Books/University of Nebraska Press); (original mass market paperback novel) Brett Cogburn for *This Side of Hell: A Widowmaker Jones Western* (Pinnacle/Kensington); (romance novel) Susanna Lane for *Imperfect Promise* (Five Star Publishing); (juvenile fiction) S.J. Dahlstrom for *Cow Boyhood: The Adventures of Wilder Good, #7* (Paul Dry Books); (juvenile nonfiction) Steph Lehmann for *Montana History for Kids in 50 Objects: With 50 Fun Activities!* (Farcountry Press); (children's picture book) Emily Crawford Wilson (author) and Jeanne Bowman (illustrator) for *Charlie Russell and the Gnomes of Bull Head Lodge* (South Dakota Historical Society Press); (short fiction) David Heska Wanbli Weiden for "Skin" in *Midnight Hour: A Chilling Anthology of Crime Fiction from 20 Authors of Color* (Crooked Lane Books); (short nonfiction) Shane Dunning for "The Right Man to Do a Wrong Thing: Charlie Thex, the Bear Creek Sheep Raid, and the Primacy of Fear" in *Montana: The Magazine of Western History* (Summer 2021: Vol. 71, No. 2); (poem) karla k. morton for "Cimarron Herd" in *Politics of the Minotaur* (Texas Review Press); (drama script) Lee Martin for *Last Shoot Out* (Feifer Worldwide); (first nonfiction book) Anne MacKinnon for *Public Waters: Lessons from Wyoming for the American West* (University of New Mexico Press); (first novel) Chase Pletts for *The Loving Wrath of Eldon Quint* (Inkshares).

Stella Prize (A$50,000, about $33,400). For the best fiction or nonfiction book by an Australian woman. *Sponsor:* Wilson Foundation. *Winner:* Evelyn Araluen for *Dropbear* (University of Queensland Press).

Wallace Stevens Award ($100,000). To recognize outstanding and proven mastery in the art of poetry. *Offered by:* Academy of American Poets. *Winner:* Marilyn Nelson.

Bram Stoker Awards. For superior horror writing. *Offered by:* Horror Writers Association. *Winners (2022):* To be announced. *Winners (2021):* (novel) Stephen Graham Jones for *My Heart is a Chainsaw* (Gallery/Saga Press); (first novel) Hailey Piper for *Queen of Teeth* (Strangehouse Books); (young adult novel) Erica Waters for *The River Has Teeth* (HarperTeen); (graphic novel) Alessandro Manzetti (author) and Stefano Cardoselli (author and illustrator) for *The Inhabitant of the Lake* (Independent Legions Publishing); (long fiction) Jeff Strand for *Twentieth Anniversary Screening* (self-published); (short fiction) Lee Murray for "Permanent Damage" in *Attack from the '80s* (Raw Dog Screaming Press); (fiction collection) Gemma Files for *In That Endlessness, Our End* (Grimscribe Press); (screenplay) Mike Flanagan, James Flanagan, and Jeff Howard for *Midnight Mass:* "Book VI: Acts of the Apostles" (Intrepid Pictures); (anthology) Ellen Datlow for *When Things Get Dark: Stories Inspired by Shirley Jackson* (Titan Books); (nonfiction) Michael Knost for *Writers Workshop of Horror 2* (Hydra Publications); (short nonfiction) Angela Yuriko Smith for "Horror Writers: Architects of Hope" in *The Sirens Call* (Halloween 2021: Issue 55); (poetry collection) Christina Sng, Angela Yuriko Smith, Lee Murray, and Geneve Flynn for *Tortured Willows: Bent. Bowed. Unbroken.* (Yuriko Publishing).

Stonewall Book Awards. *Offered by:* American Library Association's Gay, Lesbian, Bisexual, and Transgender Round Table. *Winners:* (Barbara Gittings Literature Award) Rivers Solomon for *Sorrowland* (MCD/Farrar, Straus and Giroux); (Israel Fishman Nonfiction Award) Akwaeke Emezi for *Dear Senthuran: A Black Spirit Memoir* (Riverhead Books); (Mike Morgan and Larry Romans Children's and Young Adult Literature Award) (children) Kyle Lukoff for *Too Bright to See* (Dial Books for Young Readers); (young adult) Malinda Lo for *Last Night at the Telegraph Club* (Dutton Books for Young Readers).

Story Prize ($20,000). For a collection of short fiction. *Offered by: Story* magazine. *Winner (2021–2022):* Brandon Taylor for *Filthy Animals* (Riverhead Books).

Flora Stieglitz Straus Awards. For nonfiction books that serve as an inspiration to young readers. *Offered by:* Bank Street College of Education and the Florence M. Miller Memorial Fund. *Winner:* Warren Binford for *Hear My Voice/Escucha mi voz: The Testimonies of Children Detained at the Southern Border of the United States* (Workman).

Theodore Sturgeon Memorial Award. For the year's best short science fiction. *Offered by:* Gunn Center for the Study of Science Fiction. *Winner:* Nalo Hopkinson for "Broad Dutty Water: A Sunken Story" in *The Magazine of Fantasy & Science Fiction* (November/December 2021).

Sunburst Awards for Canadian Literature of the Fantastic (C$1,000). To Canadian writers with a speculative fiction novel or book-length collection of speculative fiction published any time during the previous calendar year. Not awarded in 2022.

Sunday Times Audible Short Story Award (United Kingdom) (£30,000, about $37,300). To an author from any country for an English-language story of 6,000 words or fewer. Not awarded in 2022.

Sunday Times Charlotte Aitken Young Writer of the Year Award (United Kingdom) (£5,000, about $6,200). For a full-length published or self-published (in book or e-book formats) work of fiction, nonfiction, or poetry by a British or Irish author ages 18–35. *Winner (2022):* To be announced. *Winner (2021):* Cal Flyn for *Islands of Abandonment* (William Collins).

Tanizaki Prize (Japan) (1 million yen, about $8,450). For a full-length work of fiction or drama by a professional writer. *Offered by:* Chuokoron-Shinsha, Inc. *Winner:* Banana Yoshimoto for *Miton to fubin.*

Sydney Taylor Body-of-Work Award. Recognizes an author or entity who has made a substantial contribution over time to the genre of Jewish children's literature. *Winner:* Jane Yolen.

Sydney Taylor Book Awards. For a distinguished contribution to Jewish children's literature. *Offered by:* Association of Jewish Libraries. *Winners:* (picture book) Chana Stiefel (author) and Susan Gal (illustrator) for *The Tower of Life: How Yaffa Eliach Rebuilt Her Town in Stories and Photographs* (Scholastic); (middle grade) Mari Lowe for

Aviva vs. the Dybbuk (Arthur A. Levine, an imprint of Levine Querido); (young adult) Sacha Lamb for *When the Angels Left the Old Country* (Arthur A. Levine, an imprint of Levine Querido).

Sydney Taylor Manuscript Award ($1,000). For the best fiction manuscript appropriate for readers ages 8–13, both Jewish and non-Jewish, revealing positive aspects of Jewish life and written by an unpublished author. Not awarded in 2022.

Theatre Library Association Award. See Richard Wall Memorial Award.

Dylan Thomas Prize (United Kingdom) (£30,000, about $37,300). For a published or produced literary work in the English language, written by an author younger than 30. *Offered by:* Swansea University. *Winner:* Patricia Lockwood for *No One Is Talking about This* (Bloomsbury Circus).

Henry David Thoreau Prize for Literary Excellence in Nature Writing. *Offered by:* Thoreau Society of Concord. *Winner:* Jane Goodall.

Thriller Awards. *Offered by:* International Thriller Writers. *Winners:* (hardcover novel) S.A. Cosby for Razorblade Tears (Flatiron Books); (first novel) Amanda Jayatissa for *My Sweet Girl* (Berkley); (paperback original) Jess Lourey for *Bloodline* (Thomas & Mercer); (short story) Scott Loring Sanders for "The Lemonade Stand" in *Ellery Queen Mystery Magazine* (January/February 2021); (young adult) Courtney Summers for *The Project* (Wednesday Books); (e-book original novel) E.J. Findorff for *Blood Parish* (self-published); (audio book) *Razorblade Tears* by S.A. Cosby, narrated by Adam Lazarre-White (Macmillan).

Thurber Prize for American Humor ($5,000). For a humorous book of fiction or nonfiction. *Offered by:* Thurber House. *Winner (2021):* James McBride for *Deacon King Kong* (Riverhead Books).

Tom-Gallon Trust Award (United Kingdom) (£1,000, about $1,200). For a short story. *Offered by:* Society of Authors. *Sponsor:* Authors' Licensing and Collecting Society. *Winner:* Kanya D'Almeida for "I Cleaned the ___".

Paul Torday Memorial Prize (United Kingdom) (£1,000, about $1,200). For a first novel by an author age 60 or older. *Offered by:* Society of Authors. *Winner:* Jane Fraser for *Advent* (Honno: Welsh Women's Press).

Betty Trask Prize and Awards (United Kingdom). To Commonwealth writers younger than 35 for "romantic or traditional" first novels. *Offered by:* Society of Authors. *Winners:* (Betty Trask Prize, £10,000, about $12,500) Will McPhail for *In: The Graphic Novel* (Sceptre/Hodder & Stoughton); (Betty Trask Awards, £5,000, about $6,200) Megan Nolan for *Acts of Desperation* (Vintage Publishing), Natasha Brown for *Assembly* (Penguin Books), Caleb Azumah Nelson for *Open Water* (Penguin Books), A.K. Blakemore for *The Manningtree Witches* (Granta Books).

Kate Tufts Discovery Award ($10,000). For a first or very early book of poetry by an emerging poet. *Offered by:* Claremont Graduate University. *Winner:* Torrin A. Greathouse for *Wound from the Mouth of a Wound* (Milkweed Editions).

Kingsley Tufts Poetry Award ($100,000). For a book of poetry by a midcareer poet. *Offered by:* Claremont Graduate School. *Winner:* Divya Victor for *Curb* (Nightboat Books).

21st Century Award. See Carl Sandburg Literary Awards.

UKLA Children's Book Awards (United Kingdom). *Sponsor:* United Kingdom Literacy Association. *Winners:* (ages 3–6+) (tie) Nadia Shireen for *Barbara Throws a Wobbler* (Puffin) and Tom Percival for *The Invisible* (Simon & Schuster); (ages 7–10+) Katya Balen for *October, October* (Bloomsbury); (ages 11–14+) Ibi Zoboi and Yusef Salaam for *Punching the Air* (HarperCollins); (information, ages 3–14+) Dr. Jess Wade (author) and Melissa Castrillón (illustrator) for *Nano: The Spectacular Science of the Very (Very) Small* (Walker Books).

Ungar German Translation Award ($1,000). Awarded biennially for a distinguished literary translation from German into English that has been published in the United States. *Offered by:* American Translators Association. *Winner (2021):* Philip Boehm.

John Updike Award ($10,000). Biennial prize to a writer in midcareer whose work has demonstrated consistent excellence. *Offered by:* American Academy of Arts and Letters. *Winners (2021):* Stephen Adly Guirgis and Diane Seuss.

VCU/Cabell First Novelist Award ($5,000). For a first novel published in the previous year. *Offered by:* Virginia Commonwealth University. *Winner:* Dawnie Walton for *The Final Revival of Opal and Nev* (Simon & Schuster).

Vivian Awards. *Offered by:* Romance Writers of America. Not awarded in 2022.

Harold D. Vursell Memorial Award ($20,000). To a writer whose work merits recognition for the quality of its prose style. *Offered by:* American Academy of Arts and Letters. *Winner:* Joshua Cohen.

Amelia Elizabeth Walden Award ($5,000). To honor a book relevant to adolescents that has enjoyed a wide teenage audience. *Sponsor:* Assembly on Literature for Adolescents, National Council of Teachers of English. *Winner:* Jeff Zentner for *In the Wild Light* (Crown Books for Young Readers/Random House).

Richard Wall Memorial Award (formerly the Theatre Library Association Award). To honor an English-language book of exceptional scholarship in the field of recorded performance, including motion pictures, television, and radio. *Offered by:* Theatre Library Association. *Winner:* Chris Grosvenor for *Cinema on the Front Line: British Soldiers and Cinema in the First World War* (University of Exeter Press).

George Washington Book Prize ($50,000). To recognize an important new book about America's founding era. *Offered by:* Washington College and the Gilder Lehrman Institute of American History. *Winner:* Bruce A. Ragsdale for *Washington at the Plow: The Founding Farmer and the Question of Slavery* (Belknap Press/Harvard University Press).

Waterstones Debut Fiction Prize (£5,000, about $6,200). *Offered by:* Waterstones. *Winner:* Tess Gunty for *The Rabbit Hutch* (Oneworld Publications).

Hilary Weston Writers' Trust Prize for Nonfiction (C$60,000) (Canada). *Offered by:* Writers' Trust of Canada. *Winner:* Dan Werb for *The Invisible Siege: The Rise of Coronaviruses and the Search for a Cure* (Crown).

E.B. White Award. See American Academy of Arts and Letters E.B. White Award.

E.B. White Read-Aloud Awards. For children's books with particular appeal as read-aloud books. *Offered by:* American Booksellers Association/Association of Booksellers for Children. Not awarded in 2022.

Whiting Writers' Awards ($50,000). For emerging writers of exceptional talent and promise. *Offered by:* Mrs. Giles Whiting Foundation. *Winners:* (poetry) Ina Cariño, Anthony Cody, Claire Schwartz; (fiction) Claire Boyles, Rita Bullwinkel, Megha Majumdar, Nana Nkweti; (nonfiction) Anaïs Duplan, Alexis Pauline Gumbs, Jesse McCarthy.

Walt Whitman Award ($5,000). To a U.S. poet who has not published a book of poems in a standard edition. *Offered by:* Academy of American Poets. *Winner:* Kweku Abimbola for *Saltwater Demands a Psalm* (Graywolf Press).

Richard Wilbur Award ($1,000 and publication by the University of Evansville Press). For a book-length poetry collection. Not awarded in 2022.

Thornton Wilder Prize for Translation ($20,000). Awarded every two years to a practitioner, scholar, or patron who has made a significant contribution to the art of literary translation. *Offered by:* American Academy of Arts and Letters. *Winner (2022):* Edith Grossman.

Robert H. Winner Memorial Award ($2,500). To a midcareer poet older than 40 who has published no more than one book of poetry. *Offered by:* Poetry Society of America. *Winner:* Didi Jackson.

George Wittenborn Memorial Book Awards. To North American art publications that represent the highest standards of content, documentation, layout, and format. *Offered by:* Art Libraries Society of North America (ARLIS/NA). *Winners:* Pamela A. Parmal, Jennifer M. Swope, and Lauren D. Whitley for *Fabric of a Nation: American Quilt Stories* (Museum of Fine Arts Boston).

Thomas Wolfe Prize and Lecture. To honor writers with distinguished bodies of work. *Offered by:* Thomas Wolfe Society and University of North Carolina–Chapel Hill. *Winner:* Percival Everett.

Thomas Wolfe Fiction Prize ($1,000). For a short story that honors Thomas Wolfe. *Offered by:* North Carolina Writers Network. *Winner:* Alan Sincic for "God of the Gator."

Helen and Kurt Wolff Translator's Prize ($10,000). For an outstanding translation from German into English, published in the United States. *Offered by:* Goethe Institut Inter Nationes, New York. *Winner:* Vincent Kling for *The Strudlhof Steps* by Heimito von Doderer (New York Review Books).

Women's Prize for Fiction (United Kingdom) (formerly the Bailey's Women's Prize for Fiction) (£30,000, about $37,400). For the best novel written by a woman and published in the United Kingdom. *Winner:* Ruth Ozeki for *The Book of Form and Emptiness* (Canongate Books).

World Fantasy Awards. For outstanding fantasy writing. *Offered by:* World Fantasy Convention. *Winners:* (novel) Tasha Suri for *The Jasmine Throne* (Orbit); (novella) Premee Mohamed for *And What Can We Offer You Tonight* (Neon Hemlock); (short fiction) Lauren Ring for "(emet)" in *The Magazine of Fantasy & Science Fiction* (July/August 2021); (anthology) Oghenechovwe Donald Ekpeki (editor) for *The Year's Best African Speculative Fiction (2021)* (Jembefola); (collection) Usman T. Malik for *Midnight Doorways: Fables from Pakistan* (Kitab); (best artist) Tran Nguyen; (special award, professional) Marjorie Liu and Sana Takeda for *Monstress Volume Six: The Vow* (Image Comics); (special award, nonprofessional) Tonia Ransom, for *Nightlight: A Horror Fiction Podcast.*

Writers' Trust Engel Findley Award (C$25,000) (Canada). To a Canadian writer predominantly of fiction, for a body of work. *Offered by:* Writers' Trust of Canada. *Sponsors:* Writers' Trust Board of Directors, Pitblado Family Foundation, and Michael Griesdorf Fund. *Winner:* Shani Mootoo.

Writers' Trust Fiction Prize. See Atwood Gibson Writers' Trust Fiction Prize.

Writers' Trust/McClelland & Stewart Journey Prize (C$10,000) (Canada). To a new, developing Canadian author for a short story first published in a Canadian literary journal during the previous year. *Offered by:* Writers' Trust of Canada. *Sponsor:* McClelland & Stewart. Not awarded in 2022.

Writers' Trust Shaughnessy Cohen Prize for Political Writing (C$25,000) (Canada). For literary nonfiction that captures a political subject of relevance to Canadian readers. *Offered by:* Writers' Trust of Canada. *Winner:* Joanna Chiu for *China Unbound:*

A New World Disorder (House of Anansi Press).

YALSA Award for Excellence in Nonfiction. For a work of nonfiction published for young adults (ages 12–18). *Offered by:* American Library Association's Young Adult Library Services Association. *Winner:* Gail Jarrow for *Ambushed!: The Assassination Plot against President Garfield* (Calkins Creek, an imprint of Astra Books for Young Readers).

Yoto Carnegie Medal (United Kingdom) (formerly the CILIP Carnegie Medal; £5,000, about $6,200, plus £500, about $620, worth of books donated to a library of the winner's choice). For the outstanding children's book of the year. *Offered by:* CILIP: The Chartered Institute of Library and Information Professionals. *Winner:* Katya Balen for *October, October* (Bloomsbury).

Yoto Kate Greenaway Medal (United Kingdom) (formerly the CILIP Kate Greenaway Medal and Colin Mears Award; £5,000, about $6,200, plus £500, about $620, worth of books donated to a library of the winner's choice). For children's book illustration. *Offered by:* CILIP: The Chartered Institute of Library and Information Professionals. *Winner:* Danica Novgorodoff for *Long Way Down: The Graphic Novel* (Faber).

Young Lions Fiction Award ($10,000). For a novel or collection of short stories by an American younger than 35. *Offered by:* Young Lions of the New York Public Library. *Winner:* Kalani Pickhart for *I Will Die in a Foreign Land* (Two Dollar Radio).

Young People's Poet Laureate ($25,000). For lifetime achievement in poetry for children. Honoree holds the title for two years. *Offered by:* Poetry Foundation. *Winner (2022):* Elizabeth Acevedo.

Morton Dauwen Zabel Award ($10,000). Awarded biennially, in rotation, to a progressive and experimental poet, writer of fiction, or critic. *Offered by:* American Academy of Arts and Letters. *Winner (2022):* Patricia Lockwood (literature).

Zoetrope Short Fiction Prizes. *Offered by:* Zoetrope: All-Story. *Winners:* (first, $1,000) Emily Crossen for "Egg"; (second, $500) Cleo Qian for "Chicken. Film. Youth."; (third, $250) Robert Yune for "Baghdad, Florida."

Charlotte Zolotow Award. For outstanding writing in a picture book published in the United States in the previous year. *Offered by:* Cooperative Children's Book Center, University of Wisconsin–Madison. *Winners:* Michelle Edwards for *Me and the Boss: A Story about Mending and Love*, illustrated by April Harrison (Anne Schwartz Book/ Random House).

Part 6
Directory of Organizations

Directory of Library and Related Organizations

Networks, Consortia, and Other Cooperative Library Organizations

This list is taken from the current edition of *American Library Directory* (Information Today, Inc.), which includes additional information on member libraries and primary functions of each organization.

United States

Alabama

Alabama Health Libraries Assn., Inc. (AL-HeLa), Lister Hill Lib., Univ. of Alabama, Birmingham 35294-0013. SAN 372-8218. Tel. 205-975-8313, fax 205-934-2230. *Pres.* Andrea Wright.

Library Management Network, Inc. (LMN), 1405 Plaza St. S.E., Suite 309, Decatur 35603. SAN 322-3906. Tel. 256-822-2371. *Pres.* Derrick Griffey.

Marine Environmental Sciences Consortium, Dauphin Island Sea Laboratory, 101 Bienville Blvd., Dauphin Island 36528. SAN 322-0001. Tel. 251-861-2141, fax 251-861-4646, e-mail disl@disl.org. *Exec. Dir.* John Valentine.

Network of Alabama Academic Libraries, c/o Alabama Commission on Higher Education, 100 N. Union St., Montgomery 36104. SAN 322-4570. Tel. 334-242-2211, fax 334-242-0270. *Exec. Dir.* Sheila Snow.

Alaska

Alaska Library Network (ALN), P.O. Box 230051, Anchorage 99523-0051. SAN 371-0688. Tel. 907-205-5362, e-mail info@aklib.net. *Exec. Dir.* Steve Rollins.

California

49-99 Cooperative Library System, c/o Southern California Lib. Cooperative, 254 N. Lake Ave., Suite 874, Pasadena 91101. SAN 301-6218. Tel. 626-359-6111. *Exec. Dir.* Christine Powers.

Bay Area Library and Information Network (BayNet), 1462 Cedar St., Berkeley 94702. SAN 371-0610. Tel. 415-355-2826, e-mail infobay@baynetlibs.org. *Pres.* Marisela Meskus.

Califa, 330 Townsend St., Ste. 133, San Francisco 94107. Tel. 888-239-2289, fax 415-520-0434, e-mail califa@califa.org. *Exec. Dir.* Paula MacKinnon.

Gold Coast Library Network, 3437 Empresa Dr., Suite C, San Luis Obispo 93401-7355. Tel. 805-543-6082, fax 805-543-9487. *Admin. Dir.* Maureen Theobald.

National Network of Libraries of Medicine–Region 5, University of Washington, Health Sciences Building, Room T230, Box 357155, 1959 NE Pacific St., Seattle 98195-7155. SAN 372-8234. Tel. 206-543-8262. *Exec. Dir.* Cathy Burroughs.

Northern California & Nevada Medical Library Group (NCNMLG), Barton Memorial Hospital Lib., 2170 South Ave., South Lake Tahoe 96150. SAN 370-0445. Tel. 530-543-5844, fax 530-541-4697. *Senior Exec. Coord.* Laurie Anton.

Northern California Assn. of Law Libraries (NOCALL), 268 Bush St., #3736, San Francisco, CA 94104. E-mail admin@nocall. org. *Pres.* Jeremy Sullivan.

Northern and Central California Psychology Libraries (NCCPL), 1453 Mission St, San Francisco 94103. SAN 371-9006. Tel. 415-575-6180. *Pres.* Scott Hines.

Peninsula Libraries Automated Network (PLAN), 32 West 25th Avenue, Suite 201, San Mateo, CA 94403. SAN 371-5035. Tel. 650-349-5538, fax 650-349-5089. *CEO* Carol Frost.

Santa Clarita Interlibrary Network (SCILNET), College of the Canyons, 26455 Rockwell Canyon Road, Santa Clarita 91355. SAN 371-8964. Tel. 661-362-3758, fax 661-362-2719. *Libn.* John Stone.

Serra Cooperative Library System, Serra c/o SCLC, 254 N. Lake Ave., Suite 874, Pasadena 91101. SAN 301-3510. Tel. 626-359-6111. *Dir.* Christine Powers.

Southern California Library Cooperative (SCLC), 254 N. Lake Ave., Suite 874, Pasadena 91101. SAN 371-3865. Tel. 626-359-6111. *Dir.* Christine Powers.

Colorado

Colorado Alliance of Research Libraries, 3801 E. Florida Ave., Suite 515, Denver 80210. SAN 322-3760. Tel. 303-759-3399, fax 303-759-3363. *Exec. Dir.* George Machovec.

Colorado Assn. of Law Libraries, c/o William A. Wise Law Library, 2450 Kittredge Loop Dr., 402 UCB, Boulder 80309. SAN 322-4325. Tel. 303-492-7535, fax 303-492-2707. *Pres.* Catherine Dunn.

Colorado Council of Medical Librarians (CCML), 12950 E. Montview Blvd., A0003, Aurora 80045. SAN 370-0755. Tel. 303-724-2124, fax 303-724-2154. *Pres.* Emily Petersen.

Colorado Library Consortium (CLiC), 7400 E. Arapahoe Rd., Suite 75, Centennial 80112. SAN 371-3970. Tel. 303-422-1150, fax 303-431-9752. *Exec. Dir.* Jim Duncan.

Connecticut

Bibliomation, 24 Wooster Ave., Waterbury 06708. Tel. 203-577-4070, fax 203-577-4077. *Exec. Dir.* Carl DeMilia.

Connecticut Library Consortium, 234 Court St., Middletown 06457-3304. SAN 322-0389. Tel. 860-344-8777, fax 860-344-9199, e-mail clc@ctlibrarians.org. *Exec. Dir.* Ellen Paul.

CTW Library Consortium, Olin Memorial Lib., 252 Church St., Middletown 06459-6065. SAN 329-4587. Tel. 860-685-3887, fax 860-685-2661. *Libn. for Collaborative Projects* Lorri Huddy.

Libraries Online, Inc. (LION), 100 Riverview Center, Suite 252, Middletown 06457. SAN 322-3922. Tel. 860-347-1704, fax 860-346-3707. *Exec. Dir.* Joseph Farara.

Library Connection, Inc., 599 Matianuck Ave., Windsor 06095-3567. Tel. 860-937-8261, fax 860-298-5328. *Systems Librn.* Sam Cook.

District of Columbia

Association of Research Libraries, 21 Dupont Circle N.W., Suite 800, Washington 20036. Tel. 202-296-2296, fax 202-872-0884. *Exec. Dir.* Mary Lee Kennedy.

Council for Christian Colleges and Universities, 321 8th St. N.E., Washington 20002. SAN 322-0524. Tel. 202-546-8713, fax 202-546-8913, e-mail council@cccu.org. *Pres.* Shirley V. Hoogstra.

FEDLINK/Federal Library and Information Network, c/o Federal Lib. and Info. Center Committee, 101 Independence Ave. S.E., Washington 20540-4935. SAN 322-0761. Tel. 202-707-4800, fax 202-707-4818, e-mail flicc@loc.gov. *Mgr.* Melissa Blaschke.

Washington Theological Consortium, 415 Michigan Ave. N.E., Suite 105, Washington 20017. SAN 322-0842. Tel. 202-832-2675, fax 202-526-0818, e-mail wtc@washtheocon.org. *Exec. Dir.* Larry Golemon.

Florida

Consortium of Southern Biomedical Libraries (CONBLS), c/o Harriet F. Ginsburg Health Sciences Library, 6850 Lake Nona Blvd., Orlando 32867. SAN 370-7717. *Chair* Nadine Dexter.

Florida Library Information Network, R.A. Gray Bldg., State Library and Archives of Florida, 500 South Bronough St., Tallahassee 32399-0250. SAN 322-0869. Tel. 850-245-6600, fax 850-245-6744, e-mail library@dos.myflorida.com. *Bureau Chief* Cathy Moloney.

Florida Virtual Campus, 1753 W Paul Dirac Dr., Tallahassee 32310. Tel. 850-922-6044, fax 850-922-4869. *Dir. of E-Resources* Rachel Erb.

Library and Information Resources Network, P.O. Box 4755, Clearwater, 33758. Tel. 727-536-0214, fax 727-530-3126. *Pres. & CEO* Andrew Anderson.

Midwest Archives Conference (MAC), 2598 E Sunrise Blvd., Suite 2104, Fort Lauderdale 33304. E-mail membership@midwestarchives.org. *Pres.* Tamar Chute.

Northeast Florida Library Information Network (NEFLIN), 2233 Park Ave., Suite 402, Orange Park 32073. Tel. 904-278-5620, fax 904-278-5625, e-mail office@neflin.org. *Exec. Dir.* Brad Ward.

Panhandle Library Access Network (PLAN), Five Miracle Strip Loop, Suite 8, Panama City Beach 32407-3850. SAN 370-047X. Tel. 850-233-9051, fax 850-235-2286. *Exec. Dir.* Charles Mayberry.

SEFLIN/Southeast Florida Library Information Network, Inc., Wimberly Lib., Office 452, Florida Atlantic Univ., 777 Glades Rd., Boca Raton 33431. SAN 370-0666. Tel. 561-208-0984, fax 561-208-0995. *Exec. Dir.* Brock Peoples.

Southwest Florida Library Network (SWFLN), 13120 Westlinks Terrace, Unit 3, Fort Myers 33913. Tel. 239-313-6338, fax 239-313-6329. *Dir.* Brian Chase.

Tampa Bay Library Consortium, Inc., P.O. Box 75498, Tampa 33675. SAN 322-371X. Tel. 813-622-8252, fax 813-628-4425. *Exec. Dir.* Jim Walther.

Tampa Bay Medical Library Network, Medical Lib., Department 7660, 501 Sixth Ave. South, Saint Petersburg 33701. SAN 322-0885. Tel. 727-767-8557. *Interim Chair* Deanna Stevens.

Three Rivers Regional Library Consortium, 176 S.W. Community Cir., Mayo 32066. Tel. 386-294-3858, e-mail hello@3riverslibrary.com. *Dir.* Dale Collum.

Georgia

Association of Southeastern Research Libraries (ASERL), c/o Robert W. Woodruff Library, 540 Asbury Circle, Suite 316, Atlanta 30322-1006. SAN 322-1555. Tel. 404-727-0137. *Exec. Dir.* John Burger.

Atlanta Regional Council for Higher Education (ARCHE), 141 E. College Ave., Box 1084,

Decatur 30030. SAN 322-0990. Tel. 404-651-2668, fax 404-880-9816, e-mail arche@atlantahighered.org. *Exec. Dir.* Tracey Brantley.

GOLD Georgia Resource Sharing for Georgia's Libraries (GOLD), c/o Georgia Public Lib. Service, 1800 Century Pl. N.E., Suite 150, Atlanta 30345-4304. SAN 322-094X. Tel. 404-235-7128, fax 404-235-7201. *Project Mgr.* Elaine Hardy.

LYRASIS, 3390 Peachtree Road N.E., Ste. 400, Atlanta 30326-1108. SAN 322-0974. Tel. 800-999-8558, fax 404-892-7879. *CEO* Robert Miller.

Public Information Network for Electronic Services (PINES), 2872 Woodcock Blvd., Suite 250, Atlanta 30341. Tel. 404-235-7200. *Prog. Mgr.* Terran McCanna.

Hawaii

Hawaii-Pacific Chapter, Medical Library Assn. (HPC-MLA), Health Sciences Lib., Honolulu 96813. SAN 371-3946. Tel. 808-692-0810, fax 808-692-1244. *Chair* Krystal Kakimoto.

Idaho

Cooperative Information Network (CIN), 8385 N. Government Way, Hayden 83835-9280. SAN 323-7656. Tel. 208-772-5612, fax 208-772-2498.

Library Consortium of Eastern Idaho (LCEI), 113 S. Garfield, Pocatello 83204-3235. SAN 323-7699. Tel. 208-237-2192. *Pres.* Esther Melander.

LYNX Consortium, c/o Boise Public Lib., 715 S. Capitol Ave., Boise 83702-7195. SAN 375-0086. Tel. 208-384-4238, fax 208-384-4025. *Dir.* Kevin Booe.

Illinois

American Theological Library Assn., 200 S. Wacker Dr., Ste. 3100, Chicago, 60606-5829. Tel. 872-310-4200. *Exec. Dir.* John F. Kutsko.

Assn. of Chicago Theological Schools (ACTS), Univ. of St. Mary of the Lake, 1000 E. Maple Ave., Mundelein 60060-1174. SAN 370-0658. Tel. 773-947-6300. *Coord.* Jennifer Ould.

Big Ten Academic Alliance, 1819 S. Neil St., Suite D, Champaign 61820-7271. Tel. 217-333-8475, fax 217-244-7127, e-mail btaa@staff.cic.net. *Exec. Dir.* Keith A. Marshall.

406 / Directory of Library and Related Organizations

Center for Research Libraries, 6050 S. Kenwood, Chicago 60637-2804. SAN 322-1032. Tel. 773-955-4545, fax 773-955-4339. *Pres.* Gregory Eow.

Consortium of Academic and Research Libraries in Illinois (CARLI), 1704 Interstate Dr., Champaign 61822. SAN 322-3736. Tel. 217-244-7593, fax 217-244-7596, e-mail support@carli.illinois.edu. *Sr. Dir.* Anne Craig.

East Central Illinois Consortium (ECIC), c/o CARLE Foundation Hospital, 611 W. Park St., Urbana 61801. SAN 322-1040. Tel. 217-383-3311, 217-383-4513. *Coord.* Frances Drone-Silvers.

Illinois Library and Information Network (IL-LINET), c/o Illinois State Lib., Gwendolyn Brooks Bldg. 300 S. Second St., Springfield 62701-1796. SAN 322-1148. Tel. 217-785-5600. *Dir.* Greg McCormick.

LIBRAS, Inc., North Park Univ., 3225 W. Foster Ave., Chicago 60625-4895. SAN 322-1172. Tel. 773-244-5584, fax 773-244-4891. *Pres.* Matthew Ostercamp.

Network of Illinois Learning Resources in Community Colleges (NILRC), P.O. Box 5365, Buffalo Grove 60089. Tel. 262-287-8017. *Bus. Mgr.* Lois Bruno.

System Wide Automated Network (SWAN), 800 Quail Ridge Dr., Westmont 60559. Tel. 844-792-6542. *Exec. Dir.* Aaron Skog.

Indiana

Consortium of College and University Media Centers (CCUMC), Indiana Univ., 306 N. Union St., Bloomington 47405-3888. SAN 322-1091. Tel. 812-855-6049, fax 812-855-2103, e-mail ccumc@ccumc.org. *Exec. Dir.* Aileen Scales.

Evergreen Indiana Consortium, Indiana State Lib., 315 W. Ohio St., Indianapolis 46202. Tel. 317-234-6624, fax 317-232-0002. *Coord.* Anna Goben.

Indiana Library Federation, 941 E. 86th St., Ste. 260, Indianapolis, 46240. Tel. 317-257-2040. *Exec. Dir.* Lucinda Nord.

Iowa

National Network of Libraries of Medicine–Greater Midwest Region (NN/LM-GMR), c/o Hardin Library for the Health Sciences, 600 Newton Road, Iowa City, 52242. SAN

322-1202. Tel. 319-353-4479. *Dir.* Linda Walton.

Polk County Biomedical Consortium, c/o Broadlawns Medical Center Lib., Des Moines 50314. SAN 322-1431. Tel. 515-282-2394, fax 515-282-5634. *Treas.* Elaine Hughes.

State of Iowa Libraries Online (SILO), State Lib. of Iowa, Des Moines 50319. SAN 322-1415. Tel. 515-281-4105, fax 515-281-6191. *State Libn.* Michael Scott.

Kansas

Greater Western Library Alliance, 5200 W. 94th Terrace, Ste. 200, Prairie Village 66027. Tel. 913-370-4422. *Exec. Dir.* Joni Blake.

State Library of Kansas/Statewide Resource Sharing Div., 300 S.W. 10 Ave., Room 312-N., Topeka 66612-1593. SAN 329-5621. Tel. 785-296-3296, fax 785-368-7291. *Exec. Dir.* Jeff Hixon.

Kentucky

Appalachian College Assn., 3816 Camelot Dr., Lexington 40517. Tel. 859-986-4584, fax 859-986-9549. *Pres.* Beth Rushing.

Assn. of Independent Kentucky Colleges and Universities (AIKCU), 484 Chenault Rd., Frankfort 40601. SAN 322-1490. Tel. 502-695-5007, fax 502-695-5057. *Pres.* Gary S. Cox.

Kentuckiana Metroversity, Inc., 200 W. Broadway, Suite 800, Louisville 40202. SAN 322-1504. Tel. 502-897-3374, fax 502-895-1647.

Kentucky Medical Library Assn., University of Louisville Bldg. D, Rm 110A, 500 S. Preston St., Louisville 40292. SAN 370-0623. Tel. 502-852-8530. *Contact* Tiffney Gipson.

Louisiana

Health Sciences Library Assn. of Louisiana (HSLAL), 433 Bolivar St., New Orleans 70112. SAN 375-0035. Tel. 504-568-5550. *Pres.* Rebecca Bealer.

Loan SHARK, State Lib. of Louisiana, 701 N. Fourth St., Baton Rouge 70802. SAN 371-6880. Tel. 225-342-4918, fax 225-219-4725, e-mail ill@state.lib.la.us. *Admin.* Kytara Christophe.

Louisiana Library Network (LOUIS), 1201 N. Third St., Suite 6-200, Baton Rouge 70802.

E-mail louisresources@regents.la.gov. *Exec. Dir.* Terri Gallaway.

New Orleans Educational Telecommunications Consortium, 2045 Lakeshore Dr., Suite 541, New Orleans 70122. Tel. 504-524-0350, e-mail noetc@noetc.org. *Dir.* Michael Adler.

Maryland

Maryland Interlibrary Loan Organization (MILO), c/o Enoch Pratt Free Lib., Baltimore 21201-4484. SAN 343-8600. Tel. 410-396-5498, fax 410-396-5837, e-mail milo@prattlibrary.org. *Mgr.* Emma E. Beaven.

National Network of Libraries of Medicine (NNLM), National Lib. of Medicine, Bldg. 38, 8600 Rockville Pike, Room B1-E03, Bethesda 20894. SAN 373-0905. Tel. 301-496-4777, fax 301-480-1467. *Head, National Network Coordinating Office* Amanda J. Wilson.

National Network of Libraries of Medicine–Southeastern Atlantic Region (NN/LM-SEA), Univ. of Maryland Health Sciences and Human Services Lib., 601 W. Lombard S., Baltimore 21201-1512. SAN 322-1644. Tel. 410-706-2855, fax 410-706-0099, e-mail hshsl-nlmsea@hshsl.umaryland.edu. *Dir.* Mary Tooey.

Southeastern Chapter of the American Assn. of Law Libraries (SEAALL), c/o University of Baltimore School of Law, 1420 N. Charles St., Baltimore 21201. *Pres.* Charles Pipins.

U.S. National Library of Medicine (NLM), 8600 Rockville Pike, Bethesda 20894. SAN 322-1652. Tel. 301-594-5983, fax 301-402-1384, e-mail custserv@nlm.nih.gov. *Coord.* Martha Fishel.

Washington Research Library Consortium (WRLC), 901 Commerce Dr., Upper Marlboro 20774. SAN 373-0883. Tel. 301-390-2000, fax 301-390-2020. *Exec. Dir.* Mark Jacobs.

Massachusetts

Boston Library Consortium, Inc., 401 Edgewater Place, Suite 600, Wakefield 01880. SAN 322-1733. Tel. 781-876-8859, fax 781-623-8460, e-mail admin@blc.org. *Exec. Dir.* Susan Stearns.

Boston Theological Interreligious Consortium, P.O. Box 391069, Cambridge 02139. Tel. 207-370-5275, e-mail btioffice@boston theological.org. *Exec. Dir.* Stephanie Edwards.

Cape Libraries Automated Materials Sharing Network (CLAMS), 270 Communication Way, Unit 4E, Hyannis 02601. SAN 370-579X. Tel. 508-790-4399, fax 508-771-4533. *Exec. Dir.* Gayle Simundza.

Central and Western Massachusetts Automated Resource Sharing (C/W MARS), 67 Millbrook St., Suite 201, Worcester 01606. SAN 322-3973. Tel. 508-755-3323 ext. 30, fax 508-755-3721.

Fenway Libraries Online, Inc. (FLO), c/o Wentworth Institute of Technology, 550 Huntington Ave., Boston 02115. SAN 373-9112. Tel. 617-989-5032. *Exec. Dir.* Walter Stein.

Massachusetts Health Sciences Libraries Network (MAHSLIN), Lamar Soutter Lib., Univ. of Massachusetts Medical School, Worcester 01655. SAN 372-8293. http://nahsl.libguides.com/mahslin/home. *Pres.* Stephanie Friree Ford.

Merrimack Valley Library Consortium, 4 High St., North Andover 01845. SAN 322-4384. Tel. 978-557-1050, fax 978-557-8101. *Exec. Dir.* Eric C. Graham.

Minuteman Library Network, 10 Strathmore Rd., Natick 01760-2419. SAN 322-4252. Tel. 508-655-8008, fax 508-655-1507. *Exec. Dir.* Susan McAlister.

National Network of Libraries of Medicine–New England Region (NN/LM-NER), Univ. of Massachusetts Medical School, 55 Lake Ave. N., Room S4-241, Worcester 01655. SAN 372-5448. Tel. 800-338-7657, fax 508-856-5977. *Dir.* Elaine Martin.

North of Boston Library Exchange, Inc. (NOBLE), 42-A Cherry Hill Drive, Danvers 01923. SAN 322-4023. Tel. 978-777-8844, fax 978-750-8472, e-mail staff@noblenet. org. *Exec. Dir.* Ronald A. Gagnon.

SAILS Library Network, 10 Riverside Dr., Suite 102, Lakeville 02347. SAN 378-0058. Tel. 508-946-8600, fax 508-946-8605, e-mail support@sailsinc.org. *Exec. Dir.* Deborah K. Conrad.

Michigan

Detroit Area Library Network (DALNET), 5150 Anthony Wayne Dr., Detroit 48202. Tel. 313-577-6789, fax 313-577-1231, info@dalnet.org. *Exec. Dir.* John E. Sterbenz, Jr.

Lakeland Library Cooperative, 4138 Three Mile Rd. N.W., Grand Rapids 49534-1134.

SAN 308-132X. Tel. 616-559-5253, fax 616-559-4329. *Dir.* Carol Dawe.

The Library Network (TLN), 41365 Vincenti Ct., Novi 48375. SAN 370-596X. Tel. 248-536-3100, fax 248-536-3099. *Dir.* Steven Bowers.

Michigan Health Sciences Libraries Assn. (MHSLA), 1407 Rensen St., Suite 4, Lansing 48910. SAN 323-987X. Tel. 517-394-2774, fax 517-394-2675. *Pres.* Jill Turner.

Mideastern Michigan Library Cooperative, 503 S. Saginaw St., Suite 839, Flint 48502. SAN 346-5187. Tel. 810-232-7119, fax 810-232-6639. *Dir.* Eric Palmer.

Mid-Michigan Library League, 201 N Mitchell, Suite 302, Cadillac 49601-1835. SAN 307-9325. Tel. 231-775-3037, fax 231-775-1749. *Dir.* Sheryl L. Mase.

Midwest Collaborative for Library Services, 1407 Rensen St., Suite 1, Lansing 48910. Tel. 800-530-9019, fax 517-492-3878. *Exec. Dir.* Scott Garrison.

Southeastern Michigan League of Libraries (SEMLOL), Lawrence Technological Univ., 21000 W. Ten Mile Rd., Southfield 48075. SAN 322-4481. Tel. 810-766-4070, fax 248-204-3005. *Treas.* Gary Cocozzoli.

Southwest Michigan Library Cooperative, 401 Dix St., Ostego 49078. SAN 308-2156. Tel. 269-657-3800, e-mail aestelle@otsegoli brary.org. *Dir.* Andrea Estelle.

Suburban Library Cooperative (SLC), 44750 Delco Blvd., Sterling Heights 48313. SAN 373-9082. Tel. 586-685-5750, fax 586-685-5750. *Dir.* Tammy Turgeon.

Upper Peninsula of Michigan Health Sciences Library Consortium, c/o Marquette Health System Hospital, 580 W. College Ave., Marquette 49855. SAN 329-4803. Tel. 906-225-3429, fax 906-225-3524. *Lib. Mgr.* Janis Lubenow.

Upper Peninsula Region of Library Cooperation, Inc., 1615 Presque Isle Ave., Marquette 49855. SAN 329-5540. Tel. 906-228-7697, fax 906-228-5627. *Treas.* Suzanne Dees.

Valley Library Consortium, 3210 Davenport Ave., Saginaw 48602-3495. Tel. 989-497-0925, fax 989-497-0918. *Exec. Dir.* Randall Martin.

White Pine Library Cooperative, 429 N. State St., Ste. 207, Caro 48723. Tel. 989-793-7126. *Dir.* Kate Van Auken.

Minnesota

Capital Area Library Consortium (CALCO), c/o Minnesota Dept. of Transportation, Lib. MS155, 395 John Ireland Blvd., Saint Paul 55155. SAN 374-6127. Tel. 651-296-5272, fax 651-297-2354. *Libn.* Shirley Sherkow.

Central Minnesota Libraries Exchange (CMLE), Miller Center, Room 130-D, Saint Cloud 56301-4498. SAN 322-3779. Tel. 320-308-2950, fax 320-654-5131, e-mail cmle@stcloudstate.edu. *Exec. Dir.* Mary Wilkins-Jordan.

Cooperating Libraries in Consortium (CLIC). See MNPALS.

Metronet, 1619 Dayton Ave., Suite 314, Saint Paul 55104. SAN 322-1989. Tel. 651-646-0475, fax 651-649-3169, e-mail information@metrolibraries.net. *Exec. Dir.* Ann Walker Smalley.

Metropolitan Library Service Agency (MELSA), 1619 Dayton Ave., No. 314, Saint Paul 55104-6206. SAN 371-5124. Tel. 651-645-5731, fax 651-649-3169, e-mail melsa@melsa.org. *Exec. Dir.* Ken Behringer.

MINITEX, Univ. of Minnesota–Twin Cities, 60 Wilson Library, 309 19th Ave. S., Minneapolis 55455-0439. SAN 322-1997. Tel. 612-624-4002, fax 612-624-4508. *Dir.* Valerie Horton.

Minnesota Library Information Network (MnLINK), Univ. of Minnesota–Twin Cities, Minneapolis 55455-0439. Tel. 800-462-5348, fax 612-624-4508. *Info. Specialist* Nick Banitt.

Minnesota Theological Library Assn. (MTLA), Luther Seminary Lib., 2375 Como Ave., Saint Paul 55108. SAN 322-1962. Tel. 651-641-3447. *Exec. Dir.* Sandra Oslund.

MNPALS, Minnesota State Univ. Mankato, 3022 Memorial Library, Mankato 56001. Tel. 507-389-2000, fax 507-389-5488. *Exec. Dir.* Johnna Horton.

Northern Lights Library Network (NLLN), 1104 7th Ave. S., Box 136, Moorhead 56563. SAN 322-2004. Tel. 218-477-2934. *Exec. Dir.* Kathy Brock Enger.

Prairielands Library Exchange, 109 S. 5th St., Marshall 56258. SAN 322-2039. Tel. 507-532-9013, fax 507-532-2039, e-mail info@sammie.org. *Exec. Dir.* Shelly Grace.

Southeastern Libraries Cooperating (SELCO), 2600 19th St. N.W., Rochester 55901-0767.

SAN 308-7417. Tel. 507-288-5513, fax 507-288-8697. *Exec. Dir.* Ann Hutton.

Twin Cities Biomedical Consortium (TCBC), c/o Fairview Univ. Medical Center, 2450 Riverside Ave., Minneapolis 55455. SAN 322-2055. Tel. 612-273-6595, fax 612-273-2675. *Mgr.* Colleen Olsen.

Mississippi

Central Mississippi Library Council (CMLC), c/o Millsaps College Lib., 1701 N. State St., Jackson 39210. SAN 372-8250. Tel. 601-974-1070, fax 601-974-1082. *Chair* Justin Huckaby.

Mississippi Electronic Libraries Online (MELO), Mississippi State Board for Community and Junior Colleges, Jackson 39211. Tel. 601-432-6518, fax 601-432-6363, e-mail melo@colin.edu. *Dir.* Audra Kimball.

Missouri

Health Sciences Library Network of Kansas City (HSLNKC), Univ. of Missouri–Kansas City Health Sciences Lib., 2411 Holmes St., Kansas City 64108-2792. SAN 322-2098. Tel. 816-235-1880, fax 816-235-6570. *Pres.* Cindi Kerns.

Kansas City Library Service Program (KC-LSP), 14 W. 10 St., Kansas City 64105. Tel. 816-701-3520, fax 816-701-3401, e-mail kc-lspsupport@kclibrary.org. *Lib. Systems and Service Prog. Mgr.* Melissa Carle.

Mid-America Library Alliance/Kansas City Metropolitan Library and Information Network, 15624 E. 24 Hwy., Independence 64050. SAN 322-2101. Tel. 816-521-7257, fax 816-461-0966. *Exec. Dir.* Jane Mulvihill-Jones.

Missouri Evergreen, c/o Poplar Bluff Public Library, 318 N. Main St., Poplar Bluff 63901. Tel. 573-203-4680. *Chair* Sue Szostak.

Mobius, 111 E. Broadway, Suite 220, Columbia 65203. Tel. 877-366-2487, fax 541-264-7006. *Exec. Dir.* Donna Bacon.

Saint Louis Regional Library Network, 1190 Meramec Station Rd., Suite 207, Ballwin 63021. SAN 322-2209. Tel. 800-843-8482, fax 636-529-1396, e-mail slrln@amigos.org. *Pres.* Nina O'Daniels.

Western Council of State Libraries, 1190 Meramec Station Rd., Suite 207, Ballwin 63021-6902. Tel. 972-851-8000, fax 636-529-1396.

Montana

Treasure State Academic Information and Library Services (TRAILS), Montana State Univ., P.O. Box 173320, Bozeman 59717. Tel. 406-994-4432, fax 406-994-2851. *Coord.* Pamela Benjamin.

Nebraska

ICON Library Consortium, McGoogan Lib. of Medicine, Univ. of Nebraska, Omaha 68198-6705. Tel. 402-559-7099, fax 402-559-5498. *Exec. Secy.* Cindy Perkins.

Nevada

Information Nevada, Interlibrary Loan Dept., Nevada State Lib. and Archives, 100 N. Stewart St., Carson City 89701-4285. SAN 322-2276. Tel. 775-684-3360, fax 775-684-3330. *Asst. Admin., Lib. and Development Svcs.* Tammy Westergard.

New Hampshire

Council of State Library Agencies in the Northeast (COSLINE), c/o New Hampshire State Library, 20 Park St., Concord 03301. SAN 322-0451. Tel. 603-5271-2397, fax 603-271-6826. *Pres.* Michael York.

GMILCS, Inc., 31 Mount Saint Mary's Way, Hooksett 03106. Tel. 603-485-4286, fax 603-485-4246, e-mail helpdesk@gmilcs.org. *Systems Admin.* Kevin French.

Librarians of the Upper Valley Coop. (LUV Coop), c/o Converse Free Library, 38 Union St., Lyme 03768. SAN 371-6856. Tel. 603-795-4622. *Coord.* Judith G. Russell.

Merri-Hill-Rock Library Cooperative, c/o Sandown Public Lib., 305 Main St., P.O. Box 580, Sandown 03873. SAN 329-5338. E-mail director@sandownlibrary.us. *Chair* Deborah Hoadley.

New Hampshire College and University Council, 3 Barrell Court, Suite 100, Concord 03301-8543. SAN 322-2322. Tel. 603-225-4199, fax 603-225-8108. *Pres.* Thomas R. Horgan.

Nubanusit Library Cooperative, c/o Frost Free Lib., 28 Jaffrey Rd., Marlborough 03455. SAN 322-4600. *Chair* Kristin Readel.

Rochester Area Librarians, c/o Milton Free Public Lib., 13 Main St., Milton Mills 03852. E-mail mfpl@metrocast.net. *Dir.* Betsy Baker.

New Jersey

Basic Health Sciences Library Network (BHSL), Overlook Hospital Health Science Lib., 99 Beauvoir Ave., Summit 07902. SAN 371-4888. Tel. 908-522-2886, fax 908-522-2274. *Coord.* Pat Regenberg.

Bergen County Cooperative Library System (BCCLS), 21-00 Route 208 S., Ste. 130, Fair Lawn 07410. Tel. 201-498-7300, fax 201-489-4215, e-mail bccls@bccls.org. *Exec. Dir.* David Hanson.

Burlington Libraries Information Consortium (BLINC), 5 Pioneer Blvd., Westampton 08060. Tel. 609-267-9660, fax 609-267-4091, e-mail hq@bcls.lib.nj.us. *Dir.* Ranjna Das.

Libraries of Middlesex Automation Consortium (LMxAC), 27 Mayfield Ave., Edison 08837. SAN 329-448X. Tel. 732-750-2525, fax 732-750-9392. *Exec. Dir.* Eileen M. Palmer.

LibraryLinkNJ, New Jersey Library Cooperative, 44 Stelton Rd., Suite 330, Piscataway 08854. SAN 371-5116. Tel. 732-752-7720, fax 732-752-7785. *Exec. Dir.* Susanne Sacchetti.

Morris Automated Information Network (MAIN), 16 Wing Dr., Suite 212, Cedar Knolls 07927. SAN 322-4058. Tel. 973-862-4606, fax 973-512-2122. *Exec. Dir.* Phillip Berg.

Morris-Union Federation, 214 Main St., Chatham 07928. SAN 310-2629. Tel. 973-635-0603, fax 973-635-7827. *Exec. Dir.* Karen Brodsky.

New Jersey Health Sciences Library Network (NJHSN), Overlook Hospital Lib., 99 Beauvoir Ave., Summit 07902. SAN 371-4829. Tel. 908-522-2886, fax 908-522-2274. *Lib. Mgr.* Patricia Regenberg.

New Jersey Library Network, Lib. Development Bureau, 185 W. State St., Trenton 08608. SAN 372-8161. Tel. 609-278-2640 ext. 152, fax 609-278-2650. *Admin.* Ruth Pallante.

Virtual Academic Library Environment (VALE), NJEdge/NJIT, 218 Central Ave., GITC 3902, Newark 07102-1982. Tel. 855-832-3343. *Prog. Mgr.* Melissa Lena.

New Mexico

Estacado Library Information Network (ELIN), 509 N. Shipp, Hobbs 88240. Tel. 505-397-9328, fax 505-397-1508.

New Mexico Consortium of Academic Libraries, c/o Donnelly Library, 802 National Ave., Las Vegas. SAN 371-6872. *Pres.* Poppy Johnson-Renval.

New York

Academic Libraries of Brooklyn, Long Island Univ. Lib. LLC 517, One University Plaza, Brooklyn 11201. SAN 322-2411. Tel. 718-488-1081, fax 718-780-4057. *Dir.* Ingrid Wang.

Associated Colleges of the Saint Lawrence Valley, SUNY Potsdam, 288 Van Housen Extension, Potsdam 13676-2299. SAN 322-242X. Tel. 315-267-3331, fax 315-267-2389. *Admin. Coord.* Ben Dixon.

Brooklyn–Queens–Staten Island–Manhattan–Bronx Health Sciences Libns. (BQSIMB), 150 55th St., Brooklyn 11220. Tel. 718-630-7200, fax 718-630-8918. *Pres.* Sheryl Ramer Gesoff.

Capital District Library Council (CDLC), 28 Essex St., Albany 12206. SAN 322-2446. Tel. 518-438-2500, fax 518-438-2872. *Exec. Dir.* Kathleen Gundrum.

Central New York Library Resources Council (CLRC), 5710 Commons Park Dr., East Syracuse 13057. SAN 322-2454. Tel. 315-446-5446, fax 315-446-5590. *Exec. Dir.* Marc Wildman.

CONNECTNY, Inc., 6721 U.S. Highway 11, Potsdam 13676. Tel. 716-930-7752. *Exec. Dir.* Julia Proctor.

Library Assn. of Rockland County (LARC), P.O. Box 917, New City 10956-0917. Tel. 845-359-3877, e-mail president@rocklandlibraries.com.

Library Consortium of Health Institutions in Buffalo (LCHIB), Abbott Hall, SUNY at Buffalo, 3435 Main St., Buffalo 14214. SAN 329-367X. Tel. 716-829-3900 ext. 143, fax 716-829-2211, e-mail hubnet@buffalo.edu; ulb-lchib@buffalo.edu. *Exec. Dir.* Martin E. Mutka.

Long Island Library Resources Council (LILRC), 627 N. Sunrise Service Rd., Bellport 11713. SAN 322-2489. Tel. 631-675-1570. *Dir.* Tim Spindler.

Medical and Scientific Libraries of Long Island (MEDLI), c/o Palmer School of Lib. and Info. Science, Brookville 11548. SAN 322-4309. Tel. 516-299-2866, fax 516-299-4168. *Pres.* Claire Joseph.

Metropolitan New York Library Council (METRO), 599 Eleventh Ave., 8th Fl., New York 10036. SAN 322-2500. Tel. 212-228-2320, fax 212-228-2598, e-mail info@metro.org. *Exec. Dir.* Nate Hill.

New England Law Library Consortium (NELLCO), 756 Madison Ave., Suite 102, Albany 12208. SAN 322-4244. Tel. 518-694-3025, fax 518-694-3027. *Exec. Dir.* Corie Dugas.

Northeast Foreign Law Libraries Cooperative Group, c/o Fordham University School of Law, 5th Flr., 150 W. 62nd St., New York 10023. Tel. 212-636-6913. *Librn.* Janet Kearney.

Northern New York Library Network, 6721 U.S. Hwy. 11, Potsdam 13676. SAN 322-2527. Tel. 315-265-1119, fax 315-265-1881, e-mail info@nnyln.org. *Exec. Dir.* Meg Backus.

Rochester Regional Library Council, 3445 Winton Pl., Ste. 204, Rochester 14623. SAN 322-2535. Tel. 585-223-7570, fax 585-223-7712, e-mail rrlc@rrlc.org. *Exec. Dir.* Laura Ousterhout.

South Central Regional Library Council, 108 N. Cayuga St., Clinton Hall, 3rd Floor, Ithaca 14850. SAN 322-2543. Tel. 607-273-9106, fax 607-272-0740, e-mail scrlc@scrlc.org. *Exec. Dir.* Mary-Carol Lindbloom.

Southeastern New York Library Resources Council (SENYLRC), 21 S. Elting Corners Rd., Highland 12528-2805. SAN 322-2551. Tel. 845-883-9065, fax 845-883-9483. *Exec. Dir.* Tessa Killian.

SUNYConnect, Office of Lib. and Info. Services, Office of Library & Information Services, SUNY Administration Plaza, 353 Broadway, Albany 12246. Tel. 518-443-5577, fax 518-443-5358. *Asst. Provost for Lib. and Info. Svcs.* Carey Hatch.

United Nations System Electronic Information Acquisitions Consortium (UNSEIAC), c/o United Nations Lib., New York 10017. SAN 377-855X. Tel. 212-963-3000, fax 212-963-2608, e-mail unseiac@un.org. *Coord.* Amy Herridge.

Westchester Academic Library Directors Organization (WALDO), 118 N. Bedford Rd., Ste 100, Mount Kisco 10549. Fax 914-729-1966. *Pres.* Maureen Clements.

Western New York Library Resources Council, 4950 Genesee St., Buffalo 14225. SAN 322-2578. Tel. 716-633-0705, fax 716-633-1736. *Exec. Dir.* Sheryl Knab.

North Carolina

Carolina Consortium, Walter Clinton Jackson Library, 320 College Avenue, Rm. 224G, Greensboro 27412-0001. Tel. 336-256-1216, e-mail bucknall@uncg.edu. *Chief Negotiator* Tim Bucknall.

North Carolina Community College System, 200 W. Jones St., Raleigh 27603-1379. SAN 322-2594. Tel. 919-807-7100, fax 919-807-7165. *Pres.* Peter Hans.

Northwest AHEC Library at Hickory, Catawba Medical Ctr., 810 Fairgrove Church Rd., Hickory 28602. SAN 322-4708. Tel. 828-326-3662, fax 828-326-3484. *Dir.* Karen Lee Martinez.

Northwest AHEC Library Information Network, Wake Forest Univ. School of Medicine, Medical Center Blvd., Winston-Salem 27157-1060. SAN 322-4716. Tel. 336-713-7700, fax 336-713-7701.

Triangle Research Libraries Network, Wilson Lib., CB No. 3940, Chapel Hill 27514-8890. SAN 329-5362. Tel. 919-962-8022, fax 919-962-4452. *Exec. Dir.* Lisa Croucher.

Western North Carolina Library Network (WNCLN), c/o Appalachian State Univ., 218 College St., Boone 28608. SAN 376-7205. Tel. 828-262-2774, fax 828-262-3001. *Libn.* Ben Shirley.

North Dakota

Central Dakota Library Network, Morton Mandan Public Lib., Mandan 58554-3149. SAN 373-1391. Tel. 701-667-5365, e-mail mortonmandanlibrary@cdln.info.

Ohio

Assn. of Christian Librarians (ACL), P.O. Box 4, Cedarville 45314. Tel. 937-766-2255, fax 937-766-5499, e-mail info@acl.org. *Pres.* Leslie Starasta.

Christian Library Consortium (CLC), c/o ACL, P.O. Box 4, Cedarville 45314. Tel. 937-766-2255, fax 937-766-5499, e-mail info@acl.org. *Coord.* Beth Purtee.

Consortium of Ohio Libraries, P.O. Box 38, Cardington 43315-1116. E-mail Info@info.cool-cat.org. *Chair* Lisa Murray.

Consortium of Popular Culture Collections in the Midwest (CPCCM), c/o Popular Culture Lib., Bowling Green 43403-0600. SAN 370-5811. Tel. 419-372-2450, fax 419-372-7996. *Head Libn.* Nancy Down.

Five Colleges of Ohio, 173 West Lorain Street, Room 208, Oberlin College, Oberlin 44074. Tel. 440-775-5500, e-mail info@ohio5.com. *Exec. Dir.* Sarah Stone.

Northeast Ohio Regional Library System (NEO-RLS), 1737 Georgetown Rd., Ste. B, Hudson 44236. SAN 322-2713. Tel. 330-655-0531, fax 330-655-0568. *Exec. Dir.* Betsy Lantz.

NORWELD (formerly Northwest Regional Library System), 181½ S. Main St., Bowling Green 43402. SAN 322-273X. Tel. 419-352-2903, fax 419-353-8310. *Exec. Dir.* Arline V. Radden.

OCLC Online Computer Library Center, Inc., 6565 Kilgour Place, Dublin 43017-3395. SAN 322-2748. Tel. 614-764-6000, fax 614-718-1017, e-mail oclc@oclc.org. *Pres. & CEO* Skip Pritchard.

Ohio Health Sciences Library Assn. (OHSLA), Medical Lib., South Pointe Hospital, Warrensville Heights 44122. Tel. 216-491-7454, fax 216-491-7650. *Pres.* Mary Pat Harnegie.

Ohio Library and Information Network (Ohio-LINK), 1224 Kinnear Rd., Columbus 43215. SAN 374-8014. Tel. 614-485-6722, fax 614-228-1807, e-mail info@ohiolink.edu. *Exec. Dir.* Amy Pawlowski.

Ohio Network of American History Research Centers, Ohio Historical Society Archives–Lib., Columbus 43211-2497. SAN 323-9624. Tel. 614-297-2510, fax 614-297-2546, e-mail reference@ohiohistory.org. *Exec. Dir.* Jackie Barton.

Ohio Public Library Information Network (OPLIN), 2323 W. 5 Ave., Suite 130, Columbus 43204. Tel. 614-728-5252, fax 614-728-5256, e-mail support@oplin.org. *Exec. Dir.* Don Yarman.

OHIONET, 1500 W. Lane Ave., Columbus 43221-3975. SAN 322-2764. Tel. 614-486-2966, fax 614-486-1527. *Exec. Officer* Nancy S. Kirkpatrick.

Serving Every Ohioan Library Center, SEO, 40780 Marietta Rd., Caldwell 43724. SAN 356-4606. Tel. 740-783-5705, fax 800-446-4804. *Dir.* John Stewart.

Southeast Ohio and Neighboring Libraries (SWON), 10250 Alliance Rd., Suite 112, Cincinnati 45242. SAN 322-2675. Tel. 513-751-4422, fax 513-751-0463, e-mail info@swonlibraries.org. *Exec. Dir.* Cassondra Vick.

Southeast Regional Library System (SERLS), 252 W. 13 St., Wellston 45692. SAN 322-2756. Tel. 740-384-2103, fax 740-384-2106. *Dir.* Jay Burton.

Southwestern Ohio Council for Higher Education (SOCHE), Miami Valley Research Park, 3155 Research Blvd., Suite 204, Dayton 45420-4015. SAN 322-2659. Tel. 937-258-8890, fax 937-258-8899, e-mail soche@soche.org. *Exec. Dir.* Cassie Barlow.

Oklahoma

Mid-America Law Library Consortium (MALLCO), 800 N. Harvey Ave., Oklahoma City 73102. Tel. 405-208-5393, e-mail mallcoexecutivedirector@gmail.com. *Exec. Dir.* Susan Urban.

Oklahoma Health Sciences Library Assn. (OHSLA), HSC Bird Health Science Lib., Univ. of Oklahoma, Oklahoma City 73190. SAN 375-0051. Tel. 405-271-2285 ext. 48755, fax 405-271-3297. *Exec. Dir.* Joy Summers-Ables.

Oregon

Chemeketa Cooperative Regional Library Service, 4000 Lancaster Dr. N.E., Rm. 9/136, Salem 97305-1453. SAN 322-2837. Tel. 503-399-5165, fax 503-399-7316, e-mail contact@cclrs.org. *Dir.* John Goodyear.

Library Information Network of Clackamas County (LINCC), 1810 Red Soils Court, #110, Oregon City 97045. SAN 322-2845. Tel. 503-723-4888, fax 503-794-8238. *Lib. Network Mgr.* Kathryn Kohl.

Orbis Cascade Alliance, 2300 Oakmont Way, Eugene 97401. SAN 377-8096. Tel. 541-246-2470. *Exec. Dir.* Kim Armstrong.

Washington County Cooperative Library Services, 111 N.E. Lincoln St., MS No. 58, Hillsboro 97124-3036. SAN 322-287X. Tel. 503-846-3222, fax 503-846-3220.

Pennsylvania

Berks County Library Assn. (BCLA), c/o Berks County Public Libraries, 1040 Berks Rd., Leesport 19533. SAN 371-0866. Tel.

610-478-9035, 610-655-6350. *Pres.* Amy Resh.

Central Pennsylvania Consortium (CPC), c/o Franklin & Marshall College, Goethean Hall 101, Lancaster 17604. SAN 322-2896. Tel. 717-358-2896, fax 717-358-4455, e-mail cpc@ dickinson.edu. *Exec. Asst.* Kathy Missildine.

Central Pennsylvania Health Sciences Library Assn. (CPHSLA), Office for Research Protections, Pennsylvania State Univ., 212 Kern Graduate Bldg., University Park 16802. SAN 375-5290. Fax 814-865-1775. *Pres.* Helen Houpt.

Eastern Mennonite Associated Libraries and Archives (EMALA), 2215 Millstream Rd., Lancaster 17602. SAN 372-8226. Tel. 717-393-9745, fax 717-393-8751. *Chair* John Weber.

Greater Philadelphia Law Library Assn. (GPLLA), P.O. Box 335, Philadelphia 19105. SAN 373-1375. *Pres.* Lori Strickler Corso.

HSLC/Access PA (Health Science Libraries Consortium), 3600 Market St., Suite 550, Philadelphia 19104-2646. SAN 323-9780. Tel. 215-222-1532, fax 215-222-0416, e-mail support@hslc.org. *Exec. Dir.* Maryam Phillips.

Interlibrary Delivery Service of Pennsylvania (IDS), c/o Bucks County IU, No. 22, 705 N Shady Retreat Rd., Doylestown 18901. SAN 322-2942. Tel. 215-348-2940 ext. 1625, fax 215-348-8315, e-mail ids@bucksiu.org. *Admin. Dir.* Pamela Dinan.

Keystone Library Network, 2300 Vartan Way, Ste. 207, Harrisburg 17110. Tel: 717-720-4208. *Interim Coord.* Richard Riccardi.

Lehigh Valley Assn. of Independent Colleges, 1309 Main St., Bethlehem 18018. SAN 322-2969. Tel. 610-625-7888, fax 610-625-7891. *Exec. Dir.* Diane Dimitroff.

Montgomery County Library and Information Network Consortium (MCLINC), 520 Virginia Dr., Fort Washington 19034. Tel. 610-238-0580. *Exec. Dir.* Michelle Kehoe.

National Network of Libraries of Medicine–Middle Atlantic Region (NN/LM-MAR), Univ. of Pittsburgh, 3550 Terrace St., 200 Scaife Hall, Pittsburgh 15261. Tel. 412-684-2065, fax 412-648-1515, e-mail nnlmmar@ pitt.edu. *Exec. Dir.* Renae Barger.

Partnership for Academic Library Collaboration and Innovation (PALCI; formerly Pennsylvania Academic Library Consortium),

1005 Pontiac Road, Suite 330, Drexel Hill, PA 19026. Tel. 215-567-1755. *Exec. Dir.* Jill Morris.

Pennsylvania Library Assn., 220 Cumberland Pkwy, Suite 10, Mechanicsburg 17055. Tel. 717-766-7663, fax 717-766-5440. *Exec. Dir.* Christi Buker.

Philadelphia Area Consortium of Special Collections Libraries (PACSCL), P.O. Box 22642, Philadelphia 19110-2642. Tel. 215-985-1445, fax 215-985-1446, e-mail lblanchard@pacscl.org. *Exec. Dir.* Laura Blanchard.

Southeastern Pennsylvania Theological Library Assn. (SEPTLA), c/o Biblical Seminary, 200 N. Main St., Hatfield 19440. SAN 371-0793. Tel. 215-368-5000 ext. 234. *Pres.* Patrick Milas.

State System of Higher Education Library Cooperative (SSHELCO), c/o Bailey Lib., Slippery Rock 16057. Tel. 724-738-2630, fax 724-738-2661. *Coord.* Mary Lou Sowden.

Tri-State College Library Cooperative (TCLC), c/o Rosemont College Lib., 1400 Montgomery Ave., Rosemont 19010-1699. SAN 322-3078. Tel. 610-525-0796, e-mail office@ tclclibs.org. *Coord.* Mary Maguire.

Rhode Island

Library of Rhode Island Network, One Capitol Hill, Providence 02908. Tel. 401-574-9300, fax 401-574-9320. *Chief of Library Svc.* Karen Mellor.

Ocean State Libraries (OSL), 300 Centerville Rd., Suite 103S, Warwick 02886-0226. SAN 329-4560. Tel. 401-738-2200, e-mail sup port@oslri.net. *Exec. Dir.* Stephen Spohn.

RILINK, 317 Market St., Warren 02885. SAN 371-6821. Tel. 401-245-4998. *Exec. Dir.* Dorothy Frechette.

South Carolina

Partnership Among South Carolina Academic Libraries (PASCAL), 1122 Lady Street, Suite 300, Columbia 29201. Tel. 803-734-0900, fax 803-734-0901. *Exec. Dir.* Rick Moul.

South Carolina AHEC, c/o Medical University of South Carolina, 1 South Park Circle, Suite 203, Charleston 29407. SAN 329-3998. Tel. 843-792-4431, fax 843-792-4430. *Exec. Dir.* David Garr.

Tennessee

Knoxville Area Health Sciences Library Consortium (KAHSLC), Univ. of Tennessee Preston Medical Lib., 1924 Alcoa Hwy., Knoxville 37920. SAN 371-0556. Tel. 865-305-9525, fax 865-305-9527. *Pres.* Cynthia Vaughn.

Tennessee Health Science Library Assn. (THeSLA), Holston Valley Medical Center Health Sciences Lib., 130 W. Ravine Rd., Kingsport 37660. SAN 371-0726. Tel. 423-224-6870, fax 423-224-6014. *Pres.* Sandy Oelschlegel.

Tenn Share, P.O. Box 331871, Nashville 37203-7517. Tel. 615-669-8670, e-mail execdir@tenn-share.org. *Exec. Dir.* Jenifer Grady.

Texas

Abilene Library Consortium, 3305 N. 3 St., Suite 301, Abilene 79603. SAN 322-4694. Tel. 325-672-7081, fax 325-672-7082. *Exec. Dir.* Edward J. Smith.

Amigos Library Services, Inc., 4901 LBJ Freeway, Suite 150, Dallas 75244-6179. SAN 322-3191. Tel. 972-851-8000, fax 972-991-6061, e-mail amigos@amigos.org. *Chief Prog. Officer* Tracy Byerly.

Council of Research and Academic Libraries (CORAL), P.O. Box 6733, San Antonio 78212. SAN 322-3213. Tel. 210-710-4475. *Pres.* Michelea Mason.

Del Norte Biosciences Library Consortium, El Paso Community College, El Paso 79998. SAN 322-3302. Tel. 915-831-4149, fax 915-831-4639. *Coord.* Becky Perales.

Harrington Library Consortium, 413 E. 4 Ave., Amarillo 79101. SAN 329-546X. Tel. 806-378-6037, fax 806-378-6038. *Dir.* Amanda Barrera.

Health Libraries Information Network (Health LINE), 3500 Camp Bowie Blvd. LIB-222, Fort Worth 76107-2699. SAN 322-3299. E-mail dfwhealthline@gmail.com. *Pres.* Michele Whitehead.

National Network of Libraries of Medicine–South Central Region (NN LM-SCR), c/o UNT Health Science Center, Gibson D. Lewis Library, Room 310, 3500 Camp Bowie Blvd., Fort Worth 76107. SAN 322-3353. Tel. 713-799-7880, fax 713-790-7030, e-mail nnlm-scr@exch.library.tmc.edu. *Dir.* Brian Leaf.

Partners Library Action Network (PLAN), 5806 Mesa Dr., Ste. 375, Austin 78731. Tel. 512-583-0704, e-mail: info@libaction.net. *Exec. Dir.* Eric Lashley.

South Central Academic Medical Libraries Consortium (SCAMeL), c/o Lewis Lib.-UNTHSC, 3500 Camp Bowie Blvd., Fort Worth 76107. SAN 372-8269. Tel. 817-735-2380, fax 817-735-5158. *Chair* Kelly Gonzalez.

Texas Council of Academic Libraries (TCAL), VC/UHV Lib., 2602 N. Ben Jordan, Victoria 77901. SAN 322-337X. Tel. 361-570-4150, fax 361-570-4155. *Chair* Cate Rudowsky.

TEXSHARE—Texas State Library and Archives Commission, 1201 Brazos St., Austin 78701. Tel. 512-463-5455, fax 512-936-2306, e-mail texshare@tsl.texas.gov. *Dir. and State Libn.* Mark Smith.

Utah

National Network of Libraries of Medicine–MidContinental Region (NN/LM-MCR), Spencer S. Eccles Health Sciences Lib., Univ. of Utah, Salt Lake City 84112-5890. SAN 322-225X. Tel. 801-587-3650, fax 801-581-3632. *Dir.* Catherine Soehner.

Utah Academic Library Consortium (UALC), Univ. of Utah, Salt Lake City 84112. SAN 322-3418. Tel. 801-581-7701, 801-581-3852, fax 801-585-7185, e-mail UALCmail@library.utah.edu. *Chair* Wendy Holliday.

Vermont

Catamount Library Network, 43 Main St., Springfield 05156. *Mailing Address:* Ten Court St., Rutland 05701-4058. *Pres.* Amy Howlett.

Collaborative Libraries of Vermont (CLOVER), Vermont Dept. of Libraries, 60 Washington St., Ste. 2, Barre 05641. Tel. 802-636-0040. *Ref. Libn.* April Shaw.

Virginia

American Indian Higher Education Consortium (AIHEC), 121 Oronoco St., Alexandria 22314. SAN 329-4056. Tel. 703-838-0400, fax 703-838-0388, e-mail info@aihec.org. *Pres. & CEO* Carrie Billy.

Lynchburg Information Online Network (LION), 2315 Memorial Ave., Lynchburg 24503. SAN 374-6097. Tel. 434-381-6311, fax 434-381-6173. *Systems Admin.* Lisa Broughman.

Richmond Academic Library Consortium (RALC), James Branch Cabell Lib., Virginia Commonwealth Univ., 901 Park Ave., Richmond 23284. SAN 322-3469. Tel. 804-828-1110, fax 804-828-1105. *Pres.* Christopher Richardson.

Southwestern Virginia Health Information Librarians, Sentara RMH Virginia Funkhouser Health Sciences Library, 2010 Health Campus Dr., Harrisonburg 22801. SAN 323-9527. Tel. 540-689-1772, fax 540-689-1770, e-mail mdkhamph@sentara.com. *Libn.* Megan Khamphavong.

Virginia Independent College and University Library Assn., c/o Elizabeth G. McClenney, Roanoke College—Fintel Library, 220 High St., Salem 24153. SAN 374-6089. Tel. 540-375-2508. *Chair* Elizabeth G. McClenney.

Virginia Tidewater Consortium for Higher Education (VTC), 4900 Powhatan Ave., Norfolk 23529. SAN 329-5486. Tel. 757-683-3183, fax 757-683-4515, e-mail lgdotolo@aol.com. *Pres.* Lawrence G. Dotolo.

Virginia's Academic Library Consortium (VIVA). George Mason University, 4400 University Dr., Fenwick 5100, Fairfax 22030. Tel. 703-993-4652, fax 703-993-4662. *Dir.* Anne Osterman.

Washington

Assn. for Rural and Small Libraries, P.O. Box 33731, Seattle 98133. Tel. 206-453-3579. *Exec. Dir.* Kate Laughlin.

National Network of Libraries of Medicine–Pacific Northwest Region (NN/LM-PNR), T-344 Health Sciences Bldg., Univ. of Washington–Seattle 98195. SAN 322-3485. Tel. 206-543-8262, fax 206-543-2469, e-mail nnlm@u.washington.edu. *Assoc. Dir.* Catherine Burroughs.

Washington Community & Technical College Library Consortium (WACTCLC), c/o Big Ben Community College, 7662 Chanute St. NE, Moses Lake 98837. Tel. 509-760-4474. *Mgr.* Wade Guidry.

West Virginia

Mid-Atlantic Law Library Cooperative (MALLCO), College of Law Lib., West Virginia Univ., Morgantown 26506-6135. SAN 371-0645. Tel. 304-293-7641, fax 304-293-6020. *Lib. Dir.* Lynn Maxwell.

Wisconsin

Fox River Valley Area Library Consortium (FRVALC), c/o Polk Lib., Univ. of Wisconsin–Oshkosh, 800 Algona Blvd., Oshkosh 54901. SAN 322-3531. Tel. 920-424-3348, 920-424-4333, fax 920-424-2175. *Coord.* Holly Egebo.

NorthEast Wisconsin Intertype Libraries, Inc. (NEWIL), c/o Nicolet Federated Library System, 1595 Allouez Ave. Suite 4, Green Bay 54311. SAN 322-3574. Tel. 920-448-4410, fax 920-448-4420. *Coord.* Jamie Matczak.

Southeastern Wisconsin Health Science Library Consortium, Veterans Admin. Center Medical Lib., Milwaukee 53295. SAN 322-3582. Tel. 414-384-2000 ext. 42342, fax 414-382-5334. *Coord.* Kathy Strube.

Southeastern Wisconsin Information Technology Exchange, Inc. (SWITCH), 6801 North Yates Rd., Milwaukee 53217. Tel. 414-382-6710. *Coord.* Jennifer Schmidt.

Wisconsin Library Services (WILS), 1360 Regent St., No. 121, Madison 53715-1255. Tel. 608-216-8399, e-mail information@wils.org. *Dir.* Stef Morrill.

Wisconsin Public Library Consortium (WPLC), c/o WILS, 1360 Regent St., No. 121, Madison 53715-1255. Tel. 608-216-8399, e-mail information@wils.org. *Dir.* Stef Morrill.

Wisconsin Valley Library Service (WVLS), 300 N. 1 St., Wausau 54403. SAN 371-3911. Tel. 715-261-7250, fax 715-261-7259. *Dir.* Marla Rae Sepnafski.

WISPALS Library Consortium, c/o Gateway Technical College, 3520 30th Ave., Kenosha 53144-1690. Tel. 262-564-2602, fax 262-564-2787. *Chair* Scott Vrieze.

Wyoming

WYLD Network, c/o Wyoming State Lib., 2800 Central Ave., Cheyenne 82002-0060. SAN 371-0661. Tel. 307-777-6333, e-mail support@wyldnetwork.com. *State Libn.* Jamie Marcus.

Canada

Alberta

The Alberta Library (TAL), 623 Seven Sir Winston Churchill Sq. N.W., Edmonton T5J

2V5. Tel. 780-414-0805, fax 780-414-0806, e-mail admin@thealbertalibrary.ab.ca. *CEO* Grant Chaney.

Council of Prairie and Pacific University Libraries (COPPUL), c/o High Density Library, University of Calgary, 150 B–11711 85th St. N.W., Calgary T3R 1J3. Tel. 403-220-2414. *Exec. Dir.* Vivian Stieda.

NEOS Library Consortium, Cameron Lib., 5th Fl., Edmonton T6G 2J8. Tel. 780-492-0075, fax 780-492-8302. *Mgr.* Anne Carr-Wiggin.

British Columbia

British Columbia Electronic Library Network (BCELN), WAC Bennett Lib., 7th Fl., Simon Fraser Univ., Burnaby V5A 1S6. Tel. 778-782-7003, fax 778-782-3023, e-mail office@eln.bc.ca. *Exec. Dir.* Anita Cocchia.

Center for Accessible Post-Secondary Education Resources, Langara College Library, 100 W. 49th Ave., Vancouver V5Y 2Z6. SAN 329-6970. Tel. 604-323-5639, fax 604-323-5544, e-mail caperbc@langara.bc.ca. *Dir.* Patricia Cia.

Electronic Health Library of British Columbia (e-HLbc), c/o Bennett Lib., 8888 University Dr., Burnaby V5A 1S6. Tel. 778-782-5440, fax 778-782-3023, e-mail info@ehlbc.ca. *Exec. Dir.* Anita Cocchia.

Northwest Library Federation, 12495 Budds Rd., Prince George V2N 6K7. Tel. 250-988-1860, e-mail director@nwlf.ca. *Dir.* Anna Babluck.

Public Library InterLINK, 5489 Byrne Rd., No 158, Burnaby V5J 3J1. SAN 318-8272. Tel. 604-517-8441, fax 604-517-8410, e-mail info@interlinklibraries.ca. *Exec. Dir.* Michael Burris.

Manitoba

Manitoba Library Consortium, Inc. (MLCI), c/o Lib. Admin., Univ. of Winnipeg, 515 Portage Ave., Winnipeg R3B 2E9. SAN 372-820X. Tel. 204-786-9801, fax 204-783-8910. *Chair* Heather Brydon.

Nova Scotia

Maritimes Health Libraries Assn. (MHLA-AB-SM), W.K. Kellogg Health Sciences Lib., Halifax B3H 1X5. SAN 370-0836. Tel. 902-494-2483, fax 902-494-3750. *Libn.* Shelley McKibbon.

NOVANET, The Consortium of Nova Scotia Academic Libraries, 120 Western Pkwy., No. 202, Bedford B4B 0V2. SAN 372-4050. Tel. 902-453-2470, fax 902-453-2369, e-mail office@novanet.ca. *Mgr.* Bill Slauenwhite.

Ontario

Canadian Assn. of Research Libraries (Association des Bibliothèques de Recherche du Canada), 203-309 Cooper St., Ottawa K2P 0G5. SAN 323-9721. Tel. 613-482-9344, fax 613-562-5297, e-mail info@carl-abrc.ca. *Exec. Dir.* Susan Haigh.

Canadian Health Libraries Assn. (CHLA-AB-SC), 468 Queen St. E., LL-02, Toronto M5A 1T7. SAN 370-0720. Tel. 416-646-1600, fax 416-646-9460, e-mail info@chla-absc.ca. *Exec. Dir.* Perry Ruehlen.

Canadian Heritage Information Network, 1030 Innes Rd., Ottawa K1B 4S7. SAN 329-3076. Tel. 613-998-3721, fax 613-998-4721, e-mail pch.rcip-chin.pch@canada.ca. *Dir.* Bruno Lemay.

Canadian Research Knowledge Network (CRKN), 11 Holland Ave., Suite 301, Ottawa K1Y 4S1. Tel. 613-907-7040, fax 866-903-9094. *Exec. Dir.* Clare Appavoo.

Health Science Information Consortium of Toronto, c/o Gerstein Science Info. Center, Univ. of Toronto, 9 King's College Circle, Toronto M5S 1A5. SAN 370-5080. Tel. 416-978-6359, fax 416-971-2637. *Exec. Dir.* Lori Anne Oja.

Ontario Council of University Libraries (OCUL), 130 Saint George St., Toronto M5S 1A5. Tel. 416-946-0578, fax 416-978-6755. *Exec. Dir.* John Barnett.

Ontario Library Consortium (OLC), c/o Brant Public Lib., 12 William St., Paris M3L 1K7. *Pres.* Kelly Bernstein.

Perth County Information Network (PCIN), c/o Stratford Public Lib., 19 St. Andrew St., Stratford N5A 1A2. Tel. 519-271-0220, fax 519-271-3843, e-mail webmaster@pcin.on.ca. *CEO* Sam Coglin.

Toronto Health Libraries Assn. (THLA), 3409 Yonge St., Toronto M4N 2L0. SAN 323-9853. Tel. 416-485-0377, fax 416-485-6877, e-mail medinfoserv@rogers.com. *Pres.* Zack Osborne.

Woodstock Hospital Regional Library Services, Woodstock General Hospital, 310

Juliana Dr., Woodstock N4V 0A4. SAN 323-9500. Tel. 519-421-4233 ext. 2735, fax 519-421-4236. *Contact* Bailey Urso.

Quebec

Assn. des Bibliothèques de la Santé Affiliées a l'Université de Montréal (ABSAUM), c/o Health Library, University of Montreal, Pavillon Roger-Gaudry, 2900 Blvd. Edouard-Montpetit, 6e Etage, Salle L-623, Montreal H3C 3J7. SAN 370-5838. Tel. 514-343-6826, fax 514-343-2350. *Librn.* Natalie Clairoux.

Réseau BIBLIO de l'Ouatouais, 2295 Saint-Louis St., Gatineau, Quebec J8T 5L8. SAN 319-6526. Tel. 819-561-6008. *Exec. Gen.* Sylvie Thibault.

Saskatchewan

Consortium of Academic and Special Libraries of Saskatchewan (CASLS), Courthouse, 2425 Victoria Ave., Regina S4P 3M3. *Mailing address:* P.O. Box 5032, Regina S4P 3M3. *Chair* Melanie Hodges Neufeld.

Library and Information-Industry Associations and Organizations, U.S. and Canada

AIIM—The Association for Information and Image Management

President and CEO, Tori Miller Liu
Chief Operating Officer, Georgina Clelland
8403 Colesville Rd., Suite 1100, Silver Spring, MD 20910
800-477-2446, 301-587-8202, fax 301-587-2711, e-mail hello@aiim.org
World Wide Web https://www.aiim.org
European Office: Broomhall Business Centre, Lower Broomhall Farm, Broomhall Ln., Worcester
WR5 2NT, UK
Tel. 44-1905-727600, fax 44-1905-727609, e-mail info@aiim.org

Objective

AIIM is an international authority on enterprise content management, the tools and technologies that capture, manage, store, preserve, and deliver content in support of business processes. It was founded in 1943.

Officers (2023)

Chair Ron Cameron, KnowledgeLake; *V.Chair* Karen Hobert, Cisco; *Treas.* Rikkert Engels, Xillio; *Past Chair* Kramer Reeves, WorkRelay.

Board Members

Alyssa Blackburn, Tim Brady, Jason Cassidy, Lorelei Chernyshov, Rob Gerbrandt, Chris McNulty, Alan Pelz-Sharpe, David Quackenbush, Marko Sillanpaa, Julia Sweeney.

Publication

The AIIM Blog.

American Association of Law Libraries

Executive Director, Vani Ungapen
230 West Monroe St., Suite 2650, Chicago, IL 60606
312-939-4764, fax 312-431-1097, e-mail vungapen@aall.org
World Wide Web https://www.aallnet.org

Our Mission

The American Association of Law Libraries advances the profession of law librarianship and supports the professional growth of its members through leadership and advocacy in the field of legal information and information policy.

Membership

4,000 members. For law librarians and other legal information professionals of any professional sector. Dues (Indiv.) $281; (Ret.) $70; (Student) $70. Year. March–February.

Officers (2022–2023)

Pres. Elizabeth Adelman; *V.P.* June Hsiao Liebert; *Secy.* Mary Jenkins; *Treas.* Miriam Childs; *Past Pres.* Diane Rodriguez.

Board of Directors

Kristina Alayan, Andre Davison, Susan David Demaine, Michelle Hook Dewey, Stacy Etheredge, Kristina Niedringhaus.

Publications

AALL EBriefing.
AALL ENewsletter (mo.).
AALL Weekly ENewsletter.

AALL Spectrum (bi-mo.; free; digital only starting 2021).
AALL State of the Profession Report (print, digital, or print-digital bundle).
Law Library Journal (q.; digital; free).
AALL Biennial Salary Survey and Organizational Characteristics (biennial; memb. only online; print e-mail orders@aall.org).
Index to Foreign Legal Periodicals (print or online).
AALL White Papers (digital).
Guide to Fair Practices for Legal Publishers.
KnowItAALL (memb. only; digital; free).
LegalTrac.
Principles and Practices for Licensing Electronic Sources.
Universal Citation Guide.

American Indian Library Association

Executive Director, Heather Devine-Hardy (Eastern Shawnee)
E-mail hhdevine@gmail.com
World Wide Web https://ailanet.org

Objective

To improve library and information services for American Indians. Founded in 1979; it affiliated with the American Library Association in 1985.

Membership

Any person, library, or organization interested in working to improve library and information services for American Indians may become a member. Dues (Inst.) $40; (Indiv.) $20; (Student) $10.

Officers (2022–2023)

Pres. Richenda Hawkins; *V.P., Pres.-Elect* Allison Waukau (Menominee/Navajo); *Secy.* Doris Watts; *Treas.* Liana Juliano; *Immed. Past Pres.* Aaron LaFromboise; *Past Pres.* Cindy Hohl; *Memb.-at-Large* Danielle Burbank (Diné), Valarie Kingsland, Stacy Wells (Choctaw Nation).

Publication

AILA Newsletter (bi-ann.; memb. and nonmemb.; electronic; print: memb. only). *Ed.* George Gottschalk.

American Library Association

Executive Director, Tracie D. Hall
225 N. Michigan Ave, Suite 1300
Chicago, IL 60601
312-944-6780, 800-545-2433, fax 312-440-9374, e-mail ala@ala.org
World Wide Web https://www.ala.org

Objective

The object of the American Library Association (ALA) shall be to promote library service and librarianship. The mission of ALA is to provide leadership for the development, promotion, and improvement of library and information services and the profession of librarianship in order to enhance learning and ensure access to information for all. It was founded in 1876.

Membership

Memb. (Indiv.) 51,842; (Inst.) 5,189; (Corporate) 146; (Total) 57,177. Any person, library, or other organization interested in library service and librarians. Dues (Indiv.) 1st year, $75; 2nd year, $114; 3rd year and later, $150; (Trustee and Assoc. Memb.) $68; (Lib. Support Staff) $54; (Student) $40; (International Indiv.) $90; (Non-Salaried/In Transition/Retired) $54; (Inst.) $175 and up, depending on population served.

Divisions

See the separate entries that follow: American Assn. of School Libns.; Assn. for Lib. Service to Children; Assn. of College and Research Libs.; Core: Leadership, Infrastructure, Futures; Public Lib. Assn.; Reference and User Services Assn.; United for Libraries; Young Adult Lib. Services Assn.

Officers (2022–2023)

Pres. Lessa Kanani'opua Pelayo-Lozada; *Pres.-Elect* Emily Drabinski; *Treas.* Peter Hepburn; *Past Pres.* Patty Wong.

Board Members

Latrice Booker *(2020–2023)*; Kathy Carroll *(2022–2025)*; Sara Dallas *(2022–2025)*; Ana Elisa de Campos Salles *(2021–2024)*; Sam Helmick *(2021–2024)*; Larry Neal *(2020–2023)*; Alexandra Rivera *(2020–2023)*; Christina Rodriques *(2021–2024)*.

Round Table Chairs

Ethnic and Multicultural Information Exchange (EMIERT). Dr. Andrea Jamison.
Film and Media (FMRT). Tiffany Hudson.
Games and Gaming Round Table (GameRT). Rebecca Strang.
Government Documents Round Table (GODORT). Kian Flynn.
Graphic Novel and Comics (GNCRT). Moni Barrette.
Intellectual Freedom (IFRT). Angela Lynn Ocana.
International Relations (IRRT). Safi Safiullah.
Learning Round Table (LearnRT). Amanda E. Standerfer.
Library History (LHRT). Emily Spunaugle.
Library Instruction (LIRT). Becca Neal.
Library Research (LRRT). Dr. Karen F. Kaufmann.
Library Support Staff Interests (LSSIRT). Danielle M. Ponton (staff liaison).
Map and Geospatial Information (MAGIRT). Kevin Dyke.
New Members (NMRT). Annice Sevett.
Rainbow Round Table (RRT). Dontaná D. McPherson-Joseph.
Retired Members (RMRT). Rocco A. Staino.
Social Responsibilities (SRRT). April Sheppard.
Sustainability. Tina Chan.

Committee Chairs

Accreditation. Dr. Athena Salaba.

ALA-Children's Book Council Joint. Dr. Nicole A. Cooke.

American Libraries Advisory. Dr. Jason K. Alston.

Appointments. Emily Drabinski

Awards. Nicole LaMoreaux.

Budget Analysis and Review. Dr. Karen G. Schneider.

Chapter Relations. Brianna Hoffman.

Code of Conduct. Dr. Sheri Edwards and Daniella Smith.

Committee on Committees. Holly Robison (staff liaison).

Conference. Jennifer L. Ferriss.

Constitution and Bylaws. Brian E.C. Schottlaender.

Council Orientation. Dr. Jules Shore.

Diversity. Carla Y. Davis-Castro.

Diversity, Literacy, and Outreach Services Advisory. Suzan Antoinette Alteri and Jennifer Shimada.

Education. Dr. Sandy Hirsh.

Election. Bradley J. Kuykendall.

Human Resource Development and Recruitment Advisory. Kim Copenhaver.

Information Technology Advisory. Edward L. Sanchez.

Information Technology Policy Advisory. Sukrit Goswami

Intellectual Freedom. Lesliediana Jones.

International Relations. Julius C. Jefferson, Jr.

Legislation. Ed Garcia.

Library Advocacy. Dr. Steven D. Yates.

Literacy. Gwendolyn N. Weaver.

Membership. Miranda Henry Bennett.

Nominations. Aliqae Geraci.

Organization. Andrew K. Pace.

Policy Monitoring. Toni Negro.

Professional Ethics. Johana Emperatriz Orellana Cabrera.

Public and Cultural Programs Advisory. Kathy Zappitello.

Public Awareness. Loida A. Garcia-Febo.

Publishing. Heather M. Campbell.

Research and Statistics. Dr. Kimberley Bugg.

Resolutions. Rodney E. Lippard.

Rural, Native, and Tribal Libraries of All Kinds. Kevin Strowder (staff liaison).

Scholarships and Study Grants. Teresa Ann Copeland.

Status of Women in Leadership. Shatha Baydoun.

Sustainability. Matthew Bollerman.

Training, Orientation, and Leadership Development. Nicole Spoor.

Publications

American Libraries (6x a year; memb.; organizations in U.S., Canada, and Mexico $74; elsewhere $84; single copy $7.50).

Booklist (22 a year, with digital edition access to current and past issues of *Book Links* and 24/7 access to *Booklist Online*; U.S. and Canada $169.50; foreign $188).

Library Studies, Issues and Trends report.

Library Technology Reports (8x a year, online and print $340, non-U.S. $385).

Smart Libraries Newsletter (mo., online, and print $101, non-U.S. $111).

American Library Association
American Association of School Librarians

Executive Director, Sylvia Knight Norton
225 N. Michigan Ave., Ste. 1300, Chicago, IL 60601
312-280-4382, 800-545-2433 ext. 4382, fax (312) 280-5276, e-mail snorton@ala.org
World Wide Web https://www.ala.org/aasl, e-mail aasl@ala.org

Objective

The American Association of School Librarians (AASL) empowers leaders to transform teaching and learning. Established in 1951 as a separate division of the American Library Association (ALA), AASL understands the current realities and evolving dynamics of the professional environment and is positioned to help members achieve universal recognition of school librarians as indispensable educational leaders. AASL publishes standards for the profession—*National School Library Standards for Learners, School Librarians, and School Libraries* (2018, its latest)—providing a comprehensive approach through integrated frameworks consisting of four domains (Think, Create, Share, Grow) and six Shared Foundations (Inquire, Include, Collaborate, Curate, Explore, Engage).

Membership

Memb. 5,900+. Open to all school librarians, librarians, libraries, interested individuals, and business firms, with requisite membership in ALA.

Board of Directors (2022–2023)

Pres. Kathy Lester, East Middle School, School Librarian, Michigan; *Pres.-Elect* Courtney Pentland, North Star High School, School Librarian, Nebraska; *Secy.-Treas.* Juan Rivera, A. Philip Randolph Campus High School, School Librarian, New York; *Past Pres.* Jennisen Lucas, Park County School District #6, District Librarian, Wyoming; *Div. Councilor* Nora Wiltse, School Librarian, Illinois; *Dirs.* Lori Donovan, Cathi Fuhrman, Amanda Kordeliski, Jennifer Sharp.

Section Leadership

AAS/ESLS. Pamela R. Moore, Rebecca J. Morris, Jenna Spiering, Joyce Valenza.
AAS/ISS. Hannah Byrd Little, Neha Thakkar, Amanda Lucas, Maegen Rose.
AASL/SPVS. Jenny Takeda, Lindsey Kimery, Cherity Pennington, Jennifer Sturge.
(Subcommittees may be found on section websites.)

Committee Chairs

AASL/ALSC/YALSA Joint Committee on School/Public Library Cooperation. Sylvia Knight Norton (staff liaison).
Annual Conference. Allison Cline (staff liaison).
Association of American University Presses Book Selection. Catherine Kerns.
Awards. Cynthia Zervos, Allison Cline (staff liaison).
Budget and Finance. Erika Long, Sylvia Knight Norton (staff liaison).
Bylaws and Organization. Robbie Leah Nickel.
CAEP Coordinating Committee. Mary Ann Harlan.
Knowledge Quest. Sarah Searles, Meg Featheringham.
Leadership Development. Kathy Carroll.
Legacy. Cassandra Barnett, Allison Cline (staff liaison).
Member Engagement. Allison Cline (staff liaison).
National Conference. Allison Cline (staff liaison).
Practice. Laura Hicks and Amanda Kordeliski.
Professional Learning. Buffy Edwards, Jennifer Habley (staff liaison).
Publications. Stephanie Book (staff liaison).
School Library Event Promotion Committee. Lisa Brackel.

School Library Research. Audrey Church, Elizabeth Burns.

School Librarian Preparation National Recognition. Judy T. Bevins.

Standards. Sylvia Knight Norton (SL).

Editorial Board Chairs

Knowledge Quest Editorial Board. Sarah Searles (chair). Meg Featheringham (editor).

School Library Research Editorial Board. Audrey Church and Elizabeth Burns (co-editors).

Task Force Chairs

School Librarian Preparation Program National Recognition. Judy T. Bivens.

Awards Committee Chairs

ABC-CLIO Leadership Grant. Cynthia Zervos.

Best Digital Tools for Teaching and Learning. Samuel Northern.

Chapter of the Year Award. Brittany Tignor.

Collaborative School Library Award. Stacy Brown.

Distinguished School Administrator Award. Sarah Hunicke.

Frances Henne Award. Martha Pangburn.

Innovative Reading Grant. Alexa Lalejini.

Inspire Collection Development Grant. Nicolle Mazzola.

Inspire Special Event Grant. Zandra Lopez.

Intellectual Freedom Award. Christy James.

National School Library of the Year Award. Phoebe Warmack.

Research Grant. Allison Cline (staff liaison).

Roald Dahl Miss Honey Social Justice Award. Allison Cline (staff liaison)

Publications

Knowledge Quest (bi-mo.; memb.; nonmemb. $50 per year; outside U.S. $60 per year; https://knowledgequest.aasl.org/subscription). *Ed.* Meg Featheringham. E-mail mfeatheringham@ala.org.

School Library Research (electronic, free, at http://www.ala.org/aasl/slr). *Ed.* Meg Featheringham. E-mail mfeatheringham@ala.org.

American Library Association
Association for Library Service to Children

Executive Director, Alena Rivers
225 N. Michigan Ave., Suite 1300

Chicago, IL 60601
800-545-2433 ext. 2163, alsc@ala.org
World Wide Web https://www.ala.org/alsc

Objective

The Association for Library Service to Children (ALSC) develops and supports the profession of children's librarianship by enabling and encouraging its practitioners to provide the best library service to our nation's children. It was founded in 1901.

ALSC is interested in the improvement and extension of library services to children in all types of libraries. It is responsible for the evaluation and selection of book and nonbook library materials and for the improvement of techniques of library service to children from preschool through the eighth grade of junior high school age, when such materials and techniques are intended for use in more than one type of library. ALSC has specific responsibility for the following:

- Continuous study and critical review of activities assigned to the division
- Conduct of activities and carrying on of projects within its area of responsibility
- Cooperation with all units of the American Library Association whose interests and activities have a relationship to library service to children
- Interpretation of library materials for children and of methods of using such materials with children, to parents, teachers, and other adults, and representation of librarians' concern for the production and effective use of good children's books to groups outside the profession
- Stimulation of the professional growth of its members and encouragement of participation in appropriate type-of-library divisions
- Planning and development of programs of study and research in the area of selection and use of library materials for children for the total profession
- Development, evaluation, and promotion of professional materials in its area of responsibility

Membership

Memb. 3,797. Open to anyone interested in library services to children. Dues in addition to ALA membership (Regular) $50; (Student) $20; (Non-salaried/Ret.) $35; (Associate) $25.

Address correspondence to the ALSC Office, http://www.ala.org/alsc/aboutalsc/contact.

Officers (2022–2023)

Pres. Amy E. Koester; *V.P./Pres.-Elect.* Dr. Jonda C. McNair; *Past Pres.* Lucia Martinez Gonzalez; *Div. Councilor* Kimberly Anne Patton; *Fiscal Officer* Robbin Ellis Friedman.

Board Members

Jaime Lee Eastman (*2022–2025*), Maria F. Estrella (*2022–2025*), Ariana Augustine Sani Hussain (*2020–2023*), Sada Mozer (*2021–2024*), Tori Ann A. Ogawa (*2021–2024*), Georgina M. Rivas-Martinez (*2021–2024*), Soraya Anne-Machel Silverman-Montano (*2020–2023*), Meredith C. Steiner (*2020–2023*).

Committee Chairs

AASL/ALSC/YALSA Interdivisional Committee on School/Public Library Cooperation. Nan Trowell Brown.

BIOPC (Black, Indigenous and/or People of Color) Discussion Group. Alia R. Jones, Hanna Lee.

Budget. Christopher A. Biss-Brown.

Children and Libraries Editorial Advisory. Amalia Elizabeth Butler and Jacqueline R. Kociubuk.

Children and Technology. Manuela Victoria Aronofsky and Tina L. Bartholoma.

Children's Collections Management Discussion Group. Stephanie D. Bange (consultant).

Children's Literature Lecture Award. Todd Krueger (consultant).

Early Childhood Programs and Services. Meg Beade Stowe and Jessica N. Smith.

Early and Family Literacy. Ruth Guerrierpierre and Rachel Godwin Payne.

Education. Meagan Albright and Casey O'Leary.

Excellence for Early Learning Digital Media. Maria Dolores Vega.

Intellectual Freedom. Andrew Medlar and Maria Francesca Trivisonno.

Library Service to Underserved Children and Their Caregivers. Tammie J. Benham and Melody T. Leung

Managing Children's Services. Uma S. Nori and Kristin Kelly Williamson.

Membership. Aryssa F. Damron and Allison M. Knight.

Nominating and Leadership Development–2024. Elisa Gall and Susan Dove Lempke.

Notable Children's Books. April Rachelle Roy.

Notable Children's Digital Media. Dr. Danilo M. Baylen and Melanie A. Lyttle.

Notable Children's Recordings. Rebecca (Becki) B. Bishop.

Organizational Effectiveness. Michelle Ng and Dr. Jo Phillips.

Preschool Services Discussion Group. Dr. Tess Prendergast.

Program Coordinating. Ericka Brunson-Rochette and Tanya A. Prax.

Public Awareness and Advocacy. Emily Mroczek and Ana-Elba Pavon.

Quicklists Consulting. Dr. Emily Rose Aguilo-Perez and Destinee Renee Sutton.

School-Age Programs and Services. Emily L. Nichols and Stephanie C. Prato.

Task Force Chairs

Diversifying Revenue Streams Task Force. Nina Lindsay.

Equity, Diversity, and Inclusion (EDI) within ALSC Implementation. Naphtali Faris (consultant).

National Institute Planning. Jessica Fredrickson.

Awards Committee Chairs

Mildred L. Batchelder Award 2024. Natalie R. Ziarnik.

Pura Belpré Award 2024. Eileen Makoff.

Randolph Caldecott Award 2024. Kathie L. Meizner.

Children's Literature Legacy Award Selection Committee–2024. Caroline Ward.

Excellence for Early Learning Digital Media. Maria Dolores Vega.

Theodor Seuss Geisel Award 2024. Gwen Vanderhage.

Mock Awards Elections Tool Kit Task Force. Edith Campbell.

John Newbery Award 2024. Amber Lea Creger.

Odyssey Award 2024. Kirby McCurtis.

Professional Recognition and Scholarships. Elizabeth A. Burns and Rachel Fryd.

Programs and Services Recognition. Stephanie Luyt and Maren C. Ostergard.

Robert F. Sibert Informational Book Award 2024. Joyce R. Laiosa.

Publications

ALSC Matters! (q., electronic; open access).

Children and Libraries: The Journal of the Association for Library Service to Children (q.; print and online; memb.; nonmemb. $50; intl. $60).

American Library Association
Association of College and Research Libraries

Executive Director, Robert Jay Malone
225 N. Michigan Ave, Suite 1300, Chicago, IL 60601
312-280-2523, 800-545-2433 ext. 2523, fax 312-280-2520, e-mail acrl@ala.org
World Wide Web https://www.ala.org/acrl

Objective

The Association of College and Research Libraries (ACRL) is a forum for and an advocate of academic and research librarians and library personnel. The object of the association is to provide leadership for the development, promotion, and improvement of academic and research library resources and services and to advance learning, research, and scholarly communication. It was founded in 1940.

Membership

Memb. 9,108. For information on dues, see American Library Association entry.

Officers (2022–2023)

Pres. Erin L. Ellis, Indiana University; *V.P.* Beth McNeil, Dean of Libraries, Purdue University; *Budget and Fin. Chair* Joe Mocnik, Dean and Professor, Kansas State University Libraries; *Div. Councilor* Kara M. Whatley, University Librarian, California Institute of Technology; *Past Pres.* Julie Ann Garrison, Western Michigan University.

Board of Directors

Toni Anaya (*2020–2024*), Jessica Brangiel (*2020–2024*), Walter Butler (*2022–2026*), Kim Copenhaver (*2019–2023*), Cinthya Ippoliti (*2019–2023*), Mary Mallery (*2021–2025*), Yasmeen L. Shorish (*2021–2025*), Rebecca Miller Waltz (*2022–2026*), Robert (Jay) Malone (ex officio).

Committee Chairs

ACRL Coordinating. John P. Culshaw.

ACRL Contributed Papers. Dr. Erla P. Heyns and Brad L. Warren.

ACRL Experience and Inclusion. Emily Daly and Katelyn Quirin Manwiller.

ACRL Invited Presentations. Federico Martinez-Garcia, Jr. and Lisa M. Stillwell.

ACRL Keynote Speakers. Heidi Steiner Burkhardt and Alexia Hudson-Ward.

ACRL Lightning Talks. Brett Cloyd and Orlando Duffus.

ACRL Local Arrangements. Carrie Donovan and Dennis J. Smith.

ACRL Panel Sessions. Bethann Zani Rea and Constance M. Wade.

ACRL Poster Sessions. Angie Cox and Alyssa Koclanes.

ACRL Roundtable Discussions Committee. Sarah Bankston and Caroline Fuchs.

ACRL Scholarships. Willie Miller and Rita Marie Suarez.

ACRL Virtual Conference. Rachel Besara and Dr. Michelle Demeter.

ACRL Workshops. Matthew P. Ciszek and Christine E. Woods.

ACRL/CORE Interdivisional Academic Library Facilities Survey. Dr. Anne Marie Casey and Eric A. Kidwell.

Appointments. Mark A. Puente.

Budget and Finance. Dr. Joe Mocnik.

Communities of Practice Assembly. Elizabeth R. Fox.

Equity, Diversity, and Inclusion. Je Lee Salvador.

External Liaisons. Kathleen H. Flynn.

Government Relations. Dr. Kevin W. Walker.

Immersion Program. Margot Conahan (staff liaison).

Information Literacy Frameworks and Standards. Lori Townsend.

Dr. E.J. Josey Spectrum Scholar Mentor. Marquel Anteola.

Leadership Recruitment and Nomination. Marilyn N. Ochoa.

Liaisons Assembly. Tracey A. Allen Overbey.

Membership. Jill Sodt.

New Roles and Changing Landscapes. Amy Dye-Reeves.

President's Program Planning. Dr. Beth McNeil (board liaison).

Professional Development. Matthew Weirick Johnson

Professional Values. Marcela Yael Isuster.

Publications Coordinating. Candice C. Dahl.

Research Planning and Review. Michael Flierl.

Research and Scholarly Environment. Sandra Aya Enimil.

Section Membership. Joyce Garczynski.

Standards. Amy Dye-Reeves.

Student Learning and Information Literacy. Melissa Nicole Mallon.

Value of Academic Libraries. Dr. Jung Mi Scoulas.

Publications/Editorial Board Chairs

Academic Library Trends and Statistics Survey. Devin Savage.

ACRL/CORE Interdivisional Academic Library Facilities Survey. Dr. Anne Marie Casey and Eric A. Kidwell.

Choice. Elizabeth Fronk.

C&RL. Kristen Grace Totleben.

C&RL News. Dr. Leo S. Lo.

New Publications Advisory. Heidi Steiner Burkhardt.

Project Outcome for Academic Libraries. Jennifer Arnold.

Publications in Librarianship. Dr. Mark E. Shelton.

RBM: A Journal of Rare Books, Manuscripts, and Cultural Heritage. Dr. Richard Saunders.

Resources for College Libraries. Tammera M. Race.

Task Force Chairs

ACRL/ALA/ARL IPEDS Advisory. Devin Savage.

Awards Process Implementation. Lori Goetsch and John A. Lehner.

Diversity Alliance. Position open.

Member Accommodation/Compensation. Position open.

National Survey of Student Engagement (NSSE) Information Literacy Module Review. Maoria Kirker.

Nominations and Policies Audit. Position open.

Discussion Group Conveners

Assessment. Dr. Susanna M. Cowan, Anita Riley Hall, and Megan Hodge.

Balancing Baby and Book. Laura Bornella.

Copyright. Laura G. Burtle and Cheryl Ann Coyle.

First-Year Experience. Kimberly Shotick.

Heads of Public Services. Delores Carlito and Mira P. Waller.

Hip Hop Librarian Consortium. Lauren Carlton (staff liaison).

Human Resources and Organizational Development. Michele Lynn Mikkelsen.

Language and Linguistics. Katie E. Gibson.

Leadership. Russell S. Michalak.

Librarians from Very Small Academic Institutions. Linda Kern and Linda M. Kramer.

Librarianship in For-Profit Educational Institutions. Mary A. Snyder.

Scholarly Communication. Ashley D.R. Sergiadis.

Student Retention. Nicole Helregel.

Interest Group Conveners

Academic Library Services to Graduate Students. Victor Dominguez Baeza and Matt Ogborn.

Academic Library Services to International Students. Katie Odhner.

Access Services. Lesley Brown and H.J. Pedelty.

African-American Studies Librarians. Valerie Amele Tagoe.

Asian, African, and Middle Eastern Studies. Deepa Banerjee.

Contemplative Pedagogy. Sharon Ladenson.

Digital Badges. Dr. Michael Gutierrez.

Evidence Synthesis Methods. Dr. Zahra Premji.

Health Sciences. Dr. Rosaline Y. Odom.

History Librarians. Jessica Sheara Epstein.

Image Resources. Sarah E. Huber.

Library Marketing and Outreach. Jillian Christine Eslami.

Research Assessment and Metrics. Thane Chambers.

Residency. Kalani J. Adolpho.
Technical Services. Laurie Palumbo.
Universal Accessibility. Trisha Prevett Whiteman.
Virtual Worlds. Carla Downer Pritchett.

Awards Committee Chairs

Academic/Research Librarian of the Year Award. Marielle Veve.
Hugh C. Atkinson Memorial Award. Rebecca L. Mugridge.
Excellence in Academic Libraries Awards. Julie Ann Garrison.

Section Chairs

Anthropology and Sociology (ANSS). Elizabeth R. Fox.
Arts Section. Carla-Mae Crookendale.
College Libraries Section (CLS). Dr. Kimberley Bugg.
Community and Junior College Libraries Section (CJCLS). Victoria Ames Hart.
Digital Scholarship Section. Pamella R. Lach.
Distance and Online Learning Section (DOLS). Chimene Elise Tucker.
Education and Behavioral Sciences Section (EBSS). Samantha Godbey.
European Studies Section (ESS). Brian Vetruba.
Instruction Section (IS). Carrie Forbes.
Literatures in English Section (LES). Kristina M. De Voe.

Politics, Policy and International Relations Section (PPIRS). Mary Kathryn Oberlies.
Rare Books and Manuscripts (RBMS). Melissa Hubbard.
Science and Technology Section (STS). Bonnie L. Fong.
University Libraries Section (ULS). Maura Seale.
Women and Gender Studies Section (WGSS). Caitlin Shanley.

Publications

Choice (12 a year; $513; Canada and Mexico $551; other international $660). *Ed.* Elizabeth Fronk.
Choice Reviews-on-Cards (requires subscription to *Choice* or *Choice Reviews* $576; Canada and Mexico $618; other international $713).
C&RL (6 a year; open access online-only). *Ed.* Kristen Grace Totleben.
C&RL News (11 a year; memb.; nonmemb. $58; Canada and other PUAS countries $63; other international $68). *Ed.* Dr. Leo S. Lo.
RBM: A Journal of Rare Books, Manuscripts, and Cultural Heritage (s. ann.; $52; Canada and other PUAS countries $58; other international $69). *Ed.* Richard Saunders. Southern Utah Univ., 351 W. University Blvd. Gerrald R. Sherratt Lib., Cedar City, UT 84720-2415. Tel. 435-865-7947, fax 435-865-8152, e-mail rsaunders@suu.edu.

American Library Association
CORE: Leadership, Infrastructure, Futures

Interim Executive Director, Julie Reese
225 N. Michigan Ave, Suite 1300, Chicago, IL 60601
800-535-2433, e-mail core@ala.org
World Wide Web https://www.ala.org/core

Vision

Core members play a central role in every library, shaping the future of the profession through community building, advocacy, and learning.

Mission

To cultivate and amplify the collective expertise of library workers in core functions through building, advocacy, and learning.

Membership

Memb. 5,931. For information on dues, see the American Library Association (ALA) entry.

Officers (2022–2023)

Pres. Margaret Heller; *Pres.-Elect* Wendy Tressler; *Past Pres.* Lindsay Anne Cronk; *Div. Councilor* Rachel Fleming; *Chair of Advocacy Coord.* Morag Boyd; *Chair of Budget & Finance* Cara Mia Calabrese; *Chair of Org. & Bylaws* Don Perry Allgeier.

Board of Directors

Andrea Berstler *(2022–2025)*, Lauren Corbett *(2022–2025)*, Tyler Dzuba *(2021–2023)*, Thomas Lamanna, II *(2022–2025)*, Evviva R. Weinraub Lajoie *(2021–2023)*, Alexandra P. Rivera (executive board liaison, *2020–2023)*.

Committee Chairs

Advocacy Coordination. Morag Boyd.
Appointments. Wendy Tressler.
Awards and Scholarships Coordination. Maggie Dull and Gabrielle Somnee Wiersma.
Budget and Finance. Cara Mia Calabrese.
Bylaws and Organization. Don Perry Allgeier.
Committee Recognizing Excellence in Children's and Young Adult Science Fiction. Athina Livanos-Propst.
Communications Coordination. Braegan Abernethy.
Competencies Development. Nancy A. Cunningham and Caroline Fuchs.
Conference Program Coordination. Lacie Griffin and Dr. Patrice-Andre (Max) Prud'homme.
Content Coordination. Dale Poulter.
Continuing Education Coordination. Paromita Biswas.
CORE Reading Club Facilitation. Miranda Henry Bennett.
Diversity and Inclusion. Cara Mia Calabrese and Carrye Kay Syma.
Exchange Planning. Julie Reese (staff liaison).
Federated Authentication. Thomas P. Dowling.
Forum Planning. Thomas Ferren (staff liaison).
Fundraising and Sponsorships. Tabatha Farney and Joseph Yue.
Interest Group Coordination. Dennis J. Smith.

International Relations. Christopher Scott Dieckman.
Leadership Development and Mentoring. Kathy M. Irwin and Maurini R. Strub.
LibGuides Project Team. Jenny Levine (staff liaison).
Member Engagement Coordination. George E. Gottschalk, IV.
Nominating Committee. Christopher J. Cronin.
Preservation Outreach Committee. Jessica Bitely and Sean M. Ferguson.
Publications Coordination. Jeremy J. Myntti.
Standards. Melissa M. Brooks.
Top Technology Trends. Kate Delaney.
Web. Kelly J. Sattler.

Awards Committees

ALA John Cotton Dana Library Public Relations Award. Gregg Dodd.
Hugh C. Atkinson Memorial Award. Rebecca L. Mugridge.
Christian Larew Memorial Scholarship. Regina Beach-Bertin.
CORE Margaret Mann Citation. Dr. Karen Snow.
CORE/OCLC Frederick G. Kilgour Award for Research in Library and Information Technology. Heather Getsay and Angela R. Maranville.
CORE PR Xchange Awards. Markaaron Polger.

Editorial Boards

ITAL. Ken Varnum.
LL&M. Elizabeth Nelson.
LRTS. Dr. Rachel E. Scott.
Monographs. Kimberley A. Edwards.

Interest Group Chairs

Artificial Intelligence and Machine Learning in Libraries. Mary B. Aycock.
Authority Control. Casey B. Cheney.
Bibliographic Conceptual Models. Thomas M. Dousa and Nathan B. Putnam.
Book and Paper. Carrie Beyer.
Cartographic Resources Cataloging (CORE/MAGIRT). Amy Swanson.
Catalog Form and Function. Jenny Levine (staff liaison).

Catalog Management. Jeanette Kalchik and Cindy Tian.

Cataloging and Classification Research. Cynthia A. Romanowski and Cindy Tian.

Cataloging Norms. Bela Gupta and Dr. Shuzhen Zhao.

Chief Collection Development Officers of Large Research Libraries. Kizer S. Walker.

Collection Development Issues for the Practitioner. Jenny Levine (staff liaison).

Collection Evaluation and Assessment. Arthur Aguilera, Keri Prelitz, and Rachel Stephanie Wells.

Collection Management in Public Libraries. Jenny Levine (staff liaison).

Competencies and Education for a Career in Cataloging. Faye Mazzia and Dr. Athena Salaba.

Consortium Management. Tracy Byerly.

Copy Cataloging. Dean Bergstrom, Jr. and Lori Dekydtspotter.

Creative Ideas in Technical Services. Laura A. Sill.

Dialogue with Directors. Shelly McCoy and Denise Shorey.

Digital Conversation. Bethann Zani Rea.

Ebooks. Stacy Rene Judy Tomaszewski.

Electronic Resources. Christine Davidian.

Faceted Subject Access. Scott M. Dutkiewicz.

Heads of Library Technology. Jenny Levine (staff liaison).

Imagineering. Athina Livanos-Propst.

Instructional Technologies. Melissa Johnson.

Library Consulting. Val Edwards.

Library Facilities and Interiors. Gili Meerovitch.

Library Leaders and Managers. Cinthya Ippoliti and Dr. Erik Nordberg.

Library Storage. Cathy Martyniak.

Linked Data. Kevin M. Ford and Becky Skeen.

Maker Technology. Leanne Nay.

MARC Formats Transition. Keiko Suzuki.

Metadata. Mingyan Li.

Middle Managers. Jeffrey Scott Bullington and Carissa Ann Tomlinson.

Newspaper. Brian Geiger.

Open Access. Erin Elizabeth Owens.

Open-Source Systems. Robert Wilson.

Preservation Administration. Mark Coulbourne and Kim Knox Norman.

Project Management. Kristen Clark and Nicole Lewis.

Promoting Preservation. Elizabeth A. Stone.

Public Libraries Technical Services. Jenny Levine (staff liaison).

Publisher-Vendor-Library Relations. Ajaye Bloomstone, Claire Holloway, and Megan Sullivan.

Role of the Professional Librarian in Technical Services. Amy L. Fry and Marina Morgan.

Solo Practitioners. Jenny Levine (staff liaison).

Technical Services Managers in Academic Libraries. Nerissa Lindsey and Alexander Whelan.

Technical Services Workflow Efficiency. Sai Deng and Caroline Saccucci.

WebServices4Lib. Chris Cabrera Thompson.

Publications

Information Technologies and Libraries (4 a year). *Ed.* Ken Varnum.

Library Leadership and Management (4 a year). *Ed.* Elizabeth Nelson.

Library Resources and Technical Services (4 a year). *Ed.* Dr. Rachel E. Scott.

American Library Association
Public Library Association

Executive Director, Mary Davis Fournier
225 N. Michigan Ave., Suite 1300, Chicago, IL 60601
312-280-5752, 800-545-2433 ext. 5752, fax 312-280-5029, e-mail pla@ala.org
World Wide Web https://www.pla.org

The Public Library Association (PLA) the has specific responsibility for:

- Conducting and sponsoring research about how the public library can respond to changing social needs and technical developments

- Developing and disseminating materials useful to public libraries in interpreting public library services and needs

- Conducting continuing education for public librarians by programming at national and regional conferences, by publications such as the newsletter, and by other delivery means
- Establishing, evaluating, and promoting goals, guidelines, and standards for public libraries
- Maintaining liaison with relevant national agencies and organizations engaged in public administration and human services, such as the National Association of Counties, the Municipal League, and the Commission on Postsecondary Education
- Maintaining liaison with other divisions and units of the American Library Association (ALA) and other library organizations, such as the Association for Library and Information Science Education and the Urban Libraries Council
- Defining the role of the public library in service to a wide range of user and potential user groups
- Promoting and interpreting the public library to a changing society through legislative programs and other appropriate means
- Identifying legislation to improve and to equalize support of public libraries

PLA enhances the development and effectiveness of public librarians and public library services. This mission positions PLA to:

- Focus its efforts on serving the needs of its members
- Address issues that affect public libraries
- Commit to quality public library services that benefit the general public

The goals of PLA are:

- Advocacy and Awareness: PLA is an essential partner in public library advocacy.
- Leadership and Transformation: PLA is the leading source for learning opportunities to advance transformation of public libraries.
- Literate Nation: PLA will be a leader and valued partner of public libraries' initiatives to create a literate nation.
- Organizational Excellence: PLA is positioned to sustain and grow its resources to advance the work of the association.

Membership

Memb. 8,800+. Open to all ALA members interested in the improvement and expansion of public library services to all ages in various types of communities.

Officers (2022–2023)

Pres. Dr. Maria Taesil Hudson McCauley, Cambridge Public Library, Cambridge, MA; *Pres.-Elect* Sonia Alcántara-Antoine, Baltimore County Public Library, Baltimore, MD; *Past Pres.* Melanie Huggins, Richland Library, Columbia, SC; *Div. Councilor* Stephanie Chase, Libraries of Eastern Oregon and Consultant, Constructive Disruption, Portland, OR; *Fiscal Officer* Clara Nalli Bohrer, West Bloomfield Township Public Library, West Bloomfield, MI; *Exec. Dir.* Mary Davis Fournier, PLA/American Library Association, Chicago, IL. E-mail mfournier@ala.org (ex officio).

Board of Directors

Michael Colford (*2022–2025*), Erica Freudenberger (*2021–2024*), Mary Ellen Icaza (*2022–2025*), Candice Wing-Yee Mack (*2021–2024*), Dr. Brandy A. McNeil (*2020–2023*), Dara Hanke Schmidt (*2020–2023*).

Committee Chairs

Advocacy and Strategic Partnerships. Maureen Langley.
Annual Conference Program Subcommittee. Kimberly J. Johnson.
Budget and Finance. Clara Nalli Bohrer.
Conference. Melanie Wilson Huggins.
Continuing Education Advisory Group. Krista D. Riggs and Roosevelt Weeks.
Digital Literacy. Angela Craig and Kelvin Antonio Watson.
Equity, Diversity, Inclusion and Social Justice. Tamara M. King and Peggy P. Tseng.

Family Engagement. Rebecca Simone Shaknovich and Dr. Zachary Lee Stier.
Leadership Development. Derek E. Wolfgram.
Measurement, Evaluation and Assessment. Daniel Hensley and Jerianne Thompson.
Membership Advisory Group. Cindy Hohl and Rachel Nowell.
Nominating. Michelle M. Jeske.
Public Libraries Advisory. Martha Hutzel.
Technology. David Lee King.

Publication

Public Libraries (6 a year; memb.; nonmemb. $65; Canada and Mexico $75; Int'l. $100). *Ed.* Kathleen Hughes, PLA, 225 N. Michigan Ave., Suite 1300, Chicago, IL 60601. E-mail khughes@ala.org.

American Library Association
Reference and User Services Association

Executive Director, Bill Ladewski
225 N. Michigan Ave, Suite 1300, Chicago, IL 60601
800-545-2433 ext. 4395, 312-280-4395, fax 312-280-5273,e-mail bladewski@ala.org or rusa@ala.org
World Wide Web https://www.ala.org/rusa

Objective

The Reference and User Services Association (RUSA) is responsible for stimulating and supporting excellence in the delivery of general library services and materials and the provision of reference and information services, collection development, readers' advisory, and resource sharing for all ages in every type of library.

The specific responsibilities of RUSA are:

- Conduct of activities and projects within the association's areas of responsibility
- Encouragement of the development of librarians engaged in these activities and stimulation of participation by members of appropriate type-of-library divisions
- Synthesis of the activities of all units within the American Library Association (ALA) that have a bearing on the type of activities represented by the association
- Representation and interpretation of the association's activities in contacts outside the profession
- Planning and development of programs of study and research in these areas for the total profession
- Continuous study and review of the association's activities

Membership

Memb. 2,600+

Officers (2022–2023)

Pres. Cynthia A. Johnson; *Pres.-Elect* Joseph Yue; *Past Pres.* Christina Pryor; *Div. Councilor* Alesia M. McManus.

Board of Directors

Nanette Wargo Donohue (*2022–2023*); Adebola Fabiku (*2022–2023*); Kelly Anne McCusker (*2022–2023*); Angela K. O'Neal (*2022–2024*); Dr. Chad J. Pearson (*2021–2024*); Jenny L. Presnell (*2023*); Lauren Reiter (*2022–2024*); Candice Townsend (*2022–2023*); Bill Ladewski (ex officio).

Committee Chairs

Access to Information. Position open.
Accessibility Assembly. Lauren Sarah Kehoe.
AFL-CIO/ALA Labor. Shuntai Sykes (staff liaison).
Budget and Finance. Jennifer McElroy.
Conference Program Coordinating. Fatima K. Perkins.

Leadership Council. Cynthia A. Johnson.
Member Engagement. Meredith Knoff and
Tami Sandberg.
Nominating. Courtney Greene McDonald.
President's Program Planning. Elizabeth De
Coster and Lori Lysiak.
Professional Development. Dr. Michael Holt
and Daniel Clark Mack.
Professional Resources. Kayla Jean Kuni.
RUSA Reference & User Services Quarterly
Editorial Board. Barry Trott.
Volunteer Development. Larayne J. Dallas.

RUSA Sections

Business Reference and Services Section
(BRASS). https://www.ala.org/rusa/business-
reference-and-services-section-brass-com
mittees.
Collection Development and Evaluation Section (CODES). https://www.ala.org/rusa/
collection-development-and-evaluation-
section-codes-committees.
Emerging Technologies Section (ETS). https://
www.ala.org/rusa/emerging-technologies-
section-ets-committees.
History Section (HS). https://www.ala.org/
rusa/history-section-hs-committees.

Reference Services Section (RSS). https://www.
ala.org/rusa/reference-services-section-
rss-committees.
Sharing and Transforming Access to Resources
Section (STARS). https://www.ala.org/rusa/
sharing-and-transforming-access-resources-
section-stars-committee.
(Subcommittees may be found on section websites.)

Awards Committee Chairs

Achievement Awards and Grants. Jason Mat-
thew Coleman.
Andrew Carnegie Medal for Excellence in Fic-
tion and Nonfiction. Bill Ladewski.
Awards Coordinating Committee. Emily Nel-
son Decker.
John Sessions Memorial Award. Janet T.
O'Keefe.

Publications

Reference & User Services Quarterly (online
only at http://journals.ala.org/index.php/rusq)
(memb.).
RUSA Update (q., online newsletter, at http://
www.rusaupdate.org).

American Library Association
United for Libraries: Association of Library Trustees, Advocates, Friends, and Foundations

Executive Director, Beth Nawalinski
600 Eagleview Blvd., Suite 300, Exton, PA 19341
800-545-2433, ext. 2161, fax 215-545-3821, e-mail bnawalinski@ala.org or united@ala.org
World Wide Web https://www.ala.org/united

Objective

United for Libraries was founded in 1890 as
the American Library Trustee Association
(ALTA). It was the only division of the American Library Association (ALA) dedicated to
promoting and ensuring outstanding library
service through educational programs that develop excellence in trusteeship and promote
citizen involvement in the support of libraries.
ALTA became an ALA division in 1961. In
2008 the members of ALTA voted to expand
the division to more aggressively address the

needs of friends of libraries and library foundations, and through a merger with Friends
of Libraries USA (FOLUSA), it became the
Association of Library Trustees, Advocates,
Friends and Foundations (ALTAFF). In 2012
members voted to add "United for Libraries"
to its title.

Membership

Memb. 5,000. Open to all interested persons
and organizations. Dues (prorated to match

ALA membership expiration) $55; (student with ALA membership) $20.

Officers (2022–2023)

Pres. Gordon Baker; *V.P./Pres.-Elect* Deborah Doyle; *Secy.* Kathleen McEvoy; *Past Pres.* Charity Tyler; *Div. Councilor* Andrea Lapsley; *Fiscal Officer* Amandeep Kochar.

Board of Directors

Trustees at Large Chris Chanyasulkit, Mary Soucie, Patricia A. Shlonsky, Janet Segal. *Friends at Large* Steven Yates, Ari Brooks, Camille McCutcheon, Ben Carter. *Foundations at Large* Kathy Selking, Toledo Lucas County (Ohio) Public Library; Marie Ciepiela, Friends of the San Francisco (California) Public Library; Brenda Langstraat Bui, Chicago Public Library Foundation; Lauren Trujillo, Santa Barbara (California) Public Library Foundation. *Corporate at Large* Gary Kirk, Tech Logic; Steve Laird, Data Axle Reference Solutions; Skip Dye, Penguin Random House. *Board Members at Large* Nicolle Davies, Maura Deedy, Alan Fishel, Kathy Kosinski, Peter Pearson. *Lifetime Board Member* Pat Schuman.

Committee and Task Force Chairs

Awards & Honors Committee. Position open. Finance Committee. Position open. Governance Committee. Position open. Leadership Development Committee. Position open. Membership Committee. Position open. Nominating Committee. Position open. Partnership & Fundraising Committee. Position open. Programs Committee. Position open. Public Policy & Advocacy Committee. Position open.

Publications

All Ages Welcome: Recruiting and Retaining Younger Generations for Library Boards, Friends Groups, and Foundations.
The Complete Library Trustee Handbook.
Even More Great Ideas for Libraries and Friends.
The Good, the Great, and the Unfriendly: A Librarian's Guide to Working with Friends Groups.
A Library Board's Practical Guide to Hiring Outside Experts by Christine Lind Hage, Mary Pergander, and Jean Tabor.
A Library Board's Practical Guide to Self-Evaluation by Nicholas Spillios and Sally G. Reed.
Getting Grants in Your Community by Sally Gardner Reed and Beth Nawalinski.
Making Our Voices Heard: Citizens Speak Out for Libraries by Sally Gardner Reed and Beth Nawalinski.
Proving Your Library's Value: Persuasive, Organized, and Memorable Messaging.

American Library Association
Young Adult Library Services Association

Interim Executive Director, LaMoya Burks
225 N. Michigan Ave, Chicago, IL 60601
312-280-4390, 800-545-2433 ext. 4390, fax 312-280-5276, e-mail yalsa@ala.org
World Wide Web https://www.ala.org/yalsa
YALSA blog https://yalsa.ala.org/blog, The Hub https://yalsa.ala.org/thehub,
Wiki https://wikis.ala.org/yalsa, Twitter https://twitter.com/yalsa
Facebook https://www.facebook.com/YALSA

Objective

In every library in the nation, high-quality library service to young adults is provided by a staff that understands and respects the unique informational, educational, and recreational needs of teenagers. Equal access to information, services, and materials is recognized as a right, not a privilege. Young adults are actively involved in the library decision-making process. The library staff collaborates and cooperates with other youth-serving agencies to provide a holistic, community-wide network of activities and services that support healthy youth development.

To ensure that this vision becomes a reality, the Young Adult Library Services Association (YALSA):

- Advocates extensive and developmentally appropriate library and information services for young adults ages 12–18
- Promotes reading and supports the literacy movement
- Advocates the use of information and digital technologies to provide effective library service
- Supports equality of access to the full range of library materials and services, including existing and emerging information and digital technologies, for young adults
- Provides education and professional development to enable its members to serve as effective advocates for young people
- Fosters collaboration and partnerships among its individual members with the library community and other groups involved in providing library and information services to young adults
- Influences public policy by demonstrating the importance of providing library and information services that meet the unique needs and interests of young adults
- Encourages research and is in the vanguard of new thinking concerning the provision of library and information services for youth

Membership

Memb. 3,600+. Open to anyone interested in library services for and with young adults. For information on dues, see the American Library Association (ALA) entry.

Officers (2022–2023)

Pres. Franklin Escobedo; *Pres.-Elect* Coleen Seisser; *Div. Councilor* Elizabeth Nebeker; *Fiscal Officer* Kate Denier; *Secy.* Joel Shoemaker; *Past Pres.* Kelly Czarnecki.

Board of Directors

Josie Laine Andrews, Susannah Goldstein, Matt Layne, Melissa Malanuk, Abby Phillips, Stacey Shapiro, Melanie Wachsmann, LaMoya N. Burks (board liaison), Morgan Brickey-Jones (ex officio), Ziba Pérez (ex officio), Siva Ramakrishnan (ex officio), Gail Tobin (ex officio).

Committee Chairs

AASL/ALSC/YALSA Committee on School and Public Library Cooperation. Nan Brown (AASL).
Annual Conference Marketing and Local Arrangements. Position open.

Board Development. Kelly Czarnecki.
Division and Membership Promotion. Position open.
Education Advisory. Yvette Garcia.
Executive Committee. Franklin Escobedo.
Financial Advancement. Gail Tobin.
Hub Advisory Board. Stephanie Johnson.
Organization and Bylaws Committee. Position open.
Research Committee. Position open.
Research Journal Advisory Board. Position open.
Selection List Oversight Committee. Position open.
Social Media Marketing. Kristen Caldwell and Caitlyn Seale.
Teen Civic Engagement. Rachel McDonald.
Teens' Top Ten. Kathy Dejnowski.
YALS/YALSAblog Editorial Advisory. Position open.

Task Force Chairs

Amazing Audiobooks Blogging Team. Jennifer Sutton.
Best Fiction Blogging Team. Jodeana Kruse.
CORE/YALSA Toolkit. Position open.
Evaluating Volunteer Resources. Position open.
Graphic Novel Selection Blogging Team. Kelley Blue.
Mid-Winter Marketing and Local Arrangements. Position open.

President's Implementation. Franklin Escobedo.
Quick Picks Blogging Team. Jessica Lorentz Smith.
Teen Programming HQ. Position open.
YA Symposium Planning and Marketing Task Force. Position open.

Awards Committee Chairs

ALSC/Booklist/YALSA Odyssey Award Committee. Kirby McCurtis (ALSC).
Alex Award Committee. David Saia.
Book Awards Committees' Oversight Committee. Ninah Moore (staff liaison).
Margaret Edwards Committee. Valerie Davis.
Michael L. Printz Award. Courtney Waters.
Morris Award Committee. Kim Farnsworth.
Nonfiction Award. Janet Hilbun.

Publications

Journal of Research on Libraries and Young Adults (q.) (online, open source, peer-reviewed). *Ed.* Denise Agosto. E-mail yalsaresearch@gmail.com.
Young Adult Library Services (*YALS*) (q.) (online only; member; nonmember $70; foreign $70). *Ed.* Yolanda Hood. E-mail yalseditor@gmail.com.

ARMA International

Executive Director, Nathan Hughes
312 SW Greenwich Dr, Suite 515

Lee's Summit, MO 64082
913-444-9174, 844-565-2120, fax 913-257-3855, e-mail headquarters@armaintl.org
World Wide Web https://www.arma.org

Objective

To be the driving force that enables organizations to harness the strategic power of information, empowering the community of information professionals to advance their careers, organizations, and the profession. ARMA International is committed to finding innovative ways to provide our personal and professional communities with guidance, learning, development, and opportunity. We value the open exchange of ideas, good governance, free flow of information, and thought leadership by seeking diversity, inclusivity, and equity in all its forms. The membership of ARMA International has reached a consensus that the association's most unique value to the information community is derived from the following: (1) professional standard-setting and best practice frameworks; (2) current news, events, and industry trends; (3) a network of local chapters providing opportunities for in-person training and leadership development; (4) certification preparation and continuing education.

Membership

More than 6,000 in 30+ countries besides its U.S. base. Annual dues (Professional) $175; (Assoc.) $95. Chapter dues vary.

Officers (2022–2023)

Pres. Wendy McLain, Valero Energy Corporation. E-mail wendy.mclain@armaintl.org; *Pres.-Elect* Margaret Hermesmeyer, PNC Financial Services Group. E-mail margaret. hermesmeyer@armaintl.org; *Treas.* Michael Landau, NetApp. E-mail michael.landau@armaintl.org; *Past Pres.* Michael Haley, Cohasset Associates. E-mail michael.haley@armaintl. org.

Board of Directors

Tyrene Bada, Megan Butcher, Cindy Chmura, Melonie Jones, Ellie Kim, Neal Schubert.

Publications

Implementing the Generally Accepted Recordkeeping Principles (PDF).
inDEPTH newsletter (bi-mo. memb.).
INFORMATION: The Comprehensive Overview of the Information Profession (PDF).
Information Management (IM) (bi-mo., memb., e-magazine https://magazine.arma.org). *Ed.* Nick Inglis. Tel. 913-312-5567, e-mail nick. inglis@armaintl.org.
Records and Information Management: Fundamentals of Professional Practice, 3rd Edition (PDF).
RIM and IG Around the World (mo.).

Art Libraries Society of North America

Executive Director, Cambria Happ
4 Lan Drive, Suite 310, Westford, MA 01886
978-674-6211, 800-817-0621, fax 414-768-8001, e-mail n.short@arlisna.org
World Wide Web https://www.arlisna.org

Objective

The objective of the Art Libraries Society of North America (ARLIS/NA) is to foster excellence in art librarianship and visual resources curatorship for the advancement of the visual arts. It was established in 1972.

Membership

Memb. 1,000+. Dues (Business Affiliate) $250; (Introductory) $100 (two-year limit); (Indiv.) $150; (Student) $50 (three-year limit); (Ret.) $75; (Unemployed/Bridge) $50. Year. Jan. 1–Dec. 31. Membership is open to all those interested in visual librarianship, whether they be professional librarians, students, library assistants, art book publishers, art book dealers, art historians, archivists, architects, slide and photograph curators, or retired associates in these fields.

Officers (2022–2023)

Pres. Rebecca Price, University of Michigan. Tel. 734-647-5274; *V.P./Pres.-Elect* Rachel Resnik, Massachusetts College of Art and Design; *Secy.* Sarah Carter, Indiana University; *Treas.* Karyn M Hinkle, University of Kentucky Libraries, Lucille C. Little Fine Arts Library; *Past Pres.* Mark Pompelia, Rhode Island School of Design. Tel. 401-709-5935.

Board Members

Carla-Mae Crookendale, Stephanie H. Grimm, Pierre B. Landry, Kai Alexis Smith, Roger Lawson.

Committee Chairs

Advocacy and Public Policy. Sal Hamerman.
Anti-Racism. Rebecca M. Price.
Awards. Courtney L. Stine.
Cataloging Advisory. William T. Blueher.
Conference Planning Advisory. Rebecca M. Price.
Development. Allison R. Benedetti.
Diversity and Inclusion. Alex Watkins.
Documentation. Emilee Mathews.
Finance. Matthew Gengler.
International Relations. Laurel M. Bliss.
Membership. Gilda B. Santana.
Nominating. Lindsay M. King.
Professional Development. Courtney A. Hunt.
Strategic Planning. Suzanne Rackover and Amy Trendler.

Editorial Board Chair

Roger Lawson.

Awards Committee Chairs

Awards Chair: Courtney L. Stine.
ARLIS/NA Applauds. Claire C. Payne.
Conference Attendance and Travel Awards. Courtney L. Stine.
Distinguished Service. Katharine Keller.
Melva J. Dwyer Award. Pierre Landry.
Wolfgang M. Freitag Internship Award. Gwen Mayhew.

International Relations Study Tour Scholarship. Position open.
Samuel H. Kress Foundation Award for International Travel. Mark Pompelia.
Gerd Muehsam Award. Gwen Mayhew.
Robertson Rare Book School Scholarship. Position open.
Sotheby's Institute of Art Research Award. Position open.
H.W. Wilson Foundation Research Award. Heather Gendron.
George Wittenborn Memorial Book Award. Cara A. List.
Worldwide Books Award for Electronic Resources. Heather Gendron.
Worldwide Books Award for Publications. Heather Gendron.

Publications

ARLIS/NA Multimedia & Technology Reviews (bi-mo.; memb.). Eds. Virginia Kerr, Alexandra Alisa Provo, Karina Wratschko. E-mail arlisna.mtr@gmail.com.
ARLIS/NA Research and Reports.
ARLIS/NA Reviews (bi-mo.; memb.). Eds. Megan Macken; Terrie Wilson, e-mail wilso398@msu.edu.
Art Documentation (2 a year; memb., subscription). Ed. Judy Dyki. E-mail jdyki@cranbrook.edu.
Miscellaneous others (request current list from headquarters).

Asian/Pacific American Librarians Association

Executive Director, Alanna Aiko Moore
P.O. Box 1598, San Pedro, CA, 90733
310-377-9584 x237, e-mail ed@apalaweb.org
World Wide Web https://www.apalaweb.org

Objective

To provide a forum for discussing problems and concerns of Asian/Pacific American librarians, to provide a forum for the exchange of ideas by Asian/Pacific American librarians and other librarians, to support and encourage library services to Asian/Pacific American communities, to recruit and support Asian/Pacific American librarians in the library/information science professions, to seek funding for scholarships in library/information science programs for Asian/Pacific Americans, and to provide a vehicle whereby Asian/Pacific American librarians can cooperate with other associations and organizations having similar or allied interests. It was founded in 1980, incorporated in 1981, and affiliated with the American Library Association in 1982.

Membership

Memb. approximately 300. Dues (Corporate) $250; (Inst.) $70; (Lib. Support Staff) $20; (Life) $400; (Personal) $35 (one-year limit); (Ret.) $20 (one-year limit); (Student) $15 (Unemployed) $20. Open to all librarians and information specialists of Asian/Pacific descent working in U.S. libraries and information centers and other related organizations and to others who support the goals and purposes of the association. Asian/Pacific Americans are defined as people residing in North America who self-identify as Asian/Pacific American.

Officers (2022–2023)

Pres. Annie Pho; *V.P./Pres.-Elect* Jaena Rae Cabrera; *Secy.* Rebecca Martin and Jenay Dougherty; *Treas.* Kat Bell; *Past Pres.* Ray Pun; *Memb.-at-Large* Tarida Anantachai *(2021–2023)*, Keno Catabay *(2022–2023)*, Danilo M. Bayen *(2022–2024)*, Kiyoko Shiosaki *(2022–2024)*.

Committee Chairs

Constitution and Bylaws. Jennifer Chan and Iliana Burgos.
Family Literacy Focus. Becky Leathersich, Patty Sumire McGowan, and Sarah Nguyễn.
Finance and Fundraising. Ding Yi and Tobias Makowski.
Literature Awards. Helen Look, Zoë McLaughlin, and Candice Mack.
Media and Publicity. Silvia Lew and Amanda Cheung.
Membership. Maria (Pontillas) Shackles.
Mentorship. Yen Tran and Arya Hackney.
Nominating. Raymond Pun.
Program Planning. Susie Lee and Elaine Tai.
Scholarships and Awards. Ayshea Khan and Kathleen Baril.
Statement and Advocacy. Nicole Marconi and Angela Kent.

Publication

APALA Newsletter (2–3 a year).

Association for Information Science and Technology

Executive Director, Lydia Middleton
673 Potomac Station Drive, Suite 155, Leesburg, VA
301-495-0900, e-mail asist@asist.org
World Wide Web https://www.asist.org

Objective

The Association for Information Science and Technology (ASIS&T) provides a forum for the discussion, publication, and critical analysis of work dealing with the design, management, and use of information, information systems, and information technology. The mission of ASIS&T is to advance research and practice in information science and technology.

Membership

Regular Memb. (Indiv.) 1,100; (Student) 500; (Student Developing) $15; Dues (Professional) $150; (Professional Developing) $25; (Early Career and Ret.) $75; (Student) $45.

Officers (2022–2023)

Pres. Abebe Rorissa, University of Tennessee, Knoxville, TN; *Pres.-Elect* Crystal Fulton, University College, Dublin, Ireland; *Treas.* Ina Fourie, Univ. of Pretoria, Pretoria, South Africa; *Parliamentarian* Chris Cunningham, North Carolina Central University, Durham, NC; *Past Pres.* Naresh Agarwal, Simmons University, Boston, MA.

Board of Directors

Joan Bartlett *(2021–2024)*, Maria Bonn *(2021–2024)*, Jia Tina Du *(2021–2024)*, Lisa Hussey *(2022–2024)*, Aylin Imeri *(2022–2025)*, Dan Wu *(2020–2023)*.

Committee Chairs

Awards and Honors. Isto Huvila.
Budget and Finance. Ina Fourie.
Executive. Abebe Rorissa.
Governance. William Edgar.
History. Jenny Bossaller.
Membership. Ashraf Sharif.
Nominations. Naresh Agarwal.
Professional Development. Anthony Chow.
Publications. Andiswa Mfengu.
Research Engagement. Stephann Makri.
Standards. Mark Needleman and Timothy
Dickey.

Publications

Inside ASIS&T newsletter (bi-mo.).

Periodicals

Journal of the Association for Information Science and Technology. (JASIST) (mo.). Available with ASIS&T membership or from Wiley Blackwell.
Bulletin of the Association for Information Science and Technology (bi-mo.; memb.; online only).
Proceedings of the ASIS&T Annual Meeting. Available from ASIS&T.
Annual Review of Information Science & Technology (ARIST).

Association for Library and Information Science Education

Executive Director, Michaela Sawicki
4 Lan Dr., Suite 310, Westford, MA 01886
978-674-6190, e-mail office@alise.org
World Wide Web https://www.alise.org

Objective

The Association for Library and Information Science Education (ALISE) is an independent, nonprofit professional association whose mission is to promote excellence in research, teaching, and service for library and information science education through leadership, collaboration, advocacy, and dissemination of research. Its enduring purpose is to promote research that informs the scholarship of teaching and learning for library and information science, enabling members to integrate research into teaching and learning. The association provides a forum in which to share ideas, discuss issues, address challenges, and shape the future of education for library and information science. Founded in 1915 as the Association of American Library Schools, it has had its present name since 1983.

Membership

Memb. 700+ in four categories: Personal, Institutional, International Affiliate Institutional, and Associate Institutional. Dues (Indiv. full-time) $155; (Emerging Professional/Part-Time/Ret.) $85; (Student) $40; (Inst. varies, based on school budget) $400–$2,900; (Inst. Int'l./Assoc.) $350. Personal membership is open to anyone with an interest in the association's objectives.

Officers (2022–2023)

Pres. Rong Tang, Simmons University. E-mail rong.tang@simmons.edu; *Pres.-Elect* Lucy Santos Green, University of South Carolina. E-mail lgreen2@mailbox.sc.edu; *Secy.-Treas.* Shimelis Assefa, University of Denver. E-mail Shimelis.Assefa@du.edu; *Past Pres.* Lisa O'Connor, University of North Carolina–Greensboro. E-mail lgoconno@uncg.edu.

Directors

Monica Colon-Aguirre, Daniella Smith, Mega Subramaniam.

Publications

Journal of Education for Library and Information Science (JELIS) (q.; online only; memb.; nonmemb. $139 individual subscription; $360 institutional subscription).

Eds. John M. Budd and Denice Adkins. E-mail jeliseditor@alise.org.
Library and Information Science Education Statistical Report (ann.; electronic; memb.; nonmemb. $135).

ALISE Book Series. *Eds.* Jaya Raju and Dietmar Wolfram. E-mail jaya.raju@uct.ac.za.

Association for Rural and Small Libraries

Executive Director, Kate Laughlin
P.O. Box 33731, Seattle, WA, 98133. Tel. 206-453-3579 e-mail info@arsl.org
World Wide Web https://www.arsl.org
Twitter @RuralLibAssoc

Objective

The Association for Rural and Small Libraries (ARSL) was established in 1978, in the department of library science at Clarion University of Pennsylvania, as the Center for Study of Rural Librarianship.

ARSL is a network of people throughout the United States dedicated to the positive growth and development of libraries. ARSL believes in the value of rural and small libraries and strives to create resources and services that address national, state, and local priorities for libraries situated in rural communities.

Its objectives are:

- To organize a network of members concerned about the growth and development of useful library services in rural and small libraries
- To provide opportunities for the continuing education of members
- To provide mechanisms for members to exchange ideas and to meet on a regular basis
- To cultivate the practice of librarianship and to foster a spirit of cooperation among members of the profession, enabling them to act together for mutual goals
- To serve as a source of current information about trends, issues, and strategies
- To partner with other library and non-library groups and organizations serving rural and small library communities
- To collect and disseminate information and resources that are critical to this network

- To advocate for rural and small libraries at the local, state, and national levels

Membership

Dues (Indiv. varies, based on salary) $15–$49; (Inst.) $150; (Business) $200; (Affiliate) $150.

Officers (2022)

Pres. Jennie Garner, North Liberty Library, North Liberty, IA; *V.P./Pres.-Elect* Patrick Bodily, Independence Public Library, Independence, OR; *Secy.* Amanda Doherty, Mt. Pulaski Public Library District, Mt. Pulaski, IL; *Treas.* Erin Busbea, Columbus-Lowndes Public Library System, MS; *COSLA Rep.* Wendy Knapp, State Library of Ohio, Columbus, OH; *Past Pres.* Bailee Hutchinson, Altus Public Library, Altus, OK.

Directors

Phillip Carter, Krist Obrist, Crystal Schimpf, Erin Silva, Kate Laughlin (ex officio).

Committee Chairs

Advocacy. Elizabeth "Beth" Anderson and Tyler Hahn.
Conference. Elisa Cruz and Janine Miller.
Continuing Education. Joy Worland and Annice Sevett.
Finance. Erin Busbea.

Governance. Shannon Schultz and John A. Clexton.
Marketing and Communications. Shellie Zeigler and Callie Cortner.

Membership. Jennifer Stevenson.
Partnership. Noah Lenstra and Madeline Jarvis.
Scholarship. Kip Roberson and Savannah Kitchens.

Association of Academic Health Sciences Libraries

Executive Director, Louise Miller
2150 N. 107 St., Suite 205, Seattle, WA 98133
206-209-5261, fax 206-367-8777, e-mail office@aahsl.org
World Wide Web https://www.aahsl.org

Objective

The Association of Academic Health Sciences Libraries (AAHSL) comprises the libraries serving the accredited U.S. and Canadian medical schools belonging to or affiliated with the Association of American Medical Colleges. Its goals are to promote excellence in academic health science libraries and to ensure that the next generation of health practitioners is trained in information-seeking skills that enhance the quality of healthcare delivery, education, and research. It was founded in 1977.

Membership

Memb. 150+. Full membership is available to nonprofit educational institutions operating a school of health sciences that has full or provisional accreditation by the Association of American Medical Colleges. Full members are represented by the chief administrative officer of the member institution's health sciences library. Associate membership (and nonvoting representation) is available to organizations having an interest in the purposes and activities of the association. For dues information, contact the association.

Officers (2022–2023)

Pres. Nadine Dexter, Harriet F. Ginsburg Health Sciences Library, University of Central Florida College of Medicine. Tel. 407-266-1421; *Pres.-Elect* Stephanie Fulton, Medical Sciences Library, Texas A&M University. Tel. 979-845-7540; *Secy./Treas.* Megan von Isenburg, Medical Center Library & Archives, Duke University. Tel. 919-660-1148; *Past Pres.* Melissa De Santis, Strauss Health Sciences Library, University of Colorado. Tel. 303-724-2152.

Board of Directors

Fatima Barnes, Gabe Rios, Darell Schmick.

Committee Chairs

Assessment and Statistics. Matthew Wilcox.
Diversity, Equity and Inclusion. Bart Ragon.
Future Leadership. Teresa Knott.
Joint Legislation. Maggie Ansell.
New and Interim Directors. Debra Rand.
Nominating. Nadine Dexter.
Program and Education. Kate Flewelling.
Scholarly Communication. Beth Ketterman.

Task Force Chairs

Competency-Based Medical Education. Amy Blevins.

Association of Christian Librarians

Executive Director, Janelle Mazelin
P.O. Box 4, Cedarville, OH 45314
937-766-2255, fax 937-766-5499, e-mail info@acl.org
World Wide Web https://www.acl.org
Facebook https://www.facebook.com/ACLibrarians
Twitter @ACLibrarians

Objective

The mission of the Association of Christian Librarians (ACL) is to strengthen libraries through professional development of evangelical librarians, scholarship, and spiritual encouragement for service in higher education. ACL is a growing community that integrates faith, ministry, and academic librarianship through the development of members, services, and scholarship. It was founded in 1957.

Membership

Memb. 600+ individual and 200+ institutional members. Membership is open to those who profess the Christian faith as outlined by the association's statement of faith and are employed at an institution of higher education. Associate memberships are available for non-librarians who both agree with ACL's statement of faith and are interested in libraries or librarianship. Dues (Indiv. 1st Year) $40; (Ret. Libn., Lib. School Student) $35; (Varies, based on income) $40–$120.

Officers

Pres. (2022–2023) Linda Poston, Messiah University; *V.P. (2017–2023)* Nate Farley, Univ. of Northwestern–St. Paul; *Secy. (2020–2023)* Denise Nelson, Point Loma Nazarene Univ.; *Treas. (2019–2025)* Rodney Birch, Northwest Nazarene Univ.; *Past Pres. (2020–2022)* Leslie Starasta, Lincoln Christian University; *Dirs.-at-Large* Eric Bradley *(2020–2023)*, Sarah Davis *(2020–2023)*, Erinn Huebner *(2021–2024)*, Robin Lang *(2022–2025)*, Jeanette Parker *(2022–2025)*, Jaime Pitt *(2021–2024)*.

Section Chairs

Bible Core. Jon Jones.
Liberal Arts. Garrett Trott.
Seminary. Debra Bradshaw.

Publications

The Christian Librarian. (2 a year; memb.; nonmemb. $30). *Ed.* Garrett Trott.
Christian Periodical Index (q.; electronic).
Librarian's Manual (English or Spanish; electronic or print; $40).
Library Guidelines for ABHE Colleges and Universities (memb.).

Association of Independent Information Professionals

President, Denise Carter
8550 United Plaza Blvd., Suite 1001, Baton Rouge, LA 70809
225-408-4400, e-mail office@aiip.org
World Wide Web https://aiip.org
Facebook https://www.facebook.com/officialaiip
Twitter @AIIP

Objective

Members of the Association of Independent Information Professionals (AIIP) are owners of firms providing such information-related services as online and manual research, document delivery, database design, library support, consulting, writing, and publishing. The objectives of the association are:

- To advance the knowledge and understanding of the information profession
- To promote and maintain high professional and ethical standards among its members
- To encourage independent information professionals to assemble to discuss common issues
- To promote the interchange of information among independent information professionals and various organizations
- To keep the public informed of the profession and of the responsibilities of the information professional

Membership

Memb. 200+. Dues (Full) $200; (Assoc.) $200; (Student) $50; (Supporting) $500; (Ret.) $75; (Emeritus) $50.

Officers (2022–2023)

Pres. Denise Carter, DCision Consult; *Pres. Elect* Janel Kinlaw, Refining Workflow; *Secy.* Regina Maxwell, Maxwell Research Services; *Treas.* Roger Magnus, Roger Magnus Research; *Past Pres.* Karen Klein, Fulcrum Information Resources.

Directors

Membership, Susan Baerwald; Professional Development, Maureen Shields.

Publications

"AIIP Connections" (blog).
Member Directory (ann.).
Professional papers series.

Association of Jewish Libraries

President, Michelle Margolis
P.O. Box 1118, Teaneck, NJ 07666
201-371-3255, e-mail info@jewishlibraries.org
World Wide Web https://jewishlibraries.org
Facebook https://www.facebook.com/jewishlibraries
Twitter @JewishLibraries

Objective

The Association of Jewish Libraries (AJL) is an international professional organization that fosters access to information and research in all forms of media relating to all things Jewish. The association promotes Jewish literacy and scholarship and provides a community for peer support and professional development.

AJL membership is open to individuals and libraries, library workers, and library supporters. There are two divisions within AJL: RAS (Research Libraries, Archives, and Special Collections) and SSCPL (Synagogue, School Center and Public Libraries). The diverse membership includes libraries in synagogues, JCCs, day schools, yeshivot, universities, Holocaust museums, and the Library of Congress. Membership is drawn from North America and places beyond, including China, the Czech Republic, the Netherlands, Israel, Italy, South Africa, Switzerland, and the United Kingdom. AJL conducts an annual conference in the United States or Canada in late June.

Goals

The association's goals are to:

- Maintain high professional standards for Judaica librarians and recruit qualified individuals into the profession
- Facilitate communication and the exchange of information on a global scale
- Encourage quality publication in the field in all formats and media—print, digital, and so forth—and to stimulate publication of high-quality children's literature
- Facilitate and encourage the establishment of Judaica library collections
- Enhance information access for all through the application of advanced technologies
- Publicize the organization and its activities in all relevant venues: stimulate awareness of Judaica library services among the public at large, promote recognition of Judaica librarianship within the wider library profession, and encourage recognition of Judaica library services by other organizations and related professions
- Ensure continuity of the association through sound management, financial security, effective governance, and a dedicated and active membership

Membership

Memb. 600. Year: Oct. 1–Sept. 30. Dues (Indiv.) $77; (First-year Lib. School Student) Free; (Second/third-year Lib. School Student) $36; (Ret./unemployed) $36; (Large Inst.) (Greater than 100 FTE/includes personal membership) $118; (Small Inst.) (100 or fewer FTE/ includes 1 personal membership) $90; (Corporate) $118.

Board of Directors

Pres. Michelle Margolis; *V.P./Pres.-Elect* Sean Boyle; *V.P. Development* Jackie Ben-Efraim; *V.P. Membership* Sharon Benamou; *Secy.* Rivka Yerushalmi; *Treas.* Andrew Lillien; *RAS Pres.* Yermiyahu Ahron Taub; *RAS V.P.* Eitan Kensky; *SSCPL Pres.* Rebecca Levitan; *SSCPL V.P.* Aviva Rosenberg; *Past Pres.* Kathleen Bloomfield, Seal Beach, CA 90740 e-mail kathybloomfield@gmail.com; *Parliamentarian* Joy Kingsolver.

Council Members

Paula Breger, Joseph Galron, Haim Gottschalk, Rachel Leket-Mor, Amalia Levi, Rachel Kamin, Heidi Rabinowitz, Anjelica Ruiz, Laura Schutzman, Sheryl Stahl, Sally Steigletz.

Committee Chairs

Accreditation. Shaindy Kurzmann.
Advertising. Jackie Ben-Efriam.
Cataloging. Neil Frau-Cortes.
Conference Stipends. Lenore Bell.
Endowment. Jackie Ben-Efraim and Andrew Lillian.
Librarianship and Education. Haim Gottschalk.
Member Relations. Heidi Rabinowitz.
Public Relations. Paula Breger.
Publications. Laura Schutzman.
Strategic Planning. Sean Boyle.
Web. Sheryl Stahl.

Editorial Board Chairs

AJL News and Reviews. Sally Stieglitz.
Conference Proceedings Compiler. Elana Gensler.
Judaica Librarianship. Rachel Leket-Mor.

Awards Committee Chairs

Fanny Goldstein Merit Award. Lisa Silverman.
Jewish Fiction Award. Paula Breger.
KarBen Scholarship. Rebecca Levitan.
Reference and Bibliography Awards. Eitan Kensky.
Student Scholarship. Tina Weiss.
Sydney Taylor Book Award. Martha Simpson.
Sydney Taylor Manuscript Award. Aileen Grossberg.

Publications

AJL Conference Proceedings.
AJL News and Reviews (q., digital; memb.).
Ed. Sally Stieglitz. Tel. 631-6751-570, ext. 2005, e-mail sstieglitz@lilrc.org.

Judaica Librarianship (annual, digital).
Ed. Rachel Leket-Mor, Arizona State Univ. Libs. E-mail rachel.leket-mor@asu.edu.

Affiliate Liaisons

American Library Association (ALA). Emily Bergman and Susan Kusel.
American Theological Library Association (ATLA). Sheryl Stahl.
Association for Jewish Studies (AJS). Rachel Greenblatt.
Catholic Library Association (CATHLA). Daniel Stuhlman.
International Liaison. Amalia Levi.

Association of Research Libraries

Executive Director, Mary Lee Kennedy
21 Dupont Circle N.W., Suite 800, Washington, DC 20036
202-296-2296, fax 202-872-0884, e-mail webmgr@arl.org
World Wide Web https://www.arl.org

Objective

The Association of Research Libraries (ARL) is a nonprofit organization of 125 research libraries in Canada and the United States whose mission is to advance research, learning, and scholarly communication. ARL fosters the open exchange of ideas and expertise; advances diversity, equity, and inclusion; and pursues advocacy and public policy efforts that reflect the values of the library, scholarly, and higher education communities. ARL forges partnerships and catalyzes the collective efforts of research libraries to enable knowledge creation and to achieve enduring and barrier-free access to information.

Membership

Memb. 125. Membership is institutional. Dues: $30,605 for 2022.

Officers

Pres. Susan Parker, University Librarian, University of British Columbia; *V.P./Pres.-Elect* Trevor A. Dawes, Vice Provost for Libraries and Museums and May Morris University Librarian, University of Delaware; *Treas.* Bob Fox, Dean of University Libraries, University of Louisville; *Past Pres.* K. Matthew Dames, Edward H. Arnold University Librarian, Univ. of Notre Dame.

Board of Directors

Rhea Ballard-Thrower, University of Illinois–Chicago (*2023–2025*); Tamar Evangelestia-Dougherty, Smithsonian Libraries and Archives (*2023–2025*); Melissa Just, University of Saskatchewan (*2021–2024*); Sara Lowman, Rice University (*2023–2024*); Robert McDonald, University of Colorado–Boulder (*2020–*

2023); Lisa O'Hara, University of Manitoba (*2021–2024*); Joseph A. Salem, Jr., Duke University (*2023–2025*); Lorelei Tanji, University of California–Irvine (*2021–2024*).

Advisory Group, Task Force, and Working Group Chairs

Advocacy and Public Policy Committee. Ann Thornton.
ARL/CARL Joint Task Force on Marrakesh Treaty Implementation. Victoria Owen.
ARL Statistics Survey Revision Task Force. Athena Jackson.
Association Meeting Program Planning Task Force. Evviva Weinraub Lajoie.
Audit Committee. Lorelei Tanji.
Code of Conduct Committee. Anne Langley.
Consultative Group to Association Meeting Program Planning Task Force. Dale Askey and Tyler Walters
Diversity, Equity, and Inclusion Committee. Greg Eow.
Diversity, Equity, and Inclusion Institute Task Force. DeLa Dos.
Finance Committee. Bob Fox.
Governance Committee. Robert McDonald.
Intensive Learning Program Selection Working Group. Consuella Askew.
Intensive Learning Program Task Force. Hilary Seo.
Kaleidoscope Program Selection Working Group. Position open.
Kaleidoscope Program Task Force. Jesus Espinoza.
Leadership and Career Development Program Selection Working Group. DeLa Dos.
Leadership and Career Development Program Task Force. Andrea Malone.
Leadership Fellows Selection Working Group. Position open.
Leadership Fellows Task Force. Hilary Seo.
Learning Network Committee. Leslie Sharp.
Member Engagement and Outreach Committee. Anne Langley.
Membership Committee. Lisa O'Hara.
Membership Model and Financial Framework Task Force. Lorelei Tanji.
Nominating Committee. K. Matthew Dames.
Program Strategy Committee. Mary Lee Kennedy.
Research and Analytics Committee. Erik Mitchell.

Scholars and Scholarship Committee. Elaine Westbrooks.

Publications

Annual Report (ann.).
ARL Academic Health Sciences Library Statistics (ann.).
ARL Academic Law Library Statistics (ann.).
ARL Annual Salary Survey (ann.).
ARL Statistics (ann.).
Research Library Issues (irregular).

ARL Membership

Nonuniversity Libraries

Boston Public Lib.; Center for Research Libs.; Lib. of Congress; National Agricultural Lib.; National Archives and Records Administration; National Lib. of Medicine; New York Public Lib.; Smithsonian Libs. and Archives.

University Libraries

Alabama; Albany (SUNY); Alberta; Arizona; Arizona State; Auburn; Boston College; Boston Univ.; Brigham Young; British Columbia; Brown; Buffalo (SUNY); Calgary; California–Berkeley; California–Davis; California–Irvine; California–Los Angeles; California–Riverside; California–San Diego; California–Santa Barbara; Case Western Reserve; Chicago; Cincinnati; Colorado–Boulder; Colorado State; Columbia; Connecticut; Cornell; Dartmouth; Delaware; Duke; Emory; Florida; Florida State; George Washington; Georgetown; Georgia; Georgia Inst. of Technology; Guelph; Harvard; Hawaii–Manoa; Houston; Howard; Illinois–Chicago; Illinois–Urbana-Champaign; Indiana–Bloomington; Iowa; Iowa State; Johns Hopkins; Kansas; Kent State; Kentucky; Laval; Louisiana State; Louisville; McGill; McMaster; Manitoba; Maryland; Massachusetts–Amherst; Massachusetts Inst. of Technology; Miami (Florida); Michigan; Michigan State; Minnesota; Missouri; Nebraska–Lincoln; New Mexico; New York; North Carolina–Chapel Hill; North Carolina State; Northwestern; Notre Dame; Ohio; Ohio State; Oklahoma; Oklahoma State; Oregon; Ottawa; Pennsylvania; Pennsylvania State; Pittsburgh; Princeton; Purdue; Queen's (Kingston, Ontario); Rice;

Rochester; Rutgers; Saskatchewan; Simon Fraser; South Carolina; Southern California; Southern Illinois–Carbondale; Stony Brook (SUNY); Syracuse; Temple; Tennessee–Knoxville; Texas–Austin; Texas A&M; Texas State; Texas Tech; Toronto; Tulane; Utah; Vanderbilt; Virginia; Virginia Commonwealth; Virginia Tech; Washington; Washington–Saint Louis; Washington State; Waterloo; Wayne State; Western; Wisconsin–Madison; Yale; York.

Association of Vision Science Librarians

Co-Chairs Deborah Goss, Scott Johnson
World Wide Web http://www.avsl.org

Objective

To foster collective and individual acquisition and dissemination of vision science information, to improve services for all persons seeking such information, and to develop standards for libraries to which members are attached. Founded in 1968.

Membership

Memb. (Indiv.) approximately 150, (Inst.) 100+.

Leadership Team

Co-Chair Deborah Goss, Massachusetts Eye and Ear Infirmary, Boston, MA; *Co-Chair* Scott Johnson, Marshall B. Ketchum University, Fullerton, CA; *Secy.* Karen Alcorn, MCPHS University, Worcester, MA; *Archivist* Natalie Bobrowska, Illinois College of Optometry Library, Chicago, IL.

Meetings

Spring and fall meetings are held each year. The annual fall meeting runs 3-4 days and is usually timed alongside the annual meeting of the American Academy of Optometry.

Atla

Executive Director, John F. Kutsko
200 S. Wacker Dr., Suite 3100, Chicago, IL 60606
888-665-2852 or 312-454-5100; e-mail connect@atla.com
World Wide Web https://www.atla.com

Mission

The mission of Atla (formerly known as the American Theological Library Association) is to foster the study of theology and religion by enhancing the development of theological and religious libraries and librarianship.

Membership

Dues (Inst.) $100–$1,000; (Indiv. varies, based on income) $35–$181.50; (Student) $35; (Affiliates) $100.

Officers (2022–2023)

Pres. Jérémie LeBlanc, Jean Leon Allie Library, Saint Paul University; *V.P.* Armin Siedlecki, Pitts Theology Library, Emory University; *Secy.* Leslie A. Engelson, University Libraries, Murray State University; *Treas.* Kristine Veldheer, Paul Bechtold Library, Catholic Theological Union; *Past Pres.* Christina Torbert, University of Mississippi Libraries.

Board of Directors

Yasmine Abou-El-Kheir, Dr. Carisse Mickey Berryhill, Kerrie Burn, Susan Ebertz, Rev. Dr. Daniel Flores, Leslie Michelle Spomer, Karl Stuzman, Matthew Thiesen.

Committee Chairs

Code of Conduct Task Force. Alexis Weiss
Conference. Vance Thomas.
Diversity, Equity, and Inclusion. David Kriegh.
Endowment. Pat Graham.
Professional Development. Becky Givens.
Scholarly Communication and Digital Initiatives. Brad Ost.

Publications

Theological Librarianship (open access journal) http://serials.atla.com/theolib.
Theology Cataloging Bulletin (open access journal) http://serials.atla.com/tcb/index.
Atla Annual Yearbook (online open access ann. serial) http://serials.atla.com/yearbook.
Atla Newsletter (mo.; online).
Atla Proceedings (online open access ann. serial) http://serials.atla.com/proceedings.
books@Atla Open Press (online open access monographs): https://books.atla.com/atlapress.

Beta Phi Mu
(International Library and Information Studies Honor Society)

Administrative Assistant, Romina Rodons
P.O. Box 292992, Davie, FL 33329
e-mail headquarters@betaphimu.org
World Wide Web https://www.betaphimu.org

Objective

To recognize distinguished achievement in and scholarly contributions to librarianship, information studies, or library education and to sponsor and support appropriate professional and scholarly projects relating to these fields. Founded at the University of Illinois in 1948.

Membership

Memb. 40,000. Eligibility for membership in Beta Phi Mu is by invitation of the faculty from institutions where the American Library Association or other recognized accrediting agency approved by the Beta Phi Mu executive board has accredited or recognized a professional degree program. Candidates must be graduates of a library and information science program and fulfill the following requirements: complete the course requirements leading to a master's degree with a scholastic average of 3.75 where A equals 4 points or complete a planned program of advanced study beyond the master's degree which requires full-time study for one or more academic years with a scholastic average of 3.75 where A equals 4.0. Each chapter or approved institution is allowed to invite no more than 25 percent of the annual graduating class, and the faculty of participating library schools must attest to their initiates' professional promise.

Officers

Pres. Adrienne Teague, Rudisill Branch, Tulsa City-County Library System. E-mail adrienne.teague@gmail.com; *V.P./Pres.-Elect* Jennifer Steele, School of Library and Information Science, University of Southern Mississippi, 118 College Dr., Hattiesburg, MS 39406. Tel. 601-266-5319, E-mail jennifer.e.steele@usm.edu; *Treas.* Vicki Gregory, School of Information, College of Arts and Sciences, University of South Florida, 4202 E. Fowler Ave., CIS 2036, Tampa, FL 33620. Tel. 813-974-3520, E-mail gregory@usf.edu; *Past Pres.* Tom Rink, Northeastern State University–Broken Arrow Campus, 3100 East New Orleans Street, Broken

Arrow, OK 74014. Tel. 918-449-6457, E-mail: rink@nsuok.edu.

Directors

At-Large Juliette Appold (*2022–2024*), Kathleen De Long (*2022–2024*), Lisa Hussey (*2021–2023*), Vanessa Reyes (*2022–2024*); *Dirs.* Kimberly M. Gay (*2021–2023*), Elizabeth Jones (*2021–2023*).

Publications

Beta Phi Mu Scholars Series. Available from Rowman & Littlefield Publishers, 4501 Forbes Blvd., Suite 200, Lanham, MD 20706. *Ed.* Andrea Falcone. E-mail bpmseries@gmail.com.

Newsletter. *The Pipeline* (biennial; electronic only). *Eds.* Adrienne Teague and Tom Rink.

Chapters

Alpha. Univ. of Illinois–Urbana-Champaign, School of Info. Sciences; *Gamma.* Florida State Univ., College of Communication and Info.; *Epsilon.* Univ. of North Carolina–Chapel Hill, School of Info. and Lib. Science; *Theta.* c/o Pratt Inst., School of Info.; *Iota.* Catholic Univ. of America, Dept. of Lib. and Info. Science; Univ. of Maryland, College of Info. Studies; *Lambda.* Univ. of Oklahoma, School of Lib. and Info. Studies; *Xi.* Univ. of Hawaii–Manoa, Lib. and Info. Science Program; *Omicron.* Rutgers Univ., Grad. School of Communication, Info., and Lib. Studies; *Pi.* Univ. of Pittsburgh, School of Info. Sciences; *Sigma.* Drexel Univ., College of Computing and Informatics; *Psi.* Univ. of Missouri–Columbia, School of Info. Science and Learning Technologies; *Omega.* San José State Univ., School of Info.; *Beta Beta.* Simmons Univ., School of Lib. and Info. Science; *Beta Delta.* State Univ. of New York at Buffalo, Dept. of Lib. and Info. Studies; *Beta Epsilon.* Emporia State Univ., School of Lib. and Info. Management; *Beta Zeta.* Louisiana State Univ., School of Lib. and Info. Science; *Beta Iota.* Univ. of Rhode Island, Grad. School of Lib. and Info. Studies; *Beta Kappa.* Univ. of Alabama, School of Lib. and Info. Studies; *Beta Lambda.* Texas Woman's Univ., School of Lib. and Info. Sciences; *Beta Mu.* Long Island Univ., Palmer School of Lib. and Info. Science; *Beta Nu.* St. John's Univ., Div. of Lib. and Info. Science; *Beta Xi.* North Carolina Central Univ., School of Lib. and Info. Sciences; *Beta Pi.* Univ. of Arizona, School of Info.; *Beta Rho.* Univ. of Wisconsin–Milwaukee, School of Info. Science; *Beta Phi.* Univ. of South Florida, School of Lib. and Info. Science; *Beta Psi.* Univ. of Southern Mississippi, School of Lib. and Info. Science; *Beta Omega.* Univ. of South Carolina, College of Lib. and Info. Science; *Beta Beta Epsilon.* Univ. of Wisconsin–Madison, School of Lib. and Info. Studies; *Beta Beta Theta.* Univ. of Iowa, School of Lib. and Info. Science; *Pi Lambda Sigma.* Syracuse Univ., School of Info. Studies; *Beta Beta Mu.* Valdosta State Univ., Lib. and Info. Science Program; *Beta Beta Nu.* Univ. of North Texas, College of Info.; *Beta Beta Omicron.* East Carolina Univ., Dept. of Interdisciplinary Professions; *Beta Beta Xi.* St. Catherine Univ., Master of Lib. and Info. Science Program.

Bibliographical Society of America

Executive Director, Erin McGuirl
67 West Street Suite 401, Unit C17, Brooklyn, NY 11222
e-mail erin.mcguirl@bibsocamer.org
World Wide Web http://www.bibsocamer.org

Objective

To promote bibliographical research and to issue bibliographical publications. Organized in 1904.

Membership

Dues (Partner) $80; (Sustaining) $125; (Leadership) $250; (Advancing) $500; (Lifetime) $1,250; (Emerging bibliographers, 35 and under) $25. Year. Jan.–Dec.

Officers

Pres. Caroline Duroselle-Melish, Folger Shakespeare Library; *V.P.* Megan Peiser, Oakland University; *Secy.* John T. McQuillen, Morgan Museum and Library; *Treas.* G. Scott Clemons, Brown Brothers Harriman; *Delegate to the ACLS* Elizabeth Denlinger, New York Public Library.

Council

(2026) Mary Crawford, Robert D. Montoya, Andrew T. Nadell, M.D., Elizabeth Ott; *(2025)* Rebecca Romney, Alice Schreyer, Kenneth Soehner, Derrick Spires; *(2024)* María Victo-

ria Fernández, Thomas Goldwasser, Adam G. Hooks, Nick Wilding.

Committee Chairs

Audit. Joan Friedman.
BibSite Editorial Group. Eric Ensley.
Development. Caroline Duroselle-Melish.
Digital Strategy Working Group. Erin McGuirl.
Events. Ashley Cataldo.
Fellowship. Emily Kader.
Fellows and Fellowship Working Group. Ryan Roberts.
Investments. Mary Crawford.
Liaisons. Nina Musinsky.
Membership. Charlotte Priddle.
New Scholars. Barbara Heritage.
Nominating. Leslie Morris.
Policy and Procedures Manual Working Group. Joan Friedman.
Publications. Derrick R. Spires.

Publication

Papers of the Bibliographical Society of America (q.; memb.). *Ed.* Jesse R. Erickson, Morgan Museum and Library. E-mail editor. pbsa@bibsocamer.org.

Bibliographical Society of Canada
(La Société Bibliographique du Canada)

President, Chris Young
360 Bloor St. W., P.O. Box 19035, Walmer, Toronto, ON M5S 3C9
E-mail secretary@bsc-sbc.ca
World Wide Web https://www.bsc-sbc.ca/en

Objective

The Bibliographical Society of Canada is a bilingual (English/French) organization that has as its goal the scholarly study of the history, description, and transmission of texts in all media and formats, with a primary emphasis on Canada, and the fulfillment of this goal through the following objectives:

- To promote the study and practice of bibliography: enumerative, historical, descriptive, analytical, and textual
- To further the study, research, and publication of book history and print culture
- To publish bibliographies and studies of book history and print culture
- To encourage the publication of bibliographies, critical editions, and studies of book history and print culture
- To promote the appropriate preservation and conservation of manuscript, archival, and published materials in various formats
- To encourage the utilization and analysis of relevant manuscript and archival sources as a foundation of bibliographical scholarship and book history
- To promote the interdisciplinary nature of bibliography and to foster relationships with other relevant organizations nationally and internationally
- To conduct the society without purpose of financial gain for its members and to ensure that any profits or other accretions to the society shall be used in promoting its goal and objectives

Membership

The society welcomes as members all those who share its aims and wish to support and participate in bibliographical research and publication. Dues (Reg.) $80; (Student) $35; (Ret.) $50; (Inst.) $100; (Life) $1,000.

Executive Council (2022–2023)

Pres. Christopher Young. E-mail president@bsc-sbc.ca; *1st V.P.* Svetlana Kochkina. E-mail vice_president_1@bsc-sbc.ca; *2nd V.P.* Isabelle Robitaille. E-mail vice_president_2@bsc-sbc.ca; *Secy.* Mary Kandiuk. E-mail secretary@bsc-sbc.ca; *Assoc. Secy.* Position open; *Treas.* Tom Vincent. E-mail treasurer@bsc-sbc.ca; *Assoc. Treas.* Meaghan Scanlon; *Past Pres.* Karen Smith. E-mail past_president@bsc-sbc.ca.

Councilors

(2020–2023) Christopher Lyons, Chelsea Shriver, Danielle Van Wagner; *(2021–2024)* Mathieu Bouchard, Myron Groover, Christina Ionescu; *(2022–2025)* Heather Dean, Danielle Fuller, Karina Vernon.

Committee Chairs

Awards. Danielle Van Wagner.
Communications. Chris Young.
Fellowships. Chelsea Shriver.
Publications. Ruth Panofsky.
Special Collections Interest Group. Scott Schofield and Christopher Lyons.

Publications

Bulletin (s. ann). *Ed.* Ellen Forget.
Journal Manager. Sarah Severson.
Papers of the Bibliographical Society of Canada / Cahiers de la Société Bibliographique du Canada (s. ann.). *Ed.* Position open; *Review Ed.* (English) Rachel Harris; *Review Ed.* (French) Philippe Rioux.

Black Caucus of the American Library Association

President, Nichelle M. Hayes
P.O. Box 174, New York, NY 10159-0174
646-721-1358
World Wide Web https://www.bcala.org

Mission

The Black Caucus of the American Library Association (BCALA) serves as an advocate for the development, promotion, and improvement of library services and resources for the nation's African American community and provides leadership for the recruitment and professional development of African American librarians. It was founded in 1970.

Membership

Membership is open to any person, institution, or business interested in promoting the development of library and information services for African Americans and other people of African descent and willing to maintain good financial standing with the organization. The membership is currently composed of librarians and other information professionals; library support staff; and libraries, publishers, authors, vendors, and other library-related organizations in the United States and abroad. Dues (Lifetime) $500; (Corporate) $200; (Inst.) $60; (Reg.) $45; (Library Support Staff) $20; (Student) $10; (Ret.) $25.

Officers

Pres. Nichelle M. Hayes; *V.P./Pres.-Elect* Jason Alston; *Secy.* Michele Fenton; *Asst. Secy.* Naomi Dunsen-White; *Treas.* Wanda K. Brown; *Past Pres.* Shauntee Burns-Simpson.

Board Members

(2021–2023) Tiffani Carter, Yolanda Gleason, Denise Lyles, Tracey A. Overbey, Tracy Scott, Jessica Tingling; *(2022-2024)* Tamela Chambers, Rudolph Clay, LaKeshia Darden, Leslie Etienne, Taryn Fouche, Laura Johnson, Brenda Johnson-Perkins, Olanike Olaniyi.

Committee Chairs

Affiliates. Tiffany Alston.
ALA Relations. Latrice Booker
Awards. John Page.
Budget and Finance. Stanton Biddle and Wanda Kay Brown.
Constitution and Bylaws. Jos Holman.
Fundraising. Shauntee Burns-Simpson, Kelvin Watson, and Richard Ashby.
History. Rhonda Evans and Dr. Sibyl Moses.
International Relations. Eboni M. Henry and Vivian Bordeaux.
Marketing and Public Relations. Kim Brown-Harden.
Membership and Recruitment. Rudolph Clay.
National Conference. Tracey Hunter Hayes.
Nomination and Election. Richard E. Ashby.
Professional Development. Ana Ndumu.
President's Advisory. Shauntee Burns-Simpson.
Programs. Shauntee Burns-Simpson and Nichelle M. Hayes.
Publications. Nichelle M. Hayes.
Services to Children and Families of African Descent. Karen Lemmons.
Technology Advisory. Zakia Ringgold.

Awards Committee Chairs

Literary Awards. Gladys Smiley Bell.
Dr. E.J. Josey Scholarship. Derek Mosley and Yolanda Gleason.

Publication

BCALA News (3 a year; memb.). *Ed.* Nichelle M. Hayes.

Canadian Association for Information Science (L'Association Canadienne des Sciences de l'Information)

President, Rebekah (Becky) Willson
info@cais-acsi.ca

World Wide Web https://cais-acsi.ca

Objective

To promote the advancement of information science in Canada and encourage and facilitate the exchange of information relating to the use, access, retrieval, organization, management, and dissemination of information.

Membership

Institutions and individuals interested in information science and involved in the gathering, organization, and dissemination of information (such as information scientists, archivists, librarians, computer scientists, documentalists, economists, educators, journalists, and psychologists) and who support Canadian Association for Information Science (CAIS) objectives can become association members.

Officers

Pres. Rebekah (Becky) Willson, McGill University; *V.P./Pres.-Elect* Julia Bullard, University of British Columbia; *Secy.* Mark Ambrogio, Western University; *Treas.* Michael Ridley, Western University; *Past Pres./Comm. Dir.* Sarah Polkinghorne, University of Alberta; *Memb.-at-Large* Danica Pawlick-Potts.

Board Members

Membership Dir. Philippe Mongeon, Dalhousie University; *Webmaster* Position open; *Student Rep.* Danica Facca, Western University; *Practitioner Rep.* Mary Greenshields, European University Institute; *Event Coord.* Alex Mayhew, Western University; *Memb.-at-Large* Paulette Rothbauer, Western University.

Publication

Canadian Journal of Information and Library Science. (q.; memb.; print; online). For nonmember subscription information, visit https://ojs.lib.uwo.ca/index.php/cjils. *Ed.* Heather Hill, Information and Media Studies, Western University. E-mail cjils@cais-acsi.ca.

Canadian Association of Research Libraries (Association des Bibliothèques de Recherche du Canada)

Executive Director, Susan Haigh
309 Cooper St., Suite 203, Ottawa, ON K2P 0G5
613-482-9344 ext. 101, e-mail info@carl-abrc.ca
World Wide Web https://www.carl-abrc.ca
Twitter @carlabrc

Membership

The Canadian Association of Research Libraries (CARL), established in 1976, is the leadership organization for the Canadian research library community. The association's members are the 29 major academic research libraries across Canada together with Library and Archives Canada and the National Research Council Canada, National Science Library.

Membership is institutional and is open primarily to libraries of Canadian universities that have doctoral graduates in both the arts and the sciences. CARL is an associate member of the Association of Universities and Colleges of Canada (AUCC) and is incorporated as a not-for-profit organization under the Canada Corporations Act.

Mission

The association provides leadership on behalf of Canada's research libraries and enhances their capacity to advance research and higher education. It promotes effective and sustainable scholarly communication and public policy that enables broad access to scholarly information.

Officers (2021–2023)

Pres. Vivian Lewis, McMaster University, Hamilton, ON; *V.P.* Brett Waytuck, University of Regina, Regina, SK; *Secy.* Dr. Guylaine Beaudry, Concordia University, Montréal, PQ; *Treas.* Lesley Balcom, Harriet Irving Library, University of New Brunswick, Fredericton, NB.

Board of Directors

Amber Lannon, Carleton University, Ottawa, ON (Ontario Region Representative); Dr.

Mary-Jo Romaniuk, University of Calgary, Calgary, AB (Western Region Representative).

Committee Chairs

Advancing Research. Talia Chung.
Impact. Mary-Jo Romaniuk.
Policy and Advocacy. Susan Parker.
Strengthening Capacity. Melissa Just.

Member Institutions

National Members

Lib. and Archives Canada, National Research Council Canada

Regional Members

Univ. of Alberta, Univ. of British Columbia, Brock Univ., Univ. of Calgary, Carleton Univ., Concordia Univ., Dalhousie Univ., Univ. of Guelph, Univ. Laval, McGill Univ., McMaster Univ., Univ. of Manitoba, Memorial Univ. of Newfoundland, Univ. de Montréal, Univ. of New Brunswick, Univ. of Ottawa, Univ. du Québec à Montréal, Queen's Univ., Univ. of Regina, Ryerson Univ., Univ. of Saskatchewan, Université de Sherbrooke, Simon Fraser Univ., Univ. of Toronto, Univ. of Victoria, Univ. of Waterloo, Western Univ., Univ. of Windsor, York Univ.

Catholic Library Association

Executive Director, Melanie Talley
8550 United Plaza Blvd., Suite 1001, Baton Rouge, LA 70809
225-408-4417, e-mail cla2@cathla.org
World Wide Web https://www.cathla.org

Objective

The promotion and encouragement of Catholic literature and library work through cooperation, publications, education, and information. Founded in 1921.

Membership

Memb. 1,000. Dues $25–$500. Year. July–June.

Officers

Pres. Kathryn Shaughnessy, e-mail shaugh nk@stjohns.edu; *V.P./Treas.* Bro. Andrew J. Kosmowski, SM, e-mail kosmowskia1@uday-ton.edu; *Past Pres.* Jack Fritts, 5700 College Rd., Lisle, IL 60532. Tel. 630-829-6060, e-mail jfritts@ben.edu.

Board Members

Eva Gonsalves, Kathy Harty, Elyse Hayes, Jean McManus.

Section Chairs

Academic Libraries, Archives and Library Education. Bro. Andrew J. Kosmowski, SM.
Children and High School/Young Adult. Eva Gonsalves.
Parish and Community Library Services. Phyllis Petre.

Committee Chairs

Conference. Kathy Harty and Elyse Hayes.
Continuing Education. Kathryn Shaughnessy and Jack Fritts.
Finance. Bro. Andrew Kosmowski.
Manual Revision & Timeline. Kathy Harty.
Membership. Mary Coll, Bailee Curtis, and Kathryn Shaughnessy.
Publications. Jack Fritts and Elyse Hayes.
Social Communications & Multimedia. Kathryn Shaughnessy and Sigrid Kelsey.

Publication

Catholic Library World (q.; memb.; nonmemb. $100 domestic, $125 international). *General Ed.* Sigrid Kelsey. E-mail sigridkelsey@gmail.com.

Chief Officers of State Library Agencies

Executive Director, Jeremy Johannesen
201 E. Main St., Suite 1405, Lexington, KY 40507
859-514-9150, fax 859-514-9166, e-mail info@cosla.org
World Wide Web https://www.cosla.org
Twitter @COSLA_US

Objective

Chief Officers of State Library Agencies (CO-SLA) is an independent organization of the chief officers of state and territorial agencies designated as the state library administrative agency and responsible for statewide library development. Its purpose is to identify and address issues of common concern and national interest, to further state library agency relationships with federal government and national organizations, and to initiate cooperative action for the improvement of library services to the people of the United States.

COSLA's membership consists solely of these top library officers, variously designated as state librarian, director, commissioner, or executive secretary. The organization provides a continuing mechanism for dealing with the problems and challenges faced by these officers. Its work is carried on through its members, a board of directors, and committees.

Officers (2021–2023)

Pres. Julie Walker, State Librarian, Georgia Public Library Services. Tel. 404-406-4519, e-mail jwalker@georgialibraries.org; *V.P./Pres.-Elect* Nicolle Davies, Asst. Comm., Colorado State Library. Tel. 303-866-6733, e-mail davies_n@cde.state.co.us; *Secy.* Jennifer Nelson, State Librarian, New Jersey State Library. Tel. 612-819-6453, e-mail jnelson@njstatelib.org; *Treas.* Jamie Ritter, State Librarian, Tennessee State Library & Archives. Tel. 615-741-7996, e-mail james.ritter@tn.gov; *Past Pres.* Jennie Stapp, State Libn., Montana State Lib. Tel. 406-444-3116, e-mail jstapp2@mt.gov.

Directors

Mary Soucie, State Librarian, North Dakota State Library. Tel. 701-328-4654, e-mail msoucie@nd.gov; Michael Scott, State Librarian, Iowa State Library. Tel. 515-242-5062, e-mail michael.scott@iowa.gov; Jeremy Johannesen, Executive Director, Chief Officers of State Library Agencies (COSLA). Tel. 859-514-9826, e-mail jjohannesen@cosla.org (ex officio).

Chinese American Librarians Association

Executive Director Michael Bailou Huang
E-mail michael.b.huang@stonybrook.edu
World Wide Web https://cala-web.org

Objective

To enhance communications among Chinese American librarians as well as between Chinese American librarians and other librarians, to serve as a forum for discussion of mutual problems and professional concerns among Chinese American librarians, to promote Sino-American librarianship and library services, and to provide a vehicle whereby Chinese American librarians can cooperate with other associations and organizations having similar or allied interests.

Membership

Memb. approximately 600. Membership is open to anyone interested in the association's goals and activities. Dues (Reg.) $30; (International/Student/Nonsalaried/Overseas) $15; (Inst.) $100; (Affiliated) $100; (Life) $300.

Officers (2021–2024)

Pres. Ray Pun. E-mail raypun101@gmail.com; *V.P./Pres.-Elect* Vincci Kwong. E-mail vkwong@iusb.edu; *Treas.* Ying Liao. E-mail cairo_liao@hotmail.com; *Past Pres.* Wenli Gao. E-mail wgao5@central.uh.edu; *Incoming V.P./Pres.-Elect* Guoying Liu. E-mail gliu@uwindsor.ca.

Board of Directors

(*2020–2023*) Leping He, Yan He, Amy Jiang, Mingyan Li, Le Yang; (*2021–2024*) Ying Zhang, Michael Huang, Katherina Lee, Lei Jin, Xiaoyu Duan; (*2022–2025*) Lian Ruan, Meng Qu, Feng-Ru Sheu, Anthony Chow, Yang Zeng.

Chapter Presidents (2022–2023)

NCA: Yi Liang; SCA: Hong Cheng; GMA: Yanhong Wang; MW: Meng Qu; NE: Cindy Li; SE: Jia He; SW: Fen Lu; Canada: Qing Zou; Asia-Pacific: Katherina Lee.

Committee Chairs

Assessment and Evaluation. Jia Mi.
Awards. Lei Jin and Feng-Ru Sheu.
Conference Program & Local Arrangement. Ray Pun.
Constitution and Bylaws. Lei Jin.
Election. Michael Bailou Huang.
International Relations. Qinghua Xu.
Membership. Grace Liu and Edward Junhao Lim.
Mentorship Programming. Ning Zou and Min Tong.
Nominating. Wenli Gao.
Public Relations/Fundraising. Weiling Liu.
Web Committee. Yifan Huang.

Publications

CALA Newsletter (2 a year; memb.; online). *Eds.* Xiping Liu. E-mail xliu47@uh.edu; Esther DeLeon. E-mail esther.deleon@ttu.edu.
International Journal of Librarianship (IJoL). *Eds.* Xiaoai Ren. E-mail xren@valdosta.edu; Yongming Wang. E-mail wangyo@tcnj.edu.

Coalition for Networked Information

Executive Director, Clifford A. Lynch
21 Dupont Circle, Suite 800, Washington, DC 20036
202-296-5098, fax 202-872-0884, e-mail clifford@cni.org
World Wide Web https://www.cni.org
Facebook https://www.facebook.com/cni.org
Twitter @cni_org
YouTube https://www.youtube.com/user/cnivideo
Vimeo http://vimeo.com/cni

Mission

The Coalition for Networked Information (CNI) promotes the transformative promise of networked information technology for the advancement of scholarly communication and the enrichment of intellectual productivity.

Membership

Memb. 240+. Membership is institutional. Dues $8,660. Year. July–June.

Staff

Exec. Dir. Clifford A. Lynch. E-mail clifford@cni.org; *Assoc. Exec. Dir.* Joan K. Lippincot. E-mail joan@cni.org; *Asst. Exec. Dir.* Diane Goldenberg-Hart. E-mail diane@cni.org; *Admin. Asst.* Sharon Adams. E-mail sharon@cni.org; *Systems Coord.* Maurice-Angelo F. Cruz. E-mail angelo@cni.org; *Office Mgr.* Jacqueline J. Eudell. E-mail jackie@cni.org; *Communications Coord.* Paige Pope. E-mail paige@cni.org.

Steering Committee Members

Dale Askey, University of Alberta (*2021–2024*); Lisa R. Carter, University of Wisconsin–Madison (*2022–2025*); Daniel Cohen, Northeastern University (*2022–2023*); Jenn Stringer, (representing EDUCAUSE) University of California–Berkeley (*2020–2023*); Ann Thornton (representing ARL) Columbia University (*2020–2023*); Cheryl Washington (representing EDUCAUSE) University of California–Davis (*2022–2025*); Keith Webster, Carnegie Mellon University (*2022–2023*); Mary Lee Kennedy, Association of Research Libraries (ex officio); Clifford A. Lynch, Coalition for Networked Information (ex officio); John O'Brien, EDUCAUSE, (ex officio).

Publications

CNI-ANNOUNCE (https://www.cni.org/resources/follow-cni/cni-announce)
CNI Executive Roundtable Reports (https://www.cni.org/tag/executive-roundtable-report).

Council on Library and Information Resources

President, Charles Henry
1800 Diagonal Road, Suite 600, Alexandria, VA 22314
E-mail contact@clir.org
World Wide Web https://www.clir.org
Twitter @CLIRnews

Objective

In 1997 the Council on Library Resources (CLR) and the Commission on Preservation and Access (CPA) merged and became the Council on Library and Information Resources (CLIR). CLIR is an independent, nonprofit organization that forges strategies to enhance research, teaching, and learning environments in collaboration with libraries, cultural institutions, and communities of higher learning.

CLIR promotes forward-looking collaborative solutions that transcend disciplinary, institutional, professional, and geographic boundaries in support of the public good. CLIR identifies and defines the key emerging issues relating to the welfare of libraries and the constituencies they serve, convenes the leaders who can influence change, and promotes collaboration among the institutions and organizations that can achieve change. The council's interests embrace the entire range of information resources and services from traditional library and archival materials to emerging digital formats. It assumes a particular interest in helping institutions cope with the accelerating pace of change associated with the transition into the digital environment.

While maintaining appropriate collaboration and liaison with other institutions and organizations, CLIR operates independently of any particular institutional or vested interests. Through the composition of its board, it brings the broadest possible perspective to bear upon defining and establishing the priority of the issues with which it is concerned.

ian and Archivist of Canada Emeritus; *Pres.* Charles Henry; *Treas.* John Price Wilkin, Univ. of Illinois–Urbana-Champaign.

Board of Directors

Edward Ayers, University of Richmond; Michele Casalini, Casalini Libri; Christopher Celenza, Johns Hopkins University; Dan Cohen, Northeastern University; Tess Davis, Antiquities Coalition; Kurt De Belder, Leiden University; Kathleen Fitzpatrick, Michigan State University; Fenella France, Library of Congress; Michael A. Keller, Stanford University; W. Joseph King, Lyon College; Carol Mandel, New York University Division of Libraries; Max Marmor, Samuel H. Kress Foundation; Asma Naeem, Baltimore Museum of Art; Richard Ovenden, University of Oxford; Sandra Phoenix, HBCU Library Alliance; Winston Tabb, Johns Hopkins University; Ben Vinson III, Case Western Reserve University; Sohair Wastawy, The Information Guild.

Address correspondence to headquarters.

Officers

Chair Buhle Mbambo-Thata, National Univ. of Lesotho; *V.Chair* Guy Berthiaume, Librar-

Publications

Annual Report.
CLIR Issues (bi-mo.; electronic).

EveryLibrary

Executive Director, John Chrastka
P.O. Box 406, 45 E. Burlington St.,
Riverside, IL 60546
312-574-5098
E-mail info@everylibrary.org
World Wide Web https://www.everylibrary.org | https://action.everylibrary.org
Facebook https://www.facebook.com/EveryLibrary
LinkedIn https://www.linkedin.com/company/3801587
Twitter @EveryLibrary

Object

EveryLibrary is a national political action committee for libraries. Organized as a 501(c)4, the organization provides pro bono advising and consulting to libraries about

their funding requests, either when it appears on a ballot or through a municipal funding partner. Its school-library-focused digital activism platform Save School Librarians works to support school librarian positions and budgets for school library programs. Its national network in 2021 included more than 355,000 Americans. EveryLibrary's mission is to "build voter support for libraries" at all levels of government, and it works to fulfill that mission as a completely donor-supported organization.

Board Members

Jeannie Allen, Lori Bowen Ayer, Peter Bromberg, John Chrastka, Harmony V. Faust, Erica Findley, Brian D. Hart, Gary Kirk, Kathleen McEvoy, Patrick Sweeney.

EveryLibrary Institute, NFP

Executive Director, John Chrastka

P.O. Box 406, 45 E. Burlington St.,

Riverside, IL 60546

312-574-5098

E-mail info@everylirbaryinstitute.org
World Wide Web https://www.everylibraryinstitute.org
Facebook https://facebook.com/everylibraryinstitute
Twitter @ELInstituteNFP

Objective

The EveryLibrary Institute, NFP is a public policy and tax policy think tank for libraries that is focused on the future of public library and school library funding in the United States and abroad. Its nonprofit 501(c)3 mission is to develop research, programmatic opportunities, trainings, fiscal sponsorships, and scholarship that advance the image and impact of libraries and librarians to the general public and policymakers. Domestically, this includes publishing its journal, supporting public outreach and education across the EveryLibrary network, and providing crowdfunding services through its Fund Libraries platform. Internationally, it partners with CILIP, the Chartered Institute for Library and Information Professionals, to host the Libraries Deliver outreach campaign about libraries in England.

Board Members

K.C. Boyd, John Chrastka, Kyle Courtney, Trevor A. Dawes, Erica Findley, Britten Follett, Amy Garmer, Fran Glick, Kafi Kumasi, Steve Potter, Rivkah Sass, Cal Shepard, Maureen Sullivan, Patrick Sweeney, Jill Hurst-Wahl, Lance Werner.

Publication

The Political Librarian (irreg.; open access). *Ed.* Christopher Stewart.

Federal Library and Information Network

Manager, Melissa Blaschke
Library of Congress, 101 Independence Ave. SE

Washington, DC 20540-4935
202-707-2457, e-mail mebl@loc.gov
World Wide Web https://www.loc.gov/flicc
Twitter @librarycongress

Objective

The Federal Library and Information Network (FEDLINK) is an organization of federal agencies working together to achieve optimum use of the resources and facilities of federal libraries and information centers by promoting common services, coordinating and sharing available resources, and providing continuing professional education for federal library and information staff. FEDLINK serves as a forum for discussion of the policies, programs, procedures, and technologies that affect federal libraries and the information services they provide to their agencies, Congress, the federal courts, and the public.

Membership

The FEDLINK voting membership is composed of representatives of the following U.S. federal departments and agencies: each of the national libraries (the Library of Congress, National Agricultural Library, National Library of Education, National Library of Medicine, and National Transportation Library); each cabinet-level executive department, as defined in 5 U.S.C. § 101; additional departments and agencies (the Defense Technical Information Center; departments of the Air Force, Army, and Navy; Executive Office of the President; Government Accountability Office; General Services Administration; Government Printing Office; Institute of Museum and Library Services; National Aeronautics and Space Administration; National Archives and Records Administration; National Technical Information Service [Department of Commerce]; Office of Management and Budget; Office of Personnel Management; Office of Scientific and Technical Information [Department of Energy]; Office of the Director of National Intelligence; and Smithsonian Institution); the U.S. Supreme Court and Administrative Office of the U.S. Courts; the District of Columbia; and other federal independent agencies and government corporations.

Address correspondence to the executive director.

Publication

FEDLINK Bulletin (bi-wk.; electronic).

Librarians, Archivists, and Museum Professionals in the History of the Health Sciences

President, Polina Ilieva
E-mail lamphhs.org@gmail.com
World Wide Web www.lamphhs.org

Objective

Librarians, Archivists, and Museum Professionals in the History of the Health Sciences (LAMPHHS; formerly ALHHS/MeMA) was established exclusively for educational purposes, to serve the professional interests of librarians, archivists, and other specialists actively engaged in the librarianship of the history of the health sciences by promoting the exchange of information and by improving the standards of service.

Membership

Memb. approximately 150. Dues $15.

Officers (2022–2024)

Pres. Polina Ilieva, Archives and Special Collections, UCSF Library, San Francisco, California. E-mail polina.ilieva@ ucsf.edu; *V.P.* Keith C. Mages, Robert L. Brown History of Medicine Collection, University at Buffalo, Buffalo, New York. E-mail kcmages@buffalo.edu; *Secy.* Carrie Meyer, University of Nebraska Medical Center, Omaha, Nebraska. E-mail carrie.meyer@unmc.edu; *Treas.* Tegan Kehoe, Paul S. Russell, M.D., Museum of Medical History and Innovation, Boston, Massachusetts General Hospital, Boston, Massachusetts. E-mail lamphhs.treasurer@gmail.com. *Memb.-at-Large* Mary Hague-Yearl, Megan Keller Young, Nicole Topich, Rebecca Williams.

Committee Chairs

Annual Meeting Local Arrangements. Tamara Barnes.
Annual Meeting Program. Christopher Ryland.
Archivist. Jodi Koste.
Communications. Carrie Meyer.
Membership Directory. Carrie Meyer.
Nominating. Rachel Ingold.
Travel Scholarships. Brandon T. Pieczko.
Website. Sara Alger and Meghan Kennedy.

Awards Committee Chairs

Publications Awards. Nicole Milano.
Recognition Awards. Brooke Guthrie.

Publication

Watermark (q.; memb.). *Ed.* Stephen E. Novak. Augustus C. Long Health Sciences Library, Columbia University. E-mail sen13@cumc.columbia.org.

Medical Library Association

Executive Director, Kevin Baliozian
233 South Wacker Drive, 44th Floor, Chicago, IL 60606
312-419-9094, fax 312-419-8950, e-mail websupport@mail.mlahq.org
World Wide Web https://www.mlanet.org
Twitter @MedLibAssn

Objective

The Medical Library Association (MLA) is a nonprofit professional education organization with nearly 4,000 health sciences information professional members and partners worldwide. MLA provides lifelong educational opportunities, supports a knowledge base of health information research, and works with a global network of partners to promote the importance of high-quality information for improved health to the healthcare community and the public.

Membership

Memb. (Inst.) 400+; (Indiv.) 3,200+, in more than 50 countries. Dues (Indiv.) $75–$225; (Student) $50; (Int'l.) $150; (Affiliate) $140; (Inst.) $325–$880. Year. Institutional members are medical and allied scientific libraries. Individual members are people who are (or were at the time membership was established) engaged in professional library or bibliographic work in medical and allied scientific libraries or people who are interested in medical or allied scientific libraries. Members can be affiliated with one or more of MLA's more than 20 special-interest sections and its regional chapters.

Officers

Pres. Shannon D. Jones, Medical University of South Carolina; *Pres.-Elect* Amy Blevins, Indiana University School of Medicine; *Secy.* Heather N. Holmes, Medical University of

South Carolina; *Treas.* J. Dale Prince, Louisiana State University Health Sciences Center-New Orleans; *Past Pres.* Kristine M. Alpi, Oregon Health & Science Univ.; *Exec. Dir.* Kevin Baliozian. Med. Lib. Assn.

Board of Directors

Tara Douglas-Williams, Emily J. Hurst, Adela V. Justice, Janna C. Lawrence, Brenda M. Linares, Keith Pickett, Tony Nguyen.

Committee Chairs

Awards. Brittany R. Heer.
Books Panel. Heather Jett.
Bylaws. David Charles Duggar and Amy Gische Lyons.
Credentialing. Rachel Helbing.
Diversity, Equity, and Inclusion. Jessica Sender.
Education: Health Information Professionalism Curriculum. Elizabeth Irish.
Education: Information Management Curriculum. Erin E. Reardon.
Education: Information Services Curriculum. Julie K. Gaines.
Education: Instruction and Instructional Design Curriculum. Danielle M Westmark.
Education: Leadership and Management Curriculum. Debra Werner.
Education: Research and Evidence-Based Practice Curriculum. Andrea C. Kepsel.
Education: Steering. Stephanie M. Swanberg.
Finance. J. Dale Prince.
Grants and Scholarships. Lisa A. Adriani.
History. Gregory Laynor and Ansley Stuart.
Joseph Leiter NLM/MLA Lectureship. Caitlin Bakker.
Membership. Timothy L. Kenny.
National Program. Liz Kellermeyer and Emily Vardell.
Nominating. Kristine M. Alpi.
Professional Recruitment and Retention. Alexandria Leigh Brackett.

Editorial Board Chairs

JMLA Editors-in-Chief. Jill Boruff and Michelle Kraft.
MLAConnect Ed. Christine Willis.

Task Force Chairs

125-Year Retrospective Task Force. Michelle R. Lieggi.
Archives Task Force. Brandon Pieczko.
Joint MLA/AAHSL Legislative Task Force. Margaret Ansell.
Most Notable Workgroup. Sally Gore.
Societal Issues Task Force. Irene (Rena) Machowa Lubker.
Special Program Committee for Collection Development/Resource Sharing. Michael A. Wood.
Vision 2048 Task Force. Charlotte Beyer.

Awards Committee Chairs

Virginia L. and William K. Beatty Volunteer Service. Erin Elizabeth Ware.
Estelle Brodman Award for the Academic Medical Librarian of the Year. Lisa M. Acuff.
Chapter Project of the Year. Rebecca S. Graves.
Lois Ann Colaianni Award for Excellence and Achievement in Hospital Librarianship. Mary Beth McAteer.
Consumer Health Librarian of the Year Award Jury. Laura M. Lipke.
Louise Darling Medal for Distinguished Achievement in Collection Development in the Health Sciences. Beth Edson.
Janet Doe Lectureship. Amy Suiter.
Ida and George Eliot Prize. Lorraine Chun.
Fellows and Honorary Members. Elaine Russo Martin.
Carla J. Funk Governmental Relations. Jeanne Strausman.
T. Mark Hodges International Service. Maria Lopez (staff liaison).
Lucretia W. McClure Excellence in Education. David W. Petersen.
Erich Meyerhoff Prize. Heather Edmonds.
Research Advancement in Health Sciences Librarianship Awards Jury. Jessica A. Koos.
Daniel T. Richards Prize Jury. Mary A. Hyde.
Rising Stars Award. Emily Jones.
Rittenhouse Award. Suzanne Fricke.
Frank Bradway Rogers Information Advancement. Maria Lopez (staff liaison).

Grants, Scholarships, and Fellowships Juries

Ysabel Bertolucci MLA Annual Meeting Grant. Maria Lopez (staff liaison).
Naomi C. Broering Hispanic Heritage Grant. Jaclyn Morales.
Collection Development Professional Development Grant. Deidre (Dede) Rios.
Continuing Education Grant. Joseph Harzbecker.
Cunningham Memorial International Fellowship. Andrew Todd.
EBSCO MLA Annual Conference Support. Maria Lopez (staff liaison).
Financial Support Jury: Annual Conference and Exhibits. Pamela R. Herring.
Financial Support Jury: CE Passport. Zoe Pettway Unno.
Eugene Garfield Research Fellowship. Kimberly R. Powell.
Mary K. Haver Consumer Health Professional Development Grant. Nell Aronoff.
David A. Kronick and Charles W. Sargent Visiting Fellowship. Andrew Todd.
Librarians Without Borders Ursula Poland International Scholarship. Heidi Reis.

Donald A.B. Lindberg Research Fellowship. Karen Gau.
MLA Doctoral Fellowship. Maria Lopez (staff liaison).
MLA Hospital Libraries Professional Development Grant. Loren Hackett.
MLA Medical Informatics Career Development Grant. Amy Christine Studer.
MLA Research, Development, and Demonstration Project Grant. Jennifer Sullivan.
MLA Scholarships (including for underrepresented students). Melinda Johnson.
Research Training Institute Jury. Tara R. Malone.
Harriet L. Steuernagel Continuing Education Grant Jury. Melanie J. Norton.

Publication

Journal of the Medical Library Association (q.; electronic version, free to all through PubMed Central). *Eds.-in-Chief* Jill T. Boruff and Michelle Kraft. E-mail jmla@journals.pitt.edu.

Music Library Association

President, Paula Hickner
8401 Greenway Blvd, Suite 100, Middleton, WI 53562
608-836-5825, fax 608-831-8200, e-mail mla@areditions.com
World Wide Web https://www.musiclibraryassoc.org
Facebook https://www.facebook.com/Music.Library.Association
Twitter @musiclibassoc
Vimeo https://vimeo.com/musiclibraryassoc

Objective

The Music Library Association provides a professional forum for librarians, archivists, and others who support and preserve the world's musical heritage. To achieve this mission, it:

• Provides leadership for the collection and preservation of music and information about music in libraries and archives

• Develops and delivers programs that promote continuing education and professional development in music librarianship

• Ensures and enhances intellectual access to music for all by contributing to the development and revision of national and international codes, formats, and other standards for the bibliographic control of music

• Ensures and enhances access to music for all by facilitating best practices for housing, preserving, and providing access to music

• Promotes legislation that strengthens music library services and universal access to music

• Fosters information literacy and lifelong learning by promoting music reference services, library instruction programs, and publications

- Collaborates with other groups in the music and technology industries, government, and librarianship to promote its mission and values

Membership

Memb. 1,200+. Dues (Inst.) $175; (Indiv.) $140; (Ret.) $105; (Paraprofessional) $75; (Student) $65. (Foreign, add $10.) Year. July 1–June 30.

Officers

Pres. Paula Hickner. E-mail paula.hickner@uky.edu; *V.P./Pres.-Elect*; Paula Hickner. E-mail paula.hickner@uky.edu; *Recording Secy.* Veronica Wells. E-mail vmalzalde@gmail.com; *Chief Fin. Officer* Serena Vaquilar. E-mail serena.vaquilar@wayne.edu; *Asst. Chief Fin. Officer* Elizabeth Hille Cribbs. E-mail eliza bethhillecribbs@gmail.com; *Past Pres.* Liza Vick. E-mail lizavick@upenn.edu.

Board of Directors

(2022–2024) Parliamentarian Ray Heigemeir; *Fiscal Officer* Katie Buehner; *Planning and Reports Officer* Sonia Archer-Capuzzo. *(2023–2025) Asst. Parliamentarian* Angela Pratesi; *Asst. Fiscal Officer* Rahni Kennedy; *Asst. Planning and Reports Officer* Houman Behzadi; Student/Early Career Rep. Blaine Brubaker.

Committee Chairs

Archives and Special Collections. Maristella J. Feustle.
Career Development and Services. Emma Dederick and Timothy Sestrick.
Career Development and Services: New Members Forum. Karen I. McCool.
Cataloging and Metadata. Rebecca Belford.
Development. Sara White.
Education. Brendan Higgins.
Emerging Technologies and Services. Amy S. Jackson.

Finance. Marci Cohen.
Inclusion, Diversity, Equity, and Accessibility. Z. Sylvia Yang and Will Scharfenberger.
Legislation. Kathleen L. DeLaurenti and Peter Shirts.
Membership. Lisa Shiota.
Music Library Advocacy. Linda B. Fairtile.
Nominating. Bruce J. Evans.
Oral History. Catherine Hammer and Sara Wallace.
Planning. Scott M. Stone.
Preservation. Alice M. Carli.
Program. Carlos E. Peña.
Public Libraries. Kristine E. Nelsen.
Public Services. Andrea L. Beckendorf.
Publications. Deborah A. Campana.
Resource Sharing and Collection Development. Stephanie Bonjack.
Web. Kerry C. Masteller.

Awards Committee Chairs

Best of Chapters. Lynne C. Jaffe.
Conference Travel Grants. Andrea I. Morris.
Lenore Coral IAML Travel Grant. Position open.
Diversity Scholarship. Ellen Ogihara.
Dena Epstein Award for Archival and Library Research in American Music. Anita S. Breckbill.
Gerboth and Bradley Award. Nara L. Newcomer.
Publications. Ryan Johnson.

Publications

Basic Manual Series. *Ed.* Melanie Zeck.
Basic Music Library. *Ed.* Daniel Boomhower.
Index and Bibliography Series (irreg.; price varies). *Ed.* Lois Kuyper-Rushing.
MLA *Newsletter.* (6 a year; memb.). *Ed.* Jacey Kepich.
Music Cataloging Bulletin (mo.; online subscription only, $35). *Ed.* Kirk-Evan Billet.
Notes (q.; memb.). *Ed.* Jonathan J. Sauceda.
Technical Reports and Monographs in Music Librarianship (irreg.; price varies). *Ed.* Anna E. Kijas.

NASIG

President, Dana Sinclair
PMB 305, 1902 Ridge Road, West Seneca, NY 14224-3312
716-324-1859, e-mail: info@nasig.org
World Wide Web: https://nasig.org
Twitter: @NASIG
Facebook: https://www.facebook.com/groups/2399345882
Instagram: https://www.instagram.com/nasig_official
LinkedIn: https://www.linkedin.com/groups/149102
YouTube: https://www.youtube.com/channel/UCVvnh_CzXS8YgftuvIypTiQ

Vision and Mission

Established in 1985, NASIG is an independent organization working to advance and transform the management of information resources. NASIG's goal is to facilitate and improve the distribution, acquisition, and long-term accessibility of information resources in all formats and business models. There are three key components to the organization's mission:

- NASIG supports a dynamic community of professionals including, but not limited to, librarians, publishers, and vendors engaging in understanding one another's perspectives and improving functionality throughout the information resources life cycle with an emphasis on scholarly communications, serials, and electronic resources.
- NASIG provides a rich variety of conference and continuing education programming to encourage knowledge sharing among its members and to support their professional and career development.
- NASIG promotes the development and implementation of best practices and standards for the distribution, acquisition, and long-term accessibility of information resources in all formats and business models throughout their life cycle. In addition to developing best practices, NASIG supports the development of standards by NISO, an affiliated organization.

Membership

Memb. 525. For any person, library, or organization interested in information resources and scholarly communication. Dues (Indiv. based on salary range) $75–$100; (Ret.) $25; (Student) Free; (Lifetime) $1,000/one time; (Inst.) $195.

Executive Board (2022–2023)

Pres. Dana Sinclair, SUNY Old Westbury; *V.P./ Pres.-Elect* Courtney McAllister, Atypon; *Past Pres.* Ted Westervelt, Library of Congress; *Sec.* Willa Tavernier, Indiana University–Bloomington; *Treas.* Shannon Keller, U.S. Department of State; *Memb.-at-Large* Xiaoyan Song, North Carolina State University; Sonali Sugrim, Queens College; Treasa Bane, University of Wisconsin–Madison; Moon Kim, University of British Columbia; Mary Ann Jones, Kennesaw State University; Ilda Cardenas, California State University–Fullerton; Steve Oberg (ex officio).

Committee Chairs

Archivist. Peter Whiting.
Awards and Recognition. Emily Ray.
Bylaws. Maria Aghazarian and Christian Lear.
Communications. Amanda Bullington and Sofia Slutskaya.
Conference Coordinator. Anna Creech.
Conference Planning. Christian Burris and Steve Kelley.
Conference Proceedings Editors. Caitlin Harrington.
Continuing Education. Amy Carlson and Kate Hill.
Digital Preservation. Alicia Wise and Michelle Polchow.
Equity and Inclusion. Diana Reid.

Evaluation and Assessment. Victoria Koger.
Membership Services. Suzy Kozaitis.
Mentoring and Student Outreach. Juliya Borie.
Newsletter. Position open.
Nominations and Elections. Danielle Williams.
Open Initiatives. Melissa Hart Cantrell.
Program Planning. Sarah Dennis and Jennifer Zuccaro.
Registrar. Stephanie J. Adams.
Standards. Jessica Scott and Jacque Brellenthin.

Task Force Chair

Vendor and Publisher Engagement. Kristy White.

Publications

Conference Proceedings (currently published in two issues of *Serials Librarian*).
Core Competencies for Electronic Resources Librarians.
Core Competencies for Print Serials Management.
Core Competencies for Scholarly Communication Librarians.
NASIG Newsletter.
Various NASIGuides.
NASIG Blog.
NASIG Jobs Blog.

Meetings

Annual conference held in the summer. Continuing education events and webinars throughout the year.

National Association of Government Archives and Records Administrators

Executive Director, Johnny Hadlock
1400 L Street NW, LBBY 2 #34375, Washington, DC 20005
202-938-1988, e-mail info@nagara.org
World Wide Web https://www.nagara.org
Twitter @InfoNAGARA

Objective

Founded in 1984, the National Association of Government Archives and Records Administrators (NAGARA) is a nationwide association of local, state, and federal archivists and records administrators and others interested in improved care and management of government records. NAGARA promotes public awareness of government records and archives management programs, encourages interchange of information among government archives and records management agencies, develops and implements professional standards of government records and archival administration, and encourages study and research into records management problems and issues.

Membership

Most NAGARA members are federal, state, and local archival and records management agencies. Dues (Org.) $225–$750 dependent on number of contacts; (NARA Employees Indiv.) $40; (Students/Ret.) $50; (All other Indiv.) $89.

Officers (2022–2023)

Pres. Jennifer Green, City of Oklahoma, jennifer.green@okc.gov; *Pres.-Elect* Jen Haney Conover, Warren County (Ohio) Records Center & Archives; *V.P.* Holly Dolan, Denton County, Texas; *Secy.* Megan Wheaton-Book, Vermont State Archives & Records Administration; *Treas.* Pari J. Swift, Ohio State University; *Past Pres.* Patricia C. Franks, San José State Univ. E-mail patricia.franks@sjsu.edu.

Board of Directors

Tara Bell, Shante Ellis, Anne Frantilla, JA Pryse, Lindsey Rambow, Dennis Riley, Kristopher Stenson.

Publication

Newsletter (q.; memb.; electronic).

National Information Standards Organization

Executive Director, Todd Carpenter
3600 Clipper Mill Rd., Suite 302, Baltimore, MD 21211-1948
301-654-2512, e-mail nisohq@niso.org
World Wide Web https://www.niso.org

Objective

The National Information Standards Organization (NISO) fosters the development and maintenance of standards that facilitate the creation, persistent management, and effective interchange of information so that it can be trusted for use in research and learning. To fulfill this mission, NISO engages libraries, publishers, information aggregators, and other organizations that support learning, research, and scholarship through the creation, organization, management, and curation of knowledge. NISO works with intersecting communities of interest and across the entire life cycle of an information standard. NISO standards apply both traditional and new technologies to the full range of information-related needs, including discovery, retrieval, repurposing, storage, metadata, business information, and preservation.

NISO also develops and publishes recommended practices, technical reports, white papers, and information publications. NISO holds regular educational programs on standards, technologies, and related topics where standards-based solutions can help solve problems. These programs include webinars, online virtual conferences, in-person forums, and teleconferences.

Experts from the information industry, libraries, systems vendors, and publishing participate in the development of NISO standards and recommended practices. The standards are approved by the consensus body of NISO's voting membership, representing libraries, publishers, vendors, government, associations, and private businesses and organizations. NISO is supported by its membership and grants.

NISO is a not-for-profit association accredited by the American National Standards Institute (ANSI) and serves as the U.S. Technical Advisory Group Administrator to ISO/TC 46 Information and Documentation as well as the secretariat for ISO/TC 46/SC 9, Identification and Description.

Membership

Voting Members: 80+. Open to any organization, association, government agency, or company willing to participate in and having substantial concern for the development of NISO standards. Library Standards Alliance Members: 60+. Open to any academic, public, special, or government-supported library interested in supporting the mission of NISO.

Officers

Chair; Maria Stanton, Atla; *V. Chair* Karim Boughida, Stony Brook University; *Treas.* Wayne Strickland, NTIS; *Past Chair* Mary Sauer-Games, OCLC, Inc.

Directors

Ryan Bernier, Jonathan Clark, Trevor A. Dawes, Angela Ecklund, Patricia Ginnis, Salwa Ismail, Rebecca McCloud, Alison Mudditt, Rhonda Ross, Greg Suprock, Robert Wheeler.

Staff

Exec. Dir. Todd Carpenter; *Assoc. Exec. Dir.* Nettie Lagace; *Dir. of Business Devt. and Comm.* Mary Beth Barilla; *Dir. of Strategic Initiatives* Jason Griffey; *Education Prog. Mgr.& DEIA Advocate* Kimberly Gladfelter Graham; *Asst. Standards Program Mgr.* Keondra Bailey;

Comm. Events Coord. Sara Groveman; *Office Mgr.* Lisa Jackson; *Consultant* Betsy Fanning.

Publications

Information Standards Quarterly (back issues available in open access from the NISO website).

NISO's published standards, recommended practices, and technical reports are available free of charge as downloadable PDF files from the NISO website (http://www.niso.org). Hardcopy documents are available for sale from the website.

For additional NISO publications, see the article "NISO Standards" in this volume.

Patent and Trademark Resource Center Association

President, Dave Zwicky
Reference Department, University of Delaware Library, Newark, DE 19717-5267
World Wide Web https://ptrca.org

Objective

The Patent and Trademark Resource Center Association (PTRCA) provides a support structure for the more than 80 patent and trademark resource centers (PTRCs) affiliated with the U.S. Patent and Trademark Office (USPTO). The association's mission is to discover the interests, needs, opinions, and goals of the PTRCs and to advise USPTO in these matters for the benefit of PTRCs and their users and to assist USPTO in planning and implementing appropriate services. Founded in 1983 as the Patent Depository Library Advisory Council, its name was changed to the Patent and Trademark Depository Library Association in 1988. It became an American Library Association affiliate in 1996. In 2011 the association was renamed the Patent and Trademark Resource Center Association.

Membership

Open to any person employed in a patent and trademark resource center library whose responsibilities include the patent and trademark collection. Affiliate membership is also available. Dues (Reg.) $65; (Student) $10.

Officers (2022–2023)

Pres. Dave Zwicky, West Lafayette, IN; *V.P./ Pres.-Elect* J. Donna Arment, Durango, CO; *Secy.* Tallie Casucci, Salt Lake City, UT; *Treas.* Jim Miller, College Park, MD; *Past Pres.* Sharyl Overhiser, Philadelphia, PA.

Directors

Academic Libraries Division Reps. Suzanne Reinman *(2021–2023)*, Jared Hoppenfeld *(2022–2024)*; *Public Libraries Division Reps.* James Bettinger *(2021–2023)*, Stella Mittelbach *(2022–2024)*.

Committee Chairs (2022–2023)

Bylaws. Marian Armour-Gemman.

Conferences. Sharyl Overhiser.
Database. Lisha Li.
Election. Position open.
Membership and Mentoring. John Schlipp.
Programs. Rebecca (Missy) Murphey.
Publications. Suzanne Reinman.

Publication

PTRCA Journal. Electronic at https://ptrca.org/newsletters.

Polish American Librarians Association

President, Ewa Barczyk
984 N. Milwaukee Avenue, Chicago, IL 60642
World Wide Web http://palalib.org

Objective

Founded in 2009, the mission of the Polish American Librarians Association (PALA) is to positively affect services provided to library patrons of Polish descent and individuals interested in Polish culture.

The organization's vision is:

- To enhance professional knowledge by developing forums for discussion and networks of communication among library staff working with Polish collections and patrons of Polish origin
- To promote understanding and respect among all cultures by expanding the means to access reliable, current information about Polish and Polish American culture
- To promote Polish American librarianship
- To provide opportunities for cooperation with other library associations

Membership

Membership is open to librarians, students of library schools, library support staff, and others who support the vision of PALA. Dues $50 (one-time dues to support the goals of PALA).

Officers

Pres. Ewa Barczyk, Golda Meir Lib., Univ. of Wisconsin–Milwaukee, 2311 E. Hartford Ave., Milwaukee, WI. Tel. 414-412-5456, e-mail ewa@uwm.edu; *Secy.* Paulina Poplawska, New Ulm Public Lib., New Ulm, MN. E-mail ppoplawska@tds.lib.mn.us; *Treas.* Bernadetta Koryciarz, Niles-Maine District Lib., 6960 Oakton St., Niles, IL 60714. Tel. 847-663-6642, e-mail bkorycia@nileslibrary.org; *Past Pres.* Leonard Kniffel (dec.). *Dirs.-at-Large* Iwona Bozek, Krystyna Matusiak, Hanna Przybylski, Marianne Ryan.

REFORMA (National Association to Promote Library and Information Services to Latinos and the Spanish-Speaking)

President, Romelia Salinas
P.O. Box 71651, Los Angeles CA 90071
E-mail admin@reforma.org
World Wide Web https://www.reforma.org

Objective

Promoting library services to the Spanish-speaking for nearly 40 years, REFORMA, an affiliate of the American Library Association, works in a number of areas to advance the development of library collections that include Spanish-language and Latino-oriented materials, the recruitment of more bilingual and bicultural professionals and support staff, the development of library services and programs that meet the needs of the Latino community, the establishment of a national network among individuals who share its goals, the education of the U.S. Latino population in regard to the availability and types of library services, and lobbying efforts to preserve existing library resource centers serving the interest of Latinos.

Membership

Memb. 800+. Membership is open to any person who is supportive of the goals and objectives of REFORMA. Dues (Indiv.) $10–$50; (Int'l.) Free; (Life) $450; (Inst.) $100–$250. Year.

Executive Committee (2022–2023)

Pres. Romelia Salinas, Mt. San Antonio College. E-mail president@reforma.org; *V.P./Pres.-Elect* David López, OC Public Libraries. E-mail vice-president@reforma.org; *Secy.* Alma Ramos-McDermott, Avalon Elementary School. E-mail secretary@reforma.org; *Treas.* Denice Adkins, Univ. of Missouri. E-mail treasurer@reforma.org; *Past Pres.* Nicanor Diaz, Denver Public Library. E-mail past-president@reforma.org; *Memb.-at-Large* Alda Allina Migoni, Library of Congress. E-mail at-large-rep@reforma.org; *Chapter Reps.* Adriana Blancarte-Hayward, New York Public Library. E-mail chapter-east-region@reforma.org; Balladolid (Dolly) Lopez, California State University–Fresno. E-mail chapter-west-region@reforma.org; Taylor Charron Schwab, Denver Public Library. E-mail chapter-central-region@reforma.org.

Committee Chairs

Awards. Karen Centeno-Casillas.
Children and Young Adult Service Committee (CAYASC). Jenny Lizarraga.
Education. Bob Diaz.
Finance. Nicanor Diaz.
Fundraising. Kenny Garcia.
International Relations. Loida Garcia-Febo.
Legislative. Shaira Rock.
Membership. Tess Tobin
Mentoring. Position open.
Nominations. Kenny Garcia.
Organizational Development and New Chapters. Manny Figueroa.
Program. David López.
Public Relations. Celia Avila and Florencia Díaz.
REFORMA National Conferences Coordinating Committee. Abigail Morales and Roxana Benavides.
Research. Dr. Michele A.L. Villagran.
Scholarship. Michael Gutierrez.
Technology. Madeline Peña (web manager) and Edwin Rodarte.
Translations. Camilo Jimenez-Alfonso.

Publication

REFORMA (e-newsletter). *Ed.* Libbhy Romero.

Meetings

General membership and board meetings take place at the American Library Association Midwinter Meeting and Annual Conference and Exhibition.

Scholarly Publishing and Academic Resources Coalition

Executive Director, Heather Joseph
1201 Connecticut Ave. N.W., P.O. 607/608, Washington, DC 20036
202-630-5090, e-mail sparc@sparcopen.org
World Wide Web https://sparcopen.org
Twitter @SPARC_NA

Objective

SPARC, the Scholarly Publishing and Academic Resources Coalition, is a global organization that promotes expanded sharing of scholarship in the networked digital environment. It is committed to faster and wider sharing of outputs of the research process to increase the impact of research, fuel the advancement of knowledge, and increase the return on research investments.

Launched as an initiative of the Association of Research Libraries (ARL), SPARC has become a catalyst for change. Its pragmatic focus is to stimulate the emergence of new scholarly communication models that expand the dissemination of scholarly research and equip libraries for the inexorable growth in research output. Action by SPARC in collaboration with stakeholders—including authors, publishers, and libraries—builds on the unprecedented opportunities created by the networked digital environment to advance the conduct of scholarship.

SPARC's role in stimulating change focuses on the following:

- Educating stakeholders about the problems facing scholarly communication and the opportunities for them to play a role in achieving positive change
- Advocating policy changes that advance scholarly communication and explicitly recognize that dissemination of scholarship is an essential, inseparable component of the research process
- Incubating demonstrations of new publishing and sustainability models that benefit scholarship and academe

SPARC is an advocate for changes in scholarly communication that benefit more than the academic community alone. Founded in 1997 and now operating independently of ARL,

SPARC has expanded to represent more than 800 academic and research libraries in North America, the United Kingdom, Europe, and Japan.

Membership

Memb. 240+ institutions. SPARC membership is open to international academic and research institutions, organizations, and consortia that share an interest in creating a more open and diverse marketplace for scholarly communication. Dues are scaled by membership type and budget. For more information, visit SPARC's website at https://sparcopen.org/become-a-member, SPARC Europe at https://sparcopen.org/people/sparc-europe, SPARC Japan at http://www.nii.ac.jp/sparc, or SPARC Africa at https://sparcopen.org/people/sparc-africa.

Steering Committee

Jennifer Beamer, Gwen Bird, Chris Bourg, Jonathan O. Cain, Vicki Coleman, Karen Estlund, Scarlet Galven, Harriet Green, Lorraine Harricombe, April Hathcock, Heather Joseph, Mary Lee Kennedy, Yuan Li, Lisa Macklin, Vince Mussehl, Torsten Reimer, Ariana Santiago, Virginia Steel, Yasmeen Shorish, Catherine Steeves.

Staff

Open Education Cdtr. Aisha Abdullah. E-mail aisha@sparcopen.org.; *Dir., Open Education* Nicole Allen. E-mail nicole@sparcopen.org; *Open Education Project Mgr.* Hailey Babb. E-mail hailey@sparcopen.org; *VPO for U.S. Repository Network* Tina Baich; *HELIOS Prog. Mgr.* Caitlin Carter. E-mail caitlin@sparcopen. org; *Senior Consultant* Raym Crow. E-mail crow@sparcopen.org; *VPO for Negotiations*

Scarlet Galvan; *VPO for Privacy & Surveillance* Michele Gibney; *Chief Operating Officer* Val Hollister. E-mail val@sparcopen.org; *Exec. Dir.* Heather Joseph. E-mail heather@sparcopen.org; *Community Mgr., Open Research Funders Group,* Erin McKiernan. E-mail erin@sparc.open.org; *Prog. & Oper. Specialist* Ilana Melker. E-mail ilana@sparcopen.org; *Open & Equitable Civic Science Fellow* Eunice Mercado-Lara. E-mail eunice@sparcopen.org; *VPO for Open Models* Moriana Molchanov Garcia; *Open Education Conference Mgr.* Briana O'Neal. E-mail briana@sparcopen.org; *Dir. of Programs and Engagement* Nick Shockey. E-mail nick@sparcopen.org; *Instructor, Open Educ. Leadership Program* Tanya Spilovoy. E-mail leadership@sparcopen.org; *Manager of Public Policy and Advocacy* Katie Steen. E-mail katie@sparcopen.

org; *Consultant* Greg Tananbaum. E-mail greg@sparcopen.org.

Publications

Open Educational Resources (OER) State Policy Playbook (2021–2022 ed.) (https://sparcopen.org/our-work/oer-state-policy-playbook).

SPARC Landscape Analysis and Roadmap for Action (2021 update) by Claudio Aspesi (lead author), Nicole Allen, Raym Crow, Valerie Hollister, Heather Joseph, Joseph McArthur, Nick Shockey, Katie Steen, Marty Lentz (report editor). (https://sparcopen.org/wp-content/uploads/2021/10/2021-Landscape-Analysis-101421.pdf).

Society for Scholarly Publishing

Executive Director, Melanie Dolechek
1120 Route 73, Suite 200, Mount Laurel, NJ 08054
856-439-1385, fax 856-439-0525, e-mail info@sspnet.org
World Wide Web https://www.sspnet.org
Twitter @ScholarlyPub

Objective

To draw together individuals involved in the process of scholarly publishing. This process requires successful interaction of the many functions performed within the scholarly community. The Society for Scholarly Publishing (SSP) provides the leadership for such interaction by creating opportunities for the exchange of information and opinions among scholars, editors, publishers, librarians, printers, booksellers, and all others engaged in scholarly publishing.

Membership

Memb. 1,000+. Open to all with an interest in the scholarly publishing process and dissemination of information. Dues (Indiv. Renewal) $200; (Libn.) $85; (Early Career New) $60; (Student) $40; (Supporting Organization) $2,195; (Sustaining Organization) $5,747; (Intl. Indiv.) $50; (Intl. Early Career) $25; (Intl. Libn.) $25; (Intl. Student); $10. Year. Jan.–Dec.

Officers

Pres. Miranda Walker, Wolters Kluwer; *Pres.-Elect* Randy Townsend, PLOS; *Secy./Treas.* Emelie Delquie, Copyright Clearance Ctr.; *Past Pres.* Alice Meadows, NISO.

Board of Directors

Meredith Adinolfi, Chhavi Chauhan, Mike Di Natale, Gabe Harp, Hannah Heckner, Sai Konda, Charlotte Roh, Sara Rouhi, Tao Tao, David Crotty (ex officio), Melanie Dolechek (ex officio).

Committee Chairs

Advancement. Kim Smilay and Chelsea Tharp.
Annual Meeting Program. Emily Farrell, Lori Carlin, and Tim Lloyd.
Audit. Gabriel P. Harp and Cason Lynley.
Career Development. Michelle M. English, Karen G. Stanwood, and Sanjay Tangri.

Community Engagement. Megan M. McCarty, Sarah McKenna, and Jessica Lawrence-Hurt.
Diversity, Equity, Inclusion, and Accessibility. Allison Leung, Dr. Rebecca Kirk, and Shaina Lange.
Education. Sophie Reisz and Jeff Lang.
Finance. Emilie Delquie and Dr. Anna Wetterberg.
Marketing & Communications. Jennifer Regala, Michael Casp, and Mike Groth.
Membership. Sharon M. Mattern Büttiker and Beth Craanen.
Task Force. Lisa Janicke Hinchliffe.
TSK Cabinet. Susan Kesner and Simone Taylor.

Publications

Learned Publishing (memb.). Published by the Association of Learned and Professional Society Publishers (ALPSP) in collaboration with SSP. *Ed.* (N.A.) Lette Y. Conrad.
The Scholarly Kitchen (moderated blog). *Ed.* David Crotty.

Meetings

An annual meeting is held in late May/early June.

Society of American Archivists

Executive Director, Jacqualine Price Osafo
17 N. State St., Suite 1425, Chicago, IL 60602
312-606-0722, toll-free 866-722-7858, fax 312-606-0728, e-mail saahq@archivists.org
World Wide Web https://www2.archivists.org
Twitter @archivists_org

Object

Founded in 1936, the Society of American Archivists (SAA) is North America's oldest and largest national archival professional association. Representing more than 6,000 individual and institutional members, SAA promotes the value and diversity of archives and archivists and is the preeminent source of professional resources and the principal communication hub for American archivists.

Membership

Memb. 6,200+. Dues (Indiv.) $80–$325, graduated according to salary; (Assoc.) $115; (Ret.) $77; (Student/Bridge) $55; (Inst.) $340; (Sustaining Inst.) $595.

Officers

Pres. Terry Baxter, Multnomah County Records Program. E-mail president@archivists.org; *V.P./Pres.-Elect* Helen Wong Smith, Hamilton Library, University of Hawaii–Mānoa; *Treas.* Shamila Bhatia, National Archives at College Park.

Leadership

Exec. Dir. Jacqualine Price Osafo; *Dir. of Operations* Cherie Newell; *Dir. of Training & Org. Development* Rana Hutchinson Salzmann; *Asst. Dir. of Publishing* Abigail Christian; *Foundation & Development Mgr.* Astoria Edwards; *Governance Prog. Mgr.* Felicia Owens; *Education Mgr.* Akila Ruffin; *Mgr./Svc. Ctr.* Carlos L. Delgado; *Member Svc./Accounting Specialist* Shavon Lewis; *Marketing & Comm. Specialist* Julia Pillard; *Education & Annual Meeting Specialist* Michael Santiago; *Editorial & Prog. Coord.* Hannah Stryker.

SAA Council

Krystal Appiah, Stephen R. Curley, Joyce Gabiola, Jasmine Jones, Dominique Luster, Derek P. Mosley, Tonia Sutherland. Dr. Lydia Tang,

Rachel E. Winston; Jacqualine Price Osafo (ex officio).

Committee Chairs

American Archivist Editorial Board. Amy Cooper Cary.
Appointments. Tomaro Taylor.
Archival Reparation. Jaime Arsenault and Ricardo Punzalan.
Awards. Megan Keller Young and Jane LaBarbara.
Diversity. Erin Baucom.
Education. Jennifer Wachtel.
Ethics and Professional Conduct. Cliff Hight and Nikki Lynn Thomas.
Finance. Sharmila Bhatia.
Host. Michelle Ganz and Mitch Toda.
Membership. Brittany Newberry.
Nominating. Louis Jones.
Program. María Matienzo and Shannon O'Neill.
Public Awareness. Katherine Barbera.
Public Policy. Krista Ferrante.
Publications Board. Stacie Williams.
Research, Data, and Assessment. Chris Marino and Sarah Pratt Martin.
Selection of SAA Fellows. Meredith Evans.

Standards. Jodi Allison-Bunnell and Kira Dietz.

Task Force and Working Groups Chairs

Archival Compensation Task Force. Dominique Luster (board liaison).
A*CENSUS II Working Group. Position open.
Crisis, Disaster, and Tragedy Response Working Group. Kara McClurken and Vanessa St. Oegger-Menn.
Dictionary Working Group. Rosemary Flynn.
Intellectual Property Working Group. Aprille McKay.

Publications

American Archivist (s. ann.; $289). *Ed.* Amy Cooper Cary. Tel (414) 288-5901, e-mail AmericanArchivist@archivists.org; *Reviews Eds.* Rose Buchanan and Stephanie Luke. Tel. (217) 333-0798, e-mail ReviewsEditor@archivists.org.
Archival Outlook (bi-mo.; memb.).
In the Loop e-newsletter (bi-wk.).

Software and Information Industry Association

Interim President, Christopher Mohr
1620 I Street NW, Suite 501, Washington D.C. 20005
202-289-7442, fax 202-289-7097
World Wide Web https://www.siia.net
Twitter @SIIA

The Software and Information Industry Association (SIIA) was formed January 1, 1999, through the merger of the Software Publishers Association (SPA) and the Information Industry Association (IIA).

Membership

Memb. 800+ companies. Open to companies that develop software and digital information content. For details on membership and dues, see the SIIA website at https://www.siia.net.

Leadership

Interim Pres., Sr. V.P. for Intellectual Property and Gnl. Cnsl. Christopher Mohr. Tel. 202-789-4442. E-mail cmohr@siia.net; *Senior V.P. and Managing Dir., FISD* Tom Davin; *Chief Financial Officer* Carl Walker; *Sr. V.P., Global Public Policy* Paul Lekas.

Special Libraries Association

Managing Director, Monica Evans-Lombe
1660 International Drive, Suite 600, McLean, VA 22102
703-647-4900, fax 703-506-3266, e-mail mevans-lombe@sla.org
World Wide Web https://www.sla.org
Twitter @SLAhq

Mission

The Special Libraries Association (SLA) promotes and strengthens its members through learning, advocacy, and networking initiatives.

Strategic Vision

SLA is a global association of information and knowledge professionals who are employed in every sector of the economy. Its members thrive where data, information, and knowledge intersect, and its strategic partners support SLA because they believe in the association's mission and the future of its members. SLA's goal is to support information professionals as they contribute, in their varied and evolving roles, to the opportunities and achievements of organizations, communities, and society.

Membership

Memb. 9,000+ in 75 countries. Dues (Org.) $750; (Indiv.) $100–$200; (Student/Intl./Salary less than $18,000 income per year) $50; (Ret.) $100.

Officers (2023)

Pres. Seema Rampersad, British Library, London, England. E-mail seemaramper-sad@hotmail.com; *Pres.-Elect* John DiGilio, Sidley Austin, LLP, California. E-mail jdigilio@gmail.com; *Treas.* Eugene Giudice, Dentons US, LLP, Illinois. E-mail eugenegiudice@gmail.com; *Past Pres.* Catherine Lavallée-Welch, Bishop's Univ., Sherbrooke, PQ. E-mail clw@ubishops.ca.

Directors

Anne Barker (*2022–2024*), JonLuc Christensen (*2022–2024*), PK Jain (*2020–2023*), Heather Kotula (*2022–2024*), Kendra Levine (*2022–2024*), James Manasco (*2023–2025*), Jim Miller (*2020–2023*), Christine Pelosi (*2023–2025*), Julie Snyder (*2020–2023; Board Secretary*), Ty Webb (*2022–2023*).

Council, Committee, and Subcommittee Chairs

Annual Conference. Nabi Hasan and Andy Shimp.
Awards and Honors. Tara Grove.
Community Finance. Position open.
Community Support. Christine Geluk.
Content. Nathan Rosen.
Education. Nabi Hasan.
Finance. Eugene Giudice.
Governing Policies, Documents and Bylaws. Julie Snyder.
Innovations Challenge Implementation. Position open.
Leadership Cultivation. Nabi Hasan and Laura Walesby.
Membership. Anne Barker and Jon-Luc Christensen (board liaisons).
Nominating. Leslie Reynolds.
Professional Development. Alison Senkevitch.
Strategy and Culture. John DiGilio.
Students and New Professionals. Laura Walesby.
Technology Support. Christine Geluk.

Theatre Library Association

President, Diana King
c/o New York Public Library for the Performing Arts
40 Lincoln Center Plaza, New York, NY 10023
E-mail theatrelibraryassociation@gmail.com
World Wide Web https://www.tla-online.org
Twitter @theatrelibassn

Objective

To further the interests of collecting, preserving, and using theater, cinema, and performing arts materials in libraries, museums, and private collections. Founded in 1937.

Membership

Memb. 300. Dues (Indiv.) $50; (Student/Nonsalaried) $25; (Inst.) $75; (Sustaining) $150. Year. Jan.–Dec.

Officers

Pres. Diana King, University of California–Los Angeles. E-mail diking@library.ucla.edu; *V.P.* Karin Suni, Free Library of Philadelphia; *Exec. Secy.* Dale Stinchcomb, Houghton Library, Harvard University. E-mail dstinchcomb@fas.harvard.edu; *Treas.* Sophie Glidden-Lyon, La MaMa. E-mail sophie.gliddenlyon@gmail.com; *Past Pres.* (ex officio) Francesca Marini, Texas A&M University. E-mail fmarini@tamu.edu.

Board of Directors

(2021–2023) Kristin Dougan Johnson, Suzanne Lipkin, David Nochimson, Gabriella Steinberg; *(2022–2024)* Stephanie Bonjack, Arianne Hartsell-Gundy, Mary Huelsbeck, Megan Reichelt; *(2023–2025)* Drew Barker, Aravindi Gajanayake, Kylie Goetz.

Committee Chairs

Book Awards. Suzanne Lipkin and Annemarie van Roessel.
Conference Planning. Diana King.
Membership. William Daw.
Nominating. Stephanie Bonjack and Arianne Hartsell-Gundy.
Professional Awards. Drew Barker.
Publications. Mary Huelsbeck.
Strategic Planning. Diana King.
Website Editorial. Eric Colleary and William Daw.

Publications

Broadside Archive (digital back issues).
Performing Arts Resources (occasional) see http://www.tla-online.org/publications/performing-arts-resources/performing-arts-resources-volumes for links to subscription and https://www.proquest.com/products-services/iipa_ft.html for database from ProQuest.

Urban Libraries Council

President and CEO, Brooks Rainwater
1333 H St. N.W., Suite 1000 West, Washington, DC 20005
202-750-8650, e-mail info@urbanlibraries.org
World Wide Web http://www.urbanlibraries.org
Facebook https://www.facebook.com/UrbanLibrariesCouncil
Twitter @UrbanLibCouncil

Objective

Since 1971 the Urban Libraries Council (ULC) has worked to strengthen public libraries as an essential part of urban life. A member organization of North America's leading public library systems, ULC serves as a forum for research widely recognized and used by public- and private-sector leaders. Its members are thought leaders dedicated to leadership, innovation, and the continuous transformation of libraries to meet community needs.

ULC's work focuses on helping public libraries to identify and utilize skills and strategies that match the challenges of the 21st century.

Membership

Membership is open to public libraries and to corporate partners specializing in library-related materials and services. The organization also offers associate memberships. Annual membership dues for libraries are based on the size of a library's operating budget (local + state).

Officers (2022–2023)

Chair Karl Dean; *V.Chair/Chair-Elect* Roosevelt Weeks; *Secy./Treas.* Michelle VonderHaar; *Past Chair* Dr. Mary J. Lomax-Ghirarduzzi; *Memb.-at-Large* Pilar Martinez.

Board Members

Dr. Michele Bria, Joey Crawford, Heidi Daniel, Grace Nordhoff, Skye Patrick, Jesus Salas, Meghann Silverthorn, Rebecca Stavick.

State, Provincial, and Regional Library Associations

The associations in this section are organized under three headings: United States, Canada, and Regional. Both the United States and Canada are represented under Regional associations.

United States

Alabama

Memb. 1,200. Publication. *ALLA COMmunicator* (q.).

Pres. Amanda Melcher, University of Montevallo. Tel. 205-665-6104, e-mail melcheras@montevallo.edu; *Pres.-Elect* Matt Layne, S.C. O'Neal Library & Technology Center, J.F. Drake State Technical College; *Secy.* Danny Stewart, Pell City Public Library; *Treas.* Jessica Hayes, Auburn University at Montgomery; *Memb.-at-Large* (Central Alabama) Emily Allee, Birmingham Public Library. Tel. 205.226.3720, emily.allee@cobpl.org; (North Alabama) Craig Scott, Gadsden Public Library. Tel. 256-549-4699, ext. 2120, e-mail craig@gadsdenlibrary.org; (South Alabama) Wendy Congairdo, Thomas B. Norton Public Lib., 221 W. 19th Ave., Gulf Shores 36542. Tel. 251-968-1176, e-mail wcongiardo@hotmail.com. *Past Pres.* Laura Pitts, Scottsboro Public Library. Tel. 256-574-4335, e-mail laurap@scottsboro.org; *Assn. Admin.* (ex officio) Angela Moore, Alabama Lib. Assn., 6030 Monticello Dr., Montgomery 36117. Tel. 334-414-0113, e-mail alladmin@allanet.org.

Address correspondence to administrator. Alabama Lib. Assn., 6030 Monticello Dr., Montgomery 36117. Tel. 334-414-0113, e-mail allibraryassoc@gmail.com.

World Wide Web https://www.allanet.org.

Alaska

Memb. 450+. Publication. *Newspoke* (q.) (online at http://akla.org/newspoke).

Pres. Jessica Ieremia; *Pres.-Elect* Rachel Nash; *Secy.* Catherine Melville; *Treas.* Samantha Blanquart; *Conference Coords.* Deborah Rinio and Paul Adasiak; *ALA Rep.* Rebecca Moorman; *PNLA Rep.* Sorrel Goodwin; *Past Pres.* Jonas Lamb.

Address correspondence to the secretary. Alaska Lib. Assn., P.O. Box 81084, Fairbanks 99708. E-mail akla@akla.org.

World Wide Web https://akla.org.

Arizona

Memb. 1,000. Term of Office. Nov.–Nov. Publication. *AzLA Newsletter* (6x yearly).

Pres. Lisa Lewis. E-mail president@azla.org; *Pres.-Elect* Casey Van Haren. E-mail president.elect@azla.org; *Secy.* Terry Ann Lawler. E-mail secretary@azla.org; *Treas.* Natalie Menges. E-mail treasurer@azla.org; *Northern Regional Rep.* Pamela Galovich; *Central Regional Rep.* Shelley Reddy; *Southern Regional Rep.* Bob Diaz; *ALA Councilor* Liz Garcia; *MPLA Rep.* Amber Kent; *Past Pres.* John "Jack" Walsh. E-mail past.president@azla.org.

Address correspondence to Arizona 7760 E State Route 69, Suite C5 #385. Prescott Valley, AZ 86314. Tel. 928-288-2011, e-mail admin@azla.org.

World Wide Web https://www.azla.org.

Arkansas

Memb. 600. Publication. *Arkansas Libraries* (4x yearly).

Pres. Carol Coffey, Central Arkansas Library System, Main Library, Little Rock 72201. Tel. 501-918-3008, e-mail president@arlib.org; *Pres.-Elect* Taylor Vanlandingham, John Brown University, 2000 W. University St., Siloam Springs 72761. Tel. 479-524-1527, e-mail president-elect@arlib.org; *Secy.* Jessica Riedmueller, University of Central Arkansas, 201 Donaghey Avenue, Conway 72035. Tel. 501-450-5233, e-mail secretary@arlib.org; *Treas.* Kathleen Ashmore, Lonoke County Library System, 909 West Main St., Cabot 72023. Tel. 406-480-6249, e-mail info@arlib.org; *ALA Councilor* Crystal Gates, North Little Rock Public Library System, 2801 Orange Street, North Little Rock 72114. Tel. 501-404-2919, e-mail crystal.gates@lamanlibrary.org; *SELA State Rep.* J.P. Myrick, East Central Arkansas Regional Library, 410 Merriman Avenue, East Wynne 72396. Tel. 870-587-0587, e-mail jpaul@ecarls.org; *Past Pres.* Rachel Shankles, 891 Hwy 7, Bismarck 71929. Tel. 501-276-4949, e-mail past-president@arlib.org; *Members-at Large* John McGraw, Faulkner County Library System, 1900 Tyler Street, Conway 72032. Tel. 501-450-4983, e-mail johnam cgraw@gmail.com; Jessica Kirk, Arkansas State Library, 900 West Capitol Ave., Suite 100, Little Rock 72201. E-mail j.kirk_arla@pm.me; Jennifer Wann, Arkansas State Library, 900 West Capitol Ave., Suite 100, Little Rock 72201; Tel. 501-682-5288, e-mail jennwann@outlook.com; Simone Kirk, Star City Library, 200 E. Wiley St., Star City 71667. E-mail starcitylibrary@gmail.com; *Non-Voting: Parlaimentarian* Amber Wilson. E-mail amberc@uca.edu.

Address correspondence to Arkansas Lib. Assn., P.O. Box 3821, Little Rock 72203. Tel. 406-480-6249, e-mail info@arlib.org.

World Wide Web https://arlib.org.

California

Memb. 2,500.

Pres. Gary Shaffer, Glendale Library Arts & Culture District. E-mail gshaffer@glendaleca.gov; *V.P./Pres.-Elect* Shawn M. Thrasher, Ontario City Library. E-mail sthrasher@ontarioca.gov; *Treas.* Nichole Brown, Oakland Public Library. E-mail treasurer@cla-net.org; *Secy.* Genesis Hansen, City of Mission Viejo. E-mail ghansen@cityofmissionviejo.org *Past Pres.* Jené Brown, Los Angeles Public Library. E-mail jbrown@lapl.org.

Address correspondence to California Lib. Assn., 1055 E. Colorado Blvd., 5th Floor, Pasadena 91106. Tel. 626-204-4071, e-mail info@cla-net.org.

World Wide Web https://www.cla-net.org.

Colorado

Pres. Tiah Frankish, Adams 12 Five Star Schools. E-mail tfrankish@gmail.com; *Pres.-Elect* Jenn Cook, Garfield County Public Library District. E-mail jcook@gcpld.org; *Secy.* Sandy Hancock, Pikes Peak Library District. E-mail shancock@ppld.org; *Treas.* Nanette Fisher, Anythink Libs. E-mail nfisher@

anythinklibraries.org; *Membs.-at-Large* Christine Dyar, Arapahoe Libraries. E-mail cdyar@ald.lib.co.us; Sarah Hulsey, Summit County Library, Main Library. E-mail sarah.hulsey@summitcountyco.gov. *Past Pres.* Ryan F. Buller, Univ. of Denver. E-mail ryan.buller@du.edu.

Address correspondence to Colorado Assn. of Libs., P.O. Box 740905, Arvada 80006-0905. Tel. 303-463-6400, e-mail cal@cal-webs.org.

World Wide Web https://cal-webs.org.

Connecticut

Memb. 1,000+. Term of Office. July–June. Publication. *CLA Today* (6x yearly; online). E-mail editor@ctlibrarians.org.

Pres. Douglas C. Lord. E-mail dlord@chboothlibrary.org; *V.P./Pres.-Elect* Sarah McCusker. E-mail smccusker@townofcantonct.org; *Recording Secy.* Danielle Duffy Valenzano, Milford Public Lib. E-mail dvalenzano@milfordct.gov; *Treas.* Margaret Khan. E-mail mkhan@coventryct.org; *Past Pres.* Colleen Balie. E-mail cbailie@westhavenlibrary.

Address correspondence to Connecticut Lib. Assn., 55 North Main St., Unit 49, Belchertown 01007. Tel. 860-346-2444, e-mail mscheier@ctlibraryassociation.org.

World Wide Web https://ctlibraryassociation .org.

Delaware

Memb. 200+. Publication. *DLA Bulletin* (q.; online). E-mail Nicole.Ballance@lib.de.us.

Pres. Rachel Culver, Georgetown Public Library, 123 West Pine Street, Georgetown 19947. Tel. 302-856-7958, e-mail rachel.jackson@lib.de.us; *V.P./Conference Chair* Anne Hiller-Clark, Delaware Division of Libraries. Tel. 302-257-3018, email anne.hillerclark@delaware.gov; *Secy.* Katherine Goff, Delaware Technical Community College, Terry Campus. E-mail kgoff1@dtcc.edu; *Treas.* Jaclyn Hale, Delaware Division of Libraries, 121 Martin Luther King Jr. Blvd. N., Dover 19901. Tel. 302-257-3004, e-mail jaclynhaledla@gmail.com; *ALA Councilor* Tameca Beckett, Delaware State University, William C. Jason Library Reference and Access Services Librarian, 1200 N. DuPont Highway, Dover 19901. Tel. 302-857-7886, e-mail tbeckett@desu.edu; *Delaware State Libn.* Annie Norman, Delaware Div. of Libs., 121 Martin Luther King Jr. Blvd.

N., Dover 19901. Tel. 302-257-3001, fax 302-739-6787, e-mail annie.norman@state.de.us; *Pres., Friends of Delaware Libs.* Kay Bowes. E-mail kaybowes@gmail.com; *Past Pres.* Jen Wilson, New Castle Public Library. Tel. 302-328-1995, e-mail jennifer.wilson@lib.de.us.

Address correspondence to Delaware Lib. Assn., c/o Delaware Division of Libs., 121 Martin Luther King Jr. Blvd. N., Dover 19901. E-mail dla@lib.de.us.

World Wide Web https://dla.lib.de.us.

District of Columbia

Memb. 300+. Term of Office. July–June.
Pres. Milea Pickett. E-mail president@dcla.org; *V.P.* Angela Falkenberg. E-mail vice_presi dent@dcla.org; *Secy.* Leah Richardson. E-mail secretary@dcla.org; *Treas.* Kevin Washburn. E-mail treasurer@dcla.org; *ALA Councilor* KC Boyd. E-mail ala_councilor@dcla.org; *Past Pres.* Tracy Sumler. E-mail past_president@ dcla.org.

Address correspondence to DC Library Association, Unit 1653, Washington, DC 20013.

World Wide Web https://dcla.org.

Florida

Memb. (Indiv.) 1,000+. Publication. *Florida Libraries* (s. ann.).
Pres. Shane Roopnarine, University of Central Florida; *V.P./Pres.-Elect* Douglas Crane, Palm Beach County Library System; *Secy.* Marina Morgan, Roux Library, Florida Southern College; *Treas.* Nancy Fredricks, Pasco County Library System; *Past Pres.* Phyllis Gorshe, Dunedin Public Library; *State Libn.* Amy Johnson, Division of Lib. and Info. Svcs. E-mail Amy.Johnson@dos.myflorida.com; *ALA Councilor* Heather Sostrom, SJC-BOCC Branch Manager, Anastasia Island Branch.

Address correspondence to the executive director. Florida Lib. Assn., 545 E. Tennessee St., #103, Tallahassee 32308. Tel. 850-270-9205, e-mail admin@flalib.org.

World Wide Web https://www.flalib.org.

Georgia

Memb. 800+. Publication. *Georgia Library Quarterly* (q., online).
Pres. Rebecca Ballard, Athens Regional Library System. E-mail president@georgiali

braryassociation.org; *1st V.P./Pres.-Elect* John Mack Freeman, Georgia Institute of Technology. E-mail vicepresident@georgialibraryas sociation.org; *2nd V.P./Membership* Richard Coleman, West Georgia Regional Library System. E-mail membership@georgialibraryasso ciation.org; *2nd V.P. Marketing and Branding* Deborah Hakes, Georgia Public Library Service. E-mail marketing@georgialibraryasso ciation.org; *Secy.* Betty Wright, Fulton County Library System. E-mail secretary@georgiali braryassociation.org; *Treas.* Justin Nobles, West Georgia Regional Library System. E-mail treasurer@georgialibraryassociation.org. *Past Pres.* Karen Manning, Georgia Institute of Technology. E-mail pastpresident@georgiali braryassociation.org.

Address correspondence to Georgia Lib. Assn., 1502 W Broadway, Suite 102, Madison, WI 53713. Tel. 912-376-9155, e-mail member services@georgialibraryassociation.org.

World Wide Web https://gla.georgialibraries .org.

Hawaii

Memb. 250. Publication. *KoleKole* (3x yearly).
Pres. Carina Chernisky, James & Abigail Campbell Library, University of Hawaii–West Oahu; *V.P.* Sunyeen "Sunny" Pai, Lama Library, Kapi'olani Community College; *Secy.* Stephanie Robertson, Joseph F. Smith Library, Brigham Young University–Hawaii; *Treas.* Joy Oehlers, Lama Library, Kapi'olani Community College; *Past Pres.* Joy Jenny Silbiger, State Law Librarian & Access to Justice.

Address correspondence to Hawai'i Lib. Assn., P.O. Box 4441, Honolulu 96812-4441. E-mail hawaii.library.association@gmail.com.

World Wide Web https://www.hawaiili braryassociation.org.

Idaho

Memb. 420. Term of Office. Oct.–Oct.
President Lance McGrath, College of Idaho, Caldwell. E-mail idaholibrariespresident@ gmail.com; *V.P.* Mary DeWalt, Ada Community Library, Boise. E-mail idaholibrariesvicepresi dent@gmail.com; *Secy.* Jennifer Hills, Twin Falls Public Library, Twin Falls. E-mail idaho librariessecretary@gmail.com; *Treas.* Shelly Garland, Caldwell Public Library, Caldwell. E-mail idaholibrariestreasurer@gmail.com;

Membership Engagement Chair Ross Sempek, College of Southern Idaho, Twin Falls. E-mail idaholibrariesmemberchair@gmail.com. Address correspondence to Idaho Lib. Assn., 3046 W. Tubac Drive, Meridian 83646. World Wide Web https://idaholibraries. wildapricot.org.

Illinois

Memb. 3,000. Publication. *ILA Reporter* (bi-mo.; online).

Pres. Heather Jagman, DePaul University Library; *V.P./Pres.-Elect* Ryan Johnson, O'Fallon Public Library; *Treas.* Julie M. Milavec, Downers Grove Public Library; *ALA Councilor* Paul Mills, Fountaindale Public Library District; *Past Pres.* Jeanne Hamilton, Bloomington Public Library.

Address correspondence to the executive director. Illinois Lib. Assn., 33 W. Grand Ave., Suite 401, Chicago 60654-6799. Tel. 312 644-1896, fax 312 644-1899, e-mail ila@ila.org. World Wide Web https://www.ila.org.

Indiana

Indiana Lib. Federation. Memb. 2,000+. Publication. *Focus on Indiana Libraries* (mo.; memb.).

Pres. Christopher Proctor. Indiana University Southeast. E-mail president@ilfonline. org; *V.P.* Diane Rogers, Ben Davis 9th Grade Center; *Secy.* Cheryl Blevens, Indiana State University; *Treas.* Lynn Hobbs, Pendleton Community Public Library; *Asst. Treas.* Trista Smith, Newburgh Chandler Public Library; *ALA Councilor* Jos N. Holman, Tippecanoe County Public Library, 627 South St., Lafayette 47901; *Past Pres.* Michael Williams, Indianapolis Public Library, 40 E. Saint Clair St., Indianapolis 46204. Tel. 317-275-4302; *Exec. Dir.* Lane Valeyo. Tel. 317-257-2040, ext. 101, e-mail exec@ilfonline.org.

Address correspondence to Indiana Lib. Federation, 6510 Telecom Drive, Suite 200, Indianapolis 46278. Tel. 317-257-2040, fax 317-257-1389, e-mail askus@ilfonline.org. World Wide Web https://www.ilfonline.org.

Iowa

Memb. 1,600+. Publication. *Catalyst* (bi-mo., online).

Pres. Sam Helmick, Iowa City Public Library; *V.P.* Julie Finch, Iowa City Public Library; *Secy.* Eric Jennings, University of Northern Iowa; *Treas.* Megan Klein-Hewett, Ames Public Library; *Parliamentarian* Tyler Hahn, Cherokee Public Library; *ALA Councilor* Amanda Vazquez, Dubuque County Library; *Past Pres.* Sarah Uthoff, Kirkwood Community College.

Address correspondence to Iowa Lib. Assn., 6919 Vista Dr., West Des Moines 50266. Tel. 515-282-8192.

World Wide Web https://www.iowalibrary association.org.

Kansas

Kansas Lib. Assn. Memb. 1,500. Term of Office. July–June. Publication. *Kansas Libraries!* (6x yearly; online). E-mail kilbmag@gmail. com.

Pres. Shanna Smith-Ritterhouse; *1st V.P.* Sean Bird; *2nd V.P.* Melany Wilks; *Secy.* Sean Stacey; *Treas.* Terri Wojtalewicz, Lancing Community Library; *Exec. Secy.* Dawn Krause; *Parliamentarian* Dan Ireton; *ALA Councilor* Heather Van Dyne, Allen Community College; *Past Pres.* Holly Mercer, Southwest Kansas Lib. System.

Address correspondence to the president. Kansas Lib. Assn., P.O. Box 463, Manhattan 66505. Tel. 785-370-3544.

World Wide Web https://kslibassoc.org.

Kentucky

Memb. 1,600. Publication. *Kentucky Libraries Journal* (q.).

Pres. Mark Adler; *Pres.-Elect* Adele Koch; *Secy.* Andrew Adler; *Past Pres.* Kandace Rodgers.

Address correspondence to the president. Andrew Adler. 1588 Leestown Rd., Suite 130-310, Lexington 40511. Tel. 502-863-8405. info@kla.memberclicks.net.

World Wide Web https://www.klaonline.org.

Louisiana

Memb. 1,000+. Term of Office. July–June. Publication. *Louisiana Libraries* (q.).

Pres. Lora Amsberryaugier. E-mail lamsberr@uno.edu; *1st V.P.* Kenya Iverson. E-mail kenya.iverson@lsuhs.edu; *2nd V.P.* Trina Kirk. E-mail tmkirk@rpl.org; *Secy.* Kayla Kalnasy.

E-mail llakalnasy@gmail.com; Treas. Giovanni Tairov. E-mail gtairov@gmail.com; ALA Councilor Vivian McCain. Tel. 318-513-5508, e-mail straitviv@gmail.com; Parliamentarian Chris Achee. E-mail cachee@myapl.org; Past Pres. Jeremy Bolom. E-mail llabolom@gmail.com.

Address correspondence to Louisiana Lib. Assn., 1190 Meramec Station Rd., Suite 207, Ballwin, MO 63021. Tel 800-969-6562, ext. 3, fax 972-991-6061, e-mail lla@amigos.org. World Wide Web https://llaonline.org.

Maine

Maine Lib. Assn. Memb. 950. Publication. MLA to Z (q., online).

Pres. Wynter Giddings, Curtis Memorial Lib., 23 Pleasant St., Brunswick 04011. Tel. 207-725-3542, e-mail giddingswynter@gmail.com; V.P. Sonya Durney. E-mail vicepresident@mainelibraries.org; Secy. Anna Faherty, USM Lewiston-Auburn College. Tel. 207-753-6545, e-mail secretary@mainelibraries.org; Treas. Amy Wisehart, Ellsworth Public Lib., 20 State Street, Ellsworth, 04605. E-mail awisehart@ellsworthlibrary.net; Past Pres. Jennifer Alvino, Windham Public Lib., 217 Windham Center Rd., Windham 04062. Tel. 207-892-1908, e-mail jaalvino@windhammaine.us; Membs.-at-Large Meg Gray, Bangor Public Library. Tel. 207-947-8336, ext. 129; Kate Wing, George J. Mitchell Department of Special Collections & Archives, Bowdoin College and Curtis Memorial Library, Brunswick. E-mail katemwing@gmail.com; ALA Councilor Kara Reiman, Maine State Lib., 64 State House Station, Augusta, 04333. Tel. 207-287-5660, e-mail kara.reiman@maine.gov; NELA Rep. Michelle Sampson, York Public Lib., 15 Long Sands Rd., York 03909. Tel. 207-363-2818, e-mail msampson@york.lib.me.us.

Address correspondence to Maine Lib. Assn., 55 Main St., Unit 49, Belchertown, MA 01007. Tel. 207-744-7919. E-mail mainelibrary@gmail.com.

World Wide Web https://www.mainelibraries.org.

Maryland

Maryland Lib. Assn. Memb. 1,000+. Term of Office. July–July. Publication. The Crab (q., memb., online).

Pres. Nay Keppler, Howard County Library System, Charles E. Miller Branch, 9421 Frederick Rd., Ellicott City 21042. Tel. 410-313-1950, e-mail nay.keppler@hclibrary.org; V.P./ Pres.-Elect Kenneth Wayne Thompson, Charles County Public Library, 2 Garrett Ave., La Plata 20646. Tel. 301-943-9001, e-mail kthompson@ccplonline.org; Secy. Conni Strittmatter, Baltimore County Public Library, 6105 Kenwood Avenue, Rosedale 21237. Tel. 410-887-6047, e-mail cstrittmatter@bcpl.net; Treas. Carl Olson, Towson Univ., Cook Lib., 8000 York Rd., Towson 21252. Tel. 410-704-3267, e-mail colson@towson.edu; ALA Councilor David Dahl, Univ. of Maryland. Tel. 301-314-0395, e-mail ddahl1@umd.edu; Conference Dir. Kelsey Hughes, Howard County Library System, Savage Branch, 9525 Durness Ln., Laurel 20723. Tel. 410-313-0760, e-mail kelsey.hughes@pgcmls.info; Past Pres. Mary Anne Bowman, St. Mary's County Public Lib., 23250 Hollywood Rd., Leonardtown 20650. Tel. 301-475-2846, ext. 1015, fax 410-884-4415, e-mail mabowman@stmalib.org; Exec. Dir. Joshua Stone, Maryland Lib. Assn., 1401 Hollins St., Baltimore 21223. Tel. 410-947-5090, e-mail jstone@mdlib.org.

Address correspondence to Maryland Lib. Assn., 1401 Hollins St., Baltimore 21223. Tel. 410-947-5090, fax 410-947-5089, e-mail mla@mdlib.org.

World Wide Web https://www.mdlib.org.

Massachusetts

Massachusetts Lib. Assn. Memb. (Indiv.) 1,000; (Inst.) 100.

Pres. Kim Hewitt, Waltham Public Library. E-mail president@masslib.org; V.P. Michelle Filleul, Reading Public Library. E-mail vice-president@masslib.org; Secy. Tina McAndrew, Randall Library, Stow 01775. Tel. 978-640-4490, e-mail secretary@masslib.org; Treas. Bernadette Rivard, Bellingham Public Lib., Bellingham. E-mail treasurer@masslib.org; Past Pres. Joanne Lamothe, Sandwich Public Lib. E-mail pastpresident@masslib.org.

Address correspondence to Massachusetts Lib. Assn., P.O. Box 901, Bellingham 02019. Tel. 781-698-7764, e-mail manager@masslib.org.

World Wide Web https://mla.wildapricot.org.

Michigan

Memb. 1,200+.
Pres. Scott Duimstra, Capital Area District Libraries; *Secy./Treas.* Kristin Shelley, East Lansing Public Library; *State Librarian* Randy Riley, Library of Michigan; *Past Pres.* Erica Trowbridge, Michigan Association of School Librarians (MASL); *ALA Councilor* Tashia Miller, University of Michigan; *Exec. Dir.* Deborah E. Mikula, Michigan Lib. Association. Tel. 517-394-2774, ext. 224, e-mail dmikula@milibraries.org.

Address correspondence to the executive director. Michigan Lib. Assn., 3410 Belle Chase Way, Suite 100, Lansing 48911. Tel. 517-394-2774, e-mail MLA@milibraries.org.

World Wide Web https://www.milibraries.org.

Minnesota

Memb. 1,100. Term of Office. (*Pres., Pres.-Elect*) Jan.–Dec. Publication. *Roundup* (mo., online).

Pres. Julia Carlis, Washington County Library; *Pres.-Elect* Jodi Grebinoski, Virginia Public Library; *Secy.* Leticia Snow, St. Peter Public Library; *Treas.* Karen Pundsack, Great River Regional Library; *Past Pres.* Steve Harsin, Southeastern Libraries Cooperating; *Memb.-at-Large* Belle Nelson, Minnesota State University–Mankato; *ALA Chapter Councilor* Hannah Buckland, Minnesota Dept. of Education; *Exec. Dir.* Joy DesMarais-Lanz. E-mail office@mnlibraryassociation.org.

Address correspondence to the executive director. 1611 County Road B West, Suite 315, Saint Paul 55113. Tel. 612-294-6549, e-mail office@mnlibraryassociation.org.

World Wide Web https://www.mnlibraryassociation.org.

Mississippi

Memb. 625. Term of Office. Jan.–Dec. Publication. *Mississippi Libraries* (q.).

Pres. Stephen Parks, State Law Lib. of Mississippi. Tel. 601-359-3612; *V.P.* Philip Carter, Starkville-Oktibbeha Public Library System. Tel. 662-323-2766, ext. 7; *Secy.* Ryda Worthy, South Mississippi Regional Library. Tel. 601-736-5516; *Treas.* Audrey Beach, Mississippi Delta Community College. Tel. 662-246-6353;

Parliamentarian Patsy C. Brewer, Waynesboro-Wayne County Library. Tel. 601-735-2268; *ALA Councilor* Amanda Clay Powers, Fant Memorial Library. Tel. 662-329-7332; *Past Pres.* Mara Polk, Central Mississippi Regional Lib. System. Tel. 601-825-0100; *Admin.* Paula Bass, P.O. Box 13687, Jackson 39236-3687. Tel. 601-981-4586, e-mail info@misslib.org.

Address correspondence to the administrator. Mississippi Lib. Assn., P.O. Box 13687, Jackson 39236-3687. Tel. 601-981-4586, e-mail info@misslib.org.

World Wide Web https://mla42.wildapricot.org.

Missouri

Memb. 800+. Term of Office. Jan.–Dec. Publication. *MO INFO* (bi-mo.).

Pres. Otter Bowman, Daniel Boone Regional Library. E-mail mlapresident@molib.org; *Pres.-Elect* Kimberly Moeller, University of Missouri–Columbia; *Secy.* Tiffany Davis, St. Louis Public Library; *Treas.* Jason Phinney, Windsor Branch, Jefferson County Library; *Asst. Treas.* Andrea Johnson, St. Louis County Library; *Memb. Comm. Chair* Christina Pryor, University of Missouri–Columbia; *Membs.-at-Large* Rachelle Brandel, Missouri Baptist University; Dawn Mackey, Kansas City Public Lib.; *ALA Councilor* Margaret Conroy, Daniel Boone Regional Lib.; *Past Pres.* Claudia Young, Missouri River Regional Lib.

Address correspondence to the president. Missouri Lib. Assn., 1190 Meramec Station Rd., Suite 207, Ballwin, 63021-6902. E-mail mlapresident@molib.org.

World Wide Web http://molib.org.

Montana

Memb. 600. Term of Office. July–June. Publication. *Focus* (bi-mo.).

Pres. Angela Archuleta, KW-Vina Elementary School; *Secy./Treas./Pres.-Elect* Kelly Reisig, Sidney-Richland County Public Library; *ALA Rep.* Matt Beckstrom, Lewis & Clark Lib., 120 S. Last Chance Gulch, Helena 59601; *Past Pres.* Kit Stephenson, Bozeman Public Lib.; *Exec. Dir.* Kirk Vriesman, Montana Lib. Assn., P.O. Box 823, Arlee, MT 59821. Tel. 406-579-3121, e-mail kirkv@mtlib.org.

Address correspondence to the executive director. Montana Lib. Assn, P.O. Box 823,

Arlee, MT 59821. Tel. 406-579-3121. E-mail kirkv@mtlib.org.

World Wide Web https://mlai.wildapricot.org.

Nebraska

Term of Office. Jan.–Dec.

Pres. Holli Duggan. E-mail nlapresident@nebraskalibraries.org; *Pres.-Elect* Tammi Thiem. E-mail nlapresidentelect@nebraska libraries.org; *Secy.* Kelly Warehime. E-mail nlasecretary@nebraskalibraries.org; *Treas.* Anneka Ramirez. E-mail nlatreasurer@nebras kalibraries.org; *ALA Councilor* Brenda Ealey. E-mail nla-ala@nebraskalibraries.org; *Past Pres.* Emily Nimsakont. E-mail nlapastpresi dent@nebraskalibraries.org; *Exec. Dir.* Ginger Jelinek. E-mail nlaexecutivedirector@nebras kalibraries.org.

Address correspondence to the executive director. Nebraska Lib. Assn., P.O. Box 21756, Lincoln 68542-1756.

World Wide Web https://nebraskalibraries.or/.

Nevada

Memb. 450. Term of Office. Jan.–Dec. Publication. *Nevada Libraries* (q.).

Pres. Tammy Westergard, State of Nevada. E-mail tammywestergard@yahoo.com; *Pres.-Elect* Position open; *Exec. Secy.* Carla Land, Las Vegas–Clark County Lib. District. E-mail bookdiva@gmail.com; *Treas.* Dana Friesen. E-mail danasfriesen@gmail.com; *Finance* Morgan Tiar, Washoe County Lib. System. E-mail matiar@washoecounty.us; *State Libn.* Mike Strom, Nevada State Lib. Administrator. E-mail mstrom@admin.nv.gov; *ALA Delegate* Amy Geddes, Lyon County Lib. District. E-mail ageddes@lyon-county.org; *Past Pres.* Marcie Smedley, Henderson Libraries. E-mail mlsmedley@hendersonlibraries.com.

Address correspondence to the executive secretary.

World Wide Web https://nevadalibraries.org.

New Hampshire

Memb. 600+.

Pres. Mindy Atwood, Abbott Library, 11 Soonipi Circle/P.O. Box 314, Sunapee 03782. Tel. 603-763-5513; e-mail director@abbot

tlibrary.org; *V.P.* Deb Hoadley; *Secy.* Corinne Chronopoulos; *Treas.* Jessica Delangie. E-mail treasurer@nhlibrarians.org; *ALA Councilor* Amy Lappin; *Past Pres.* Denise M. van Zanten, Manchester City Lib., 405 Pine Street, Manchester 03104. Tel. 603-624-6550, ext. 3329, e-mail dvanzant@manchesternh.gov.

Address correspondence to New Hampshire Lib. Assn., c/o New Hampshire State Lib., 20 Park St., Concord 03301-6314. E-mail nhlaex ecutive@googlegroups.com.

World Wide Web https://nhlibrarians.org.

New Jersey

Memb. 1,800. Term of Office. July–June. Publication. *New Jersey Libraries NEWSletter* (q.). E-mail newsletter_editor@njlamembers.org.

Pres. Jessica Trujillo, Montclair Public Library. E-mail jbmtrujillo@gmail.com; *1st V.P./Pres.-Elect* Carina Gonzalez, Piscataway Public Library. E-mail librariancarina@gmail.com; *2nd V.P.* Allen McGinley, Westfield Memorial Library. E-mail allen.mcginley@gmail.com; *Secy.* Heather Dalal, Rider University. E-mail hdalal@rider.edu; *Treas.* Allan Kleiman, Edison Public Library. E-mail akleiman@edi sonpubliclibrary.org; *ALA Councilor* Laverne Mann, Cherry Hill Public Library. E-mail lmann@chplnj.org; *Past Pres.* Kate Jaggers, Highland Park Public Lib. E-mail librari ankatej@gmail.com; *Exec. Dir.* Brett Bonfield. E-mail njladirector@njla.org.

Address correspondence to New Jersey Lib. Assn., 163 US Hwy 130 N., Bldg. 1, Suite 1C, Bordentown 08505. Tel. 609-482-1282, fax 609-379-6278, e-mail njladirector@njla.org.

World Wide Web https://www.njla.org.

New Mexico

Memb. 550. Term of Office. Apr.–Apr. Publication. *NMLA Newsletter* (bi-mo., online). E-mail newsletter@nmla.org.

Pres. Kate Alderete. E-mail president@nmla.org; *V.P./Pres.-Elect* Ruben Aragón. E-mail vicepresident@nmla.org; *Secy.* Sarah Obenauf. E-mail secretary@nmla.org; *Treas.* Kelli Murphy. E-mail treasurer@nmla.org; *Membs.-at-Large* Julia Kelso. E-mail library director@vglibrary.org; Cassandra Osterloh. E-mail cassandra.osterloh@state.nm.us; Ellen Bosman. E-mail ebosman@nmsu.edu; Anne Lefkosfsky. E-mail alefkofsky@cabq.gov;

ALA-APA Councilor Nadia M Orozco-Sahi. E-mail alacouncilor@nmla.org.

Address correspondence to New Mexico Lib. Assn., P.O. Box 26074, Albuquerque 87125. Tel. 505-400-7309, e-mail contact@nmla.org. World Wide Web https://nmla.org.

New York

Memb. 4,000. Term of Office. Nov.–Nov. Publication. *The ebulletin* (6x yearly, online). *Pres.* Arlene LaVerde, Townsend Harris High School; *Pres.-Elect* Lisa Kropp, Lindenhurst Memorial Library; *Treas.* Kelly Harris, John Jermain Memorial Library; *Treas.-Elect* Frank McKenna, Seaford Public Library; *ALA Chapter Councilor* Keturah Cappadonia, Southern Tier Library System; *Past Pres.* Beth Merkle, The Strong Museum of Play; *Exec. Dir.* AnnaLee Dragon, New York Lib. Assn., 6021 State Farm Rd., Guilderland 12084. Tel. 518-432-6952, fax 518-427-1697, e-mail director@nyla.org.

Address correspondence to New York Lib. Assn., 6021 State Farm Rd., Guilderland 12084. Tel. 518-432-6952, fax 518-427-1697, e-mail info@nyla.org.

World Wide Web https://www.nyla.or.

North Carolina

Memb. 1,100. Term of Office. Oct.–Oct. Publication. *North Carolina Libraries* (1–2x yearly, online).

Pres. Libby Stone. E-mail president@ncla online.org; *V.P./Pres.-Elect* Dawn Behrend. E-mail vicepresident@nclaonline.org; *Secy.* Jenneffer Sixkiller. E-mail secretary@nclaon line.org; *Treas.* Lara Luck. E-mail treasurer@ nclaonline.org; *Treas.-Elect* Kate Engelbrecht. E-mail treasurer.elect@nclaonline.org; *ALA Councilor* Siobhan Loendorf. E-mail sloen dorf@catawbacountync.gov; *Past Pres.* Lorrie Russell. E-mail pastpresident@nclaonline.org.

Address correspondence to North Carolina Lib. Assn., 265 Eastchester Dr., Suite 133, #364, High Point 27262. E-mail nclaonline@ gmail.com.

World Wide Web https://nclaonline.org.

North Dakota

Memb. (Indiv.) 300+. Term of Office. Sept.–Sept. Publication. *The Good Stuff* (q.). *Ed.*

Shannon Yarbrough. E-mail shannon.yar brough@und.edu.

Pres. Kerrianne Boetcher, Ward County Public Library. E-mail kerrianne.boetcher@ co.ward.nd.us; *Pres.-Elect* Tammy Kruger, State Library. E-mail tkruger@nd.gov. *Secy.* Tonya Palmer, Grand Forks Public Library. E-mail tonya.palmer@gflibrary.com; *Treas.* Aaron Stefanich, Grand Forks Public Library. E-mail aaron.stefanich@gflibrary.com; *Past Pres.* Will Martin, Chester Fritz Library, University of North Dakota. E-mail william.d.martin@und.edu; *ALA Councilor* Sara Westall, School of Medicine and Health Sciences, University of North Dakota. E-mail sara.westall@und.edu; *State Libn.* Mary J. Soucie, North Dakota State Lib. E-mail msou cie@nd.gov.

Address correspondence to the president. North Dakota Lib. Assn., 604 E. Boulevard Ave., Bismarck 58505.

World Wide Web https://ndla.info.

Ohio

Memb. 2,700+. Term of Office. Jan.–Dec. Publication. *OLC News* (online).

Chair Laura Lee Wilson, Huron County Community Library. Tel. 419-933-2544; *V. Chair/Chair-Elect* Sarah Clevidence, Findlay-Hancock County Public Library. Tel. 419-434-1474; *Secy./Treas.* Mary Ellen Icaza, Stark County District Library. Tel. 330-458-2700; *Immediate Past Chair* Tom Dillie, Minerva Public Lib. Tel. 330-868-4101; *ALA Councilor*, Nick Tepe, Athens County Public Libraries. Tel. 740-737-6003; *Exec. Dir.* Michelle Francis. Tel. 614-410-8092, ext. 105, e-mail mfran cis@olc.org.

Address correspondence to the executive director. Ohio Lib. Council, 495 Metro Place South, Suite 350, Dublin 43017. Tel. 614-410-8092.

World Wide Web https://olc.org.

Oklahoma

Memb. 500–600. Term of Office. July–June.

Pres. Tim Miller. E-mail president@oklibs. org; *V.P./Pres.-Elect* Dana Belcher. E-mail president-elect@oklibs.org; *Secy.* Bailee Hutchinson. E-mail secretary@oklibs.org; *Treas.* Michael Hull. E-mail treasurer@oklibs. org; *ALA Councilor* Kelly Sitzman. E-mail ala_councilor@oklibs.org; *Past Pres.* Cherity Pennington. E-mail finance@oklibs.org. Address correspondence to Oklahoma Lib. Assn., 1190 Meramec Station Rd., Suite 207, Ballwin, MO 63021-6902. Tel. 800-969-6562, ext. 5, fax 636-529-1396, e-mail ola@amigos. org. World Wide Web https://www.oklibs.org.

Oregon

Memb. (Indiv.) 1,000+. Publications. *OLA Hotline.* (bi-w.). E-mail olahotline@olaweb.org; *OLA Quarterly* (q.). *Pres.* Star Khan, Driftwood Public Library. E-mail olapresident@olaweb.org; *V.P./ Pres.-Elect* Brittany Young, Lane County Law Library. E-mail olavp@olaweb.org; *Secy.* Adrienne Doman Calkins, Sherwood Public Library. E-mail olasecretary@olaweb.org. *Treas.* Stuart Levy, Parkrose High School. E-mail olatreasurer@olaweb.org; *Memb.-at-Large* Ericka Brunson-Rochette, Deschutes Public Library. E-mail erickab@dpls.lib. or.us; *ALA Rep.* Kirsten Brodbeck-Kenney, Driftwood Public Library. E-mail olachaptercouncilor@olaweb.org; *Past Pres.* Arlene Weible, State Lib. of Oregon. E-mail olapastpresident@olaweb.org. Address correspondence to Oregon Lib. Assn., P.O. Box 3067, La Grande 97850. Tel. 541-962-5824, e-mail ola@olaweb.org. World Wide Web https://www.olaweb.org.

Pennsylvania

Memb. 1,900+. Term of Office. Jan.–Dec. Publication. *PaLA Bulletin* (q.). *Pres.* Melissa Rowse; *1st V.P.* Melissa Rowse; *2nd V.P. (Kalahari Conference)* Rose Chiocchi; *2nd V.P. (Harrisburg Conference)* Carolyn Blatchley; *3rd V.P. (Membership Chair)* Dana Barber; *Treas.* Kate Cummings; *ALA Councilor* Robbin Degeratu; *Past Pres.* Jen Knisely; *Exec. Dir.* Christi Buker. Pennsylvania Lib. Assn., 220 Cumberland Pkwy., Suite 10, Mechanicsburg 17055. Tel. 717-766-7663, e-mail christi@palibraries.org. Address correspondence to the executive director. Pennsylvania Lib. Assn., 220 Cumberland Parkway, Suite 10, Mechanicsburg 17055. Tel. 717-766-7663, fax 717-766-5440. World Wide Web https://www.palibraries. org.

Rhode Island

Memb. (Indiv.) 350+; (Inst.) 50+. Term of Office. June–June. Publication. *RILA Bulletin* (6x yearly). *Pres.* Beatrice Pulliam, Providence Public Library. Tel. 401-455-8101, e-mail president@rilibraries.org; *V.P.* position open; *Secy.* Celeste Dyer, Cumberland Public Lib. Tel. 401-333-2552, e-mail secretary@rilibraries. org; *Treas.* Sam Simas, Providence Public Library. Tel. 401-455-8101, e-mail treasurer@rilibraries.org; *Membs.-at-Large* Megan Hamlin-Black, Rhode Island State Libn. Tel. 401-330-3184, e-mail mblack@sos.ri.gov; Lisa Richter, Salve Regina University; *ALA Councilor* Ed Garcia, Cranston Public Library; *Past Pres.* Julie Holden, Cranston Public Library. Tel. 401-943-9080, ext. 101, e-mail pastpresident@rilibraries.org. Address correspondence to Rhode Island Lib. Assn., P.O. Box 6765, Providence 02940. World Wide Web https://www.rilibraries. org.

South Carolina

Memb. 350+. Term of Office. Jan.–Dec. Publication. *South Carolina Libraries Journal* (s.-ann., online). *Pres.* Melanie Huggins, Richland Library. Tel. 803-929-3422, e-mail mhuggins@richland library.com; *1st V.P./Conference Chair* Jimmie Epling, Darlington County Library System, Tel. 843-398-4940, e-mail jimmie.epling@ darlington-lib.org; *2nd V.P./Membership Chair* Kelly Jones, Richland Library. Tel. 803-929-2633, e-mail kjones@richlandlibrary.com; *Secy.* Tomeka Jackson, Clemson University. Tel. 864-656-2682, e-mail tomekaj@clemson.edu; *Treas.* Sarah Schroeder, Richland Library. Tel. 803-929-3468, e-mail sclatreasurersc@gmail.com; *ALA Councilor* Joshua Greer, Beaufort County Library. Tel. 843-255-6462, e-mail jgreer@ bcgov.net; *Past Pres.* Megan Palmer, Clemson Univ. Tel. 864-656-5179, e-mail mpalme4@ clemson.edu. *Exec. Sec.* Donald Wood, South Carolina Lib. Association, P.O. Box 1763, Columbia, 29202. Tel. 803-252-1087, fax 803-252-0589, e-mail scla@capconsc.com. Address correspondence to the executive secretary. South Carolina Lib. Assn., P.O. Box 1763, Columbia 29202. Tel. 803-252-1087, e-mail scla@capconsc.com. World Wide Web https://www.scla.org.

South Dakota

Memb. (Indiv.) 450+; (Inst.) 60+. Publication. *Book Marks* (q.).
Pres. Jamie Formanek, Watertown Regional Library. E-mail jformanek@watertownsd.us; *V.P./Pres.-Elect* Sarah Jones-Lutter, Redfield Carnegie Library. E-mail sarahejones.22@gmail.com; *Recording Secy.* Daniel Burniston, Edith B. Siegrist Vermillion Public Library. E-mail Daniel.Burniston@vermillionpublicli brary.org; *Exec. Secy./Treas.* Krista Ohrtman, Mikkelsen Library, Augustana University, Sioux Falls. E-mail SDLibraryAssociation@gmail.com; *ALA Councilor* Danielle De Jager-Loftus, University of South Dakota, Vermillion. E-mail Danielle.Loftus@usd.edu; *Past Pres.* Shari Theroux, HM Briggs Lib, South Dakota State University, Brookings. E-mail Shari.Theroux@sdstate.edu.

Address correspondence to the executive secretary. South Dakota Lib. Assn., Mikkelsen Lib., 2001 S. Summit Ave., Sioux Falls 57197. Tel. 605-743-0889.

World Wide Web https://www.sdlibraryas sociation.org.

Tennessee

Memb. 600+. Term of Office. July–June. Publications. *Tennessee Libraries* (q.; online); *TLA Newsletter* (q.; online).
Pres. Dwight Hunter. E-mail dwight.hunt er@chattanoogastate.edu; *V.P./Pres.-Elect* Rhonda Tippitt. E-mail Rtippitt@sevierlibrary. org; *Recording Secy.* Holly Hebert. E-mail holly.hebert@mtsu.edu; *Past Pres.* Sharon Edwards. E-mail sharonedwards405@gmail. com; *Exec. Dir.* Cathy Farley. E-mail exdirtla@gmail.com.

Address correspondence to the executive director. Tennessee Lib. Assn., P.O. Box 6297, Sparta 38583. Tel. 931-607-1182, e-mail exdirtla@gmail.com.

World Wide Web https://www.tnla.org.

Texas

Memb. 6,000. Term of Office. Apr.–Apr. Publication. *Texas Library Journal* (q).
Pres. Mary Woodard, Mesquite ISD; *Pres.-Elect* Gretchen Pruett, New Braunfels Public Library; *Treas.* Dianna Morganti, Texas A&M University; *ALA Councilor* Dorcas Hand,

Students Need Libraries in HISD; *Past Pres.* Daniel Burgard, University of North Texas Health Science Center; *Exec. Dir.* Shirley Robinson, Texas Lib. Assn., 3420 Executive Center Dr., Suite 301, Austin 78731. Tel. 512-328-1518, ext. 151, e-mail shirleyr@txla.org.

Address correspondence to the executive director. Texas Lib. Assn., 3420 Executive Center Dr., Suite 301, Austin 78731. Tel. 512-328-1518, e-mail tla@txla.org.

World Wide Web https://txla.org.

Utah

Memb. 650. Publication. *Utah Libraries News* (q.; online).
Pres. Marissa Bischoff, Harold B. Lee Library, Brigham Young University. E-mail maris-sa_bischoff@byu.edu; *Pres.-Elect* Patrick Hoecherl, Salt Lake City Public Library; *Exec. Treas.* Allen Arnoldsen. E-mail allen_ar noldsen@byu.edu; *ALA Chapter Councilor* Trish Hull, Kearns Branch, Salt Lake County Library. E-mail thull@slcolibrary.org; *Past Pres.* Rita Christensen, Orem Public Library. E-mail rchristensen@orem.org; *Exec. Dir.* Mindy Hale. E-mail mhale@ula.org.

Address correspondence to the executive director.

World Wide Web https://ula.org.

Vermont

Memb. 300+. Publication. *VLA News* (q.).
Pres. Kelly McCagg, Burnham Memorial Library, 898 Main St., Colchester 05446. Tel. 802-264-5660, e-mail president@vermontlibraries. org; *V.P./Pres.-Elect* Bryn Geffert, University of Vermont, David W. Howe Memorial Library, 538 Main Street, Burlington 05405. Tel. 802-656-2020, e-mail vicepresident@vermontli braries.org; *Secy.* Barbara Ball, Windsor Public Library, 43 State St., Windsor 05089. Tel. 802-674-2556, e-mail secretary@vermontlibraries. org; *Treas.* Lisa Milchman, Norwich Public Library, P.O. Box 290, Norwich 05055. Tel. 802-649-1184, e-mail treasurer@vermontlibraries. org; *Past Pres.* Michael D. Roy, Middlebury College, Middlebury 05753. Tel. 802-443-5490, e-mail mdroy@middlebury.edu.

Address correspondence to Vermont Lib. Assn., P.O. Box 803, Burlington 05402.

World Wide Web https://www.vermontli braries.org.

Virginia

Memb. 950+. Term of Office. Oct.–Oct. Publication. *Virginia Libraries* (ann.).

Pres. Kimberly Knight, Alexandria Library. E-mail kknight@alexlibraryva.org; *Pres.-Elect* Nan Carmack, Library of Virginia; *2nd V.P.* Zach Elder, Massanutten Regional Library. E-mail zacharyelder@gmail.com; *Secy.* Rebecca Purdy, Central Rappahannock Regional Library; *Treas.* Kyle Binaxas, Suffolk Public Library. E-mail k.binaxas@gmail.com; *ALA Councilor* Kerri Copus, Montgomery-Floyd Regional Library System; *Past Pres.* K.T. Vaughan, Washington & Lee University. E-mail kvaughan@wlu.edu; *Exec. Dir.* Lisa Varga, Virginia Lib. Assn., P.O. Box 56312, Virginia Beach 23456. Tel. 757-689-0594, e-mail vla.lisav@cox.net.

Address correspondence to the executive director. Virginia Lib. Assn., P.O. Box 56312, Virginia Beach 23456. Tel. 757-689-0594, fax 757-447-3478, e-mail vla.lisav@cox.net.

World Wide Web https://www.vla.org.

Washington

Memb. (Indiv.) 742, (Inst.) 47. Publication. *Alki: The Washington Library Association Journal* (3x yearly, online).

Pres. Johanna Jacobsen Kiciman, University of Washington. E-mail jmjk@uw.edu; *V.P./ Pres.-Elect* Sarah Logan, Camas School District. E-mail sarah.logan@camas.wednet.edu; *Treas.* Muriel Wheatley, Timberland Regional Lib. E-mail mwheatley@trl.org; *ALA Councilor* Steven Bailey, King County Lib. System. E-mail sbailey@kcls.org; *Past Pres.* Ahniwa Ferrari, The Evergreen State College. E-mail ferraria@evergreen.edu; *Exec. Dir.* Brianna Hoffman, Washington Lib. Association. E-mail brianna@wla.org.

Address correspondence to the executive director. Washington Lib. Assn., P.O. Box 33808, Seattle 98133. Tel. 206-823-1138, e-mail info@wla.org.

World Wide Web https://www.wla.org.

West Virginia

Memb. 700+.

Pres. Angela Strait, Marshall University Library; *1st V.P.* Megan Tarbett, Putnam County Library; *2nd V.P.* Angela Arthur, Cox Landing Library; *Secy.* Larissa Cason, Marion County Public Library; *Treas.* Erika Connelly, Kanawha County Public Library; *Past Pres.* Breana Roach Bowen, Cabell County Public Library. Tel. 304-528-5700, fax 304-528-5701, e-mail breana.bowen@cabell.lib.wv.us; *ALA Councilor* Majed Khader, Marshall University. Tel. 304-696-3121, fax 304-696-5219, e-mail khader@marshall.edu; *Exec. Secy.* Kerry Trahan, Marion County Public Library.

Address correspondence to the executive director at wvlaexedir@gmail.com.

World Wide Web https://wvla.org.

Wisconsin

Memb. 1,900. Term of Office. Jan.–Dec. Publication. *WLA eNewsletter* (3–4x yearly; online).

Pres. Kris Turner. E-mail kris.turner@wisc.edu; *V.P.* Desiree Bongers, Ripon Public Lib., Ripon. E-mail dbongers@riponlibrary.org; *Secy.* Katherine Freund, Little Chute Library, Little Chute. E-mail kfreund@littlechutelibrary.org; *Treas.* Rachel Arndt. E-mail rachel.arndt27@gmail.com; *ALA Councilor* Kristina Gómez. E-mail kgomez@madisonpubliclibrary.org; *Past Pres.* Nyama Reed. E-mail n.reed@wfblibrary.org; *Exec. Dir.* Laura Sauser. E-mail sauser@wisconsinlibraries.org.

Address correspondence to Wisconsin Lib. Assn., P.O. Box 6437, 112 Owen Rd., #6437, Monona 53716. Tel. 608-245-3640, e-mail wla@wisconsinlibraries.org.

World Wide Web https://www.wisconsinlibraries.org.

Wyoming

Memb. 450+. Term of Office. Oct.–Oct. Publication. Newsletter (ann.; August).

Pres. Conrrado Saldivar, Wyoming State Library. Tel. 307-777-6330, e-mail conrrado.saldivar@wyo.gov; *V.P.* Darcy Acord. E-mail darcylippacord@gmail.com; *Secy./Treas.* Chelsie Troutman, Natrona County Library. Tel. 307-577-7323, e-mail ctroutman@natronacountylibrary.org; *ALA Councilor* Lisa Scroggins, Natrona County Library. Tel. 307-237-4935, ext. 115, e-mail lscroggins@natronacountylibrary.org; *Membs.-at-Large* Angela Jordan, Teton County Library. Tel. 307-733-2164, ext. 3258, e-mail ajordan@tclib.org; Susan Parkins, Laramie County Library Sys-

tem. Tel. 307-773-7228, e-mail sparkins@
lclsonline.org; *Past Pres.* Katrina Brown,
Casper College Goodstein Foundation Library.
Tel. 307-268-2036, e-mail katrina.brown@
caspercollege.edu; *Communications Advisor*
Elizabeth Thorson, Laramie County Lib. System. Tel. 307-773-7230, e-mail ethorson@
lclsonline.org (ex officio); *State Librarian* Jamie Markus, Wyoming State Library. Tel. 307-
777-5914, e-mail jamie.markus@wyo.gov (ex
officio).

Address correspondence to Wyoming Lib.
Assn., 1190 Meramac Station Rd., Suite 207,
Ballwin, MO 63201. Tel. 800-969-6562, ext. 6,
e-mail wla@amigos.org.

World Wide Web https://wyla.org.

Canada

Alberta

Memb. 800+. Term of Office. May–April.

Pres. Jessica Knoch, Yellowhead Regional
Library. E-mail president@laa.ca; *1st V.P.*
Haley Amendt; *2nd V.P.* Megan Ginther; *Treas.*
Charla Majeran, Tofield School. E-mail treas
urer@laa.ca; *Past Pres.* Kirk MacLeod, Alberta
Law Libraries; *Dirs.* Kait McClary, Shortgrass
Library System; Jocie Wilson, Yellowhead Re-
gional Library; Jessie Pepin; *Comm. Officer*
Lorisia MacLeod, The Alberta Library. E-mail
info@laa.ca.

Address correspondence to Lib. Assn. of
Alberta, c/o The Alberta Library, #623, 7 Sir
Winston Churchill Sq. NW, Edmonton, AB,
T5J 2V.

World Wide Web https://www.laa.ca.

British Columbia

Memb. 750+. Term of Office. April–April.
Publication. *BCLA Perspectives* (q.; online).

Pres. Todd Mundle, Kwantlen Polytechnic
University Library; *Incoming Pres.* Tracey
Therrien, Nelson Public Library; *Recording
Secy.* Rina Hadziev, BCLA Executive Director;
Treas. Donald Taylor, SFU Library; *Incoming
Treas.* Sarah Felkar, West Vancouver Memorial
Library; *Past Pres.* Chris Middlemass, Van-
couver Public Lib.; *Exec. Dir.* Rina Hadziev.
E-mail execdir@bcla.bc.ca.

Address correspondence to the executive
director. British Columbia Lib. Assn., P.O. Box
19008 Rocky Point PO, Port Moody V3H 0J1.
E-mail bclaoffice@bcla.bc.ca.

World Wide Web https://bclaconnect.ca.

Manitoba

Memb. 500+. Term of Office. May–May.

Pres. Melanie Sucha; *V.P.* Sarah Lee; *Secy.*
Caralie Heinrichs. E-mail secretary@mla.
mb.ca; *Treas.* Position open; *Past Pres.* Position open.

Address correspondence to Manitoba Lib.
Assn., 606-100 Arthur St., Winnipeg R3B 1H3.
E-mail secretary@mla.mb.ca.

World Wide Web https://mla.mb.ca.

Ontario

Memb. 5,000+. Publication. *Open Shelf* (mo.,
multimedia).

Pres. Melanie Mills, Huron University College, Western University. E-mail mela-nie.
mills@uwo.ca; *V.P./Pres.-Elect* S.S. Ahmad,
Green Beacon; *Treas.* Lori Hallahan, Seneca
College. E-mail lori-ann.hallahan@senecacol
lege.ca; *Past Pres.* Sabrina Saunders, The Blue
Mountains Public Lib. E-mail ssaunders@
thebluemountains.ca; *Exec. Dir.* Shelagh Pat-
erson, Ontario Lib. Assn. E-mail spaterson@
accessola.com.

Address correspondence to Ontario Lib.
Assn., 2080 Danforth Ave., Toronto M4C 1J9.
Tel. 877-340-1730, e-mail info@accessola.
com.

World Wide Web https://accessola.com.

Quebec

Memb. (Indiv.) 100+. Term of Office. May–
April. Publication. *ABQLA Bulletin* (3x
yearly).

Pres. Barbara Whiston and Maria Ressina;
V.P. Nicholas Lobraico; *Treas.* Taylor Gam-
mon; *Past Pres.* Position open.

Address correspondence to the president.
Assn. des Bibliothecaires du Quebec/Quebec
Lib. Assn., C.P. 26717, CPS Beaconsfield H9W
6G7.

World Wide Web https://abqla.qc.ca/en.

Saskatchewan

Memb. 200+.

Pres. Amy Rankin, CMP Resource Centre,
P.O. Box 6500, Regina. Tel. 639-625-3537,

e-mail amy.rankin@rcmp-grc.gc.ca; *V.P. Engagements and Communications* Riane La-Paire, National Network for Equitable Library Service (NNELS); *V.P. Advocacy and Development* Morgan Kelly, Southeast Regional Library; *Treas.* Michele Fedyk, Regina Public Library; *Past Pres.* Alison Jantz, RCMP Resource Centre; *Exec. Dir.* Tina Kleisinger, Saskatchewan Lib. Assn., #15–2010 7th Ave, Regina S4R 1C3. Tel. 306-780-9413, fax 306-780-9447, e-mail tkleisinger@saskla.ca.

Address correspondence to the executive director. Saskatchewan Lib. Assn., 10-2010 7th Ave., Regina S4R 1C3. Tel. 306-780-9413, fax 306-780-3633, e-mail tkleisinger@saskla.ca.

World Wide Web https://saskla.ca.

Regional

Atlantic Provinces: N.B., N.L., N.S., P.E.I.

Memb. (Indiv.) 320+.

Pres. Cate Carlyle, Mount Saint Vincent University, Halifax, Nova Scotia. E-mail president@apla.ca; *V.P./Pres.-Elect* Krystal Dionne, Charlottetown Library Learning Centre, Charlottetown, PE. E-mail president-elect@apla.ca; *V.P. Nova Scotia* Agnieszka Hayes, Acadia University, Wolfville, NS. E-mail ns@apla.ca; *V.P. New Brunswick* Chantale Saulnier, New Brunswick Public Library Service, Fredericton, NB. E-mail nb@apla.ca; *V.P. Newfoundland and Labrador* Susan Cleyle, Memorial University of Newfoundland, St. John's, NL. E-mail nl@apla.ca; *V.P. Prince Edward Island* Emily MacIsaac, Holland College, Charlottetown, PE. E-mail pe@apla.ca; *V.P. Membership* Jason Lee, Cape Breton University, Sydney, NS. E-mail membership@apla.ca; *Treas.* Margaret Vail, St. Francis Xavier University, Antigonish, NS. E-mail treasurer@apla.ca; *Secy.* Evelyn Trainer, Chignecto Central Regional Centre for Education, Truro, NS. E-mail secretary@apla.ca; *Past President* Marc Harper, Bibliothèque Champlain, 18 avenue Antonine-Maillet (local 164), Moncton, NB E1A 3E9. Tel. 506-858-4154, e-mail past-president@apla.ca.

Address correspondence to Atlantic Provinces Lib. Assn., Dalhousie Univ., Kenneth C. Rowe Mgt. Bldg., 6100 University Ave., Suite 4010, P.O. Box 15000, Halifax, NS B3H 4R2. E-mail president@apla.ca or secretary@apla.ca.

World Wide Web https://www.apla.ca.

Mountain Plains: Ariz., Colo., Kan., Mont., Neb., Nev., N.D., N.M., Okla., S.D., Utah, Wyo.

Memb. 700. Term of Office. Oct.–Oct. Publication. *MPLA Newsletter* (6x yearly, online).

Pres. Amadee Ricketts, Cochise County Library, 1415 W. Melody Lane, Building C, Bisbee, AZ, 85603. E-mail president@mpla.us; *V.P./Pres.-Elect* Robin Hastings, 4317 W. 6th Street, Lawrence, KS, 66049. E-mail vice-president@mpla.us; *Secy.* Luise Davis, Douglas County Public Library, 1625 Library Lane, Minden, NV, 89423. E-mail secretary@mpla.us; *Past Pres.* Brenda Hemmelman, South Dakota State Library, 800 Governors Drive, Pierre, SD 57501. Tel. 605-773-5075, fax 605-773-6962, e-mail pastpresident@mpla.us; *Exec. Secy.* Judy Kulp, 14293 West Center Dr., Lakewood, CO 80228. Tel. 303-985-7795, e-mail execsecretary@mpla.us.

Address correspondence to the executive secretary. Mountain Plains Lib. Assn., 14293 West Center Drive, Lakewood, Colorado 80228. Tel. 303-985-7795, e-mail execsecretary@mpla.us.

World Wide Web https://mpla.us.

New England: Conn., Maine, Mass., N.H., R.I., Vt.

Memb. (Indiv.) 650+. Term of Office. Nov.–Oct. Publication. "NELA News" (blog).

Pres. Bethany Klem, Dover Town Library, Dover, MA. Tel. 413-323-5925, ext. 102, e-mail president@nelib.org; *V.P.* Maisam Nouh, Innovative, part of Clarivate. Tel. 413-323-5925, ext. 103, e-mail vice-president@nelib.org; *Secy.* Lynn Harlan, Bangor Public Library, Bangor, ME. Tel. 413-323-5925, ext. 106, e-mail secretary@nelib.org; *Treas.* Bernie Prochnik, Bath Public Library, NH. Tel. 413-323-5925, ext. 105, e-mail treasurer@nelib.org; *Past Pres.* Kimberly Usselman, Hobrook Public Library, Holbrook, MA. Tel. 413-323-5925, ext. 104, e-mail past-president@nelib.org; *Members-at-Large* Heather Backman, Weymouth Public Library, Weymouth, MA. Tel. 413-323-5925, ext. 107, e-mail member-at-large-2@nelib.org; Gail Hurley, Connecticut State Library, Hartford, CT. Tel. 413-323-5925, ext. 107, e-mail member-at-large-1@nelib.org; *Admin.* Robert Scheier, NELA Office, 55 N. Main St., Unit 49, Belchertown, MA 01007. Tel. 413-323-5925, ext. 100, e-mail rscheier@nelib.org.

Address correspondence to the administrator. New England Lib. Assn., 55 N. Main St., Unit 49, Belchertown, MA 01007. Tel. 413-323-5925, e-mail rscheier@nelib.org.

World Wide Web https://www.nelib.org.

Pacific Northwest: Alaska, Idaho, Mont., Ore., Wash., Alb., B.C.

Memb. 170+. Term of Office. Aug.–Aug. Publication. *PNLA Quarterly.*

Pres. Gavin Woltjer, Billings Public Library, Billings, MT; *Vice-Pres./Pres.-Elect* Position open; *2nd V.P./Membership Chair* Duncan Lotoski, Peace Library System, Grande Prairie, Alberta; *Secy.* Christina Brischetto, Kids Read Books, Randle, WA; *Treas.* Dawn Lowe-Wincentsen, Shoreline Community College, Shoreline, WA; *Past Pres.* Nicole Thode, Tumwater Timberland Lib., Thurston County, WA.

Address correspondence to Pacific Northwest Lib. Assn., 1430 Willamette Street, #764, Eugene, OR 97401.

World Wide Web https://pnla.org.

Southeastern: Ala., Ark., Fla., Ga., Ky., La., Miss., N.C., S.C., Tenn., Va., W.Va.

Memb. 500. Publication. *The Southeastern Librarian* (*SELn*) (q.; online, open access).

Pres. Melissa Dennis, University of Mississippi, University, MS. E-mail president@selaonline.org; *Pres.-Elect* Crystal Gates, William F. Laman Public Lib, North Little Rock, AR. E-mail president.elect@selaonline.org; *Secy.* Kristin Rogers, University of Mississippi, MS. E-mail secretary@selaonline.org; *Treas.* Vicki Gregory, University of South Florida (Professor Emeritus), Tampa, FL. E-mail treasurer@selaonline.org; *Archivist* Camille McCutcheon, Univ. of South Carolina Upstate, Spartanburg, SC. E-mail archivist@selaonline.org; *Past Pres.* Tim Dodge, Auburn University Libraries, Auburn, AL.

Address correspondence to Southeastern Lib. Assn., Admin. Services, P.O. Box 30703, Savannah, GA 31410. Tel. 912-999-7979, e-mail selaadminservices@selaonline.org.

World Wide Web https://selaonline.org.

State and Provincial Library Agencies

The state library administrative agency in each of the U.S. states will have the latest information on its state plan for the use of federal funds under the Library Services and Technology Act (LSTA). The directors and addresses of these state agencies are listed below.

United States

Alabama

Nancy Pack, Dir., Alabama Public Lib. Svc., 6030 Monticello Dr., Montgomery 36117. Tel. 334-213-3900, fax 334-213-3993, e-mail npack@apls.state.al.us. World Wide Web https://aplsws2.apls.state.al.us.

Alaska

Freya Anderson, Head of Information Services, Alaska State Lib., P.O. Box 110571, Juneau 99811-0571. Tel. 907-465-1315, fax 907-465-2151, e-mail freya.anderson@alaska.gov. World Wide Web https://library.alaska.gov.

Arizona

Holly Henley, State Libn. and Dir. of Lib. Svcs., Arizona State Lib., Archives and Public Records, 1901 W. Madison St., Phoenix 85009. Tel. 602-542-6200. World Wide Web https://azlibrary.gov.

Arkansas

Jennifer Chilcoat, State Libn., Arkansas State Lib., 900 W. Capitol, Suite 100, Little Rock 72201. Tel. 501-682-2053, e-mail jennifer.chilcoat@ade.arkansas.gov. World Wide Web https://www.library.arkansas.gov.

California

Greg Lucas, State Libn., California State Lib., P.O. Box 942837, Sacramento, 94237-0001. Tel. 916-323-9759, fax 916-323-9768, e-mail csl-adm@library.ca.gov. World Wide Web https://www.library.ca.gov.

Colorado

Katy Anthes, Commissioner, Colorado State Lib., 201 E. Colfax Ave., Denver 80203-1799. Tel. 303-866-6600, fax 303-830-0793, e-mail commissioner@cde.state.co.us. World Wide Web http://www.cde.state.co.us/cdelib.

Connecticut

Deborah Schander, State Libn., Connecticut State Lib., 231 Capitol Ave., Hartford 06106. Tel. 860-757-6510, fax 860-757-6503, e-mail deborah.schander@ct.gov. World Wide Web https://ctstatelibrary.org.

Delaware

Annie Norman, Dir., Delaware Division of Libs., 121 Martin Luther King Jr. Blvd. N., Dover 19901. Tel. 302-257-3001, fax 302-739-6787, e-mail annie.norman@delaware.gov. World Wide Web https://libraries.delaware.gov.

District of Columbia

Richard Reyes-Gavilan, Exec. Dir., District of Columbia Public Lib., 901 G Street, NW, Suite 301, Washington, DC 20001. Tel. 202-727-1101, fax 202-727-1129, e-mail rrg@dc.gov. World Wide Web https://www.dclibrary.org.

Florida

Amy L. Johnson, State Libn. and Div. Dir., Division of Lib. and Info. Svcs., R.A. Gray Bldg., 500 S. Bronough St., Tallahassee 32399-0250. Tel. 850-245-6600, fax 850-245-6622, e-mail info@dos.myflorida.com. World Wide Web https://dos.myflorida.com/library-archives.

Georgia

Julie Walker, State Libn., Georgia Public Lib. Svc., 2872 Woodcock Boulevard, Suite 250, Atlanta 30341. Tel. 404-235-7200, e-mail jwalker@georgialibraries.org. World Wide Web https://georgialibraries.org.

Hawaii

Stacy A. Aldrich, State Libn., Hawaii State Public Lib. System, Office of the State Libn., 44 Merchant St., Honolulu 96813. Tel. 808-586-3704, fax 808-586-3715, e-mail stlib@librarieshawaii.org. World Wide Web https://www.librarieshawaii.org.

Idaho

Stephanie Bailey-White, State Libn., Idaho Commission for Libs., 325 W. State St., Boise 83702. Tel. 208-639-4145, fax 208-334-4016, e-mail stephanie.bailey-white@libraries.idaho.gov. World Wide Web https://libraries.idaho.gov.

Illinois

Alexi Giannoulias, Secy. of State/State Libn.., Illinois State Lib., Gwendolyn Brooks Bldg., 300 S. Second St., Springfield 62701-1796. Tel. 217-785-5600, fax 217-785-4326, e-mail islinfo@ilsos.net. World Wide Web https://www.ilsos.gov/departments/library/home.html.

Indiana

Jacob Speer, State Libn., Indiana State Lib., 315 W. Ohio St., Indianapolis 46202. Tel. 317-232-3675, e-mail jspeer@library.in.gov. World Wide Web https://www.in.gov/library.

Iowa

Michael Scott, State Libn., State Lib. of Iowa, 1112 E. Grand Ave., Des Moines 50319-0233. Tel. 800-248-4483, fax 515-281-6191, e-mail Michael.Scott@iowa.gov. World Wide Web https://www.statelibraryofiowa.gov.

Kansas

Ray C. Walling, State Libn., Kansas State Lib., Capitol Bldg., 300 S.W. 10th Ave., Rm. 312-N, Topeka 66612. Tel. 785-296-5437, e-mail cindy.roupe@ks.gov. World Wide Web https://kslib.info.

Kentucky

Beth Milburn, Deputy Commissioner, Kentucky Dept. for Libs. and Archives, 300 Coffee Tree Rd., P.O. Box 537, Frankfort 40602-0537. Tel.
502-564-8325, e-mail beth.milburn@ky.gov. World Wide Web https://www.kdla.ky.gov.

Louisiana

Rebecca Hamilton, State Libn., State Lib. of Louisiana, 701 N. 4th St., P.O. Box 131, Baton Rouge 70821-0131. Tel. 225-342-4923, fax 225-219-4804, e-mail rhamilton@crt.la.gov. World Wide Web https://www.state.lib.la.us.

Maine

Lori Fisher, State Libn., Maine State Lib., 64 State House Sta., Augusta 04333-0064. Tel. 207-287-5600, fax 207-287-5624, e-mail lori.fisher@maine.gov. World Wide Web https://www.maine.gov/msl.

Maryland

Irene M. Padilla, State Libn., Maryland State Lib., 25 S. Charles St., Suite 1310, Baltimore 21201. Tel. 667-219-4800, fax 667-219-479, e-mail elizabeth.fletcher@maryland.gov. World Wide Web https://www.marylandlibraries.org.

Massachusetts

James Lonergan, Dir., Massachusetts Board of Lib. Commissioners, 90 Canal St., Suite 500, Boston, 02114. Tel. 617-725-1860, ext. 222, fax 617-725-0140, e-mail james.lonergan@state.ma.us. World Wide Web https://mblc.state.ma.us.

Michigan

Randy Riley, State Libn., Lib. of Michigan, 702 W. Kalamazoo St., P.O. Box 30007, Lansing 48909-7507. Tel. 517-335-1517, e-mail rileyr1@michigan.gov. World Wide Web https://www.michigan.gov/libraryofmichigan.

Minnesota

State Libn. and Dir. of State Lib. Svcs., Minnesota State Lib. Agency, Div. of State Lib. Svcs., MN Dept. of Educ., 400 NE Stinson Blvd., Minneapolis 55413. Tel. 651-582-8200, e-mail mde.lst@state.mn.us. World Wide Web https://education.mn.gov/MDE/dse/Lib/sls.

Mississippi

Lori Barnes, Chair, Mississippi Lib. Commission, 3881 Eastwood Dr., Jackson 39211. Tel.

601-432-4038, e-mail hbivins@mlc.lib.ms.us. World Wide Web http://www.mlc.lib.ms.us.

Missouri

Robin Westphal, State Libn., Missouri State Lib., 600 W. Main St., P.O. Box 387, Jefferson City 65101. Tel. 573-526-4783, e-mail robin.westphal@sos.mo.gov. World Wide Web http://www.sos.mo.gov/library.

Montana

Jennie Stapp, State Libn., Montana State Lib., P.O. Box 201800, 1201 11th Avenue, Helena 59620. Tel. 406-444-3115, e-mail jstapp2@mt.gov. World Wide Web https://msl.mt.gov.

Nebraska

Rodney G. Wagner, Dir., Nebraska Lib. Commission, 1200 N St., Suite 120, Lincoln 68508-2023. Tel. 402-471-2045, fax 402-471-2083, e-mail rod.wagner@nebraska.gov. World Wide Web http://www.nlc.nebraska.gov.

Nevada

Mike Strom, Admin., Nevada State Lib. and Archives, 100 N. Stewart St., Carson City 89701. Tel. 775-684-3410, fax 775-684-3311, e-mail mstrom@admin.nv.gov. World Wide Web https://nsla.nv.gov/home.

New Hampshire

Michael York, State Libn., New Hampshire State Lib., 20 Park St., Concord 03301. Tel. 603-271-2397, e-mail michael.york@dncr.nh.gov. World Wide Web https://www.nh.gov/nhsl.

New Jersey

Jennifer R. Nelson, State Libn., New Jersey State Lib., an affiliate of Thomas Edison State Univ., P.O. Box 520, Trenton 08625-0520. Tel. 609-278-2640 ext. 101, fax 609-278-2652, e-mail jnelson@njstatelib.org. World Wide Web https://www.njstatelib.org.

New Mexico

Eli Guinnee, State Libn., New Mexico State Lib., 1209 Camino Carlos Rey, Santa Fe 87507-5166. Tel. 505-476-9762, e-mail Eli.Guinnee@state.nm.us. World Wide Web https://www.nmstatelibrary.org.

New York

Lauren Moore, State Libn., New York State Lib., Cultural Educ. Ctr., 222 Madison Ave., Albany 12230. Tel. 518-474-5930, fax 518-474-5786, e-mail statelibrarian@nysed.gov. World Wide Web https://www.nysl.nysed.gov.

North Carolina

Michelle Underhill, State Libn., State Lib. of North Carolina, Administrative Section, 4640 Mail Svc. Ctr., Raleigh 27699-4600; 109 E. Jones St., Raleigh 27601. Tel. 919-814-6784, fax 919-733-8748, e-mail michelle.underhill@ncdcr.gov. World Wide Web https://statelibrary.ncdcr.gov.

North Dakota

Mary J. Soucie, State Libn., North Dakota State Lib., 604 E. Boulevard Ave., Dept. 250, Bismarck 58505-0800. Tel. 701-328-4654, fax 701-328-2040, e-mail msoucie@nd.gov. World Wide Web http://www.library.nd.gov.

Ohio

Wendy Knapp, State Libn., 274 E. First Ave., Suite 100, Columbus 43201. Tel. 616-644-6843, e-mail jward@library.ohio.gov. World Wide Web https://library.ohio.gov.

Oklahoma

Natalie Currie, Dir., Oklahoma Dept. of Libs., 200 N.E. 18th St., Oklahoma City 73105-3298. Tel. 405-521-2502, fax 405-525-7804, e-mail natalie.currie@libraries.ok.gov. World Wide Web https://oklahoma.gov/libraries.html.

Oregon

Wendy Cornelisen, State Libn., State Lib. of Oregon, 250 Winter St., N.E., Salem 97301. Tel. 503-378-4367, fax 503-585-8059, e-mail wendy.cornelisen@slo.oregon.gov. World Wide Web https://www.oregon.gov/Library.

Pennsylvania

Susan Banks, Deputy Secy. of Educ., Commissioner of Libs., and State Libn., State Lib.

of Pennsylvania, Commonwealth Keystone Bldg., Plaza Lib. (Museum Plaza Wing), 400 North St., Harrisburg 17120-0211. Tel. 717-787-2646, fax 717-772-3265, e-mail ra-edocldeptysecty@pa.gov. World Wide Web https://www.statelibrary.pa.gov/Pages/default.aspx.

Rhode Island

Karen Mellor, Chief of Lib. Services, Rhode Island Office of Lib. and Info. Svcs., One Capitol Hill, Providence 02908. Tel. 401-574-9304, fax 401-574-9320, e-mail karen.Mellor@olis.ri.gov. World Wide Web https://olis.ri.gov.

South Carolina

Leesa M. Aiken, Dir., South Carolina State Lib., 1500 Senate St., Columbia 29201. Tel. 803-734-8668, fax 803-734-8676, e-mail laiken@statelibrary.sc.gov. World Wide Web https://www.statelibrary.sc.gov.

South Dakota

George Seamon, State Libn., South Dakota State Lib., MacKay Bldg., 800 Governors Dr., Pierre 57501. Tel. 605-773-3131, option 6, fax 605-773-6962, e-mail brenda.hemmelman@state.sd.us. World Wide Web https://library.sd.gov.

Tennessee

State Libn. and Archivist, Tennessee State Lib. and Archives, 1001 Rep. John Lewis Way N., Nashville 37219. Tel. 615-741-2764, e-mail ask@tsla.libanswers.com. World Wide Web https://sos.tn.gov/tsla.

Texas

Gloria Meraz, Dir. and Libn., Texas State Lib. and Archives Commission, 1201 Brazos St., Austin 78701; P.O. Box 12927, Austin 78711-2927. Tel. 512-463-5460, fax 512-463-5436, e-mail director.librarian@tsl.texas.gov. World Wide Web https://www.tsl.texas.gov.

Utah

Chaundra Johnson, State Libn., Utah State Lib. Div., 250 N. 1950 W., Suite A, Salt Lake City 84116-7901. Tel. 801-715-6770, fax 801-715-6767, e-mail crjohns@utah.gov. World Wide Web https://library.utah.gov.

Vermont

Catherine Delneo, State Libn., Vermont State Lib., 60 Washington St., Suite 2, Barre, VT 05641. Tel. 802-636-0040, e-mail catherine.delneo@vermont.gov. World Wide Web https://libraries.vermont.gov/state_library.

Virginia

Sandra Treadway, Libn. of Virginia, Lib. of Virginia, 800 E. Broad St., Richmond 23219-8000. Tel. 804-692-3535, fax 804-692-3556, e-mail sandra.treadway@lva.virginia.gov. World Wide Web https://www.lva.virginia.gov.

Washington

Sara Jones, State Libn., Washington State Lib., Office of the Secretary of State, Point Plaza E., 6880 Capitol Blvd., Tumwater 98501; P.O. Box 42460, Olympia 98504-2460. Tel. 360-704-5276, e-mail sara.jones@sos.wa.gov. World Wide Web https://www.sos.wa.gov/library.

West Virginia

Karen Goff, Dir./State Libn., West Virginia Lib. Commission Cultural Ctr., Bldg. 9, 1900 Kanawha Blvd. E., Charleston 25305. Tel. 304-558-2041 ext. 2084, fax 304-558-2044, e-mail karen.e.goff@wv.gov. World Wide Web https://librarycommission.wv.gov/Pages/default.aspx.

Wisconsin

Ben Miller, Dir., Div. for Libs. and Tech., Wisconsin Dept. of Public Instruction, 125 S. Webster St., Madison 53703; P.O. Box 7841, Madison 53707-7841. Tel. 608-224-6168, fax 608-267-9207, e-mail benjamin.miller@dpi.wi.gov. World Wide Web https://dpi.wi.gov/libraries.

Wyoming

Jamie Markus, State Libn., Wyoming State Lib., 2800 Central Ave., Cheyenne 82002. Tel. 307-777-5914, e-mail jamie.markus@wyo.gov. World Wide Web https://library.wyo.gov.

American Samoa

Emma Solaita Malele, Territorial Libn., Feleti Barstow Public Lib., Box 997687, Pago Pago 96799. Tel. 684-633-5816, fax 684-633-5823, e-mail feletibarstow@feletibarstow.info. World Wide Web https://www.feletibarstow.org.

Federated States of Micronesia

Augustine Kohler, Ntl. Historic Preservation Officer, Office of National Archives, Culture, and Historic Preservations, PS175, Palikir, Pohnpei State 96941. Tel. 691-320-2343, fax 691-320-5632, e-mail hpo@mail.fm. World Wide Web https://www.fsmgov.org.

Guam

Sandra Stanley, Admin. Officer, Guam Public Lib. System, 254 Martyr St., Hagatna 96910-5141. Tel. 671-475-4765, fax 671-477-9777, e-mail sandra.stanley@guampls.guam.gov. World Wide Web https://gpls.guam.gov.

Northern Mariana Islands

Erlinda Naputi, Lib. Dir., CNMI Joeten-Kiyu Public Lib., P.O. Box 501092, Saipan 96950. Tel. 670-235-7322, fax 670-235-7550, e-mail ecnaputi@gmail.com. World Wide Web https://cnmilib.org.

Palau

Sinton Soalablai, Chief, Div. of School Mgt., Palau Ministry of Educ., Madalaii Box 189, Koror, Palau 96940. Tel. 680-488-2570, fax 680-488-2380, e-mail ssoalablai@palaumoe.net. World Wide Web https://www.palaugov.pw/executive-branch/ministries/education.

Puerto Rico

National Library of Puerto Rico, Institute of Puerto Rican Culture, Box 9024184, San Juan, Puerto Rico 00902-4184. Tel. 787-724-0700, 787-724-8393, e-mail info@icp.pr.gov. World Wide Web https://www.icp.pr.gov/bnpr.

Republic of the Marshall Islands

Wisse Amram, Exec. Dir., Alele Museum, Lib. and National Archives, P.O. Box 629, Majuro 96960. Tel. 011-692-625-3372, fax 011-692-625-3226, World Wide Web https://www.alele.org.

U.S. Virgin Islands

Arlene Pinney-Benjamin, Acting Dir., The Division of Libraries, Archives and Museums, c/o Florence Augusta Williams Public Lib., 1122 King St. Christiansted, St. Croix 00820. Tel. 340-773-5715, fax 340-773-5327, e-mail arlene.benjamin@dpnr.vi.gov. World Wide Web https://www.usvipubliclibraries.com.

Canada

Alberta

Diana Davidson, Dir., Alberta Public Lib. Svcs., Municipal Affairs, 8th fl., 10405 Jasper Ave., Edmonton T5J 4R7. Tel. 780-415-0284, fax 780-415-8594, e-mail diana.davidson@gov.ab.ca or libraries@gov.ab.ca. World Wide Web https://www.alberta.ca/public-library-services.aspx.

British Columbia

Mari Martin, Dir., Libs. Branch, Ministry of Educ., P.O. Box 9831, Stn. Prov. Govt., Victoria V8W 9T1. Tel. 250-886-2584, fax 250-953-4985, e-mail Mari.Martin@gov.bc.ca. World Wide Web https://www2.gov.bc.ca/gov/content/sports-culture/arts-culture/public-libraries/tool-resources-library-administrators/about-the-libraries-branch.

Manitoba

Trevor Surgenor, Dir., Public Lib. Services Branch, Manitoba Culture, Sport and Heritage Dept., B10 - 340 9th St., Brandon R7A 6C2. Tel. 204-726-6590, fax 204-726-6868, e-mail trevor.surgenor@gov.mb.ca. World Wide Web https://www.gov.mb.ca/chc/pls/index.html.

New Brunswick

Ella Nason, Acting Exec. Dir., New Brunswick Public Libs., Provincial Office, 570 Two Nations Crossing, Suite 2, Fredericton E3A 0X9. Tel. 506-453-2354, fax 506-444-4064, e-mail ella.nason@gnb.ca. World Wide Web https://www2.gnb.ca/content/gnb/en/departments/nbpl.html.

Newfoundland and Labrador

Andrew Hunt, Exec. Dir., Provincial Info. and Lib. Resources Board, 48 St. George's Ave., Stephenville A2N 1K9. Tel. 709-643-0900, fax 709-643-0925, e-mail ahunt@nlpl.ca. World Wide Web https://nlpl.ca.

Northwest Territories

Brian Dawson, Territorial Libn., Northwest Territories Public Lib. Services, 75 Woodland Dr., Hay River X0E 1G1. Tel. 867-874-6531, fax 867-874-3321, e-mail brian_dawson@gov.nt.ca. World Wide Web https://www.ece.gov.nt.ca/en/services/nwt-public-libraries.

Nova Scotia

Director, Provincial Lib., Nova Scotia Provincial Lib., 6016 University Ave., 5th Fl., Halifax B3H 1W4. Tel. 902-424-2457, fax 902-424-0633, e-mail nspl@novascotia.ca. World Wide Web https://library.novascotia.ca.

Nunavut

Ron Knowling, Mgr., Nunavut Public Lib. Svcs., P.O. Box 270, Baker Lake X0C 0A0. Tel. 867-793-3353, fax 867-793-3360, e-mail rknowling@gov.nu.ca. World Wide Web https://publiclibraries.nu.ca.

Ontario

Rob Lavery, Ontario Ministry of Tourism, Culture and Sport, 438 University Avenue, 6th Floor, Toronto, Ontario M5G 2K8. Tel. 416-314-7154, fax 416-212-1802, e-mail rob.lavery@ontario.ca. World Wide Web https://www.ontario.ca/page/ontario-public-libraries.

Prince Edward Island

Kathleen Simmonds, Dir., Libs. and Archives, Education and Lifelong Learning, Sullivan Bldg., 16 Fitzroy St., 1st Fl., Charlottetown, PE CIA 7N8. Tel. 902-314-5523, fax 902-894-0342, e-mail kesimmonds@gov.pe.ca. World Wide Web https://www.princeedwardisland.ca/en/topic/libraries-and-archives.

Quebec

Marie Grégoire, Chairman and CEO, Bibliothèque et Archives Nationales du Québec (BAnQ), 475, Boulevard de Maisonneuve Est, Montreal, H2L 5C4. Tel. 800-363-9028 or 514-873-1100, e-mail pdg@banq.qc.ca. World Wide Web https://www.banq.qc.ca/accueil/index.html.

Saskatchewan

Alison Hopkins, Provincial Libn./Exec. Dir., Provincial Lib. and Exec. Dir., Ministry of Educ., 409A Park Street, Regina, SK, S4N 5B2. Tel. 306-787-2976, fax 306-787-2029, e-mail alison.hopkins@gov.sk.ca. World Wide Web https://www.saskatchewan.ca/residents/education-and-learning/library-system-in-saskatchewan.

Yukon Territory

Melissa Yu Schott, Dir. of Public Libs., Community Development Div., Dept. of Community Svcs., Government of Yukon, 1171 Front Street, Whitehorse, Y1A 0G9. Tel. 867-667-5811, e-mail Melissa.YuSchott@yukon.ca. World Wide Web https://yukon.ca/en/arts-and-culture/yukon-public-libraries.

State School Library Associations

Alabama

Youth Services and School Libns. Div., Alabama Lib. Assn. (ALLA). Memb. 600+.

Chair Caitlin Rogers, The Altamont School. E-mail crogers@altamontschool.org; *Chair-Elect* Cristina Castor, Homewood Public Lib. E-mail cristina.castor@homewoodpubliclibrary.org.

Address correspondence to the Youth Services and School Libns. Div., ALLA, 6030 Monticello Dr., Montgomery 36117. Tel. 334-414-0113, e-mail allaadmin@allanet.org.

World Wide Web https://www.allanet.org/youth-services-and-school-library-division-yssld-.

Alaska

Alaska Assn. of School Libns. (AkASL). Memb. 100+. Publication. *The Puffin* (continuing basis online at http://akasl.org/puffin-news.) Submissions e-mail akasl.puffin@gmail.com.

Pres. Katie Conover Clark. E-mail akasl.presidentelect@gmail.com; *Secy.* Jessica Tonnies. E-mail akasl.secretary@gmail.com; *Treas.* Janet Madsen. E-mail janet.madsen@alaska.gov; *Past Pres.* Pam Verfaillie (Valdez).

Address correspondence to AkASL, P.O. Box 101085, Anchorage, 99510-1085, e-mail akasl.webmaster@gmail.com.

World Wide Web http://www.akasl.org.

Arizona

Teacher-Libn. Div., Arizona Lib. Assn. (AZLA). Memb. 1,000. Term of Office. Jan.–Dec.

Co-Chair Jean Kilker, Maryvale High School, 3415 N. 59th Ave., Phoenix 85033. Tel. 602-764-2134, e-mail jkilker@phoenixunion.org; *Co-Chair* Judi Moreillon, Tel. 520-603-4868, e-mail info@storytrail.com.

Address correspondence to the chairpersons, AZLA, c/o Arizona Lib. Assn., 7760 E. State Route 69, Suite C5 #385, Prescott Valley 86314. Tel. 928-288-2011, e-mail admin@azla.org.

World Wide Web https://www.azla.org/AZYASummit.

Arkansas

Arkansas Assn. of School Libns. (ARASL), div. of Arkansas Lib. Assn.

Chair Rachel Shankles, 891 Hwy. 7, Bismarck 71929. Tel. 501-276-4949, e-mail arasl.chair@gmail.com; *Past Chair* Daniel Fouts II, Osceola High School, 2800 W. Semmes Ave., Osceola 72370. Tel. 870-563-1863, e-mail dfouts@glaucus.org.

Address correspondence to the chairperson via e-mail.

World Wide Web https://arasl.weebly.com.

California

California School Lib. Assn. (CSLA). Memb. 1,200+. Publications. *CSLA Journal* (2x yearly). *Ed.* Mary Ann Harlan, San José State Univ. E-mail maryann.harlan@sjsu.edu; *CSLA Newsletter* (10x yearly, memb., via e-mail).

(State Board)

Pres. Rosan Cable, Pacifica High School, Garden Grove, CA. E-mail president_rosan@csla.net; *Pres.-Elect* Rene Hohls. E-mail president_rene@csla.net; *Secy.* Lori Broger-Mackey, Columbus Middle School, Canoga Park, CA. E-mail secretary@csla.net; *Treas.* Melissa Misenhimer, Portola High School, Irvine, CA. E-mail treasurer@csla.net; *Past Pres.* Nina Jackson, Franklin Classical Middle School, 540 Cerritos Ave., Long Beach 90802. E-mail njcatsandbooks@gmail.com.

Address correspondence to CSLA, 6444 E. Spring St., No. 237, Long Beach 90815-1553. Tel./fax 888-655-8480, e-mail info@csla.net.

World Wide Web http://csla.net.

Colorado

Colorado Assn. of Libs. School Library Interest Group. Memb. 18+.

Chair Terri Brungardt, Widefield School Dist. 3. E-mail brungardtt@wsd3.org.

Address correspondence to Colorado Assn. of Libs., P.O. Box 740905, Arvada 80006-0905. Tel. 303-463-6400.

World Wide Web https://cal-webs.org/School_Libraries_Interest_Group.

Connecticut

Connecticut Assn. of School Libns. (CASL). Memb. 500+. Term of Office. July–June. *Pres.* Melissa Thom. E-mail President@ctcasl.org; *V.P.* Jenny Lussier. E-mail Vicepresident@ctcasl.org; *V.P. Intern* Valerie DiLorenzo. E-mail VPIntern@ctcasl.org; *Recording Secy.* Maria Frederick. E-mail Secretary@ctcasl.org; *Treas.* Laura Hedenberg. E-mail treasurer@ctcasl.org; *Past Pres.* Barbara Johnson. E-mail bjohnson@ctcasl.org.

Address correspondence to the president. CASL, 4 Wotton Lane, Burlington 06013. World Wide Web https://casl.wildapricot.org.

Delaware

Delaware Assn. of School Libns. (DASL), div. of Delaware Lib. Assn. Memb. 100+. Publications. *DASL Newsletter* (online; irreg.); column in *DLA Bulletin* (2x yearly).

Pres. Katelynn Scott, Alfred G. Waters Middle School, 1235 Cedar Lane Rd., Middletown 19709. Tel. 302-449-3490 ext. 2134, e-mail katelynn.scott@appo.k12.de.us; *V.P./Pres.-Elect* Patty Brown, Everett Meredith Middle School, 504 S. Broad St., Middletown 19709. Tel. 302-378-5001, e-mail patricia.brown@appo.k12.de.us; *Secy.* Patty Crilley, Old State Elementary School, 580 Tony Marchio Dr., Townsend 19734. Tel. 302-378-6720, e-mail Patricia.Crilley@appo.k12.de.us; *Treas.* Jaclyn Hale, Dover Public Lib., 35 Loockerman Plz., Dover 19901. Tel. 302-736-7185, e-mail jaclyn.haledla@gmail.com; *Past Pres.* Kim Read, St. George's Technical High School, 555 Hyatt's Corner Rd., Middletown 19709, Tel. 302-449-3360, e-mail kim.read@nccvt.k12.de.us.

Address correspondence to the president, DASL, c/o Delaware Lib. Assn., Delaware Division of Libs., 121 Martin Luther King, Jr. Blvd. N., Dover 19901. World Wide Web https://dla.lib.de.us/divisions/dasl.

District of Columbia

District of Columbia Assn. of School Libns. (DCASL). Memb. 8. Publication. *Newsletter* (4x yearly).

Dir. Christopher Stewart; *Assistant Dir.* Angela Falkenberg.

Address correspondence to DCASL, DC Library Association, Unit 1653, Washington, DC 20013. Tel. 301-502-4203, e-mail contactdcasl@gmail.com.

World Wide Web https://dcla.org/School-Library-Section.

Florida

Florida Assn. for Media in Educ. (FAME). Memb. 1,400+. Term of Office. Nov.–Oct. Publication. *Florida Media Quarterly* (q.; memb.). *Ed.* Okle Miller. E-mail okle.miller@gmail.com.

Pres. Kathleen Daniels; *Pres.-Elect* Kris Smith; *Secy.* Brandi Gutch; *Treas.* Angela Michael; *Parliamentarian* Vic Burke; *Past Pres.* Michelle Jarrett.

Address correspondence to FAME, P.O. Box 941169, Maitland 32794-1169. Tel. 863-585-6802, e-mail FAME@floridamediaed.org.

World Wide Web https://www.floridamediaed.org.

Georgia

Georgia Lib. Media Assn. (GLMA). Memb. 700+.

Pres. Ashley Sherman. E-mail president@glma-inc.org; *Pres.-Elect* Meggan Ford; *Secy.* Sarah Sansbury; *Treas.* Lora Taft. E-mail treasurer@glma-inc.org; *Past Pres.* Martha Bongiorno.

Address correspondence to GLMA, P.O. Box 148, Waverly Hall 31831. E-mail info@glma-inc.org.

World Wide Web https://www.glma-inc.org.

Hawaii

Hawaii Assn. of School Libns. Memb. (HASL). 145. Term of Office. June–May.

Pres. Caitlin Ramirez, Mokapu Elementary; *V.P. Programming* Caitlin Ramirez, Mokapu Elementary; *VP Programming* Danielle Fujii, Kalaheo High School; *VP Membership* Elodie Arellano, Ahuimanu Elementary; *Secy.* Daphne Miyashiro, Kalani High School; *Treas.* Renea Ruark, Kaimuki High School.

Address correspondence to HASL, P.O. Box 29691 Honolulu 96820. E-mail hasl.contactus@gmail.com.

World Wide Web https://haslhawaii.weebly.com.

Idaho

School Libs. Services and Consulting, Idaho Commission for Libs. (ICfL).
School Library Action Planning Committee: School Lib. Consultant Jeannie Standal. Tel. 208-639-4139, e-mail jeannie.standal@libraries.idaho.gov; Kit Anderson, Teton High School, Teton School Dist.; Sherrilynn Bair, Snake River School Community Lib.; Dennis Hahs, Rocky Mountain High School, Joint School Dist #2; Lynn Johnson, Mountain View School Dist.; Kiersten Kerr, Coeur d'Alene School Dist.; Susan Tabor-Boesch, Wood River Middle School.

Address correspondence to Jeannie Standal, Idaho Commission for Libs. 325 W. State St., Boise 83702. Tel. 208-334-2150, fax 208-334-4016, e-mail jeannie.standal@libraries.idaho.gov.

World Wide Web https://libraries.idaho.gov/school-libraries.

Illinois

Assn. of Illinois School Lib. Educators (AISLE). Memb. 1,000. Term of Office. July–June. Publications. Newsletter (4x yearly). *Ed.* David P. Little. E-mail newsletter@aisled.org.
Pres. Christy Semande, Canton USD #66, Canton. E-mail president@aisled.org; *Pres.-Elect* Mary Jo Matousek. E-mail preselect@aisled.org; *Secy.* Joanna Marek, La Grange School Dist. 105. E-mail secretary@aisled.org; *Treas.* Michelle Glatt. E-mail; treasurer@aisled.org; *Past Pres.* Anna Kim, Chappell Elementary, Chicago. E-mail pastpres@aisled.org; *Exec. Secy.* Carolyn Kinsella. E-mail execsecretary@aisled.org.

Address correspondence to Assn. of Illinois School Lib. Educators. P.O. Box 110, Seneca 61360. Tel./fax 815-357-6023, e-mail execsecretary@aisled.org.

World Wide Web https://www.aisled.org.

Indiana

Assn. of Indiana School Lib. Educators (AISLE), affiliation of the Indiana Lib. Federation.
Chair Emily Wilt, Chesterton High School. E-mail ewilt@duneland.k12.in.us; *Chair Elect* Position Open; *Past Chair* Diane Rogers, Ben Davis 9th Grade Ctr. Tel. 317-988-7577; *Secy.* Ben Moore, Summit Middle School.

Address correspondence to AISLE, c/o Indiana Lib. Federation, 6510 Telecom Drive, Suite 200, Indianapolis 46278. Tel. 317-257-2040, e-mail info@ilfonline.org.

World Wide Web https://www.ilfonline.org.

Iowa

Iowa Assn. of School Libns. (IASL), div. of the Iowa Lib. Assn. Memb. 180+. Term of Office. Jan.–Jan.
Pres. Ron Frascht, Lewis Central Community School District, Council Bluffs; *V.P./ Pres.-Elect* Position Open; *Secy./Treas.* Lisa Newgard, Orchard Hill Elementary, Cedar Falls; *Past Pres.* Michelle Kruse, Cedar Rapids Middle School. E-mail michelle.kruse.2011@gmail.com; *Membs.-at-Large* Diana Geers, Carrie Teske.

Address correspondence to the president, IASL, c/o the Iowa Lib. Assn., 6919 Vista Dr., W. Des Moines 50266. Tel. 515-282-8192.

World Wide Web https://www.iasl-ia.org.

Kansas

Kansas Assn. of School Libns. (KASL). Memb. 600.
Pres. Rachel Yoder. E-mail rachel.yoder@usd460.org; *1st V.P.* Position Open; *2nd V.P.* Kristy Oborny. E-mail korborny@usd489.com; *Secy.* Rachel Hodges. E-mail hodgesrac@gmail.com; *Treas.* Amanda Harrison. E-mail amanda.harrison@mcpherson.com; *Past Pres.* Gail Becker. E-mail gbecker@usd259.net.

Address correspondence to the president, KASL, c/o Kansas Lib. Assn., P.O. Box 463, Manhattan 66505. Tel. 785-370-3544.

World Wide Web https://www.ksschoolli brarians.org.

Kentucky

Kentucky Assn. of School Libns. (KASL), section of Kentucky Lib. Assn. Memb. 600+. Publication. "KASL Blog." (blog) http://www.kaslblog.com.
Pres. Jen Gilbert. E-mail jennifer.gilbert@eminence.kyschools.us; *Pres.-Elect* Carrie Wilkerson. E-mail carrie.wilkerson@daviess.kyschools.us; *Secy.* Lindsy Serrano. E-mail lserrano@stfrancisschool.org; *Treas.* Fred Tilsley. E-mail tilsley.kasl@gmail.com; *Past Pres.* Deidra Bowling-Meade. E-mail deidra.bowl ingmeade@ashland.kyschools.us.

Address correspondence to the president. World Wide Web http://www.kasl.us.

Louisiana

Louisiana Assn. of School Libns. (LASL), section of the Louisiana Lib. Assn. Memb. 230. Term of Office. July–June.
Pres. Kim "Lovie" Howell, Benton Middle School. E-mail kim.howell@bossierschools. org; *1st V.P.* Amanda Jones, Live Oak Middle School. E-mail amanda.jones@lpsb.org; *2nd V.P.* Tammy Chaffin, French Settlement High School. E-mail tammy.chaffin@lpsb.org; *Secy.* Kelsye Baudoin, Belle Place Elementary School. E-mail kebaudoin@iberiaschools.org; *Parliamentarian* Tiffany Whitehead, Episcopal School Library. E-mail librariantiff@gmail. com; *Past-Pres.* Amanda Blanco, Lafayette High School.

Address correspondence to LASL, c/o Louisiana Lib. Assn., 1190 Meramec Station Rd., Suite 207, Ballwin, MO 63021. Tel. 1-800-969-6562 ext. 3, e-mail lla@amigos.org. World Wide Web http://laslonline.weebly.com.

Maine

Maine Assn. of School Libs. (MASL). Memb. 200+.
Pres. Jennifer Stanbro, Skillin Elementary, South Portland; *Pres.-Elect* Heather Perkinson, Greely High School; *Secy.* Cathy Potter, Falmouth Middle School, Falmouth; *Treas.* Amy Denecker–Windham High School; *Past Pres.* Amanda Kozaka, Cape Elizabeth Middle School. E-mail akozaka@capeelizabethschools.org.

Address correspondence to the president, MASL, c/o Maine State Lib. Assn., 64 State House Station, Augusta 04333-0004. E-mail maslibraries@gmail.com. World Wide Web http://www.maslibraries.org.

Maryland

Maryland Assn. of School Libns (MASL). Publication. Newsletter (mo.; online).
Pres. Tatanisha Love, Loch Raven Technical Academy, Baltimore County Public Schools. E-mail presidentelect@maslmd.org; *Pres.-Elect* Donna Mignardi, Calvert High School,

Calvert County Public Schools. E-mail presidentelect@maslmd.org; *Secy.* Beau Williams, Snow Hill Middle School, Worcester County Public Schools. E-mail secretary@maslmd.org; *Treas.* Brittany Tignor, Snow Hill High School, Worcester County Public Schools. E-mail treasurer@maslmd.org; *Past Pres.* Lindsey Weaver, West Frederick Middle School, Frederick County Public School. E-mail pastpresident@maslmd.org; *Membs.-at-Large*, Stacy Nunn, Winland Elementary School, Baltimore County Public Schools. E-mail memberatlarge@maslmd.org; Sally Wolfe, Sunderland Elementary School, Calvert County Public Schools. E-mail memberatlarge@maslmd.org.

Address correspondence to the secretary via 111 Tail of the Fox Drive, Ocean Pines 21811. Tel. 410-929-1181, e-mail secretary@maslmd.org.
World Wide Web https://www.maslmd.org.

Massachusetts

Massachusetts School Lib. Assn. (MSLA). Memb. 800. Publication. *MSLA Forum* (irreg.; online). Eds. Katherine Steiger, Reba Tierney.
Pres. Jennifer Varney, MLKing, Jr. School, Cambridge. E-mail jvarney@maschoolibraries.org; *Pres. Elect* Barb Fecteau, Beverly High School. E-mail bfecteau@maschoolibraries.org; *Secy.* Emma Kwon, Weston Elementary Schools. E-mail ekwon@maschoolibraries.org; *Treas.* Michelle Fontaine. E-mail mfontaine@maschoolibraries.org; *Past Pres.* Laura Luker, Pioneer Valley Chinese Immersion Charter, Hadley. E-mail lluker@maschoolibraries.org.

Address correspondence to Emily Kristofek, office manager, P.O. Box 336. Wayland, MA 01778. Tel. 508-276-1697, e-mail ekristofek@maschoolibraries.org.
World Wide Web https://www.maschoolibraries.org.

Michigan

Michigan Assn. of School Librarians (formerly Michigan Assn. for Media in Education (MAME)). Memb. 1,200. Publication. *Media Matters!* newsletter (mo.). Eds. Beverly Banks. E-mail beverlybanks@wlcsd.org and Jonathan Richards. E-mail jrichards@vanburenschools.net.
Pres. Carma Roesch, Clinton Community Schools, 341 E. Michigan Ave., Clinton

49236. E-mail croesch@mimasl.org; *Pres.-Elect* C Carrie Betts. E-mail cbetts@mimasl.org; *V.P. Continuing Ed.* Cheri Dobbs, Detroit Country Day School, Beverly Hills. Tel. 248-430-1246, e-mail cdobbs@dcds.edu; *V.P. Regions and SIGS* Katherine Montei, Oakview Middle School, 917 Lake George Road, Oakland 48363. Tel. 248-693-0321 ext. 8306, e-mail Katherine.Montei@lok12.org; *Secy.* Kelly Hincks. E-mail khincks@mimasl.org; *Treas.* Lisa Kelley, Rochester Community Schools, University Hills, 600 Croydon, Rochester Hills 48309. Tel. 248-726-4404, e-mail lkelley@mimasl.org; *Past Pres.* Erica Trowbridge, Oakridge Public Schools, 5493 E. Hall Rd., Muskegon 49442. E-mail etrowbridge@mimasl.org; *Exec. Secy.* Teri Belcher. E-mail tbelcher@mimame.org.

Address correspondence to Michigan Association of School Librarians, 520 S. Creyts Rd., Lansing 48917. E-mail mame@mimame.org.

World Wide Web http://www.mimasl.org.

Minnesota

Info. and Technology Educators of Minnesota (ITEM) (formerly Minnesota Educ. Media Organization). Memb. 400+. Term of Office. July–June.

Co-Pres. Janeen Perrizo, St. Charles Public Schools. E-mail jperrizo@schs.k12.mn.us; *Co-Pres.* Tami Rhea, Dover-Eyota Public Schools; *Secy.* Sarah Rose, Minneapolis Public Schools; *Past Co-Pres.* Sara Florin, Centennial Public Schools; *Past Co-Pres.* Ashley Krohn, Minneapolis Public Schools; Marie Hydukovich, South Saint Paul Public Schools.

Address correspondence to ITEM, P.O. Box 130555, Roseville 55113. Tel. 651-771-8672, e-mail admin@mnitem.org.

World Wide Web https://www.mnlibraryassociation.org/page/ITEM.

Mississippi

School Lib. Section, Mississippi Lib. Assn. (MLA). Memb. 1,300.

School Lib. Section Chair Angela Mullins, Simpson Central School/Simpson County School Dist. Tel. 601-847-2630, e-mail angel amullins39073@gmail.com.

Address correspondence to School Lib. Section, MLA, P.O. Box 13687, Jackson 39236-3687. Tel. 601-981-4586, e-mail info@misslib.org.

World Wide Web http://www.misslib.org/page-1860236.

Missouri

Missouri Assn. of School Libns. (MASL). Memb. 1,000. Term of Office. July–June.

Pres. Melissa Corey, Robidoux Middle School, St. Joseph School Dist. E-mail melissa.corey@sjsd.k12.mo.us; *1st V.P.* Tom Bober, Ralph M. Captain Elementary, School District of Clayton. E-mail tombob-er@clayton schools.net; *2nd V.P.* Matt King, Discovery Elementary, Orchard Farm School District. E-mail mking@ofr5.com; *Secy.* Jenn Baldwin, East Newton High School, East Newton R-VI School District. E-mail baldwinj@eastnewton.org; *Treas.* Tamie Williams, Neosho School District. E-mail williamstamie@neoshosd.org; *AASL Delegate* Hope Hunter, St. James R-1. E-mail hope.j.hunter@gmail.com; *Past Pres.* Kris Baughman, Eastwood Hills Elementary School, Raytown C-2 School Dist. E-mail kris.baughman@raytownschools.org.

Address correspondence to MASL, P.O. Box 2107, Jefferson City 65102. Tel. 573-893-4155, fax 573-635-2858, e-mail info@maslonline.org.

World Wide Web https://maslonline.org.

Montana

School Lib. Div., Montana Lib. Assn. (MLA). Memb. 200+.

Co-Chair Chani Craig, Whitefish Middle School Library; *Co-Chair* Shelley O'Rourke, North Middle School, Great Falls; *MLA Exec. Dir.* Kirk Vriesman, Montana Library Association, P.O. Box 823, Arlee, MT 59821. E-mail kirkv@mtlib.org.

Address correspondence to the MLA executive director, P.O. Box 823, Arlee, 59821.

World Wide Web https://mlai.wildapricot.org/SLD.

Nebraska

Nebraska School Libns. Assn. (NSLA). Memb. 300+. Term of Office. July–June. Publication. *NSLA News* (blog; mo.).

Pres. Kelly Kenny. E-mail NSLApres@gmail.com; *Pres.-Elect* Chris Haeffner; *Secy.* Jess Winter; *Treas.* Beth Wilson. E-mail treasurernsla@gmail.com; *Past Pres.* Crys Bauermeister. E-mail cbauermeister@gmail.com; *Exec. Secy.* Carole Matthews. E-mail con tactnsla@gmail.com.

Address correspondence to the executive secretary via e-mail.

World Wide Web https://www.neschoolli brarians.org.

Nevada

Nevada School and Children Libns. Section (NSCLS) of the Nevada Lib. Assn. (NLA). Memb. 120.

Chair Susan Thurnbeck, Las Vegas–Clark County Lib. Dist. E-mail susantnvlibrary@ gmail.com; *Past Chair* Larry Johnson, Las Vegas–Clark County Lib. Dist.; *Exec. Secy.* NLA Carla Land, Las Vegas–Clark County Lib. District. E-mail bookdiva@gmail.com.

Address correspondence to the chair, NLA School and Children Libns. Section, via e-mail.

World Wide Web https://nevadalibraries. org/Handbook-NSCLS.

New Hampshire

New Hampshire School Lib. Media Assn. (NSHLMA). Memb. 250+. Term of Office. July–June. Publication. *NHSLMA Newsletter* (irreg.; online).

Pres. Kristin Whitworth, Dover High School. E-mail president@nhslma.org; *V.P.* Jennifer Toth, Atkinson Academy, Timberlane Regional School District. E-mail vicepresident@nhslma.org; *Secy.* Mindi Charles, New Boston Central School, New Boston School District. E-mail secretary@nhslma.org; *Treas.* Audra Lewis, Horne Street School, Dover. E-mail treasurer@nhslma.org; *Past Pres.* Justine Thain, Hooksett School Dist., Hooksett. E-mail past-president@nhslma.org.

Address correspondence to the president, NHSLMA, P.O. Box 418, Concord 03302-0418. E-mail nhslma@gmail.com.

World Wide Web https://nhslma.wildapri cot.org.

New Jersey

New Jersey Assn. of School Libns. (NJASL). Memb. 1,000+. Term of Office. Aug. 1–July 31. Publication. *Bookmark Newsletter* (mo.; memb.). *Ed.* Casey Schaffer. E-mail book mark@njasl.org.

Pres. Ewa Dziedzic-Elliott, Lawrence Township High School, Lawrence. E-mail president@njasl.org; *Pres.-Elect.* Beth Raff, Mt. Tabor Elementary School, Parsippany-Troy Hills School District. E-mail presidentelect@ njasl.org; *V.P.* Karen Grant, Ewing Township Public Schools. E-mail vp@njasl.org; *Recording Secy.* Jessica Piazza, Harmony Township School. E-mail secretary@njasl.org; *Treas.* Elizabeth (Beth) Willoughby, Dunellen Public Schools. E-mail treasurer@njasl.org; *Membs.-at-Large* Iveth Mollinedo Yelegen, Steve Tetreault. E-mail membersatlarge@njasl.org; *Past Pres.* Lisa Straubinger, T. Baldwin Demarest School, Old Tappan. E-mail pastpresident@ njasl.org.

Address correspondence to the recording secretary, NASL, P.O. Box 1460, Springfield 07081.

World Wide Web https://njasl.org.

New York

Section of School Libns., New York Lib. Assn. (NYLA). Memb. 800+. Term of Office. Nov.–Oct. Publication. *School Library Update* (3x yearly; memb. online).

Pres. Madelyn Haussner, E-mail nfogod dess@gmail.com; *Pres.-Elect* Maureen Squire, E-mail maureen.squier@questar.org; *Secy.* Jessica Regitano. E-mail jlregitano@gmail. com; *Treas.* Sue Padjen. E-mail spadjen@ esmschools.org; *V.P. of Conferences* Annarose Foley. E-mail annarose.foley@icsd.k12.ny.us; *V.P. of Communications* Sharon Fox. E-mail sharonfoxlibrarian@gmail.com; *Past Pres.* Lisa Perkowski. E-mail lehnski16@gmail. com.

Address correspondence to the Section of School Libns., NYLA, 6021 State Farm Rd., Guilderland 12084. Tel. 518-432-6952, fax 518-427-1697, e-mail info@nyla.org.

World Wide Web https://www.nyla. org/4DCGI/cms/review.html?Action=CMS_ Document&DocID=136&MenuKey=ssl.

North Carolina

North Carolina School Lib. Media Assn. (NCSLMA). Memb. 1,000+. Term of Office. Nov.–Oct.

Pres. Jennifer Abel. E-mail jenniferabel@ ncslma.org; *Pres.-Elect* Kristy Sartain. E-mail kristysartain@ncslma.org; *Secy.* Scott Summers.

E-mail scottsummers@ncslma.org; *Treas.* Bitsy Griffin. E-mail bitsygriffin@ncslma.org; *Past Pres.* Jenny Umbarger. E-mail jennyum barger@ncslma.org.

Address correspondence to the president, NCSLMA, 151 NC Hwy. 9, Suite B-188, Black Mountain, 28711.

World Wide Web https://ncslma.wildapricot. org.

North Dakota

School Lib. and Youth Svcs. section of the North Dakota Lib. Assn. (NDLA). Memb. 100.

Chair Jennifer Hess, Eagles Elementary School, Fargo Public Schools. E-mail hes sj@fargo.k12.nd.us; *Chair-Elect* Kimberly Mosely, Williston Schools. E-mail kimberly. mosley@willistonschools.org; *Secy.* Carmen Redding, North Dakota State Lib. E-mail Carmen.Redding@k12.nd.us; *Past Chair* Sharri Mosser, North Dakota State Lib. E-mail ssandwick@nd.gov.

Address correspondence to the School Lib. and Youth Svcs. Section, NDLA, 604 E. Boulevard Ave., Bismarck 58505.

World Wide Web https://ndla.info/School-Library-and-Youth-Services.

Ohio

Ohio Educ. Lib. Media Assn. (OELMA). Memb. 1,000.

Pres. Gayle Schmuhl, Walsh Jesuit High School. E-mail president@oelma.org; *V.P.* Lisa Barnes Prince, Manchester Local Schools. E-mail vicepresident@oelma.org; *Secy.* Emily Colpi, Mariemont City Schools. E-mail secretary@oelma.org; *Treas.* Sarah Thornbery, Springboro Community Schools. E-mail treas urer@oelma.org *Past Pres.* Karen Gedeon, Cuyahoga Falls City Schools. E-mail pastpresi dent@oelma.org.

Address correspondence to OELMA, 675 Alpha Drive, Suite E and K, Highland Heights, OH 44143. Tel. 614-647-3487.

World Wide Web https://www.oelma.org.

Oklahoma

Oklahoma School Libns. Div., Oklahoma Lib. Assn. (OLA). Memb. 200+.

Chair Dr. Alesha Baker. E-mail oksl@ oklibs.org; *Chair-Elect* Molly Dettmann.

E-mail mdettmann@norman.k12.ok.us; *Secy.* Latasha McKinney; *Treas.* Lisa Battige. E-mail Lisabattige@gmail.com; *Past Chair* Ashleigh Dautermann.

Address correspondence to the chairperson, School Libns. Div., OLA, 1190 Meramec Station Rd., Suite 207, Ballwin, MO 63021-6902. Tel. 800-969-6562 ext. 5, fax 636-529-1396.

World Wide Web https://www.oklibs.org/ page/OKSL.

Oregon

Oregon Assn. of School Libs. (OASL). Memb. 600. Publication. *Interchange* (3x yearly). Coord. Ed. Dana Berglund. E-mail interchange@ oasl.olaweb.org.

Pres. Jessica Lorentz Smith, Bend Senior High School. E-mail president@oasl.olaweb. org; *V.P./Pres.-Elect* Ayn Frazee, Franklin High School, Portland Public Schools. E-mail presidentelect@oasl.olaweb.org; *Secy.* Jenny Takeda, Beaverton School District. E-mail secretary@oasl.olaweb.org; *Treas.* Jen Maurer, State Library of Oregon. E-mail treasur er@oasl.olaweb.org; *Past Pres.* Grace Butler, Whitman Elementary School. E-mail past-president@oasl.olaweb.org; *Membs.-at-Large* Laura Axton, Portland Public Schools. E-mail region4@oasl.olaweb.org; Elaine Ferrell-Burns, Portland Public Schools/Portland State University. E-mail reading@oasl.olaweb.org.

Address correspondence to the president, OASL, c/o Oregon Lib. Assn., P.O. Box 3067, La Grande 97850. Tel. 541-962-5824, e-mail president@oasl.olaweb.org.

World Wide Web https://www.olaweb.org/ oasl-home.

Pennsylvania

Pennsylvania School Libns. Assn. (PSLA). Memb. 800+. Publication. *PSLA Pulse* (blog).

Pres. Laura Aimee Emerson, Floyd C. Fretz Middle School, Bradford Area School District. E-mail aemerson@psla.org; *Pres.-Elect.* Leah Lindemann, Blackhawk High School, Blackhawk School District. E-mail llindemann@ psla.org; *V.P.* Sarah DeMaria, Hempfield High School, Hempfield School District. E-mail sdemaria@psla.org; *Secy.* Elizabeth Henry, Lampeter-Strasburg School District. E-mail secretary@psla.org; *Treas.* Jeffrey Weiss, Bradford Area High School, Bradford Area

School Dist. E-mail pslatreasurer@gmail. com; *Past Pres.* Laura Ward, Fox Chapel Area School Dist. E-mail lward@psla.org.

Address correspondence to the president, PSLA, Hershey Square #125, 1152 Mae St., Hummelstown 17036.

World Wide Web https://www.psla.org.

Rhode Island

School Libns. of Rhode Island, section of the Rhode Island Lib. Assn. (RILA). Memb. 350+. Publication. *SLRI Update* (irreg.; online).

Pres. Joan Eldredge-Mouradjian. E-mail jmouradjian@nssk12.org; *V.P.* Mary Moen. E-mail mary_moen@uri.edu; *Secy.* Marianne Mirando. E-mail mmirando@westerly.k12. ri.us; *Past Pres.* Deanna Brooks. E-mail slri. prez@gmail.com.

Address correspondence to the president, School Libns. of Rhode Island, RILA, P.O. Box 6765, Providence 02940.

World Wide Web https://rilibraries.org/slri.

South Carolina

South Carolina Assn. of School Libns. (SCASL). Memb. 900. Term of Office. July–June. Publication *SCASL Messenger* (q., online, memb.). *Ed.* Anya Bonnette. E-mail anya. bonnette@ocsd5.net.

Pres. Tamara Cox. E-mail president@scasl. net; *Pres.-Elect* Michelle Spires. E-mail presi dent.elect@scasl.net; *Secy.* Gloria Coleman. E-mail secretary@scasl.net; *Treas.* Tiffany Anderson; *Past Pres.* Katherine Malmquist.

Address correspondence to SCASL, P.O. Box 2442, Columbia 29202. Tel./fax 803-492-3025.

World Wide Web https://www.scasl.net.

South Dakota

South Dakota School Lib. Media Section, South Dakota Lib. Assn. (SDLA). Memb. 140+. Term of Office. Oct.–Sept.

Chair Kris O'Brien, Watertown High School, Watertown. E-mail korey.erickson@ k12.sd.us; *Past Chair* Korey Erickson, Sioux Falls Public Schools, Sioux Falls. E-mail korey.erickson@k12.sd.us.

Address correspondence to the chairperson. South Dakota School Lib. Media Section,

SDLA, Mikkelsen Lib., 2001 S. Summit Ave., Sioux Falls 57197. Tel. 605-743-0889.

World Wide Web https://www.sdlibraryas sociation.org/page/Sections.

Tennessee

Tennessee Assn. of School Libns. (TASL). Memb. 450. Term of Office. Jan.–Dec. Publication. *TASL Talks* (wk.; blog).

Pres. Katelyn Jernigan; *Pres.-Elect* Dustin Hensley; *Secy.* Heather Alexander; *Treas.* Mallory Nygard; *Past Pres.* Katie Capshaw.

Address correspondence to the president, P.O. Box 10516, Knoxville 37919.

World Wide Web https://www.tasltn.org.

Texas

Texas Assn. of School Libns. (TASL), div. of Texas Lib. Assn. Memb. 4,500+. Term of Office. Apr.–Mar.

Chair Lucy Podmore. E-mail lucy.podmore@ nisd.net; *Chair-Elect* Brooke King. E-mail brookebeesonking@gmail.com; *Secy.* Andrea Keller. E-mail akbusybee@gmail.com; *Councilor* Amanda Hunt. E-mail ahunt@nbisd.org; *Alternate Councilor* Emma McDonald. E-mail EMc donald@mesquiteisd.org; *Independent Schools Chair* Abby Harrison. E-mail harrisona@green hill.org; *Social Media Chair* Heather Horner. E-mail hornorh@gmail.com; *Past Chair & Web Admin.* Jill Bellomy. E-mail jillbellomy@ gmail.com; *TLA Exec. Dir.* Shirley Robinson. E-mail shirleyr@txla.org.

Address correspondence to the chairperson, TASL, c/o Texas Lib. Assn., 3420 Executive Center Dr., Suite 301, Austin 78731. Tel. 512-328-1518, fax 512-328-8852.

World Wide Web https://www.txla.org/ groups/tasl.

Utah

Utah Educ. Lib. Media Assn. (UELMA). Memb. 500+. Publication. *UELMA Works* (q.).

Pres. Michele Edgley, Salt Lake City. E-mail michele.edgley@slcschools.org; *Pres.-Elect* Gretchen Zaitzeff, Canyons. E-mail gretchen.zaitzeff@canyonsdistrict.org; *Secy.* Beth Tanner; *Past Pres.* Tricia Fenton, Granite School District; *Exec. Dir.* Davina Sauthoff. E-mail executivedirector@uelma.org.

Address correspondence to the executive director.

World Wide Web https://uelma.org.

Vermont

Vermont School Lib. Assn. (VSLA). Memb. 220+. Term of Office. May–May.

Pres. Charles Dabritz. E-mail cdabritz@bsdvt.org; *Pres.-Elect* Ericka Behrsing. E-mail ebehrsing@sbschools.net; *Secy.* Shannon De-Santis Gile. E-mail shannon.desantis@lsuu.org; *Treas.* Megan Sutton. E-mail msutton@acsdvt.org; *Past Pres.* Meg Allison.

Address correspondence to VSLAmembership@gmail.com.

World Wide Web https://vsla.wildapricot.org.

Virginia

Virginia Assn. of School Libns. (VAASL). Memb. 1,200. Term of Office. Nov.–Nov. Publication. *VAASL Voice* (q.; memb.).

Pres. Nathan Sekinger. E-mail president@vaasl.org; *Pres.-Elect* Kelly Passek. E-mail presidentelect@vaasl.org; *Secy.* Jennifer Cooper. E-mail secretary@vaasl.org; *Treas.* Christine Ware. E-mail Treasurer@vaasl.org; *Past Pres.* Judy Deichman. E-mail pastpresident@vaasl.org; *Exec. Dir.* Margaret Baker. E-mail executive@vaasl.org.

Address correspondence to the executive director, VAASL, P.O. Box 2015, Staunton 24402-2015. Tel. 540-416-6109, e-mail executive@vaasl.org.

World Wide Web https://www.vaasl.org.

Washington

School Lib. Div., Washington Lib. Assn. (WLA). Memb. 700+. Term of Office. Apr.–Apr.

Chair Elizabeth Roberts, Bellevue School District. E-mail elizabeth.k.roberts@gmail.com; *V. Chair/Chair-Elect* Sam Harris, Charles Wright Academy. E-mail s.kathleen.harris@gmail.com.

Address correspondence to WLA School Lib. Div., P.O. Box 33808, Seattle 98133. Tel. 206-823-1138, e-mail info@wla.org.

World Wide Web https://www.wla.org/school-libraries.

West Virginia

School Lib. Div., West Virginia Lib. Assn. (WVLA). Memb. 50. Term of Office. Nov.–Nov.

Chair Leigh Ann Hood, East Park Elementary, 805 Pittsburgh Ave., Fairmont 26554. Tel. 304-534-0927, e-mail lahood@k12.wv.us; *Past Chair* Lynda Suzie Martin, Brookhaven Elementary, 147 Estate Dr., Morgantown 26508. Tel. 304-282-0147, e-mail librarynbct@gmail.com.

Address correspondence to the chairperson, WVLA School Lib. Div., P.O. Box 1432, Morgantown 26507.

World Wide Web https://wvla.org.

Wisconsin

Wisconsin Educ. Media and Technology Assn. (WEMTA). Memb. 800+.

Pres. Tina Birkett; *Pres.-Elect* Jennifer Griffith; *V.P.* Kay Koepsel-Benning; *Secy.* Dawn Totzke; *Treas.* Emily Dittmar; *Past Pres.* Raquel Rand.

Address correspondence to WEMTA, 1502 W. Broadway, Suite 102, Madison, WI 53713. Tel. 608-588-6006, e-mail wemta@wemta.org.

World Wide Web https://www.wemta.org.

Wyoming

School Lib. Interest Group, Wyoming Lib. Assn. (WLA). Memb. 100+.

Co-Chair Melissa Brumsted Snider, Teton County School Dist. Tel. 307-733-3020; *Co-Chair* Megan Bietz, Campbell County School Dist. Tel. 307-682-7289; *Secy.* Maggie Unterseher, Weston County School Dist. #1. Tel. 307-629-0190.

Address correspondence to the chairperson, SLIG, c/o WLA, 1190 Meramac Station Rd., Suite 207, Ballwin MO 63201.

World Wide Web https://wyla.org/School-Library-Interest-Group.

International Library Associations

International Association of Law Libraries

Mark Engsberg, President
P.O. Box 5709, Washington, DC 20016
E-mail president@iall.org
World Wide Web https://iall.org

Objective

The International Association of Law Libraries (IALL) is a worldwide organization of librarians, libraries, and other persons or institutions concerned with the acquisition and use of legal information emanating from sources other than their jurisdictions and from multinational and international organizations.

IALL's purpose is to facilitate the work of librarians who acquire, process, organize, and provide access to foreign legal materials. IALL has no local chapters but maintains liaison with national law library associations in many countries and regions of the world.

Membership

More than 400 members in more than 50 countries on five continents.

Officers

Pres. Mark Engsberg, Emory University School of Law, Atlanta, GA 30341. Tel. 404-727-6983, e-mail president@iall.org; *V.P.* Kerem Kahvecioglu, Haciahment Mahellesi, Istanbul, Turkey. Tel: 90 212 311 5157, e-mail vicepresident@iall.org; *Secy.* Trung Quach, High Court of Australia, Parkes, Australia. Tel. 61 2 6270 6834; *Treas.* Jean Wenger, Chicago-Kent College of Law, Chicago, IL 60661. Tel. 312-906-5610, fax 312-906-5679; *Past Pres.* Kurt Carroll, Library of Congress, Washington, DC 20540. Tel. 202-707-5080.

Board of Directors

Rebecca J. Five Bergstrøm, University of Oslo Law Library, Oslo, Norway. Tel. 4722859306; Vanessa Blackmore, New South Wales Department of Communities and Justice, Sydney, Australia. Tel. 612 9230 8675; Yee Xin Chai, C.J. Koh Law Library, National University of Singapore. Tel. 65 6601 7163; Sonia Crenn, International Committee of the Red Cross Library, Geneva, Switzerland. Tel. 41 22 730 20 30; Claudia Holland, Max Planck Institute for Comparative and International Private Law, Hamburg, Germany. Tel. 49 40 419 00 – 226; Lyonette Louis-Jacques, D'Angelo Law Library, University of Chicago Law School, Chicago, IL. Tel. 773-702-9612; David Wills, Squire Law Library, University of Cambridge, Cambridge, United Kingdom. Tel. 44 (0)1223 330071.

Publication

International Journal of Legal Information (*IJLI*) (3x yearly; memb.).

International Association of Music Libraries, Archives, and Documentation Centres

Anders Cato
Slots- og Kulturstyrelsen, Danish Agency for Culture and Palaces
Hammerichsgade 14, DK-1611 Copenhagen V, Denmark
Tel: +45 5376 6337, e-mail secretary@iaml.info
World Wide Web https://www.iaml.info

Objective

The objective of the International Association of Music Libraries, Archives, and Documentation Centres (IAML) is to promote the activities of music libraries, archives, and documentation centers and to strengthen the cooperation among them; to promote the availability of all publications and documents relating to music and further their bibliographical control; to encourage the development of standards in all areas that concern the association; and to support the protection and preservation of musical documents of the past and the present.

Membership

Memb. approximately 1,700 in about 40 countries worldwide.

Officers

Pres. Pia Shekhter, Gothenburg Univ. Lib., Sweden. E-mail president@iaml.info; *V.P.s* Jürgen Diet, Bayerische Staatsbibliothek, Munich; Jane Gottlieb, The Juilliard School, New York; Anna Pensaert, Cambridge Univ. Lib. and the Pendlebury Lib. of Music; Rupert Ridgewell, British Lib., London; *Secy.-Gen.* P. Anders Cato, Danish Agency for Culture and Palaces, Copenhagen, Denmark. E-mail secretary@iaml.info; *Treasurer* Kimmy Szeto, Baruch College, City University of New York, USA. E-mail treasurer@iaml.info; *Past Pres.* Stanislaw Hrabia, Uniwersytet Jagiellonski, Kraków, Poland.

Publication

Fontes Artis Musicae (q.; memb.). *Ed.* James P. Cassaro, Univ. of Pittsburgh, B-30 Music Bldg., Pittsburgh, PA 15260. Tel. 412-624-4131, e-mail fontes@iaml.info.

Institutional Sections

Archives and Music Documentation Centres. *Chair* Joseph Hafner, McGill Library, Montréal, Canada. E-mail archives@iaml.info.

Broadcasting and Orchestra Libraries. *Chair* Sabina Benelli, Teatro alla Scala, Milan, Italy. E-mail broadcasting-orchestra@iaml.info.

Libraries in Music Teaching Institutions. *Chair* Charles Peters, William & Gayle Cook Music Lib., Indiana Univ., Bloomington, IN. E-mail teaching@iaml.info.

Public Libraries. *Chair* Blanka Ellederová, Municipal Lib. of Prague, Czech Republic. E-mail public-libraries@iaml.info.

Research Libraries. *Chair* Ruprecht Langer, Deutsche Nationalbibliothek, Leipzig, Germany. E-mail research-libraries@iaml.info.

Subject Sections

Audio-Visual Materials. *Chair* Zane Grosa, National Library of Latvia, Riga. E-mail ajustice@usc.edu.

Bibliography. *Chair* Stefan Engl, Österreichische Nationalbibliothek, Vienna, Austria. E-mail bibliography@iaml.info.

Cataloguing. *Chair* Kimmy Szeto, Baruch College, New York, USA. E-mail cataloguing@iaml.info.

Service and Training. *Chair* Katherine Penner, University of Manitoba, Canada. E-mail service@iaml.info.

International Association of School Librarianship

Jill Hancock, Executive Director
P.O. Box 684, Jefferson City, MO 65102
Tel. 573-635-2173, e-mail iasl@c2pro.solutions
World Wide Web https://iasl-online.org

Mission and Objectives

The mission of the International Association of School Librarianship (IASL) is to provide an international forum for those interested in promoting effective school library programs as viable instruments in the education process. IASL also provides guidance and advice for the development of school library programs and the school library profession. IASL works in cooperation with other professional associations and agencies.

Membership is worldwide and includes school librarians, teachers, librarians, library advisers, consultants, education administrators, and others who are responsible for library and information services in schools. The membership also includes professors and instructors in universities and colleges where there are programs for school librarians and students who are undertaking such programs.

The objectives of IASL are to advocate the development of school libraries throughout all countries; to encourage the integration of school library programs into the instruction and curriculum of the school; to promote the professional preparation and continuing education of school library personnel; to foster a sense of community among school librarians in all parts of the world; to foster and extend relationships between school librarians and other professionals in connection with children and youth; to foster research in the field of school librarianship and the integration of its findings with pertinent knowledge from related fields; to promote the publication and dissemination of information about successful advocacy and program initiatives in school librarianship; to share information about programs and materials for children and youth throughout the international community; and to initiate and coordinate activities, conferences, and other projects in the field of school librarianship and information services. IASL was founded in 1971.

Membership

Approximately 825.

Officers

Pres. Jennifer Branch-Mueller, University of Alberta, Edmonton, Canada. E-mail jbranch@ualberta.ca; *V.P. Assn. Operations* Fredrik Ernerot, School Library West, Gothenburg, Sweden. E-mail fredrik.ernerot@grundskola.goteborg.se; *V.P. Assn. Relations* Annie Tam, Independent Schools Foundation Academy, Hong Kong, China. E-mail atam@isf.edu.hk; *V.P. Advocacy and Promotion* Zakir Hossain, ICS Inter-Community School, Zurich, Switzerland. E-mail zakir.researchtl@gmail.com; *Treas.* Katy Manck, Independent Book Reviewer, Gilmer, Texas.

Regional Board of Directors

Sophia Adeyeye, Africa; Dr. Chavvi Jain, Asia; Eleanor Duggan, East Asia; Meghan Harper, North America; Mark-Jeffery O'Niel Deans, Latin America/Caribbean; Antonija Lujanac, Europe; Sevgi Arioglu, North Africa/Middle East; Dr. Kay Oddone, Oceania; Corinne Hertel, International Schools.

Publications

School Libraries Worldwide (http://www.iasl-online.org/publications/slw/index.html), the association's refereed research and professional journal (online only; 2x yearly; memb.).

IASL Newsletter (http://www.iasl-online.org/publications/newsletter.html) (print; 4x yearly; memb.).

International Association of University Libraries

Rita Pape, Office Manager
Zum Ehrenhain 34, 22885 Barsbüttel, Germany
Tel. +49-40-670 882-80, email iatul@cpo-hanser.de
World Wide Web https://www.iatul.org

Objective

The main objective of the International Association of Scientific and Technological University Libraries (IATUL) is to provide a forum where library directors and senior managers can meet to exchange views on matters of current significance and to provide an opportunity for them to develop a collaborative approach to solving problems. IATUL also welcomes into membership organizations that supply services to university libraries, if they wish to be identified with the association's activities.

Membership

260 in 60 countries.

Officers

Pres. Dr. Anna Walek, GUT Library, Gdańsk University of Technology, Poland. E-mail anna.walek@pg.edu.pl; *V.P.* Dr. Charles Eckman, Otto G. Richter Library, University of Miami, USA. E-mail ceckman@miami.edu; *Secy.* Kate Robinson, University of Bath, United Kingdom. E-mail liskmr@bath.ac.uk; *Treas.* Mag. Gerda Winkler, Universitiy Library, Free University of Bozen-Bolzano, Italy. E-mail library@unibz.it.

Board Members

Kara Jones, American University of Sharjah. E-mail kjones@aus.edu; Xinwan Li, Shanghai Jiao Tong University. E-mail lixinwan@sjtu.edu.cn; Liliana Luchi, Universidad Austral. E-mail lluchi@austral.edu.ar; Ujala Satgoor, University of Cape Town, South Africa. E-mail ujala.satgoor@uct.ac.za.

Publication

IATUL Conference Proceedings (https://www.iatul.org/publications/proceedings).

International Council on Archives

Fina Solà i Gasset, President
60 rue des Francs-Bourgeois, 75003 Paris, France
Tel. 33-1-40-27-63-06, fax 33-1-42-72-20-65, e-mail ica@ica.org
World Wide Web https://www.ica.org/en

Objective

The mission of the International Council on Archives (ICA) is to establish, maintain, and strengthen relations among archivists of all lands and among all professional and other agencies or institutions concerned with the custody, organization, or administration of archives, public or private, wherever located. ICA was established in 1948.

Membership

Approximately 1,900 in nearly 200 countries and territories.

Officers

Pres. Fina Solà i Gasset, Maritim Museum, Barcelona, Spain; *V.P.* Meg Phillips, U.S.

Board Members

Hamad bin Mohammed al-Dhawyani, Oman; Françoise Banat-Berger, France; Avril Belfon, Trinidad and Tobago; Alexander Lukas Bieri, Switzerland; Caroline Brown, United Kingdom; Yolanda Cagigas Ocejo, Spain; Montserrat Canela Garayoa, Switzerland; Søren Bitsch Christensen, Denmark; Emma de Ramon Acevedo, Chile; Charles Farrugia, Malta; Emilie Gagnet Leumas, United States; Becky Haglund Tousey, United States; Jeff James, United Kingdom; James Lowry, United States; Guoqiang Lu, China; Victorino M. Manalo, Philippines; Vitor Manoel Marques da Fonseca, Brazil; Paolo Massa, Italy; Mathias Massode, Benin; Noa Petueli Tapumanaia, Tuvalu; Fina Solà i Gasset, Spain; Atakilty Assefa Asgedom, Ethiopia (ex officio).

Publications

Comma (print and online; 2x yearly; memb.).
Flash (online only; 2x yearly; memb.).
ICA e-newsletter (online only; mo.).
Conference Papers and Proceedings.

International Federation of Film Archives
(Fédération Internationale des Archives du Film)

Michael Loebenstein, Secretary-General
Secretariat, 42 rue Blanche, B-1060 Brussels, Belgium
Tel. 32-2-538-30-65, fax 32-2-534-47-74, e-mail info@fiafnet.org
World Wide Web https://www.fiafnet.org

Objective

Founded in 1938, the International Federation of Film Archives (FIAF) brings together not-for-profit institutions dedicated to rescuing films and any other moving-image elements considered both as cultural heritage and as historical documents.

FIAF is a collaborative association of the world's leading film archives whose purpose has always been to ensure the proper preservation and showing of motion pictures. Almost 90 member archives in more than 50 countries collect, restore, and exhibit films and cinema documentation spanning the entire history of film.

FIAF seeks to promote film culture and facilitate historical research, to help create new archives around the world, to foster training and expertise in film preservation, to encourage the collection and preservation of documents and other cinema-related materials, to develop cooperation between archives, and to ensure the international availability of films and cinema documents.

Officers

Pres. Frédéric Maire; *V.P.* Chalida Uabumrungjit; *Secy.-Gen.* Michael Loebensten; *Treas.* Jon Wengström.

Address correspondence to Christophe Dupin, Senior Administrator, FIAF Secretariat. E-mail c.dupin@fiafnet.org.

Publications and Databases

FIAF Bulletin Online.
FIAF Directory (print).
International Index to Film Periodicals database (OVID, ProQuest).
Journal of Film Preservation. Ed. Elaine Burrows. E-mail jfp.editor@fiafnet.org.
Treasures from the Film Archives database.
Extensive selection of books through the FIAF Bookshop.

International Federation of Library Associations and Institutions

Prins Willem-Alexanderhof 5, 2595 BE The Hague, Netherlands
Tel. 31-70-314-0884, fax 31-70-383-4827, e-mail ifla@ifla.org
World Wide Web https://www.ifla.org

Objective

The objective of the International Federation of Library Associations and Institutions (IFLA) is to promote international understanding, cooperation, discussion, research, and development in all fields of library activity, including bibliography, information services, and the education of library personnel, and to provide a body through which librarianship can be represented in matters of international interest. IFLA is the leading international body representing the interests of library and information services and their users. It is the global voice of the library and information profession. IFLA was founded in 1927.

Officers

Pres. Barbara Lison, Stadtbibliothek, Bremen, Germany. E-mail barbara.lison@stadtbibliothek.bremen.de; *Pres.-Elect* Antonia Arahova, General Council for Libraries, Ministry of Education and Religious Affairs, Greece; *Treas.* Perry Moree, ZB - Library of Zeeland, Netherlands; *Past Pres.* G Christine Mackenzie, Australia.

Governing Board

At-Large Kirsten Boelt, Denmark; Jonathan Hernández Pérez, Mexico; Yasuyo Inoue, Japan; Ayub Khan, United Kingdom; Mandla Ntombela, South Africa; *Chair, Professional Council* Adjoa Boateng, Germany; *Chair, Regional Council* Nthabiseng Kotsokoane, South Africa; Chair, *Management of Library Assns. Section* Position open.

Publications

IFLA Annual Report.
IFLA Journal (4x yearly).
IFLA Trend Reports.
IFLA Professional Reports.
IFLA Publications Series.
IFLA Series on Bibliographic Control.
Global Studies in Libraries and Information (irreg. series).
Access and Opportunity for All: How Libraries Contribute to the United Nations 2030 Agenda.

American Membership

Associations

American Lib. Assn., Assn. for Lib. and Info. Science Educ., Assn. of Research Libs., Chief Officers of State Lib. Agencies, Medical Lib. Assn., Special Libs. Assn., Urban Libs. Council, Chinese American Libns. Assn., Polish American Lib. Assn.

Institutional Members

More than 100 libraries and related institutions are institutional members or consultative bodies and sponsors of IFLA in the United States (out of a total of more than 1,000 globally), and more than 100 are individual affiliates (out of a total of more than 300 affiliates globally).

International Organization for Standardization

Sergio Mujica, Secretary-General
ISO Central Secretariat, Chemin de Blandonnet 8, CP 401 1214 Vernier, Geneva, Switzerland
Tel. 41-22-749-01-11, fax 41-22-733-34-30, e-mail central@iso.org
World Wide Web https://www.iso.org/home.html

Objective

Founded in 1947, the International Organization for Standardization (ISO) is a worldwide federation of national standards bodies that currently comprises members from 164 countries and 785 technical committees and subcommittees working on various aspects of standards development. The objective of ISO is to promote the development of standardization and related activities in the world with a view to facilitating international exchange of goods and services and to developing cooperation in the spheres of intellectual, scientific, technological, and economic activity. The scope of ISO covers international standardization in all fields except electrical and electronic engineering standardization, which is the responsibility of the International Electrotechnical Commission (IEC). The results of ISO's technical work are published as international standards.

Officers

Pres. Ulrika Francke, Sweden; *V.P.s* Christoph Winterhalter, Germany *(Policy)*, Sauw Kook Choy, Singapore *(Technical Management)*, Mitsuo Matsumoto, Japan *(Finance)*; *Treas.* Jacqueline Curzon, Switzerland; *Past Pres.* Eddy Njoroge, Kenya; *Secy.-Gen.* Sergio Mujica, Chile.

Technical Work

The technical work of ISO is carried out by groups of experts collaborating worldwide, representing every imaginable sector, from soaps to spacecraft, from MP3 to coffee. Among its technical committees are:

ISO/TC 46—Information and documentation (Secretariat, Association Française de Normalization, 11 rue Francis de Pressensé, 93571 La Plaine Saint-Denis, Cedex, France). Scope: Standardization of practices relating to libraries, documentation and information centers, indexing and abstracting services, archives, information science, and publishing.

ISO/TC 37—Language and terminology (Secretariat, Standardization Administration of China, No. 9 Madian Donglu, Haidian District, Beijing 100088, China). Scope: Standardization of descriptions, resources, technologies, and services related to terminology, translation, interpreting, and other language-based activities in the multilingual information society.

ISO/IEC JTC 1—Information technology (Secretariat, American National Standards Institute, 1899 L St. NW, 11th Fl., Washington, DC 20036). Scope: Standardization in the field of information technology.

Publications

ISO Annual Report.
ISOfocus (6x yearly).
Extensive selection of titles on the ISO website (https://www.iso.org/publication-list.html).

Foreign Library Associations

The following is a list of regional and national library associations around the world. A more complete list can be found in *International Literary Market Place* (Information Today, Inc.).

Regional

Africa

Standing Conference of Eastern, Central, and Southern African Lib. and Info. Assns. (SCECSAL), c/o General-Secretary, Uganda Library and Information Association, P.O. Box 5894, Kampala, Uganda. Tel. +256-772-488937, +256-782-617623, +256-782-42204, e-mail info@ulia.or.ug, World Wide Web https://www.scecsal.org.

The Americas

Assn. of Caribbean Univ., Research, and Institutional Libs. (ACURIL), P.O. Box 23317, San Juan, Puerto Rico 00931-3317. Tel. 787-612-9343, e-mail executivesecretariat@acuril.org, World Wide Web https://acuril.org. *Pres.* Jeannette Lebrón Ramos; *Exec. Secy.* Elizabeth Pierre-Louis.

Seminar on the Acquisition of Latin American Lib. Materials (SALALM), c/o SALALM Secretariat, Latin American Lib., 422 Howard Tilton Memorial Lib., Tulane Univ., 7001 Freret St., New Orleans, LA 70118-5549. Tel. 504-247-1366, fax 504-247-1367, e-mail salalm@tulane.edu, World Wide Web https://salalm.org. *Exec. Dir.* Hortensia Calvo. E-mail hcalvo@tulane.edu.

Asia

Congress of Southeast Asian Libns. (CONSAL), Razathingaha Road, Uottra Thiri TSP, Naypyitaw, Myanmar. Tel. 95 67 418427, fax 95 67 418426, e-mail info@consalxvii.org.

The Commonwealth

Commonwealth Lib. Assn. (COMLA), P.O. Box 144, Mona, Kingston 7, Jamaica. Tel. +1-876-978-2274, fax +1-876-927-1926, e-mail comla72@yahoo.com, World Wide Web https://www.commonwealthofnations.org/commonwealth-directory/organisations-by-sector/libraries. *Interim Pres.* Elizabeth Watson, University of the West Indies, Cave Hill Campus, Barbados; *Hon. Exec. Secy.* Norma Y Amenu-Kpodo (Jamaica).

U.K. Library and Archives Group on Africa (SCOLMA), c/o Sarah Rhodes, Bodleian Social Science Lib., Univ. of Oxford, Manor Rd. Bldg., Manor Rd., Oxford OX1 3UQ, England. Tel. 01865-277162, World Wide Web http://scolma.org. *Chair* Lucy McCann, Weston Library, Bodleian Libraries, Broad Street, Oxford, OX1 3BG, England. E-mail *Secy.* Sarah Rhodes.

Europe

European Bureau of Library, Information and Documentation Associations (EBLID), c/o EBLIDA Secretariat, Koninklijke Bibliotheek (National Library of the Netherlands), Prins Willem-Alexanderhof 5, 2595 BE, The Hague. Tel. 31 (0) 70 3140137, e-mail eblida@eblida.org, World Wide Web http://www.eblida.org. *Dir.* Giuseppe Vitiello.

Ligue des Bibliothèques Européennes de Recherche (LIBER) (Assn. of European Research Libs.), P.O. Box 90407, 2509 LK The Hague, Netherlands. Tel. 31-70-314-07-67, fax 070-314-01-97, e-mail liber@kb.nl, World Wide Web https://libereurope.eu. *Pres.* Jeannette Frey; *V.P.* Julien Roche; *Secy.-Gen.* Anja Smit; *Exec. Dir.* Astrid Verheusen.

National

Argentina

ABGRA (Asociación de Bibliotecarios Graduados de la República Argentina) (Assn. of Graduate Libns. of Argentina), Paraná 918, 2do Piso, C1017AAT Buenos Aires. Tel. 54-11-4811-0043, fax 54-11-4816-3422, e-mail info@abgra.org.ar, World Wide Web https://

abgra.org.ar. *Pres.* Maria Silvia LaCorazza; *Secy. Gen.* Jessica Soledad Castaño.

Australia

Australian Lib. and Info. Assn., Box 6335, Kingston, ACT 2604. Tel. 61-2-6215-8222, fax 61-2-6282-2249, e-mail enquiry@ alia.org.au, World Wide Web https://www. alia.org.au. *Pres.* Vicki Edmunds. E-mail ALIABoard@alia.org.au.

Australian Society of Archivists, P.O. Box 576, Crows Nest, NSW 1585. Tel. 61-2-6190-7983, e-mail office@archivists.org. au, World Wide Web https://www.archivists. org.au. *Pres.* Nicola Laurent; *V.P.* Hannah Hibbert; *Gen. Mgr.* James Polley.

National and State Libs. Australia (NSLA), 9-11 Napier Close, Deakin ACT 2600, Australia. Tel. 03 8664 7512, e-mail info@nsla. org.au, World Wide Web https://www.nsla. org.au. *Chair* Vicki McDonald; *Exec. Officer* Barbara Lemon.

Austria

Österreichische Gesellschaft für Dokumentation und Information (Austrian Society for Documentation and Info.), c/o Österreichische Computer Gesellschaft OCG, Wollzeile 1, 1010 Vienna. E-mail office@oegdi. at, World Wide Web http://oegdi.at. *Chair* Gerhard Frohlich.

Vereinigung Österreichischer Bibliothekarinnen und Bibliothekare (VOEB) (Assn. of Austrian Libns.), Universitätsbibliothek Graz, Universitätsplatz 3, 8010 Graz. E-mail voeb@ub.tuwein.ac.at, World Wide Web https://www.univie.ac.at/voeb/php. *Interim Presidents* Pamela Stückler and Eva Ramminger. *Secy.* Markus Lackner.

Bangladesh

Bangladesh Assn. of Libns., Info. Scientists and Documentalists (BALID), House # 67/B (3rd floor), Road # 9/A, Dhanmondi, Dhaka-1209, Bangladesh. E-mail balidbd@ gmail.com, info@balidbd.org, World Wide Web https://www.balid.org. *Chair* Muhammad Hossam Haider Chowdhury.

Belgium

Archief-en Bibliotheekwezen in België (Belgian Assn. of Archivists and Libns.),

Royal Library of Belgium, Boulevard de l'Empereur 2, 1000 Brussels. Tel. 2-519-53-93, fax 2-519-56-10, e-mail abb@kbr. be, World Wide Web http://www.archibib. be. *Pres.* Marc Libert; *Admin. Secy.* Anja Marginet

Assn. Belge de Documentation/Belgische Vereniging voor Documentatie (Belgian Assn. for Documentation), 4 Boulevard de l'Empereur, 1000 Bruxelles. Tel. 2-675-58-62, fax 2-672-74-46, e-mail abdbvd@ abd-bvd.be, World Wide Web https://www. abd-bvd.be/fr. *Pres.* Sara Decoster. E-mail sara.decoster.pro@gmail.com; *Secy. Gen.* Guy Delsaut. E-mail delsautg@gmail.com.

Association des Professionales des Bibliothèques Francophones de Belgique (APBFB), Rue Nanon 98, 5002 Namur. Tel. 32-492-31-09-41, e-mail info@apbfb.be, World Wide Web http://www.apbfb.be. *Pres.* Françoise Dury.

Vlaamse Vereniging voor Bibliotheek-, Archief-, en Documentatiewezen (Flemish Assn. of Libns., Archivists, and Documentalists), Statiestraat 179, B-2600 Berchem, Antwerp. Tel. 3-281-44-57, e-mail vvbad@ vvbad.be, World Wide Web https://www. vvbad.be. *Coord.* Jessica Jacobs. E-mail jessica.jacobs@vvbad.be.

Bolivia

Centro Nacional de Documentación Científica y Tecnológica (National Scientific and Technological Documentation Center), Av. Mariscal Santa Cruz 1175, Esquina c Ayacucho, La Paz. Tel. 02-359-583, fax 02-359-586, e-mail iiicndct@huayna.umsa.edu.bo, World Wide Web http://www.bolivian.com/ industrial/cndct.

Bosnia and Herzegovina

Drustvo Bibliotekara Bosne i Hercegovine (Libns. Society of Bosnia and Herzegovina), Zmaja od Bosne 8B, 71000 Sarajevo. Tel. 33-275-301, e-mail nubbih@nub.ba, World Wide Web https://www.nub.ba. *Pres.* Ismet Ovcina. E-mail ured.direktora@ nub.ba.

Botswana

Botswana Lib. Assn., Box 1310, Gaborone. Tel. 267-732-31047, e-mail secretary@bla.org.bw,

Pres. Lynn Jabril. E-mail president@bla.org. bw, World Wide Web https://www.facebook. com/BotsLibAssociation.

Brunei Darussalam

Persatuan Perpustakaan Negara Brunei Darussalam (National Lib. Assn. of Brunei), c/o Class 64 Lib., SOASC, Jalan Tengah, Bandar Seri Begawan BS8411. Fax 2-222-330, e-mail pobox.bla@gmail.com, World Wide Web http://bruneilibraryassociation. wordpress.com.

Cameroon

Assn. des Bibliothécaires, Archivistes, Documentalistes et Muséographes du Cameroun (Assn. of Libns., Archivists, Documentalists, and Museum Curators of Cameroon), BP 12092, Yaoundé. Tel. 237-2-22-22-28-98, e-mail abadcameroun@gmail.com, World Wide Web http://www.abadcam. sitew.com. *Pres.* Alim Garga. E-mail a_garga@yahoo.fr.

Chile

Colegio de Bibliotecarios de Chile (Chilean Lib. Assn.), Avda. Diagonal Paraguay 383, Torre 11, Oficina 122, 6510017 Santiago. Tel. 2-222-5652, e-mail cbc@bibliotecarios. cl, World Wide Web http://www.bibliote carios.cl. *Pres.* María Angélica Fuentes Martínez.

China

Library Society of China, c/o National Library of China, 33 Zhongguancun Nandajie, Hai Dian District, Beijing 100081. Tel: 4006006988, (+86 10) 88545426. Email: webmaster@nlc.cn, World Wide Web http://www.nlc.cn/newen. *Secy. Gen.* Wang Yanhang.

Colombia

Asociación Colombiana de Bibliotecólogos y Documentalistas (Colombian Assn. of Libns. and Documentalists), Calle 21, No. 6-58, Oficina 404, Bogotá D.C. Tel. 1-282-3620, fax 1-282-5487, e-mail secretaria@ ascolbi.org, World Wide Web http://www. ascolbi.org. *Dir.* Monica Sandoval.

Croatia

Hrvatsko Knjiznicarsko Drustvo (Croatian Lib. Assn.), c/o National and Univ. Lib., Hrvatske bratske zajednice 4, 10 000 Zagreb. Tel./fax 1-615-93-20, e-mail hkd@nsk.hr, World Wide Web http://www.hkdrustvo.hr. *Pres.* Dijana Machala; *Secy.* Andreja Tominac.

Cuba

Asociación Cubana de Bibliotecarios (AS-CUBI) (Lib. Assn. of Cuba), P.O. Box 6670, Havana. Tel. 7-555-442, fax 7-816-224, e-mail ascubi@bnjm.cu, World Wide Web http://ascubi.blogspot.com. *Chair* Margarita Bellas Vilariño. E-mail ascubi@bnjm.cu.

Cyprus

Cyprus Association of Librarians - Information Scientists (KEVEP), T.Th. 21100, 1501 Nicosia, Cyprus. Tel. 99-277-758, e-mail kebepcy@gmail.com, World Wide Web http://kebep.blogspot.com.

Czech Republic

Svaz Knihovniku a Informacnich Pracovniku Ceske Republiky (SKIP) (Assn. of Lib. and Info. Professionals of the Czech Republic), National Library of the Czech Republic, Mariánské náměstí 190/5, 110 00 Prague 1. Tel. 420-221-663-379, fax 420-221-663-175, e-mail skip@nkp.cz, World Wide Web https://www.skipcr.cz. *Chair Mgr.* Roman Giebisch.

Denmark

Arkivforeningen (Archives Society), Ingrid Nostberg, Vestfoldmuseene IKS, Department Vestfoldarkivet, 3205 Sandefjord. Tel. 958 21 501, e-mail post@arkivarforeningen. no, World Wide Web http://www.arkivar foreningen.no. *Chair* Ingrid Nostberg.
Danmarks Biblioteksforening (Danish Lib. Assn.), Vartov, Farvergade 27D, 1463 Copenhagen K. Tel. 3325-0935, fax 3325-7900, e-mail db@db.dk, World Wide Web http://www.db.dk. *Chair* Steen Bording Andersen. E-mail steen.a@aarhus.dk. *Dir.* Michel Steen-Hansen. E-mail msh@db.dk.
Danmarks Forskningsbiblioteksforening (Danish Research Lib. Assn.), c/o University of Southern Denmark, Studiestræde 6, 1455

Copenhagen K. Tel. 45-4220-2177, e-mail secretariat@dfdf.dk, World Wide Web http://www.dfdf.dk. *Chair* Karin Englev. E-mail kabe@kb.dk.

Dansk Musikbiblioteks Forening (Assn. of Danish Music Libs.), c/o Helene Olsen, Sundby Library, Jemtelandsgade 2300, Copenhagen S. E-mail sekretariat@dmbf.nu, World Wide Web https://www.dmbf.nu.

Ecuador

Asociación Ecuatoriana de Bibliotecarios (Ecuadoran Lib. Assn.), c/o Casa de la Cultura Ecuatoriana, Casillas 87, Quito. E-mail asoecubiblio@gmail.com, World Wide Web http://aeb-nacional.blogspot.com.

El Salvador

Asociación de Bibliotecarios de El Salvador (ABES) (Assn. of Salvadorian Libns.), Residencial La Cima, Avenida 7, Calle 5 house # 15G, San Salvador. Tel. 503-2212-7600, e-mail abeselsalvador@gmail.com, World Wide Web https://bibliotecarios-de-el-salvador.webnode.es. *Pres.* Claudia Oviedo.

Finland

Suomen Kirjastoseura (Finnish Lib. Assn.), Runeberginkatu 15 A 6, 00100 Helsinki. Tel. 44-522-2941, e-mail info@fla.fi, World Wide Web http://www.fla.fi. *Exec. V.P.* Rauha Maarno. E-mail rauha.maarno@fla.fi.

France

Association des Archivistes Français (Assn. of French Archivists), 8 rue Jean-Marie Jego, 75013 Paris. Tel. 1-46-06-39-44, fax 1-46-06-39-52, e-mail secretariat@archivistes.org, World Wide Web http://www.archivistes.org.

Association des Bibliothécaires de France (Assn. of French Libns.), 31 rue de Chabrol, F-75010 Paris. Tel. 1-55-33-10-30, fax 1-55-30-10-31, e-mail info@abf.asso.fr, World Wide Web http://www.abf.asso.fr. *Pres.* Hélène Brochard; *Gen. Secy.* Mélanie Roson.

Association des Professionnels de l'Information et de la Documentation (Assn. of Info. and Documentation Professionals), 25 rue Claude Tillier, 75012 Paris. Tel. 06-81-39-

82-14, e-mail adbs@adbs.fr, World Wide Web http://www.adbs.fr. *Secy. Gen.* Valérie Rostowski.

Germany

Arbeitsgemeinschaft der Spezialbibliotheken (Assn. of Special Libs.), c/o German-French Institute (dfi) – France Library, Asperger Str. 30, 71634 Ludwigsburg. Tel. +49-7141-930338, e-mail geschaeftsstelle@aspb.de, World Wide Web http://aspb.de. *Chair* Monika Sommerer.

Berufsverband Information Bibliothek (Assn. of Info. and Lib. Professionals), P.O. Box 13 24, 72703 Reutlingen. Tel. 7121-3491-0, fax 7121-3491-34, e-mail mail@bib-info.de, World Wide Web http://www.bib-info.de. *Chair* Ute Engelkenmeier.

Deutsche Gesellschaft für Informationswissenschaft und Informationspraxis eV (German Society for Information Science and Practice eV), Windmühlstr. 3, 60329 Frankfurt-am-Main. Tel. 69-43-03-13, fax 69-490-90-96, e-mail mail@dgi-info.de, World Wide Web http://www.dgi-info.de. *Pres.* Margarita Reibel-Felten.

Deutscher Bibliotheksverband eV (German Lib. Assn.), Fritschestr. 27–28, 10585 Berlin. Tel. 30-644-98-99-10, fax 30-644-98-99-29, e-mail dbv@bibliotheksverband.de, World Wide Web http://www.bibliotheksverband.de. *Dir.* Barbara Schleihagen.

VdA—Verband Deutscher Archivarinnen und Archivare (Assn. of German Archivists), Woerthstr. 3, 36037 Fulda. Tel. 661-29-109-72, fax 661-29-109-74, e-mail info@vda.archiv.net, World Wide Web http://www.vda.archiv.net. *Chair* Ralf Jacob; *Managing Dir.* Thilo Bauer.

Verein Deutscher Bibliothekare eV (Society of German Libns.), University and State Library, 06108 Hall, August-Bebel-Str. 13, Saxony-Anhalt. Tel. 09131-85-22150, e-mail geschaeftsstelle@vdb-online.org, World Wide Web http://www.vdb-online.org. *Chair* Konstanze Söllner. E-mail chairman@vdb-online.org.

Ghana

Ghana Lib. Assn., Box GP 4105, Accra. Tel. 244-17-4930, e-mail info@gla-net.org, World Wide Web http://gla-net.org. *Pres.* Comfort Asare.

Greece

Enosis Hellinon Bibliothekarion (Association of Greek Librarians), Akadimias 84, PC 106 78, Athens. Tel./fax 210-330-2128, e-mail info-eebep@eebep.gr, World Wide Web http://www.eebep.gr. *Pres.* Dr. Anthi Katsirikou; *Gen. Secy.* Eleni Molfesi.

Guyana

Guyana Lib. Assn., c/o Department of Public Information, Area 'B' Homestretch Ave., D'Urban Park, Georgetown. Tel. 592-226-6715, fax 592-227-4052, e-mail info@dpi.gov.gy, World Wide Web https://dpi.gov.gy/tag/guyana-library-association.

Hong Kong

Hong Kong Lib. Assn., GPO Box 10095, Hong Kong, China. E-mail hkla@hkla.org, World Wide Web http://www.hkla.org. *Pres.* Wilson Chu. E-mail president@hkla.org. *Membership Secy.* Bernice Chan. E-mail membership@hkla.org.

Hungary

Magyar Könyvtárosok Egyesülete (Assn. of Hungarian Libns.), 1827 Budapest, Budavári Palota Building F. Tel./fax 1-311-8634, e-mail mke@oszk.hu, World Wide Web http://www.mke.info.hu. *Chair* Dr. Ágnes Hajdu; *Secy. Gen.* Judit Gerencsér.

Iceland

Upplysing—Felag bokasafns-og upplysingafraeoa (Information—The Icelandic Lib. and Info. Science Assn.), Mailbox 8865, 128 Reykjavík. Tel. 354-864-6220, e-mail upplysing@upplysing.is, World Wide Web http://www.upplysing.is. *Chair* Þórný Hlynsdóttir. E-mail chairman@upplysing.is.

India

Indian Assn. of Special Libs. and Info. Centres, P-291, CIT Scheme 6M, Kankurgachi, Kolkata 700-054. Tel. 33-2362-9651, e-mail iaslic@vsnl.net, World Wide Web http://www.iaslic1955.org.in. *President* Narendra Lahkar; *Gen. Secy.* Abhijit Kumar.

Indian Lib. Assn., A/40-41, Flat 201, Ansal Bldg., Mukerjee Nagar, New Delhi 110009.

Tel./fax 11-2765-1743, e-mail dvs-srcc@re diffmail.com, World Wide Web http://www.ilaindia.net. *Pres.* B.D. Kumbar; *Gen. Secy.* O.N. Chaubey.

Indonesia

Ikatan Pustakawan Indonesia (Indonesian Lib. Assn.), Jl. Salemba Raya, RT.8/RW.8, Kramat Senen, Kota Jakarta Pusat, DKI Jakarta 10430. Tel. (021) 3900944, World Wide Web http://ipi.web.id. *Chair* T. Syamsul Bahri.

Ireland

Cumann Leabharlann na hEireann (Lib. Assn. of Ireland), c/o 138–144 Pearse St., Dublin 2. E-mail honsecretary@libraryassociation.ie, World Wide Web http://www.libraryassociation.ie. *Pres.* Cathal McCauley. E-mail president@libraryassociation.ie. *Hon. Secy.* Niall O'Brien. E-mail honsecretary@libraryassociation.ie.

Israel

Israeli Center for Libs., 22 Baruch Hirsch St., P.O. Box 801, 51108 Bnei Brak. Tel. 03-6180151, fax 03-5798048, e-mail meida@gmail.com or icl@icl.org.il, World Wide Web http://www.icl.org.il. *Chair* Moshe Perl.

Italy

Associazione Italiana Biblioteche (Italian Lib. Assn.), Biblioteca Nazionale Centrale, Viale Castro Pretorio 105, 00185 Rome RM. Tel. 6-446-3532, fax 6-444-1139, e-mail segreteria@aib.it, World Wide Web http://www.aib.it.

Jamaica

Lib. and Info. Assn. of Jamaica, P.O. Box 125, Kingston 5. Tel./fax 876-927-1614, e-mail liajapresident@yahoo.com, World Wide Web https://www.facebook.com/groups/147277112846.

Japan

Info. Science and Technology Assn., 1-11-14, Shinkawa, Chuo-ku, Tokyo 104-0033. Tel. 81-3-6222-8506, fax 81-3-6222-8107, e-mail infosta@infosta.or.jp, World Wide Web http://www.infosta.or.jp. Nihon Toshokan Kyokai (Japan Lib. Assn.), 1-11-14 Shinkawa, Chuo-ku, Tokyo 104 0033. Tel. 3-3523-0811, fax 3-3523-0841, e-mail info@jla.or.jp, World Wide Web http://www.jla.or.jp. *Chair* Mitsuhiro Oda. Senmon Toshokan Kyogikai (Japan Special Libs. Assn.), c/o Japan Lib. Assn., Bldg. F6, 1-11-14 Shinkawa Chuo-ku, Tokyo 104-0033. Tel. 3-3537-8335, fax 3-3537-8336, e-mail jsla@jsla.or.jp, World Wide Web http://www.jsla.or.jp. *Co-Chairs* Akio Mimura and Toru Ishida.

Jordan

Jordan Lib. and Info. Assn., P.O. Box 6289, Amman 11118. Tel./fax 00962-64629412, World Wide Web http://jlia.org/component/content/en. *Pres.* Dr. Naguib Al-Sharbaji.

Kenya

Kenya Assn. of Lib. and Info. Professionals (formerly Kenya Lib. Assn.), Buruburu, P.O. Box 49468-00100 Nairobi. Tel. 20-733-732-799, e-mail info@kenyalibraryassociation.or.ke, World Wide Web http://www.kenyalibraryassociation.or.ke.

Korea (Republic of)

Korean Lib. Assn., 201 Banpo-daero (Banpo-dong), Seocho-gu, Seoul. Tel. 2-535-4868, fax 2-535-5616, e-mail license@kla.kr, World Wide Web http://www.kla.kr. *Pres.* Nam Young-joon.

Laos

Association des Bibliothécaires Laotiens (Lao Lib. Assn.), c/o Direction de la Bibliothèque Nationale, Ministry of Educ., BP 704, Vientiane. Tel. 21-21-2452, fax 21-21-2408, e-mail bailane@laotel.com.

Latvia

Latvian Libns. Assn., c/o Latvian National Lib., Mukusalas iela 3, Riga, LV-1423. Tel. 67806100, fax 67280851, e-mail lnb@lnb.lv, World Wide Web http://www.lnb.lv. *Dir.* Andris Vilks. E-mail andris.vilks@lnb.lv.

Lebanon

Lebanese Lib. Assn., P.O. Box 113/5367, Beirut. Tel. 1-786-456, e-mail leblibassociation@gmail.com, World Wide Web https://www.facebook.com/LebaneseLibraryAssociation. *Pres.* Fawz Abdallah. E-mail fabdallas@gmail.com.

Lithuania

Lietuvos Bibliotekininkų Draugija (Lithuanian Libns. Assn.), Gedimino pr. 51, Vilnius, LT-01504. Tel. 370-5-231-8585, e-mail lbd.sekretore@gmail.com, World Wide Web http://www.lbd.lt. *Chair* Jolita Stephonaitiene. E-mail jolita.stephonaitiene@lnb.lt.

Luxembourg

Association Luxembourgeoise des Bibliothécaires, Archivistes, et Documentalistes (ALBAD) (Luxembourg Assn. of Libns., Archivists, and Documentalists), c/o National Lib. of Luxembourg, BP 295, L-2012 Luxembourg. Tel. 352-621-46-14-15, World Wide Web http://www.albad.lu. *Pres.* Estelle Beck. E-mail presidence@albad.lu; *Secy. Gen.* Bernard Linster. E-mail secretarie@albad.lu.

Malaysia

Persatuan Pustakawan Malaysia (Libns. Assn. of Malaysia), P.O. Box 12545, 50782 Kuala Lumpur. Tel./fax 3-2694-7390, e-mail pustakawan55@gmail.com, World Wide Web http://ppm55.org. *Pres.* Dr. Rashidah binti Bolhassan. E-mail rashidahb@sarawak.gov.my.

Mali

Association Malienne des Bibliothécaires, Archivistes et Documentalistes (Mali Assn. of Libns., Archivists, and Documentalists) (AMBAD), BP E4473, Bamako. Tel. 20-29-94-23, fax 20-29-93-76, e-mail dnambko@afribone.net.ml.

Malta

Malta Lib. and Info. Assn. (MaLIA), c/o Univ. of Malta Lib., Msida MSD 2080.

E-mail info@malia-malta.org, World Wide Web https://www.facebook.com/malia.malta.

Mauritania

Association Mauritanienne des Bibliothécaires, Archivistes, et Documentalistes (Mauritanian Assn. of Libns., Archivists, and Documentalists), c/o Bibliothèque Nationale, BP 20, Nouakchott. Tel. 525-18-62, fax 525-18-68, e-mail bibliothequenationale@yahoo.fr.

Mauritius

Mauritius Lib. Assn., Quatre Bornes, Mauritius 230. Tel. 230 5769 7392, fax 454-9553, e-mail mauritiuslibassociation@gmail.com, World Wide Web https://www.facebook.com/Mauritius-Library-Association-MLA-1429 91592578201.

Mexico

Asociación Mexicana de Bibliotecarios (Mexican Assn. of Libns.), Angel Urraza 817-A, Colonia Del Valle, Benito Juárez, Mexico DF, CP 03100. Tel. 55-55-75-33-96, e-mail correo@ambac.org.mx, World Wide Web http://www.ambac.org.mx. *Chair* Brenda Cabral Vargas; *V.P.* María Guadalupe Vega Díaz.

Myanmar

Myanmar Lib. Assn., Room 003, Diamond Jubilee Hall, Yangon University, Yangon, Myanmar. Tel. 95-9-420728446, e-mail libraryassociation@mlamyanmar.org, World Wide Web http://myanmarlibraryassociation.org. *Pres.* Daw Ah Win.

Namibia

Namibia Information Workers Assn., P.O. Box 308, Windhoek. Tel. 264-8148-10713, e-mail niwaassociation@gmail.com. *Contact* Ms. Namutenya Hamwaalwa, e-mail hnamutenya@gmail.com.

Nepal

Nepal Lib. Assn., KVPL, Bhrikuti Mandap, Kathmandu. Tel. 01-4221163, e-mail nepal libraryassociation@gmail.com, World Wide Web https://nla.org.np. *Pres.* Indra Prasad Adhikari; *Gen. Secy.* Reshma Dangol.

The Netherlands

KNVI—Koninklijke Nederlandse Vereniging van Informatieprofessionals (Royal Dutch Association of Information Professionals), Ambachtsstraat 15, 3861 RH Nijkerk. Tel. 033-2473427, e-mail info@knvi.nl, World Wide Web http://knvi.nl.

New Zealand

New Zealand Lib. Assn. (LIANZA), 70 Molesworth St., Wellington 6140. Tel. 027-347-5326, e-mail officeadmin@lianza.org.nz, World Wide Web http://www.lianza.org.nz. *Pres.* Erica Rankin.

Nicaragua

Asociación Nicaragüense de Bibliotecarios y Profesionales Afines (ANIBIPA) (Nicaraguan Assn. of Libns.), Bello Horizonte, Tope Sur de la Rotonda 1/2 cuadra abajo, J-11-57, Managua. Tel. 277-4159, e-mail anibipa@hotmail.com. World Wide Web https://www.facebook.com/ANIBIPA.

Nigeria

National Lib. of Nigeria, Plot 274 Sanusi House, Central Business District, Abuja. Tel. 09-234-6773, e-mail info@nln.gov.ng, World Wide Web https://www.nln.gov.ng. *Chair* Prof. Zaynab Alkali.

Norway

Arkivar Foreningen (Assn. of Archivists), Vestfoldmuseene IKS. department Vestfoldarkivet, 3205 Sandefjord. Tel. 936 56 026, e-mail post@arkivarforeningen.no, World Wide Web http://www.arkivarforeningen. no. *Chair* Ingrid Nøstberg.

Norsk Bibliotekforening (Norwegian Lib. Assn.), Universitetsgata 14, 0164 Oslo. Tel. 23 24 34 30, e-mail nbf@norskbib liotekforening.no, World Wide Web https:// norskbibliotekforening.no. *Dir.* Vidar Lund; *Gen. Secy.* Ann Berit Hulthin. E-mail abh@norskbibliotekforening.no.

Panama

Asociación Panameña de Bibliotecarios (Lib. Assn. of Panama), c/o Biblioteca Interamericana Simón Bolívar, Estafeta

Universitaria, Panama City. E-mail biblis2@arcon.up.ac.pa, Tel. 507-6527-1904, e-mail ocastillos@hotmail.com, World Wide Web https://www.facebook.com/asociacionpanamenabibliotecarios/info.

Paraguay

Asociación de Bibliotecarios Graduados del Paraguay (Assn. of Paraguayan Graduate Libns.), Facultad Politécnica, Universidad Nacional de Asunción, 2160 San Lorenzo. Tel. 21-585-588, e-mail abigrap@pol.una.py, World Wide Web https://www.facebook.com/AGCIPy.

Peru

Asociación Peruana de Archiveros y Gestores de la Información (Peruvian Assn. of Archivists and Info. Managers), Av. Manco Capac No. 1180, Dpto 201, La Victoria, Lima. Tel. 51-934-182079, e-mail contacto@archiverosdelperu.org, World Wide Web http://archiverosdelperu.org. Pres. Ricardo Arturo Moreau Heredia.

Philippines

Assn. of Special Libs. of the Philippines, c/o Goethe-Institut Philippinen, G/4-5/F Adamson Centre, 121 Leviste St., Salcedo Village, 1227 Makati City. Tel. 2-840-5723, e-mail aslplibrarians@gmail.com, World Wide Web https://aslplibrarians.org/home. Pres. Eugene Jose T. Espinoza.

Philippine Libns. Assn., Room 301, National Lib. Bldg., T. M. Kalaw St., 1000 Ermita, Manila. Tel. 525-9401. World Wide Web http://plai.org.ph. Pres. Emma Rey.

Poland

Stowarzyszenie Bibliotekarzy Polskich (Polish Libns. Assn.), al Niepodleglosci 213, 02-086 Warsaw. Tel. 22-608-28-24, e-mail biuro@sbp.pl, World Wide Web http://www.sbp.pl. Dir. Aldona Zawałkiewicz. E-mail a.zawalkiewicz@sbp.pl; Secy. Małgorzata Dargiel-Kowalska. E-mail m.dargielkowalska@sbp.pl.

Portugal

Associação Portuguesa de Bibliotecários, Arquivistas e Documentalistas (Portuguese Assn. of Libns., Archivists, and Documentalists), Praça Dr. Nuno Pinheiro Torres 10-A, 15500 246 Lisbon. Tel. +351-218-161-980, e-mail bad@bad.pt, World Wide Web http://www.apbad.pt. Pres. Ana Paula Gordo.

Puerto Rico

Sociedad de Bibliotecarios de Puerto Rico (Society of Libns. of Puerto Rico), Apdo 22898, San Juan 00931-2898. Tel./fax 787-764-0000, World Wide Web https://sociedadbibliotecariospr.wordpress.com. Pres. Juan Ramón Soto Rosa.

Russia

Rossiiskaya Bibliotechnaya Assotsiatsiya (Russian Lib. Assn.), 18 Sadovaya St., St. Petersburg 191069. Tel./fax 812-110-5861, e-mail rba@nlr.ru, World Wide Web http://www.rba.ru. Exec. Secy. Trushina Irina Aleksandrovna.

Senegal

Association Sénégalaise des Bibliothécaires, Archivistes et Documentalistes (Senegalese Assn. of Libns., Archivists, and Documentalists), BP 2006, Dakar RP, Université Cheikh Anta Diop, Dakar. Tel. 77-651-00-33, fax 33-824-23-79, e-mail asbadsn@gmail.com.

Serbia

Jugoslovenski Bibliografski Informacijski Institut, Terazije 26, 11000 Belgrade. Tel. 11-2687-836, fax 11-2687-760.

Sierra Leone

Sierra Leone Assn. of Archivists, Libns., and Info. Scientists, 7 Percival Street, Freetown. Tel. 022-220-758.

Singapore

Lib. Assn. of Singapore, National Lib. Board, 100 Victoria St., No. 14-01, Singapore 188064. Tel. 6332-3255, fax 6332-3248, e-mail lassec@las.org.sg, World Wide Web http://www.las.org.sg. Pres. Dr. Sadie-Jane Nunis. E-mail president@las.org.sg.

Slovenia

Zveza Bibliotekarskih Društev Slovenije (Union of Assns. of Slovene Libns.), Turjaöka 1, 1000 Ljubljana. Tel. 1-2001-176, fax 1-4257-293, e-mail info@zbds-zveza. si, World Wide Web http://www.zbds-zveza. si. *Pres.* Damjana Vovk. E-mail damjana. vovk@nuk.uni-lj.si.

South Africa

Lib. and Info. Assn. of South Africa, P.O. Box 1598, Pretoria 0001. Tel. 27 (0) 12-328-2010, 27 (0) 12-323-4912, fax 27 (0) 12-323-1033, e-mail liasa@liasa.org.za, World Wide Web http://www.liasa.org.za. *Pres.* Naziem Hardy. E-mail naziem.hardy@ capetown.gov.za.

Spain

Federación Española de Archiveros, Bibliotecarios, Arqueólogos, Museólogos y Documentalistas (ANABAD) (Spanish Federation of Assns. of Archivists, Libns., Archaeologists, Museum Curators, and Documentalists), de las Huertas, 37, 28014 Madrid. Tel. 91-575-1727, fax 91-578-1615, e-mail anabad@anabad.org, World Wide Web http://www.anabad.org. *Pres.* José María Nogales Herrera.

Sri Lanka

Sri Lanka Lib. Assn., Sri Lanka Professional Centre 275/75, Stanley Wijesundara Mawatha, Colombo 7. Tel./fax 11-258-9103, e-mail slla@slltnet.lk, World Wide Web https://www.slla.lk. *Pres.* Dr. Ananda Tissa. E-mail president@slla.lk; *Gen. Secy.* M P P Dilhani. E-mail gs@slla.lk.

Sweden

Foreningen for Archiv & Informationsforvaltening (Society of Archives and Records Management in Sweden—FAI), c/o Foreningshuset Sedab AB, Virkesvägen 26, 120 30 Stockholm. Tel. 08-121 513 21, e-mail info@fai.nu, World Wide Web https:// fai.nu. *Pres.* Katarina Ekelof.

Svensk Biblioteksförening (Swedish Lib. Assn.), Oxtorgsgrand 2, 111 57 Stockholm. Tel. 08-545-132-30, fax 8-545-132-31, e-mail info@svbib.se, World Wide Web http:// www.biblioteksforeningen.se. *Pres.* Johanna Hansson; *Secy. Gen.* Karin Linder.

Svensk Förening för Informationsspecialister (Swedish Assn. for Info. Specialists), c/o Föreningshuset Sedab, Virkesvägen 26, 120 30 Stockholm. E-mail info@sfis.nu, World Wide Web http://www.sfis.nu. *Chair* Elisabeth Hammam Lie.

Switzerland

Verein Schweizer Archivarinnen und Archivare (Assn. of Swiss Archivists), Schweizerisches Bundesarchiv, Büro Pontri GmbH, Solohurnstr. 13, Postfach CH-3322, Urtenen Schönbühl. Tel. 41-31-312-26-66, fax 41-31-312-26-68, e-mail info@vsa-aas.ch, World Wide Web http://www.vsa-aas.org.

Taiwan

Lib. Assn. of the Republic of China (LAROC), 20 Zhongshan South Rd., Taipei 10001. Tel. 2-2361-9132, fax 2-2370-0899, e-mail lac@ msg.ncl.edu.tw, World Wide Web http:// www.lac.org.tw.

Tanzania

Tanzania Lib. Assn., P.O. Box 33433, Dar es Salaam. Tel./fax 255-744-296-134, e-mail info@tla.or.tz, World Wide Web http:// www.tla.or.tz.

Thailand

Thai Lib. Assn., 1346 Songkhon 5 Road (between Sri Burapha Road 8-9), Klong Chan, Bang Kapi, Bangkok 10240. Tel. 02-734-9022, fax 02-734-9021, e-mail tla2497@ gmail.com, World Wide Web http://tla.or.th.

Trinidad and Tobago

Lib. Assn. of Trinidad and Tobago, P.O. Box 1275, Port of Spain. Tel. 868-687-0194, e-mail latt46@gmail.com, World Wide Web http://www.latt.org.tt. *Pres.* Beverly Ann Williams.

Turkey

Türk Kütüphaneciler Dernegi (Turkish Libns. Assn.), Necatibey Cad Elgun Sok 8/8, 06440

Kizilay, Ankara. Tel. 312-230-13-25, fax 312-232-04-53, e-mail tkd.dernek@gmail. com, World Wide Web https://kutuphaneci. org.tr. *Pres.* Ali Fuat Kartal.

Uganda

Uganda Lib. and Info. Assn., P.O. Box 25412, Kampala. Tel. 256-704-885-246, e-mail secretariat@ulia.org.ug. World Wide Web https://www.facebook.com/Uganda-Library-and-Information-Association-1799 98355458703.

Ukraine

Ukrainian Lib. Assn., a/c 62, Kiev, 03057. Tel. 380-44-383-14-32, e-mail info@ula.org.ua, World Wide Web https://ula.org.ua/en. *Pres.* Oksana Brui; *Exec. Dir.* Yaroslava Soshynska.

United Kingdom

Archives and Records Assn., UK and Ireland (formerly the Society of Archivists), Prioryfield House, 20 Canon St., Taunton TA1 1SW, England. Tel. 1823-327-077, fax 1823-271-719, e-mail societyofarchivists@archives.org.uk, World Wide Web https://www.archives.org.uk. *Chief Exec.* John Chambers; *Chair* Lisa Snook.

Bibliographical Society, Institute of English Studies, Senate House, Malet St., London WC1E 7HU, England. E-mail admin@bibsoc.org.uk, World Wide Web http://www.bibsoc.org.uk. *Pres.* James Raven. E-mail president@bibsoc.org.uk.

Chartered Institute of Lib. and Info. Professionals (CILIP), 7 Ridgmount St., London WC1E 7AE, England. Tel. 20-7255-0500, fax 20-7255-0501, e-mail info@cilip.uk, World Wide Web http://www.cilip.org.uk.

School Lib. Assn., 1 Pine Court, Kembrey Park, Swindon SN2 8AD, England. Tel. 1793-530-166, fax 1793-481-182, e-mail info@sla.org.uk, World Wide Web http://

www.sla.org.uk. *Chair* Sue Bastone; *Chief Exec.* Allison Tarrant.

Scottish Lib. and Info. Council, 175 W. George St., Glasgow G2 2LB, Scotland. Tel. 141-202-2999, e-mail info@scottishlibraries.org, World Wide Web http://www.scottishlibraries.org. *Chair* Ian Ruthven.

Society of College, National, and Univ. Libs. (SCONUL) (formerly Standing Conference of National and Univ. Libs.), 94 Euston St., London NW1 2HA, England. Tel. 20-7387-0317, fax 20-7383-3197, e-mail info@sconul.ac.uk, World Wide Web http://www.sconul.ac.uk. *Exec. Dir.* Ann Rossiter.

Uruguay

Agrupación Bibliotecológica del Uruguay (Uruguayan Lib. and Archive Science Assn.) and Asociación de Bibliotecólogos del Uruguay (Uruguayan Libns. Assn.), Eduardo V. Haedo 2255, CP 11200, Montevideo. Tel. 2409-9989, e-mail abu@adinet.com.uy, World Wide Web https://www.abu.net.uy. *Pres.* Alicia Ocaso Ferreira.

Vietnam

Hôi Thu-Vien Viet Nam (Vietnam Lib. Assn.), National Lib. of Vietnam, 31 Trang Thi, Hoan Kiem, 10000 Hanoi. Tel. 43-9366596, e-mail info@nlv.org.vn, World Wide Web http://www.vla.org.vn. *Chair* Nguyen Huu Gioi.

Zambia

Lib. and Info. Assn. of Zambia, P.O. Box 50183 Ridgeway, Lusaka. Tel. 260-965-024914, e-mail liaz@zambia.co.zm, World Wide Web https://zambia.co.zm.

Zimbabwe

Zimbabwe Lib. Assn., ZimLA Midlands Branch, P.O. Box 1521, Gweru. Tel. 263-773-568-837, e-mail information@zimla.org.zw, World Wide Web https://zimbabwereads.org/zimla.

Directory of Book Trade and Related Organizations

Book Trade Associations, United States and Canada

For more extensive information on the associations listed in this section, see the annual edition of *Literary Market Place* (Information Today, Inc.).

AIGA—The Professional Assn. for Design, 228 Park Ave South, Suite 58603, New York, NY 10003. Tel. 212-807-1990, fax 212-807-1799, e-mail general@aiga.org, World Wide Web https://www.aiga.org. *Pres.* Manuhuia Barcham; *Chapter Relations Mgr.* Riian Kant-McCormick.

American Book Producers Assn. (ABPA), 31 West 8th Street, #2, New York, NY 10011. Tel. 212-944-6600, e-mail office@ABPA online.org, World Wide Web https://abpa online.org. *Pres.* Richard Rothschild; *V.P./ Treas.* Nancy Hall; *Admin.* Michael Centore.

American Booksellers Assn., 333 Westchester Ave. Suite S202, White Plains, NY 10604. Tel. 800-637-0037, fax 914-417-4013, e-mail info@bookweb.org, World Wide Web https://www.bookweb.org. *Pres.* Christine Onorati, WORD Bookstores, Brooklyn, NY & Jersey City, NJ; *Co-V.P.* Kelly Estep, Carmichael's Bookstore & Carmichael's Kids, Louisville, KY; *Co-V.P.* Angela María Spring, Duende District, Albuquerque, NM and Washington, DC. *CEO* Allison Hill. E-mail allisonhill@bookweb.org.

American Literary Translators Assn. (ALTA), University of Arizona, Esquire Building #205, 1230 N. Park Ave., Tucson, AZ 85721. World Wide Web https://literarytranslators. org. *Exec. Dir.* Elisabeth Jaquette. E-mail elisabeth@literarytranslators.org.

American Printing History Assn., Box 4519, Grand Central Sta., New York, NY 10163-4519. World Wide Web https://printinghisto ry.org. *Pres.* J. Fernando Peña; *Treas.* David Goodrich; *Board Secy.* Meghan Constantinou; *Exec. Secy.* Lyndsi Barnes. E-mail secretary@printinghistory.org.

American Society for Indexing, 1628 E. Southern Ave., No. 9-223, Tempe, AZ 85282. Tel. 480-245-6750, e-mail info@asindex ing.org, World Wide Web https://www.asin dexing.org. *Pres.* Gina Guilinger. E-mail president@asindexing.org; *V.P./Pres.-Elect.* Theresa Duran. E-mail presidentelect@ asindexing.org; *Exec. Dir.* Gwen Henson. E-mail gwen@asindexing.org.

American Society of Journalists and Authors, 355 Lexington Ave., 15th Fl., New York, NY 10017-6603. Tel. 212-997-0947, fax 212-937-2315, e-mail asjaoffice@asja.org, World Wide Web https://www.asja.org. *Pres.* Emily Paulsen. E-mail president@ asja.org; *V.P.* Lisa Rabasca Roepe. E-mail vicepresident@asja.org; *Exec. Dir.* James Brannigan.

American Society of Media Photographers, Four Embarcadero Center, Suite 1400, San Francisco, CA 94111. Tel. 877-771-2767, fax 231-946-6180, e-mail asmp@vpconnec tions.com, World Wide Web https://www. asmp.org. *Chair* Michael Shay. E-mail chair@asmp.org; *V. Chair* Gabriella Marks; *CEO* James Edmund Datri. E-mail jdatri@ asmp.org.

American Translators Assn., 225 Reinekers Lane, Suite 590, Alexandria, VA 22314. Tel. 703-683-6100, fax 703-683-6122, e-mail ata@atanet.org, World Wide Web https:// www.atanet.org. *Pres.* Madalena Sánchez

Zampaulo; *Pres.-Elect* Veronika Demichelis; *Secy.* Alaina M. Brandt; *Treas.* John M. Milan; *Exec. Dir.* Kelli C. Baxter. E-mail kelli@atanet.org.

Antiquarian Booksellers Assn. of America, 155 Water Street, Floor 6, Suite 7, Brooklyn, NY 11201. Tel. 212-944-8291, fax 212-944-8293, World Wide Web https://www.abaa.org. *Pres.* Sheryl Jaeger; *V.P.* Alexander Akin; *Secy.* Elizabeth Young; *Treas.* Peter Blackman; *Exec. Dir.* Susan Benne. E-mail sbenne@abaa.org.

Assn. Media and Publishing Network, 620 I Street NW, Suite 501, Washington D.C. 20005. Tel. 202-289-7442, World Wide Web https://www.siia.net/amp-network. *Interim Pres.* Christopher Mohr.

Assn. of American Publishers, 1730 Pennsylvania Avenue NW, Washington, DC 20006. Tel. 202-347-3375, fax 202-347-3690, World Wide Web https://publishers.org. *Pres./CEO* Maria A. Pallante. E-mail ceo@publishers.org. *Chair* Julia Reidhead; *V. Chair* Brian Napack; *Treas.* Jeremy North.

Assn. of University Presses, 1412 Broadway, Suite 2135, New York, NY 10018. Tel. 212-989-1010, fax 212-989-0275, e-mail info@aupresses.org, World Wide Web https://aupresses.org. *Pres.* Charles Watkinson, Univ. of Michigan Press; *Pres.-Elect* Jane Bunker, Cornell Univ. Press; *Treas.* Amy Schultz, Stanford Univ. Press; *Exec. Dir.* Peter Berkery. Tel. 917-288-5594, e-mail pberkery@aupresses.org.

Assn. of Canadian Publishers, 401 Richmond Street W., Studio 257A, Toronto, ON M5V 3A8. Tel. 416-487-6116, fax 416-487-8815, e-mail admin@canbook.org, World Wide Web https://publishers.ca. *Pres.* Ruth Linka, Orca Book Publishers, Victoria, BC; *V.P.* Leigh Nash, House of Anansi Press, Toronto, ON; *Treas.* Brian Lam, Arsenal Pulp Press, Victoria, BC; *Exec. Dir.* Jack Illingworth. Tel. 416-487-6116 ext. 2340, e-mail jack_illingworth@canbook.org.

Audio Publishers Assn., 333 Hudson Street Suite 503, New York, NY 10013. Tel. 646-688-3044, e-mail info@audiopub.org, World Wide Web https://www.audiopub.org. *Pres.* Ana Maria Allessi; *V.P.* Samantha Edelson; *Secy.* Laura Gachko; *Treas.* Lee Jarit; *Exec. Dir.* Michele Cobb. E-mail mcobb@audiopub.org.

Authors Guild, 31 E. 32 Street, 7th Floor, New York, NY 10016. Tel. 212-563-5904, e-mail staff@authorsguild.org, World Wide Web https://www.authorsguild.org. *Pres.* Laura Pedersen; *V.P.s* Wendy Strothman and Scott Turow; *Secy.* Roxana Robinson; *Treas.* Robert Pesce; *Exec. Dir.* Mary Rasenberger.

Book Industry Study Group, 232 Madison Ave., Suite 1400, New York, NY 10016. Tel. 646-336-7141, e-mail info@bisg.org, World Wide Web https://bisg.org. *Chair* Kathleen Reid, Elsevier; *V.Chair* Joshua Tallent, Firebrand Technologies; *Secy.* Andrea Fleck-Nisbet, Independent Book Publishers Association; *Treas.* Joe Matthews, Independent Publishers Group; *Exec. Dir.* Brian O'Leary. Tel. 646-336-7141, e-mail brian@bisg.org.

Book Manufacturers' Institute (BMI), 7282 55th Avenue East, #147, Bradenton, FL 34203. Tel. 386-986-4552, fax 386-986-4553, World Wide Web https://www.bmibook.com. *Pres.* David McCree, Lakeside Book Company; *V.P.* Mark Levin, HP, Inc.; *Treas.* Suzanne Wiersma, Wallaceburg Bookbinding; *Exec. Dir./Secy.* Matthew J. Baehr.

Bookbuilders West. See Publishing Professionals Network.

California Independent Booksellers Alliance, 100 Black Diamond Road, Stonyford, CA 95979. Tel. 415-561-7686, e-mail info@caliballiance.org, World Wide Web https://caliballiance.org/default.aspx. *Pres.* Melinda Powers; *Pres.-Elect* Mary Williams; *Treas.* Mimi Hannan; *Secy.* Bridget Schinnerer; *Co-Exec. Dirs.* Ann Seaton, e-mail ann@caliballiance.org, and Kristin Rasmussen, e-mail kristin@caliballiance.org.

Canadian International Standard Numbers (ISNs) Agency, c/o Lib. and Archives Canada, 550 de la Cité Boulevard, Gatineau, Quebec J8T 0A7. Tel. 866-578-7777 (toll-free), 819-994-6872, e-mail isbn@bac-lac.gc.ca, World Wide Web https://library-archives.canada.ca/eng/services/publishers/Pages/publishers.aspx.

Canadian Printing Industries Assn., 4000 Blvd Industriel, Laval, QC H7L 4R9. World Wide Web https://cpia-aci.ca. *Chair* Richard Kouwenhoven, Tel. 604-438-2456, e-mail richard@hemlock.com; *Assoc. Mgr.* Gerry Lacombe, e-mail admin@cpia-aci.ca.

Children's Book Council, 54 W. 39 St., 14th Fl., New York, NY 10018. Tel. 917-890-7416, e-mail cbc.info@cbcbooks.org, World Wide Web https://www.cbcbooks.org. Chair Francesco Sedita; Vice Chair Alvina Ling; Treas. Terry Borzumato-Greenberg; Secy. Karen Walsh; Exec. Dir. Carl Lennertz.

Community of Literary Magazines and Presses, 154 Christopher St., Suite 3C, New York, NY 10014. Tel. 212-741-9110, e-mail info@clmp.org, World Wide Web https://www.clmp.org. Chair Nicole Dewey; Exec. Dir. Mary Gannon. E-mail mgannon@clmp.org.

Copyright Society, 1 E. 53 St., 8th Fl., New York, NY 10022. Tel. 212-354-6401, World Wide Web https://copyrightsociety.org. Pres. Casey Chisick; V.P./Pres.-Elect Daniel Cooper; Secy. Erica Carter; Treas. Allison Roach; Exec. Dir. Kaitland E. Kubat.

Educational Book and Media Assn., P.O. Box 3363, Warrenton, VA 20188. Tel. 540-318-7770, e-mail info@edupaperback.org, World Wide Web https://www.edupaperback.org. Pres. Ben Conn; V.P. Marin Foster; Treas. Susan Marston; Secy. Don Reinbold; Exec. Dir. Brain Gorg.

Evangelical Christian Publishers Assn., 9633 S. 48 St., Suite 140, Phoenix, AZ 85044. Tel. 480-966-3998, fax 480-966-1944, e-mail info@ecpa.org, World Wide Web https://www.ecpa.org. Pres./CEO Jeff Crosby; Chair Dan Kok; V. Chair Paul Santhouse; Secy. Barb Sherrill; Treas. Dan Baker.

Graphic Artists Guild, 2248 Broadway, Suite 1341, New York, NY 10024. Tel. 212-791-3400, e-mail admin@graphicartistsguild.org, World Wide Web https://www.graphicartistsguild.org. Interim Pres. Yanique DaCosta. E-mail president@graphicartistsguild.org; Secy. Jacqueline McCarthy.

Great Lakes Independent Booksellers Assn., 3123 Andrea Court, Woodridge, IL 60517. Tel. 630-841-8129, e-mail larry@gliba.org, World Wide Web https://www.gliba.org. Pres. Tim Smith; V.P. Alyson Turner; Treas. Melissa Weisberg; Secy. David Underwood; Exec. Dir. Larry Law.

Guild of Book Workers, 521 Fifth Ave., New York, NY 10175. Tel. 212-292-4444, e-mail communications@guildofbookworkers.org, World Wide Web https://guildofbookworkers.org. Pres. Kate Levy. E-mail president@guildofbookworkers.org; V. Pres. Henry Hebert. E-mail vicepresident@guildofbookworkers.org; Secy. Lindsey Jackson. E-mail secretary@guildofbookworkers.org; Treas. Lawrence Houston. E-mail treasurer@guildofbookworkers.org.

Horror Writers Assn., P.O. Box 56687, Sherman Oaks, CA 91413. E-mail hwa@horror.org, World Wide Web https://horror.org. Pres. John Edward Lawson. E-mail president@horror.org; V.P. Meghan Arcuri. E-mail vp@horror.org; Secy. Becky Spratford. E-mail secretary@horror.org; Treas. Maxwell I. Gold. E-mail treasurer@horror.org; Admin. Brad Hodson. E-mail admin@horror.org.

Independent Book Publishers Assn., 1020 Manhattan Beach Blvd., Suite 204, Manhattan Beach, CA 90266. Tel. 310-546-1818, fax 310-546-3939, e-mail info@ibpa-online.org, World Wide Web https://www.ibpa-online.org. Chair Karen Pavlicin, Elva Resa Publishing; Treas. Victoria Sutherland, Foreword Reviews; Secy. Kathryn Sparks, American Academy of Pediatrics; CEO Andrea Fleck-Nisbet.

International Standard Book Numbering U.S. Agency, c/o R.R. Bowker, 26 Main Street, Suite 102, Chatham, NJ 07928. Tel. 856-399-7495, e-mail isbn-san@bowker.com, World Wide Web http://www.isbn.org. Dir., Identifier Svcs. Beat Barblan.

Jewish Book Council, 520 Eighth Ave., 4th Fl., New York, NY 10018. Tel. 212-201-2920, fax 212-532-4952, e-mail info@jewishbooks.org, World Wide Web https://www.jewishbookcouncil.org. Pres. Elisa Spungen Bildner; Co-Pres. Joy Greenberg; V.P.s, Alan Kadish, Deborah Miller, Dana Raucher; Secy. Tracy Brown; Treasurer Lilian Stern; Exec. Dir. Naomi Firestone-Teeter.

Midwest Independent Publishers Assn. (MIPA), P.O. Box 580475, Minneapolis, MN 55458-0475. Tel. 651-917-0021, World Wide Web https://mipa.org. Pres. Nayt Rundquist, New Rivers Press, Tel. 218-477-5870, e-mail president@mipa.org; V.P. Paul Nylander, Illustrada Design, Tel. 612-325-1228, e-mail vicepresident@mipa.org; Secy. Ron Peterson, PTB Books, e-mail secretary@mipa.org; Treas. Joshua Weber, Calumet Editions, e-mail treasurer@mipa.org; Exec. Dir. Jennifer Baum, e-mail bookawards@mipa.org.

Miniature Book Society. Tel. 619-226-4441, e-mail member@mbs.org, World Wide Web https://www.mbs.org. *Pres.* Tony Firman; *V.P.* Kim Herrick; *Secy.* Cynthia Cosgrove; *Treas.* Sherry Bruning.

Minnesota Book Publishers' Roundtable. E-mail information@publishersroundtable.org, World Wide Web https://publishersround table.org. *Pres.* Allison Juda, Bearport Publishing. E-mail president@publish ersroundtable.org; *V.P.* Melissa York, Redleaf Press. E-mail vice.president@pub lishersroundtable.org; *Secy.* Cathy Broberg, Hazelden Betty Ford Foundation. E-mail CBroberg@Hazeldenbettyford.org; *Treas.* Paul Nylander, illustrada design. E-mail treasurer@publishersroundtable.org.

Mountains and Plains Independent Booksellers Assn., P.O. Box 746, Denver, CO 80201. Tel. 800-752-0249, e-mail info@moun tainsplains.org, World Wide Web https:// www.mountainsplains.org. *Pres.* Stephanie Schindhelm; *Vice Pres.* Cristina Rodriguez; *Secy.* Allison Senecal; *Treas.* Brian Contine; *Exec. Dir.* Heather Duncan. E-mail heather@ mountainsplains.org.

National Assn. of College Stores, 528 E. Lorain St., Oberlin, OH 44074. Tel. 800-622-7498, 440-775-7777, fax 440-775-4769, e-mail info@nacs.org, World Wide Web https:// www.nacs.org. *Pres. and Treas.* Andy Dunn; *Pres.-Elect* Ella Van Nort; *CEO* Eric Schlechenmayer. E-mail eschlichenmayer@ nacs.org.

National Book Foundation, 90 Broad St., Suite 604, New York, NY 10004. Tel. 212-685-0261, fax 212-213-6570, e-mail national book@nationalbook.org, World Wide Web https://www.nationalbook.org. *Chair* David Steinberger, Arcadia Publishing; *V. Chair* Fiona McCrea, Graywolf Publishing; *Secy.* Calvin Sims, CNN; *Treas.* Elpidio Villarreal; *Exec. Director* Ruth Dickey. E-mail rdickey@nationalbook.org.

National Coalition Against Censorship (NCAC), 19 Fulton St., Suite 407, New York, NY 10038. Tel. 212-807-6222, fax 212-807-6245, e-mail ncac@ncac.org, World Wide Web https://ncac.org. *Dirs.* Jon Anderson, Chris Finan, Eric M. Freedman, Robie Harris, Michael Jacobs, Mitchell Kaplan, Randall Kennedy, Emily Knox, Gina Maria Leonetti, Barbara Marcus, Larry Siems, Oren J. Teicher, Emily Whitfield; *Exec. Dir.* Chris Finan. E-mail chris@ncac.org.

New Atlantic Independent Booksellers Assn. (NAIBA), 2667 Hyacinth St., Westbury, NY 11590. Tel. 516-333-0681, fax 516-333-0689, e-mail naibabooksellers@gmail.com, World Wide Web https://www.naiba.com. *Pres.* Hannah Oliver Depp, Loyalty Bookstores; *V.P.* Erin Matthews, The Last Word; *Secy.* Adlai Yeomans, White Whale Bookstore; *Treas.* Amanda Zirn Hudson, Bethany Beach Books; *Exec. Dir.* Eileen Dengler. E-mail eileen@naiba.com.

New England Independent Booksellers Assn. (NEIBA), One Beacon Street, 15th Floor, Boston, MA 02108. Tel. 617-547-3642, fax 617-830-8768, e-mail beth@neba.org, World Wide Web https://newenglandbooks. org. *Pres.* Emily Russo, Print: A Bookstore, Portland, ME; *V.P.* Kelsy April, Savoy Bookshop & Cafe, Westerly, RI, Bank Square Books, Mystic, CT, and Title IX, New London, CT; *Treas. & Clerk* Meghan Hayden, River Bend Bookshop, Glastonbury, CT; *Exec. Dir.* Beth Ineson. E-mail beth@neba.org.

News Media Alliance, 4401 N. Fairfax Drive, Suite 300, Arlington, VA 22203. Tel. 571.366.1000, e-mail info@newsmediaal liance.org, World Wide Web https://www. newsmediaalliance.org. *Chair* Maribel Perez Wadsworth; *Vice Chair* Debby Krenek; *Treas.* Mike Riggs; *Secy.* Rebecca Grossman-Cohen; *Interim CEO & CFO* Robert Walden.

PEN American Center, Div. of International PEN, 588 Broadway, Suite 303, New York, NY 10012. Tel. 212-334-1660, fax 212-334-2181, e-mail pen@pen.org, World Wide Web https://pen.org. *Pres.* Ayad Akhtar; *Exec. V.P.* Markus Dohle; *V.P.s* Masha Gessen, Tracy Higgins; *Treas.* Yvonne Marsh; *CEO* Susanne Nossel. E-mail snossel@pen. org.

Publishing Professionals Network (formerly Bookbuilders West), c/o Postal Annex, 274 Redwood Shores Parkway, Box 129, Redwood City, CA 94065-1173. E-mail oper ations@pubpronetwork.org, World Wide Web https://pubpronetwork.org. *Pres.* Dave Peattie. E-mail dave@bookmatters.com; *V.P.* Roberta Morris; *Treas.* Kelly Lee. E-mail klee@bkpub.com.

Romance Writers of America, 5315-B Cypress Creek Parkway, #111, Houston, TX

77069. Tel. 832-717-5200, e-mail info@rwa.org, World Wide Web https://www.rwa.org. *Pres.* Clair Brett. E-mail president@rwa.org; *Secy.* Jacki Renée. E-mail secretary@rwa.org; *Treasurer* Brooke Wills. E-mail treasurer@rwa.org; *Exec. Dir.* Leslie Scantlebury. E-mail leslie.scantlebury@rwa.org.

Science Fiction and Fantasy Writers of America, PO Box 215, San Lorenzo, CA 94580. World Wide Web https://www.sfwa.org. *Pres.* Jeffe Kennedy. E-mail president@sfwa.org; *V.P.* Tobias S. Buckell. E-mail tobias.buckell@sfwa.org; *Secy.* Adam Rakunas. E-mail secretary@sfwa.org; *CFO* Nathan Lowell. E-mail cfo@sfwa.org. *Exec. Dir.* Kate Baker, E-mail office@sfwa.org

SIBA (formerly Southern Independent Booksellers Alliance), 51 Pleasant Ridge, Asheville, NC 28805. Tel. 803-994-9530, e-mail siba@sibaweb.com, World Wide Web https://sibaweb.com. *Exec. Dir.* Linda-Marie Barrett, E-mail lindamarie@sibaweb.com.

Society of Children's Book Writers and Illustrators (SCBWI), 4727 Wilshire Blvd., Suite 301, Los Angeles, CA 90010. Tel. 256-634-6982, e-mail support@scbwi.zendesk.com, World Wide Web https://www.scbwi.org. *Exec. Dir.* Sarah Baker, E-mail sarahbaker@scbwi.org.

Society of Illustrators (SI), 128 E. 63 St., New York, NY 10065. Tel. 212-838-2560, fax 212-838-2561, e-mail info@societyillustrators.org, World Wide Web https://societyillustrators.org. *Pres.* Leslie Cober; *Secy.* Sara Gomez Woolley; *Treas.* David Reuss; *Exec. Dir.* Anelle Miller. E-mail anelle@societyillustrators.org.

Southern Independent Booksellers Alliance. See SIBA.

Western Writers of America, c/o Candy Moulton, 271 CR 219, Encampment, WY 82325 Tel. 307-329-8942, e-mail wwa.moulton@gmail.com, World Wide Web https://westernwriters.org. *Pres.* Phil Mills, Jr.; *V.P.* Melody Groves; *Secy./Treas.* Rocky Gibbons; *Exec. Dir.* Candy Moulton.

Women's National Book Assn., P.O. Box 237, FDR Sta., New York, NY 10150. Tel. 866-610-WNBA (9622), e-mail info@wnba-books.org, World Wide Web https://wnba-books.org. *Pres.* Natalie Obando-Desai; e-mail nationalpresidentWNBA@gmail.com; *Co-V.P.s* Elise Marie Collins and NC Weil; *Secy.* Dayna Bennett; *Treas.* Leah Pierre.

International and Foreign Book Trade Associations

For Canadian book trade associations, see the preceding section, "Book Trade Associations, United States and Canada." For a more extensive list of book trade organizations outside the United States and Canada, with more detailed information, consult International Literary Market Place (Information Today, Inc.), which also provides extensive lists of major bookstores and publishers in each country.

International

Afro-Asian Book Council, 4259/3, Ansari Road, Darya Ganj, New Delhi 110 002, India. Tel. 91-11-45355555, fax 91-11-23275542, e-mail aabookcouncil@gmail.com, World Wide Web http://www.aabookcouncil.org. *Secretary-General* Ramesh Mittal. E-mail rkmittal@dkagencies.com; *Dir.* Pranav Gupta. E-mail pgprintsindia@gmail.com.

Centro Regional para el Fomento del Libro en América Latina y el Caribe (CERLALC) (Regional Center for Book Promotion in Latin America and the Caribbean), Calle 70, No. 9-52, Bogotá, Colombia. Tel. 571-518-70-70, e-mail cerlalc@cerlalc.com, World Wide Web https://cerlalc.org. *Dir.* Andrés Ossa.

Federation of European Publishers, Chaussee d'Ixelles 29/35, Box 4, 1050 Brussels, Belgium. Tel. 32-2-770-11-10, fax 32-2-771-20-71, e-mail info@fep-fee.eu, World Wide Web https://fep-fee.eu. *Pres.* Peter Kraus vom Cleff; *Dir.* Anne Bergman-Tahon.

International Board on Books for Young People (IBBY), Nonnenweg 12, Postfach CH-4009, Basel, Switzerland. Tel. 41-61-272-29-17, fax 41-61-272-27-57, e-mail ibby@ibby.org, World Wide Web https://www.ibby.org. *Pres.* Sylvia Vardell; *Exec. Dir.* Carolina Ballester.

International League of Antiquarian Booksellers (ILAB), c/o Rue Toepffer 5, Case postale 499, 1211 Geneva 12, Switzerland. E-mail secretariat@ilab.org, World Wide Web https://ilab.org. *Pres.* Mario Giupponi; *Exec. Secy.* Angelika Elstner.

International Publishers Assn. (Union Internationale des Editeurs), 23 ave. de France, CH-1202 Geneva, Switzerland. Tel. 41-22-704-1820, fax 41-22-704-1821, e-mail info@internationalpublishers.org, World Wide Web https://www.internationalpublishers.org.

Pres. Karine PANSA; *Secy.-Gen.* José Borghino.

STM: The International Assn. of Scientific, Technical, and Medical Publishers, Prins Willem-Alexanderhof 5, 2595 BE The Hague, The Netherlands. Tel. 31-70-314-09-30, fax 31-70-314-09-40, e-mail info@stm-assoc.org, World Wide Web https://www.stm-assoc.org. *CEO* Caroline Sutton.

National

Argentina

Cámara Argentina del Libro (Argentine Book Assn.), Av. Belgrano 1580, 4 piso, C1093AAQ Buenos Aires. Tel. 54-11-4381-8383, fax 54-11-4381-9253, e-mail cal@editores.org.ar, World Wide Web http://www.editores.org.ar. *Pres.* Martín Gremmelspacher.

Fundación El Libro (Book Foundation), Yrigoyen 1628, 5 piso, C1089AAF Buenos Aires. Tel. 54-11-4370-0600, fax 54-11-4370-0607, e-mail fundacion@el-libro.com.ar, World Wide Web https://www.el-libro.org.a. *Pres.* Gabriel Waldhuter; *Admin. Dir.* José Gutiérrez Brianza.

Australia

Australian and New Zealand Assn. of Antiquarian Booksellers (ANZAAB), 40 Charlotte St. (Ground Floor), Brisbane, Q 4000. E-mail admin@anzaab.com, World Wide Web https://anzaab.com. *Pres.* Douglas Stewart.

Australian Booksellers Assn., 828 High St., Unit 9, Kew East, Vic. 3102. Tel. 3-9859-7322, fax 3-9859-7344, e-mail mail@aba.org.au, World Wide Web https://www.booksellers.org.au. *CEO* Robbie Egan.

Australian Publishers Assn., 60/89 Jones St., Ultimo, NSW 2007. Tel. 2-9281-9788, e-mail apa@publishers.asn.au, World Wide Web https://www.publishers.asn.au. *Pres.* James Kellow.

Austria

Hauptverband des Österreichischen Buchhandels (Austrian Publishers and Booksellers Assn.), Grünangergasse 4, A-1010 Vienna. Tel. 43-1-512-15-35, fax 43-1-512-84-82, e-mail office@hvb.at, World Wide Web https://www.buecher.at. *Pres.* Benedikt Föger.

Verband der Antiquare Österreichs (Austrian Antiquarian Booksellers Assn.), Grünangergasse 4, A-1010 Vienna. Tel. 1-512-1535-14, e-mail sekretariat@hvb.at, World Wide Web https://www.buecher.at/antiquar.

Belgium

Boek.be (formerly Vlaamse Boekverkopersbond, Flemish Booksellers Assn.), Te Buelaerlei 37, 2140 Borgerhout. Tel. 03-230-89-23, fax 3-281-22-40, World Wide Web http://www.boek.be/over-boekbe.

Brazil

Câmara Brasileira do Livro (Brazilian Book Assn.), Rua Cristiano Viana 91, Pinheiros-São Paulo-SP, CEP: 05411-000. Tel./fax 11-3069-1300, e-mail cbl@cbl.org.br, World Wide Web https://cbl.org.br. *Pres.* Sevani Matos.

Sindicato Nacional dos Editores de Livros (Brazilian Publishers Assn.), Rue da Ajuda 35/18th Fl., 20040-000 Rio de Janeiro-RJ. Tel. 21-99472-6066, 21-2533-0399, fax 21-2533-0422, e-mail snel@snel.org.br, World Wide Web https://snel.org.br. *Pres.* Dante Jose Alexandre Cid.

Chile

Câmara Chilena del Libro AG (Chilean Assn. of Publishers, Distributors, and Booksellers), Av. Libertador Bernardo O'Higgins 1370, Oficina 501, Santiago. Tel. 2-672-0348, fax 2-687-4271, e-mail prolibro@tie.cl, World Wide Web https://camaradellibro.cl. *Pres.* Eduardo Castillo.

Colombia

Câmara Colombiana del Libro (Colombian Book Assn.), Calle 35, No. 5A 05, Bogotá.

Tel. 57-1-323-01-11, fax 57-1-285-10-82, e-mail camlibro@camlibro.com.co, World Wide Web https://camlibro.com.co. *Exec. Pres.* Emiro Aristizábal; *Secy.-Gen.* Manuel José Sarmiento Ramírez.

Czech Republic

Svaz ceských knihkupcu a nakladatelu (Czech Publishers and Booksellers Assn.), Fugnerovo nameisti 1808/3, Prague 2, 120 00. Tel. 420-227-660-644, e-mail sckn@sckn.cz, World Wide Web https://www.sckn.cz. *Dir.* Marcela Turečková. E-mail tureckova@sckn.cz.

Denmark

Danske Boghandlerforening (Danish Booksellers Assn.), Slotsholmsgade 1 B, 1216 Copenhagen K. Tel. 45-32-54-2255, fax 45-32-54-0041, e-mail info@boghandlerne.dk, World Wide Web https://boghandlerforeningen.dk. *Chair* Lone Haagerup; *Vice Chair* Trine Thougaard

Danske Forlæggerforening (Danish Publishers Assn.), Stock Exchange, Slotsholmsgade 1, 1217 Copenhagen K. Tel. 45-33-15-66-88, e-mail info@danskeforlag.dk, World Wide Web https://www.danskeforlag.dk. *Chair* Morten Hesseldahl; *Dir.* Christine Bødtcher-Hansen.

Ecuador

Câmara Ecuatoriana del Libro, N29-61 Eloy Alfaro and England, 9th Floor, Quito. Tel. 593-2-2553311, fax 593-2-2553314, e-mail info@celibro.org.ec, World Wide Web https://www.celibro.org.ec/pagina. *Pres.* Oswaldo Almeida Mora.

Egypt

General Egyptian Book Organization (GEBO), 1194 Corniche El Nil, Ramlet Boulaq, Book Authority Building, Cairo 1194. Tel. 2-577-5367, e-mail info@gebo.gov.eg, World Wide Web http://www.gebo.gov.eg.

Estonia

Estonian Publishers Assn., Roosikrantsi 6-207, 10119 Tallinn. Telephone 372-644-9866, fax 372-617-7550, e-mail info@estbook.

com, World Wide Web http://www.estbook. com. *CEO* Kaidi Urmet.

Finland

Kirjakauppaliitto Ry (Booksellers Association of Finland), Eteläranta 10, 00130 Helsinki. Tel. 040-689-9112, e-mail toimisto@kir jakauppaliitto.fi, World Wide Web https:// kirjakauppaliitto.fi. *Managing Director* Laura Karlsson. E-mail laura.karlsson@kir jakauppaliitto.fi.

Suomen Kirjasaatio (Finnish Book Foundation). Eteläranta 10, FI-00130 Helsinki. Tel. 358 9 228 77 255, World Wide Web https:// kustantajat.fi. *Chair Timo Julkunen*; Mgr. Sakari Laiho.

France

Bureau International de l'Edition Française (BIEF) (International Bureau of French Publishing), 115 blvd. Saint-Germain, F-75006 Paris. Tel. 01-44-41-13-13, fax 01-46-34-63-83, e-mail info@bief.org, World Wide Web https://www.bief.org. *Pres.* Antoine Gallimard. *New York Branch* French Publishers Agency, 30 Vandam Street, Suite 5A, New York, NY 10013. Tel./fax 212-254-4540, World Wide Web https://www.french rights.com.

Cercle de la Librairie (Circle of Professionals of the Book Trade), 35 rue Grégoire-de-Tours, F-75006 Paris. Tel. 01-44-41-28-00, fax 01-44-41-28-65, e-mail support@electre.com, World Wide Web https://accueil.electre.com.

Syndicat de la Librairie Française, Hotel Massa, 38 rue du Faubourg Saint-Jacques, F-75014 Paris. Tel. 01-53-62-23-10, fax 01-53-62-10-45, e-mail contact@syndicat-librarie.fr, World Wide Web https://www. syndicat-librairie.fr/accueil. *Admin. Secy.* Gaëlle Sacase. E-mail g.sacase@syndicat-librairie.fr.

Syndicat National de la Librairie Ancienne et Moderne (SLAM) (National Assn. of Antiquarian and Modern Booksellers), 4 rue Gît-le-Coeur, F-75006 Paris. Tel. 01-43-29-46-38, fax 01-43-25-41-63, World Wide Web https://slamlivrerare.org. *Pres.* Jean-Marc Dechaud; *Secy.-Gen.* Charles-Henri de Boissieu.

Syndicat National de l'Edition (SNE) (National Union of Publishers), 115 Blvd. Saint-Germain, F-75006 Paris. Tel. 01-44-41-40-50, fax 01-44-41-40-77, World Wide Web https://www.sne.fr. *Pres.* Vincent Montagne.

Germany

Börsenverein des Deutschen Buchhandels e.V. (Stock Exchange of German Booksellers), Braubachstr. 16, 60311 Frankfurt-am-Main. Tel. 49-69-1306-0, fax 49-69-1306-201, e-mail info@boev.de, World Wide Web https://www.boersenverein.de. *Chair* Karin Schmidt-Friderichs.

Verband Deutscher Antiquare e.V. (German Antiquarian Booksellers Assn.), Geschäftsstelle, Seeblick 1, 56459 Elbingen. Tel. 49-0-6435-90-91-47, fax 49-0-6435-90-91-48, e-mail buch@antiquare.de, World Wide Web https://www.antiquare.de/aktuelles. *Chair* Sibylle Wieduwilt. E-mail s.wieduwilt@ antiquare.de.

Hungary

Magyar Könyvkiadók és Könyvterjesztök Egyesülése (Assn. of Hungarian Publishers and Booksellers), Kertész u. 41. I /4, 1073 Budapest. Tel. 06-1-343-2538, e-mail mkke@mkke.hu, World Wide Web https:// mkke.hu. *Pres.* Katalin Gál.

Iceland

Félag Islenskra Bókaútgefenda (Icelandic Publishers Assn.), Brautarholti 8, 105 Reykjavik. Tel. 517-7200, e-mail fibut@fibut.is, World Wide Web http://www.fibut.is. *Chair* Heidar Ingi Svannsson; *Man. Dir.* Benedikt Kristjánsson.

India

Federation of Indian Publishers, Federation House, 18/1C Institutional Area, Aruna Asaf Ali Marg, New Delhi 110067. Tel. 11-2696-4847, fax 11-2686-4054, e-mail fippresi dent@gmail.com, World Wide Web https:// www.fiponline.org. *Exec. Dir.* Shri. Ramesh K. Mittal.

Indonesia

Ikapi (Indonesian Publisher Association), Ikapi Building, Jalan Kalipasir, No. 32, Cikini,

Central Jakarta, 10340. Tel. 62 21 314 1907, e-mail sekretariat@ikapi.org, World Wide Web https://www.ikapi.org. *Chair* Arys Hilman Nugraha; *Secy.* Novi Arsianti.

Ireland

Publishing Ireland/Foilsiu Eireann (formerly CLÉ: The Irish Book Publishers' Assn.), 63 Patrick St., Dun Laoghaire, Co Dublin. Tel. 353-1-639-4868, e-mail info@publishingireland.com, World Wide Web https://www.publishingireland.com. *Pres.* Ruth Hallinan; *Gen. Mgr.* Orla McLoughlin.

Israel

Israeli Association of Book Publishers, 29 Carlebach St., 67132 Tel Aviv. Tel. 3-561-4121, fax 3-561-1996, e-mail info@tbpai.co.il, World Wide Web https://www.tbpai.co.il. *Chair* Benjamin Trivaks.

Italy

Associazione Italiana Editori (Italian Publishers Assn.), Corso di Porta Romana 108, 20122 Milan. Tel. 2-89-28-0800, fax 2-89-28-0860, e-mail info@aie.it, World Wide Web https://www.aie.it. *Pres.* Ricardo Franco Levy.

Associazione Librai Antiquari d'Italia (Antiquarian Booksellers Assn. of Italy), Via Luigi Cadorna 22, 22100 Como. Tel. 39-349-0748229; e-mail alai@alai.it, World Wide Web https://www.alai.it. *Pres.* Gabriele Maspero.

Japan

Antiquarian Booksellers Assn. of Japan, Kokusai Hamamatsucho Bldg., 9th Floor, 1-9-18 Kaigan, Minato-ku, Tokyo, 105-0022. Tel. 81-3-6367-6070, fax 81-3-6367-6196, e-mail abaj@abaj.gr.jp, World Wide Web http://www.abaj.gr.jp. *Chair* Ichiro Kitazawa.

Japan Assn. of International Publications, 1-1-13-4F Kanda, Jimbocho, Chiyodakku, Tokyo 101-0051. Tel. 3-5479-7269, fax 3-5479-7307, e-mail office@jaip.jp, World Wide Web https://www.jaip.jp/en. *Exec. Dir.* Mark Gresham.

Japan Book Publishers Assn., 5th Fl., Shuppan-Club Building 1-32, Kanda-Jimbocho,

Chiyoda-ku, Tokyo, 101-0051. Tel. 81-0-3-6273-7065, fax 81-0-3-6811-0959, e-mail research@jbpa.or.jp, World Wide Web http://www.jbpa.or.jp. *Pres.* Masaru Onodera.

Kenya

Kenya Publishers Assn., P.O. Box 42767, Nairobi 00100. Tel. 254-724-255848, e-mail info@kenyapublishers.org, World Wide Web https://www.facebook.com/kenyapublishersassociation. *Chair* Lawrence Njagi.

Korea (Republic of)

Korean Publishers Assn., Publishing Culture Center, 6 Samcheong-ro (Sagan-dong), Jongno-gu, Seoul. Tel. 2-733-8402, fax 2-738-5414, e-mail webmaster@kpa21.or.kr, World Wide Web http://kpa21.or.kr/?ckattempt=1. *Chair* Yoon Cheol-ho.

Latvia

Latvian Publishers' Assn., Baznicas iela 37-3, LV-1010 Riga. Tel./fax 67-217-730, e-mail lga@gramatizdeveji.lv, World Wide Web https://www.gramatizdeveji.lv. *Pres.* Renāte Punka; *Exec. Dir.* Marika Celma.

Lithuania

Lithuanian Publishers Assn., Vokiečių st. 18A, LT 01130, Vilnius. Tel. 370-675-75692, fax 370-670-32287, e-mail info@lla.lt, World Wide Web https://lla.lt/lt. *Pres.* Lolita Varanavičienė; *Exec. Dir.* Rūta Elijošaitytė-Kaikarė.

Malaysia

Malaysian Book Publishers' Assn., No. 7-6, Block E2, Jl PJU 1/42A, Dataran Prima, 47301 Petaling Jaya, Selangor. Tel. 3-7880-5840, fax 3-7880-5841, e-mail info@mabopa.com.my, World Wide Web http://www.mabopa.com.my. *Pres.* Arief Hakim Sani Rahmat.

Mexico

Cámara Nacional de la Industria Editorial Mexicana (Mexican Publishers' Assn.), Holanda No. 13, Col. San Diego Churubusco, Deleg.

Coyoacán, 04120 Mexico DF. Tel. 155-56-88-20-11, fax 155-56-04-31-47, e-mail contacto@caniem.com, World Wide Web https://caniem.online. *Pres.* Juan Luis Arzoz Arbide. E-mail presidencia@caniem.com.

The Netherlands

KVB—Koninklijke Vereeniging van het Boekenvak (Royal Society for the Book Trade), P.O. Box 12040, AA Amsterdam-Zuidoost. Tel. 020-430-9115, e-mail info@kvb.nl, World Wide Web https://kvb.nl. *Dirs.* M.K.J. David and A. Schroën.

Nederlands Uitgeversverbond (Royal Dutch Publishers Assn.), Postbus 12040, 1100 AA Amsterdam. Tel. 20-430-9150, fax 20-430-9199, e-mail info@mediafederatie.nl, World Wide Web https://mediafederatie.nl. *Chair* Derk Haank; *Dir.* Peter Stadhouders. E-mail pstadhouders@mediafederatie.nl.

Nederlandsche Vereeniging van Antiquaren (Netherlands Assn. of Antiquarian Booksellers), P.O. Box 503, 4200 AM Gorinchem. Tel. 31-0-114-3142-09, fax 31-0-114-e-mail rashi@xs4all.nl, World Wide Web https://nvva.nl. *Gen. Secy.* Ingrid Oey.

Nederlandse Boekverkopersbond (Dutch Booksellers Assn.), Hamburgerstraat 28a, 512 NS, Utrecht. Tel. 088-600-9500, e-mail info@boekbond.nl, World Wide Web https://www.boekbond.nl. *Chair* Jan Peter Prenger.

New Zealand

Booksellers New Zealand, Ground Floor, Red Shield House, 79 Boulcott St., Wellington 6011. Tel. 4-472-1908, fax 4-472-1912, e-mail info@booksellers.co.nz, World Wide Web https://www.booksellers.co.nz. *Chair* Juliet Blyth. E-mail juliet.blyth@booksellers.co.nz. *CEO* Dan Slevin. E-mail dan.slevin@booksellers.co.nz.

Nigeria

Nigerian Publishers Assn., 1st Floor Premium House, Opp. Evans Brothers (Nig. Publishers) Ltd., Jericho, GPO Box 2541, Dugbe, Ibadan, Oyo States. Tel. 234-816-248-9037, e-mail nigerianpublishers@ymail.com, World Wide Web https://www.facebook.com/nigerianpublishers. *Pres.* Adedapo Gbadega.

Norway

Norske Bokhandlerforening (Norwegian Booksellers Association), Sehesteds gate 6, 0164 Oslo. Tel. 47-22-39-68-00, e-mail firmapost@bokhandlerforeningen.no, World Wide Web https://bokhandlerforeningen.no. *Chair* Hans Antonsen; *Dir.* Anne Schiøtz. E-mail direktor@bokhandlerforeningen.no.

Norske Forleggerforening (Norwegian Publishers Assn.), Sehesteds gate 6, 0164 Oslo. Tel. 22-00-75-80, fax 22-33-38-30, e-mail dnf@forleggerforeningen.no, World Wide Web https://forleggerforeningen.no. *Chair* Edmund Austigard; *Admin. Dir.* Heidi Austlid.

Peru

Cámara Peruana del Libro (Peruvian Publishers Assn.), Av. Cuba 427, Jesús María, Apdo. 10253, Lima 11. Tel. (511) 265-0735, fax (511) 265-0735, e-mail cp-libro@cpl.org.pe, World Wide Web https://cpl.org.pe. *Pres.* José Wilfredo Del Pozo Alarcón.

Philippines

Philippine Educational Publishers Assn., Phoenix Building, 927 Quezon Ave., Quezon City. Tel. (632) 376-4041 local 334, fax (632) 376-4031, e-mail pepasecretariat@gmail.com, World Wide Web http://www.pepa.org.ph. *Pres.* Jose Paolo M. Sibal.

Poland

Władze Stowarzyszenie Księgarzy Polskich (Assn. of Polish Booksellers), ul. Złota 65/25, 00-819 Warsaw. Tel./fax 0-22-827-93-81, e-mail skp@ksiegarze.org.pl, World Wide Web http://ksiegarze.org.pl. *Chair* Zofia Szpojankowska; *Gen. Secy.* Katarzyna Balicka-Więckowska.

Portugal

Associação Portuguesa de Editores e Livreiros (Portuguese Assn. of Publishers and Booksellers), Av. dos Estados Unidas da America 97, 6 Esq., 1700-167 Lisbon. Tel. 21-843-51-80, e-mail geral@apel.pt, World Wide Web https://www.apel.pt. *Exec. Dir.* Pedro Sobral. *Gen. Secy.* Bruno Pires Pacheco.

Russia

Assn. of Book Publishers of Russia, 101000, Lubyanka, Luchnikov per., D.4, p. 1, Moscow. Tel. 7-926-900-85-27, e-mail aski book@gmail.com, World Wide Web http://www.aski.ru. Pres. Chechenev Konstantin Vasilievich.

Rossiiskaya Knizhnaya Palata (Russian Book Chamber), Zvezdny boulevard 17, building 1, 129085, Moscow. Tel. 495-688-96-89, fax 495-688-99-91, e-mail info@bookchamber.ru, World Wide Web https://www.bookchamber.ru.

Singapore

Singapore Book Publishers Assn., 9 Jurong Town Hall Road, 02-02 Trade Association Hub, Jurong Town Hall, Singapore 609431. Tel. 65-6957-7093, e-mail info@singapore bookpublishers.sg, World Wide Web https://www.singaporebookpublishers.sg. *President* Max Phua. E-mail schoppert@nus.edu.sg; *Exec. Dir.* Cecilia Woo.

Slovenia

Zdruzenie Zaloznikov in Knjigotrzcev Slovenije Gospodarska Zbornica Slovenije (Assn. of Publishers and Booksellers of Slovenia), Dimičeva 13, SI-1504 Ljubljana. Tel. 386-1-5898-000, fax 386-1-5898-100, e-mail info@gzs.si, World Wide Web https://www.gzs.si/zbornica_knjiznih_zaloznikov_in_knjigotrzcev. *Pres.* Tibor Šimonka; *Gen. Mgr.* Aleš Cantarutti.

South Africa

Publishers Assn. of South Africa (PASA), House Vincent, Wynberg Mews, 10 Brodie Rd., Wynberg, Cape Town 7800. Tel. 21-762-9083, fax 21-762-2763, e-mail pasa@publishsa.co.za, World Wide Web http://www.publishsa.co.za. *Chair* Brian Wafawarowa; *Exec. Dir.* Mpuka Radinku.

South African Booksellers Assn. (formerly Associated Booksellers of Southern Africa), Regus Business Centre, 2 Fir Street, Observatory, 7925, Cape Town. Tel. 27 21 003 8098, e-mail saba@sabooksellers.com, World Wide Web https://www.sabooksellers.com. *Pres.* Melvin Kaabwe. E-mail melvin.kaabwe@vanschaik.com.

Spain

Federación de Gremios de Editores de España (Federation of Spanish Publishers Assns.), Calle de Cea Bermúdez 44, 28003 Madrid. Tel. 91-534-51-95, fax 91-535-26-25, e-mail fgee@fge.es, World Wide Web http://www.federacioneditores.org. *Acting Pres.* D. Daniel Fernandez; *Secy.* Antonio María Ávila.

Sweden

Svenska Förläggareföreningen (Swedish Publishers Assn.), c/o Svenska Publisher AB, Kungstensgatan 38, 2 tr, 113 59 Stockholm. Tel. 8-736-19-40, e-mail info@forlaggare.se, World Wide Web https://forlaggare.se. *Chair* Jesper Monthán.

Switzerland

Swiss Booksellers and Publishers Association (SBVV), Limmatstrasse 111, Postfach 8031, Zürich. Tel. 44-421-36-00, fax 44-421-36-18, e-mail info@sbvv.ch, World Wide Web https://www.sbvv.ch. *Pres.* Thomas Kramer. E-mail t.kramer@scheidegger-spiess.ch; *Gen. Mgr.* Tanja Messerli. E-mail tanja.messerli@sbvv.ch.

Thailand

Publishers and Booksellers Assn. of Thailand, 83/159 Soi Ngam Wong Wan 47 (Chinnaket 2), Thung Song Hong, Lak Si, Bangkok 10210. Tel. 2-954-9560-4, fax 02-954-9565-6, e-mail info@pubat.or.th, World Wide Web https://pubat.or.th.

Uganda

Uganda Publishers Assn., P.O. Box 7732, Kampala. Tel. 256-752-707327. World Wide Web https://www.facebook.com/UgandaPublishers.

United Kingdom

Antiquarian Booksellers Assn., 21 John Street, London WC1N 2BF, England. Tel. 44-0-20-8004-9512, e-mail admin@aba.org.uk, World Wide Web https://aba.org.uk. *Pres.* Deborah Coltham.

Assn. of Learned and Professional Society Publishers, Egale 1, 80 St Albans Road,

Watford, Hertfordshire WD17 1DL England. Tel. 44 (0)1245 260571, e-mail admin@alpsp.org, World Wide Web https://www.alpsp.org. *Chair* Jamie Humphrey; *Chief Exec.* Wayne Sime.

Booktrust, G8 Battersea Studios, 80 Silverthorne Rd., Battersea, London SW8 3HE, England. Tel. 020 7801 8800, e-mail query@booktrust.org.uk, World Wide Web https://www.booktrust.org.uk. *Pres.* Michael Morpurgo; *Chief Exec.* Diana Gerald.

Publishers Assn., 50 Southwark Street, London SE1 1UN, England. Tel. 44 0 20 7378 0504, e-mail mail@publishers.org.uk, World Wide Web https://www.publishers.org.uk. *Pres.* Nigel Newton.

Scottish Book Trust, Sandeman House, Trunk's Close, 55 High St., Edinburgh EH1 1SR, Scotland. Tel. 131-524-0160, e-mail info@scottishbooktrust.com, World Wide Web https://www.scottishbooktrust.com.

Welsh Books Council (Cyngor Llyfrau Cymru), Castell Brychan, Aberystwyth, Ceredigion SY23 2JB, Wales. Tel. 1970-624-151, fax 1970-625-385, e-mail info@wbc.org.uk, World Wide Web https://llyfrau.cymru/en. *Hon. Counsel* Gwydion Hughes.

Uruguay

Cámara Uruguaya del Libro (Uruguayan Publishers Assn.), Colón 1476, Apdo. 102, 11000 Montevideo. Tel. 2-916-93-74, fax 2-916-76-28, e-mail gerencia@camaradellibro.com.uy, World Wide Web https://www.camaradellibro.com.uy. *Chair* Alicia Guglielmo.

Venezuela

Cámara Venezolana del Libro (Venezuelan Publishers Assn.), Av. Andrés Bello, Centro Andrés Bello, Torre Oeste 11, piso 11, of. 112-0, Caracas 1050. Tel. 212-793-1347, fax 212-793-1368, e-mail cavelibro@gmail.com, World Wide Web https://www.facebook.com/CamaradelLibro.

Zimbabwe

Zimbabwe Book Publishers Assn., P.O. Box 3041, Harare. Tel. 263-77-706-4272, e-mail danielle.zbpa@gmail.com. World Wide Web https://www.facebook.com/zimbabwebookpublishers.

National Information Standards Organization (NISO)

NISO, the National Information Standards Organization, a nonprofit association accredited by the American National Standards Institute (ANSI), identifies, develops, maintains, and publishes technical standards to manage information in today's continually changing digital environment. NISO standards apply to both traditional and new technologies and to information across its whole lifecycle, from creation through documentation, use, repurposing, storage, metadata, and preservation. The following listing includes NISO standards of interest to readers of *Library and Book Trade Almanac*.

Content and Collection Management

ANSI/NISO Z39.2-1994 (R2016)	Information Interchange Format ISBN 978-1-937522-70-4
ANSI/NISO Z39.4-2021	Criteria for Indexes ISBN 978-1-950980-14-7
ANSI/NISO Z39.14-1997 (R2015)	Guidelines for Abstracts ISBN 978-1-937522-44-5
ANSI/NISO Z39.18-2005 (R2010)	Scientific and Technical Reports— Preparation, Presentation, and Preservation ISBN 978-1-937522-21-6
ANSI/NISO Z39.19-2005 (R2010)	Guidelines for the Construction, Format, and Management of Monolingual Controlled Vocabularies ISBN 978-1-937522-22-3
ANSI/NISO Z39.23-1997 (S2015)	Standard Technical Report Number Format and Creation ISBN 978-1-937522-45-2
ANSI/NISO Z39.29-2005 (R2010)	Bibliographic References ISBN 978-1-937522-26-1
ANSI/NISO Z39.32-1996 (R2012)	Information on Microfiche Headers ISBN 978-1-937522-29-2
ANSI/NISO Z39.41-1997 (S2015)	Placement Guidelines for Information on Spines ISBN 978-1-937522-46-9

ANSI/NISO Z39.43-1993 (R2017)   Standard Address Number (SAN) for the Publishing Industry
ISBN 978-1-937522-75-9

ANSI/NISO Z39.48-1992 (R2009)   Permanence of Paper for Publications and Documents in Libraries and Archives
ISBN 978-1-937522-30-8

ANSI/NISO Z39.71-2006 (R2011)   Holdings Statements for Bibliographic Items
ISBN 978-1-937522-31-5

ANSI/NISO Z39.73-1994 (R2012)   Single-Tier Steel Bracket Library Shelving
ISBN 978-1-937522-32-2

ANSI/NISO Z39.74-1996 (R2012)   Guides to Accompany Microform Sets
ISBN 978-1-937522-40-7

ANSI/NISO Z39.78-2000 (R2018)   Library Binding
ISBN 978-1-937522-86-5

ANSI/NISO Z39.84-2005 (R2010)   Syntax for the Digital Object Identifier
ISBN 978-1-937522-34-6

ANSI/NISO Z39.85-2012   The Dublin Core Metadata Element Set
ISBN 978-1-937522-14-8

ANSI/NISO Z39.86-2005 (R2012)   Specifications for the Digital Talking Book
ISBN 978-1-937522-35-3

ANSI/NISO Z39.96-2021   JATS: Journal Article Tag Suite, version 1.3
ISBN 978-1-950980-13-0

ANSI/NISO Z39.98-2012   Authoring and Interchange Framework for Adaptive XML Publishing Specification
ISBN 978-1-937522-07-0

ANSI/NISO Z39.102-2022   STS: Standards Tag Suite, Version 1.2
ISBN 978-1-950980-23-9

ANSI/NISO Z39.104-2022   CRediT, Contributor Roles Taxonomy
ISBN 978-1-950980-18-5

ANSI/NISO/ISO 12083-1995 (R2009)   Electronic Manuscript Preparation and Markup
ISBN 978-1-880124-20-8

Standards for Discovery to Delivery

ANSI/NISO Z39.19-2005 (R2010)   Guidelines for the Construction, Format, and Management of Monolingual Controlled Vocabularies
ISBN 978-1-937522-22-3

ANSI/NISO Z39.50-2003 (S2014)   Information Retrieval (Z39.50) Application Service Definition and Protocol Specification
ISBN 978-1-937522-42-1

ANSI/NISO Z39.83-1-2012	NISO Circulation Interchange Part 1: Protocol (NCIP), version 2.02 ISBN 978-1-937522-03-2
ANSI/NISO Z39.83-2-2012	NISO Circulation Interchange Protocol (NCIP) Part 2: Implementation Profile 1, version 2.02 ISBN 978-1-937522-04-9
ANSI/NISO Z39.85-2012	The Dublin Core Metadata Element Set ISBN 978-1-937522-14-8
ANSI/NISO Z39.87-2006 (R2017)	Data Dictionary—Technical Metadata for Digital Still Images ISBN 978-1-937522-76-6
ANSI/NISO Z39.88-2004 (R2010)	The OpenURL Framework for Context-Sensitive Services ISBN 978-1-937522-38-4
ANSI/NISO Z39.89-2003 (S2014)	The U.S. National Z39.50 Profile for Library Applications ISBN 978-1-937522-43-8
ANSI/NISO Z39.99-2017	ResourceSync Framework Specification ISBN 978-1-937522-73-5

Business Information

ANSI/NISO Z39.7-2013	Information Services and Use: Metrics and Statistics for Libraries and Information Providers—Data Dictionary ISBN 978-1-937522-15-5
ANSI/NISO Z39.93-2014	The Standardized Usage Statistics Harvesting Initiative (SUSHI) Protocol ISBN 978-1-937522-47-6

Preservation and Storage

ANSI/NISO Z39.32-1996 (R2012)	Information on Microfiche Headers ISBN 978-1-937522-29-2
ANSI/NISO Z39.48-1992 (R2009)	Permanence of Paper for Publications and Documents in Libraries and Archives ISBN 978-1-937522-30-8
ANSI/NISO Z39.73-1994 (R2012)	Single-Tier Steel Bracket Library Shelving ISBN 978-1-937522-32-2
ANSI/NISO Z39.78-2000 (R2018)	Library Binding ISBN 978-1-937522-86-5

In Development/NISO Initiatives

NISO develops new standards, reports, and best practices on a continuing basis to support its ongoing standards development program. NISO working groups are currently developing or exploring the following:

- Collection Description Specification (NISO Z39.91-200x)
- Content Profile/Linked Document (NISO Z39.105-202x)
- Criteria for Indexes (NISO Z39.4-201x)
- Digital Bookmarking and Annotation (NISO Z39.97-201x)
- Information Retrieval Service—Description Specification (NISO Z39.92-200x)
- Information Services and Use Metrics & Statistics for Libraries and Information Providers—Data Dictionary (NISO Z39.7-201x)
- Permanence of Paper for Publications and Documents in Libraries and Archives (ANSI/NISO Z39.48-201x)
- Scientific and Technical Reports—Preparation, Presentation, and Preservation (ANSI/NISO Z39.18-2005 [R201x])
- Standard Interchange Protocol (SIP) (NISO Z39.100-201x)
- Standards-Specific Ontology (SSOS) (NISO Z39.103-201x)

NISO Recommended Practices

A Framework of Guidance for Building Good Digital Collections, 3rd ed., 2007
ISBN 978-1-880124-74-1

NISO RP-2005-01	Ranking of Authentication and Access Methods Available to the Metasearch Environment ISBN 978-1-880124-89-5
NISO RP-2005-02	Search and Retrieval Results Set Metadata ISBN 978-1-880124-88-8
NISO RP-2005-03	Search and Retrieval Citation Level Data Elements ISBN 978-1-880124-87-1
NISO RP-2006-01	Best Practices for Designing Web Services in the Library Context ISBN 978-1-880124-86-4
NISO RP-2006-02	NISO Metasearch XML Gateway Implementers Guide ISBN 978-1-880124-85-7
NISO RP-6-2012	RFID in U.S. Libraries ISBN 978-1-937522-02-5
NISO RP-7-2012	SERU: A Shared Electronic Resource Understanding ISBN 978-1-937522-08-7
NISO RP-8-2008	Journal Article Versions (JAV) ISBN 978-1-880124-79-6
NISO RP-9-2014	KBART: Knowledge Bases and Related Tools ISBN 978-1-937522-41-4

NISO RP-10-2010	Cost of Resource Exchange (CORE) Protocol ISBN 978-1-880124-84-0
NISO RP-11-2011	ESPReSSO: Establishing Suggested Practices Regarding Single Sign-On ISBN 978-1-880124-98-7
NISO RP-12-2012	Physical Delivery of Library Resources ISBN 978-1-937522-01-8
NISO RP-14-2014	NISO SUSHI Protocol: COUNTER-SUSHI Implementation Profile ISBN 978-1-937522-45-2
NISO RP-15-2013	Recommended Practices for Online Supplemental Journal Article Materials ISBN 978-1-937522-12-4
NISO RP-16-2013	PIE-J: The Presentation and Identification of E-Journals ISBN 978-1-937522-05-6
NISO RP-17-2013	Institutional Identification: Identifying Organizations in the Information Supply Chain ISBN 978-1-937522-11-7
NISO RP-19-2020	Open Discovery Initiative: Promoting Transparency in Discovery ISBN 978-1-950980-08-6
NISO RP-20-2014	Demand Driven Acquisition of Monographs ISBN 978-1-937522-44-5
NISO RP-21-2013	Improving OpenURLs Through Analytics (IOTA): Recommendations for Link Resolver Providers ISBN 978-1-937522-18-6
NISO RP-22-2015	Access License and Indicators ISBN 978-1-937522-49-0
NISO RP-22-2021	Access & License Indicators (2021 Revision) ISBN 978-1-950980-17-8
NISO RP-23-2015	Protocol for Exchanging Serial Content (PESC) ISBN 978-1-937522-66-7
NISO RP-24-2019	Transfer Code of Practice, version 4.0 ISBN 978-1-937522-90-2
NISO RP-25-2016	Outputs of the NISO Alternative Assessment Project ISBN 978-1-937522-71-1
NISO RP-26-2019	KBART Automation: Automated Retrieval of Customer Electronic Holdings ISBN 978-1-937522-91-9
NISO RP-27-2019	Resource Access in the 21st Century ISBN 978-1-937522-99-5
NISO RP-29-2022	E-Book Bibliographic Metadata Requirements in the Sale, Publication, Discovery, Delivery, and Preservation Supply Chain ISBN 978-1-950980-01-7

NISO RP-30-2020	Manuscript Exchange Common Approach (MECA) ISBN 978-1-950980-02-4
NISO RP-31-2021	Reproducibility Badging and Definitions ISBN 978-1-950980-03-1
NISO RP-32-2019	JATS4R Subject & Keyword Guidelines ISBN 978-1-950980-04-8
NISO RP-33-2020	NISO JATS4R Ethics Statements ISBN 978-1-950980-05-5
NISO RP-35-2020	JATS4R Preprint Citations ISBN 978-1-950980-07-9
NISO RP-36-2020	JATS4R Data Citations ISBN 978-1-950980-09-3
NISO RP-37-2021	JATS4R Funding, Version 1.3 ISBN 978-1-950980-15-4
NISO RP-38-2021	Content Platform Migrations ISBN 978-1-950980-11-6
NISO RP-39-2021	JATS4R Peer Review Materials ISBN: 978-1-950980-12-3
NISO RP-40-2021	JATS4R Software Citations, Version 1.0 ISBN 978-1-950980-16-1
NISO RP-41-2023	Video and Audio Metadata Guidelines 978-1-950980-19-2
NISO RP-42-2022	JATS4R Permissions, Version 2 978-1-950980-20-8
NISO RP-43-2022	JATS4R Abstracts, Version 1.0 978-1-950980-21-5

NISO Technical Reports

NISO TR-01-1995	Environmental Guidelines for the Storage of Paper Records by William K. Wilson ISBN 978-1-800124-21-5
NISO TR-02-1997	Guidelines for Indexes and Related Information Retrieval Devices by James D. Anderson ISBN 978-1-880124-36-X
NISO TR-03-1999	Guidelines for Alphabetical Arrangement of Letters and Sorting of Numerals and Other Symbols by Hans H. Wellisch ISBN 978-1-880124-41-6
NISO TR-04-2006	Networked Reference Services: Question/Answer Transaction Protocol ISBN 978-1-880124-71-0

NISO TR-05-2013 IOTA Working Group Summary of Activities and
        Outcomes
        ISBN 978-1-937522-17-9

NISO TR-06-2017 Issues in Vocabulary Management
        ISBN 978-1-937522-79-7

Other NISO Publications

The Case for New Economic Models to Support Standardization
 by Clifford Lynch
 ISBN 978-1-880124-90-1

The Exchange of Serials Subscription Information
 by Ed Jones
 ISBN 978-1-880124-91-8

The Future of Library Resource Discovery
 by Marshall Breeding
 ISBN 978-1-937522-41-4

Information Standards Quarterly (ISQ) [NISO quarterly open access
 magazine]
 ISSN 1041-0031

Internet, Interoperability and Standards—Filling the Gaps
 by Janifer Gatenby
 ISBN 978-1-880124-92-5

Issues in Crosswalking Content Metadata Standards
 by Margaret St. Pierre and William P. LaPlant
 ISBN 978-1-880124-93-2

Making Good on the Promise of ERM: A Standards and Best Practices
 Discussion Paper
 by the ERM Data Standards and Best Practices Review Steering Committee
 ISBN 978-1-9357522-00-1

Metadata Demystified: A Guide for Publishers
 by Amy Brand, Frank Daly, and Barbara Meyers
 ISBN 978-1-880124-59-8

The Myth of Free Standards: Giving Away the Farm
 by Andrew N. Bank
 ISBN 978-1-880124-94-9

NISO Newsline (free monthly e-newsletter)
 ISSN 1559-2774

NISO Working Group Connection (free quarterly supplement to *Newsline*)
Patents and Open Standards
 by Priscilla Caplan
 ISBN 978-1-880124-95-6

The RFP Writer's Guide to Standards for Library Systems
 by Cynthia Hodgson
 ISBN 978-1-880124-57-4

Streamlining Book Metadata Workflow
by Judy Luther
ISBN 978-1-880124-82-6

Understanding Metadata: What Is Metadata, and What Is It For?: A Primer
by Jenn Riley
ISBN 978-1-937522-72-8

*Up and Running: Implementing Z39.50: Proceedings of a Symposium
Sponsored by the State Library of Iowa*
edited by Sara L. Randall
ISBN 978-1-880124-33-8

Z39.50: A Primer on the Protocol
ISBN 978-1-880124-35-2

Z39.50 Implementation Experiences
ISBN 978-1-880124-51-2

NISO standards are available at https://www.niso.org/publications/standards.

Recommended Practices, technical reports, white papers, and other publications are available on the NISO website at https://www.niso.org/publications.

For more information, contact NISO, 3600 Clipper Mill Rd., Suite 302, Baltimore, MD 21211. Tel. 301-654-2512, e-mail nisohq@niso.org, World Wide Web https://www.niso.org.

Calendar, 2023–2028

This listing contains information on association meetings and promotional events that are, for the most part, national or international in scope. U.S. state and regional library association meetings are also included.

Due to evolving approaches regarding public gatherings, many conferences scheduled for 2023 and into 2024 have been rescheduled or moved to a virtual or hybrid format. The calendar indicates where meetings are scheduled to be held as virtual only. Events with cities listed are expected to include an in-person component; hybrid meetings that offer both an in-person gathering and a virtual component are indicated by (H) next to the meeting location.

A web URL is included for each event. For meetings scheduled in 2023 and early 2024, the URL will often deliver a dedicated event webpage; for meetings further in the future, the URL may point to event basics, including date, venue, and contact information. Future dates and venues that have not been finalized are indicated by TBA (to be announced). To confirm the status of a particular conference as well as its start and end dates, please refer to the sponsoring organization's website or contact the association directly.

For information on additional book trade and promotional events, see *Literary Market Place* and *International Literary Market Place*, published by Information Today, Inc., and other library and book trade publications such as *Library Journal*, *School Library Journal*, and *Publishers Weekly*. The American Library Association (ALA) keeps an online calendar at https://www.ala.org/conferencesevents/planning-calendar. An Information Today, Inc. events calendar can be found at https://www.infotoday.com/calendar.asp.

2023

June

5–16	Assn. of American University Presses https://aupresses.org/programs-events/ annual-meeting/aupresses-2023	Virtual
6–8	Assn. of Christian Librarians http://www.acl.org/index.cfm/conference	Cedarville, OH
15–18	Beijing International Book Fair https://www.bibf.net/en	Beijing, China
19–22	Assn. of Jewish Libraries https://jewishlibraries.org/2023- digital-conference	Virtual

22–23	Computing Conference	London, UK
	https://saiconference.com/Computing	
22–27	American Library Assn. Annual Conference	Chicago, IL
	https://2023.alaannual.org	
25–30	IEEE International Symposium on Information Theory	Taipei, Taiwan
	https://isit2023.org	

July

5–7	Assn. of European Research Libraries	Budapest, Hungary
	https://liberconference.eu	
15–18	American Assn. of Law Libraries (AALL)	Boston, MA
	https://www.aallnet.org/conference	
17–21	International Assn. of School Librarianship	Rome, Italy
	https://iasl-online.org/page-1863733	
19–25	Hong Kong Book Fair	Hong Kong
	https://hkbookfair.hktdc.com/en/ About-Book-Fair/Fair-Details.html	
20–23	Comic-Con International	San Diego, CA
	https://comic-con.org/cci	

August

12–28	Edinburgh International Book Festival	Edinburgh, UK
	https://www.edbookfest.co.uk	
21–25	International Federation of Library Assns. (IFLA) General Conf. and Assembly	Rotterdam, The Netherlands
	https://2023.ifla.org	
26–29	Society of American Archivists	Washington, DC (H)
	https://www2.archivists.org/am2023	

September

27–29	Ohio Library Council	Cincinnati, OH
	https://conventionexpo.olc.org	
27–29	South Dakota Library Assn.	Rapid City, SD
	https://www.sdlibraryassociation.org/page/ Conference2023	
28–Oct. 1	Gothenburg Book Fair	Gothenburg, Sweden
	https://goteborg-bookfair.com	

October

1–4	Pennsylvania Library Assn. https://www.palibraries.org/page/2023ConferencePrelim	Pocono Manor, PA
4–6	Georgia Libraries Conference https://gla.georgialibraries.org/glc	Athens, GA
11–13	Iowa Library Assn. https://www.iowalibraryassociation.org/index.php/conference	Dubuque, IA
11–13	North Dakota Library Assn. https://ndla.info/NDLA-Annual-Conference	Fargo, ND
12–14	Colorado Library Assn. https://cal-webs.wixsite.com/calcon2023	Loveland, CO
13–15	Arkansas Library Assn. https://www.arlib.org/conference	Hot Springs, AR
15–17	New England Library Assn. https://nela2023.godaddysites.com	Springfield, MA
16–20	North Carolina Library Assn. https://nclaonline.org/conference	Winston-Salem, NC
17–19	Internet Librarian Connect https://internet-librarian.infotoday.com/2023/default.aspx	Virtual
18–22	Frankfurt Book Fair https://www.buchmesse.de/en	Frankfurt, Germany
19–20	Arizona Library Assn. https://www.azla.org/Conference	Fort McDowell, AZ
19–21	American Assn. of School Librarians (AASL) National Conference http://www.ala.org/aasl/conferences/events	Tampa, FL
21–25	International Conference on Information and Knowledge Management (CIKM) https://cikm2023.github.io	Birmingham, UK
22–24	Virginia Library Assn. https://www.vla.org/2023-vla-annual-conference	Chantilly, VA
24–26	Illinois Library Assn. https://www.ila.org/events/annual-conference	Springfield, IL
24–26	International Conference of Indigenous Archives, Libraries, and Museums https://www.atalm.org/node/573	Oklahoma City, OK
25–27	New Mexico Library Assn. https://nmla.wildapricot.org/Conferences	Albuquerque, NM

26–29	Helsinki Book Fair https://kirjamessut.messukeskus.com/ ?lang=en	Helsinki, Finland
26–29	Krakow International Book Fair https://ksiazka.krakow.pl/en	Krakow, Poland
27–31	Assn. for Information Science and Technology (ASIS&T) https://www.asist.org/am23	London, UK

November

1–4	New York Library Assn. https://www.nyla.org/4DCGI/cms/ review.html?Action=CMS_Document& DocID=281&MenuKey=conf_info	Saratoga Springs, NY
6–9	KM World https://www.kmworld.com/Conference/ 2023	Washington, DC
8–12	Buch Wein International Book Fair https://www.buchwien.at	Vienna, Austria
17–19	China Shanghai International Children's Book Fair http://www.ccbookfair.com/en	Shanghai, China
25–Dec. 3	Guadalajara International Book Fair https://www.fil.com.mx	Guadalajara, Mexico

December

| 10–13 | International Conference on
Information Systems (ICIS)
https://icis2023.aisconferences.org | Hyderabad, India |

2024

January

| 3–6 | Hawaii International Conference on System
Sciences
https://hicss.hawaii.edu/#!future-
conferences/ctld | Honolulu, HI |
| 19–22 | American Library Assn. LibLearnX: The
Library Learning Experience (LLX)
https://2024.alaliblearnx.org/ | Baltimore, MD |

March

1–3	Washington Library Assn. https://www.wla.org/conferences-events	Spokane, WA
12–14	Computers in Libraries https://www.infotoday.com/conferences.asp	Arlington, VA
12–14	London Book Fair https://www.londonbookfair.co.uk/en-gb/help/ venue-and-travel.html	London, UK

April

16–19	Texas Library Assn. https://txla.org/annual-conference/general- information/future-dates	San Antonio, TX

May

22–25	U.S. Book Show https://usbookshow.com	New York, NY (H)

June

11–13	Assn. of American University Presses https://aupresses.org/programs-events/ annual-meeting/save-the-date	Montréal, QC
27–July 2	American Library Assn. Annual Conference http://www.ala.org/conferencesevents/node/7	San Diego, CA

July

20–23	American Assn. of Law Libraries https://www.aallnet.org/conference/about/ future-meetings	Chicago, IL

September

25–27	South Dakota Library Assn. https://www.sdlibraryassociation.org/page/ Conference	Aberdeen, SD

October

2–4	Nebraska Library Assn. https://nebraskalibraries.org/meetinginfo. php?p_or_f=f	TBA
6–9	Pennsylvania Library Assn. https://www.palibraries.org/page/ More_Conf	Harrisburg, PA

8–10	Illinois Library Assn. https://www.ila.org/events/future-ila-annual-conferences	Peoria, IL
16–20	Frankfurt Book Fair https://www.buchmesse.de/en	Frankfurt, Germany

November

6–9	New York Library Assn. https://www.nyla.org/4DCGI/cms/review. html?Action=CMS_Document&DocID= 281&MenuKey=conf_info	Syracuse, NY

December

15–18	International Conference on Information Systems (ICIS) https://aisnet.org/page/ICISPage	Bangkok, Thailand

2025

January

24–27	American Library Assn. LibLearnX: The Library Learning Experience (LLX) https://www.ala.org/conferencesevents/ ala-upcoming-annual-and-liblearnx -conferences	Phoenix, AZ

April

1–4	Texas Library Assn. https://txla.org/annual-conference/general- information/future-dates	Dallas, TX
10–12	Washington Library Assn. https://www.wla.org/conferences-events	Tacoma, WA

June

TBA	Assn. of American University Presses https://aupresses.org/programs-events/ annual-meeting/save-the-dates	Virtual
26–July 1	American Library Assn. Annual Conference https://www.ala.org/conferencesevents/ ala-upcoming-annual-and-liblearnx- conferences	Philadelphia, PA

July

19–22   American Assn. of Law Libraries (AALL)   Portland, OR
https://www.aallnet.org/conference/about/
future-meetings

October

1–3   South Dakota Library Assn.   Grand Forks, SD
https://www.sdlibraryassociation.org/page/
Conference

15–19   Frankfurt Book Fair   Frankfurt, Germany
https://www.buchmesse.de/en

16–18   American Assn. of School Librarians   St. Louis, MO
(AASL) National Conference
http://www.ala.org/aasl/conferences/events

November

5–8   New York Library Assn.   Saratoga Springs, NY
https://www.nyla.org/4DCGI/cms/review.
html?Action=CMS_Document&DocID
=281&MenuKey=conf_info

December

14–17   International Conference on Information   Nashville, TN
Systems (ICIS)
https://aisnet.org/page/ICISPage

2026

January

23–26   American Library Assn. LibLearnX: The   National Harbor, MD
Library Learning Experience (LLX)
https://www.ala.org/conferencesevents/
ala-upcoming-annual-and-liblearnx-
conferences

March

30–April 2   Texas Library Assn.   Houston, TX
https://txla.org/annual-conference/general-
information/future-dates

June

13–15   Assn. of American University Presses   Seattle, WA
https://aupresses.org/programs-events/
annual-meeting/save-the-dates

25–30   American Library Assn. Annual Conference   Chicago, IL
https://www.ala.org/conferencesevents/
ala-upcoming-annual-and-liblearnx-
conferences

September

20–22   South Dakota Library Assn.   Pierre, SD
https://www.sdlibraryassociation.org/page/
Conference

October

7–11   Frankfurt Book Fair   Frankfurt, Germany
https://www.buchmesse.de/en

14–16   Mountain Plains Library Association   La Vista, NE
Conference
https://nebraskalibraries.org/meetinginfo.
php?p_or_f=f

November

4–7   New York Library Assn.   Saratoga Springs, NY
https://www.nyla.org/4DCGI/cms/review
.html?Action=CMS_Document&DocID
=281&MenuKey=conf_info

December

13–16   International Conference on Information   Lisbon, Portugal
Systems (ICIS)
https://aisnet.org/page/ICISPage

2027

March

30–Apr. 2   Texas Library Assn.   Dallas, TX
https://txla.org/annual-conference/general-
information/future-dates

April

7–10   Assn. of College and Research Libraries   Portland, OR
http://www.ala.org/acrl/conferences

June

24–29	American Library Assn. Annual Conference https://www.ala.org/conferencesevents/ ala-upcoming-annual-and-liblearnx -conferences	New Orleans, LA

October

6–10	Frankfurt Book Fair https://www.buchmesse.de/en	Frankfurt, Germany
27–30	New York Library Assn. https://www.nyla.org/4DCGI/cms/review .html?Action=CMS_Document&DocID =281&MenuKey=conf_info	Syracuse, NY

2028

April

24–27	Texas Library Assn. https://txla.org/annual-conference/ general-information/future-dates	San Antonio, TX

June

22–27	American Library Assn. Annual Conference https://www.ala.org/conferencesevents/ ala-upcoming-annual-and-liblearnx -conferences	Denver, CO

Acronyms

A

AACR2. Anglo-American Cataloging Rules

AAHSL. Association of Academic Health Sciences Libraries

AALL. American Association of Law Libraries

AAP. Association of American Publishers

AAPB. American Archive of Public Broadcasting

AASHE. Association for the Advancement of Sustainability in Higher Education

AASL. American Association of School Librarians

AAU. Association of American Universities

ABA. Acquisitions and Bibliographic Access Directorate

ABA. American Booksellers Association

ABAA. Antiquarian Booksellers' Association of America

ABOS. Association of Bookmobile and Outreach Services

ABPA. American Book Producers Association

ACL. Association of Christian Librarians

ACOS. Advisory Committee on Standards (IFLA)

ACP. Association of Canadian Publishers

ACRL. Association of College and Research Libraries

ACURIL. Association of Caribbean University, Research, and Institutional Libraries

AFSIC. Alternative Farming Systems Information Center

AgLaw. Agricultural Law Information Partnership

AGLINET. Agricultural Libraries Network

AgNIC. Agriculture Network Information Collaborative

AGRICOLA. AGRICultural On-Line Access

AIGA. Professional Association for Design

AIIM. Association for Information and Image Management

AIIP. Association of Independent Information Professionals

AILA. American Indian Library Association

AJL. Association of Jewish Libraries

ALA. American Library Association

ALCTS. Association for Library Collections and Technical Services

ALD. American Library Directory

ALIA. Australian Library and Information Association

ALIC. Archives Library Information Center

ALISE. Association for Library and Information Science Education

ALS. Academic Libraries Survey

ALSC. Association for Library Service to Children

ALTA. American Literary Translators Association

AM&P. Association Media and Publishing

ANSI. American National Standards Institute

AOMR. ALA Offices and Member Relations

APA. Audio Publishers Association

APALA. Asian/Pacific American Librarians Association

APLU. Association of Public and Land-grant Universities

APPC. Advocacy and Public Policy Committee's (ARL)

AR. Augmented reality

ARL. Association of Research Libraries

ARLIS/NA. Art Libraries Society of North America

ARMA International (formerly the Association of Records Managers and Administrators)

ARP. American Rescue Plan

ARSL. Association for Rural and Small Libraries

ASDAL. Association of Seventh-Day Adventist Librarians

ASGCLA. Association of Specialized Government and Cooperative Library Agencies

ASI. American Society for Indexing

ASIS&T. Association for Information Science and Technology

ASJA. American Society of Journalists and Authors

ATA. American Translators Association

ATALM. Association of Tribal Archives, Libraries, and Museums

Atla. (formerly American Theological Library Association)

AUPresses. Association of University Presses

AVSL. Association of Vision Science Librarians

AWIC. Animal Welfare Information Center

B

BARD. Braille and Audio Reading Download

BCALA. Black Caucus of the American Library Association

BIBCO. Bibliographic Record Cooperative

BIPOC. Black, Indigenous, and People of Color

BISAC. Book Industry Systems Advisory Committee

BISG (formerly Book Industry Study Group)

BLC. Boston Library Consortium

BMI. Book Manufacturers' Institute

BSA. Bibliographical Society of America

BSC-SBC. Bibliographical Society of Canada

BtP. By the People

C

C&I. Cataloging and indexing

C&RL. *College & Research Libraries*

CAFS. Center for Agriculture and Food Systems

CAIS-ACSI. Canadian Association for Information Science

CALA. Chinese American Librarians Association

CALL. Canadian Association of Law Libraries

CARES Act. Coronavirus Aid, Relief, and Economic Security Act

CARL-ABRC. Canadian Association of Research Libraries

CASE. Copyright Alternative in Small-Claims Enforcement Act

CAUL. Council of Australia University Librarians

CBC. Children's Book Council

CCB. Copyright Claims Board

CCC. Copyright Clearance Center

CCD. Common Core of Data

CDL. Controlled Digital Lending

CDO. Collection Development Office

CFUW. Canadian Federation of University Women

CGP. Catalog of U.S. Government Publications

CIKM. International Conference on Information and Knowledge Management

CIP. Cataloging in Publication

CLA. Catholic Library Association

CLIR. Council on Library and Information Resources

CLLE. Center for Learning, Literacy, and Engagement

CLM. Committee on Copyright and Other Legal Matters (IFLA)

CMD. Collection Management Division

CMO. Communications and Marketing Office (ALA)

CNI. Coalition for Networked Information

COAR. SPARC/Confederation of Open Access Repositories

COMLA. Commonwealth Library Association

CONSAL. Congress of Southeast Asian Libraries

CONSER. Cooperative Online Serials

CORE. Leadership, Infrastructure, Futures

COSLA. Chief Officers of State Library Associations

CPC. Cost per Circ

CPI. Consumer Price Index

CRN. Civics Renewal Network

CRO. Chapter Relations Office (ALA)

CRRSAA. Coronavirus Response and Relief Supplemental Appropriations Act

CRS. Congressional Research Service

CSH. Canadian Subject Headings

CUI. Controlled unclassified information

D

DAMS. Digital Asset Management System
DC-PAL. Dynamic Coalition on Public
    Access in Libraries
DDC. Dewey Decimal Classification
DEI. Diversity, Equity, and Inclusion
DEL. Documenting Endangered
    Languages
DLF. Digital Library Federation
DLME. Digital Library of the Middle East
DMCA. Digital Millennium Copyright Act
DoD IACs. Department of Defense
    Information Analysis Centers
DoD. Duplication on Demand
DPLA. Digital Public Library of America
DSD. Digitization Services Directorate
DTIC. Defense Technical Information
    Center

E

EBLIDA. European Bureau of Library,
    Information and Documentation
    Associations
ECIP. Electronic Cataloging in Publication
    Program
ECLS. Early Childhood Longitudinal
    Study
EDI. Equity, Diversity, and Inclusion
ELS. Education Longitudinal Study
ELSIA. European Libraries and Sustainable
    Development Implementation and
    Assessment
EMIERT. Ethnic and Multicultural Information
    and Exchange Round Table
ENSUBLIB. Environment, Sustainability
    and Libraries (IFLA)
ERA. Electronic Records Archives
ERIC. Education Resources Information
    Center
ERT. Exhibits Round Table

F

FAB. FEDLINK Advisory Board
FAFLIG. Federal and Armed Forces
    Libraries Interest Group
FAIFE. Freedom of Access to Information
    and Freedom of Expression (IFLA)
FDLD. Federal Depository Library
    Directory

FDLP. Federal Depository Library Program
FEDLINK. Federal Library and Information
    Network
FIAF. International Federation of Film
    Archives
FMRT. Film and Media Round Table
FNIC. Food and Nutrition Information
    Center
FOIA. Freedom of Information Act
FRCs. Federal Records Centers
FSRIO. Food Safety Research Information
    Office

G

GameRT. Games and Gaming Round Table
GBA. Green Book Alliance
GDPR. General Data Protection Regulation
GLBTRT. Gay, Lesbian, Bisexual, and
    Transgendered Round Table
GNCRT. Graphic Novel and Comics Round
    Table
GODORT. Government Documents Round
    Table
GPO. U.S. Government Publishing Office

H

HBCU. Historically Black Colleges and
    Universities
HEERF. Higher Education Emergency
    Relief Fund
HESI. Higher Education Sustainability
    Initiative
HRDR. Office for Human Resource
    Development and Recruitment

I

IACs. Information Analysis Centers
IAL. Innovative Approaches to Literacy
IALL. International Association of Law
    Libraries
IAML. International Association of
    Music Libraries, Archives and
    Documentation Centres
IASL. International Association of School
    Librarianship
IATUL. International Association of
    Scientific and Technological
    University Libraries

IAU. International Association of Universities

IBBY. International Board on Books for Young People

IBPA. Independent Book Publishers Association

ICA. International Council on Archives

ICIS. International Conference on Information Systems

ICP. International Cataloging Principles

ICSD. International Conference on Sustainable Development

IFLA. International Federation of Library Associations and Institutions

IFRT. Intellectual Freedom Round Table

ILA. International Literacy Association

ILAB. International League of Antiquarian Booksellers

IMLS. Institute of Museum and Library Services

IPA. International Publishers Association

IPEDS. Integrated Postsecondary Education Data System

IRO. International Relations Office (ALA)

IRRT. International Relations Round Table

ISBD. International Standard Bibliographical Description

ISBN. International Standard Book Number

ISLD. International Sustainable Library Development interest group

ISNs. Canadian International Standard Numbers

ISO. International Organization for Standardization

ISOO. Information Security Oversight Office

ISSN. International Standard Serial Number

J

JCLC. National Joint Conference of Librarians of Color

JDR&E. *Journal of DoD Research and Engineering*

JELIS. *Journal of Education for Library and Information Science*

L

LAC. Library and Archives Canada

LAMPHHS. Librarians, Archivists, and Museum Professionals in the History of the Health Sciences (formerly ALHHS)

LARC. Library and Research Center

LC. Library of Congress

LCA. Library Copyright Alliance

LCDP. Leadership and Career Development Program

LCI. Leading Change Institute

LearnRT. Learning Round Table (formerly CLENERT)

LHRT. Library History Round Table

LIBER. Association of European Research Libraries (Ligue des Bibliotheques Européennes de Recherche)

LIRT. Library Instruction Round Table

LIS. Library and information science

LITA. Library and Information Technology Association

LJ. *Library Journal*

LLAMA. Library Leadership and Management Association

LLX. Library Learning Experience

LMPI. Library Materials Price Index

LOC. Library of Congress

LRM. Library Reference Model

LRRT. Library Research Round Table

LSCM. Library Services and Content Management

LSSIRT. Library Support Staff Interests Round Table

LSTA. Library Services and Technology

LTC. Libraries Transforming Communities

M

MAGIRT. Map and Geospatial Information Round Table

MARC. Machine Readable Cataloging

MARS. Material Acquisition Request Service

MeSH. Medical Subject Headings

METRO. Metropolitan New York Library Council

MFA. Museums for America

MIPA. Midwest Independent Publishers Association

MLA. Maryland Library Association

MLA. Medical Library Association

MLA. Music Library Association

MLIS. Master of Library and Information Science

MLSA. Museum and Library Services
Act
MMLIS. Master of Management in Library
and Information Science
MPA. Association of Magazine Media
MPLA. Mountain Plains Library Association

N

NAC. National Archives Catalog
NACO. Name Authority Cooperative
NACS. National Association of College
Stores
NAGARA. National Association of
Government Archives and Records
Administrators
NAIBA. New Atlantic Independent
Booksellers Association
NAL. National Agricultural Library
NALC. National Agricultural Law Center
NALDC. National Agricultural Library
Digital Collection
NALT. National Agricultural Library
Thesaurus
NARA. National Archives and Records
Administration
NASIG (formerly North American Serials
Interest Group)
NCAC. National Coalition Against
Censorship
NCES. National Center for Education
Statistics
NCTE. National Council of Teachers of
English
NDC. National Declassification Center
NDNP. National Digital Newspaper
NDSA. National Digital Stewardship
Alliance
NEH. National Endowment for the
Humanities
NEIBA. New England Independent
Booksellers Association
NHES. National Household Education
Survey
NHPRC. National Historical Publications
and Records Commission
NIH. National Institutes of Health
NILPPA. National Impact of Library Public
Programs Assessment
NISIC. National Invasive Species
Information Center
NISO. National Information Standards
Organization

NIST. National Institute of Standards and
Technology publications
NLE. National Library of Education
NLM. National Library of Medicine
NLS. National Library Service for the Blind
and Print Disabled
NLW. National Library Week
NLWD. National Library Workers Day
NMRT. New Members Round Table
NNLM. Network of the National Library of
Medicine
NPA. Norwegian Publishers Association
NTIS. National Technical Information
Service
NTPS. National Teacher and Principal
Survey
NTRL. National Technical Reports Library
NYPL. New York Public Library

O

OCIO. Office of the Chief Information
Officer (LC)
OCLC. Online Computer Library Center
ODL. Office of Digital Humanities
ODLOS. Office for Diversity, Literacy and
Outreach Services (ALA)
OECD. Organisation for Economic
Co-operation and Development
OGIS. Office of Government Information
Services
OIB. USSBY Outstanding International
Books
OIF. Office for Intellectual Freedom
OLOS. Office for Literacy and Outreach
Services
OLS. Office of Library Services
ORFG. Open Research Funders Group

P

PALA. Polish American Librarians
Association
PCC. Program for Cooperative
Cataloging
PCPAC. Public and Cultural Programs
Advisory Committee (ALA)
PENS. Public Law Electronic Notification
Service
PLA. Public Library Association
PLS. Public Library Survey
PMC. PubMed Central

PPAO. Public Policy and Advocacy Office (ALA)
PPO. Public Programs Office (ALA)
PRH. Penguin Random House
PSLF. Public Service Loan Forgiveness
PTRCA. Patent and Trademark Resource Center Association

R

RBMS. Rare Books and Manuscripts Section (ACRL)
RDA. Resource Description and Access
RDaF. NIST Research Data Framework
REALM. REopening Archives, Libraries, and Museums
REFORMA. National Association to Promote Library and Information Services to Latinos and the Spanish-Speaking
RIC. Rural Information Center
RMS. Research Management and Support
RNTLOAK. Rural, Native and Tribal Libraries of All Kinds (ALA)
RRS. Researcher and Reference Services Division (LC)
RRT. Rainbow Round Table
RUSA. Reference and User Services Association
RWA. Romance Writers of America

S

SAA. Society of American Archivists
SACO. Subject Authority Cooperative
SALALM. Seminar on the Acquisition of Latin American Library Materials
SAN. Standard Address Number
SASS. Schools and Staffing Survey
SCBWI. Society of Children's Book Writers and Illustrators
SCCR. Standing Committee on Copyright and Related Rights (IFLA)
SCECSAL. Standing Conference of Eastern, Central, and Southern African Libraries and Information Associations
SCOLMA. U.K. Library and Archives Group on Africa
SDGs. Sustainable Development Goals

SDSN. Sustainable Development Solutions Network
SI. Society of Illustrators
SIBA (formerly Southern Independent Booksellers Alliance)
SIGL. Stitching IFLA Global Libraries
SIIA. Software and Information Industry Association
SLA. Special Libraries Association
SLAA. State Library Administrative Agency
SLIDE. School Librarian Investigation—Decline or Evolution?
SORT. Staff Organization Round Table
SPARC. Scholarly Publishing & Academic Resources Coalition
SRA. Sequence Read Archive
SRRT. Social Responsibilities Round Table
SSP. Society for Scholarly Publishing
ST&B. Science, Technology and Business Division (LC)
STEAM. Science, Technology, Engineering, Arts, and Mathematics
STEM. Science, Technology, Engineering, and Mathematics
STM. International Association of Scientific, Technical, and Medical Publishers
SU. Simultaneous use

T

TDR. Trustworthy Digital Repository
TLA. Theatre Library Association
TOME. Toward an Open Monograph Ecosystem
TPS. Teaching with Primary Sources
TRAIL. Technical Report Archive & Image Library

U

ULC. Urban Libraries Council
UMLS. Unified Medical Language System
USAIN. United States Agricultural Information Network
USBBY. United States Board on Books for Young People
USPPI. U.S. Periodical Price Index

V

VHP. Veterans History Project

W

WAIC. Water and Agriculture Information
Center
WIPO. World Intellectual Property
Organization
WLIC. World Library and Information
Congress

WNBA. Women's National Book
Association

Y

YALSA. Young Adult Library Services
Association

Index

Note: Pages numbers followed by "t" represent tables. The Directory of Organizations (Part 6) is not included in the index.